A HANDBOOK OF PROCESS TRACING METHODS

A Handbook of Process Tracing Methods demonstrates how to better understand decision outcomes by studying decision *processes*, through the introduction of a number of exciting techniques. Decades of research have identified numerous idiosyncrasies in human decision behavior, but some of the most recent advances in the scientific study of decision making involve the development of sophisticated methods for understanding decision process—known as process tracing. In this volume, leading experts discuss the application of these methods and focus on the best practices for using some of the more popular techniques, discussing how to incorporate them into formal decision models.

This edition has been expanded and thoroughly updated throughout, and now includes new chapters on mouse tracking, protocol analysis, neurocognitive methods, the measurement of valuation, as well as an overview of important software packages. The volume not only surveys cutting-edge research to illustrate the great variety in process tracing techniques, but also serves as a tutorial for how the novice researcher might implement these methods.

A Handbook of Process Tracing Methods will be an essential read for all students and researchers of decision making.

List of Editors

Michael Schulte-Mecklenbeck is a senior lecturer for methods at the University of Bern Business School and an Adjunct Researcher at the Max Planck Institute for Human Development in Berlin.

Anton Kühberger is Professor of Psychology at the University of Salzburg.

Joseph G. Johnson is Department Chair and Professor of Psychology at Miami University, Ohio.

A HANDBOOK OF PROCESS TRACING METHODS

Second Edition

Edited by
Michael Schulte-Mecklenbeck, Anton Kühberger,
and Joseph G. Johnson

NEW YORK AND LONDON

Second edition published 2019
by Routledge
52 Vanderbilt Avenue, New York, NY 10017

and by Routledge
2 Park Square, Milton Park, Abingdon, Oxon, OX14 4RN

Routledge is an imprint of the Taylor & Francis Group, an informa business

© 2019 selection and editorial matter, Michael Schulte-Mecklenbeck, Anton Kühberger, and Joseph G. Johnson; individual chapters, the contributors

The right of the Michael Schulte-Mecklenbeck, Anton Kühberger, and Joseph G. Johnson to be identified as the authors of the editorial material, and of the authors for their individual chapters, has been asserted in accordance with sections 77 and 78 of the Copyright, Designs and Patents Act 1988.

All rights reserved. No part of this book may be reprinted or reproduced or utilised in any form or by any electronic, mechanical, or other means, now known or hereafter invented, including photocopying and recording, or in any information storage or retrieval system, without permission in writing from the publishers.

Trademark notice: Product or corporate names may be trademarks or registered trademarks, and are used only for identification and explanation without intent to infringe.

First edition published by Routledge 2015

Library of Congress Cataloging-in-Publication Data
A catalog record has been requested for this book

ISBN: 978-1-138-06420-1 (hbk)
ISBN: 978-1-138-06421-8 (pbk)
ISBN: 978-1-315-16055-9 (ebk)

Typeset in Bembo
by Newgen Publishing UK

Printed and bound by CPI Group (UK) Ltd, Croydon, CR0 4YY

CONTENTS

List of Contributors	*viii*
Acknowledgments	*xviii*

Introduction	1

1	Eye Fixations as a Process Trace *J. Edward Russo*	4
2	Pervasive Eye-Tracking for Real-World Consumer Behavior Analysis *Andreas Bulling and Michel Wedel*	27
3	Investigating Pupil Dilation in Decision Research *Joseph Tao-yi Wang and Wei James Chen*	45
4	A Primer on Eye-Tracking Methodology for Behavioral Science *Jacob L. Orquin and Kenneth Holmqvist*	53
5	Increasing Reproducibility of Eye-Tracking Studies: The EyeGuidelines *Susann Fiedler, Michael Schulte-Mecklenbeck, Frank Renkewitz,* *and Jacob L. Orquin*	65
6	(Re)Visiting the Decision Factory: Observing Cognition with MouselabWEB *Martijn C. Willemsen and Eric J. Johnson*	76
7	Comparing Process Tracing Paradigms: Tracking Attention via Mouse and Eye Movements *Ana M. Franco-Watkins, Hayden K. Hickey, and Joseph G. Johnson*	96

vi Contents

8 Mouse-Tracking: A Practical Guide to Implementation and Analysis 111
Pascal J. Kieslich, Felix Henninger, Dirk U. Wulff, Jonas M. B. Haslbeck,
and Michael Schulte-Mecklenbeck

9 Mouse-Tracking: Detecting Types in Movement Trajectories 131
Dirk U. Wulff, Jonas M. B. Haslbeck, Pascal J. Kieslich, Felix Henninger,
and Michael Schulte-Mecklenbeck

10 Mouse-Tracking to Understand Real-Time Dynamics of Social Cognition 146
Benjamin S. Stillerman and Jonathan B. Freeman

11 Measuring Electrodermal Activity and Its Applications in Judgment and
Decision-Making Research 161
Bernd Figner, Ryan O. Murphy, and Paul Siegel

12 Response Times as Identification Tools for Cognitive Processes
Underlying Decisions 184
Mario Fifić, Joseph W. Houpt, and Jörg Rieskamp

13 A Practical Guide for Automated Facial Emotion Classification 198
Sabrina Stöckli, Michael Schulte-Mecklenbeck, Stefan Borer,
and Andrea C. Samson

14 EEG and ERPs as Neural Process Tracing Methodologies in
Decision-Making Research 217
Mary E. Frame

15 Decision Neuroscience: fMRI Insights into Choice Processes 234
Vinod Venkatraman and Crystal Reeck

16 Probing the Decisional Brain with Noninvasive Brain Stimulation 249
Nadège Bault, Elena Rusconi, and Giorgio Coricelli

17 Verbal Reports and Decision Process Analysis 270
Rob Ranyard and Ola Svenson

18 Thinking Aloud during Superior Performance on Tasks Involving
Decision Making 286
K. Anders Ericsson and Jerad H. Moxley

19 Tracking Free Information Access: The Method of Active
Information Search 302
Oswald Huber, Anton Kühberger, and Michael Schulte-Mecklenbeck

Contents **vii**

20 Uncovering the Anatomy of Search Without Technology 313
   Dirk U. Wulff and Ralph Hertwig

21 Process Tracing, Sampling, and Drift Rate Construction 326
   Neil Stewart and Timothy L. Mullett

22 Using Multiple Methods to Elicit Choices and to Identify Strategies 341
   Ulrich Hoffrage and Nils Reisen

23 Testing Cognitive Models by a Joint Analysis of Multiple Dependent
   Measures Including Process Data 356
   Andreas Glöckner and Marc Jekel

24 Using Process Tracing Data to Define and Test Process Models 374
   Joseph G. Johnson and Mary E. Frame

Index *388*

CONTRIBUTORS

Nadège Bault obtained a PhD in Cognitive Neuroscience from the University of Lyon in 2010. Dr. Bault's research focuses on decision-making and learning processes in social environments.

Stefan Borer is a research assistant pursuing his master studies in computer science.

Andreas Bulling is Full Professor of Human-Computer Interaction and Cognitive Systems at the University of Stuttgart, Germany. From 2013–2018 he was a Senior Researcher at the Max Planck Institute for Informatics and an Independent Research Group Leader at the Cluster of Excellence on Multimodal Computing and Interaction at Saarland University, Germany, and previously a Feodor Lynen Research Fellow and a Marie Curie Research Fellow in the Computer Laboratory at the University of Cambridge, UK. His research interests are in novel computational methods as well as ambient and on-body systems to sense, model, and analyze everyday social and interactive non-verbal human behavior, specifically gaze and physical behavior. Andreas Bulling received his PhD in Information Technology and Electrical Engineering from ETH Zurich, in 2010, and his MSc in Computer Science from the Karlsruhe Institute of Technology, in 2006. He received an ERC Starting Grant in 2018.

Wei James Chen is a research fellow at the ShenZhen University, formerly associated with the Marketing Department at the CUHK and the Krajbich Neuroeoconmics lab.

List of Contributors   ix

Giorgio Coricelli is a Professor of Economics and Psychology at the University of Southern California. He studies human behaviors emerging from the interplay of cognitive and emotional systems.

K. Anders Ericsson is presently Conradi Eminent Scholar and Professor of Psychology at Florida State University. Currently he studies the measurement of expert performance in domains, such as music, chess, nursing, law enforcement, and sports, and how expert performers attain their superior performance by acquiring complex cognitive mechanisms and physiological adaptations through extended deliberate practice. His recent popular book (2016) *Peak: Secrets from the new science of expertise* was co-authored with Robert Pool.

Susann Fiedler is a psychologist and behavioral economist. Since 2014 she has been leading the Gielen-Leyendecker Research Group at the Max Planck Institute for Research on Collective Goods focusing on the cognitive processes underlying economic decision making. Her recent work has been examining the influence of social value orientation on information search and integration in social dilemma situations. She is also interested in the underlying cognitive and affective processes involved in risky choices and has been conducting research centered on measuring physiological components which reflect such processes.

Mario Fifić is an Associate Professor in the Department of Psychology at Grand Valley State University, Michigan. He directs the Cognitive Science and Decision-Making laboratory. His research focuses on the development of a highly diagnostic and sophisticated methodology for uncovering mental architecture, known as systems factorial technology (SFT). SFT allows for precise determination of the fundamental properties of mental processes underlying cognitive operations in categorization, face detection, reading, and visual/memory search.

Bernd Figner works as associate professor at the Behavioural Science Institute at Radboud University where he heads the Decision, Development, and Psychopathology lab. His research focuses on the psychological and neural processes underlying risky and intertemporal decisions in healthy adults as well as developing and clinical populations.

Mary E. Frame is a Research Psychologist at Wright State Research Institute working as part of the Multi-Domain Integrated Intelligence, Surveillance, and Reconnaissance research group at the Air Force Research Laboratory (AFRL). Her research expertise focuses on leveraging process tracing methods across a variety of higher order cognitive processes and decision making in an applied research setting. Her primary areas of study are decision making, human-machine teaming, metrics development, and time series analysis of electroencephalography (EEG), eye tracking, mouse tracking, and physiological data. Dr. Frame obtained her MA and PhD in Psychology from Miami University and her BS in Psychology and Criminal Justice from Baldwin Wallace University.

Ana M. Franco-Watkins is Professor and Chair in the Department of Psychology at Auburn University. Her research interests include judgment and decision making, broadly, and using attention and eye-tracking methods to address basic and applied questions.

Jonathan B. Freeman is Associate Professor of Psychology and Neural Science at New York University and Director of the Social Cognitive & Neural Sciences Lab. He studies split-second social perception, primarily how we use facial cues to categorize other people into social groups, perceive their emotion, and infer their personality. He treats social perception as fundamentally dynamic, examining how visual processes may be shaped by stereotypes and biases, prior knowledge and beliefs, and other aspects of social cognition. He uses several brain and behavior-based techniques (e.g., neuroimaging, real-time behavioral measures, computational modeling) to study the interplay of visual and social processes in perceptual and interpersonal decisions, including the roles of specific facial features, social context, and individual differences. He is additionally interested in how initial perceptions influence downstream behavior and real-world outcomes. He is also the developer of the data collection and analysis software, MouseTracker.

Andreas Glöckner is Professor of Social Psychology at the University of Cologne and senior research fellow at the Max Planck Institute for Research on Collective Goods, Bonn. He is President of the European Association for Decision Making and editor in chief of the journal *Judgment and Decision Making*. Andreas Glöckner studied psychology at the University of Heidelberg and at the University of Oregon, Eugene. After receiving his PhD in Psychology from University of Erfurt, he was head of the Max Planck Research Group Intuitive Experts in Bonn and held professor positions at the Universities of Göttingen and Hagen. His research focuses on decision making and social dilemmas with a special interest in methodology and cognitive processes. Aside from basic research, Andreas Glöckner also explores implications of psychological findings for legal institutions and public policy.

Jonas M. B. Haslbeck is a PhD student at the Psychosystems lab at the University of Amsterdam. Jonas' research focus is on modeling psychological disorders as complex systems, both from a statistical and a dynamical systems perspective.

Felix Henninger is a cognitive scientist and research software engineer, working at the Universities of Mannheim and Koblenz-Landau. He investigates the processes underlying decisions and judgments, with a focus on risky choices. As a developer and advocate for open science, he builds tools that make transparent and robust research easier. For process tracing in particular, he has helped build several software packages that make this kind of research more accessible, and the experiment builder lab.js, which allows researchers to create and run experiments in the browser.

Ralph Hertwig works at the Max Planck Institute for Human Development in Berlin and heads the Center for Adaptive Rationality. His research focuses on models of bounded rationality, models of decisions from experience, and evidence-based policy interventions (boosts).

Hayden K. Hickey is a PhD student at Auburn University studying Industrial-Organizational Psychology. His research interests include decision making in organizations, using eye-tracking technology to investigate heuristics and biases, as well as the role of perceived effort in fairness norms.

Ulrich Hoffrage received his PhD (Dr. phil.) in 1995 at the University of Salzburg (Austria) with his dissertation on the overconfidence phenomenon. He is one of the founding members of the ABC Research Group (Adaptive Behavior and Cognition) at the Max Planck Institute of Human Development in Berlin. Since 2005 he is Professor of Decision Theory at the Faculty of Business and Economics at the University of Lausanne, Switzerland.

Kenneth Holmqvist now works at Regensburg University, Germany. He is most known for his method research and for his book, *Eye tracking: a comprehensive guide to methods, paradigms, and measures*. He founded the Scandinavian Workshop on Applied Eye Tracking, and also arranged it so that the eye-tracking group in Lund could jointly organize ECEM 2013 in Lund. In 2008, he started the international LETA training courses in eye-tracking methodology which has taught more than 650 scholars around the world.

Joseph W. Houpt is an Associate Professor in the Department of Psychology at Wright State University. His research examines human performance in basic and applied contexts through mathematical cognitive modeling.

Oswald Huber is Professor Emeritus of Psychology at the University of Fribourg, Switzerland.

Marc Jekel is a psychologist at Universität zu Köln in Germany interested in how people search and integrate probabilistic information and how they learn to do both better. He uses artificial neural networks, evidence accumulation models, prospect theory, and other formal models to describe and predict choices, decision times, eye fixations, and other measures.

Eric J. Johnson is holder of the Norman Eig Chair of Business, and Director of the Center for Decision Sciences at Columbia Business School. His research examines the interface between Behavioral Decision Research, Economics and the decisions made by consumers, managers, and their implications for public policy, markets, and marketing.

Joseph G. Johnson is Professor in the Department of Psychology at Miami University. His interests include mathematical and computational modeling of cognitive processes, and testing those models with process-tracing methods. His topic areas currently include preferential choice, risky behaviors, and stress and decision making. He uses multiple behavioral methods as well as psychophysiological measures including pupil and eye-tracking, ECG, EEG, salivary cortisol, and more. He has also served as Director of Undergraduate Research at Miami and held Fellowships at a Max Planck Institute (ABC, Berlin) and Hanse Wissenschaftskolleg (Delmenhorst).

Pascal J. Kieslich is a psychologist working at the Experimental Psychology Lab, University of Mannheim, Germany. In his research, he investigates how people make decisions in different domains, including social dilemmas and decisions under risk. He has developed the mousetrap software packages for creating and analyzing mouse-tracking experiments. As a statistical consultant, he has contributed to research projects from different disciplines, including Clinical Psychology, Social Psychology, and Radiology.

Anton Kühberger Professor of Psychology at the Deptartment of Psychology and a member of the Centre for Cognitive Neuroscience at the University of Salzburg. He has done extensive research in judgment and decision making, especially in the context of risk and uncertainty. His recent interests include improving methodology, and questions of the transparency of psychological research.

Jerad H. Moxley graduated with a BA in History and Psychology from Murray State University and a PHD in Cognitive Psychology from Florida State University. Jerad works as a data analyst and instructor for the Center on Aging and Behavioral Research at Weill Cornell Medicine.

List of Contributors xiii

Timothy L. Mullett attained his PhD in Psychology and Neuroscience at the University of Nottingham. He has since spent time at the University of Warwick, University of Cambridge, and the University of Bath, and he is now an Assistant Professor in the Behavioural Science Group at Warwick Business School. His research investigates how people form preferences and make decisions. He uses a variety of methods, including eye tracking, neuroimaging, cognitive modelling, and big data analysis.

Ryan O. Murphy is the Head of Decision Sciences at Morningstar Investment Management where he researches how people make decisions and think about trade-offs, especially concerning time, money, and risk. His research interests are interdisciplinary bringing together insights and methods from experimental economics and mathematical psychology.

Jacob L. Orquin is Professor at Aarhus University and his main research interest is the role of eye movements in decision making.

Rob Ranyard is a freelance researcher and Visiting Professor affiliated to the Centre for Decision Research, Leeds University Business School. His research training was at the University of Stirling, from where he graduated in 1972 with a PhD on the Psychology of Decision Making. He has held various research and lecturing posts in psychology, including Professor of Psychology at the University of Bolton from 2001 to 2014. He has undertaken psychological research using a range of methods, published widely on economic psychology and decision research, and is currently the President of the International Association for Research into Economic Psychology.

Crystal Reeck is an Assistant Professor at Temple University's Fox School of Business. Combining both neuroscience and behavioral approaches, her research examines how emotions influence decision making and how different strategies help people manage that influence. She has published her research in peer-reviewed journals that span multiple fields, including Science, Trends in Cognitive Sciences, and Proceedings of the National Academy of Sciences. Dr. Reeck completed both her Bachelor's and Master's degrees at Stanford University. She holds a PhD in Psychology and Neuroscience from Duke University and completed her post-doctoral training at Columbia Business School.

Nils Reisen holds a PhD in Psychology and now works as a product manager and consultant at Creaholic in Biel, Switzerland. He develops tools that enable employees to do better work and to improve their collaboration and their working environment based on feedback.

Frank Renkewitz is research fellow at the Center for Empirical Research and Economic Behavior (CEREB) at the University of Erfurt, Germany. His research focus is on decision making and research methods in psychology.

Jörg Rieskamp is the Director of the Center for Economic Psychology at the University of Basel, Switzerland. He develops and tests cognitive theories of judgment and decision making.

Elena Rusconi is Full Professor in Psychobiology and Physiological Psychology at the University of Trento (Italy).

J. Edward Russo is S.C. Johnson Family Professor of Management in the Johnson College of Business and a member of the Field of Cognitive Studies at Cornell University. Professor Russo earned a BS in Mathematics from Caltech, and an MS in Mathematics and a PhD in Cognitive Psychology from the University of Michigan. He has published over four score research articles and two books, focused mainly on how people make decisions and how to help them make better decisions. He is a Fellow of the Association for Psychological Science and of the American Association for the Advancement of Science.

Andrea C. Samson is Assistant Professor at the Faculty of Psychology of the Swiss Distance Learning University and at the Institute of Special Education of the University of Fribourg, Switzerland. She has a strong focus on affective processes in psychopathology (developmental disorders including autism spectrum disorders and intellectual disabilities) and does research on positive emotions, emotion regulation, and the role of play and games. She is also using novel technologies (virtual reality) to assess and remediate emotional competences.

List of Contributors xv

Michael Schulte-Mecklenbeck is a senior lecturer for research methods at the University of Bern Business School and an Adjunct Researcher at the Max Planck Institute for Human Development in Berlin. He wants to understand how people make decisions, loves process tracing methods and is a fan of open science and replication Studies. Michael enjoys the Swiss mountains on a road bike or on skis.

Paul Siegel is a clinical psychologist, and Associate Professor of Psychology at Purchase College of the State University of New York. His research focuses on very brief exposures to masked stimuli in the study and treatment of fear-related disorders.

Neil Stewart works in the field of behavioral and economic science, and applies this research to problems in the real world. Right now he is working on consumer decision making using credit card transaction data, on criminal and other bad behavior using crime and incident records, and on a mathematical model of consumer decision making called decision by sampling. Stewart uses a mixture of laboratory experiments, field experiments, and data science techniques applied to large data sets.

Benjamin S. Stillerman is a PhD student at New York University. His research is concerned with the interaction between intergroup processes, like stereotyping and dehumanization, and visual perception.

Sabrina Stöckli is postdoc at the Institute of Marketing and Management at the University of Bern. Stöckli is primarily interested in consumer behavior, behavioral change, and social influence with past research centered on the influence of unconscious perception on consumers' emotions, intentions, and behavior.

Ola Svenson is Professor Emeritus at Stockholm University and senior research scientist at Decision Research. He is one of the pioneers who introduced a process perspective and the think-aloud method in behavioral decision research. Ola Svenson and Rob Ranyard started the European Group for Process Tracing of Decision Making, EGPROC together with researchers from Sweden, Great Britain, and Poland. The group has met annually since 1981. Svenson's Differentiation and Consolidation theory is a coherence theory describing decision rules and how decision problems are reconstructed before and after a decision. In the early 1970s he discovered the time saving bias and his research includes studies of judgment and decision making, mental arithmetics, risk analysis, traffic safety, nuclear safety, and other topics.

Vinod Venkatraman is an Associate Professor of Marketing at Fox School of Business, Temple University. His research involves the use of behavioral, eye-tracking, neurophysiological, and neuroimaging methodologies to study the effects of task environment, state variables, and individual traits on decision preferences and consumer behavior. A core emphasis of his research is in the application of findings from the laboratory to real-world decisions in the areas of financial decision making, public policy, and marketing communications. He received the Early Career Award from the Society of Neuroeconomics in 2016 for his contributions to the area of decision neuroscience.

Joseph Tao-yi Wang received his BS degree in Mathematics with minors in Foreign Languages (English) and Economics from National Taiwan University in 1998. He received his PhD in Economics from University of California, Los Angeles in 2005, after which he became a postdoctoral scholar in economics at the Division of Humanities and Social Sciences, California Institute of Technology. In 2007, he joined the Department of Economics, National Taiwan University, as an Assistant Professor, became an Associate Professor in 2010, and a Professor in 2014. His current research interests include economic experiments that test theory, economic theory inspired by experiments, and the human reasoning process that leads to economic decisions.

Michel Wedel is the Pepsico Chaired Professor of Consumer Science at the Robert H. Smith School of Business, and a Distinguished University Professor at the University of Maryland. He holds the Henri Theil Visiting Chair in Marketing and Econometric at the Econometric Institute of the Erasmus University. Wedel has improved the understanding of consumer behavior and marketing decision making through the development and application of statistical and econometric methods. Wedel published three books, seven software packages, more than 175 peer reviewed articles, and over 20 book chapters. His work has been cited over 20,000 times. Wedel's work has received several best paper awards, and he received the Muller award for outstanding contributions to the social sciences from the Royal Dutch Academy of the Sciences, and both the Churchill and Parlin awards for lifetime contributions to marketing research from the American Marketing Association. He is a fellow of the American Statistical Association, the American Marketing Association, and the Institute for Operations research and Management Science.

Martijn C. Willemsen is an Associate Professor of Human Decision Making in Interactive Systems at Eindhoven University of Technology, The Netherlands. He researches the cognitive aspects of Human-Technology Interaction, with a strong focus on judgment and decision making in online environments. His applied research focuses on how online decisions can be supported by recommender systems, and includes domains such as movies, health-related decisions and energy-saving measures. From a more theoretical perspective, he has a special interest in process-tracing technologies to capture and analyze in detail information processing of decision makers.

Dirk U. Wulff is a researcher at the Center for Cognitive and Decision Sciences, University of Basel. Dirk studies learning mechanisms and the cognitive representations they create and develops methods to help other researchers to do the same.

ACKNOWLEDGMENTS

We would like to thank the following people who helped in making this book awesome.

Sophie Crowe and Ceri McLardy – Routledge Psychology
Tatiana Bremova-Ertl – cover
Geraldine Neeser – proof reading
Andrea Pfander and the PH Bern Medienwerkstatt – cover
Christian Salic – photography
Kelly Winter – Newgen Publishing
Cedric Zurbrügg – cover (hand model)

INTRODUCTION

Michael Schulte-Mecklenbeck, Anton Kühberger,
and Joseph G. Johnson

There is nothing so theoretical as a good method.

Greenwald, 2012, p. 99

This is the second edition of what was called A *Handbook of Process Tracing Methods for Decision Research.* The first edition of the handbook had 9 chapters and which, according to Google Scholar, have been cited over 500 times since their publication in 2011 (retrieved February, 2019). This revised edition serves as an update of established chapters, but, importantly, it is also an extended edition containing various new chapters. These additions demonstrate the ever-growing interest in process tracing methods during the intervening years and the increasing variety of research methods interested in a perspective going beyond investigating simple choices. In fact, not only do existing methods benefit from new applications, but many new methods have also been developed—one indication for this growth is the nearly tripled number of chapters and topics covered in this edition. This volume extends and deepens the discussion of topics presented before (e.g., mouselab, eye-tracking, or self-report methods) and adds new topics (e.g., mouse-tracking, sampling, and EEG). Beyond the inclusion of new chapters this edition also includes integrative chapters discussing the combination of different process tracing methods and emphasizing the importance of computational modeling of process data.

This book should be, as the name suggests, treated like a handbook. By this we mean that one will, most likely, not read it from first to last page but directly jump to the relevant methods for ones' research question. In preparing this edition a big question that came up was how to organize the different methods into larger groups or sections. Schulte-Mecklenbeck et al. (2017) suggest a structure of process tracing methods on two axes - *temporal resolution* (what is the minimal resolution a method can deliver) and *distortion risk* (how likely does the application of a method distort the measured process), resulting in four stylized groups of process tracing techniques shown in Figure 0.1. We move through this excellent suggestion in the following order: Interactive measures (Chapters 1–10: eye-tracking, mouselab, mouse-tracking); peripheral psychophysiology together with neural techniques (Chapters 11–16: electrodermal responses, reaction time, video classification, EEG, fMRI, TMS); and subjective reports (Chapters 17–19, verbal data, AIS). We conclude with topics that were not considered by Schulte-Mecklenbeck et al. (2017): sampling (Chapters 20–21) and multi-method approaches (Chapters 22–24).

2 Introduction

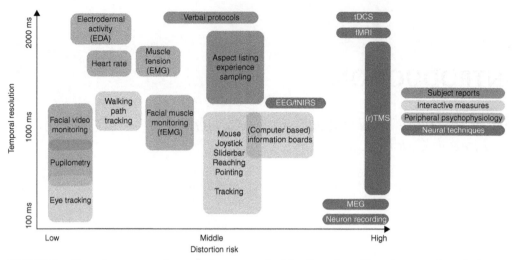

FIGURE 0.1 Map of process tracing techniques organized by distortion risk and temporal resolution.

We begin the interactive methods section with exploring the history of eye-tracking (Chapter 1), followed by a glimpse into the future (Chapter 2), describing the application of mobile eye-trackers in psychology, marketing or informatics. Chapter 3 deals with the measurement and interpretation of pupil dilation and how such data can be utilized. The remaining two chapters in this section discuss methodological details in eye-tracking studies, including design decisions, potential pitfalls when running an eye-tracking study, and their solutions (Chapter 4) and standards for reporting to improve reproducibility (Chapter 5). In the next chapter, we re-visit the decision factory to learn more about mouselab (Chapter 6), which is an inexpensive analogue to eye-tracking. The two methods are explicitly compared in Chapter 7 to assist researchers who might be facing a choice between them.

A relatively new method, mouse-tracking, is represented by a set of chapters that stand as important new contributions in this edition—reflecting a substantial increase in use of this method in decision research. Rather than merely surveying work using this method, the chapters here provide practical guidelines for setting up and running mouse-tracking studies with free software tools (Chapter 8), explore the common assumption of continuity in movement trajectories in mouse-tracking (Chapter 9), and provide an overview of the method including historical context, theoretical issues, and links to other measures such as neural activity; Chapter 10).

Our treatment of methods involving psychophysiology begins with two chapters expanded from the previous edition, including usage of skin conductance (Chapter 11) and the benefits of advanced reaction time analyses for process tracing (Chapter 12). These are followed by a new chapter on automatic video based emotion classification (Chapter 13), demonstrating the advances of computer technology and machine learning in our field. We then focus more specifically on neural techniques, including a new chapter on using EEG and ERPs (Chapter 14), in addition to revised chapters explaining the role of fMRI as a means to investigate decision making processes (Chapter 15) and demonstrating what can be learned from invasive methods such as rTMS and tDCS (Chapter 16).

All the methods up to this point need apparatuses that, in some cases, become very technical. In contrast, the subject reports section features three chapters covering verbal data. As one of the oldest process-tracing methods, it is inspected from a historical point of view in Chapter 17.

In Chapter 18, we see how a specific and interesting research topic (expertise) benefits from, and is heavily influenced by, verbal data. This section concludes with a structured approach to utilize verbal data as a dependent variable (Chapter 19). Continuing with other "low-tech" experiments, sampling techniques are introduced to better understand decisions from experience (in contrast to description, Chapter 20) and sampling information in a diffusion model framework (Chapter 21).

We conclude with an entirely new section consisting of three chapters that advocate for an integrative approach in utilizing process data. Chapter 22 describes the advantages of combining methods, such as by bringing together verbal protocols, eye-tracking and mouselab (Chapter 22). Similarly, Chapter 23 describes the efficient testing of theories using multiple dependent measures. Chapter 24 shows how to use process data to inform cognitive (computational) models of decision making.

Some stylized facts about this edition of the handbook: The 24 chapters were contributed by 49 authors, from 12 different countries and have 202014 words in them. Preparation time for the handbook was 3 years (from the first email sent to receiving the printed version of the handbook).

We would like to thank the authors for their contributions, discussions and the insights into their work—all of which were delivered on time, in some cases.

References

Greenwald, A. G. (2012). There is nothing so theoretical as a good method. *Perspectives on Psychological Science, 7*(2), 99–108.

Schulte-Mecklenbeck, M., Johnson, J.G., Böckenholt, U., Goldstein, D., Russo, J., Sullivan, N., & Willemsen, M. (2017). Process tracing methods in decision making: On growing up in the 70ties. *Current Directions in Psychological Science, 26*(5), 442–450.

1

EYE FIXATIONS AS A PROCESS TRACE

J. Edward Russo

The eye is our preeminent sense for acquiring information from the external environment, and nearly all such acquisition is accomplished when the eye fixates on an object. The eye has evolved so that its movement to the next fixation point is the fastest of all external information acquisition behaviors. Its unique value has led humans to rely on it for nearly all intellective tasks. Without vision can one imagine the development of writing, and without writing, the development of civilization?[1]

One such intellective task is decision making, or more generally judgment and decision making (JDM). Almost every decision involves the acquisition of visual information. The main exceptions occur when all the needed information is purely auditory like music or is retrieved from long-term memory, that is, via internal rather than external search. Tracking the eye during a decision yields a series of fixations on different units of the available information.

Such a sequence of fixations brings unique advantages. Because it is the least effortful of information acquisition responses ("metabolically cheap" in the biological phrasing of Spivey, Richardson, & Dale, 2009, p. 237), a fixation sequence provides a detailed trace of the information acquired. Indeed, an eye movement to reacquire information is so cheap that it can sometimes substitute for the use of working memory as a storage and retrieval system (Droll & Hayhoe, 2007; Maxcey-Richard, & Hollingworth, 2013). Further, eye fixations can be recorded nonreactively, and they are difficult to censor. Both properties derive in part because eye movements are fast and largely automatic. No manual response can compare in detail, cost, and veridicality, even pointing a computer mouse (although this information acquisition technology is widespread and useful; see Chapters 6–10).

At the same time, there are barriers. The greatest of these was the availability of an eye-tracking apparatus. That barrier has changed substantially over the last decade, with accurate eye trackers now costing only a few hundred dollars (Lejarraga, Schulte-Mecklenbeck, & Smedema, 2016; Titz, Scholz, & Sedlmeier, 2017). Indeed, the supply of eye-tracking apparatus probably exceeds the demand—for the first time in history. The biggest remaining barrier is the task of interpreting the recorded sequence of fixations. A fixation tells researchers where individuals are looking, not what they are thinking. However, it is the latter that is needed for the development and testing of explanations of observed JDM phenomena.

Fundamentals of Eye Movements and Measurement Technology

Types of Eye Movements

Saccades

For JDM studies and cognition more generally, one type of eye movement is the most relevant: saccades (Henderson, 2006). These are rapid, voluntary movements of widely different amplitude from one object of regard to another. Historically, the broad reliance on a sequence of saccades to accomplish most cognitive tasks was not appreciated until the end of the 19th century. Instead, the eye was thought to move more continuously, especially in such common visual tasks as scanning scenes, search, and reading. Unlike most of our movements, we do not notice our own eyes move. For example, you have no awareness of your own saccades as you read this sentence, but you can clearly observe another reader's eyes leap from one word to another and down to the next line. Such movement was labeled "par saccade" by the French physiologist Javal, and can be translated roughly as movement "by fits and starts", with the single word "saccade"[2] corresponding to something like the English words "jerk" or "leap" (Wade, 2007).

See Wade and Tatler (2005) for comprehensive histories of eye movement research and the much earlier detailed review in Chapter 2 of Yarbus (1967). The performance capabilities of saccades are well documented (e.g., Carpenter, 1988; Becker, 1991). These movements are rapid, reaching a peak velocity of 700° per sec for longer movements. When acceleration and deceleration are incorporated, a 2° saccade that is typical in reading takes about 25 msec, while a 6° movement that might occur in scanning a visual scene requires about 35 msec.

An important characteristic of saccades is the "suppression" of vision during movement (Matin, 1974; Thiele, Henning, Buischik, & Hoffman, 2002).[3] During a saccade, essentially no information can be acquired, certainly not the recognition of alphanumeric characters in typical JDM tasks.[4]

Among voluntary movements, saccades are so effortless that they usually go unnoticed. Thus, we recognize errors in other voluntary movements like motor "missteps", but there are no "misfixations". We may fixate something anticipated to be interesting and then find that it is not, but the error is one of prediction, not one of incorrectly executing a saccadic movement. Even when the movement is aimed imperfectly, the control system of the eye rapidly corrects its aim and accomplishes the necessary adjustment so effortlessly that the correction is no more recognized than the original saccade. In contrast, a misstep while walking, even when it is corrected in time to avoid tripping, is often a more conscious action, likely eliciting embarrassment when done in a public situation.

Non-Saccadic Movements

There are other movements of the eyes besides saccades. In vergence movements, the eyes jointly focus on a single point or object of regard. They contribute to both visual acuity and depth perception. Smooth pursuit movements allow the eye to track an object that follows a continuous trajectory. Such movements maintain the target at a fixed point on the retina, usually the fovea, in order to attain sufficient resolution for such ordinary actions as walking over uneven terrain. Nystagmus movements enable constant focus on an object of regard when the head moves. Such compensatory movements are essential to vision as observers move through their environment. There are also very small movements (tremors, drifts, and flicks) that will, in most cases, not concern JDM researchers. For a more detailed description of the varieties of eye movements, see Kowler (1995; 2011) or Duchowski (2017, especially Chapter 4).

Methods for Tracking Eye Movements

Since the late 1800s researchers have wanted to track eye movements (Yarbus, 1967; see also Alpern, 1962). Early techniques were often intrusive, for example, making plaster of Paris casts that fit over the eyeball (Delabarre, 1898). Over the next century, the success of eye fixations as process data was largely driven by better instruments and techniques. For instance, direct contact with the eye and other methods typically required immobilization of the head. These methods gave way to ones in which the eye-tracking apparatus can be mounted on the head, today achieved with unobtrusive glasses (see Chapter 2). The concern of JDM researchers is mainly functional, what the available apparatus can do, and not how it does it. Nonetheless, it should not be forgotten that sometimes the "how" constrains the "what", even in JDM studies. For instance, a glasses-mounted eye tracker used while a consumer traverses a supermarket aisle offers limited ability to identify which elements of package facings are fixated or even exactly which packages are fixated if the latter are small.

Hardware

The most popular eye-tracking system uses a video camera, pointed at the eye, often illuminated with infrared light, to record its corneal reflection. Some devices also record the reflected image off the back surface of the lens for additional resolution. Other methods currently in use are electro-oculography, a reflecting contact lens on the sclera (the white of the eye), and tracking the limbus which is the border between the iris and sclera. Thorough reviews of the available eye-tracking technologies are provided by Duchowski (2017), Holmqvist et al. (2011) and Liversedge, Gilchrist, and Everling (2011).

The ideal system, which various laboratories and commercial firms have essentially achieved, provides excellent resolution and high recording frequency, as well as being head mounted (or unobtrusively placed) so that it is able to track the eye even as the head moves. The latter capability is especially valuable in dynamic environments like those faced by airplane pilots or automobile drivers (e.g., Lee, 2009; Friedrich, Russwinkel, & Mohlenbrink, 2017). There are also some common decisions, such as supermarket purchases, where the consumer's progress through a rich and changing environment requires allowance for head motion.

Nonetheless, current systems are more than adequate for nearly all JDM studies, often not even requiring researchers to modify their preferred visual display of the stimulus.[5]

Software

Software has become an increasingly important part of the technology of eye movement tracking. It has greatly facilitated the recording of eye position. It has also enabled the automation of both the distinction of fixations from movements (e.g., Blingnaut, 2008) and the identification of areas of interest (e.g., Hessels, Kemner, van den Boomen, & Hooge, 2016). Current software also enables gaze-initiated changes in the stimulus (Duchowski, Cournia, & Murphy, 2004; Glaholt, Rayner, & Reingold, 2012; McConkie & Rayner, 1975; Rayner, 1975; Rosen, 1975). That is, as a function of where a participant is looking, another part of the visual display is changed. For instance, to test the number of letters in the "perceptual span" while reading, a letter N spaces ahead is altered. Only if this is noticed, does its position lie within the perceptual span.[6] These systems enable various other stimulus manipulations like a moving window in which all but the "window" is occluded or masked (Bertera & Rayner, 2000; Bradshaw, Nettleton, Wilson, & Nathan, 1984; Franco-Watkins & Johnson, 2011; Franco-Watkins, Davis, & Johnson, 2016; Rayner, Smith, Malcolm, & Henderson,

2009). They also permit the serial presentation of stimuli to the fovea (i.e., without eye movements) and the magnification of a portion of the stimulus, termed foveated imaging/rendering (Miellet, O'Donnell, & Sereno, 2009). Some of the most intriguing current and potential JDM research using eye fixations involves the software of eye-tracking systems.

Object of Regard

The most direct use of eye fixations is to identify the objects of regard in a visual environment. To simplify the presentation, this section is partitioned into applications where objects of regard are treated as individual entities and those where a distribution of fixations over multiple objects is the primary focus.

Individual Objects of Regard

A sense of the variety and importance of applications of eye fixations can be conveyed by considering content areas only marginally related to JDM. For example, Mello-Thoms, Nodine, and Kundel (2002; Kundel & Nodine, 1978) found all cases when there was visual evidence of breast cancer (a "lesion" present in an X-ray) but radiologists failed to report it. In 59% of those cases, the lesion had been fixated (yet not reported as seen). Similarly, Fischer, Richards, Berman, and Krugman (1989) showed that when viewing cigarette advertisements, three out of seven adolescents never fixate the mandated warning.

Predicted Fixations

Eye fixation data can be used to test an object of regard that has been predicted from theory or from some standard of comparison. For instance, in an unusual test of the "just world hypothesis", eye fixations revealed that good (bad) behavior influenced the fixation to the corresponding visual location even before the appearance of the actual good (bad) outcome (Callan, Ferguson, & Bindemann, 2013). The success of many magic tricks depends on the misdirection of visual attention, something naturally verified by recording an observer's eye fixations. In an unusual application of predicted fixations, Tatler and Kuhn (2007) tested the trick of making a lighted cigarette "disappear". Briefly, attention is drawn to one hand while the other hand removes the cigarette from the mouth of the magician (who was Kuhn). Then, just before it reaches the table in front of him, the lit cigarette is dropped onto his lap. By the time that the subject's gaze returns to the hand that held the cigarette, the latter has "disappeared". Video recording of the subject's gaze confirmed the misdirection of attention away from the cigarette when it was dropped out of sight. That is, eye fixations away from a crucial object of regard, the dropped cigarette, verified the misdirection hypothesis. In a broader statement of the value of predicted objects of regard, Henderson (2017) argues that fixations in viewing complex scenes are better understood as the result of knowledge-based predictions than as the result of attraction due to stimulus properties like brightness or shape.

Sometimes the prediction of the object of regard comes from a comparison with the eye fixations of experts. Thus, although laparoscopic surgery has many advantages, it removes tactile feedback and forces the surgeon to rely more on visual information. Law, Atkins, Kirkpatrick, Lomax, and Mackenzie (2004) found that novices fixated the laparoscope more often than did experts, while the latter were better able to maintain their gaze continuously on the target in the patient's body. Similar comparisons between the eye fixations of experts and novices are reported for chess by Sheridan and Reingold (2014; also Reingold & Charness, 2005) and for a computer game by Underwood (2005). The standard of comparison may also be the eye fixations of normal individuals when contrasted to a clinical population. Senju, Southgate, White, and Frith (2009) recorded eye fixations during a false belief task to show that adults with Asperger's syndrome are less able to recognize the mental state of another person.

Reading

The most frequent application of eye-tracking has very likely been the experimental study of reading. Excellent reviews are available, so no summary of the field is attempted here (Radach & Kennedy, 2004; Rayner & Liversedge, 2011; van Gompel, Fischer, Murray, & Hill, 2007). However, the contribution of eye-tracking to reading research (and to the diagnosis of reading problems like dyslexia, e.g., Benfatto et al., 2016) should be acknowledged, where it has been called "an indispensable technology" (Radach & Kennedy, 2004, p. 13). For instance, a long-standing question is temporal overlap. During the current fixation might some processing of the last fixation's material still be occurring and, more controversially, some processing of the next fixation based on information obtained via a "parafoveal preview" (i.e., peripheral perception)? Although such an overlap of processing across fixations has been modeled (e.g., Reichle, Pollatsek, & Rayner, 2007; Russo, 1978; for a review see Radach, Reilly, & Inhoff, 2007), only eye fixations can provide the needed empirical answers. That answer is affirmative to both questions. Hold-over processing from the prior fixation was not unexpected (e.g., Morrison, 1984). However, the less obvious "preview" processing of the next fixation relied importantly on eye fixations to demonstrate its presence (e.g., Rayner & Duffy, 1986). In a preference task for scenes, Nuthmann (2017) found the same "successor effect" in which image characteristics of the next fixation's location affected the duration of the current fixation. Recent techniques for studying reading have usefully augmented eye fixations by both concurrent and retrospective verbal protocols (e.g., Brand-Gruwel, Kammerer, van Meeuwen, & van Gog, 2017).

Distribution of Fixations

In almost all JDM and (other relatively complex) tasks, multiple fixations are needed to address the research questions. This section reviews the simplest cases of multiple fixations, their distribution over the stimulus. It also focuses on the common inference that the fixation's frequency signals importance. The more complex analysis of the order of fixations is considered in the following section.

In some tasks, the balance of fixations is the main focus, while in others, it is the absence of fixations that is more interesting. For example, in one of the earliest uses of eye fixation recording in a decision task, van Raaij (1977) observed housewives as they chose one of 13 brands of coffee described by four attributes each. He found that only 80% of brands received even a single fixation and only about half of all the available brand-attribute values were seen. This result confirmed (with the least effortful of all information acquisition actions) that in one common environment, much of the available information was ignored.

A common application of eye fixations where differences in distribution are crucial is scene analysis. For example, in viewing works of art (and to no one's surprise), fixations tend to congregate on the more informative elements of a picture, such as internal boundaries (Yarbus, 1967). When a picture's main content is a person, fixations are concentrated on the face, especially the eyes, nose, and mouth. Further, the components of a scene receive different fixation frequencies when the processing instructions differ. For instance, Yarbus varied instructions to estimate people's ages vs their "material circumstances" (1967, p. 192), and Boutet, Lemieux, Goulet, and Collin (2017) changed the relevance of different information while discriminating faces. As unsurprising as these results may be, they provide a useful confirmation of expectations that were based only on anecdotal evidence. For more recent work on picture/scene scanning, see Hsiao and Cottrell (2008), or Malcolm, Groen, and Baker (2016).

In an applied domain more familiar to some JDM researchers, the attention-attracting characteristics of print advertisements were identified as early as the 1940s (Karslake, 1940; McNamara, 1940; for reviews of "visual marketing" see Pieters & Wedel, 2007; Duchowski, 2017). Wedel and Pieters (2000) recorded the eye fixations of 88 female consumers as they flipped through two consumer magazines that contained 236 pages and 65 full-page advertisements. The apparatus enabled head movements, so the viewing situation approximated a natural at-home environment. All fixation locations in the advertisements were classified into three categories: text, pictures, and the brand name or brand identity. One finding was that brand occupied the least area of the typical advertisement (6–7%) but received the highest ratio of fixations to area (3:1). This result and others like it (see later) are useful to advertisers who wish to determine, first, whether the brand has been seen and, second, whether the surrounding material designed to draw and hold the viewer's attention was also viewed.

In a related study, Janiszewski (1998) showed actual catalog pages to typical purchasers and reported that larger displays drew more fixations. Furthermore, the total fixation duration on a product significantly predicted sales. Of course, the causal assertion that total duration on each product influences the preference for a product cannot be established. However, successful catalog sales have to begin with a successful competition for visual attention. Related work on "yellow pages" telephone books has been performed by Lohse (1997) and Lohse and Wu (2001).

Fixation Frequency as an Index of Importance

Maybe the most common conceptually driven use of fixation locations is interpreting the relative frequency of fixations as relative importance. That is, more fixations on an object, such as a choice alternative, indicate greater importance or value. For instance, in a medical diagnosis task, Jahn and Braatz (2014) found that the proportion of fixations corresponds to a symptom's causal strength. In a more traditional JDM task, Reisen, Hoffrage, and Mast (2008) used a standard alternative-by-attribute matrix to display information for a consumer choice (mobile telephones). They found that the frequency of fixations on attributes correlates highly with the rank order of importance ratings of those attributes. Kim, Seligman, and Kable (2012) used eye fixations to confirm one of the oldest JDM anomalies, the preference reversal phenomenon (Lichtenstein & Slovic, 1971; Slovic & Lichtenstein, 1983). As expected, the amounts in a gamble were fixated more frequently during bidding while the probabilities were fixated more often during choices.

In another consumer choice study, the display consisted of six alternatives (Russo & Rosen, 1975). Eye fixations were recorded and categorized (as explained later) into isolated (i.e., single) fixations and those in multialternative comparisons. Importantly for this discussion, the utility of each alternative was estimated separately from the choices. The correlation between the frequencies of isolated/single fixations and the utilities of the fixated alternatives was essentially zero. In contrast, the number of fixations in comparisons was monotonically related to those two alternatives' combined utilities. The authors concluded that the processing during the comparisons was sensitive to the alternatives' values, whereas those values were irrelevant to the processing of single fixations which "were used mainly in a search capacity" (p. 273).

Fixation Order

In decisions, especially those with many alternatives, the first fixation on an option indicates that it has been recognized and initially evaluated. Maybe more important is the last fixation. It seems natural to interpret this as the alternative's elimination, or at least its implicit elimination. Thus, first and last fixations can uniquely indicate important aspects of the decision process.

In a simulated supermarket, Russo and Leclerc (1994) had typical shoppers choose one product from a display of four shelves with four brand-sizes on each. The sequence of first fixations prior to any refixations was used to define an initial phase of screening or orientation. Parallel to the sequence of first fixations, the last fixation on each alternative would seem to reflect its elimination. A less obvious purpose for the last fixation was to use it to define a final "checking" phase of the choice process (Russo & Leclerc, 1994). That is, working back from the last fixation prior to the announcement of the chosen product, a sequence of fixations without refixations could identify a "last look" that confirmed the chosen product as superior. Russo and Leclerc used a concurrent verbal protocol to confirm both the interpretation of an initial screening phase and of a final checking phase.

Oddly, in the same study, some shoppers fixated products after they had announced their chosen brand-size and had begun to turn away from the display. This occurred in over half of the choices. These post-announcement fixations rarely included the chosen product (only 8% of fixations) or a comparison between two products (only 2% of fixations) and a remarkable one-third of them were devoted to fixating brand-sizes not seen before. These post-choice fixations were interpreted as a second checking phase, one that included some of the never seen brand-sizes.

There is a general acceptance that the first fixation is devoted to information acquisition, even if some evaluative processing is also accomplished. However, as the previous result shows, the interpretation of the last fixation is not straightforward. In some decision tasks, it will indicate the elimination of the fixated alternative from further consideration. However, in other tasks its interpretation is not so obvious but will require additional analysis and, possibly, additional data.

Time Measures

Total Fixation Time

The total time fixating an alternative is sometimes taken as an indicator of that alternative's perceived value (much like the total number of fixations discussed earlier). In other cases, the total time of a sequence of fixations can reveal an important aspect of the decision process. In the study of supermarket shoppers in which three stages were identified (Russo & Leclerc, 1994), the mean total time of the second stage, mainly associated with comparisons, was nearly 23 sec. In contrast, the times of the first (orienting and screening) and third (checking) stages were far briefer, 3.7 and 4.2 sec, respectively. Thus, nearly three-fourths of the time spent choosing a product from a shelf display of 16 brand-sizes was devoted to one stage of the choice process. Although this study illustrates the use of total time, its specific findings should not be taken as general but rather dependent on the particular task environment (see Shams, Wastlund, & Witell, 2014, for a replication in a somewhat different environment with somewhat different time allocations).

Fixation Duration

The mean fixation duration is usually interpreted as an indicator of processing depth or effort. Pieters and Warlop (1999) presented six actual containers (of shampoo) to typical consumers and found that the chosen brand receives the longest fixation durations. However, their main interest was the effects of both involvement and time pressure on the choice process. When involvement was high (by letting participants keep whichever brand they chose), they found longer fixation durations, 404 msec vs 368 msec for low involvement. Under time pressure (created by limiting exposure of the visual display of brands to only 7 sec, instead of 20 sec for the low time pressure condition), fixation durations were shorter, 354 msec vs 431 msec. In spite of these differences, across the four conditions formed by the two manipulations, the fixation durations on the chosen brand were always longer than on the non-chosen alternatives. Thus, for both involvement and item pressure, mean duration indicated the predicted change in processing depth.

In the multialternative study of Russo and Rosen (1975), the majority of refixations occurred in pair comparisons. This raised the question of what the comparisons were used for. The most obvious hypothesis was the elimination of one of the two alternatives, as in a single elimination tournament with two players in each match. In this study, utility values for the six alternatives (used cars) were assessed in advance. Then the utility difference between each pair of cars was computed. If the purpose of the pair comparisons was elimination, then the comparisons with the largest differences in utility should have been easiest and exhibited the briefest processing durations. When the mean durations were regressed on the utility differences, the result was statistically null (and in the wrong direction). Thus, the mean fixation durations indicated that the all-important pair comparisons were not used to eliminate one of the two compared alternatives. Multialternative choice is not a tournament-like series of pairwise eliminations.

What, then, were they used for? The same durations were regressed on the average utility of the alternatives in a pair. The result was strongly positive, indicating that pair comparisons were used to gain information about the relative value of both cars, with more time spent on the better pairs. The information resulting from these pairwise comparisons was then used to eventually select the best one of the six available.

Recall the supermarket study with 16 products across four shelves, and the odd situation of two final checking phases, one before and one after the announcement of the chosen product (Russo & Leclerc, 1994). The mean durations of these two checking phases were 1.01 sec and .61 sec, respectively. These were, as might be expected, significantly different, and were taken as indicating significantly different checking processes (again see Shams et al., 2014, for a replication with different results).

An open question is what to do with the duration of the saccade following a fixation. Processing of the information acquired during that fixation almost certainly continues through the following saccade, yet the duration of that processing does not include the time of the saccade (Irwin, 1998). When the processing of single fixations is all that matters as, for instance, in much of reading research, (e.g., Sereno, O'Donnell, & Rayner, 2006), the addition of the subsequent saccade's duration may not matter. However, when a sequence of several fixations forms a cognitive unit (see later), the inclusion of saccade times may improve the accuracy of the total duration of that unit (Radach & Kennedy, 2004).

Sequences of Fixations

Binary Transitions

Without minimizing the importance to JDM research of individual fixations and their distributions, many of the processes of interest cover multiple fixations in a particular sequence. The simplest and most common are transitions from one stimulus element to another. Yet even here, specific sequences of multiple transitions are sometimes needed to capture a hypothesized subprocess. The simpler binary transitions are considered first.

In JDM research the most common transitions of interest are within an alternative and between attributes or within an attribute but across alternatives. For example, do decision makers compare "by-alternative" by looking at all the attributes or features of one alternative before moving to the attribute information of the next alternative? Instead, do they compare "by-attribute" by collecting information about one feature for all alternatives before moving to the next feature? Of course, any such analysis requires that the information that describes the alternatives be segmented into attributes and, usually, presented in some form of alternative-by-attribute display. To record the object of regard unambiguously, the spacing in the array is designed so that only one cell's contents can be seen. That is, a fixation in one cell precludes peripheral perception of all other cells. Instead, these other cells might be explicitly occluded so that only one cell is exposed (e.g., Franco-Watkins & Johnson, 2011; Chapter 7). In studies of consumer choice, the alternatives are usually brands within a product category and sometimes the actual packages are displayed (e.g., Pieters & Warlop, 1999). In such cases, areas of the package can be distinguished, such as the brand name, the ingredients, and the picture. Transitions can then be tracked as if these areas were attributes.

The simplest fixation-based definition of by-alternative processing is a fixation transition across the attributes within an alternative. Similarly, a single transition within an attribute but between alternatives is defined as by-attribute processing. van Raaij (1977) recorded eye fixations on a display of 13 alternatives (brands), each described by four attributes. He found 56% of transitions were within-brand (i.e., by-alternative), but only 19% by-attribute. When compared to their chance base rates, 6% and 23% respectively, by-alternative processing was shown to dominate the choice process.

It should be noted that the reported relative frequencies of by-attribute and by-alterative processing for the van Raaij study should not be considered a general guide to the balance between these two processing modes. Thus, in the Pieters and Warlop (1999) study discussed earlier, involvement (heightened by giving participants whichever brand they chose) not only led to longer fixation durations but also to more by-brand and fewer by-attribute transitions. During decision making on the Dell website (www.dell.com), Shi, Wedel, and Pieters (2013) used eye fixation transitions and a multilevel model to infer the use of these two processing strategies. The specific balance between by-attribute and by-alternative processing naturally differs across studies as a function of such variables as the characteristics of the task environment (e.g., numbers of alternatives and of attributes) and of the decision makers (e.g., domain knowledge and motivation). Nonetheless, comparability between studies has been facilitated by well-defined measures of processing, notably processing by-attribute and by-brand (e.g., Böckenholt & Hynan, 1994; Payne, 1976).

Multiple Fixations

What constitutes a subsequence of eye fixations that can be reliably interpreted (and not merely defined) as by-alternative or by-attribute processing? One set of criteria was offered by Russo and Dosher (1983). A binary choice was presented in a 2 x 3 matrix with two used cars represented by three attributes each. To qualify as processing by-alternative, all three attributes had to be fixated without interruption (e.g., A_1-A_2-A_3 or A_1-A_2-A_1-A_3, where subscripts indicate the attributes of Alternative A). When one of the two alternatives was processed in this way, it was interpreted as a case of by-alternative evaluation. When both were processed contiguously, this sequence was interpreted as a by-alternative comparison (e.g., A_1-A_2-A_3-A_2-B_2-B_1-B_2-B_3). A corresponding distinction was made between by-attribute evaluations and by-attribute comparisons. The former were signaled by three or more fixations on the same attribute (e.g., A_1-B_1-A_1). The longer by-attribute comparisons required contiguous by-attribute evaluations of all three attributes (e.g., A_1-B_1-A_1-A_2-B_2-A_2-B_2-A_3-B_3-A_3-B_3).

These criteria may seem plausible, even natural, yet how does one know that such interpretations of fixation subsequences are, in fact, valid? Can researchers accurately infer what decision makers are thinking from what they are seeing? Such an inference usually requires a second source of data. Russo and Dosher (1983) used a retrospective verbal protocol (see Chapters 17–18) that was prompted by a replay of the eye fixation sequence. Then they computed the proportion of times when their proposed interpretation of a pattern of fixations was confirmed by the verbal report. For by-alternative processing, 78% of the evaluations were confirmed in the verbal protocol, as were 100% of the by-alternative evaluations (of which there were many fewer). The corresponding values for by-attribute processing were 89% for evaluations and 86% for comparisons. Although these values were not always 100%, it should be noted that the verbal protocol was not always complete. Thus, the failure to confirm an interpretation of a fixation sequence may have been due to an omission in the protocol, not to a contrary description of what the decision maker was doing.

Once the fixation sequences were validated, they could be used to classify decision makers as primarily by-alternative or primarily by-attribute processors. The majority used by-attribute processing, usually overwhelmingly so. It should be noted again that these results reflect behavior in only a single task environment. Indeed, in the same research report, subjects completed a different task, choosing between two simple gambles with each described only by an amount to be won, $, and a probability of winning, P. Because choosing the better alternative means the one with the higher expected value ($ x P), the process to calculate it requires more by-alternative transitions. Nonetheless, the attraction of by-attribute processing was strong enough that one-half of the subjects used more of it than by-alternative processing. Similar results are reported by Arieli, Ben-Ami, and Rubinstein (2011), Fiedler and Glöckner (2012), and Su et al. (2013). These results illustrate the use of sequences of eye fixations (verified by a prompted retrospective verbal protocol) to reveal decision processes.

Subsequences of eye fixations can also be defined for multiple alternatives when individual attributes are not distinguished. Russo and Rosen (1975) identified pair and triple comparisons by specific fixation sequences. A pair comparison was said to occur when three or more fixations landed on two alternatives (e.g., A-B-A or longer). Similarly, a triple comparison required that three alternatives be fixated in sequence and that at least one of them be refixated (e.g., A-B-C-B or longer). Again, prompted retrospective verbal protocols were used to verify the validity of these interpretations of fixation sequences. Of the patterns interpreted as triple comparisons, 69% received confirmation in the verbal protocol. Of the alternating sequences identified as pair comparisons, the corresponding value was 83%. Both values were judged sufficiently valid. However, longer sequences provided greater assurance of a valid interpretation. For instance, although 83% of pair comparisons were corroborated by statements in the retrospective protocols, when the sequence contained at least four fixations (i.e., A-B-A-B…), the confirmation rate increased to 95%.

As useful as individual fixations may be, it is often sequences of fixations that correspond to the parts of a theoretically proffered process. One traditional JDM question is whether the information that describes the available alternatives is processed by-alternative or by-attribute. Eye fixation sequences seem well suited to providing the needed process data. This claim is even truer when they can be validated by other data, like a verbal report, or by other information acquisition methods, like manual movements (e.g., Johnson, Schulte-Mecklenbeck, & Willemsen, 2008).

Eye Fixations as Complementary Data

Eye fixations are sometimes used to complement other data. For instance, van Gog, Paas, van Merrienboer, and Witte (2005) compared the ability of different kinds of verbal protocols to reveal various aspects of the process of trouble-shooting an electrical circuit. In addition to the obvious concurrent and retrospective protocols, they tested the value of a retrospective protocol cued by a replay of the eye fixations sequence. The results revealed the ability of such a prompted protocol to contain more information and, especially, certain kinds of information such as metacognitive statements like "I am going in the right direction".

Albertazzi (2006) nicely summarizes the results of the joint use of eye fixations and concurrent verbal protocols to elucidate the process of viewing (and describing) artistic pictures. He observes that his subjects tend to:

> make large saccades across the whole picture, picking up information from different locations to support concepts which are distributed across the picture (like "early summer" or "flying insects"). With the increasing cognitive involvement, observers and describers tend to return to certain areas, change their perspective and reformulate or recategorize the scene. It becomes clear that perception of the picture changes over time.
>
> *p. 254*

These conclusions would be more uncertain if either eye fixations or verbal protocols were used alone (see Chapters 22–24 for multimethod approaches).

Sometimes JDM researchers will be fortunate enough that the record of eye fixations by itself will enable tests of predictions. Thus, when the task requires the computation of expected value for simple gambles, the proportion of within-gamble vs between-gamble transitions can verify the predicted computation. However, many other decision processes are more complex, if for no other reason than the complexity of the task itself with multiple alternatives and their components. In these cases, eye fixations may not "speak for themselves" and yield obvious interpretations. Instead, other data may be needed to complement the fixations and complete their interpretation.

Fixations to Monitor Attention

In some experiments it is essential that visual attention conform to an instruction. The simplest requirement is that the gaze remains on a predetermined point (e.g., Liu, Abrams, & Carrasco, 2009). For instance, a constant foveal position is essential when peripheral processing is being studied. Alternatively, it may be important to identify when the eye has moved from an instructed fixation point (e.g., Day, Shyi, & Wang, 2006). Sometimes individuals are instructed not to fixate, or at least not to refixate, parts of a display. To test recognition for an added sequence of digits, Russo, Johnson, and Stephens (1989) needed the digits to be seen only once and not refixated for further processing. Monitoring participants' eye fixations enabled them both to assess compliance and to eliminate violations.

The need to control the locus of visual attention has been eliminated for some tasks by enabling changes in the stimulus display that are controlled by the current fixation, called gaze-contingent stimulus alteration. Consider the common situation of instructing the focus on a specified point in order to reduce peripheral processing. An occluding mask can be placed over all elements of the stimulus that are X° from the current object of regard. The power of such a gaze-contingent mask is that it can be imposed wherever the individual is currently looking. Thus, Jordan, Paterson, and

Kurtev (2009) use it to report a left hemisphere advantage for peripherally presented words (but not for non-words). Similarly, Calvo and Eysenck (2008) tested the impact of emotional words, but only when presented parafoveally. In both studies the important stimulus elements were guaranteed to appear at the designed distance from the fovea by using gaze-contingent software.

Gaze-contingent processing is also used to control attention by allowing only the fixated stimulus to be seen because the rest of the stimulus display is occluded (e.g., Schwedes & Wentura, 2016). Such an apparatus was used to compare a "decision moving window" with both free fixations and manual acquisitions by reporting such attentional characteristics as mean viewing duration, reacquisitions, and an index of by-alterative and by-attribute processing (Franco-Watkins & Johnson, 2011; Franco-Watkins, Davis, & Johnson, 2016; Chapter 7). These researchers reported expected results for mean duration (lowest for free fixations) and reacquisitions (lowest for manual acquisitions), but the less expected finding that the moving window and manual acquisition both exhibited more by-alternative processing than free fixations.

The Contributions of Eye Fixation Data to JDM

While eye fixations are only indicators of external attention, they are rich within that space of observations. That richness allows them to be used in two general ways. First, they can test the predictions of JDM theories whenever those theories include something close to a prediction of attention to visual stimuli. Second, they can help to generate hypotheses about the JDM processes that underlie the observed eye fixations. Researchers naturally want to hypothesize a decision process that is consistent with an observed pattern of eye fixations.

The first JDM theories were drawn from the optimality paradigm of economics and statistics. These tended to be "as if" theories in that they usually did not imply a specific sequence of information acquisitions. Nonetheless, differences in processing, such as by-alternative vs by-attribute, became part of the experimental focus of JDM. Although most often traced via manual acquisition (Payne, 1976), eye fixations were sometimes used to reveal a decision process (Russo & Rosen, 1975).

Researchers who sought process-consistent decision models adapted both sampling and connectionist theories to JDM tasks. As discussed later, both classes of models rely on patterns of attention, so were naturally compatible with testing based on eye fixations.

Testing Heuristics

The empirical test of the optimality models led to the revelation of effort-saving heuristics. Most of those that have received substantial attention do not imply a specific process of information acquisition. Nonetheless, some of these heuristics include an implied process of sequential attention. As an illustration, consider the lexicographic choice rule. The rule begins by comparing all alternatives on the single most important attribute, choosing the one that is best. If one alternative is not superior on that first attribute (i.e., if there is a tie), the rule repeats the search for a superior alternative on the second most important attribute (and then on to the third and so on). Brandstätter, Gigerenzer, and Hertwig (2006) proposed the priority heuristic, which asserts a lexicographic-like order of consideration of the attributes of simple gambles. Using eye fixations, Glöckner and Herbold (2011) showed that choices between gambles did not accord with the priority heuristic, but were better characterized by more compensatory models.

Several heuristics have been proposed for gambles, and these mental shortcuts seem especially appealing as ways to reduce the computational burden of more complex gambles. In such a situation, Venkatraman, Payne, and Huettel (2014) used eye fixations to provide evidence for a heuristic that relies mainly on the probability of winning. These authors are careful to acknowledge that the use of this heuristic depends on the task environment and not to generalize over a range of risky gambles.

Finally, consider the anchoring heuristic (see Turner & Schley, 2016, for a recent review of competing explanations of its causes). Even though the processes underlying the anchoring heuristic are largely internal, might we better understand this heuristic by using two opposing anchors (Russo & Schoemaker, 2002) and the frequency of fixations on each one? Chapman and Johnson's (1999) explanation for anchoring as a biased activation process "predicts that decision makers will give more attention to target features that are like the anchor as compared to features that are different from the anchor" (p. 122). Might such a prediction be testable by recording eye fixations on an appropriate visual display of features? Finally, how much might be learned by using gaze-contingent software to alter a display? For instance, might the exposure to the anchor itself (Mussweiler & Englich, 2005) be controlled or an anchor be changed after it had been fixated? In summary, might the availability of eye-tracking, including gaze-contingent manipulation of the stimulus, prompt experimental designs and visual displays that can provide a new class of tests?

Models Predicting Visual Attention

A class of models emerged in the psychology of perceptual choice that assumed repeated sampling (both discrete and continuous) of stimulus elements (Ratcliff, 1978; Ratcliff & McKoon, 2008). These sampling models became the drift diffusion process of decision field theory (Busemeyer & Townsend, 1993; Roe, Busemeyer, & Townsend, 2001; Mullett & Stewart, 2016; see especially the attention drift diffusion models of Krajbich, Armel, & Rangel, 2010; Fisher, 2017). They also formed the basis of decision by sampling theory (Stewart, Chater, & Brown, 2006). These models propose a more or less continuous process of evidence accumulation as attention is devoted to the elements of the available alternatives. This attention then drives the development of a relative preference until sufficient to justify the commitment to one alternative (i.e., to a decision). For instance, Krajbich et al. use the eye fixations to each of two options (food items) to drive a model of the differentiation of value over time.

The sampling models have the distinct advantage of separating stimulus encoding and response execution from the core process of evaluation of the decision alternatives. However, the assumption that looking at a unit of information drives its perceived value may not hold for any but the simplest or most familiar information. Ratcliff and McKoon (2008) warns that the sampling/diffusion:

> model should be applied only to relatively fast two-choice decisions (mean RTs less than about 1000 to 1500 msec) and only to decisions that are a single-stage decision process (as opposed to the multiple-stage processes that might be involved in, for example, reasoning tasks).
>
> *p. 875*

A second class of models that imply processes of information acquisition relies on parallel constraint satisfaction and postulates a spread of activation through a semantic network. The units of decision-relevant information are nodes in that network. Attention to a node increases its activation which, in turn, spreads to activate the nodes connected to it (Kunda & Thagard, 1996; Glöckner & Betsch, 2008). Stewart, Hermens, and Matthews (2016) found that eye fixation patterns in the choice between simple gambles were inconsistent with decision field theory, decision by sampling, and the parallel constraint satisfaction (connectionist) model (see also Mullet & Stewart, 2016). Their work will certainly not be the last word on tests of these process models, but it serves to illustrate the value of eye fixations in testing JDM theories that make predictions at the level of information acquisition.

Eye Fixations for Discovery of JDM Processes

As a second contribution to JDM research, an observed sequence of eye fixations can be used to reveal the cognitive processes associated with a decision. As one illustration of such discovery, Russo and Dosher (1983) used eye fixations in a 2 x 3 alternative-by-attribute display to reveal the "majority of confirming dimensions" heuristic (see also Riedl, Brandstätter, & Roithmayr, 2008). This shortcut was designed to ease the computational burden of trading off the values on one attribute for those on another. Each attribute's difference was approximated to +1 or -1, where the sign pointed to one or the other option. Given three attributes, one alternative always had two of them favoring it. That option then became the majority choice. The majority of attributes heuristic was revealed by a combination of eye fixations and verbal protocols.

More generally, eye fixation sequences reveal the attention component of a JDM process. Even if there is no theory that predicts such detailed behavior, the sequences of information acquisition (in the particular decision environment) may suggest elements of the underlying process. Further, if those fixation sequences are used in conjunction with a verbal protocol, and especially to prompt a retrospective verbal protocol, an even more plausible understanding of the decision process may be revealed.

The role of eye fixations in discovering (and testing) JDM theories raises the broad question of what process-based JDM theories should look like. More specifically, can theories of decision making become specific enough to predict eye fixations? Indeed, do they need to become so specific about information acquisition? Lest this requirement seem overwhelming, note that researchers need not account for every individual fixation, but only groups of fixations that form plausible cognitive units like pair comparisons. Although this chapter is not the place to attempt to address the desired nature of JDM theories (but see Chapters 23–24), there is an increasing supply of theoretical frameworks and empirical methods that offer the concepts and data for such theories.

To take just one example of a conceptual framework, JDM theories could be based on goals. These might include either the full set of goals that a decision maker seeks to achieve (e.g., van Osselaer et al., 2005; van Osselaer & Janiszewski, 2012) or the intermediate process goals and actions needed to complete the decision process (e.g., Payne, Bettman, & Johnson, 1993; Russo, Carlson, Meloy, & Yong, 2008). The challenge is to be able to link the use of a specific goal to a pattern of information processing via eye fixations. For instance, if a goal is consistency between a current preference and new information (Chaxel & Russo, 2015), might the researcher observe a pattern of fixations and refixations between the two visual elements, much like a pair comparison?

There are also new sources of process data, especially neurophysiological observations. Among the most prominent and recently applied to JDM questions are fMRI records (e.g., Plassmann, O'Doherty, & Rangel, 2007; Vaidya & Fellows, 2015; Chapter 15) and EEGs (Harris, Adolphs, Camerer, & Rangel, 2011; Venkatraman et al., 2015; Chapter 14). These methods literally link what the eyes see with what is in the head. This is not to say that the interpretation of these data is straightforward; it is not. However, they provide additional insight into the processes underlying JDM. As the application of these data to JDM tasks increases, so should their contribution.

Perception-Driven Preference

What is the power of a stimulus to influence preference? We accept that preference often drives perception in that people look more at what they prefer. However, might the opposite hold, namely that inducing people to look at a stimulus longer or more frequently increases their preference for it?

A weak version of this question, whether drawing a fixation to a target can activate its value, is easily answered in the affirmative. For instance, Lwin, Morrin, Chong, and Goh (2015) show that the combination of an olfactory stimulus and a learned semantic association to an object in an advertisement can direct the gaze to that object. That gaze led to greater recall and intent to purchase the advertised product. Similarly, Towal, Mormann, and Koch (2013) use a drift diffusion model to show that the visual saliency of food items in a crowded, multi-alternative display contributes significantly to choice. However, the more difficult question is not whether an element's visual characteristics can draw attention and thereby influence its value but whether, once an object is fixated, its value can be made to increase (or decrease) by forcing a longer duration of that fixation.

There is work, now a half century old, which reveals the power of familiarity to facilitate preference (Zajonc, 1968; 1980; see also Bornstein & D'Agostino, 1994; Winkielman & Cacioppo, 2001). Might a similar effect hold for controlled viewing time? Shimojo, Simion, Shimojo, and Scheier (2003) had participants choose their more preferred of two faces while recording eye fixations. Unsurprisingly, the preferred face received more fixations, which is the usual phenomenon of preference driving attention (as measured by eye fixations). In their second study, however, exposure to each face was controlled. They found that the face that received longer (forced) exposure was also preferred. The longer exposure was 900 msec and the shorter was 300 msec (both received multiple repetitions/trials). Thus, the usual causal direction was reversed and attention (forced visual exposure) drove preference. Armel, Beaumel, and Rangel (2008) report a similar result for food preferences when brief (300 and 900 msec) repeated stimulus exposure was controlled. Glaholt and Reingold (2011) also found an effect of longer (400 msec) vs shorter (200 msec) exposures on the preference for grayscale photographs. However, they explained their result not as attention driving preference but as the inability of observers to draw sufficient information from the briefer exposures. Finally, Pärnamets et al. (2015) randomly terminated a decision involving a complex moral judgment on one of the alternatives. They found that the alternative that was being fixated when the trial was arbitrarily ended was chosen significantly more often.

As interesting as these results are, they are not accepted by all. Orquin and Loose's (2013) review of the role of eye fixations in decisions concluded:

> that gaze allocation does not have a direct causal effect on preference formation, contrary to the predictions of the gaze cascade hypothesis (Shimojo, Simion, Shimojo, & Scheier, 2003) and the attention Drift Diffusion Model (Krajbich, Armel, & Rangel, 2010).

The reluctance to publish null replications may contribute to the visibility of results like those of Shimojo et al. and others. However, for one counterexample to the publishing of null results, Morii and Sakagami (2015) report the failure to replicate the result reported by Pärnamets et al. (2015). The ability of attention to drive preference is an intriguing, and to some troubling, JDM phenomenon that will continue to be tested, often by controlling attention via eye fixations.

Looking and Thinking

While the detail and validity of eye fixations are rightly unquestioned, they frequently must be interpreted in order to test hypotheses in JDM research. Said differently, eye fixations show where people are looking, but not what they are thinking. For instance, it is well-known that people, even professionals, can fixate a target and still not "see" it. Recall that eye fixations reveal that radiologists reading lung X-rays sometimes fixate a cancer-indicating lesion yet do not report having detected it (Mello-Thoms, Nodine, & Kundel, 2002). There seems no doubt that the radiologist acquired the visual information, but did so without the cognitive recognition of a lesion. Almost all judgments and decisions with material consequences require more than a few seconds of deliberation. As essential as information acquisition is in these decisions, it is the internal processes of what people do with the acquired information that is the greater determinant of the chosen alternative.

Even the smallest units of eye fixation data, single fixations, do not necessarily provide their own clear interpretations. Is the first fixation on a decision alternative devoted only to information acquisition? Instead, might a previously fixated alternative be recalled and a comparison process with the new alternative begun during this initial fixation?

Consider again the last fixation on an alternative during a decision. Is it an indication of an explicit elimination, or does it only reflect that more consideration of other alternatives is still needed while preserving the option of returning to reconsider the one currently fixated? Recall the simulated supermarket shelves displaying 16 products, with the chosen one announced audibly (Russo & Leclerc, 1994). In over half of these choices, products were fixated after the choice was announced. These post-announcement fixations were rarely on the chosen product (8%) and often on a product never before fixated (33%). During some of the post-announcement fixations, the viewed product must have been compared to the announced choice (held in working memory). More generally, many internal operations might be performed on the combination of the currently fixated object and those previously seen and now recalled. Franco-Watkins, Davis, and Johnson (2016) find not only a role for working memory in their estimation task, but also show that individual differences in working memory span can influence task performance. Finally, it should be recognized that the use of gaze-contingent occlusion of non-foveated viewing increases the assurance that the object of regard is also the object of attention.

Sometimes the challenge is not the absence of an interpretation of eye fixations, but the plausibility of two or more interpretations of the same observation. Recall the fixation pattern A-B-A, where each different letter signifies a fixation on a different alternative (Russo & Rosen, 1975). Verbal protocol data confirmed that most of these patterns reflected a pair comparison. However, these comparisons might have been used for two different purposes, either learning about the two alternatives' relative value or eliminating one of them. The durations of each such comparison revealed that these pair comparisons were used only to learn more about the relative values of the two alternatives. A general conclusion is that knowing where decision makers are looking does not assure that the researcher knows what they are thinking—as inconvenient as it may be for the use of eye fixations to test theory-driven predictions.

It is easy to ask too much of the record of eye fixations during a decision. As complete and non-intrusive as the fixation sequence can be, it is not self-interpreting. As much as researchers would like to assign a first fixation solely to information acquisition or the last fixation on an alternative to its implicit elimination, such straightforward interpretations are not always valid. There remains the challenge of learning what decision makers are thinking. Returning to the sampling and connectionist models that use eye fixations as measure of attention, they assume that a fixation's duration activates whatever is seen. Although this may often be true, surely there are important instances where the acquired information is not merely activated but is re-evaluated and possibly rejected. When evaluating the attributes of two possible restaurants for a romantic dinner, the decision maker may suddenly recall any number of facts that could affect their relative evaluation.

For instance, maybe the guest has most recently eaten the same food that is one restaurant's signature dish, making that option less attractive; or the realization that the weather is predicted to be cold and rainy suggests that the convenience of parking should be given greater weight. The inconvenient truth is that thinking about acquired information can, and must, mean more than its straightforward re-activation. Eye fixations may need to be augmented by other data that can complement them with respect to what decision makers are doing with the information that the sequence of eye fixations has provided.

Conclusion

Eye fixations are the primary way that humans acquire information. Improved technology has made it easier to record and analyze the sequence of fixations during many JDM tasks. Despite many applications of eye fixation recording in decisions, the method is still underutilized. One reason has been the limited number of JDM theories that require such detailed information acquisition data to test them. That dearth is changing as theories found elsewhere in psychology are being adapted to JDM phenomena and as the analysis of eye fixations leads to the development of process-based theories of other JDM phenomena. A second cause of eye fixations' underutilization is that these data reveal where decision makers are looking, but not necessarily what they are thinking. This latter barrier is being overcome in many JDM tasks by collecting additional data, such as some form of verbal protocol.

Notes

1   Civilization is sometimes defined as based on the presence of writing. For instance, Merriam-Webster's online dictionary defines civilization as "the stage of cultural development at which writing and the keeping of written records is attained".
2   English uses the original French word, saccade, sometimes preserving its French pronunciation, with the two vowel sounds like the "a" in yard, and sometimes anglicizing it to a final long "a" as in lemonade.
3   Recent works suggests that processing of information occurs not only during a saccade but even during such other movements as smooth pursuit. Kowler (2011) notes "the involvement of cues, signals, plans, attention and expectations in the preparation of pursuit are beginning to blur the classical line between pursuit and saccades" (p. 1465).
4   Interestingly, the opposite is not true. That is, in the "looks-at-nothing" phenomenon, a saccade to an empty area can facilitate recall of what was at that location (Staudte & Altmann, 2017).
5   Apparatus based on the most popular pupil-centered corneal reflections technique is manufactured inter alia by Applied Science Laboratories (www.asleyetracking.com), by Tobii Pro (www.tobiipro.com), and by Eye Tribe, which sells an inexpensive eye tracker and was purchased in 2016 by a Facebook-owned company, Oculus Rift. Typical sampling rates for systems begin at 60 Hz but rise to 500–1000 Hz with some high-fidelity systems. Spatial accuracy is typically $0.5°$ during more optimal tracking conditions (e.g., Gibaldi, Vanegas, Bex, & Maiello, 2017). However, accuracy and precision can vary depending on test and participant variables such as lighting, the range of movement, viewing angles, and distance. There are also head-mounted systems designed as lightweight, wearable eye glasses with a small recording unit that the participant wears for powering the unit and collecting and storing the data (e.g., Tobii Pro Glasses 2; www. tobiipro.com/product-listing/tobii-pro-glasses-2/). These wearable eye-tracking systems usually sacrifice some degree of temporal resolution, but enable applications in more natural environments. A sense of the growing variety of eye-tracking apparatus can be gathered from comparisons like that of Wang, Mulvey, Pelz, and Holmqvist (2017) who tested 12 different commercial eye trackers. The accuracy of even the least expensive eye trackers has been demonstrated by Titz, Scholz, and Sedlmeier (2017).
6   The technique of the moving window was used for decades prior to the more sophisticated gaze-contingent capability (e.g., Poulton, 1962).

Recommended Reading List

- Duchowski (2017): offers broad and deep views of the methods and apparatus for recording and analyzing eye movements.
- Liversedge, Gilchrist, and Everling (2011): *The Oxford Handbook of Eye Movements* covers eye movements and related methods.
- van Gompel, Fischer, Murray, and Hill (2007): they provide comprehensive coverage from the history, physiology, and modeling of eye fixations to their application to reading, scene perception, and natural environments.
- Henderson (2006): chapter reviews the role of eye fixations in cognitive science broadly, with emphasis on the technology of eye movement measurement.

References

Albertazzi, L. (2006). *Visual Thought.* Amsterdam, NL: John Benjamins.

Alpern, M. (1962). Movements of the eyes. In H. Davson (Ed.), *The eye* (Vol. 3, pp. 7–26). New York, NY: Academic Press.

Arieli, A., Ben-Ami, Y., & Rubinstein, A. (2011). Tracking decision makers under uncertainty. *American Economic Journal: Microeconomics, 3*(4), 68–76.

Armel, K. C., Beaumel, A., & Rangel, A. (2008). Biasing simple choices by manipulating relative visual attention. *Judgment and Decision Making, 3*(5), 396–403.

Becker, W. (1991). Saccades. In R. H. S. Carpenter (Ed.), *Eye movements, vision and visual dysfunction* (Vol. 8, pp. 95–137). Boca Raton, FL: CRC Press.

Benfatto, M. N., Seimyr, G. O., Ygge, J., Pansell, T., Rydberg, A., & Jacobson, C. (2016). Screening for dyslexia using eye-tracking during reading. *PloS ONE, 11*(12), e0165508.

Bertera, J. H., & Rayner, K. (2000). Eye movements and the span of effective stimulus in visual search. *Perception & Psychophysics, 62*, 576–585.

Blingnaut, P. (2008). Fixation identification: The optimum threshold for a dispersion algorithm. *Attention, Perception & Psychophysics, 71*, 881–895.

Böckenholt, U., & Hynan, L. S. (1994). Caveats on a process-tracing measure and a remedy. *Journal of Behavioral Decision Making, 7*, 103–117.

Bornstein, R. F., & D'Agostino, P. R. (1994). The attribution and discounting of perceptual fluency: Preliminary tests of a perceptual fluency/attributional model of the mere exposure effect. *Social Cognition, 12*(2), 103–128.

Boutet, I., Lemieux, C. L., Goulet, M. A., & Collin, C. A. (2017). Faces elicit different scanning patterns depending on task demands. *Attention, Perception, and Psychophysics, 79*(4), 1050–1063.

Bradshaw, J. L., Nettleton, N. C., Wilson, L., & Nathan, G. (1984). A moving video window or a mask yoked to eye movements: Experiments on letters, words and biological movement with prolonged hemifield stimulation. *International Journal of Neuroscience, 25*, 81–98.

Brand-Gruwel, S., Kammerer, Y., van Meeuwen, L., & van Gog, T. (2017). Source evaluation of domain experts and novices during Web search. *Journal of Computer Assisted Learning, 33*(3), 234–251.

Brandstätter, E., Gigerenzer, G., & Hertwig, R. (2006). The priority heuristic: Making choices without trade-offs. *Psychological Review, 113*, 409–432.

Busemeyer, J. R., & Townsend, J. T. (1993). Decision field theory: A dynamic cognition approach to decision making. *Psychological Review, 100*, 432–459.

Callan, M. J., Ferguson, H. J., & Bindemann, M. (2013). Eye movements to audiovisual scenes reveal expectations of a just world. *Journal of Experimental Psychology: General, 142*(1), 34–40.

Calvo, M. G., & Eysenck, M. W. (2008). Affective significance enhances covert attention: Roles of anxiety and word familiarity. *The Quarterly Journal of Experimental Psychology, 61*(11), 1669–1686.

Carpenter, R. H. S. (1988). Saccades. In R. H. S. Carpenter (Ed.), *Movement of the eyes* (2nd ed., pp. 69–111). London, UK: Pion Limited.

Chapman, G. B., & Johnson, E. J. (1999). Anchoring, activation, and the construction of values. *Organizational Behavior and Human Decision Processes, 79*(2), 115–153.

Chaxel, S., & Russo, J. E. (2015). Cognitive consistency: Cognitive and motivational perspectives. In E. A. Wilhelms & V. F. Reyna (Eds.), *Neuroeconomics, judgment, and decision making* (pp. 29–48). New York, NY: Psychology Press.

Day, R. F., Shyi, G. C. W., & Wang, J. C. (2006). The effect of flash banners on multiattribute decision making: Distractor or source of arousal? *Psychology & Marketing, 23*(5), 369–382.

Delabarre, E. B. (1898). A method of recording eye-movements. *American Journal of Psychology, 9*(4), 572–574.

Droll, J. A., & Hayhoe, M. M. (2007). Trade-offs between gaze and working memory use. *Journal of Experimental Psychology: Human Perception and Performance, 33*(6), 1352–1365.

Duchowski, A. T. (2017). *Eye Tracking Methodology: Theory and Practice.* New York, NY: Springer.

Duchowski, A. T., Cournia, N., & Murphy, H. (2004). Gaze-contingent displays: A review. *Cyberpsychology, Behavior, and Social Networking, 7*(6), 621–634.

Fiedler, S., & Glöckner, A. (2012). The dynamics of decision making in risky choice: An eye-tracking analysis. *Frontiers in Psychology, 3,* 1–18.

Fischer, P. M., Richards, J. W., Berman, E. J., & Krugman, D. M. (1989). Recall and eye tracking study of adolescents viewing tobacco advertisements. *Journal of the American Medical Association, 261*(1), 84–89.

Fisher, G. (2017). An attentional drift diffusion model over binary-attribute choice. *Cognition, 168,* 34–45.

Franco-Watkins, A. M., & Johnson, J. G. (2011). Decision moving window: Using eye tracking to examine decision processes. *Behavior Research Methods, 43*(3), 853–863.

Franco-Watkins, A. M., Davis, M. E., & Johnson, J. G. (2016). The ticking time bomb: Using eye-tracking methodology to capture attentional processing during gradual time constraints. *Attention Perception and Psychophysics, 78*(8), 2363–2372.

Friedrich, M., Russwinkel, N., & Mohlenbrink, C. (2017). A guideline for integrating dynamic areas of interests in existing set-up for capturing eye movement: Looking at moving aircraft. *Behavior Research Methods, 49*(3), 822–834.

Gibaldi, A., Vanegas, M., Bex, P. J., & Maiello, G. (2017). Evaluation of the Tobii EyeX eye tracking controller and Matlab toolkit for research. *Behavior Research Methods, 49*(3), 923–946.

Glaholt, M. G., & Reingold, E. M. (2011). Eye movement monitoring as a process tracing methodology in decision making research. *Journal of Neuroscience, Psychology, and Economics, 4*(2), 125–146.

Glaholt, M. G., Rayner, K., & Reingold, E. M. (2012). The mask-onset delay paradigm and the availability of central and peripheral visual information during scene viewing. *Journal of Vision, 12*(1), 1–19.

Glöckner, A., & Betsch, T. (2008). Modeling option and strategy choices with connectionist networks: Towards an integrative model of automatic and deliberative decision making. *Judgment and Decision Making, 3*(3), 215–228.

Glöckner, A., & Herbold, A. K. (2011). An eye-tracking in risky decisions: Evidence for compensatory strategies based on automatic processes. *Journal of Behavioral Decision Making, 24*(1), 71–98.

Harris, A., Adolphs, R., Camerer, C., & Rangel, A. (2011). Dynamic construction of stimulus values in the ventromedial prefrontal cortex. *PloS ONE, 6*(6), e21074.

Henderson, J. M. (2006). Eye movements. In C. Senior, T. Russell, & M. S. Gazzaniga (Eds.), *Methods in mind* (pp. 171–191). Cambridge, MA: MIT Press.

Henderson, J. M. (2017). Gaze control as prediction. *Trends in Cognitive Sciences, 21*(1), 15–23.

Hessels, R. S., Kemner, C., van den Boomen, C., & Hooge, I. T. (2016). The area-of-interest problem in eyetracking research: A noise-robust solution for face and sparse stimuli. *Behavior Research Methods, 48*(4), 1694–1712.

Holmqvist, K., Nyström, M., Andersson, R., Dewhurst, R., Jarodzka, H., & van de Weijer, J. (2011). *Eye Tracking: A Comprehensive Guide to Methods and Measures.* Oxford, UK: Oxford University Press.

Hsiao, J. W., & Cottrell, G. (2008). Two fixations suffice in face recognition. *Psychological Science, 19*(10), 998–1006.

Irwin, D. E. (1998). Lexical processing during saccadic eye movements. *Cognitive Psychology, 36*(1), 1–27.

Jahn, G., & Braatz, J. (2014). Memory indexing of sequential symptom processing in diagnostic reasoning. *Cognitive Psychology, 68*(5), 59–97.

Janiszewski, C. (1998). The influence of display characteristics on visual exploratory search behavior. *Journal of Consumer Research, 25*(3), 290–301.

Johnson, E. J., Schulte-Mecklenbeck, M., & Willemsen, M. (2008). Process models deserve process data: Comment on E. Brandstätter, G. Gigerenzer, & R. Hertwig (2006). *Psychological Review, 115*(1), 263–272.

Jordan, T. R., Paterson, K. B., & Kurtev, S. (2009). Reevaluating split-fovea processing in word recognition: Hemispheric dominance, retinal location, and the word-nonword effect. *Cognitive, Affective & Behavioral Neuroscience, 9*(1), 113–21.

Karslake, J. S. (1940). The Purdue eye-camera: A practical apparatus for studying the attention value of advertisements. *Journal of Applied Psychology, 24*, 417–440.

Kim, B. E., Seligman, D., & Kable, J. W. (2012). Preference reversals in decision making under risk are accompanied by changes in attention to different attributes. *Frontiers in Neuroscience, 6*, 109.

Kowler, E. (1995). Eye movements. In S. Kosslyn (Ed.), *An invitation to cognitive science* (Vol. 2, pp. 215–265). Cambridge, MA: MIT Press.

Kowler, E. (2011). Eye movements: The past 25 years. *Vision Research, 51*(13), 1457–1483.

Krajbich, I., Armel, C., & Rangel, A. (2010). Visual fixations and the computation and comparison of value in simple choice. *Nature Neuroscience, 13*(10), 1292–1298.

Kunda, Z., & Thagard, P. (1996). Forming impressions from stereotypes, traits, and behaviors: A parallel-constraint satisfaction theory. *Psychological Review, 103*, 284–308.

Kundel, H. L., & Nodine, C. F. (1978). Studies of eye movements and visual search in radiology. In J. W. Senders, D. F. Fisher, & R. A. Monty (Eds.), *Eye movements and the higher psychological functions* (pp. 317–328). New York, NY: Erlbaum.

Law, B., Atkins, M. S., Kirkpatrick, A. E., Lomax, A. J., & Mackenzie, C. L. (2004). Eye gaze patterns differentiate novice and experts in a virtual laparoscopic surgery training environment. In *Proceedings of the 2004 symposium on eye tracking research and applications* (pp. 41–48). ACM.

Lee, J. D. (2009). Can technology get your eyes back on the road? *Science, 324*, 344–346.

Lichtenstein, S., & Slovic, P. (1971). Reversals of preference between bids and choices in gambling decisions. *Journal of Experimental Psychology, 89*(1), 46–55.

Liu, T., Abrams, J., & Carrasco, M. (2009). Voluntary attention enhances contrast appearance. *Psychological Science, 20*(3), 354–362.

Liversedge, S. P., Gilchrist, I., & Everling, S. (2011). *The Oxford Handbook of Eye Movements.* Oxford, UK: Oxford University Press.

Lohse, G. L. (1997). Consumer eye movement patterns on yellow pages advertising. *Journal of Advertising, 26*(1), 61–73.

Lohse, G. L., & Wu, D. J. (2001). Eye movement patterns on Chinese yellow pages advertising. *Electronic Markets, 11*(2), 87–96.

Lwin, M. O., Morrin, M., Chong, C. S. T, & Goh, S. X. (2015). Odor semantics and visual cues: What we smell impacts where we look, what we remember, and what we want to buy. *Journal of Behavioral Decision Making, 29*(2–3), 336–350.

Maxcey-Richard, A. M., & Hollingworth, A. (2013). The strategic retention of task-relevant objects in visual working memory. *Journal of Experimental Psychology: Learning, Memory, and Cognition, 39*(3), 760–772.

Malcolm, G. L., Groen, I. I. A., & Baker, C. I. (2016). Making sense of real-world scenes. *Trends in Cognitive Science, 20*(11), 843–856.

Matin, E. (1974). Saccadic suppression: A review and an analysis. *Psychological Bulletin, 81*, 899–917.

McConkie, G. W., & Rayner, K. (1975). The span of the effective stimulus during a fixation in reading. *Perception & Psychophysics, 17*, 578–86.

McNamara, J. J. (1940). A new method for testing advertising effectiveness through eye movement photography. *The Psychological Record, 4*(26), 399–460.

Mello-Thoms, C., Nodine, C. F., & Kundel, H. L. (2002). What attracts the eye to the location of missed and reported breast cancers? In *Proceedings of the 2002 symposium on eye tracking research & applications* (pp. 111–117). ACM.

Miellet, S., O'Donnell, P. J., & Sereno, S. C. (2009). Parafoveal magnification: Visual acuity does not modulate the perceptual span in reading. *Psychological Science, 20*(6), 721–728.

Morii, M., & Sakagami, T. (2015). The effect of gaze-contingent stimulus elimination on preference judgments. *Frontiers in Psychology, 6,* 1–8.

Morrison, R. E. (1984). Manipulation of stimulus onset delay in reading: Evidence for parallel programming of saccades. *Journal of Experimental Psychology: Human Perception and Performance, 10,* 667–682.

Mullet, T. L., & Stewart, N. (2016). Implications of visual attention for models of preferential choice. *Decision, 3*(4), 231–253.

Mussweiler, T., & Englich, B. (2005). Subliminal anchoring: Judgmental consequences and underlying mechanisms. *Organizational Behavior and Human Decision Processes, 98,* 133–143.

Nuthmann, A. (2017). Fixation duration in scene viewing: Modeling the effects of local image features, oculomotor parameters, and task. *Psychonomic Bulletin and Review, 24*(2), 370–392.

Orquin, J. L., & Loose, S. M. (2013). Attention and choice: A review of eye movements in decision making. *Acta Psychologica, 144,* 190–206.

Pärnamets, P., Johansson, P., Hall, L., Balkenius, C., Spivey, M. J., & Richardson, D. C. (2015). Biasing moral decisions by exploiting the dynamics of eye gaze. *Proceedings of the National Academy of Sciences, 112*(13), 4170–4175.

Payne, J. W. (1976). Task complexity and contingent processing in decision making: An information search and protocol analysis. *Organizational Behavior and Human Performance, 16,* 366–387.

Payne, J. W., Bettman, J. R., & Johnson, E. J. (1993). *The Adaptive Decision Maker.* Cambridge, MA: Cambridge University Press.

Pieters, R., & Warlop, L. (1999). Visual attention during brand choice: The impact of time pressure and task motivation. *International Journal of Research in Marketing, 16,* 1–16.

Pieters, R., & Wedel, M. (2007). Information of eye movements for visual marketing: Six cornerstones. In M. Wedel & R. Pieters (Eds.), *Visual marketing: From attention to action* (pp. 43–71). New York, NY: Psychology Press.

Plassmann, H., O'Doherty, J., & Rangel, A. (2007). Orbitofrontal cortex encodes willingness to pay in everyday economic transactions. *Journal of Neuroscience, 27*(37), 9984–9988.

Poulton, E. C. (1962). Peripheral vision, refractoriness, and eye movements in fast oral reading. *British Journal of Psychology, 53*(4), 409–419.

Radach, R., & Kennedy, A. (2004). Theoretical perspectives on eye movements in reading: Past controversies, current issues, and an agenda for future research. *European Journal of Cognitive Psychology, 16*(1–2), 3–26.

Radach, R., Reilly, R., & Inhoff, A. (2007). Models of oculomotor control in reading: Toward a theoretical foundation of current debates. In R. P. G. van Gompel, M. H. Fischer, W. S. Murray, & R. L. Hill (Eds.), *Eye movements: A window on the brain* (pp. 237–269). London, UK: Elsevier.

Ratcliff, R. (1978). A theory of memory retrieval. *Psychological Review, 85,* 59–108.

Ratcliff, R., & McKoon, G. (2008). The Diffusion Decision Model: Theory and data for two-choice decision tasks. *Neural Computation, 20*(4), 873–922.

Rayner, K. (1975). The perceptual span and peripheral cues in reading. *Cognitive Psychology, 7,* 65–81.

Rayner, K., & Duffy, S. D. (1986). Lexical complexity and fixation times in reading: Effects of word frequency, verb complexity and lexical ambiguity. *Memory and Cognition, 14,* 191–201.

Rayner, K., & Liversedge, S. P. (2011). Linguistic and cognitive influences on eye movements during reading. In S. P. Liversedge, I. Gilchrist, & S. Everling (Eds.), *The Oxford handbook of eye movements* (pp. 751–766). Oxford, UK: Oxford University Press.

Rayner, K., Smith, T. J., Malcolm, G. L., & Henderson, J. M. (2009). Eye movements and visual encoding during scene perception. *Psychological Science, 20*(1), 6–10.

Reichle, E. D., Pollatsek, A., & Rayner, K. (2007). Modeling the effects of lexical ambiguity during reading. In R. P. G. van Gompel, M. H. Fischer, W. S. Murray, & R. L. Hill (Eds.), *Eye movements: A window on the brain* (pp. 271–292). London, UK: Elsevier.

Reingold, E. M., & Charness, N. (2005). Perception in chess: Evidence from eye movements. In G. Underwood (Ed.), *Cognitive processes in eye guidance* (pp. 325–353). Oxford, UK: Oxford University Press.

Reisen, N., Hoffrage, U., & Mast, F. W. (2008). Identifying decision strategies in a consumer choice situation. *Judgment and Decision Making, 3,* 641–658.

Riedl, R., Brandstätter, E., & Roithmayr, F. (2008). Identifying decision strategies: A process and outcome-based classification method. *Behavior Research Methods, 40*(3), 795–807.

Roe, R. M., Busemeyer, J. R., & Townsend, J. T. (2001). Multialternative decision field theory: A dynamic connectionist model of decision making. *Psychological Review, 108*(2), 370–392.

Rosen, L. D. (1975). *Memory influence during reprocessing.* Doctoral dissertation, University of California, San Diego, CA.

Russo, J. E. (1978). Adaptation of cognitive processes to the eye movement system. In J. W. Senders, D. F. Fisher, & R. A. Monty (Eds.), *Eye movements and the higher psychological functions* (pp. 89–112). New York, NY: Erlbaum.

Russo, J. E., Carlson, K. A., Meloy, M. G., & Yong, K. (2008). The goal of consistency as a cause of information distortion. *Journal of Experimental Psychology: General, 137*(3), 456–470.

Russo, J. E., & Dosher, B. A. (1983). Strategies for multiattribute binary choice. *Journal of Experimental Psychology: Learning, Memory, and Cognition, 9*(4), 676–696.

Russo, J. E., Johnson, E. J., & Stephens, D. L. (1989). The validity of verbal protocols. *Memory & Cognition, 17*(6), 759–769.

Russo, J. E., & Leclerc, F. (1994). An eye-fixation analysis of choice processes for consumer nondurables. *Journal of Consumer Research, 21*(2), 274–290.

Russo, J. E., & Rosen, L. D. (1975). An eye fixation analysis of multialternative choice. *Memory & Cognition, 3*(3), 267–276.

Russo, J. E., & Schoemaker, P. (2002). *Winning Decisions: Getting it Right the First Time.* New York, NY: Doubleday.

Schwedes, C., & Wentura, D. (2016). Through the eyes to memory: Fixation durations as an early indirect index of concealed knowledge. *Memory and Cognition, 44*(8), 1244–1258.

Senju, A., Southgate, V., White, S., & Frith, U. (2009). Mindblind eyes: Absence of spontaneous theory of mind in Asperger syndrome. *Science, 325,* 883–885.

Sereno, S. C., O'Donnell, P. J., & Rayner, K. (2006). Eye movements and lexical ambiguity resolution: Investigating the subordinate-bias effect. *Journal of Experimental Psychology: Human Perception and Performance, 32*(2), 335–350.

Shams, P., Wastlund, E., & Witell, L. (2014). Revisiting Russo and Leclerc. In *Proceedings of the 2014 symposium on eye tracking research and applications* (pp. 389–392). ACM.

Sheridan, H., & Reingold, E. M. (2014). Expert vs novice differences in the detection of relevant information during a chess game: evidence from eye movements. *Frontiers in Psychology, 5,* 1–6.

Shi, S. W., Wedel, M., & Pieters, F. M. G. (2013). Information acquisition during online decision making: A model-based exploration using eye-tracking data, *Management Science, 59*(5), 1009–1026.

Shimojo, S., Simion, C., Shimojo, E., & Scheier, C. (2003). Gaze bias both reflects and influences preference. *Nature Neuroscience, 6*(12), 1317–1322.

Slovic, P., & Lichtenstein, S. (1983). Preference reversals: A broader perspective. *American Economic Review, 73,* 596–605.

Spivey, M., Richardson, D. C., & Dale, R. (2009). Movements of eye and hand in language and cognition. In E. Morsella, J. Bargh, & P. M. Gollwitzer (Eds.), *The psychology of action* (Vol. 2, pp. 225–249). New York, NY: Oxford University Press.

Staudte, M., & Altmann, G. T. M. (2017). Recalling what was where when seeing nothing there. *Psychonomic Bulletin and Review,* 24(2), 400–407.

Stewart, N., Chater, N., & Brown, G. D. A. (2006). Decision by sampling. *Cognitive Psychology, 53,* 1–26.

Stewart, N., Hermens, F., & Matthews, W. J. (2016). Eye movements in risky choice. *Journal of Behavioral Decision Making, 29*(2–3), 116–136.

Su, Y., Rao, L. L., Sun, H. Y., Du, X. L., Li, X. S., & Li, S. (2013). Is making a risky based on a weighting and adding process? An eye-tracking investigation. *Journal of Experimental Psychology: Learning, Memory, and Cognition, 39*(6), 1765–1770.

Tatler, B. W., & Kuhn, G. (2007). Don't look now: The magic of misdirection. In R. van Gompel, M. Fischer, W. Murray, & R. Hill (Eds.), *Eye movement research: Insights into mind and brain* (pp. 697–714). Amsterdam, NL: Elsevier.

Thiele, A., Henning, M., Buischik, K., & Hoffman, P. (2002). Neural mechanisms of saccadic suppression. *Science, 295,* 2460–2462.

Titz, J., Scholz, A., & Sedlmeier, P. (2017). Comparing eye trackers by correlating their eye-metric data. *Behavior Research Methods, 50*(5), 1853–1863.

Towal, R. B., Mormann, M., & Koch, C. (2013). Simultaneous modeling of visual saliency and value computation improves predictions of economic choice. *Proceedings of the National Academy of Science, 110*, 3858–3867.

Turner, B. M., & Schley, D. R. (2016). The anchor integration model: A descriptive model of anchoring effects. *Cognitive Psychology, 90*, 1–47.

Underwood, J. (2005). Novice and expert performance with a dynamic control task: Scanpaths during a computer game. In G. Underwood (Ed.), *Cognitive processes in eye guidance* (pp. 303–324). Oxford, UK: Oxford University Press.

Vaidya, A. R., & Fellows, L. K. (2015). Testing necessary regional frontal contributions to value assessment and fixation-based updating. *Nature Communications, 6*, 1–12.

van Gog, T., Paas, F., van Merrienboer, J. J. G., & Witte, P. (2005). Uncovering the problem-solving process: Cued retrospective reporting versus concurrent and retrospective reporting. *Journal of Experimental Psychology: Applied, 11*(4), 237–244.

van Gompel, R. P. G., Fischer, M. H., Murray, W. S., & Hill, R. L. (2007). *Eye Movements: A Window on the Brain*. London, UK: Elsevier.

van Osselaer, S. M. J., & Janiszewski, C. (2012). A goal-based model of product evaluation and choice. *Journal of Consumer Research, 39*(2), 260–292.

van Osselaer, S. M. J., Ramanathan, S., Cohen, J. B., Dale, J. K., Herr, P. M., Janiszewski, C., … Tavassoli, N. T. (2005). Choice based on goals. *Marketing Letters, 16*(3/4), 335–346.

van Raaij, W. F. (1977). Consumer information processing for different information structures and formats. *Advances in Consumer Research, 4*(1), 176–184.

Venkatraman, V., Dimoka, A., Pavlou, P. A., Vo, K., Hampton, W., Bollinger, B., … Winer, R. S. (2015). Predicting advertising success beyond traditional measures: New insights from neurophysiological methods and market response modeling. *Journal of Marketing Research, 52*(4), 436–452.

Venkatraman, V., Payne, J. W., & Huettel, S. A. (2014). An overall probability of winning heuristic for complex risky decisions: Choice and eye fixation evidence. *Organizational Behavior and Human Decision Processes, 125*(2), 73–87.

Wade, N. J. (2007). Scanning the seen: Vision and the origins of eye-movement research. In R. P. G. van Gompel, M. H. Fischer, W. S. Murray, & R. L. Hill (Eds.), *Eye movements: A window on the brain* (pp. 31–63). London, UK: Elsevier.

Wade, N. J., & Tatler, B. W. (2005). *The moving tablet of the eye: The origins of modern eye movement research*. New York, NY: Oxford University Press.

Wang, D., Mulvey, F. B., Pelz, J. B., & Holmqvist, K. (2017). A study of artificial eyes for the measurement of precision in eye-trackers. *Behavior Research Methods, 49*(3), 947–959.

Wedel, M., & Pieters, R. (2000). Eye fixations on advertisements and memory for brands: A model and findings. *Marketing Science, 19*(4), 297–312.

Winkielman, P., & Cacioppo, J. T. (2001). Mind at ease puts a smile on the face: Psychophysiological evidence that processing facilitation elicits positive affect. *Journal of Personality and Social Psychology, 81*(6), 989–1000.

Yarbus, A. L. (1967). *Eye Movements and Vision*. New York, NY: Plenum Press.

Zajonc, R. B. (1968). Attitudinal effects of mere exposure. *Journal of Personality and Social Psychology Monograph Supplement, 9*(2), 1–27.

Zajonc, R. B. (1980). Feeling and thinking: Preferences need no inferences. *American Psychologist, 35*(2), 151–175.

2

PERVASIVE EYE-TRACKING FOR REAL-WORLD CONSUMER BEHAVIOR ANALYSIS

Andreas Bulling and Michel Wedel

Introduction

Human gaze has long held a particular fascination among researchers and practitioners alike because of its fundamental importance in human communication and interaction as well as its close links to human perception and cognition. A large body of work in the psychological and social sciences as well as in consumer behavior research has shed light on the many different ways in which a wide range of factors influence or are influenced by gaze behavior. Much of this research has been conducted in controlled laboratory settings where users sit behind a computer monitor and look at carefully designed visual stimuli. Real-world consumer behavior has, for a long time, been beyond the reach of gaze behavior research.

Methods to assess consumers' attention, their point of gaze, or the movement of their eyes over time use either sensors placed in the environment (so-called stationary eye-tracking) or worn on the head (so-called mobile eye-tracking). While early eye trackers were intrusive, cumbersome to use, and restricted data collection to short-term recordings in controlled laboratory settings, two recent developments have started to change this. First, mobile eye trackers can now be implemented as lightweight embedded systems, and therefore have become suitable for recordings in mobile daily life settings (Bulling & Gellersen, 2010; Tonsen, Steil, Sugano, & Bulling, 2017)— facilitating recordings over several hours or days and for large groups of users (Bulling, Weichel, & Gellersen, 2013; Pieters & Wedel, 2004; Steil & Bulling, 2015). Second, methods for stationary eye-tracking that only require a single off-the-shelf camera have recently improved considerably and now promise accurate eye-tracking capabilities on the millions of handheld devices, displays deployed in public, and smart appliances at home that increasingly feature integrated cameras (Sugano, Zhang, & Bulling, 2016; Wood & Bulling, 2014; Zhang, Sugano, & Bulling, 2017). Taken together, both advances give rise to a new class of *pervasive eye-tracking* systems that will enable continuous, robust, and accurate monitoring of gaze in everyday life.

The ramifications of this imminent paradigm shift are far-reaching in the social, psychological, business, and computer sciences, as well as for practice. Gaze has a long history as a modality for explicit human-computer interaction, such as for gaze-based pointing or object selection (Majaranta & Bulling, 2014), as well as in social signal processing (Adams & Kleck, 2003) and in artificial conversational agents (Vertegaal, Slagter, van der Veer, & Nijholt, 2001). Gaze also serves as a source of implicit information about users, including their behavioral context (Bulling, Ward, Gellersen,

& Tröster, 2011; Zhang, Wedel, & Pieters, 2009), intents and goals (Bednarik, Vrzakova, & Hradis, 2012; Pieters & Wedel, 2007), cognitive processes and states (Bulling & Roggen, 2011; Bulling & Zander, 2014), and even personality traits (Hoppe, Loetscher, Morey, & Bulling, 2015). With eye-tracking now moving into everyday life, gaze will also become a rich source of information on the "inner workings" of consumers—information that is difficult if not impossible to obtain from other modalities available today (see Chapters 1, 3–5). This information will become readily available at large scales in real-world environments, for example, while consumers are making purchases in brick-and-mortar and online stores, providing unprecedented insights into consumers' preference formation and decision-making processes (Stüttgen, Boatwright, & Monroe, 2012). As such, *pervasive eye-tracking, defined as the collection and utilization of gaze data in real-world settings in which consumers go about their everyday tasks*, has the potential to become a core technology to passively monitor, analyze, and actively manage consumer attention. Pervasive eye-tracking also has significant potential to facilitate, support, and enhance consumers' interactions, such as with interactive billboards or smart shelves. Figure 2.2 illustrates the spectrum of pervasive eye-tracking applications from offline to real-time.

Eye-Tracking

One of the first eye-tracking devices was developed by Huey (1898). The device consisted of a lever that was attached to a cup that was placed on the eye and that had a hole for the respondent to see through. Moving the eyes caused a pen attached to the cup to move across the surface of a drum, which recorded the eye movement. This device had obvious mechanical limitations. To alleviate these, Orschansky (1899) attached a mirror to the eye cup, and recorded the reflection of light on the mirror. It soon became clear that it was even better to record light reflected by the surface of the eye itself. Dodge first used this principle when developing his "falling plate" camera (Dodge, 1900). His eye tracker consisted of a photographic plate that was lowered gradually to record the reflection of sunlight off a white piece of cardboard placed in front of the eye. This device produced the first published trace of eye movements (Wade, 2010).

Today, eye trackers typically measure eye movements in one of three ways (see also Chapter 4; Duchowski, 2007): a) video-based infrared pupil-corneal reflection (PCR), b) measurement of the cornea-retinal standing potential between the front and the back of the human eye (Electrooculography, EOG), and c) video-based eye-tracking using head-mounted or stationary visible light video cameras (video-oculography). We call the latter systems *pervasive eye-tracking systems*. They can be further categorized depending on whether they use eye landmarks, such as pupil centers and eye corners, or directly estimate gaze direction from the eye image using machine learning techniques (Hansen & Ji, 2010). Video-based eye trackers can be either used in a stationary or mobile configuration. A typical setup consists of a video camera that records the movements of the eye(s) and a computer and software that processes, saves, and analyzes the gaze data. In stationary systems, this eye camera is often placed below the screen while in mobile systems the camera is mounted on a glasses-like frame. Mobile eye trackers additionally include an egocentric scene camera to map the user's gaze direction to the visual scene and thus facilitate subsequent analysis.

PCR-Based Eye-Tracking

Most commercial stationary eye trackers are PCR-based, and have gained popularity because they typically have high spatial and temporal precision. PCR-based eye trackers emit infrared light and use cameras to detect the reflection of the light on the cornea, the outer layer of the eye. Most devices are binocular, i.e., they detect the reflection on both eyes. The point of focus of the eyes is estimated from the relative distance between the corneal reflection(s) and the pupil center, which has to be determined through a calibration task prior to first use. Because the distance between the pupil and the corneal reflection does not change much during head movements, modern stationary eye trackers allow small head movements. PCR-based eye trackers record the x- and y-coordinates of the point of gaze with sampling rates of up to 2 kHz and a spatial resolution of $0.5°$.

Stationary eye-tracking confines users' body and head movement to a rather small virtual tracking box about half a meter away from the tracker. This requirement has, for a long time, restricted gaze recordings to controlled laboratory settings and carefully selected stimuli that were presented to participants on a computer screen for predefined durations. This approach has been increasingly criticized because principles guiding the eyes when looking at computer screens can be very different from those when engaging in everyday behavior (Foulsham, Walker, & Kingstone, 2011). Findings obtained in controlled settings may thus have limited validity for natural environments (Kingstone, Smilek, & Eastwood, 2008). Compelling evidence for these differences was provided in a study which compared eye movements of participants while exploring different real-world environments and watching videos of these environments (Marius't Hart et al., 2009). The distribution of eye movements obtained in the laboratory predicted the gaze distribution in the real world with around 60% accuracy—indicating significant differences in eye movements between laboratory and real-world situations. Mobile eye trackers (see Figure 2.1) address these challenges by allowing collection of gaze data in everyday settings and during unconstrained head and body movements, including daily activities such as making tea or sandwiches, driving, walking, playing sports, and shopping (Hayhoe & Ballard, 2005).

Mobile PCR-based eye trackers consist of lightweight glasses, in which miniature infrared (IR) cameras pointing at one or both eyes, as well as a scene camera, are built in. The IR cameras record the Purkinje reflections off the cornea as in stationary PCR-based eye trackers, while the scene

FIGURE 2.1 (left) PUPIL from Pupil Labs is an accessible, affordable, and extensible open source platform for mobile eye-tracking, gaze-based interaction, and egocentric vision research. (right) MEME from J!NS is an integrated eyewear computer for measuring eye movements using Electrooculography (EOG) and head movements using integrated inertial sensors.

camera additionally records the participant's field of view. Because the eye camera is mounted on the head and moves with it, the position of the IR source relative to the eye is nearly fixed. This allows participants to move around freely, i.e., without any constraints on head or body movements. The output of the eye tracker is a video of the participant's field of view with the 2D gaze point overlaid in real-time in the form of a cursor or cross-hair. The two most important applications of mobile eye-tracking, so far, are in the analysis of visual attention and behavior in human vision research, and for gaze-based human-computer interaction in computer science.

Video-Based Eye-Tracking Using Visible Light Cameras

While PCR-based eye trackers can provide high tracking accuracy, they do require special-purpose equipment (IR light sources and special cameras) that is not commonly available. This requirement triggered research into methods that only require off-the-shelf cameras in combination with computer vision algorithms. These video-based methods can generally be categorized as model-based or learning-based (Hansen & Ji, 2010). Model-based methods use a geometric model of the human eye as a basis for estimating the direction of gaze. The contour of the pupil and iris, which is a circle in three dimensions, takes the form of an ellipse when projected on a 2D image plane. An ellipse fitted algorithmically to the pupil and/or iris can, in turn, be used to reconstruct the original sphere in three dimensions, which allows the orientation of the eyeball to be calculated and the gaze direction to be predicted (Chen & Ji, 2008; Valenti, Sebe, & Gevers, 2012). Although model-based video-oculography methods have recently been applied in more practical scenarios (Cristina & Camilleri, 2016; Funes Mora & Odobez, 2014; Wood & Bulling, 2014), their gaze estimation accuracy is still low, since they depend on accurate eye feature detection for which high-resolution images and homogeneous bright illumination are required. This has largely prevented these methods from being widely used in real-world settings or on commodity devices.

In contrast, learning-based gaze estimation methods do not rely on explicit detection of eye features but directly map the pixel information contained in images obtained from the user to 3D gaze directions using machine learning algorithms. Because they do not rely on explicit eye feature detection, learning-based methods can handle low-resolution images and longer distances from the object of gaze. While early methods assumed a fixed head pose, more recent methods allow for free 3D head movement in front of the camera (Gao, Harari, Tenenbaum, & Ullman, 2014). An open research challenge in learning-based gaze estimation is to train gaze estimators that make minimal assumptions regarding the user, environment, or camera.

The need to collect person-specific training data represents a fundamental limitation for both model-based and learning-based gaze estimation methods. To reduce the burden on the user, several previous works used events that can be observed when the user interacts with computing systems, such as mouse clicks or key presses, as a proxy for users' on-screen gaze position. Alternatively, visual saliency maps (Sugano & Bulling, 2015) or pre-recorded human gaze patterns on defined visual stimuli (Alnajar, Gevers, Valenti, & Ghebreab, 2013) can be used as training data to learn the gaze estimation function. However, the need to acquire user input fundamentally limits the extent to which these approaches can be applied to interactive settings. Thus, another line of work aims to train gaze estimators that generalize to arbitrary users without requiring explicit user input (Funes Mora & Odobez, 2013).

Despite significant advances in such person-independent gaze estimation, all of these previous works only considered gaze estimation tasks in which training and test data are assumed to come from the same respondents. Zhang, Sugano, Fritz, and Bulling (2015, 2017, 2019) were first to study the practically most relevant but also significantly more challenging task of unconstrained gaze estimation via cross-dataset evaluation. They introduced a method based on a multimodal deep convolutional neural network that outperformed the state-of-the-art methods by a large margin. These latest methods were also shown to have significant potential for other tasks, such as estimation of audience attention (Sugano et al., 2016) or detection of eye contact in everyday settings (Zhang, Sugano, & Bulling, 2017). Later works demonstrated that large-scale methods for unconstrained gaze estimation can benefit from advances in computer graphics techniques for eye region modelling. These models can be used to synthesize large amounts of highly realistic and perfectly annotated eye region images, thereby significantly reducing both data collection and annotation efforts (Wood et al., 2015). The latest model is fully morphable and can synthesize more than 40 eye images per second on commodity hardware (Wood, Baltrušaitis, Morency, Robinson, & Bulling, 2016).

The cameras used for video-based eye-tracking typically capture video images at a frame rate of between 30 and 120 Hz. Therefore, pervasive eye trackers currently provide lower spatio-temporal precision than PCR-based systems, and face additional challenges with respect to accurate detection of fast eye movements, so-called saccades (Rayner, 1998). Studies employing pervasive eye-tracking therefore mostly report dwell times on manually defined areas of interest. Burton, Albert, and Flynn (2014) compared video-based with PCR-based eye-tracking and found that the former is less accurate especially for smaller regions of interest (around 1% of the screen or less), even more when they are located in the periphery of the computer screen. Video-based eye-tracking may underestimate dwell time by as much as 50% for these smaller areas of interest. For larger areas of interest that comprise of 5% of the screen or more, dwell times may be underestimated by about 25%. Video-based technology, however, may realize accuracies comparable to IR eye-tracking when interest focuses on hit rates, that is, percentages of participants who fixated at least once on a larger area of interest. The advantages of video-based eye-tracking are the very low cost, the possibility of eye-tracking in natural settings (at home, at work, or any other location where respondents are in front of a desktop or laptop computer), and across dispersed geographic locations. The lower spatial and temporal precision may partially be offset by using much larger samples of participants.

Information That Pervasive Eye-Tracking Systems Provide

As mentioned before, eye-tracking provides a plethora of information about the user and has, consequently, been used for a long time as both a measurement technique and input modality. Arguably, the two most important applications of eye-tracking, so far, are in the analysis of visual attention and behavior in human vision research, and for gaze-based human–computer interaction in computer science (see Figure 2.2).

Analysis of visual attention in human vision research has traditionally focused on analyzing the deployment of gaze to different areas of interest (AOIs) on a defined stimulus, e.g., a natural image, visual pattern, or website, displayed to the user on a computer monitor (see Chapters 4–5). The AOIs can be either content-based (face, text, image, object, etc.) or space-based (grid, image pixels). The analysis either involves statistically testing for differences in eye movement characteristics, or aggregating and visualizing fixations in fixation density maps (see Figure 2.3) or other graphical displays (Holmqvist et al., 2011). All of these analyses are readily provided by commercial software shipped together with the eye trackers or free software downloadable from the web. If the analysis is done for a large number of users, robust measures of potential differences in visual attention towards a given stimulus for two or more user groups can be obtained. The eye movement characteristics commonly used for statistical analysis are the average fixation duration, the total gaze duration, time until the first fixation, or the total number of fixations on a set of given AOIs (Holmqvist et al., 2011). See Pieters and Wedel (2004) for an example of this approach.

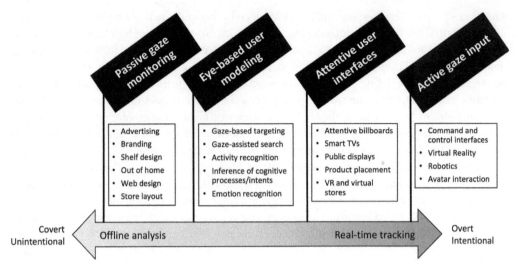

FIGURE 2.2 Spectrum of possible eye-tracking applications and use of gaze information in consumer behavior analysis and decision making (inspired by Majaranta & Bulling, 2014; Author generated).

Statistical testing provides a principled and well-established way of identifying differences in attentive behavior between AOIs. One drawback of this approach, however, is that temporal information is not considered. Scan-path analysis was devised to address this limitation and thus provides a complementary form of attention analysis (Noton & Stark, 1971; Pieters, Rosbergen, & Wedel, 1999). Scan-paths are sequences of multiple fixations on a stimulus for a given amount of time, typically no more than a few seconds. To calculate scan-paths, fixation sequences are first encoded, averaged per user if desired, and then programmatically or statistically compared to the scan-paths of other users or experimental conditions. An application to decision-making tasks, for example, was provided by Day (2010). The programmatic comparison involves calculating how similar different scan-paths are, for example using normalized scan-path similarity (Le Meur & Baccino, 2013). In addition to retaining temporal information of fixation sequences, scan-paths can also be visualized easily by overlaying the fixations and their connections with lines onto the stimulus (see Figure 2.3). The key drawbacks of this type of scan-path analysis are that visualization does not scale well to a large number of scan-paths and users and scan-path visualizations become cluttered very quickly. An alternative approach is a statistical approach to scan-path analysis, which may involve either Markov (Pieters, Rosbergen, & Wedel, 1999), or Hidden Markov Models (Liechty, Pieters, & Wedel, 2003) to describe first-order transitions between AOIs. Finally, if neither difference between individual eye movement characteristics nor temporal information of fixation sequences are desired, fixation density maps provide yet another means to summarize the eye movement data (Holmqvist et al., 2011). Further, statistical models that predict probability distributions of fixations from low-level image characteristics can be used to estimate saliency maps that display regions in the stimulus that are salient to each viewer (van der Lans, Pieters, & Wedel, 2008).

Gaze-Based Interaction

In human-computer interaction, gaze has a long history as a means for hands-free interaction with computing systems (Majaranta & Bulling, 2014; Sibert & Jacob, 2000). Gaze has, for example,

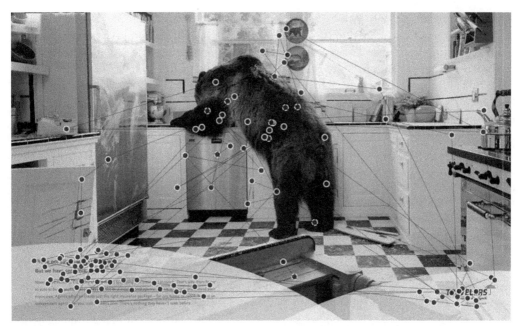

FIGURE 2.3 Eye movements of multiple participants on advertisement for Traveler (reprinted with permission of MIT Press; Fawcett, Jonathan M., Evan F. Risko, and Alan Kingstone, (eds.) *The Handbook of Attention*, Figure 25.1, p. 571, © 2015 Massachusetts Institute of Technology, published by the MIT Press.).

been used for fast, accurate, and natural interaction with ambient and body-worn devices and displays (Esteves, Velloso, Bulling, & Gellersen, 2015; Huang, Li, Ngai, & Leong, 2017; Vaitukaitis & Bulling, 2012; Wood & Bulling, 2014) for a variety of tasks including, but not limited to, pointing (Zhai, Morimoto, & Ihde, 1999), object selection and transfer (Sibert & Jacob, 2000; Stellmach & Dachselt, 2012; Turner, Alexander, Bulling, Schmidt, & Gellersen, 2013; Vidal, Bulling, & Gellersen, 2013; Zhang, Bulling, & Gellersen, 2013; Zhang, Müller, Chong, Bulling, & Gellersen, 2014), or text entry (Majaranta & Räihä, 2002). Prior work also investigated means to combine gaze input with other modalities, such as touch (Simeone, Bulling, Alexander, & Gellersen, 2016; Stellmach & Dachselt, 2012; Turner, Alexander, Bulling, & Gellersen, 2015), mouse and keyboard input (Kumar, Paepcke, & Winograd, 2007) or mid-air gestures (Velloso, Turner, Alexander, Bulling, & Gellersen, 2015). Due to the aforementioned prior limitations of eye-tracking, much of this work was done in desktop settings or, in general, settings in which users moved relatively little in front of the display. Complementing these active uses of gaze for interaction is a relatively large body of work on attentive user interfaces (Bulling, 2016; Vertegaal, 2003; Xu, Sugano, & Bulling, 2016), i.e., interfaces that monitor user attention passively and adapt to users' current attentional capacity and state in different ways. These attentive user interfaces are increasingly explored in everyday settings, in particular on public displays (Alt, Bulling, Mecke, & Buschek, 2016; Khamis, Alt, & Bulling, 2016; Khamis, Bulling, & Alt, 2015; Sugano et al., 2016; Walter, Bulling, Lindlbauer, Schüssler, & Müller, 2015).

The key underlying measure of the vast majority of all of these works is the 2D point of gaze on the display itself or, in cases in which 3D information can be related to specific objects of interests, 3D gaze direction measured using both mobile and remote eye trackers. More recently, a new line of work has started to explore machine learning approaches on top of the "raw" gaze data, i.e., methods to encode gaze into rich higher-level representations that can subsequently be linked to user behavior and, thus, be used for implicit human-computer interaction (Majaranta & Bulling, 2014). A growing body of work has demonstrated that, for example, spatio-temporal information on gaze can be used to automatically predict users' everyday activities (Bulling, Ward, & Gellersen, 2012; Bulling et al., 2011; Kunze, Bulling, Utsumi, Yuki, & Kise, 2013), also in an unsupervised fashion during full-day mobile gaze recordings (Bulling et al., 2013; Steil & Bulling, 2015), cognitive processes and states (Bulling & Roggen, 2011; Bulling & Zander, 2014; Tessendorf et al., 2011), intentions and goals (Bednarik et al., 2012), social interactions (Pfeiffer, Vogeley, & Schilbach, 2013), or even aspects of users' personality and decision-making processes (Hoppe et al., 2015).

All of these analyses rely on the 2D point of gaze on a stimulus or the 3D gaze direction as input. In addition, eye trackers may also provide other information about the user. For example, the videos of the users' faces that video-based eye trackers obtain can serve as input to emotion recognition (Cohen, Sebe, Garg, Chen, & Huang, 2003). Although not directly eye-tracking, this is a rich source of auxiliary data that may provide important information on users' underlying emotional states (see Chapter 23).

In addition, eye trackers also provide measurements of the pupil diameter (see Chapter 3), which may depend on the cognitive load and/or arousal of the respondent. The pupil tends to dilate when users are aroused or deploy more cognitive resources to process the information (Bradley, Miccoli, Escrig, & Lang, 2008). Pupil size also depends on other factors, however, including lightning conditions, because of which pupil diameter is not an unambiguous indicator of cognitive load or arousal (Loewenfeld, 1993).

Further, an image of the scene that the person is looking at can be reflected on the cornea and may thus be obtained from the corneal image recorded using mobile eye trackers (Nakazawa & Nitschke, 2012). The cornea reflects not only the incoming light, but also the entire surrounding scene over a wide field of view. The corneal reflection itself allows for the analysis of the entire field of view. It enables the reconstruction and analysis of the scene and the 3D environment of the viewer (Nishino & Nayar, 2006), and eliminates the need for a separate camera to capture the users' field of view, thus further enabling miniaturization of pervasive eye-tracking.

Other measures that are obtained as a corollary of eye-tracking are micro-saccades, blinks and vergence movements. First, micro-saccades are very small, involuntary movements of the eyes (less than 1° of visual angle) that have been shown to be associated with attentional load, onset of new or oddball visual stimuli, and the preparation of motor response (Engbert, 2006; Pastukhov & Braun, 2010; Rolfs, Kliegl, & Engbert, 2008). Despite their potential, as of yet, micro-saccades are difficult to record in everyday settings and require highly accurate and high-speed PCR-based eye trackers. Second, eye blinks are recorded as an interruption of the corneal reflection in PCR-based eye trackers and can be detected with video-based trackers (Grauman, Betke, Gips, & Bradski, 2001). An increase in blink rate, i.e., the number of blinks for a particular time duration, is associated with higher levels of arousal (Bradley, Codispoti, Cuthbert, & Lang, 2001), while a decrease can be observed during attentional focus, high cognitive load (Stern, Walrath, & Goldstein, 1984), or increased drowsiness (Caffier, Erdmann, & Ullsperger, 2003). Third, vergence eye movements are movements where both eyes turn inward or outward, in order to keep an object that moves towards or from us in focus. Vergence eye movements can thus be used to determine the distance of a visually attended object (Choi, Jung, Ban, Niitsuma, & Lee, 2006) or, if controlled voluntarily, as a means for user input (Kirst & Bulling, 2016).

All of the auxiliary measures discussed earlier provide additional information on users' underlying cognitive states and can be used together with users' gaze to model underlying cognitive states and/or traits. It may additionally enable the optimization of visual design and user interfaces, filling the void in areas such as optimization of sponsored search, movie and video clips, banner ads, product reviews, text and image search, and product comparison layouts (Pieters, Wedel, & Zhang, 2007). Bayesian models can be used to represent cognition from first principles and make predictions on how multiple unobserved attentional processes may have affected the recorded eye movements. This enables inferences on multiple underlying cognitive processes from eye movement data, and has been shown to result in accurate forecasts of downstream behavior such as memory (Wedel & Pieters, 2000), search (van der Lans et al., 2008), consideration (Chandon, Hutchinson, Bradlow, & Young, 2009), choice (Stüttgen et al., 2012), and even sales (Zhang et al., 2009) from eye movements.

Pervasive Eye-Tracking Applications in Consumer Behavior Analysis

Most recent mobile eye trackers that rely on video cameras can be implemented as lightweight and fully embedded mobile systems and therefore have become suitable for recordings in everyday settings (see Figure 2.1 for an example). Such systems now also allow, for the first time, to record gaze over long periods of time, e.g., over a full day of a person's life (Bulling et al., 2013; Steil & Bulling, 2015). The low cost of this new generation of eye-tracking systems, easy calibration, and unobtrusive measurement in natural exposure conditions are beginning to contribute to the growth of applications in practice, and theory development and testing in academic research.

Consequently, several recent works have started to explore the use of mobile eye-tracking to analyze consumer behavior in these and other natural everyday settings.

Classic work using PCR-based mobile eye-tracking (Land & Hayhoe, 2001; Land, Mennie, & Rusted, 1999; Smeets, Hayhoe, & Ballard, 1996) showed that routine goal-directed activities require continuous monitoring with the eyes and have revealed a tight linkage between eye movements and the motor actions that are performed. Eye movements during these tasks are thus mostly directed top-down towards task-relevant objects. The pioneering work of Yarbus had already shown this early on for static contexts (Yarbus, 1967). The eyes usually reach an object before any hand action towards the object, and move on to the next object before the preceding action is completed. A shift of the eyes is often followed by a movement of the head, which is followed by the movement of the hand. Thus, research with mobile eye trackers has shown that eye movements are a fundamental component of the motor pattern and are leading indicators of goal-directed motion.

Using mobile eye-tracking, research has investigated human performance in real-world tasks such as driving (Shinoda, Hayhoe, & Shrivastava, 2001), making tea (Land, Mennie, & Rusted, 1999), walking (Jovancevic-Misic & Hayhoe, 2009), and playing sports (Vickers, 2006, Vickers & Adolphe, 1997). As for consumer decision making, mobile eye trackers have been used to assess the effectiveness of in-store merchandising (Hendrickson & Ailawadi, 2014). Research with several hundreds of shoppers in multiple stores demonstrated that shoppers 1) look in a narrow window below and above eye level and as a consequence especially signage placed on the ceiling in stores is hardly noticed; 2) look at signage for about a second on average and process 3–5 words; 3) look at signage only when it is immediately relevant for and in close proximity to the shopping goal; and 4) process information on signage in the store in a left–right or top–bottom direction. Other research, using content analysis of data produced by mobile eye trackers (Harwood & Jones, 2014), has confirmed that 75–85% of fixations that shoppers make in a store fall on products, while signage receives a much lower number of fixations (0.5%). This research also revealed that the (vertical) line of sight and visual salience (brightness and color contrast) are two main factors affecting store navigation. A study on digital out-of-home advertising in public transport revealed that over

60% of participants looked at the digital screens placed in a tram during a 30-minute tram ride, fixating on it 16% of the time the screen was in their field of view (Höller, Schrammel, Tscheligi, & Paletta, 2009). While they are merely scratching the surface of applications of mobile eye-tracking, these studies illustrate how research in retail and out-of-home settings benefits from mobile pervasive eye-tracking and yields insights that would be difficult to obtain otherwise. Another area of research that can benefit from the application of mobile eye-tracking is research into multitasking and multi-screen behaviors. One study has shown that viewers preferentially attend to computer screens as compared to TV screens during media multitasking, which is manifested in longer gaze on the computer screen (Brasel & Gips, 2011). But, gaze times on both screens are limited to a few seconds only, and people switch between screens around four times per minute. Again, these insights would be very difficult to obtain without the use of pervasive eye-tracking.

Ever since the work of Yarbus (1967) it is evident that eye movements are dependent on the tasks and goals of consumers. It is increasingly recognized that decision making is embedded in perception-action cycles, and that attention plays an active role in constructing decisions (Orquin & Loose, 2013). However, most often decision making has been studied in isolation from the perception-action cycle in which it naturally occurs. A major step forward was made when recent research investigated eye movements during decision making (e.g., Glaholt & Reingold, 2011; Krajbich, Armel, & Rangel, 2010; Pieters & Warlop, 1999; Shi, Wedel, & Pieters, 2013; Shimojo, Simion, Shimojo, & Scheier, 2003), because it revealed the role of attention in decision making. This stream of research was initiated by the work of Russo and colleagues (Russo & Leclerc, 1994; Russo & Rosen, 1975) who demonstrated not only that eye movements were used to acquire information, but also how that information was used. This has been recently formalized in statistical models that describe eye movements and decisions jointly (Stüttgen et al., 2012; Yang, Toubia, & de Jong, 2015). However, in that research eye movements are still collected in a lab setting rather than a real-life decision context. Pervasive eye-tracking systems will be needed to study decision making embedded in the perception-action cycle in natural contexts. A first attempt was made by Gidlöf, Wallin, Dewhurst, and Holmqvist (2013), who extended the work by Russo and Leclerc (1994) to real-world settings, and revealed a deeper processing of the decision alternatives in the evaluation stage, as compared to lab settings.

Emerging Applications

In a few years from now, eye-tracking will likely be an integrated part of our lives, via camera-based gaze estimation incorporated in laptops and desktop computers, billboards, kiosks, smart-TVs, tablets, smartphones, and so on. The incorporation of gaze recording in everyday digital devices will help make our daily lives simpler, safer, more efficient, and more enjoyable. It may also enable the optimization of visual design and user interfaces, filling the void in areas such as optimization of sponsored search, movie and video clips, banner ads, product reviews, text and image search, and product comparison layouts (Pieters et al., 2007). The rapid development of recording technology has already begun to see innovative application and is likely to create many more opportunities (see Figure 2.2). For example, eye-tracking systems that record what users look at on their digital screens may provide hands-free access to information via gaze control, thereby facilitating interaction with electronic devices. Today, users can already deploy their gaze to activate apps, scroll through web pages, and make a selection among options by fixating on one of them, thus improving their user experience. In combination with automated image analysis, pervasive eye-tracking may allow for automatic alerts if important information is overlooked, and may use visual cues to support or even interactively direct visual search (Sattar, Müller, Fritz, & Bulling,

2015; Wedel, Yan, Siegel, & Li, 2016). As more gaze data are collected and being used for marketing purposes, privacy and security become critical issues. Privacy laws have not kept pace with data collection and processing technologies. Several governments have been enacting stricter privacy laws. But, because their gaze, emotion, and other process tracing data is considered sensitive by most consumers, respecting customers' privacy is good business practice.

In reading, selective blurring of text may improve reading speed and focus. Explanations may pop-up when eye movements indicate comprehension is slow. Much of this was already implemented in Text 2.0, which is a framework for developing web-based eye-tracking applications to facilitate interactive reading (Biedert, Buscher, Schwarz, Hees, & Dengel, 2010). Also, words and sentences that a viewer looks at longer may be included in document summaries, which can be optimized to reflect a reader's personal interests and used to develop recommendation systems that recommend new articles, texts, or reviews.

Pervasive eye-tracking will also render computer games more immersive. Waterloo Labs allows players the use of eye movements to control EyeMario (http://waterloolabs.blogspot.com/), and Formula Face (http://games.redbull.com/int/en/game/formula-face) allows gamers to use blinks, smiles, and head movements to control their game. As a player moves her head, expresses emotions, or blinks, the head and face of the avatar moves synchronously by mirroring these movements and emotions. Thus, eye, head, and facial movements are recorded and analyzed in real time to render the avatar's movements and expressions more realistic and more in tune with the user's moment-to-moment feelings, producing games that are more immersive and appealing. Optitrack's (www.naturalpoint.com/optitrack/) face capture system already accomplishes much of that.

While eye-tracking has traditionally been used to measure people's visual attention, it is increasingly becoming clear that when used along with additional measures that can be extracted from the facial images, including pupil dilation (see Chapter 3), blinks, micro-saccades, emotion expressions, scene reflection, head movements, and body movements, a much richer picture of the behavioral and cognitive state of the viewer can be obtained, including attention, location and environment, emotions, goals and intentions, activities, and social interactions. Inferring such states presents opportunities of improving visual user interfaces in a large variety of everyday contexts (Bulling, 2016; Bulling & Zander, 2014).

New virtual and augmented reality applications may also benefit greatly from routine eye movement recording. Increasingly, companies are exploiting these technologies. Augmented reality applications allow consumers to see information that is important to them, but not present in the real-world context, by overlaying digital information on top of real-world settings. Virtual reality (VR) and augmented reality (AR) allow consumers to use their digital device to try on new clothes, explore a home, hotel or museum, visit or fly over new cities and countries, or test drive a car. VR and AR are already used in an increasing number of applications in advertising and selling. For example, for virtual test driving of cars, the car manufacturer Volvo has developed smartphone applications (www.volvocars.com/intl). There are also an increasing number of applications in hospitality and travel, through which prospective customers can virtually explore hotels and hotel rooms, museums, entertainment options, and tourist destinations via 360-degree views on their smartphones. The hotel chain Mariott has developed in-room VR travel applications (http://marriott-hotels.marriott.com/). Gaming is on the forefront of virtual and augmented reality applications, with Pokemon Go as a prime example (www.pokemongo.com/), but with current developments going already beyond that. The Chinese retailer Yihaodian has developed mobile phone applications that enable its customers to browse and shop in virtual stores at any location using their smartphones (https://en.wikipedia.org/wiki/Yihaodian). Eye-tracking has already been integrated with VR technology (Pfeiffer, 2008), where it enables rendering of the virtual context based on the real-time field of view and depth of field blur. It uses the viewer's gaze to analyze what he looks at inside the virtual space with the purposes of making the aim of actions more accurate, making the virtual environment more immersive, and the interactions with actors in it more life-like (Hillaire, Lécuyer, Cozot, & Casiez, 2008).

Open Challenges

Mobile eye trackers are ideal for tracking eye movements during everyday activities in natural settings, where head, hand, and body movements need to be unconstrained. One challenge with the application of mobile eye trackers for research purposes is the analysis of data from multiple participants, because each participant has an idiosyncratic field of view at each point in time during the recording. The data resulting from pervasive eye-tracking essentially consists of movie clips of the visual field of the user, on which the gaze point is indicated. The degree of heterogeneity of the data can be extensive, each respondent having his/her own field of view at each point in time during the study. Computer vision methods are needed to process the individual data streams and aggregate them to enable the application of statistical methods that facilitate generalizable conclusions. Progress has been made in off-the-shelf software to identify and track AOIs across multiple videos, which makes quantitative analyses feasible especially when researchers have well-defined ideas about the objects and regions that are of interest in the analysis.

Another challenge is that mapping gaze to the 3D environment requires visual markers that have to be placed and detected in real time in the environment. Alternatively, sophisticated computer vision algorithms are required to detect and track objects such as displays or, in general, areas of interest in the egocentric video (Lander, Gehring, Krüger, Boring, & Bulling, 2015). Further, fully invisible integration of the eye tracker into ordinary glasses is not yet feasible due to the rather large imaging sensors currently used. The design of current mobile eye trackers can lead to low social acceptance and was shown to result in unnatural behavior of both the wearers and people they interact with (Nasiopoulos, Risko, Foulsham, & Kingstone, 2015).

Conclusion

Over the past decade, eye movement research has increasingly relied on the integration of techniques and theories from visual computing, attention research, and in-lab eye-tracking—fields that have been relatively disparate before. Visual computing has developed powerful tools that enable the extraction of basic visual features from images, segment and describe images, and recognize forms, shapes, faces, and large numbers of object classes. Attention research offers theories that explain eye movements from underlying cognitive processes while laboratory eye-tracking experiments offer methods of recording, analyzing, and interpreting eye, face, and head movements. Combined, these fields have provided unprecedented insights into people's processing of, evaluation of, and behavior towards controlled visual stimuli.

Recent advances in mobile eye-tracking as well as stationary eye-tracking using video cameras readily integrated into handheld devices and ambient displays pave the way for a new generation of pervasive eye-tracking systems that allow researchers and practitioners to understand and analyze gaze information in real-world settings. As such, pervasive eye-tracking has not only significant potential to validate and complement existing theories and findings in the previous research areas but also to uncover entirely new behavioral, cognitive, and attention phenomena and enable new applications impossible before. The ramifications of this imminent paradigm shift are transformative, in particular for applications in consumer behavior analysis and decision making in offline, online, mobile, and VR settings. With pervasive eye-tracking and analysis of gaze behavior and facial expressions becoming a commodity, gaze will provide a unique source of information on the "inner workings" of consumers. Moreover, these measures will increasingly provide input that will be used to shape our digital environment.

Recommended Reading List

- Land (2006): Early research on eye movements in everyday life
- Rayner (1998): A classic review of eye-tracking research in reading
- Wedel and Pieters (2008): A review of eye-tracking and visual attention research in marketing
- Majaranta and Bulling (2014): An introduction to eye-tracking and eye-based human-computer interaction

References

Adams Jr., R. B., & Kleck, R. E. (2003). Perceived gaze direction and the processing of facial displays of emotion. *Psychological Science, 14*(6), 644–647.

Alnajar, F., Gevers, T., Valenti, R., & Ghebreab, S. (2013). Calibration-free gaze estimation using human gaze patterns. In *Proceedings IEEE International Conference on Computer Vision* (pp. 137–144).

Alt, F., Bulling, A., Mecke, L., & Buschek, D. (2016). Attention, please! Comparing Features for Measuring Audience Attention Towards Pervasive Displays. In *Proc. ACM SIGCHI Conference on Designing Interactive Systems (DIS)* (pp. 823–828).

Bednarik, R., Vrzakova, H., & Hradis, M. (2012). What do you want to do next: A novel approach for intent prediction in gaze-based interaction. In *Proceedings of the Symposium on Eye Tracking Research and Applications* (pp. 83–90). ACM.

Biedert, R., Buscher, G., Schwarz, S., Hees, J., & Dengel, A. (2010). Text 2.0. In *CHI'10 Extended Abstracts on Human Factors in Computing Systems* (pp. 4003–4008). ACM.

Bradley, M. M., Codispoti, M., Cuthbert, B. N., & Lang, P. J. (2001). Emotion and motivation I: Defensive and appetitive reactions in picture processing. *Emotion, 1*(3), 276.

Bradley, M. M., Miccoli, L., Escrig, M. A., & Lang, P. J. (2008). The pupil as a measure of emotional arousal and autonomic activation. *Psychophysiology, 45*(4), 602–607.

Brasel, S. A., & Gips, J. (2011). Media multitasking behavior: Concurrent television and computer usage. *Cyberpsychology, Behavior, and Social Networking, 14*(9), 527–534.

Bulling, A. (2016). Pervasive attentive user interfaces. *IEEE Computer, 49*(1), 94–98.

Bulling, A., & Gellersen, H. (2010). Toward mobile eye-based human-computer interaction. *IEEE Pervasive Computing, 9*(4), 8–12.

Bulling, A., & Roggen, D. (2011). Recognition of visual memory recall processes using eye movement analysis. In *Proceedings of the 13th International Conference on Ubiquitous Computing* (pp. 455–464). ACM.

Bulling, A., Ward, J. A., & Gellersen, H. (2012). Multimodal recognition of reading activity in transit using body-worn sensors. *ACM Transactions on Applied Perception, 9*(1), 2:1–2:21.

Bulling, A., Ward, J. A., Gellersen, H., & Tröster, G. (2011). Eye movement analysis for activity recognition using electrooculography. *IEEE Transactions on Pattern Analysis and Machine Intelligence, 33*(4), 741–753.

Bulling, A., Weichel, C., & Gellersen, H. (2013). Eyecontext: Recognition of high-level contextual cues from human visual behaviour. In *Proceedings ACM SIGCHI Conference on Human Factors in Computing Systems (CHI)* (pp. 305–308).

Bulling, A., & Zander, T. O. (2014). Cognition-aware computing. *IEEE Pervasive Computing, 13*(3), 80–83.

Burton, L., Albert, W., & Flynn, M. (2014). A comparison of the performance of webcam vs. infrared eye tracking technology. In *Proceedings of the Human Factors and Ergonomics Society Annual Meeting* (Vol. 58, pp. 1437–1441). Los Angeles, CA: SAGE Publications.

Caffier, P. P., Erdmann, U., & Ullsperger, P. (2003). Experimental evaluation of eye-blink parameters as a drowsiness measure. *European Journal of Applied Physiology, 89*(3–4), 319–325.

Chandon, P., Hutchinson, J. W., Bradlow, E. T., & Young, S. H. (2009). Does in-store marketing work? Effects of the number and position of shelf facings on brand attention and evaluation at the point of purchase. *Journal of Marketing, 73*(6), 1–17.

Chen, J., & Ji, Q. (2008). 3D gaze estimation with a single camera without IR illumination. In *International Conference on Pattern Recognition (ICPR)* (pp. 1–4).

Choi, S. B., Jung, B. S., Ban, S. W., Niitsuma, H., & Lee, M. (2006). Biologically motivated vergence control system using human-like selective attention model. *Neurocomputing, 69*(4), 537–558.

Cohen, I., Sebe, N., Garg, A., Chen, L. S., & Huang, T. S. (2003). Facial expression recognition from video sequences: Temporal and static modeling. *Computer Vision and Image Understanding, 91*(1), 160–187.

Cristina, S., & Camilleri, K. P. (2016). Model-based head pose-free gaze estimation for assistive communication. *Computer Vision and Image Understanding, 149*, 157–170.

Day, R. F. (2010). Examining the validity of the Needleman–Wunsch algorithm in identifying decision strategy with eye-movement data. *Decision Support Systems, 49*(4), 396–403.

Dodge, R. (1900). Visual perception during eye movement. *Psychological Review, 7*(5), 454.

Duchowski, A. T. (2007). *Eye Tracking Methodology: Theory and Practice* (Vol. 373). London, UK: Springer.

Engbert, R. (2006). Microsaccades: A microcosm for research on oculomotor control, attention, and visual perception. *Progress in Brain Research, 154*, 177–192.

Esteves, A., Velloso, E., Bulling, A., & Gellersen, H. (2015). Orbits: Enabling gaze interaction in smart watches using moving targets. In *Proceedings ACM Symposium on User Interface Software and Technology (UIST)* (pp. 457–466).

Foulsham, T., Walker, E., & Kingstone, A. (2011). The where, what and when of gaze allocation in the lab and the natural environment. *Vision Research, 51*(17), 1920–1931.

Funes Mora, K. A., & Odobez, J. M. (2013). Person independent 3D gaze estimation from remote RGB-D cameras. In *Proceedings IEEE Int. Conf. on Image Processing* (pp. 2787–2791).

Funes Mora, K. A., & Odobez, J. M. (2014). Geometric generative gaze estimation (G3E) for remote RGB-D cameras. In *Proceedings IEEE Conf. Computer Vision and Pattern Recognition* (pp. 1773–1780).

Gao, T., Harari, D., Tenenbaum, J., & Ullman, S. (2014). *When Computer Vision Gazes at Cognition*. Cambridge, MA: Center for Brains, Minds, & Machines.

Gidlöf, K., Wallin, A., Dewhurst, R., & Holmqvist, K. (2013). Using eye tracking to trace a cognitive process: Gaze behaviour during decision making in a natural environment. *Journal of Eye Movement Research, 6*(1), 1–14.

Glaholt, M. G., & Reingold, E. M. (2011). Eye movement monitoring as a process tracing methodology in decision making research. *Journal of Neuroscience, Psychology, and Economics, 4*(2), 125–146.

Grauman, K., Betke, M., Gips, J., & Bradski, G. R. (2001). Communication via eye blinks-detection and duration analysis in real time. In *Proceedings 2001 IEEE Computer Society Conference on Computer Vision and Pattern Recognition (CVPR 2001)* (Vol. 1, pp. 1010–1017). IEEE.

Hansen, D. W., & Ji, Q. (2010). In the eye of the beholder: A survey of models for eyes and gaze. *IEEE Transactions on Pattern Analysis and Machine Intelligence, 32*(3), 478–500.

Harwood, T., & Jones, M. (2014). Mobile eye-tracking in retail research. In M. Horsley, M. Eliot, B. A. Knight, & R. Reilly (Eds.), *Current Trends in Eye Tracking Research* (pp. 183–199). London, UK: Springer.

Hayhoe, M., & Ballard, D. (2005). Eye movements in natural behavior. *Trends in Cognitive Sciences, 9*(4), 188–194.

Hendrickson, K., & Ailawadi, K. L. (2014). Six lessons for in-store marketing from six years of mobile eye-tracking research. In D. Grewal, A. L. Roggeveen, & J. Nordfält (Eds.), *Shopper Marketing and the Role of In-Store Marketing* (pp. 57–74). Bingley, UK: Emerald Group Publishing Limited.

Hillaire, S., Lécuyer, A., Cozot, R., & Casiez, G. (2008). Using an eye-tracking system to improve camera motions and depth-of-field blur effects in virtual environments. In *Virtual Reality Conference, 2008. VR'08. IEEE* (pp. 47–50). IEEE.

Höller, N., Schrammel, J., Tscheligi, M., & Paletta, L. (2009). The perception of information and advertisement screens mounted in public transportation vehicles-results from a mobile eye-tracking study. In *Proceedings of the 2nd Workshop on Pervasive Advertising* (Vol. 39).

Holmqvist, K., Nyström, M., Andersson, R., Dewhurst, R., Jarodzka, H., & van de Weijer, J. (2011). *Eye Tracking: A Comprehensive Guide to Methods and Measures*. Oxford, UK: Oxford University Press.

Hoppe, S., Loetscher, T., Morey, S., & Bulling, A. (2015). Recognition of curiosity using eye movement analysis. In *Adjunct Proceedings of the 2015 ACM International Joint Conference on Pervasive and Ubiquitous Computing and Proceedings of the 2015 ACM International Symposium on Wearable Computers* (pp. 185–188). ACM.

Huang, M. X., Li, J., Ngai, G., & Leong, H. V. (2017). Screenglint: Practical, in-situ gaze estimation on smartphones. In *Proceedings of the 2017 CHI Conference on Human Factors in Computing Systems* (pp. 2546–2557). ACM.

Huey, E. B. (1898). Preliminary experiments in the physiology and psychology of Reading. *American Journal of Psychology, 9*(4), 575–586.

Jovancevic-Misic, J., & Hayhoe, M. (2009). Adaptive gaze control in natural environments. *Journal of Neuroscience, 29*(19), 6234–6238.

Khamis, M., Alt, F., & Bulling, A. (2016). Challenges and design space of gaze-enabled public displays. In *Adjunct Proceedings ACM International Joint Conference on Pervasive and Ubiquitous Computing (UbiComp)* (pp. 1736–1745).

Khamis, M., Bulling, A., & Alt, F. (2015). Tackling challenges of interactive public displays using gaze. In *Adjunct Proceedings ACM International Joint Conference on Pervasive and Ubiquitous Computing (UbiComp)* (pp. 763–766).

Kingstone, A., Smilek, D., & Eastwood, J. D. (2008). Cognitive ethology: A new approach for studying human cognition. *British Journal of Psychology, 99*(3), 317–340.

Kirst, D., & Bulling, A. (2016). On the verge: Voluntary convergences for accurate and precise timing of gaze input. In *Proceedings of the 2016 CHI Conference Extended Abstracts on Human factors in Computing Systems* (pp. 1519–1525). ACM.

Krajbich, I., Armel, C., & Rangel, A. (2010). Visual fixations and the computation and comparison of value in simple choice. *Nature Neuroscience, 13*(10), 1292–1298.

Kumar, M., Paepcke, A., & Winograd, T. (2007). EyePoint: practical pointing and selection using gaze and keyboard. In *Proceedings of the SIGCHI Conference on Human Factors in Computing Systems* (pp. 421–430). ACM.

Kunze, K., Bulling, A., Utsumi, Y., Yuki, S., & Kise, K. (2013). I know what you are reading: Recognition of document types using mobile eye tracking. In *Proceedings IEEE International Symposium on Wearable Computers (ISWC)* (pp. 113–116). ACM.

Land, M. F. (2006). Eye movements and the control of actions in everyday life. *Progress in Retinal and Eye Research, 25*(3), 296–324.

Land, M. F., & Hayhoe, M. (2001). In what ways do eye movements contribute to everyday activities? *Vision Research, 41*(25), 3559–3565.

Land, M., Mennie, N., & Rusted, J. (1999). The roles of vision and eye movements in the control of activities of daily living. *Perception, 28*(11), 1311–1328.

Lander, C., Gehring, S., Krüger, A., Boring, S., & Bulling, A. (2015). Gazeprojector: Accurate gaze estimation and seamless gaze interaction across multiple displays. In *Proceedings of the 28th Annual ACM Symposium on User Interface Software & Technology* (pp. 395–404). ACM.

Le Meur, O., & Baccino, T. (2013). Methods for comparing scanpaths and saliency maps: strengths and weaknesses. *Behavior Research Methods, 45*(1), 251–266.

Liechty, J., Pieters, R., & Wedel, M. (2003). Global and local covert visual attention: Evidence from a Bayesian hidden Markov model. *Psychometrika, 68*(4), 519–541.

Loewenfeld, I. E. (1993). *The Pupil: Anatomy, Physiology, and Clinical Applications*. Detroit, MI: Wayne State University Press.

Majaranta, P., & Bulling, A. (2014). Eye tracking and eye-based human–computer interaction. In *Advances in Physiological Computing* (pp. 39–65). London, UK: Springer.

Majaranta, P., & Räihä, K.-J. (2002). Twenty years of eye typing: Systems and design issues. In *Proceedings of the 2002 Symposium on Eye Tracking Research & Applications* (pp. 15–22). ACM.

Marius't Hart, B., Vockeroth, J., Schumann, F., Bartl, K., Schneider, E., Koenig, P., & Einhäuser, W. (2009). Gaze allocation in natural stimuli: Comparing free exploration to head-fixed viewing conditions. *Visual Cognition, 17*(6–7), 1132–1158.

Nakazawa, A., & Nitschke, C. (2012). Point of gaze estimation through corneal surface reflection in an active illumination environment. In A. Fitzgibbon, S. Lazebnik, P. Perona, Y. Sato, & C. Schmid (Eds.), *Computer Vision – ECCV 2012* (pp. 159–172). Berlin/Heidelberg: Springer.

Nasiopoulos, E., Risko, E. F., Foulsham, T., & Kingstone, A. (2015). Wearable computing: Will it make people prosocial? *British Journal of Psychology, 106*(2), 209–216.

Nishino, K., & Nayar, S. K. (2006). Corneal imaging system: Environment from eyes. *International Journal of Computer Vision, 70*(1), 23–40.

Noton, D., & Stark, L. (1971). Eye movements and visual perception. *Scientific American, 224*(6), 34–43.

Orquin, J. L., & Loose, S. M. (2013). Attention and choice: A review on eye movements in decision making. *Acta Psychologica, 144*(1), 190–206.

Orschansky, J. (1899). Eine Methode die Augenbewegungen direct zu untersuchen. *Zentralblatt für Physiologie, 12*, 785–790.

Pastukhov, A., & Braun, J. (2010). Rare but precious: Microsaccades are highly informative about attentional allocation. *Vision Research, 50*(12), 1173–1184.

Pfeiffer, T. (2008). Towards gaze interaction in immersive virtual reality: Evaluation of a monocular eye tracking set-up. In M. Schumann, & T. Kuhlen (Eds.), *Virtuelle und Erweiterte Realität – Fünfter Workshop der GI-Fachgruppe VR/AR* (pp. 81–92). Aachen: Shaker Verlag.

Pfeiffer, U. J., Vogeley, K., & Schilbach, L. (2013). From gaze cueing to dual eye-tracking: Novel approaches to investigate the neural correlates of gaze in social interaction. *Neuroscience & Biobehavioral Reviews, 37*(10), 2516–2528.

Pieters, R., Rosbergen, E., & Wedel, M. (1999). Visual attention to repeated print advertising: A test of scanpath theory. *Journal of Marketing Research, 36*(4), 424–438.

Pieters, R., & Warlop, L. (1999). Visual attention during brand choice: The impact of time pressure and task motivation. *International Journal of Research in Marketing, 16*(1), 1–16.

Pieters, R., & Wedel, M. (2004). Attention capture and transfer in advertising: Brand, pictorial, and text-size effects. *Journal of Marketing, 68*(2), 36–50.

Pieters, R., & Wedel, M. (2007). Goal control of attention to advertising: The Yarbus implication. *Journal of Consumer Research, 34*(2), 224–233.

Pieters, R., Wedel, M., & Zhang, J. (2007). Optimal feature advertising design under competitive clutter. *Management Science, 53*(11), 1815–1828.

Rayner, K. (1998). Eye movements in reading and information processing: 20 years of research. *Psychological Bulletin, 124*(3), 372–422.

Rolfs, M., Kliegl, R., & Engbert, R. (2008). Toward a model of microsaccade generation: The case of microsaccadic inhibition. *Journal of Vision, 8*(11), 5.1–5.23.

Russo, J. E., & Leclerc, F. (1994). An eye-fixation analysis of choice processes for consumer nondurables. *Journal of Consumer Research, 21*(2), 274–290.

Russo, J. E., & Rosen, L. D. (1975). An eye fixation analysis of multialternative choice. *Memory & Cognition, 3*(3), 267–276.

Sattar, H., Müller, S., Fritz, M., & Bulling, A. (2015). Prediction of search targets from fixations in open-world settings. In *Proc. IEEE International Conference on Computer Vision and Pattern Recognition (CVPR)* (pp. 981–990).

Shi, S. W., Wedel, M., & Pieters, F. (2013). Information acquisition during online decision making: A model-based exploration using eye-tracking data. *Management Science, 59*(5), 1009–1026.

Shimojo, S., Simion, C., Shimojo, E., & Scheier, C. (2003). Gaze bias both reflects and influences preference. *Nature Neuroscience, 6*(12), 1317–1322.

Shinoda, H., Hayhoe, M. M., & Shrivastava, A. (2001). What controls attention in natural environments? *Vision Research, 41*(25–26), 3535–3545.

Sibert, L. E., & Jacob, R. J. (2000). Evaluation of eye gaze interaction. In *Proceedings of the SIGCHI Conference on Human Factors in Computing Systems* (pp. 281–288). ACM.

Simeone, A., Bulling, A., Alexander, J., & Gellersen, H. (2016). Three-point interaction: Combining bi-manual direct touch with gaze. In *Proceedings of the International Conference on Advanced Visual Interfaces (AVI)* (pp. 168–175).

Smeets, J. B., Hayhoe, M. M., & Ballard, D. H. (1996). Goal-directed arm movements change eye-head coordination. *Experimental Brain Research, 109*(3), 434–440.

Steil, J., & Bulling, A. (2015). Discovery of everyday human activities from long-term visual behaviour using topic models. In *Proceedings ACM International Joint Conference on Pervasive and Ubiquitous Computing (UbiComp)* (pp. 75–85).

Stellmach, S., & Dachselt, R. (2012). Look & touch: Gaze-supported target acquisition. In *Proceedings of the SIGCHI Conference on Human Factors in Computing Systems* (pp. 2981–2990). ACM.

Stern, J. A., Walrath, L. C., & Goldstein, R. (1984). The endogenous eyeblink. *Psychophysiology, 21*(1), 22–33.

Stüttgen, P., Boatwright, P., & Monroe, R. T. (2012). A satisficing choice model. *Marketing Science, 31*(6), 878–899.

Sugano, Y., & Bulling, A. (2015). Self-calibrating head-mounted eye trackers using egocentric visual saliency. In *Proceedings ACM Symposium on User Interface Software and Technology (UIST)* (pp. 363–372).

Sugano, Y., Zhang, X., & Bulling, A. (2016). Aggregaze: Collective estimation of audience attention on public displays. In *Proceedings of the 29th Annual Symposium on User Interface Software and Technology (UIST)* (pp. 821–831). ACM.

Tessendorf, B., Bulling, A., Roggen, D., Stiefmeier, T., Feilner, M., Derleth, P., & Tröster, G. (2011). Recognition of hearing needs from body and eye movements to improve hearing instruments. In *Proceedings of the International Conference on Pervasive Computing* (pp. 314–331).

Tonsen, M., Steil, J., Sugano, Y., & Bulling, A. (2017). Invisibleeye: Mobile eye tracking using multiple low-resolution cameras and learning-based gaze estimation. *Proceedings of the ACM on Interactive, Mobile, Wearable and Ubiquitous Technologies (IMWUT), 1*(3), 106.

Turner, J., Alexander, J., Bulling, A., & Gellersen, H. (2015). Gaze+RST: Integrating gaze and multitouch for remote rotate-scale-translate tasks. *Proceedings of the 33rd Annual ACM Conference on Human Factors in Computing Systems* (pp. 4179–4188). ACM.

Turner, J., Alexander, J., Bulling, A., Schmidt, D., & Gellersen, H. (2013). Eye pull, eye push: Moving objects between large screens and personal devices with gaze and touch. In *14th International Conference on Human-Computer Interaction (INTERACT)* (pp. 170–186). Springer.

Vaitukaitis, V., & Bulling, A. (2012). Eye gesture recognition on portable devices. In *Proceedings of the 2012 ACM Conference on Ubiquitous Computing* (pp. 711–714). ACM.

Valenti, R., Sebe, N., & Gevers, T. (2012). Combining head pose and eye location information for gaze estimation. *IEEE Transactions on Image Processing, 21*(2), 802–815.

van der Lans, R., Pieters, R., & Wedel, M. (2008). Eye-movement analysis of search effectiveness. *Journal of the American Statistical Association, 103*(482), 452–461.

Velloso, E., Turner, J., Alexander, J., Bulling, A., & Gellersen, H. (2015). An empirical investigation of gaze selection in mid-air gestural 3D manipulation. In *Human-Computer Interaction* (pp. 315–330). Springer.

Vertegaal, R. (2003). Attentive user interfaces. *Communications of the ACM, 46*(3), 30–33.

Vertegaal, R., Slagter, R., van der Veer, G., & Nijholt, A. (2001). Eye gaze patterns in conversations: There is more to conversational agents than meets the eyes. In *Proceedings of the SIGCHI Conference on Human Factors in Computing Systems* (pp. 301–308). ACM.

Vickers, J. N. (2006). Gaze of Olympic speedskaters skating at full speed on a regulation oval: Perception-action coupling in a dynamic performance environment. *Cognitive Processing, 7*(1), 102–105.

Vickers, J. N., & Adolphe, R. M. (1997). Gaze behaviour during a ball tracking and aiming skill. *International Journal of Sports Vision, 4*(1), 18–27.

Vidal, M., Bulling, A., & Gellersen, H. (2013). Pursuits: Spontaneous interaction with displays based on smooth pursuit eye movement and moving targets. In *Proceedings of the 2013 ACM International Joint Conference on Pervasive and Ubiquitous Computing* (pp. 439–448). ACM.

Wade, N. J. (2010). Pioneers of eye movement research. *i-Perception, 1*(2), 33–68.

Walter, R., Bulling, A., Lindlbauer, D., Schüssler, M., & Müller, H. J. (2015). Analyzing visual attention during whole body interaction with public displays. In *Proc. ACM International Joint Conference on Pervasive and Ubiquitous Computing (UbiComp)* (pp. 1263–1267).

Wedel, M., & Pieters, R. (2000). Eye fixations on advertisements and memory for brands: A model and findings. *Marketing Science, 19*(4), 297–312.

Wedel, M., & Pieters, R. (2008). A review of eye-tracking research in marketing. In N. Malhotra (Ed.), *Review of Marketing Research* (Vol. 4, pp. 123–147). New York, NY: M. E. Sharpe Inc.

Wedel, M., Yan, J., Siegel, E. L., & Li, H. A. (2016). Nodule detection with eye movements. *Journal of Behavioral Decision Making, 29*(2–3), 254–270.

Wood, E., Baltrušaitis, T., Morency, L. P., Robinson, P., & Bulling, A. (2016). A 3D morphable eye region model for gaze estimation. In *Proceedings of the European Conference on Computer Vision (ECCV)* (pp. 297–313). Springer.

Wood, E., Baltrušaitis, T., Zhang, X., Sugano, Y., Robinson, P., & Bulling, A. (2015). Rendering of eyes for eye-shape registration and gaze estimation. In *Proc. IEEE International Conference on Computer Vision (ICCV)* (pp. 3756–3764).

Wood, E., & Bulling, A. (2014). Eyetab: Model-based gaze estimation on unmodified tablet computers. In *Proceedings of the International Symposium on Eye Tracking Research and Applications (ETRA)* (pp. 207–210). ACM.

Xu, P., Sugano, Y., & Bulling, A. (2016). Spatio-temporal modeling and prediction of visual attention in graphical user interfaces. In *Proceedings of the 2016 CHI Conference on Human Factors in Computing Systems* (pp. 3299–3310). ACM.

Yang, L., Toubia, O., & de Jong, M. G. (2015). A bounded rationality model of information search and choice in preference measurement. *Journal of Marketing Research, 52*(2), 166–183.

Yarbus, A. L. (1967). Eye movements during perception of complex objects. In *Eye Movements and Vision* (pp. 171–211). New York, NY: Plenum Press.

Zhai, S., Morimoto, C., & Ihde, S. (1999, May). Manual and gaze input cascaded (MAGIC) pointing. In *Proceedings of the SIGCHI Conference on Human Factors in Computing Systems* (pp. 246–253). ACM.

Zhang, J., Wedel, M., & Pieters, R. (2009). Sales effects of attention to feature advertisements: A Bayesian mediation analysis. *Journal of Marketing Research, 46*(5), 669–681.

Zhang, X., Sugano, Y., & Bulling, A. (2017). Everyday eye contact detection using unsupervised gaze target discovery. In *Proceedings of the 30th Annual ACM Symposium on User Interface Software and Technology (UIST)* (pp. 193–203). ACM.

Zhang, X., Sugano, Y., Fritz, M., & Bulling, A. (2015). Appearance-based gaze estimation in the wild. In *Proceedings of the IEEE International Conference on Computer Vision and Pattern Recognition (CVPR)* (pp. 4511–4520).

Zhang, X., Sugano, Y., Fritz, M., & Bulling, A. (2019). MPIIGaze: Real-World Dataset and Deep Appearance-Based Gaze Estimation. *IEEE Transactions on Pattern Analysis and Machine Intelligence* (TPAMI), 41(1), pp. 162–175, 2019.

Zhang, X., Sugano, Y., Fritz, M., & Bulling, A. (2017). It's written all over your face: Full-face appearance-based gaze estimation. In *Proceedings of the IEEE International Conference on Computer Vision and Pattern Recognition Workshops (CVPRW)*.

Zhang, Y., Bulling, A., & Gellersen, H. (2013). Sideways: A gaze interface for spontaneous interaction with situated displays. In *Proceedings of the SIGCHI Conference on Human Factors in Computing Systems (CHI)* (pp. 851–860). ACM.

Zhang, Y., Müller, H. J., Chong, M. K., Bulling, A., & Gellersen, H. (2014). GazeHorizon: Enabling passers-by to interact with public displays by gaze. In *Proceedings of the 2014 ACM International Joint Conference on Pervasive and Ubiquitous Computing (UbiComp)* (pp. 559–563). ACM.

3

INVESTIGATING PUPIL DILATION IN DECISION RESEARCH

Joseph Tao-yi Wang and Wei James Chen

Pupil dilation or the measure of pupil diameter/size has been used in decision research starting from the 1960s (Hess & Polt, 1960, 1964; Kahneman & Beatty, 1966; Hicks, Reaney, & Hill, 1967). Since then, pupil dilation has been viewed as an index of arousal and cognitive load (Beatty, 1982). Regarding pupil dilation as an emotional reaction, Hess and Polt (1960) reported pupillary dilation responses to what they call "emotionally toned or interesting visual stimuli". Other studies reporting pupillary responses to arousal include Hicks et al. (1967), Bull and Shead (1979), and more recently Aboyoun and Dabbs (1998).

Hess and Polt (1964) first reported task-evoked pupillary responses to cognitive load, as differential pupillary dilation responses while mentally calculating the product of two one-digit or two-digit numbers. Kahneman and Beatty (1966) showed how more difficult memory tasks (memorizing numbers with more digits versus less digits) induced larger pupillary response. More recently, Bailey and Iqbal (2008) utilized pupillary responses to provide a steady stream of data to study workload changes within a single task.

For single responses, pupil dilation occurs and peaks several seconds (or hundreds msec) after stimuli were presented, with timing depending on the type of stimuli. For example, Hess (1972) reported that such dilation would occur 2–7 sec after emotional stimuli were presented and suggested faster dilation for stronger stimuli. Chapman et al. (1999) found that pupil dilation responses to pain began at 330 msec and peaked at 1250 msec after stimulus onset. Peak dilation increased significantly as pain intensity increased. Using different sounds as stimuli (baby crying, laugh, or regular office noise), Partala and Surakka (2003) showed that there was first seemingly no response for about 400 msec, and then a steep increase in pupil size peaking at 2–3 sec after stimulus onset. When performing a cognitively demanding task, pupils dilate in response to mental workload, and peak at about 1–2 sec after the onset of demand (Beatty, 1982). Pupils constrict after the task is completed, either gradually (Kahneman & Beatty, 1966; Hess, 1972) or instantly (Bernhardt, Dabbs, & Riad, 1996).

In more recent years, the finding that pupil diameter is highly correlated with neuronal activity in the Locus Coeruleus (LC; Rajkowski, Kubiak, & Aston-Jones, 1994)[1] has linked pupil dilation to neural gain. LC is a nucleus located in the pons, part of the brainstem. It has wide projections throughout the entire brain, and it is the primary source of norepinephrine (NE), which is an important neurotransmitter and neuromodulator that, among other functions, increases arousal and focuses attention. Together, the LC and the areas of the brain that are affected by NE are jointly called the LC-NE system. Since there is a positive relationship between NE and pupillary response, pupil dilation can be viewed as an indirect but noninvasive measure of NE.

In fact, Aston-Jones and Cohen (2005) proposed an integrated model, the Adaptive Gain Theory (AGT), of the LC-NE system and the exploration and exploitation trade-off. In particular, AGT predicts that the LC phasic mode (pupil dilation) is associated with exploitation behavior that optimizes current task performance, while the LC tonic mode (pupil constriction or baseline pupil) is associated with worse performance (in the current task) but broader attention that induces exploration behavior (of other rewarding tasks). Several researchers have demonstrated this effect in different contexts, including ambiguous perceptual identification (Einhäuser, Stout, Koch, & Carter, 2008), perceptual discrimination (Gilzenrat, Nieuwenhuis, Jepma, & Cohen, 2010), and gambling (Jepma & Nieuwenhuis, 2011). The link to breadth of attention has been shown in several studies including visual and semantic learning (Eldar, Cohen, & Niv, 2013), ambiguous letter identification (Eldar, Niv, & Cohen, 2016), and binary food-choice (Chen & Krajbich, 2017b).

This chapter is designed for researchers who are interested in using pupil diameter as a data input in their research but have little or no prior experience. Therefore, we cover the modern method of measuring pupil diameter, the common environmental control and experimental design that need to be considered, post-experiment data analysis, and the difficulties in interpreting pupil dilation results along with some solutions. We conclude with some examples of actual pupil dilation research.

Modern Method of Measuring Pupil Diameter

There are several different methods to measure pupil dilation (see Duchowski, 2007, for a complete review). Among these methods, one of the most reliable and noninvasive methods utilizes high-speed video cameras. In particular, video-based eye trackers put cameras and infrared illuminators in front of subjects' eyes, and videotape their pupils. This is typically performed by either placing cameras in front of the computer screen subjects are viewing (desk-mount), or by placing cameras on a head restraint similar to a bicycle helmet so they are located right in front of each eye (head-mount). Since images of the pupil are recorded, the eye tracker is able to measure pupil diameter by either counting the number of pixels of the (dark color) pupillary area or fitting an ellipse on the pupil image and calculating the length of the major axis. Note that when using video cameras, pupil diameter is usually reported in relative terms, since actual image size depends on camera position. This is in contrast to traditional methods that focus on absolute measure of pupil dilation.

As discussed in Klingner, Kumar, and Hanrahan (2008), the pixel-counting method, but not the ellipse-fitting method, is subject to the pupil foreshortening error (PFE), namely that the pupil diameter varies with the gaze direction. However, a more recent paper (Hayes & Petrov, 2016a) explicitly models the geometric relationship between gaze angle and the change in observed pupil diameter. They proposed a simple method that uses the gaze data to correct the PFE, which can reduce it by 82.5%, and a slightly more complicated method can reduce it by 97.5%.

Experimental Design

Experimental design for pupil dilation research differs from the usual eye-tracking experiments for several reasons. First of all, pupil dilation experiments generally need longer inter-trial interval (ITI, up to 2000 msec longer) and longer trial time (at least 1000 msec longer). This is because the cognitive effect on the pupil dilation has a delay of about 1000 msec and most research defines pupil dilation as a percentage relative to a pre-stimuli baseline from 1000 to 2000 msec (Beatty &

Lucero-Wagoner, 2000). For example, in a repeated binary-choice experiment, if we only want to obtain the gaze data, the ITI can be as short as possible (as long as it is sufficient for subjects to fixate at the center) and each trial can end once subjects make their decision. However, if we want to further obtain the pupil diameter data, a longer ITI will be needed to establish the baseline, and recording needs to continue for an additional 1000 to 2000 msec after subjects make their decisions.

Second, pupil dilation is heavily affected by the luminance level on the screen. This is typically handled by controlling luminance during the course of the experiment. For example, Beatty (1982) contains instructions on producing stimulus slides with comparable brightness and contrast, and most recent work (Einhäuser et al., 2008; Einhäuser, Koch, & Carter, 2010; Eldar et al., 2016; Chen & Krajbich, 2017a) use isoluminant stimuli. This is more easily done with computerized displays, but still remains a challenge in many naturally occurring settings, such as flying an airplane at night or viewing online search results that contain images of different colors. For example, Dehais, Causse, and Pastor (2008) embedded an eye tracker in a real aircraft to record pupillary responses (as well as fixations) when pilots performed different flying routines, but eventually decided to analyze pupil dilation for only a subset of the pilots to make luminance conditions comparable. Similar to the luminance problem, pupil dilation is also affected by the ambient light and noise. Hence, a common practice to handle this problem is to use a dim/dark and quiet room when running the experiment.

Lastly, as mentioned earlier, pupil diameter can be affected by the PFE. Besides the analytic method we mentioned (Hayes & Petrov, 2016a), the common practice to handle this problem is to design the experiment so that subjects always gaze at the center position on the monitor. However, this is obviously not a universal solution.

Preprocessing and Data Analysis

Video-based eye trackers report raw data (usually called the "sample report") for each instance of observation. Each record consists of a time stamp, the pupil diameter of the eye(s), the X-Y location of the left and right eye (or just one eye under monocular mode), and possible "messages" that are sent to the eye tracker. These messages are commonly used as syncing timestamps between the data recorded by the eye tracker (eye data) and by the experimental program (behavioral data).

Preprocessing

First of all, blinks are very common in the pupil data. These are usually recognized by the manufacturer's own data analysis software or by an algorithm designed by the researcher. The most common practice is to do a linear interpolation to remove the blinks, but other methods such as cubic-spline fit are also available (Mathôt, 2013). Second, the pupil data measured by the eye tracker has a high-frequency noise (Duchowski, 2007). Since pupils dilate and constrict at low frequency, it is a common practice to smooth the data with a low-pass filter. Klingner et al. (2008) provide a detailed method of how to determine the cutoff frequency for this filter. Lastly, some other corrections may be required depending on the experimental design. For example, if the experimental design does not restrict subjects to always gaze at some point on the monitor and the stimuli are not isoluminant, then the correction for the PFE and luminance level will be needed. Note that the correction for luminance is usually done by regressing out the effect of different luminance levels. This is not a very precise method; thus we recommend using isoluminant stimuli for any pupil dilation experiment.

Data Analysis

The first step of data analysis is to establish a baseline for each trial of observation. This is usually defined as the average pupil diameter of the 1000 (up to 2000) msec time interval before the trial onset. Each trial's pupil data after the trial onset is then calculated as a percentage change compared to the baseline in that trial.

There are some common static measurements that are being reported regarding the trial pupil data: mean pupil dilation, peak pupil dilation, and latency to peak (Beatty & Lucero-Wagoner, 2000). As for the dynamic measurement, the common practice is to compare the time course of pupil dilation between different experimental treatments/conditions (Hayes & Petrov, 2016b; Chen & Krajbich, 2017a).

Interpretations of Pupillary Responses

Since there are different causes that could all trigger pupillary responses, care must be taken to identify the exact cause that activated the response to avoid "reverse inference", such as may occur when interpreting functional magnetic resonance imaging (fMRI) data (Chapter 15). Here we discuss some of these issues and possible solutions.

The main interpretive challenge is to isolate the exact cause of the pupil dilation. For studies conducted to observe pupillary responses to specific tasks, this is done by designing control trials identical to the treatment trials except for only one particular factor of interest. For example, to identify the pupillary responses to (positive) affect, Partala and Surakka (2003) compared mean pupil size of trials where subjects heard a baby laughing (positive affect) with that of trials where subjects heard regular office noise (neutral). Oliveira, Aula, and Russell (2009) asked subjects to investigate three different web search results sequentially, and determine which was most relevant. They found pupillary responses to the relevance of search results when the results were each shown for exactly 5 sec. However, they also noted that their analysis was made possible by separating the search process into several stages, which is typically not the case in actual web searches.

In more naturally occurring settings, pupillary responses could be compared with other subjective or psychophysical measures, such as skin conductance (Chapter 11), heart rate variability, subjective ratings, etc. By combining the results from various measures, researchers are more likely to identify the unique cause that could explain all of them (see also Chapters 22–23). For example, Kahneman, Tursky, Shapiro, and Crider (1969) combined pupillary responses with skin conductance and heart rate to find similar responses in all three measures during information intake and processing, as well as peak responses depending on task difficulty.

In some studies, pupil dilation is used to inform interpretation and analysis of other measures; in other studies, other measurements provide more accurate interpretation of pupil dilation. For example, Siegle, Steinhauer, Stenger, Konecky, and Carter (2003) compared the time course of pupil dilation with that of the fMRI signal in the middle frontal gyrus during a digit sorting task to suggest that activity in that area indexed the working memory subtask of digit sorting. In contrast, Kang et al. (2009) found a pupillary response before seeing the answer to an interesting question, which could be attributed to either arousal due to anticipation of the answer, or frustration due to the impatience of waiting for the answer. The former interpretation was preferred because the same self-reported curiosity is also shown by fMRI to activate the ventral striatum, a region involved in anticipated reward. Another piece of evidence is the time series of pupil size, which gradually increases during the countdown and peaks immediately after the answer is displayed. This favors the anticipation story since impatience should decrease rather than increase as the remaining waiting time decreases.

In addition to combining measurements, interpretation of pupil dilation can also be aided by relevant theory that explains behavior. In particular, Wang, Spezio, and Camerer (2010) studied strategic information transmission, which consists of an informed sender (e.g., stock analyst) who sends a (possibly deceptive) message to an uninformed receiver who will then take action (e.g., invest in the stock). They find pupil dilation proportional to the size of the lie (how much subjects inflate the true state), which could be due simply to guilt, or a more complicated process (cognitive difficulty) involved in lying. Wang et al. (2010) eventually affirmed that pupil dilation is evoked by cognitive difficulty because individual differences in subject behavior are explained by a level-k model that generates heterogeneous subject types each performing different steps of thinking.

Some tasks may suggest a particular decomposition of the decision-making process which could be empirically tested (with either behavioral or psychophysical data). In fact, researchers in computer science have been performing similar decomposition of tasks using well-known modeling techniques (Card, Newell, & Moran, 1983; John & Kieras, 1996). These models of task execution also played important roles in explaining pupillary responses in human-computer interaction. For example, Iqbal Zheng, and Bailey (2004) recorded pupillary responses when subjects were performing reading comprehension, mathematical reasoning, product searching, and email classification. They found little difference in pupil dilation for simple and difficult tasks when averaged across entire trials, but they did find significant difference in "cognitive subtasks" (but not in "motor subtasks") when they decomposed the original task into several lower-level subtasks.

Applications in Decision Making

In behavioral decision making, Hochman and Yechiam (2011) report pupil dilation when subjects chose between a risky and safe lottery. They find asymmetric pupillary responses for gains (versus losses), even when subjects did not exhibit loss aversion behaviorally. They interpret this as supporting the hypothesis that a loss signals a threat in the environment and induces arousal and alertness to all outcomes. Yechiam and Hochman (2013) later propose an attentional model to explain this.

We now turn to recent examples of using pupillary response as an indicator of NE and LC-NE system activation during decision making. To begin with, Einhäuser et al. (2010) let subjects choose one of the ten seconds in a time interval to push a button, and received a reward if the chosen interval matched a random draw. The authors found maximum pupil dilation occurring 1–2 sec after the button press, and take this as supporting evidence that the neurotransmitter NE released by the LC played an important role in reaching a cognitive decision. To rule out alternative causes of pupil dilation, they conducted a series of follow-up experiments: First, they modified the task so subjects instead chose one out of five numbers between 1 and 10. When first showing these numbers in ascending order, the timing of maximum pupil dilation corresponded to the eventually chosen number. Since decisions were made at the end, the increase in pupil dilation during viewing cannot be attributed to button press. To rule out arousal due to reward, the authors also ran the same experiment without payment, yielding similar results. They even ran an instructed-pick version to rule out anticipation since the instruction to pick a particular number was only shown on the spot. This is a good example of careful experimental design for pupil dilation studies.

Preuschoff (2011) conducted a gambling task where two numbers were randomly drawn from 1 to 10 and subjects were rewarded for correctly predicting which draw is larger. By showing the two drawn numbers sequentially, the authors induced changes in risk (variance of reward), reward prediction error (RPE, actual minus expected reward), and risk prediction error (actual minus expected size of RPE) as information arrives. They find pupil dilation corresponding to risk prediction error that measures surprise (instead of expected reward) and propose a risk prediction error hypotheses of NE. Since Preuschoff (2011), much research has shown that pupil dilation signals surprise (or large prediction error) in the Iowa gambling task (Lavín, San Martín, & Rosales Jubal, 2014), while making intertemporal choices (Lempert, Glimcher, & Phelps, 2015), or playing two-person guessing games (Chen & Krajbich, 2017a).

Nassar et al. (2012) generated a random sequence from a normal distribution with known variance but unknown mean and asked subjects to guess the next number after viewing the current one. Subjects were also told that the unknown mean would change from time to time, but did not know exactly when. Intuitively, the larger the current prediction error, the more likely there was a shift; the more observations one has (after a shift), the more certain one is about the mean. Indeed, a reduced Bayesian model predicts people would estimate and respond to the likelihood the mean has shifted (change-point probability), and the relative uncertainty about the underlying true mean after a shift. The authors found that pupil change during outcome-viewing is positively correlated with change-point probability, linking in to LC phasic mode, except when the prediction was an exact hit (i.e., no change) which also triggered pupil dilation. Also, the average pupil diameter is at the highest level right after the change point (with the largest relative uncertainty), linking it to LC tonic mode.

Finally, Hayes and Petrov (2016b) let subjects play a sequence of tasks taken from Raven's Advanced Progressive Matrices (APM) under the think-aloud verbal protocols (speak out what they were thinking, see Chapters 17–19). In these tasks, subjects saw a 3x3 matrix containing eight items with various characteristics and were asked to fill in the last item that fits the pattern. Voice-recording data were used to classify subjects' thinking into pattern recognition and pattern application stages. Subjects' pupils dilate only in the pattern recognition stage, but constrict in the pattern application stage. In fact, those with higher Raven's APM scores have a higher percentage change in pupil diameter (PCPD) averaged across the pattern recognition stage.[2]

These findings indicate that pupil dilation can be very informative in many different domains; however, its interpretation should be taken carefully since there are multiple causes of pupil dilation. Nonetheless, the LC-NE system and its AGT provide a neural foundation to pupillary response, and hence, have the potential to provide a unifying framework to understand pupil dilation. After all, NE directly increases arousal, and cognitive demanding tasks could trigger the LC phasic mode to induce better performance, both increasing pupil dilation. Future work in this direction would facilitate better interpretation of pupillary responses, and more applications of pupil dilation would surely follow.

Notes

1 Although there is direct (single neuron) evidence only on primates, research with humans (Costa & Rudebeck, 2016; Joshi, Li, Kalwani, & Gold, 2016; Laeng, Sirois, Gredeback, 2012; Murphy, O'Connell, O'Sullivan, Robertson, Balsters, 2014) has shown this relationship using fMRI data.

2 Hayes and Petrov (2016b) refer to the pattern recognition stage as "exploration" and the pattern application stage as "exploitation", which may be confusing: This indicates pupil dilation during "exploration", instead of "exploitation" predicted by AGT, while they claim their results are consistent with Jepma and Nieuwenhuis (2011) which support AGT. Interestingly, they report mean PCPD averaged across segments of the same stage in a trial, instead of baseline pupil diameter used in Jepma and Nieuwenhuis (2011) to represent the LC tonic mode.

References

Aboyoun, D. C., & Dabbs, J. N. (1998). The Hess pupil dilation findings: Sex or novelty? *Social Behavior and Personality, 26*(4), 415–419.

Aston-Jones, G., & Cohen, J. D. (2005). An integrative theory of locus coeruleus-norepinephrine function: Adaptive gain and optimal performance. *Annual Review of Neuroscience, 28*(1), 403–450.

Bailey, B. P., & Iqbal, S. T. (2008). Understanding changes in mental workload during execution of goal-directed tasks and its application for interruption management. *ACM Transactions on Computer-Human Interaction, 14*(4), 1–28.

Beatty, J. (1982). Phasic not tonic pupillary responses vary with auditory vigilance performance. *Psychophysiology, 19*(2), 167–172.

Beatty, J., & Lucero-Wagoner, B. (2000). The pupillary system. In J. T. Cacioppo, L. G. Tassinary, & G. G. Berntson (Eds.), *Handbook of psychophysiology* (2nd ed., pp. 142–162). Cambridge, UK: Cambridge University Press.

Bernhardt, P. C., Dabbs, J. M., & Riad, J. K. (1996). Pupillometry system for use in social psychology. *Behavior Research Methods, Instruments, & Computers, 28*(1), 61–66.

Bull, R., & Shead, G. (1979). Pupil-dilation, sex of stimulus, and age and sex of observer. *Perceptual and Motor Skills, 49*(1), 27–30.

Card, S. K., Newell, A., & Moran, T. P. (1983). *The psychology of human-computer interaction.* Hillsdale, NJ: Lawrence Erlbaum Associates Inc.

Chapman, C. R., Oka, S., Bradshaw, D. H., Jacobson, R. C., & Donaldson, G. W. (1999). Phasic pupil dilation response to noxious stimulation in normal volunteers: Relationship to brain evoked potentials and pain report. *Psychophysiology, 36*(1), 44–52.

Chen, W. J., & Krajbich, I. (2017a). Computational modeling of epiphany learning. *Proceedings of the National Academy of Sciences, 114*(18), 4637–4642.

Chen, W. J., & Krajbich, I. (2017b). Pupil dilation and attention in value-based choice. *Working Paper.*

Costa, V. D., & Rudebeck, P. H. (2016). More than meets the eye: The relationship between pupil size and locus coeruleus activity. *Neuron, 89*(1), 8–10.

Dehais, F., Causse, M., & Pastor, J. (2008). Embedded eye tracker in a real aircraft: New perspectives on pilot/aircraft interaction monitoring. In *Proceedings from the 3rd international conference on research in air transportation.* Fairfax, VA: Federal Aviation Administration. Retrieved May 14, 2018, from http://oatao.univ-toulouse.fr/2138/

Duchowski, A. (2007). *Eye tracking methodology: Theory and practice* (Vol. 373). London, UK: Springer Science & Business Media.

Einhäuser, W., Koch, C., & Carter, O. L. (2010). Pupil dilation betrays the timing of decisions. *Frontiers in Human Neuroscience, 4*, 18.

Einhäuser, W., Stout, J., Koch, C., & Carter, O. (2008). Pupil dilation reflects perceptual selection and predicts subsequent stability in perceptual rivalry. *Proceedings of the National Academy of Sciences, 105*(5), 1704–1709.

Eldar, E., Cohen, J. D., & Niv, Y. (2013). The effects of neural gain on attention and learning. *Nature Neuroscience, 16*(8), 1146–1153.

Eldar, E., Niv, Y., & Cohen, J. D. (2016). Do you see the forest or the tree? Neural gain and breadth versus focus in perceptual processing. *Psychological Science, 27*(12), 1632–1643.

Gilzenrat, M. S., Nieuwenhuis, S., Jepma, M., & Cohen, J. D. (2010). Pupil diameter tracks changes in control state predicted by the adaptive gain theory of locus coeruleus function. *Cognitive, Affective, & Behavioral Neuroscience, 10*(2), 252–269.

Hayes, T. R., & Petrov, A. A. (2016a). Mapping and correcting the influence of gaze position on pupil size measurements. *Behavior Research Methods, 48*(2), 510–527.

Hayes, T. R., & Petrov, A. A. (2016b). Pupil diameter tracks the exploration–exploitation trade-off during analogical reasoning and explains individual differences in fluid intelligence. *Journal of Cognitive Neuroscience, 28*(2), 308–318.

Hess, E. H. (1972). Pupillometrics. In N. S. Greenfield & R. A. Sternbach (Eds.), *Handbook of psychophysiology* (pp. 491–531). New York, NY: Holt, Rinehart & Winston.

Hess, E. H., & Polt, J. M. (1960). Pupil size as related to interest value of visual stimuli. *Science, 132*(3423), 349–350.

Hess, E. H., & Polt, J. M. (1964). Pupil size in relation to mental activity during simple problem-solving. *Science, 143*(3611), 1190–1192.

Hicks, R. A., Reaney, T., & Hill, L. (1967). Effects of pupil size and facial angle on preference for photographs of a young woman. *Perceptual and Motor Skills, 24*(2), 388–390.

Hochman, G., & Yechiam, E. (2011). Loss aversion in the eye and in the heart: The autonomic nervous system's responses to losses. *Journal of Behavioral Decision Making, 24*(2), 140–156.

Iqbal, S. T., Zheng, X. S., & Bailey, B. P. (2004). Task-evoked pupillary response to mental workload in human-computer interaction. In E. Dykstra-Erickson & M. Tscheligi (Eds.), *Proceedings of the ACM conference on human factors in computing systems* (pp. 1477–1480). Vienna: ACM. Retrieved from http://dl.acm.org/citation.cfm?id=986094

Jepma, M., & Nieuwenhuis, S. (2011). Pupil diameter predicts changes in the exploration–exploitation trade-off: Evidence for the adaptive gain theory. *Journal of Cognitive Neuroscience, 23*(7), 1587–1596.

John, B. E., & Kieras, D. E. (1996). The GOMS family of user interface analysis techniques: Comparison and contrast. *ACM Transactions on Computer-Human Interaction (TOCHI), 3*(4), 320–351.

Joshi, S., Li, Y., Kalwani, R. M., & Gold, J. I. (2016). Relationships between pupil diameter and neuronal activity in the locus coeruleus, colliculi, and cingulate cortex. *Neuron, 89*(1), 221–234.

Kahneman, D., & Beatty, J. (1966). Pupil diameter and load on memory. *Science, 154*(3756), 1583–1585.

Kahneman, D., Tursky, B., Shapiro, D., & Crider, A. (1969). Pupillary, heart rate, and skin resistance changes during a mental task. *Journal of Experimental Psychology, 79*(1), 164–167.

Kang, M. J., Hsu, M., Krajbich, I. M., Loewenstein, G., McClure, S. M., Wang, J. T., & Camerer, C. F. (2009). The wick in the candle of learning: Epistemic curiosity activates reward circuitry and enhances memory. *Psychological Science, 20*(8), 963–973.

Klingner, J., Kumar, R., & Hanrahan, P. (2008). Measuring the task-evoked pupillary response with a remote eye tracker. In *Proceedings of the 2008 symposium on eye tracking research & applications* (pp. 69–72). Savannah, GA: ACM.

Laeng, B., Sirois, S., & Gredeback, G. (2012). Pupillometry: A window to the preconscious? *Perspectives on Psychological Science, 7*(1), 18–27.

Lavín, C., San Martín, R., & Rosales Jubal, E. (2014). Pupil dilation signals uncertainty and surprise in a learning gambling task. *Frontiers in Behavioral Neuroscience, 7*, 218.

Lempert, K. M., Glimcher, P. W., & Phelps, E. A. (2015). Emotional arousal and discount rate in intertemporal choice are reference dependent. *Journal of Experimental Psychology: General, 144*(2), 366–373.

Mathôt, S. (2013). *A simple way to reconstruct pupil size during eye blinks.* figshare. http://dx.doi.org/10.6084/m9.figshare.688001

Nassar, M. R., Rumsey, K. M., Wilson, R. C., Parikh, K., Heasly, B., & Gold, J. I. (2012). Rational regulation of learning dynamics by pupil-linked arousal systems. *Nature Neuroscience, 15*(7), 1040–1046.

Oliveira, F. T., Aula, A., & Russell, D. M. (2009). Discriminating the relevance of web search results with measures of pupil size. In *Proceedings of the SIGCHI conference on human factors in computing systems* (pp. 2209–2212). ACM. Retrieved from http://dl.acm.org/citation.cfm?id=1519038

Partala, T., & Surakka, V. (2003). Pupil size variation as an indication of affective processing. *International Journal of Human-Computer Studies, 59*(1), 185–198.

Preuschoff, K. (2011). Pupil dilation signals surprise: Evidence for noradrenaline's role in decision making. *Frontiers in Neuroscience, 5*, 115.

Rajkowski, J., Kubiak, P., & Aston-Jones, G. (1994). Locus coeruleus activity in monkey: Phasic and tonic changes are associated with altered vigilance. *Brain Research Bulletin, 35*(5–6), 607–616.

Siegle, G. J., Steinhauer, S. R., Stenger, V. A., Konecky, R., & Carter, C. S. (2003). Use of concurrent pupil dilation assessment to inform interpretation and analysis of fMRI data. *NeuroImage, 20*(1), 114–124.

Wang, J. T., Spezio, M., & Camerer, C. F. (2010). Pinocchio's pupil: Using eyetracking and pupil dilation to understand truth telling and deception in sender-receiver games. *The American Economic Review, 100*(3), 984–1007.

Yechiam, E., & Hochman, G. (2013). Losses as modulators of attention: Review and analysis of the unique effects of losses over gains. *Psychological Bulletin, 139*(2), 497–518.

4

A PRIMER ON EYE-TRACKING METHODOLOGY FOR BEHAVIORAL SCIENCE

Jacob L. Orquin and Kenneth Holmqvist

Eye-tracking methodology is widely used in the behavioral sciences such as judgment and decision making (JDM), marketing, or human computer interaction. In these disciplines, eye-tracking helps to understand psychological processes by enriching behavioral data such as choices with process data such as eye movements and pupil dilation. While behavioral researchers frequently apply eye-tracking, methodological research on eye-tracking is mainly conducted by vision researchers and published in vision journals. Consequently, methodological research is not always noticed by behavioral or applied researchers. In this chapter we aim to bridge the gap between methodological and behavioral eye-tracking research by providing an overview of best practices for eye-tracking research. The structure of the chapter corresponds to a typical research project beginning with research questions and progressing to experimental design, implementation of the experiment, data collection, data preprocessing and analysis, and finally interpretation of results. Throughout the chapter we focus on examples from JDM, but the issues raised here relate equally to other areas of the behavioral sciences as well.

Research Questions and Hypotheses

Eye-tracking research in JDM can be classified along a decision versus vision science dimension. Studies closer to decision science tend to use the eye tracker as a process measure, sometimes, along with other measures such as reaction time and verbal reports (e.g., Fiedler, Glöckner, Nicklisch, & Dickert, 2013). That is, these studies seek to understand decision processes and the eye tracker provides the additional process data that helps limit the space of possible decision processes. On the other end are studies more related to vision science (e.g., Mitsuda & Glaholt, 2014). These studies are more concerned with eye movements and attention processes in the context of decision making, comparing them to, for instance, eye movements in reading, visual search, or natural tasks. In between these poles, we find studies that bridge decision and vision science by modelling how eye movements influence decision-making processes (e.g., Bird, Lauwereyns, & Crawford, 2012; Krajbich, Armel, & Rangel, 2010).

A key challenge for all types of eye-tracking research in JDM, and particularly for studies using eye-tracking as a process measure, is how to derive predictions about eye movements in decision making. One approach has been to map predictions from behavioral decision theory

(BDT) directly to eye movements (Glöckner & Herbold, 2011). For instance, BDT might propose that participants using a weighted additive decision process (WADD) will search information in an alternative-wise manner whereas participants using a lexicographic process (LEX) will search information in an attribute-wise manner (Payne, Bettman, & Johnson, 1988). However, attempts to directly map predictions from BDT to eye movements have not been very successful in demonstrating the use of these decision processes (for a review see Orquin & Loose, 2013). It might be, of course, that decision makers simply do not use such processes, but a more realistic suggestion is that eye movements cannot be predicted directly from a deterministic information search model such as WADD or LEX. A recommendation for generating eye movement predictions in decision making is therefore to carefully consider eye movement control processes in their own right first and only then generate predictions from decision models. Eye movement control processes differ depending on the task and context (Rayner, 2009), but a general and useful framework distinguishes between top down and bottom up control processes. Top down control refers to situations where eye movements are driven by tasks or goals, which allow the observer to attend to what is currently relevant and ignore everything else, e.g., focusing on reading a newspaper while the TV is on. Bottom up control refers to eye movements that are driven by stimulus characteristics such as the color, contrast, or position of objects in our surroundings. The distinction between the two eye movement processes can be blurry at times. For instance, top down control predicts that a person searching for a red car will be more likely to look at red cars rather than cars in other colors. However, bottom up control could easily predict the same if red cars are more visually prominent than cars in other colors. For this reason it can be difficult to disentangle whether a specific fixation or saccade is driven more by top down or bottom up processes. In a JDM context, the complex relation between top down and bottom up processes may be part of the explanation of why it is so difficult to identify decision processes such as WADD or LEX (Schulte-Mecklenbeck, Kühberger, Gagl, & Hutzler, 2017) since these top down decision processes are intermingled with bottom up processes. Because of such complications, it can be difficult to translate a research question directly into a prediction about eye movements. Understanding eye movement control processes such as the top down and bottom up taxonomy is therefore essential to generating predictions and interpreting eye movements in many areas of behavioral research (Meißner & Oll, 2017; Orquin & Loose, 2013; Wedel & Pieters, 2008).

Experimental Design

Comparisons in Eye-Tracking

Fundamental to any experimental design is the question of what is being compared to what. To make sense of comparisons in eye-tracking we propose to distinguish between three types of comparisons. The first type, *group-level* comparisons, refers to any manipulation or measurement outside the visual stimulus. This could, for instance, be comparisons of eye movements between older or younger adults or between participants instructed to follow either WADD or LEX decision rules. Group-level comparisons generally result in changes in top down control processes. The second type, *between-stimuli* comparisons, refers to a manipulated or measured difference between at least two visual stimuli presented in separate trials. This could, for instance, be comparisons of fixations to choice options with high versus low contrast, which is useful for understanding bottom up control components in decisions. Between-stimuli comparisons can also be used for studying top down control. For instance, Orquin, Chrobot, and Grunert (2017) showed that the predictability of object locations influence top down control. However, using between-stimuli comparisons to understand top down control can be problematic. Manipulating the visual characteristics of experimental stimuli is likely to introduce confounding with bottom up factors. For example, Kuo, Hsu, and Day (2009) compared eye movements to positively and negatively framed messages, assuming that the framing effect only influences the interpretation of the choice problem. However, in changing the framing, the authors also changed the syntactical structure of the message, which can influence the reading process (Rayner, 2009) and thereby confound the findings. The third type, *within-stimulus* comparisons, refers to comparisons between at least two objects or areas of interest (AOIs) within the same visual scene or trial. Considering that most eye-tracking studies rely on two or more AOIs per trial this type of comparison is probably the most common. A typical situation in decision research is the comparison between eye movements to probabilities and pay-offs in risky gambles. Within-stimulus comparisons are used both for understanding top down and bottom up control. In risky gambles, it is generally assumed that different decision strategies will result in different eye movement patterns to probabilities and pay-offs. The challenge with this prediction is that the comparison is confounded by stimulus characteristics. It is, for instance, likely that decision makers process probabilities stated in percentages and pay-offs stated in monetary amounts differently which will bias a comparison between them (Brandstätter & Körner, 2014). Within-stimulus comparisons are also used for understanding bottom up control. For instance, Atalay, Bodur, and Rasolofoarison (2012) compared eye movements to centrally and non-centrally positioned choice options. Drawing conclusions about a single aspect of bottom up control such as position can be equally problematic since changes to stimulus characteristics are likely to influence other stimulus aspects as well. Choice options that are more centrally positioned could also by chance be more salient or larger since similarly sized objects occupy a smaller area of our visual field when positioned peripherally. Besides the three main types of comparisons, researchers can also apply any combination of these in their experimental design: *group-level-between-stimuli*, *group-level-within-stimulus*, *within-between-stimuli*, and *group-level-within-between-stimuli*. In general, the same challenges exist for combined comparisons as for simple comparisons. Table 4.1 contains an overview of the comparison types and examples of studies using them.

Fixed versus Free Exposure Time

When designing eye-tracking experiments it is necessary to consider the exposure time of stimuli. The most common approach in decision making is to use free exposure time which typically allows participants to terminate the trial by indicating their choice. An alternative approach is to use fixed exposure time which predetermines how long participants see a stimulus. A fixed exposure time has the advantage that measures such as dwell time, number of fixations, and over-time measures are directly comparable between different subjects. However, fixed exposure time may bias the eye movement process by either over- or under-exposing stimuli. That is, in a given trial the participant will either see the stimulus for a shorter or longer time than she would otherwise have wanted compared to free exposure time. This is likely to create a feeling of either time pressure or a feeling of idleness. These psychological processes are likely to influence eye movements, which may or may not be desirable, depending on the research question (for further discussion see Orquin & Holmqvist, 2018). For these reasons, it is generally preferable to use free exposure time.

Number of Trials and Sample Size

Determining an adequate number of trials and participants for an eye-tracking experiment can be daunting. The task is complicated by the fact that different types of comparisons, e.g., within- or

56 Orquin and Holmqvist

TABLE 4.1 A taxonomy of eye movement comparisons

Definition	Examples	
group-level	Comparison between at least two groups on a single AOI or scan-path. Can be either a within- or between-subjects factor (levels 3 and 2 in Figure 4.2).	van Herpen and van Trijp (2011) compare eye movements to nutrition labels (single AOI) for participants instructed with preferential shopping goals versus general or specific health shopping goals. Shimojo, Simion, Shimojo, & Scheier (2003) show that the probability of fixating the eventually chosen (versus non chosen) option increases immediately before the choice is made.
between stimuli	Comparison between at least two different stimuli on a single AOI or scan-path. Can be either a within- or between-subjects factor (level 2 in Figure 4.2).	Kuo et al. (2009) compare eye movements under positive and negative framing. Orquin et al. (2017) compare fixations to a product feature under fixed versus random positioning.
within stimulus	Comparison within a stimulus between two or more AOIs. Can only be a within-subjects factor (level 1 in Figure 4.2).	Glöckner and Herbold (2011) compare eye movements to probabilities versus pay-offs in risky gambles. Atalay et al. (2012) compare eye movements to centrally versus non centrally positioned products.
group-level-between stimuli	Crossed comparison between at least two groups and two stimuli on a single AOI or scan-path.	Orquin and Lagerkvist (2015) compare eye movements to a product feature under high versus low salience (between stimuli) and positive versus negative valence (group-level).
group-level-within stimulus	Crossed comparison between at least two groups and at least two AOIs within one stimulus.	Ashby, Dickert, and Glöckner (2012) compare eye movements between buyers and sellers (group-level) to high versus low outcomes (within stimulus) for risky gambles.
within-between stimuli	Crossed comparison between at least two stimuli and at least two AOIs within each stimulus.	Perkovic and Orquin (2018) compare eye movements between two product features (within stimulus) across three visual contingency conditions (between stimuli).
group-level-within-between stimuli	Crossed comparison between at least two groups, at least two stimuli, and at least two AOIs within each stimulus.	Kwak, Payne, Cohen, and Huettel (2015) compare eye movements between younger and older adults (group-level), between random and structured gambles (between stimuli) to high versus low outcomes (within stimulus) in risky gambles.

between-stimuli, often lead to nested data structures or mixed within-between subjects designs. Generic power analyses often provide little help with such designs and using heuristics, such as minimum 25 participants per cell, may also be inadequate. For example, vision scientists occasionally conduct eye-tracking experiments with as few as four to five participants exposed to over 1000 trials. Such studies are more common for research on cognitive processes that are constant rather than variable across participants. Generally, the more trials the fewer participants are needed, but there are limits of course. Rather than guessing at what is optimal in terms of number of trials and participants it is better to simulate the analysis. Power simulations generally involve the following steps. First, write a function that generates data according to the experimental hypotheses. Second, write a function that fits the hypothesized model to the generated data. Third, fit the model to the generated data and extract the relevant model statistics, e.g., p-values or goodness of fit measures such as AIC, BIC, or a LL-ratio test. Repeat this, for instance, 1000 times and compute the average of the relevant statistic, e.g., the percentage of iterations resulting in a p-value $< .05$. The resulting average indicates the power of the experimental design, i.e., the probability of detecting an effect given that there is one. By repeating the procedure with different number of trials and sample sizes we can estimate the minimum sample size and number of trials required to achieve a desired level of power such as 75% (for an introduction to power simulation see Bolker, 2008). Performing a power simulation can be difficult, but is often the only solution to complex experimental designs which are typical in eye-tracking research. An example of R code for this type of power simulation can be found at https://osf.io/23c6v/.

Setting Up the Experiment

Stimulus Characteristics

A crucial step in all eye-tracking studies is the development of visual stimuli. A simple rule of thumb is that an eye-tracking experiment is only as good as its visual stimuli. This is especially true for experiments based on between- or within-stimulus comparisons in which the visual stimuli operationalizes the construct of interest, e.g., salience (Itti & Koch, 2001) or emotional valence (Nummenmaa, Hyönä, & Calvo, 2006). It is therefore important to take great care when developing the visual stimuli and it is advisable to test the validity of the stimuli whenever possible. Such tests could, for instance, be validations of salience manipulations against salience models (Orquin, Bagger, & Loose, 2013) or ensuring that textual information is equally readable across AOIs (Brandstätter & Körner, 2014).

Another important aspect of stimulus development is considering the size of the stimuli. Eye trackers generally record eye positions with considerable spatial noise, which means that fixations to an object are not always recorded as falling within the boundaries of the object. When a fixation is recorded outside the AOI surrounding the object it is typically deleted leading to a false negative observation. Figure 4.1 shows an example of how recorded fixations are scattered outside and around the boundaries of objects. Using a better eye-tracking with more accuracy and precision would reduce the scattering and increase certainty about which fixations belong to which objects. We refer to the percentage of fixations to an object that are recorded within the boundaries of the object as the *capture rate* (Orquin & Holmqvist, 2018). Ideally, we want the capture rate to be 100%, i.e., all fixations to an object are recorded correctly. However, the capture rate is rarely 100% and only gets worse when we use an eye tracker with low accuracy (validity) or low precision (reliability), but also when objects are relatively small, i.e., less than 3–5 degrees of visual angle. When recording with eye trackers with poor accuracy and precision it can be necessary to increase the size of objects in order to ensure a high enough capture rate. Even for high precision eye trackers (e.g., accuracy = .5° and precision = .05°) ensuring an 80% capture rate requires a minimum stimulus size of 3.2 degrees of visual angle. Examples of R code for computing capture rates can be found at https://osf.io/5c7yt/ and for computing degrees of visual angle at https://osf.io/umnr9/. The code is easy to apply and helps compute minimum object sizes for stimulus development given a desired capture rate and the accuracy and precision of the eye tracker that will be used.

As a final issue regarding stimulus development, it is important to use counterbalancing of stimulus positions whenever possible. Also note that counterbalancing is important for other process tracing methods such as mouse tracking (see Chapters 8–10) and MouselabWEB (see Chapters 6–7). In

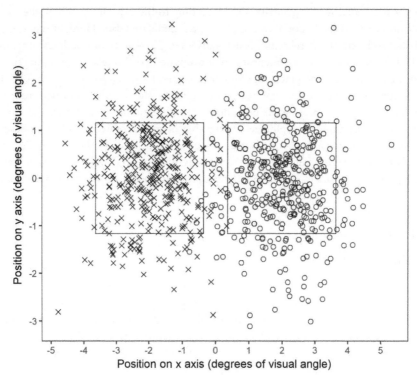

FIGURE 4.1 An example of how recorded eye movements tend to scatter around the fixated objects. Crosses and circles represent fixations to the left and right squares respectively.

studies using naturalistic stimuli this may not be feasible, but many decision studies rely on matrices for presenting choice information, e.g., columns representing choice options and rows representing choice attributes. Such studies often rely on within-stimulus comparisons, and without counterbalancing the positions of options and attributes the eye movements to each stimulus would be confounded by the respective position of that stimulus since participants generally fixate more in the middle and top left of the matrix (Orquin & Loose, 2013).

Collecting Data

The actual accuracy and precision of eye trackers depend not only on the eye tracker, but on many other factors as well. Some of these factors can be influenced by the researcher and we list several of the known factors in Table 4.2. The data quality values are reported by Holmqvist and Andersson (2017). For example, if you record participants without glasses or lenses, who have brown eyes, and do not wear make-up, the classification of fixations and saccades will be more accurate, as will the AOI analysis (see previous section). A 300% worse precision, for instance, corresponds to an artefactual increase in average fixation durations of more than 150 msec, when using a common velocity-based detection algorithm (Holmqvist & Andersson, 2017).

Preparing Data for Analysis

Before analyses are performed, eye-tracking data typically undergoes considerable preprocessing. This may consist of filtering or smoothing the data, averaging the eye positions, and classifying

A Primer on Eye-Tracking Methodology **59**

TABLE 4.2 Factors influencing eye-tracking data quality

Data Quality Factor	Explanation
Glasses	Better data quality when participants do not wear glasses. Anti-reflective glasses in particular result in accuracies of 3–10° and a noise in data three times worse than with no glasses. Scratched and dirty glasses have 1–3° inaccuracy and doubled noise, on average. Consider screening for glasses.
Contact lenses	Most remote eye trackers handle lenses well, while high-end eye trackers can have increased noise and artefacts. Overall, lenses are better than glasses for eye-tracking.
Right versus left eye recorded	Using the dominant eye yields 0.2–2° better accuracy, depending on the eye tracker. In about 70% of the cases, subjects are right-eye dominant.
Eye color	Brown eyes give better data on most eye trackers. Blue eyes result in data that is 20–80% less precise and about 0.5° less accurate than brown eyes.
Make-up	Mascara, eye-liner, and eye-shadow all affect precision (10–300% worse, depending on the eye tracker) and accuracy (0.5–3° worse). Consider whether to ask participants not to wear any make-up around the eyes.
Pupil diameter	Larger pupils result in worse accuracy (up to 2°) and more noise (up to 300% more). Consider increasing ambient light sources.
Calibration type	Better data quality with participant controlled calibration, about half a degree better accuracy.
Corner positions	Placing crucial stimuli in the corner of the eye-tracker monitor is a bad idea since corners often provide inaccurate data (up to 10° average error on some eye trackers).
Sun light	Avoid sunlight and hot light bulbs, as they are detrimental to data quality.

Adapted from Holmqvist and Andersson (2017). All increases refer to the RMS-S2S-values of the (x,y) signal for precision, and the offset between recorded (x,y) position and subjectively experienced gaze position.

fixations and saccades. These steps are often performed by default by the eye-tracker software, but it is an advantage to understand the effect of different types of preprocessing (averaging and event detection, for instance) as these may lead to different results depending on the data quality. Another important preprocessing step is assigning AOIs. There are several alternatives to using AOIs and even ways of assigning AOIs, but the vast majority of eye-tracking studies probably rely on hand-drawn AOIs (Hessels, Kemner, van den Boomen, & Hooge, 2016). One of the main challenges in assigning AOIs is to balance false negatives and false positives. Because capture rates are never 100%, fixations are often recorded as falling outside the object to which they belong (see Figure 4.1). When this occurs, a simple solution is to make the AOI larger than the object (Holmqvist et al., 2011). This, however, is only a useful solution when neighboring objects are sufficiently far away. Extending AOIs to neighboring objects increases the risk of assigning false positives, i.e., fixations that rightfully belong to the neighboring object. When objects are positioned relatively close to each other and when data quality is relatively low it is therefore advisable to use minimal AOIs that follow the perimeter of the object. When objects are positioned relatively far apart or when data quality is high it is advisable to use AOIs that are larger than the object to which they are assigned (Orquin, Ashby, & Clarke, 2016). In some cases it might be worth hand coding a number of trials to test whether the AOI margins produce more false positive or false negative fixations (Perkovic & Orquin, 2018).

Analyzing Data

Checking Data Quality

Before beginning data analyses, it is advisable to perform one or more tests of the data quality. A simple test concerns the percentage of data samples recorded by the eye tracker. In some cases the eye tracker fails to obtain a measure of the eye position, for instance during blinks, but also when a participant gazes outside the screen, moves their head, or in other ways interferes with the infrared light reflected from their eyes. It is common to exclude participants with a large proportion of missing data or alternatively, exclude trials with a large proportion of missing data. Clean data always have 2–3% lost samples, due to blinks. With increasing data loss, fixations become longer and fewer (Holmqvist & Andersson, 2017). Another simple approach is to manually inspect the scan-path for each trial to determine whether fixations have been recorded reliably and accurately (Holmqvist et al., 2011). As this approach is very time demanding an alternative is to inspect participants or trials with a relatively low percentage of fixations falling within AOIs. It is also advisable to perform more rigorous tests of missing data, for instance, to ensure that data is missing at random or missing completely at random (see for instance Orquin & Lagerkvist, 2015) or to use computational methods to determine trials with a lot of noise (high RMS-S2S values) or a high proportion of lost samples.

Eye Movement Metrics

The choice of eye movement metrics for any research question should be made during the experimental design. If there is any doubt which eye movement measures to use, this is an indicator that the research question is not sufficiently precise in terms of eye movement control processes. If in doubt about measures Holmqvist and Andersson (2017) propose the following method. First, draw the eye movements you expect onto your stimulus images. Second, based on the drawing decide whether you want to measure movement properties, position properties, latencies, or number of different events. Finally, check Chapters 13–16 of Holmqvist and Andersson (2017) for the specific measures. Research on bottom up processes often focuses on attention capture and common eye movement metrics are whether AOIs are fixated or not (fixation likelihood) and the speed with which they are fixated (saccadic latency). Research questions related to top down control can use the same metrics, but may also rely on the number of fixations or dwells (fixation or dwell count), the duration of individual fixations (fixation duration), or the order of fixations or dwells (fixation or dwell order). Besides these basic metrics, many researchers rely on transformed metrics as well. By transformed we mean any or several of the basic metrics that have been transformed or aggregated to produce a new metric. A common transformed metric is total dwell time (also referred to as total fixation duration) which is the product of fixation count and fixation duration. Another common approach is to transform fixation count or total dwell time into proportions when using within-stimulus comparisons. In general, we recommend caution when considering whether to use transformed metrics. Total dwell time can produce misleading conclusions when the underlying metrics (fixation count and duration) are correlated. For instance, when total dwell time indicates a difference between two objects, this may be due to either more or longer fixations. When total dwell time indicates no difference, this does not, however, imply that there are no differences in fixation count and duration (Orquin & Holmqvist, 2018). Fixation proportions produce the same statistical results as the original metric, but has the clear disadvantage of hiding the basic metrics. A comparison might, for instance, reveal that one object is fixated 50% more often than another, but does that mean 3 versus 2 fixations or 15 versus 10 fixations? There is an important difference between one more fixation and five more fixations that is obscured by using proportions. Besides the basic and transformed metrics, decision researchers often rely on more complex indices computed from several underlying metrics. A common index is the Search Index which computes the proportion of within alternative to within attribute-wise transitions (Payne, 1976). Complex indices are useful for highly specific tests of models and hypotheses, for instance, whether participants make decisions by searching information within alternatives as suggested by decision rules such as WADD or within attributes as suggested by the lexicographic rule (Glöckner & Herbold, 2011). Occasionally new indices are invented such as the Strategy Measure which adjusts the Search Index for the number of alternatives and attributes (Böckenholt & Hynan, 1994), or the Systematicity of Search Index which produces a measure of the randomness of a search process (Perkovic, Kaptan, & Bown, 2018). Using complex indices requires a higher degree of computation, but also imposes a higher demand for specific hypotheses and models, which is generally a good thing. As a final word on choosing metrics, it is important to remember that the fewer the better. It is unfortunately common to test multiple basic and transformed metrics without clear hypotheses which increases the risk of type I errors unnecessarily.

Eye Movement Analysis

There are a large number of ways to analyze eye movement data, each linked to an experimental design. A particularly common approach is using generalized linear mixed models (also referred to as GLMMs, multilevel or hierarchical models). This has become a widely adopted method since most eye-tracking studies use repeated measures to increase the precision and power of the study and some experimental designs such as within-stimulus comparisons necessarily produce repeated measures. To take the dependency of observations into account it is common to use GLMMs which allow for random intercepts and slopes. In plain words, a GLMM is a regression that takes into account how groupings in the data, such as participants or trials, influence the dependent variable (modelled with the random intercept) or the effect of the independent variables (modelled with the random slopes). As an example, imagine a study examining whether presenting information with numbers or symbols changes processing of risk information. Such a study would yield a between-stimuli comparison for number versus symbol conditions and a within-stimulus comparison for probabilities versus pay-offs. With 50 trials of risky gambles per participant this would lead to a three level data structure (see Figure 4.2).

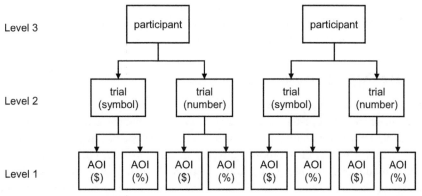

FIGURE 4.2 A typical multilevel structure of eye movement data with observations per AOI (probabilities = % versus pay-offs = $) nested within trials (symbols versus numbers) within participants.

GLMMs are suitable for the multilevel structure in eye movement data, which would yield biased estimates in standard statistical tests, but GLMMs have other advantages as well. For eye-tracking studies, it is particularly interesting to know that GLMMs can handle missing data and unbalanced designs, which occurs when researchers delete trials or participants with low data quality, which is common, as we noted earlier. These models can also handle many types of dependent variables: normally distributed (fixation duration), count variables (fixation count), or binary variables (fixation likelihood). GLMMs can be performed in SAS with PROC GLIMMIX, in SPSS with the MIXED Procedure or in R with the lme4 package (Bates, Mächler, Bolker, & Walker, 2015); for an example eye-tracking data set and R code for standard GLMMs see https://osf.io/84tex/.

Interpreting and Reporting the Study

Interpreting Eye Movements

The great promise of eye-tracking is undoubtedly the possibility of opening the black box of cognitive processes. Some understand this to mean that eye movements provide a direct insight into psychological processes. Such claims are sometimes accompanied with a reference to the eye-mind assumption which states that what is fixated is also processed at a cognitive level (Just & Carpenter, 1976). While it is true that there is a strong association between eye movements and attention (Orquin & Loose, 2013), this does not mean that we can therefore interpret fixations as attention. Attention can be overt such as when we attend to the currently fixated object or covert when we attend to an object outside fovea. Besides this challenge, fixations are not always assigned correctly (see earlier on capture rate) which makes it even less realistic to infer attention from eye movements. In general, it is worth considering whether it is necessary to make such claims at all since it is often sufficient, both in terms of theory and application, to focus on eye movements only. A second challenge in interpreting eye movements is the generalizability to external environments. Particularly applied research is often concerned with the transfer of findings to non-laboratory environments (see Chapter 2). There are, however, many reasons to suspect that eye movement patterns identified in lab studies may be difficult to transfer to other environments. For instance, in lab studies participants keep their head position fixed while moving their eyes, while in the real world people move both their head and their eyes. Furthermore, participants in the lab do not have to interact with other people or objects which can lead to quite different eye movement patterns (Foulsham, Walker, & Kingstone, 2011). In general, rather than attempt to generalize eye movements it might be better to generalize eye movement control mechanisms. For instance, finding that eye movements in decision making are driven both by bottom up and top down processes may transfer well from the lab (Orquin & Lagerkvist, 2015) to decision making in physical stores (Gidlöf, Anikin, Lingonblad, & Wallin, 2017).

Reporting Eye-Tracking Studies

Complete and transparent reporting is important to all types of studies to ensure reproducibility and progress in science. In eye-tracking research it can be challenging to know what complete and reproducible reporting includes. It is far too common for eye-tracking researchers to under-report their studies which limits reproducibility. For instance, many studies fail even to mention the name and producer of the eye tracker used, let alone the details of the fixation classification, or the average precision and accuracy, which we know may affect results. To avoid repetition, we refer the reader to Chapter 5 which proposes a reporting guideline for eye-tracking studies in decision research.

Conclusion

In this chapter, we have aimed to provide an overview of best practices for eye-tracking research in behavioral sciences. We have proposed several methodological and theoretical issues that are important to meaningful and valid eye-tracking research. In the first two sections we showed how some research questions and comparisons can introduce confounds already at the early stages of a project. In the latter sections we showed how factors such as data quality, the analytical approach, or reporting may influence the validity, generalizability, and reproducibility of the research. All issues are necessary to achieve meaningful and valid eye-tracking research, but we do not guarantee that considering these issues is sufficient. We therefore advise aspiring eye-tracking researchers to consult more comprehensive work on eye-tracking methodology and, of course, to apply critical judgment before following or deciding not to follow best practice advice.

Recommended Reading List

- Orquin and Holmqvist (2017): for further details regarding challenges to eye-tracking research.
- Orquin and Loose (2013): for a broader introduction to eye movements in decision making.
- Holmqvist et al. (2011) and Holmqvist and Andersson (2017): for a broader introduction to eye-tracking methodology.

References

Ashby, N. J. S., Dickert, S., & Glöckner, A. (2012). Focusing on what you own: Biased information uptake due to ownership. *Judgment and Decision Making, 7*(3), 254–267. Retrieved from https://search.proquest.com/openview/4db183217d6d8b00afc426ea1ba9ed4b/1?pq-origsite=gscholar&cbl=696407

Atalay, A. S., Bodur, H. O., & Rasolofoarison, D. (2012). Shining in the center: Central gaze cascade effect on product choice. *Journal of Consumer Research, 39*(4), 848–866.

Bates, D., Mächler, M., Bolker, B. M., & Walker, S. C. (2015). Fitting linear mixed-effects models using lme4. *Journal of Statistical Software, 67*(1), 1–48.

Bird, G. D., Lauwereyns, J., & Crawford, M. T. (2012). The role of eye movements in decision making and the prospect of exposure effects. *Vision Research, 60*, 16–21.

Böckenholt, U., & Hynan, L. S. (1994). Caveats on a process-tracing measure and a remedy. *Journal of Behavioral Decision Making, 7*(2), 103–117.

Bolker, B. M. (2008). *Ecological Models and Data in R*. Princeton, NJ: Princeton University Press.

Brandstätter, E., & Körner, C. (2014). Attention in risky choice. *Acta Psychologica, 152*, 166–176.

Fiedler, S., Glöckner, A., Nicklisch, A., & Dickert, S. (2013). Social value orientation and information search in social dilemmas: An eye-tracking analysis. *Organizational Behavior and Human Decision Processes, 120*(2), 272–284.

Foulsham, T., Walker, E., & Kingstone, A. (2011). The where, what and when of gaze allocation in the lab and the natural environment. *Vision Research, 51*(17), 1920–1931.

Gidlöf, K., Anikin, A., Lingonblad, M., & Wallin, A. (2017). Looking is buying. How visual attention and choice are affected by consumer preferences and properties of the supermarket shelf. *Appetite, 116*, 29–38.

Glöckner, A., & Herbold, A.-K. (2011). An eye-tracking study on information processing in risky decisions: Evidence for compensatory strategies based on automatic processes. *Journal of Behavioral Decision Making, 24*(1), 71–98.

Hessels, R. S., Kemner, C., van den Boomen, C., & Hooge, I. T. C. (2016). The area-of-interest problem in eyetracking research: A noise-robust solution for face and sparse stimuli. *Behavior Research Methods, 48*(4), 1694–1712.

Holmqvist, K., & Andersson, R. (2017). *Eye tracking: A comprehensive guide to methods, paradigms, and measures*. Lund, SWE: Lund Eye-Tracking Research Institute.

Holmqvist, K., Nyström, M., Andersson, R., Dewhurst, R., Halszka, J., & van de Weijer, J. (2011). *Eye tracking: A comprehensive guide to methods and measures*. Oxford, UK: Oxford University Press.

Itti, L., & Koch, C. (2001). Computational modelling of visual attention. *Nature Reviews Neuroscience, 2*(3), 194–203.

Just, M. A., & Carpenter, P. A. (1976). Eye fixations and cognitive processes. *Cognitive Psychology, 8*(4), 441–480.

Krajbich, I., Armel, C., & Rangel, A. (2010). Visual fixations and the computation and comparison of value in simple choice. *Nature Neuroscience, 13*(10), 1292–1298.

Kuo, F.-Y., Hsu, C.-W., & Day, R.-F. (2009). An exploratory study of cognitive effort involved in decision under framing—an application of the eye-tracking technology. *Decision Support Systems, 48*(1), 81–91.

Kwak, Y., Payne, J. W., Cohen, A. L., & Huettel, S. A. (2015). The rational adolescent: Strategic information processing during decision making revealed by eye tracking. *Cognitive Development, 36*, 20–30.

Meißner, M., & Oll, J. (2017). The promise of eye-tracking methodology in organizational research. *Organizational Research Methods*, doi.109442811774488.

Mitsuda, T., & Glaholt, M. G. (2014). Gaze bias during visual preference judgements: Effects of stimulus category and decision instructions. *Visual Cognition, 22*(1), 11–29.

Nummenmaa, L., Hyönä, J., & Calvo, M. G. (2006). Eye movement assessment of selective attentional capture by emotional pictures. *Emotion, 6*(2), 257–268.

Orquin, J. L., Ashby, N. J. S., & Clarke, A. D. F. (2016). Areas of interest as a signal detection problem in behavioral eye-tracking research. *Journal of Behavioral Decision Making, 29*(2–3), 103–115.

Orquin, J. L., Bagger, M. P., & Loose, S. (2013). Learning affects top down and bottom up modulation of eye movements in decision making. *Judgment and Decision Making, 8*(6), 700–716.

Orquin, J. L., Chrobot, N., & Grunert, K. G. (2017). Guiding decision makers' eye movements with (un)predictable object locations. *Journal of Behavioral Decision Making, 31*(3), 341–354.

Orquin, J. L., & Holmqvist, K. (2018). Threats to the validity of eye-movement research in psychology. *Behavior Research Methods, 50*(4), 1645–1656.

Orquin, J. L., & Lagerkvist, C. J. (2015). Effects of salience are both short- and long-lived. *Acta Psychologica, 160*, 69–76.

Orquin, J. L., & Loose, S. (2013). Attention and choice: A review on eye movements in decision making. *Acta Psychologica, 144*(1), 190–206.

Payne, J. W. (1976). Task complexity and contingent processing in decision making: An information search and protocol analysis. *Organizational Behavior and Human Performance, 16*(2), 366–387.

Payne, J. W., Bettman, J. R., & Johnson, E. J. (1988). Adaptive strategy selection in decision making. *Journal of Experimental Psychology: Learning, Memory, and Cognition, 14*(3), 534–552.

Perkovic, S., Kaptan, G., & Bown, N. (2018). Systematicity of search index: A new measure for exploring information search patterns. *Journal of Behavioral Decision Making, 31*(5), 673–685.

Perkovic, S., & Orquin, J. L. (2018). Implicit statistical learning in real-world environments leads to ecologically rational decision making. *Psychological Science, 29*(1), 34–44.

Rayner, K. (2009). Eye movements and attention in reading, scene perception, and visual search. *The Quarterly Journal of Experimental Psychology, 62*(8), 1457–1506.

Schulte-Mecklenbeck, M., Kühberger, A., Gagl, B., & Hutzler, F. (2017). Inducing thought processes: Bringing process measures and cognitive processes closer together. *Journal of Behavioral Decision Making, 30*(5), 1001–1013.

Shimojo, S., Simion, C., Shimojo, E., & Scheier, C. (2003). Gaze bias both reflects and influences preference. *Nature Neuroscience, 6*(12), 1317–1322.

van Herpen, E., & van Trijp, H. C. M. (2011). Front-of-pack nutrition labels. Their effect on attention and choices when consumers have varying goals and time constraints. *Appetite, 57*(1), 148–160.

Wedel, M., & Pieters, R. (2008). Eye tracking for visual marketing. *Foundations and Trends® in Marketing, 1*(4), 231–320.

5

INCREASING REPRODUCIBILITY OF EYE-TRACKING STUDIES

The EyeGuidelines

Susann Fiedler, Michael Schulte-Mecklenbeck, Frank Renkewitz, and Jacob L. Orquin

Standards are an essential part of the scientific method. They guarantee a commonly accepted approach for (reproducible) research (e.g., Asendorpf et al., 2013; Wicherts et al., 2016), ensure agreement on how data should be collected and analyzed (Gopen & Swan, 1990), and how reporting of the methods and results should be done (APA Publications and Communications Board Working Group on Journal Article Reporting Standards, 2008; Appelbaum et al., 2018). This last aspect of standards is central to this chapter that will provide a list of reporting standards meant to increase reproducibility of eye-tracking research in judgment and decision making (JDM).

In eye-tracking (see Chapters 1–5), technological advances in the last decades have lowered the prices, increased the availability, and made the application of eye-tracking technology easier. Given these shrinking barriers, many researchers have begun using the technology to describe otherwise unobservable cognitive processes in different areas of JDM research. In the last ten years alone, this has led to hundreds of published articles with contributions in various areas such as behavioral decision theory (Ashby, Johnson, Krajbich, & Wedel, 2016), organizational processes (Meißner & Oll, 2018), economic and financial decision making (Krajbich, Oud, & Fehr, 2014), marketing (Wedel & Pieters, 2007), clinical and medical decision making (Schulte-Mecklenbeck, Spaanjaars, & Witteman, 2017), and moral decision making (Fiedler & Glöckner, 2015).

For researchers to benefit from this wealth of findings, the literature has to be clear in the questions addressed, the description of the used methods, the presented results, and their interpretation (Glasziou et al., 2014). The quality and resource efficiency of a research field depends heavily on the contributions of individual publications. While eye-tracking in JDM has amassed an impressive number of studies, it may still be lacking on other more qualitative aspects. We reviewed all papers (N = 215, including 268 individual studies) using eye-tracking in JDM (broadly defined) published between 2009 and 2017. Figure 5.1 shows that the field experiences a steady increase in papers using eye-tracking as the main methodology. While in 2009 only four papers could be identified, in 2014 this number grew to 35 and stayed at this frequency up to 2017 with 37 papers.

Using this data set of papers, we additionally coded the presence or absence of a large set of reporting criteria dealing with the description of the used methodology (find further detailed analysis of this data set in Fiedler, Schulte-Mecklenbeck, Renkewitz, & Orquin, 2018). In Figure 5.2, we added a black rectangle given that a variable was reported (present) in a paper. A white rectangle was added whenever a variable was missing (not present). As we will discuss later, a report of

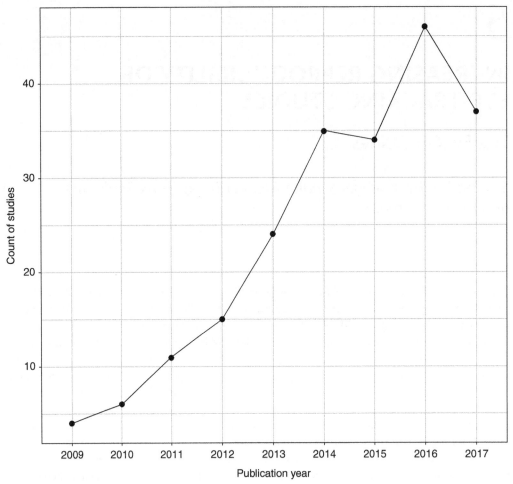

FIGURE 5.1 Overview of included studies using eye-tracking as the main methodology (author generated).

an eye-tracking study that ensures reproducibility would require that columns of papers are filled black with a few white spaces in-between at most.

The gap analysis illustrates that there are no papers reporting on all the items we suggest as a minimal standard. Approximately 70% of all experiments reported less than half of the necessary information according to the minimal reporting standard introduced later. These deficits in reporting make reproducibility and interpretation of the results difficult.

The lack of reporting transparency in eye-tracking and JDM is probably the result of insufficient and ambiguous information due to missing standards within the research community. Researchers may be looking for guidelines to assist them with eye-tracking technology and its use (e.g., designing eye-tracking compatible experiments, setting up the eye-tracker parameters) as well as in the reporting and interpretation of the resulting data (see Chapter 4). To make eye-tracking methodology a regular and more efficient tool, instructions in the form of shared standards are imperative.

The complete documentation of the research process includes a large amount of details that might not be evident to the researcher given that many methodological decisions are hiding in

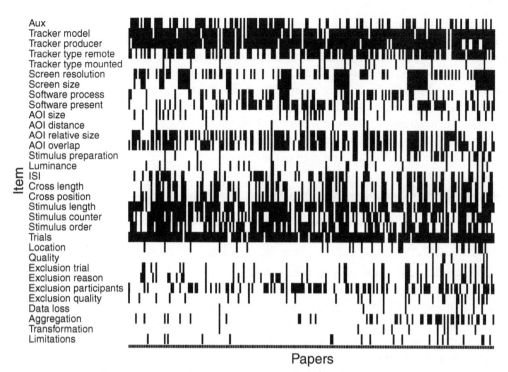

FIGURE 5.2 For each paper (tick on the x-axis) and item (described in our minimal standard) we add a black rectangle if the item is reported and a white rectangle if the item is not reported (the lists of variables corresponds to Table 4.1, Author generated).

the default settings of the eye-tracker and its software. Yet other methodological decisions might have been actively made in past research projects, but are now repeated without reflection and therefore difficult to document. This is unfortunate, since many methodological details, which may seem unimportant at first, can in fact have unintended consequences. For example, the size of area of interest (AOI) margins have been shown to influence statistical results (Orquin, Ashby, & Clarke, 2016), but despite this, most researchers fail to report AOI sizes. To avoid losing track of these methodological details, this chapter provides recommendations for transparent reporting which we hope will increase reproducibility and awareness of the many degrees of freedom in eye-tracking studies.

We address a wide set of reporting criteria across the typical sections in research papers: introduction, methods, data preprocessing, and discussion of the results. The list of reporting criteria specifies the minimum information needed for successfully reproducing a study. The list reflects the opinion of experts in the field of eye-tracking and JDM and draws on methodological considerations based on the literature published in this area between 2009 and 2017. The recommended reporting practices can be incorporated in publications with little effort and provide simultaneously hands-on advice for first time users of eye-tracking.

Development and Description of the Minimal Reporting Standard

We developed a list of all required information that would allow a researcher to reproduce the experimental setup and preprocess data in the same way as the original study. The final list of 30

68 Fiedler et al.

criteria, each of which is related to eye-tracking methodology or conceptually related to eye-movement analysis, was developed by first screening the JDM literature from 2009–2017 for papers using eye-tracking. Second, we asked an expert panel of 39 researchers who have published at least two papers (with a maximum of 20) utilizing eye-tracking in the area of JDM about the importance of each of these criteria in the context of reproducibility. Through majority voting between the experts, we generated the List of Minimal Reporting Standards (see Table 5.1). In order to give the list an intuitive structure, it is organized around the typical sections of an APA paper (see American Psychological Association, 2010). The following sections will describe best reporting practices and provide a rationale for each of the criteria.

The Introduction—Auxiliary Assumptions

The recording of eye movements provides an objective measure of the spatial orientation of the eye and pupil size at a given point in time. In most JDM experiments, this movement is used as a proxy for the underlying cognitive process and the researcher is not interested in the movement itself. This means that each observable gaze behavior will be interpreted as an indicator of an unobservable cognitive process. When making inferences about unobserved cognitive processes based on eye movements, we typically have to make assumptions about the relation between observed and unobserved variables. These auxiliary assumptions may be more or less reasonable given the setup of the stimulus material. For instance, researchers often postulate a strong relationship between the proportion of attention towards a particular information and its respective importance within the decision-making process (e.g., Jacob & Karn, 2003). However, this assumption can only be true when attention is not guided by other factors like the saliency or location of a specific stimulus. Another assumption concerning pupil behavior is that dilation reflects working memory load, but the interpretation of pupil data is strongly dependent on ruling out alternative explanations such as arousal or luminance (see Chapter 3). Such boundary conditions make it necessary to report the *auxiliary assumptions* linking the dependent measurement with the construct under investigation to allow for a clear interpretation of the later reported results.

Method

Eye Tracker

One of the most constitutive aspects of eye-tracking data is the device with which it is collected. Due to a wide variety of sampling techniques, different sampling rates (e.g., 1000 versus 30 Hz), and smoothing algorithms, eye-tracking devices differ tremendously regarding their temporal and spatial precision and accuracy. This can in some cases lead to changes in the level of dependent variables (e.g., the number of fixations might change due to these differences in measurement). Thus, by simply reporting the *model*, *producer*, and *type* of eye tracker, other researches have the chance to consult online documentation of these specific eye-tracking devices and appraise the eye tracker's quality and its fit to the respective research design.

Monitor

Most eye-tracking devices can be attached to a wide set of different monitors or even projectors. Thus, we find large heterogeneity within the measures of *screen size* and *resolution*. This information is needed to comprehend the stimulus size in degrees of visual angle and the distance between specific AOIs, allowing other researchers to recreate the original setup that will result in saccades

TABLE 5.1 Minimal Reporting Standards of 30 items for authors, editors, and reviewers of eye-tracking studies in JDM (author generated)

Studies in JDM

Introduction
A description of the auxiliary assumptions about the underlying processes of all dependent variables [Aux]

Method
 Description of the eye-tracking device
  Model (e.g., Tobi 1000) [Tracker model]
  Producer/brand [Tracker producer]
  Type (remote, head mounted) [Tracker type remote, Tracker type mounted]
 Description of the monitor
  Resolution [Screen resolution]
  Size [Screen size]
 Description of the software
  Software used to preprocess the eye-tracking data [Software process]
  Stimulus presentation software [Software present]

Material
 Description of how AOIs were defined
  Absolute size of the AOIs [AOI size]
  Relative size of AOIs and content within the AOIs [AOI relative size]
  Minimal distance between AOIs [AOI distance]
  Overlap between the AOIs [AOI overlap]
 Description of the stimulus
  Method for stimulus preparation [Stimulus preparation]
  Luminance matched [Luminance]

Procedure
 Setup
  Inter-stimulus interval [ISI]
  Length of fixation cross presentation [Cross length]
  Position of the fixation cross [Cross position]
  Length of stimulus presentation [Stimulus length]
  Counterbalancing of the position [Stimulus counter]
  Order of stimulus presentation [Stimulus order]
  Number of trials [Trials]
  Settings and locations where data was collected [Location]

Results
 Data quality
  Monitoring of data quality during experiment [Quality]
  Proportion of trials excluded for the analysis [Exclusion trial]
  Reasons for exclusion [Exclusion reason]
  Number of participants excluded from the analysis [Exclusion participants]
  Quality threshold for data exclusion [Exclusion quality]
  Percentage of lost data [Data loss]
 Dependent measures
  Aggregation method for fixations [Aggregation]
  Additional transformation of the data [Transformation]

Discussion
 Limitations
  Limitations due to the use of eye-tracking methodology [Limitations]

of similar length and AOIs of similar size. Hence, it is crucial for reproducibility to know, or make an educated guess, about the screen size and resolution. For example, reproducing a study using a screen with a different resolution or size will either distort the stimuli or change the size of the stimulus. If using a smaller screen this would mean that a larger proportion of the stimulus falls within the visual span of the observer, which could reduce the need for direct fixations (Wästlund, Shams, & Otterbring, 2018) and hence alter results.

Software

When setting up the experimental program for an eye-tracking study, researchers draw from a large pool of available programs to build their experiments. Often software solutions are directly provided by eye-tracking manufactures (e.g., Experiment Center), but over the years open source alternatives have been developed (e.g., Psychopy) featuring interfaces for many eye-tracking devices. Each stimulus presentation software and version has its own properties such as how randomization of trials is done and their presentation latencies, which can influence the data (Holmqvist et al., 2011). Reporting the used programs and potential deviations from their default settings allows other researchers to reproduce the reported work and compare their own results accounting for potential parameter deviations between experiments. In the process of data aggregation, specifically when generating individual fixations or pupil dilations from raw gaze data, a great amount of data preprocessing precede the final data set. Often these filtering, aggregation, and event detection procedures can be performed by a software package connected to the eye-tracking device. The parameter setup within these software packages or researchers' individually scripted preprocessing programs will determine the nature of the data set used in subsequent analyses. Default setups in the standard preprocessing programs differ (e.g., what is the maximum dispersion of a fixation, how is the pupil size being normalized) between eye-tracking providers and program versions. This heterogeneity in parameter setups in generating the final data set has been proven problematic already in the field of neuroscience and respective calls for full transparency and joint standards have been made (Eklund, Nichols, & Knutsson, 2016). Working with similar data structures and the resulting researchers' degrees of freedom make reporting the respective choices a necessary step also for the eye-tracking community. When using individually scripted software, releasing the respective code is highly recommended because only with the original software a full reproduction of the experiment and any preprocessing steps can be realized.

Material

Areas of Interest

The vast majority of eye-tracking research relies on AOIs for data aggregation and analysis. AOIs are defined as an area around an object of interest and all fixations falling inside the area are assigned to the object of interest. AOI definition and location has been shown to influence the data set and the respective results, which may lead to either type I or II errors (Orquin, Ashby, & Clarke, 2016). While in studies where fixation distributions do overlap (e.g., AOIs have to be close to each other given the design of the experiment), analyses benefited from smaller AOI sizes (>.5° visual angle margins), we see the opposite result for designs in which fixation distributions have no overlap. Hence, it is important to report the absolute and relative size of the AOI, the distance between the AOIs, and their potential overlap. Moreover, even more subtle issues such as the interaction between the individual eye-tracker characteristics (i.e., accuracy, precision, or filtering) and the size of the AOI can change the resulting data set and results (Holmqvist et al., 2011).

Stimuli

Eye-tracking studies are inseparable from the visual stimuli they use and besides a general description of the specifics of the stimuli, it is recommended to report the *stimulus preparation method*, e.g., the criteria for how naturalistic stimuli were selected or how artificial stimuli were generated and specific to eye-tracking research whether stimuli were *luminance matched*. Luminance matching reduces the volatility of the pupil size due to changes in light conditions and is therefore particularly, but not only, important when pupil dilation is a measure of interest, but has effects on the accuracy of the location recordings. Ruling out differences in light sources eases the interpretation of pupil data (Beatty & Lucero-Wagoner, 2000) and reduces noise when collecting eye position measures (Holmqvist et al., 2011).

Describe the Procedure

Describing the full procedure of an eye-tracking study consists of answering several questions concerning the length and form of the stimuli presentation as well as the general setup of the experiment. All of these questions influence the validity of the study and subsequently the conclusions that can be drawn from it. Reporting the *length of the inter-stimulus interval*, that is, the time between the stimulus presentation, will provide crucial information about resting phases and potential baseline measures. This information allows readers to evaluate the relative differences in pupil size conditional on the time the eye spends without stimulation. Since pupil contraction has some latency it needs time to recover to its baseline (app. 4 sec). When using a fixation cross before the stimulus presentation to focus (divert) attention on (or away from) a particular position on the screen reporting its *position* (e.g., at the middle of the screen) and *presentation length* allow for a better evaluation of the meaning of the first fixation. Similarly important for the interpretation of the data is the *length of the stimulus presentation*. For instance, a fixed exposure time of 2000 msec and a free exposure time (participants decide themselves when to continue) call for radically different interpretations of the same analysis. While in the fixed exposure time the number of fixations towards a particular AOI can be easily compared between subjects, free exposure time introduces systematic differences in invested decision effort (i.e., time invested to make the decision). To estimate the extent of potential noise in the data due to unfamiliarity with the stimulus material, additionally reporting the *number of trials* is key.

One of the most important issues when presenting multiple AOIs is the question of the position *counterbalancing*, that is, do the objects of interest switch position (e.g., between the top and bottom or left and right side of the screen)? Lack of counterbalancing could lead to confounding of eye movements to an object due to its relevance with eye movements caused by the position of the object (Orquin & Holmqvist, 2017). Similar concerns are connected to the temporal *ordering* of the stimuli (e.g., random or fixed order presentation). In the beginning of an experiment we often observe longer decision times and larger amounts of inspected information in comparison to a stronger focus and shorter decision times in later trials (e.g., Fiedler, Glöckner, Nicklisch, & Dickert, 2013). Building on this observation Orquin, Bagger, and Loose (2013) provide evidence of an increase in top down control of eye movements over time. Hence, reporting the type and temporal ordering of the stimuli in particular in within-subject designs is pertinent. To understand the external circumstance of data collection and how controlled the data collection was, it is also essential to describe the location of data collection (e.g., in a light and sound controlled laboratory vs. a mall, etc.).

Results

Dependent Measures

As part of the data preprocessing, most researchers perform one or more data aggregations and transformation steps before finally analyzing their data (see Chapter 2). These steps involve, for instance, *aggregation of fixations* (i.e., defining the minimum fixation length and maximum dispersion) or *pupil size* (i.e., algorithm used to calculate pupil size, e.g., as a difference measure to baseline or as a relative change in size) from raw data. These aggregations are often made within the preprocessing programs supplied by the eye-tracking provider. Reporting these characteristics of the data is crucial because defaults set by the providers vary greatly and decisions should be made in accordance with the stimuli used (Manor & Gordon, 2003). Besides the standard algorithms, many analyses are based on further transformations such as transition indices that, for instance, indicate the amount of within- or between-alternative search or how systematic search is (Perkovic, Bown, & Kaptan, 2018). How such metrics are computed naturally influences subsequent analyses and the correct computation is sometimes subject to debate, as seen in, for instance, the development of transition indices (Böckenholt & Hynan, 1994).

Data Quality

Data quality is essential to understanding what conclusions can be drawn from the data and the extent of our confidence in the results (Orquin & Holmqvist, 2017). Reporting on data quality in eye-tracking studies can refer to several measures most of which are common to all eye-tracking studies. These measures include: the *proportion of excluded participants* and *trials* from the analysis and the respective *reasons for these exclusions*, the percentage of data samples for which the eye tracker could not obtain the gaze position, also referred to as *lost data*, and whether *data quality was monitored* during the experiment.

Discussion—Limitations

Eye-tracking studies are subject to specific *limitations* due to methodological and theoretical factors. Methodological limitations such as poor data quality can reduce the internal or external validity of a study while theoretical limitations concern the interpretation of eye movements in terms of cognitive processes. For example, a fixation cannot always be interpreted as information processing, and likewise the absence of a fixation cannot necessarily be interpreted as the absence of processing, given that eye trackers do not measure the use of peripheral vision. Additionally, issues related to stimulus design, subject sample, and data quality have to be reported and discussed to provide a transparent picture of the warranted and unwarranted conclusions based on the data. Reporting them allows readers to derive their own conclusions with regards to the validity of the results and their interpretation.

Using the Minimal Reporting Standards as an Author

The criteria summarized earlier constitute the minimum level of reporting required to describe a JDM eye-tracking study in a reproducible way. The list is in no way exhaustive, and interested readers can see the complete list of reporting elements in Fiedler et al. (2018). Furthermore, the list also serves as a tool to increase awareness of methodological choices made while setting up eye-tracking experiments. Adopting shared standards does not only reduce the degrees of freedom in reporting and thereby decision load of the individual researcher, but also benefits the research community by generating comparable and reproducible study materials. Some authors might find that reporting all the technical information will harm the readability of their work, but given the growing use of online supplements especially for methodological information, this can be added without any compromise. To make reporting even more user friendly, we have created a template (https://goo.gl/forms/snzWHTuFRtmcA16s1) in which researchers will be guided by concrete questions through the decisions made during the design, data collection, and preprocessing stages of their experiment to collect the necessary details. The template automatically generates a PDF detailing the methodology and sends it to the email addresses provided at the beginning of the questionnaire.

Using the Minimal Reporting Standards as a Peer Reviewer and Editor

The Minimal Reporting Standards is thought of as a tool not only for researchers, but also for reviewers, editors, and funders. Promoting openness and comparability of eye-tracking research is, of course, the responsibility of individual researchers, but better research practices can also be fostered through the review system (Asendorpf et al., 2013). Editors and peer reviewers can be influential in guiding researchers to comply with reporting norms. Referring to subfield specific reporting standards, peer reviewers have the chance to influence common standards by requesting full and transparent reporting. Checking eye-tracking submissions against the Minimal Reporting Standards reduces the workload of reviewers by providing a systematic way to evaluate the reproducibility of the paper and is fair because it sets the same standards for everyone. The request for additional information with reference to the Minimal Reporting Standards in all reviews not only makes the papers more reproducible, but also highlights the changes in cultural reporting norms and disclosure practices. Hence, authors, editors, and reviewers can use the Minimal Reporting Standards to make the degrees of freedom more salient and increase reproducibility in the long run.

Conclusion

From the first design idea to the final publication, eye-tracking researchers have to make many decisions about their methods, materials, and procedures. These decisions may be more or less arbitrary, but methodological research suggests that even seemingly trivial details may have unintended consequences for the data set and results (Holmqvist et al., 2011; Orquin & Holmqvist, 2017). Transparent reporting of these details is therefore crucial to reproducibility and for others to judge the quality of the research. By developing minimum standards for reporting, this chapter provides guidance to researchers who are new to eye-tracking and helps to adjust current practices for researchers with more experience. We intend these recommendations to provide a clear answer to what should be reported in an eye-tracking study. The chapter aims to constitutes a resource for researchers pursuing open and reproducible practices and constitutes a coordination device for the eye-tracking community to come to a joint standard of reporting allowing comparison of results across wide sets of papers and topics. Evidence is accumulating that adopting checklists and minimal reporting standards like CONSORT (Turner et al., 2012), PRISMA (Moher, Liberati, Tetzlaff, Altman, & The PRISMA Group, 2009), STROBE (von Elm et al., 2007), and others improves the transparency and quality of publications in many other areas of research (Plint et al., 2006; Smidt et al., 2006). These guidelines are an integral part of the research process and are often recommended by journals and widely adopted by individual authors. Reproducibility is an important stepping stone to ensure that insights from scientific experiments stand the test of time (Open Science Collaboration, 2015). The Minimal Reporting Standards help to promote the

74 Fiedler et al.

cultural shift towards openness and transparency in science to increased reproducibility, because precise, accurate, and informative reporting is a prerequisite of reproducibility.

Recommended Reading List

- American Psychological Association (2010): The standard in Psychological Science for reporting of experiments and writing articles.
- APA Publications and Communications Board Working Group on Journal Article Reporting Standards (2008): The results of the APA working group on Journal Article Reporting Standards (JARS).
- Quintana, Alvares, and Heathers (2016): Reporting guidelines from psychiatry.

References

American Psychological Association. (2010). *Publication manual of the American Psychological Association* (6th ed.). Washington, DC: American Psychological Association.

APA Publications and Communications Board Working Group on Journal Article Reporting Standards. (2008). Reporting standards for research in psychology: Why do we need them? What might they be?. *The American Psychologist, 63*(9), 839–851.

Appelbaum, M., Cooper, H., Kline, R. B., Mayo-Wilson, E., Nezu, A. M., & Rao, S. M. (2018). Journal article reporting standards for quantitative research in psychology: The APA Publications and Communications Board task force report. *American Psychologist, 73*(1), 3–25.

Asendorpf, J. B., Conner, M., de Fruyt, F., de Houwer, J., Denissen, J. J., Fiedler, K., … & Perugini, M. (2013). Recommendations for increasing replicability in psychology. *European Journal of Personality, 27*(2), 108–119.

Ashby, N. J., Johnson, J. G., Krajbich, I., & Wedel, M. (2016). Applications and innovations of eye-movement research in judgment and decision making. *Journal of Behavioral Decision Making, 29*(2–3), 96–102.

Beatty, J., & Lucero-Wagoner, B. (2000). The pupillary system. In J. T. Cacioppo, L. G. Tassinary, & G. G. Berntson (Eds.), *Handbook of psychophysiology* (2nd ed., pp. 142–162). New York, NY: Cambridge University Press.

Böckenholt, U., & Hynan, L. S. (1994). Caveats on a process-tracing measure and a remedy. *Journal of Behavioral Decision Making, 7*(2), 103–117.

Eklund, A., Nichols, T. E., & Knutsson, H. (2016). Cluster failure: Why fMRI inferences for spatial extent have inflated false-positive rates. *Proceedings of the National Academy of Sciences, 113*(28), 7900–7905.

Fiedler, S., & Glöckner, A. (2015). Attention and moral behavior. *Current Opinion in Psychology, 6*, 139–144.

Fiedler, S., Glöckner, A., Nicklisch, A., & Dickert, S. (2013). Social value orientation and information search in social dilemmas: An eye-tracking analysis. *Organizational Behavior and Human Decision Processes, 120*(2), 272–284.

Fiedler, S., Schulte-Mecklenbeck, M., Renkewitz, F., & Orquin, J. (2018). Strengthening the reporting of eye-tracking studies in behavioral research: The EyeGuidelines. Article in preparation.

Glasziou, P., Altman, D. G., Bossuyt, P., Boutron, I., Clarke, M., Julious, S., … Wager, E. (2014). Reducing waste from incomplete or unusable reports of biomedical research. *The Lancet, 383*(9913), 267–276.

Gopen, G. D., & Swan, J. A. (1990). The science of scientific writing. *American Scientist, 78*(6), 550–558.

Holmqvist, K., Nyström, M., Andersson, R., Dewhurst, R., Jarodzka, H., & van de Weijer, J. (2011). *Eye tracking: A comprehensive guide to methods and measures.* Oxford, UK: Oxford University Press.

Jacob, R. J., & Karn, K. S. (2003). Eye tracking in human-computer interaction and usability research: Ready to deliver the promises. In J. Hyönä, R. Radach, & H. Deubel (Eds.), *The mind's eye: Cognitive and applied aspects of eye movement research* (pp. 573–605). Amsterdam, NL: Elsevier Science.

Krajbich, I., Oud, B., & Fehr, E. (2014). Benefits of neuroeconomic modeling: New policy interventions and predictors of preference. *The American Economic Review, 104*(5), 501–506.

Manor, B. R., & Gordon, E. (2003). Defining the temporal threshold for ocular fixation in free-viewing visuocognitive tasks. *Journal of Neuroscience Methods, 128*(1–2), 85–93.

Meißner, M., & Oll, J. (2018). The promise of eye-tracking methodology in organizational research: A taxonomy, review, and future avenues. *Organizational Research Methods*, doi.1094428117744882.

Moher, D., Liberati, A., Tetzlaff, J., Altman, D. G., & The PRISMA Group (2009). Preferred reporting items for systematic reviews and meta-analyses: The PRISMA statement. *PLoS Medicine*, *6*(7), 1–6.

Open Science Collaboration. (2015). Estimating the reproducibility of psychological science. *Science*, *349*(6251), 4716.

Orquin, J. L., Ashby, N. J., & Clarke, A. D. (2016). Areas of interest as a signal detection problem in behavioral eye-tracking research. *Journal of Behavioral Decision Making*, *29*(2–3), 103–115.

Orquin, J. L., Bagger, M. P., & Loose, S. M. (2013). Learning affects top down and bottom up modulation of eye movements in decision making. *Judgment and Decision Making*, *8*(6), 700–716.

Orquin, J. L., & Holmqvist, K. (2017). Threats to the validity of eye-movement research in psychology. *Behavior Research Methods*, 1–12.

Perkovic, S., Bown, N. J., & Kaptan, G. (2018). Systematicity of search index: A new measure for exploring information search patterns. *Journal of Behavioral Decision Making*, 1–13.

Plint, A. C., Moher, D., Morrison, A., Schulz, K., Altman, D. G., Hill, C., & Gaboury, I. (2006). Does the CONSORT checklist improve the quality of reports of randomised controlled trials? A systematic review. *Medical Journal of Australia*, *185*(5), 263–267.

Schulte-Mecklenbeck, M., Spaanjaars, N. L., & Witteman, C. L. M. (2017). The (in)visibility of psychodiagnosticians' expertise. *Journal of Behavioral Decision Making*, 30(1), 89–94.

Smidt, N., Rutjes, A., van der Windt, D., Ostelo, R., Bossuyt, P., Reitsma, J., … de Vet, H. (2006). The quality of diagnostic accuracy studies since the STARD statement Has it improved? *Neurology*, *67*(5), 792–797.

Turner, L., Shamseer, L., Altman, D. G., Weeks, L., Peters, J., Kober, T., … Moher, D. (2012). Consolidated standards of reporting trials (CONSORT) and the completeness of reporting of randomised controlled trials (RCTs) published in medical journals. *The Cochrane Database of Systematic Reviews*, *11*(11).

von Elm, E., Altman, D. G., Egger, M., Pocock, S. J., Gøtzsche, P. C., Vandenbroucke, J. P., & Strobe Initiative (2007). The strengthening the reporting of observational studies in epidemiology (STROBE) statement: Guidelines for reporting observational studies. *PLoS Medicine*, *4*(10), 296.

Wästlund, E., Shams, P., & Otterbring, T. (2018). Unsold is unseen … or is it? Examining the role of peripheral vision in the consumer choice process using eye-tracking methodology. *Appetite*, *120*, 49–56.

Wedel, M., & Pieters, R. (2007). A review of eye-tracking research in marketing. In N. Malhotra (Ed.), *Review of marketing research* (pp. 123–147). Armonk, NY: M.E. Sharpe.

Wicherts, J. M., Veldkamp, C. L., Augusteijn, H. E., Bakker, M., van Aert, R., & van Assen, M. A. (2016). Degrees of freedom in planning, running, analyzing, and reporting psychological studies: A checklist to avoid p-hacking. *Frontiers in Psychology*, 7(1832), 1–12.

6

(RE)VISITING THE DECISION FACTORY

Observing Cognition with MouselabWEB

Martijn C. Willemsen and Eric J. Johnson

Great progress has been made in developing descriptive models of human choice behavior, in part through the design of clever experiments that test alternative models by varying inputs. However, there are several cases where quite different processes are proposed to account for the same outcome data. One example discussed in detail later in this chapter is the choice between gambles: A stark contrast exists between integration models such as prospect theory (Kahneman & Tversky, 1979) and heuristic models such as the Priority Heuristic (Brandstätter, Gigerenzer, & Hertwig, 2006). These models are quite different in their process predictions, but yet can produce similar predictions of choice outcomes.

The kind of data that we describe in this chapter, process tracing data using Mouselab, provides a richer set of data beyond observed choices allowing researchers to sort through alternative explanations more quickly. Broadly speaking, we see two important advantages of using process data. First, process tracing facilitates the comparative evaluation of multiple theories. Though as-if models are built to predict choice outcomes, many of their assumptions have testable process level implications that can expose theoretical limitations of these models. Second, process tracing can help us understand heterogeneity among individuals. Augmenting a study with process data can greatly increase our ability to understand how individuals differ in processing strategies and how that relates to their choices.

Information Acquisition as a Process Tracing Method

By observing how information is acquired, we can make inferences about the underlying cognitive process and test existing decision models. Initial studies measured the physical retrieval of information required to solve a problem from information boards (Payne, 1976). With the introduction of more powerful personal computers in the early 1980s, computer-based information acquisition tools were developed that monitored the acquisition of information from a computer screen. Historically, several different pointing devices were used, including track balls, pointing with electronic pens, and keyboards. Because it is particularly ubiquitous, easily learned, and both fast and accurate (Card, Moran, & Newell, 1980), the computer mouse has become the dominant pointing device. People navigate through a task by moving the mouse and clicking or hovering over boxes, revealing information.

Computer-based information acquisition is often seen as analogous to eye-tracking (Chapters 1–5). Just as the eye moves, then fixates to encode an item of information, computer-based techniques allow the user to move to a location, pause, and acquire the information revealed. Because eye movements and mouse movements have shown to be correlated (Chen, Anderson, & Sohn, 2001; Goldstein, Suri, McAfee, Ekstrand-Abueg, & Diaz, 2014), this analogy seems to hold especially well for the use of mouse movements as an information acquisition method (but see Chapter 7).

Early research used information acquisition data to examine the choice of gambles (Payne & Braunstein, 1978), the setting of reservation prices for gambles using different response modes (Johnson & Schkade, 1989), the effects of time pressure on choice (Payne, Bettman, & Johnson, 1993; Rieskamp & Hoffrage, 1999), and the study of preference reversals (Schkade & Johnson, 1989). This work largely looked at aggregate measures of order of information acquisition. Many of these early studies employed the DOS-based Mouselab tool (Johnson, 1996; Payne et al., 1993). A new system intended to be used on the worldwide web was labeled MouselabWEB (Willemsen & Johnson, 2017). Similar information acquisition techniques have been developed (e.g., Jasper & Shapiro, 2002; Reisen, Hoffrage, & Mast, 2008; Schulte-Mecklenbeck, Murphy, & Hutzler, 2011).

More recent work has benefited from three developments that clearly advance the additional insights that can be gained from information acquisition methods. First, the assumptions underlying the interpretation of information acquisition have been clearly articulated with two empirically testable assumptions (Costa-Gomes, Crawford, & Broseta, 2001) about the relationship between search and cognition: *Occurrence* states that if information is used by a decision maker, it must have been acquired; *Adjacency* assumes that information acquisition is temporally proximate to information use. In other words, information is acquired rather than memorized because of limitations in short-term memory and the low cost of (re)acquisition. Second, model development has advanced beyond looking at overall patterns of search (such as the Payne Index, Payne et al., 1993; see for a discussion Böckenholt & Hynan, 1994) to models that look at this data at a fine-grained level of individual acquisitions often using multilevel modeling (e.g., Willemsen, Böckenholt, & Johnson, 2011). This allows the test of specific process predictions that originate from the underlying theories. Third, information acquisition methods can reveal how different people can use different strategies, or how strategies might vary across different decisions (Brocas, Carrillo, Wang, & Camerer, 2014; Polonio, di Guida, & Coricelli, 2015; Reeck, Wall, & Johnson, 2017). We illustrate these advances focusing on two case studies from common decision domains that test specific theoretical accounts and acknowledge individual differences.

Two Investigations: Bargaining Games and the Priority Heuristic

Johnson, Camerer, Sen, and Rymon (2002) used the original Mouselab to study the processes underlying sequential bargaining games. Two players bargain in three rounds over a pie (an amount of money) that shrinks with each round that a player rejects the offer of the other player. Suppose in the first round the pie is worth $5 and Player 1 makes the first offer. Player 2 can accept and the trial ends, or can reject the offer and move to the next round with a smaller pie ($2.50). Now Player 2 makes an offer to Player 1. Player 1 accepts or rejects, and in the latter case they enter a final third round with a smaller pie ($1.25). If Player 2 rejects Player 1's offer in the third round, neither player receives anything and the trial ends.

Purely self-interested players (who believe others are too), will backward induct to derive an optimal game-theoretic equilibrium: Player 1 offers $1.26 in the first round, which is accepted. This does not describe typical data, where actual offers are typically much higher than the equilibrium prediction and rejections are frequent. Camerer and Johnson (2004) and Johnson et al. (2002)

argue that two separate accounts could explain these deviations. A *limited cognition* account argues that many players do not apply game-theoretical reasoning using backward induction, and do not look ahead much. An *equilibrium social preference* account keeps the assumption of a game-theoretic reasoning, but includes fairness considerations and does not assume pure self-interest of the other player, who might reject offers that appear unfair.

These two accounts are not mutually exclusive, and participants might differ in the degree of fairness considerations and cognitive abilities. Looking at the actual offers alone (Camerer & Johnson, 2004) cannot distinguish between these accounts. However, if we assume occurrence and adjacency, the two theories make very different predictions. The limited cognition account suggests that players deviating strongly from equilibrium offers will not look at later rounds, since they are not using backward induction. The equilibrium social preference account suggests that players do make equilibrium computations and then adjust for fairness. These predictions are directly testable by inspecting the information acquisition process in a Mouselab display in which the actual information about the pie-sizes and which player can make the offer was hidden behind boxes that could be opened using the mouse. Johnson et al. (2002) demonstrated that the information acquisition data supported a limited cognition account in that much more attention was devoted to information on earlier rounds, rather than to the later rounds (19% did not even look once at second round information and 10% did not look at third round information). These findings strongly support a limited cognition account because participants did not inspect necessary information to calculate the equilibrium. The data also considered individual differences by identifying three types of players that differed in the number of rounds inspected, and these three groups made offers that were consistent with each level of limited cognition.

In individual choice, Johnson, Schulte-Mecklenbeck, and Willemsen (2008) examined the process predictions made by the Priority Heuristic (PH, Brandstätter et al., 2006), which demonstrates impressive predictive strength in the aggregate of choices between gambles. Though designed to predict choices, the PH also suggests an unambiguous and testable process. Brandstätter et al. (2006) did report reaction time data consistent with the PH, but Johnson et al. (2008) argued that the PH model makes more detailed process predictions that could be tested by examining information acquisition.

The PH predictions about the content and sequence of information acquisition are based on the fact that the heuristic identifies a set of reasons to be followed by the decision maker in a specific order. To illustrate, consider the process for two outcomes gambles containing gains. First, the decision maker inspects if the difference between the minimum gains of the two gambles is larger than the aspiration level (10% of the maximum gain). If so, she will stop and choose the gamble with the more attractive gain (one-reason stopping rule). If not, she inspects the difference between the two probabilities attached to the minimum gains, and to see if they differ more than 10%. If so, she stops (two-reason stopping rule) and chooses the gamble with the more attractive probability. Otherwise, she chooses the gamble with the greater maximum gain (three-reason stopping rule). An interesting characteristic of this heuristic is that to make decisions, no integration of outcomes and probabilities (e.g., calculating expected utility) are required.

Johnson et al. (2008) ran a MouselabWEB study in which they looked at gambles created to produce either a one- or three-reason stopping rule. The following process was predicted based on the PH-rules: First the decision should be divided into a reading and choice phase. In the reading phase the minimum and maximum pay-offs are identified (which need be known before the actual reasons underlying the heuristic can be considered), suggesting mostly attention to these outcomes (acquiring probabilities is unnecessary). In the choice phase most comparisons should occur between similar elements of the gambles (comparing outcomes with each other, or probabilities) as these are the comparisons proposed by the reasons, and not between outcomes and their probabilities (as an integration model would predict). The choice phase considers the reasons in the order as predicted by the heuristic, and makes specific predictions for one- and three-reason gambles. One-reason gambles require attention to minimum gains only, three-reason gambles also need maximum gains and minimum probabilities.

Overall, and in contrast with the PH predictions, Johnson et al. (2008) found the most common type of transition was between outcome and probabilities within a gamble, as predicted by integration models. In addition, specific probabilities not required by the heuristic were acquired. While there was some evidence that one- and three-reason gambles differ in ways predicted by the PH, the process data strongly argues against the idea of the PH that people avoid outcome-probability trade-offs.

Designing, Executing and Analyzing Information Acquisition Studies

Process Measures and the Design of Information Acquisition Studies

In most computer-based displays used in information acquisition studies, information about the attribute values is hidden behind boxes. As the participants move the mouse over a box, it opens and reveals the information until the participant moves the mouse out of the box again. Figure 6.1 shows one example, the MouselabWEB display used by Johnson et al. (2008). In the figure the mouse is opening the amount to win for the second outcome of gamble A.

Most computers record time and sequence of acquisitions with sufficient precision (1/60th of a second), resulting in a time-stamped event list of box openings and closings. Three important process measures can be derived from this data: acquisition time and frequency for each box (reflecting the attention paid to specific information) and transitions between boxes (potentially reflecting comparison processes between units of information).

Designing Displays

One crucial aspect of an information acquisition study is the design of the display itself (see also Chapter 4 for similar treatment in eye-tracking studies). Layout, labels, and text inside the boxes represent important design decisions that can affect choices. The principles of occurrence and

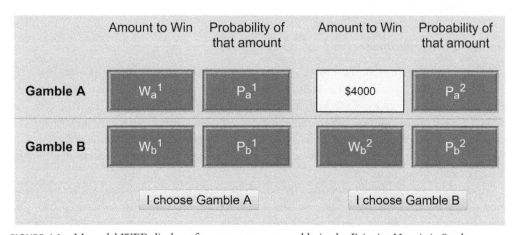

FIGURE 6.1 MouselabWEB display of a two-outcome gamble in the Priority Heuristic Study.

adjacency can help guide the design. Another concern is keeping information similar in the display as it would appear in the real word, when it is important to maintain the ecological validity of the process tracing results.

Most information acquisition studies reveal large effects of reading order, with (western) participants typically starting at the top-left box. Following the principle of occurrence, this means that information is more likely to be acquired if positioned favorably in reading order. If we are interested in the impact of different types of information, we should disentangle position from importance by systematically counterbalancing the information across the screen. However, counterbalancing is sometimes constrained by two considerations. First, attributes often have a logical order. The outcome of a lottery and its probability are naturally associated and often presented together. Second, some applications require that we maintain the order found in the real world. For example, Schulte-Mecklenbeck, Sohn, de Bellis, Martin, and Hertwig (2013) randomized the nutritional information of two dishes but always kept the name and image of the dish on top of the display. This illustrates the fact that some components of the display can be randomized as a group. Gambles could be kept together but the position counterbalanced. In contrast, displays are sometimes formatted to be equidistant between cells (e.g., Noguchi & Stewart, 2014) to equalize the effort required for each transition.

Interpretation of search is easier when respondents are looking at the information they want, not for the information they desire. Clear labeling on the boxes or in row or column headings allows participants to locate the information that they want, minimizing exploratory search. Especially when theories make clear predictions about information usage, such as the PH study, clear labeling supports the relevance of the occurrence principle, and minimizes noise.

A final consideration concerns the text contained in the cells. To strengthen adjacency, more complex information avoids the possibility that participants just memorize the contents of the boxes and use memory instead of search. Therefore, Willemsen et al. (2011) used rich stimulus descriptions: The price of a printer was composed of several components such as purchase and printing costs, all presented together in one box. Since information acquisition in a MouselabWEB is low cost, most participants prefer to acquire rather than memorize information. Empirical evidence of Adjacency is provided by frequent reacquisition of information, consistent with the observation that the respondent finds it easier to look than memorize. This was confirmed in the Asian disease study of Willemsen et al. (2011) that showed that even a box with very simple and brief information "p = 1", which in principle is easy to memorize, was acquired many times.

Executing the Experiment

Information acquisition studies are usually within-subject designs, consisting of multiple trials. To maximize task understanding and minimize effects of initial learning of the information acquisition method, one should include introductory trials that let the user test the interface and that introduce the particular display, indicating where different kinds of information can be found. We often employ a quiz after testing the interface to test for respondents' understanding of the task. For example, in the PH study respondents were asked about the largest probability and smallest pay-off for one gamble on a practice trial.

We are also concerned with potential fatigue and inattention in experimental studies involving many similar trials. The beauty of process data is that we can check this through comparisons of acquisition times and frequencies of earlier and later trials, if order of trials is counterbalanced or randomized.

Managing Information Acquisition Data

Process data becomes a good news, bad news story: the good news is that it provides a wealth of information on the behavior of the participant, potentially providing insights into their strategy. The bad news is that this wealth of information may seem overwhelming: Often hundreds of lines of data result from a single decision by a respondent, complicating data analysis and management.

Data Cleaning

The first step after data collection is to exclude participants and trials who did not engage in the task. Information acquisition can provide attention checks through many different measures, such as the time per trial, average looking time per box, and time between acquisitions. Unrealistically short trial times or very short average looking times per box might indicate low engagement, but unrealistically long trial times or long intervals between acquisitions might indicate distraction or interruptions during a trial. These checks are especially important in online information acquisition studies, where there is no immediate observation of participants' behavior and environment. In these studies, typically about 5 to 10% of the observations are removed from further analyses. However, even in controlled laboratory settings we often exclude a few percent based upon their search (or lack thereof). When using information acquisition, it is common that respondents may open boxes incidentally when the mouse moves over them. These very short (spurious) acquisitions are very unlikely to be consciously processed. A standard practice is to filter out any acquisition lasting less than about 200 msec (Card, Moran, & Newell, 1983; DiCarlo, Zoccolan, & Rust, 2012; Payne, Bettman, & Johnson, 1988).

Extracting Process Measures

The output of many process tracing tools is a list of events from the trial (including opening and closing events of the box, click events on buttons, etc.). Such event data has to be processed before it can be used to look in detail at the higher-level process measures of interest (acquisitions, times, transitions between boxes, etc.). Figure 6.2a (event list 1) shows raw event data of two participants in a 2x2 MouselabWEB display. The entry and exit events are labeled *mouseover* and *mouseout*. Processing the raw event file (into the processed event file, list 2) requires: collapsing the entry and exit time for each cell into a single event; cleaning the event data as described previously, or by combining adjacent acquisitions of like kind (when respondents jitter while entering or exiting a box); and adding additional information to each event to support further processing, such as frequency (e.g., f_A_price in Figure 6.2a, list 2), duration (e.g., t_A_price), or absolute/relative serial position (*count/Rel count*).

The Datalyser in the MouselabWEB package facilitates this initial data processing. This web-based tool accesses the data and performs the steps earlier and provides these data as standard csv (comma-separated-values) files to be imported in any statistical package for further processing and analysis.

Figure 6.2a also illustrates the process of taking the processed event file and producing a higher level summary. By having acquisitions for each box in separate columns, we can easily summarize both across and within columns. The relative counter allows for summarizing over different time periods within each trial. Figure 6.2a (list 3) shows the same event data, now aggregated over two divisions (halves), with the data of the first 50% of acquisitions (relative count <.5) in the first row and the data for the second half in the second. The column *div* indicates which half. The frequency

Event list 1: raw event data

subj	event	name	time
1	onload	body	63
1	mouseover	A_price	2046
1	mouseout	A_price	3209
1	mouseover	B_price	3211
1	mouseout	B_price	3791
1	mouseover	A_price	3858
1	mouseout	A_price	4826
1	mouseover	B_price	4875
1	mouseout	B_price	6043
1	mouseover	B_img	6045
1	mouseout	B_img	6694
1	mouseover	A_img	6712
1	mouseout	A_img	7527
1	mouseover	B_img	7529
1	mouseout	B_img	8345
1	mouseover	A_img	8378
1	mouseout	A_img	9196
1	btnClick	Camera A	9896
1	submit	submit	11567
2	onload	body	79
2	mouseover	A_img	5432
2	mouseout	A_img	5601
2	mouseover	A_price	5649
2	mouseout	A_price	6348
2	mouseover	A_img	6349
2	mouseout	A_img	7732
2	mouseover	B_img	7749
2	mouseout	B_img	8818
2	mouseover	B_price	8819
2	mouseout	B_price	9600
2	mouseover	B_img	9602
2	mouseout	B_img	11518
2	mouseover	B_price	11519
2	mouseout	B_price	11719
2	btnClick	Camera B	13206
2	submit	submit	15236

MouselabWEB 2.0 display: pointer opens a blurred box

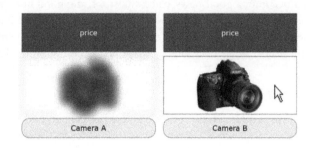

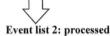

Event list 2: processed

Subj	boxname	boxin	Box time	count	Rel count	f_A_price	t_A_price	f_B_price	...
1	A_price	1983	1163	1	0.125	1	1163	0	...
1	B_price	3148	580	2	0.25	0	0	1	...
1	A_price	3795	968	3	0.375	1	968	0	...
1	B_price	4812	1168	4	0.5	0	0	1	...
1	B_img	5982	649	5	0.625	0	0	0	...
1	A_img	6649	815	6	0.75	0	0	0	...
1	B_img	7466	816	7	0.875	0	0	0	...
1	A_img	8315	818	8	1	0	0	0	...
2	A_price	5570	699	1	0.2	1	699	0	...
2	A_img	6270	1383	2	0.4	0	0	0	...
2	B_img	7670	1069	3	0.6	0	0	0	...
2	B_price	8740	781	4	0.8	0	0	1	...
2	B_img	9523	1916	5	1	0	0	0	...

Event list 3: summarized per subject across two divisions (halfs)

subj	choice	div	Maxcount	f_A_price	f_B_price	f_B_img	f_A_img	t_A_price	t_B_price	t_B_img	t_A_img
1	Camera A	1	8	2	2	0	0	2131	1748	0	0
1	Camera A	2	8	0	0	2	2	0	0	1465	1633
2	Camera B	1	5	1	0	0	1	699	0	0	1383
2	Camera B	2	5	0	1	2	0	0	781	2985	0

FIGURE 6.2A An example display and event list and the processing steps to convert raw event files into meaningful process data files, as performed by the Datalyser in MouselabWEB.

(f_xx) and time (t_xx) columns now represent the total number of acquisitions and looking time for that division. The Datalyser also produces these summarized data sets.

A third process measure which increasingly is used in process analysis is the transitions between boxes, which may reflect comparisons or information integration and are therefore often more theoretically relevant than looking frequency or time. This measure is currently not part of the output of the Datalyser, but can be generated from the processed event files, using for example R-scripts that loop through these events files to generate the transition columns. Modern packages such as Tidyverse for R (Wickham & Grolemund, 2017) allow doing such summaries with great flexibility directly on the processed event files.

Some example code snippets for R using the tidyverse framework

Load the tidyverse library and read the event-processed dataset (list 2) from the Datalyser

```
library(tidyverse)
cam <- read.csv("cam_proc.csv")
```

Summarizing the data

The code takes the *cam* data, groups it by subject and boxname and then summarizes the boxtimes using the mean function across these groups. GGplot takes the *boxtimes* data set and plots the data in a boxplot.

```
boxtimes <- cam %>% group_by(subject, boxname) %>%
summarize(boxtime=mean(boxtime))

ggplot(boxtimes, aes(y=boxtime, x=boxname))+geom_boxplot()
```

FIGURE 6.2B   R-code snippets to summarize event data using the Tidyverse framework.

Figure 6.2b provides a short impression of some R-code snippets to achieve this using the Tidyverse framework. In just a few lines of code we can produce summarized data sets for both the acquisition times as well as create a data set that summarizes the transitions between boxes. Such summarized data files (either directly from the Datalyser or using R) can be used as direct input for scripts that create Icon Graphs (see later) or for multilevel models.

Displaying Information Acquisition Data

Global measures (e.g., Payne, et al., 1993; for a review see Schulte-Mecklenbeck et al., 2017) characterize entire decisions by aggregating the frequency of acquisitions and transitions producing

Counting transitions between boxes

This script uses *mutate* to calculate a transitions variable *'trans'* (by combining two subsequent boxnames) using the lag function. The script excludes the first row per subject (counter>1) as there is no transition yet for this acquisition. GGplot plots the data, filtered for NA's produced by the first rows, separately for participant 1 (left pane) and participant 2 (right pane), showing that participant 1 mostly compares within attributes, whereas participant 2 compares within alternatives.

```
transitions<-cam %>% group_by(subject) %>%
mutate(trans=ifelse(counter>1, paste(boxname,lag(boxname),sep="-"),NA))

ggplot(filter(transitions,
!is.na(trans)))+geom_bar(aes(trans))+facet_grid(~subject)+coord_flip()
```

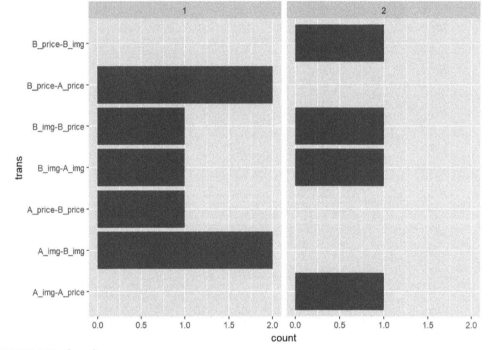

FIGURE 6.2B (cont.)

a series of global measures for each decision, such as the amount of within-option relative to between-option processing. Researchers used these measures to ask questions such as how decision strategies are affected by display sizes and layouts. But as theory and analysis have become more sophisticated, we can produce more precise process predictions and tests requiring finer grained slices of the data.

Finer Grained Representations

Information acquisition data represents a challenge in data presentation: How can we show mean acquisition time and frequencies as well as transitions between boxes in one graphical presentation? Icon Graphs (Johnson et al., 2002) can be used to represent the data using box-type icons. The height of each icon is proportional to the number of acquisitions for that item of information, and the width of the icon is proportional to the total looking time. Box size thus represents a measure of attention. For example, in Figure 6.3, which provides an Icon Graph of the games study, the top-left box represents the first round pay-off for Level 0 players. It was acquired on average 3.4 times and looked at on average for 12.44 sec in total. Arrows show the transitions between boxes, with length proportional to the frequency (low frequency arrows are omitted in the Icon Graph for purposes of clarity).

In the games study, Johnson et al. (2002) distinguished three types of players: players that do not look ahead (Level 0), players that look ahead only one round (Level 1), and players that look at all three rounds (Equilibrium) and argue that these players might differ substantially in their information acquisition strategies. Types were classified by identifying which box was looked at the longest in the first bargaining round (Figure 6.3). Level 0 players (leftmost column in Figure 6.3) looked most and longest at the first round pay-off, spent little time looking at other pay-offs, and showed the highest mean offer. Level 1 players showed an increased time of looking at round 2 and 3, and these players also gave lower mean offers in the game. Finally, players identified as equilibrium players (rightmost part of Figure 6.3) showed strategies consistent with backward induction. They concentrated on the pie-sizes of round 2 and 3 and their mean offers where closest to equilibrium values. Based on the data and on the Icon Graphs, Johnson et al. (2002) concluded that the equilibrium social preference theory could be rejected: the most "fair" offers were from Level 0 players that simply do not look ahead (and thus could not be computing equilibriums). Not only does this single Icon Graph represent a large amount of process data more transparently (compared to putting everything into one complex, chaotic table), it also helps directly in evaluating theories and in showing heterogeneity in the data.

Examining Time Dynamics and Decision Phases

Increasingly, process-based theories make predictions about what occurs as a decision evolves. A simple, efficient, and manageable way to look at dynamics is to divide the process of each participant into parts (divisions) and then summarize across participants for each division. Divisions should be set based on data density considerations as well as theoretical considerations (such as different decision stages). Data density considerations arise because we need sufficient data per division to get stable means and statistical estimates but we also require a fine enough grain to see changes over time. This will depend on the length of the task and the amount of acquisition data.

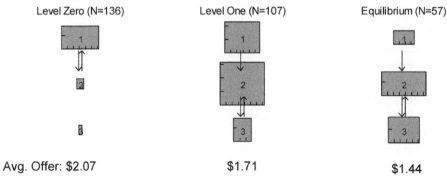

FIGURE 6.3 Icon Graphs of the Sequential Bargaining Study. Columns represent player type (with sample size), rows represent Round 1, 2, and 3 pay-offs. Ticks represent 2.0 seconds (horizontal) and 2.0 acquisitions (vertical).

In much work with MouselabWEB data divisions of 3 (thirds) or 4 (quarters) have been applied (e.g., Willemsen et al., 2011).

Theory may also inform the kinds of divisions. In the PH study, Johnson et al. (2008) used Brandstätter et al.'s distinction between a reading phase and a choice phase. A simple rule was used to identify the boundary between these two phases (all outcomes have to be inspected once, see also Klayman, 1983). Figure 6.4a depicts the predicted Icon Graph, showing predictions for both reading and choice phases, for one and three reason gambles. Figure 6.4b depicts the actual results from the experiment showing quite a few remarkable differences. First, the dominant transition is not between similar items but between outcomes and their probabilities, revealing a process that seems consistent with the integration of these two types of information. Furthermore, more attention than expected seems to be given to probabilities. Finally, the results show that the items associated with reasons in the PH are not the dominant focus of attention.

Figures 6.4a and 6.4b show convincingly that a good graphical representation of both predictions and results is very useful in understanding processes, and in conveying a complicated message to the audience in an effective way. While a good graphic representation is quite useful in describing data, we also need good statistical methods for inference.

Modeling Information Acquisition Data with Multilevel Models

The richer graphical representations of process data suggest a parallel need for methods that can reflect these more detailed characteristics of the decision process, take advantage of the repeated observations, and account for the heterogeneity in the data—multilevel modeling is a statistical approach that can satisfy all these needs. Many modern statistical packages can be used to estimate multilevel models, such as Stata or SPSS. The open source statistical package R (R Core Team, 2017) has additional libraries for the *lmer* function (Bates, Mächler, Bolker, & Walker, 2015) that can be used to run a multilevel regression and Gelman and Hill (2007) provide an excellent book on multilevel regression in R.

Multilevel Models and Random Effects

Multilevel models (Raudenbush & Bryk, 2002), also called hierarchical or mixed models, take into account heterogeneity in the data, modeling multiple interrelated levels of regression. Typically, the first level in the model represents the separate observations for each participant in each period (division). For example, in the case of the paired two-outcome gambles in the PH study, we would have eight boxes. To capture the dynamics, we divided the data into two phases. Thus a model for acquisition time would have 8x2=16 observations per participant per trial, representing 16 (repeated) dependent measures. The second level in the model captures differences among the observations across participants and can be just a random intercept for each participant, or a complex second regression equation with random slopes that estimates how coefficients in the first level regression depend on participant characteristics. For example, in the PH study a multilevel model for looking time was estimated with three coefficients with random variation over subjects, the intercept (participants vary in mean looking time), a decision phase coefficient (participants vary in how they differ between phases within a decision), and a number of reasons coefficient (participants differ in how they change strategies for problems with one or three reasons). In the multilevel model these Level 1 coefficients are assumed to differ between participants, but their variation is assumed to follow a normal distribution (with mean of 0), and we estimate the variance of this distribution based on the data, rather than estimating a separate coefficient for each participant.

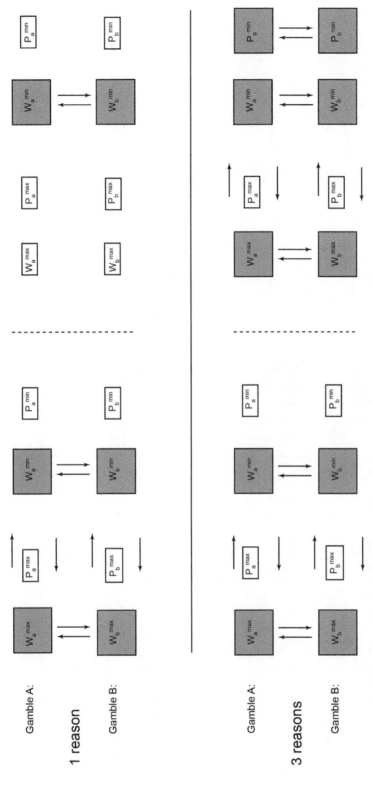

FIGURE 6.4A Prediction Icon Graph for PH process data.

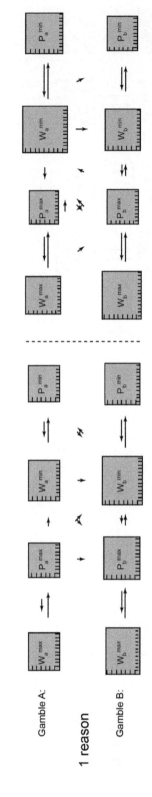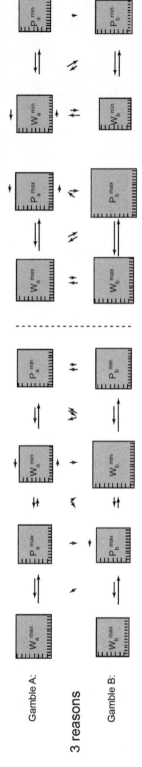

FIGURE 6.4B Results Icon Graph for PH process data. Ticks represent 400 msec (horizontal) and .5 acquisitions (vertical).

Because the dependent measures, time and frequency, are often skewed, it makes sense to apply a transformation to make them normally distributed. A log transformation is usually appropriate for time measures while a square-root transformation is often helpful with frequency data (see Willemsen et al., 2011). Alternatively, process data can be analyzed with generalized linear models, for example assuming a Poisson distribution or negative binomial when data is overdispersed as is common for frequency or transition data.

In terms of the independent variables, we can enter fixed effects present in our data (e.g., factors indicating the manipulation, display order, etc.). The power of a multilevel model is that we can run contrasts that can test specific predictions in differences in attention or transitions between boxes, which we will discuss next.

Using Contrasts in Multilevel Models

The kind of fine-grained analysis required by some theories necessitates the application of contrasts to test specific hypotheses. For example the PH study generated a specific Hypothesis 1a: "In the choice phase, one-reason gambles require that decision makers look more at the minimum outcomes than at the maximum outcomes." This means that of the eight cells, we should compare, by contrast, the acquisitions for the two minimum outcomes with those of the two maximum outcomes. A sample part of the data is shown in Figure 6.5, with this contrast (Contrast H1a, -1 for max outcomes (W^{max}, W stands for Win amount) and +1 for min outcomes W^{min}, zero otherwise). We also include some other factors to illustrate the multilevel data format. *Freq* is the dependent variable in this data. Note that this is only part of the data of one participant, for one phase.

Using contrasts, we can test other specific hypotheses (for more details and examples about the hypotheses and their tests see Johnson et al., 2008, or Willemsen et al., 2011). Note that the data in Figure 6.5 is just a transposed version of the summarized data set (in wide format) that we discussed in the process measures section (Figure 6.2). For multilevel modeling most statistical packages require each observation of each box in a separate row (long format), and they typically offer restructuring or reshape functions to do this.

Understanding Heterogeneity: Individual Differences, Random Effects, and Clustering

Information acquisition data allows us to understand how users differ in their attention allocation and how those differences relate to theories. Pachur, Schulte-Mecklenbeck, Murphy, and Hertwig (2018) estimated parameters of Cumulative Prospect Theory (CPT) at the individual level

freq	boxID	Contrast H1a	Choice phase	gambleA	prob	minOutc
0	W_a^{min}	+ 1	1	1	0	1
0	P_a^{min}	0	1	1	1	1
1	W_b^{min}	+ 1	1	0	0	1
0	P_b^{min}	0	1	0	1	1
0	W_a^{max}	-1	1	1	0	0
3	P_a^{max}	0	1	1	1	0
0	W_b^{max}	-1	1	0	0	0
1	P_b^{max}	0	1	0	1	0
3	W_a^{min}	0	0	1	0	1
2	P_a^{min}	0	0	1	1	1
0	W_b^{min}	0	0	0	0	1

FIGURE 6.5 Sample data demonstrating contrasts in a multilevel analysis.

from participants' choices and correlated these to individual differences in attention allocation to outcomes and probabilities. For example, the individual level of loss-aversion as estimated based on choices was associated with more relative attention to losses. Higher levels of outcome-sensitivity and probability-sensitivity parameters were associated with more attention to outcomes and probabilities, respectively.

We can also examine individual differences by using multilevel modeling. One way is to model heterogeneity by means of the random coefficients in the model. In the PH study, Johnson et al. (2008) modeled individual differences in transitions between outcomes and probabilities by estimating a random effect for this coefficient. The random effect was quite significant, and an index was constructed for each participant to see if participants could be individually classified at "integrating" (index larger than 1) or using the Priority Heuristic (index smaller than 1). The index had a mean of 4.47, and none of the individual-level means were significantly less than 1. Thus, all respondents seemed most consistent with a strategy that uses probabilities in the evaluation of pay-offs, but to varying degrees.

Reeck et al. (2017) used a random effects model in a study on intertemporal choice to compare variability among items and respondents. They found that participants deciding between receiving an amount now or a larger amount later differed systematically in how they searched for information. Subsequently they used K-means cluster analysis on the transition data to identify two different search strategies: comparative searchers who mostly compare across alternatives (i.e., comparing the time delay of options 1 and 2) and integrative searchers who mostly compare within an alternative (compare the time delay with the amount to receive for an option). Cluster analysis on process data has also been used to identify heterogeneity in strategic thinking in games (Brocas et al., 2014) showing that the (data-driven) clusters of which boxes were opened matched well with different levels of level-k thinking, the depth by which a player thinks ahead of his opponent. Polonio et al. (2015) used clustering to identify several types of players that attended to information differently in two-player normal-form games, using eye-tracking data. The combination of variance partitioning and cluster analysis holds great promise as a method of modeling differences.

Predicting Choice and Testing for Mediation

Finally, another important question is to what extent process data can predict choices? As-if models would model choice as being dependent mostly on the independent factors of the experimental design, but if responses are related to processing strategies, the process data should also predict responses. For example, in the PH study, Johnson et al. (2008) fit a choice model (using multilevel logistic regression) with the outcome-probability transitions as predictors. The model showed that the likelihood of choosing a specific gamble depended on the amount of outcome-probability transitions within that gamble. This is an important result as it shows that the underlying process that might drive choice was very different from what the PH predicts, since this heuristic does not consider probability-outcomes transitions as relevant. Moreover, this result suggests that the integration of probability and pay-offs that might be underlying these probability-outcomes transitions seems essential in modeling choice.

A more direct example of the link between information acquisition and choice is provided in the second study of Pachur et al. (2018). They manipulated the attention to losses and gains in a MouselabWEB study by controlling the duration each box opened and showed that these manipulations indeed influenced attention and choices of the participants as well as the resulting loss aversion parameters calculated from the choices using CPT.

If experimental manipulations affect our process data, and if process data is related to choice, mediation analysis (Pieters, 2017; Zhao, Lynch, & Chen, 2010) might help explain how manipulations cause specific cognitive processes which subsequently lead to particular choice patterns. Willemsen et al. (2011) showed that for the Asian Disease scenario, the framing manipulation as well as the order of presentation affected relative attention to the sure and risky prospect already early in the decision process, which partially mediated the effect of framing on choice. This partial mediation provided additional evidence for their Value Construction account of Loss aversion.

Evaluation of MouselabWEB as a Process Tracing Tool

Computer-based information acquisition methods such as MouselabWEB offer several advantages over think-aloud protocols (Chapters 17–18), eye movements (Chapters 1–5, Chapter 7), and other methods of recording information acquisition. The recording of information acquisition is automatic, so experiments can be run on networked computers without intervention by experimenters. In this chapter, we discussed an online variant: MouselabWEB. Online research has several advantages over laboratory studies, as they allow for large samples of very heterogeneous participants (Johnson, 2001) and the data on the underlying process allows us to check if participants were serious in performing the tasks online, outside of our control. However, even a sympathetic reader may have some concerns about this type of information acquisition data. We will now discuss two main methodological concerns.

Does Recording Information Acquisition Change the Underlying Process?

Within decision research, there is a significant literature replicating many standard phenomena, such as preference reversals, using computer-based techniques (Payne et al., 1993). Researchers have also directly compared behavior in games when players *do not* have to open boxes because they appear on the screen uncovered. Costa-Gomes et al. (2001) presented one session of their normal form games without covering up the pay-offs and noted no difference in observed choices. Willemsen et al. (2011) replicated standard framing effects and reference dependence in a MouselabWEB experiment with similar effect sizes than the original studies, despite the fact that information was hidden behind boxes and that the participant pool consisted of a much more heterogeneous sample (in terms of age and level of education) than standard lab studies.

Several studies have directly compared Mouselab to its most similar counterpart, eye-tracking (see also Chapter 7). Lohse and Johnson (1996) found some differences that were confined to tasks where the amount of information presented was much larger than that typically used in games or simple gambles. They conclude that for purposes of theory testing, the advantages of a computer-based method probably far outweigh disadvantages in most cases. Similarly, Reisen et al. (2008), in a comparison of Mouselab with eye-tracking, concluded that search patterns and proportion of information search were very similar and that eye-tracking for their interactive process tracing tool provided no benefits as eye-tracking is harder to setup, often results in calibration problems, and cannot be used online. Reeck et al. (2017) compared eye-tracking to computer-based information acquisition, and found similar differences in strategies between comparative and integrative searchers which similarly influenced the behavior of the participants.

Can Information Acquisition Data Really Tell us Something About Underlying Decision Processes?

Both Costa-Gomes et al. (2001) and Johnson et al. (2002) have run controls where participants were trained to follow game theoretic principles. For example, in the games study, several groups were trained to calculate the backward induction equilibrium and their process data was exactly what was expected. In the decision literature, Bettman, Johnson, and Payne (1990) report success in training subjects to follow various choice strategies and these strategies were reflected in their information acquisition patterns. Bröder and Schiffer (2003) showed convergent validity of process measures from a Mouselab study with a Bayesian method for assessing decision strategies in multiattribute probabilistic inferences.

Moreover, the partial mediation of process data in recent studies (e.g., Willemsen et al., 2011) illustrates that process data can reveal part of the underlying cognitive mechanisms. Stronger evidence comes from studies that actually influence decision strategies by subtle changes in information processing. For example, Sanjurjo (2015) showed that optimal order of information presentation reduced working memory load and subsequently choice errors. Reeck et al. (2017), who identified different decision strategies (using MouselabWEB) in intertemporal choice, showed in a follow-up study that by facilitating or hindering specific comparisons using a delay on the box opening, decision strategies could be partially shifted without participants' awareness, providing a direct link between information acquisition and cognitive processes.

Together, these results from multiple studies indicate that information acquisition *does* monitor cognitive process in decisions. Yet in some sense, the development of these methods has outstripped theory. Most theories do not make explicit process predictions. Yet such predictions would be very helpful in comparing theories, as our examples in this chapter have shown extensively. Examples include sequential sampling models such as Decision Field Theory (Roe, Busemeyer, & Townsend, 2001), closely related theories (Diederich, 2003; Usher & McClelland, 2004), and drift diffusion models (e.g., Krajbich, Armel, & Rangel, 2010). Since these models make different processing assumptions to explain the same choice phenomena, they benefit from empirical tests, not just of the choices made, but also of their implications for cognitive processing (see Chapters 21 and 24; also Schulte-Mecklenbeck et al., 2017). For example, Noguchi and Stewart (2014) tested several computational models on their process assumptions using an eye-tracking study.

Future Directions

Researchers have been using computers to study information acquisition for almost 30 years, and the method has proven to be amazingly robust. It has developed from a method requiring specialized laboratory computers to web-based methods capable of running hundreds of respondents a day, who are located anywhere in the world.

MouselabWEB, the method central in this chapter, was first released in 2004 and has over 1200 registered users. The current version is 1.0 with major releases in 2008 and 2010. As browsing online has moved from desktops towards mobile devices, our online research tools should also adapt to that. MouselabWEB 2.0, currently under development, uses modern responsive web techniques that adapt easily to changes in screen sizes. This allows MouselabWEB to not only run on traditional mouse-based computers, but also on mobile touch-based screens found on phones and tablets. The new version also includes an option to blur rather than hide the information in the box, which provides a more natural cue to the content of the box (see the screenshot in Figure 6.2a). The new version uses the same data structure as version 1 but differs in that the page definition is stored in a well-specified separate (JSON-formatted) file. This allows processing scripts (such as the icon graph scripts) to retrieve the layout of the display easily and process the data more automatically.

As both cognitive theories on decision making and computational models become more sophisticated, and as statistical tools such as multilevel models and data-analytic tools such as clustering are becoming more widespread and easier to use, process data will have increasing value for psychology, especially when being used online to acquire large samples of diverse participant populations.

A final challenge is the development of more precise theories linking information acquisition and cognition. Costa-Gomes et al. (2001) made a significant step in this direction when they posited the principles of Occurrence and Adjacency. These principles, while obviously overly simplistic, do allow for precise predictions linking information acquisition to purported process. We hope that further cooperation between formal descriptions of process and acquisition will lead to greater insight.

Recommended Reading List

- Wickham and Grolemund (2017): A good introduction to data processing and visualization in R (see also: http://r4ds.had.co.nz/).
- Gelman and Hill (2007): A good introduction to multilevel models using R.
- Payne, Bettman, and Johnson (1993): Insights into early work on information acquisition.
- Schulte-Mecklenbeck et al. (2017): A recent overview of information acquisition.
- www.mouselabweb.org/: For details on the free open source package MouselabWEB.

References

Bates, D., Mächler, M., Bolker, B., & Walker, S. (2015). Fitting linear mixed-effects models using lme4. *Journal of Statistical Software*, *67*(1), 1–48.

Bettman, J. R., Johnson, E. J., & Payne, J. W. (1990). A componential analysis of cognitive effort in choice. *Organizational Behavior and Human Decision Processes*, *45*(1), 111–139.

Böckenholt, U., & Hynan, L. S. (1994). Caveats on a process-tracing measure and a remedy. *Journal of Behavioral Decision Making*, *7*(2), 103–117.

Brandstätter, E., Gigerenzer, G., & Hertwig, R. (2006). The priority heuristic: Making choices without trade-offs. *Psychological Review*, *113*(2), 409–432.

Brocas, I., Carrillo, J. D., Wang, S. W., & Camerer, C. F. (2014). Imperfect choice or imperfect attention? Understanding strategic thinking in private information games. *The Review of Economic Studies*, *81*(3), 944–970.

Bröder, A., & Schiffer, S. (2003). Bayesian strategy assessment in multi-attribute decision making. *Journal of Behavioral Decision Making*, *16*(3), 193–213.

Camerer, C. F., & Johnson, E. J. (2004). Thinking about attention in games: Backward and forward induction. In I. Brocas, & J. Carillo (Eds.), *The psychology of economic decisions* (pp. 111–129). New York, NY: Oxford University Press.

Card, S. K., Moran, T. P., & Newell, A. (1980). Computer text editing: An information-processing analysis of a routine cognitive skill. *Cognitive Psychology*, *12*(1), 32–74.

Card, S. K., Moran, T. P., & Newell, A. (1983). *The psychology of human-computer interaction*. Hillsdale, NJ: Erlbaum.

Chen, M. C., Anderson, J. R., & Sohn, M. H. (2001). What can a mouse cursor tell us more? Correlation of eye/mouse movements on web browsing. In *CHI'01 extended abstracts on human factors in computing systems* (pp. 281–282). ACM.

Costa-Gomes, M., Crawford, V. P., & Broseta, B. (2001). Cognition and behavior in normal-form games: An experimental study. *Econometrica*, *69*(5), 1193–1235.

DiCarlo, J. J., Zoccolan, D., & Rust, N. C. (2012). How does the brain solve visual object recognition? *Neuron*, *73*(3), 415–434.

Diederich, A. (2003). MDFT account of decision making under time pressure. *Psychonomic Bulletin & Review*, *10*(1), 157–166.

Gelman, A., & Hill, J. (2007). *Data analysis using regression and multilevel/hierarchical models*. New York, NY: Cambridge University Press.

Goldstein, D. G., Suri, S., McAfee, R. P., Ekstrand-Abueg, M., & Diaz, F. (2014). The economic and cognitive costs of annoying display advertisements. *Journal of Marketing Research, 51*(6), 742–752.

Jasper, J. D., & Shapiro, J. (2002). MouseTrace: A better mousetrap for catching decision processes. *Behavioral Research Methods, 34*(3), 364–374.

Johnson, E. J. (1996). *The last whole MouseLab manual.* Retrieved from The Columbia Center for Excellence in E-Business website: www.cebiz.org/mouselab/mouselab.pdf

Johnson, E. J. (2001). Digitizing consumer research. *Journal of Consumer Research, 28*(2), 331–336.

Johnson, E. J., Camerer, C., Sen, S., & Rymon, T. (2002). Detecting failures of backward induction: Monitoring information search in sequential bargaining. *Journal of Economic Theory, 104*(1), 16–47.

Johnson, E. J., & Schkade, D. A. (1989). Bias in utility assessments: Further evidence and explanations. *Management Science, 35*(4), 406–424.

Johnson, E. J., Schulte-Mecklenbeck, M., & Willemsen, M. C. (2008). Process models deserve process data: Comment on Brandstätter, Gigerenzer, and Hertwig (2006). *Psychological Review, 115*, 263–272.

Kahneman, D., & Tversky, A. (1979). Prospect theory: An analysis of decisions under risk. *Econometrica, 47*, 263–291.

Klayman, J. (1983). Analysis of predecisional search patterns. In P. Humphreys, O. Svenson, & A. Vari (Eds.), *Analyzing and Aiding Decision Processes* (pp. 400–414). Amsterdam, NL: North Holland.

Krajbich, I., Armel, C., & Rangel, A. (2010). Visual fixations and the computation and comparison of value in simple choice. *Nature Neuroscience, 13*(10), 1292–1298.

Lohse, G. L., & Johnson, E. J. (1996). A comparison of two process tracing methods for choice tasks. *Organizational Behavior and Human Decision Processes, 68*(1), 28–43.

Noguchi, T., & Stewart, N. (2014). In the attraction, compromise, and similarity effects, alternatives are repeatedly compared in pairs on single dimensions. *Cognition, 132*(1), 44–56.

Pachur, T., Schulte-Mecklenbeck, M., Murphy, R. O., & Hertwig, R. (2018). Prospect theory reflects selective allocation of attention. *Journal of Experimental Psychology: General, 147*(2), 147.

Payne, J. W. (1976). Task complexity and contingent processing in decision making: An information search and protocol analysis. *Organizational Behavior and Human Performance, 16*(2), 366–387.

Payne, J. W., Bettman, J. R., & Johnson, E. J. (1988). Adaptive strategy selection in decision making, *Journal of Experimental Psychology: Learning, Memory, and Cognition, 14*(3), 534–552.

Payne, J. W., Bettman, J. R., & Johnson, E. J. (1993). *The adaptive decision maker.* New York, NY: Cambridge University Press.

Payne, J. W., & Braunstein, M. L. (1978). Risky choice: An examination of information acquisition behavior. *Memory and Cognition, 6*(5), 554–561.

Pieters, R. (2017). Meaningful mediation analysis: Plausible causal inference and informative communication. *Journal of Consumer Research, 44*(3), 692–716.

Polonio, L., di Guida, S., & Coricelli, G. (2015). Strategic sophistication and attention in games: An eye-tracking study. *Games and Economic Behavior, 94*, 80–96.

R Core Team. (2017). *R: A language and environment for statistical computing.* Retrieved from The R Foundation for Statistical Computing website: www.R-project.org/

Raudenbush, S. W., & Bryk, A. S. (2002). *Hierarchical linear models: Applications and data analysis methods* (2nd ed.). London, UK: Sage Publications.

Reeck, C., Wall, D., & Johnson, E. J. (2017). Search predicts and changes patience in intertemporal choice. *Proceedings of the National Academy of Sciences, 114*(45), 11890–11895.

Reisen, N., Hoffrage, U., & Mast, F. W. (2008). Identifying decision strategies in a consumer choice situation. *Judgment and Decision Making, 3*(8), 641–658.

Rieskamp, J., & Hoffrage, U. (1999). When do people use simple heuristics, and how can we tell? In G. Gigerenzer, P. M. Todd, & The ABC Research Group (Eds.), *Evolution and cognition. Simple heuristics that make us smart* (pp. 141–167). New York, NY: Oxford University Press.

Roe, R. M., Busemeyer, J. R., & Townsend, J. T. (2001). Multialternative decision field theory: A dynamic connectionist model of decision making. *Psychological Review, 108*(2), 370–392.

Sanjurjo, A. (2015). Search, memory, and choice error: An experiment. *PLoS ONE, 10*(6), e0126508.

Schkade, D. A., & Johnson, E. J. (1989). Cognitive processes in preference reversals. *Organizational Behavior and Human Decision Processes, 44*(2), 203–231.

Schulte-Mecklenbeck, M., Johnson, J. G., Böckenholt, U., Goldstein, D., Russo, J., Sullivan, N., & Willemsen, M. (2017). Process tracing methods in decision making: On growing up in the 70ties. *Current Directions in Psychological Science, 26*(5), 442–450.

Schulte-Mecklenbeck, M., Murphy, R. O., & Hutzler, F. (2011). Flashlight: Recording information acquisition online. *Computers in Human Behavior, 27*(5), 1771–1782.

Schulte-Mecklenbeck, M., Sohn, M., de Bellis, E., Martin, N., & Hertwig, R. (2013). A lack of appetite for information and computation. Simple heuristics in food choice. *Appetite, 71*, 242–251.

Usher, M., & McClelland, J. L. (2004). Loss aversion and inhibition in dynamical models of multialternative choice. *Psychological Review, 111*(3), 757–769.

Wickham, H., & Grolemund, G. (2017). *R for data science: Import, tidy, transform, visualize, and model data.* Sebastopol, CA: O'Reilly Media.

Willemsen, M. C., Böckenholt, U., & Johnson, E. J. (2011). Choice by value encoding and value construction: Processes of loss aversion. *Journal of Experimental Psychology: General, 140*(3), 303–324.

Willemsen, M. C., & Johnson, E. J. (2017). MouselabWEB: Monitoring information acquisition processes on the web. Retrieved from www.mouselabweb.org/

Zhao, X., Lynch, J. G., Jr., & Chen, Q. (2010). Reconsidering Baron and Kenny: Myths and truths about mediation analysis. *Journal of Consumer Research, 37*(2), 197–206.

7

COMPARING PROCESS TRACING PARADIGMS

Tracking Attention via Mouse and Eye Movements

Ana M. Franco-Watkins, Hayden K. Hickey, and Joseph G. Johnson

From the onset, judgment and decision-making research emphasized theoretical accounts for processing and valuation of prospects (e.g., Edwards, 1962; Savage, 1954). Modern decision theory assumes attentional components are present when people process and use information during decision making (e.g., Decision Field Theory: Busemeyer & Johnson, 2004; Johnson & Busemeyer, 2005; Query Theory: Weber et al., 2007). The ability to connect theory with behavior becomes stronger with the advent of technological advances. Capturing the decision process has become more tangible and concrete with the ability to measure finer-grain processes (e.g., Schulte-Mecklenbeck, Kühberger, Gagl, & Hutzler, 2017). We are constantly making new advances in methodologies, often with direct connections to brain activity (see Chapters 14–16). The focus for this chapter is on two often implemented methodologies for capturing attention in decision making via recording mouse movements (Mouselab: see Chapter 6[1]) and eye movements (see Chapters 1–5). Specifically, we provide an overview of attentional processing which is central to understanding relevant tracking methods and decision making.

Attentional Processing in Decision Making

Attention is broadly defined as a limited cognitive resource that allows an individual to perceive, process, and interpret information whether it is external to their environment or internally generated in the mind (Baddeley & Hitch, 1974; Kahneman, 1973; Pashler, 1998). It is limited as a cognitive resource because there are mental constraints as to how much information can be processed at any given time (i.e., attention bottlenecks: Pashler, 1998; and working memory limits: Baddeley, 2003; Cowan, 2012). Sometimes, attention can be involuntary such as when individuals naturally startle when attention is directed, such as, to the source of a loud noise. In deliberate decision making, the process of acquiring, processing, and evaluating information requires voluntary or directed attention. Attentional processing can be defined as the directing of one's mental resources, typically by focusing on specific elements, to process information or stimuli. Anticipating that decision makers will attend to and use information during the decision process requires specifying or measuring *attention*. In fact, the premise behind many process tracing methodologies, such as tracking mouse or eye movements, is that visual attention can be measured via eye or mouse movements, and these movements provide a mechanism to understand attention and information processing that leads to decision outcomes. For example, the implicit supposition when using mouse movements is that the mouse position can be used as a measure of attention to infer information processing in Mouselab (Chen, Anderson, & Sohn, 2001; see also Chapter 6). Furthermore, tracking eye movements is also an analog to measure voluntary visual attention to certain presented information. More specifically, as an individual directs and moves their eyes (i.e., fixation) to information presented before them (typically, on a computer screen), the location and time spent on specific information on the screen are recorded and used to infer information processing. Although there is some debate as to whether or not covert attention precedes overt orienting of the eye, the coupling of eye movements and visual attention are mandatory (Hoffman, 1998). Thus, the assumption that eye movements provide a mechanism for understanding attention to presented information is justified. Granted, any cognitive process may rely on information acquired over multiple visual samples due to working memory, so the exact nature of this processing may not always be revealed. Additionally, for methodologies that do not occlude information (such as standard eye-tracking paradigms), information in the periphery of the visual field may also affect judgment and choice (Wästlund, Shams, & Otterbring, 2018). Nonetheless, methodologies that assess attention via mouse or eye movements capture attentional processing to varying degrees, because the decision maker is presented with visual information, and normally directs their attention to that information in order to make a judgment or choice.

The eyes are the biological vehicle used to direct attentional processing to the outside world as it is experienced. Visual attention has been extensively examined for many decades with much of the emphasis on clarifying the basic processes associated with simple visual search, discrimination, and pattern recognition (see Pashler, 1998 for an overview). Characteristics of visual attention have been applied to higher-level processes in cognition (e.g., reading and scene perception; Rayner, 1998), and more recently, in decision research (e.g., Franco-Watkins & Johnson, 2011a; Glöckner & Herbold, 2011; Orquin & Loose, 2013; Schulte-Mecklenbeck et al., 2017). The premise to use visual attention as a means for information processing stems from the eye-mind assumption whereby an individual mentally processes information in their visual field (Just & Carpenter, 1980). The strong assumption of the eye-mind assumption may not always hold, as covert attention is possible and occurs (Hoffman, 1998). Notwithstanding, measuring eye or mouse movements to infer attentional processing provides many avenues to understand the mechanisms that affect decision behavior.

Eye-Tracking Technology and Measures

Eye-tracking has roots in sensation and perception research (see Chapters 1–2), with the first era of development defined by É Javal's (1878) discovery of saccade movements during the reading process and Edmund Huey's (1908) creation of laboratory devices that could capture and track eye movements. Although conducted on somewhat crude instruments (i.e., requiring contact lenses attached to aluminum pointers), attempts to measure phenomena such as saccadic suppression, saccade latency, and perceptual span size resulted in many discoveries that still hold true (Rayner, 1998). Moreover, these devices laid groundwork for less intrusive measuring instruments, which eventually utilized video cameras to trace eye movements (see Thagaseen, Dharani, Soundharya, Venkat, & Radha, 2016).

The second and third eras of eye-tracking are represented by developments in technology, leading to a mass increase in data feasibility and quality. Researchers such as Guy Thomas Buswell (1935) and Miles Tinker (1946) utilized new camera technologies to investigate reading and scene perception. Major findings from this era include applied research of eye movements in areas of education (e.g., reading improvement), with little theory-based development due to a suppressed interest in measuring cognitive processes (Rayner, 1978). The third era of eye-tracking was marked by improvements in eye movement recording systems, facilitating large amounts of data in laboratory settings via computers (Pillalamarri, Barnette, Birkmire, & Karsh, 1993), which give researchers the ability to track methods in real time to assess human–computer interactions (HCIs; Jacob, 1991). Preceding modern 21st century research, this third era of eye-tracking is categorized by an influx of data availability and an innovation for measurement techniques (Rayner, 1998). For example, it was during this time that the eye-contingent display change paradigm surfaced (McConkie & Rayner, 1975), in which changes in a participant's visual display are contingent upon his/her eye position.

The most common measures of eye movements encompass saccades (i.e., rapid simultaneous movement of both eyes) and fixations (stationary or relatively fixed eye position on a target). Much of the research in reading and scene perception has focused on gaze duration as the primary measurement of selective visual attention. Gaze duration consists of the time spent viewing the target (word or elements of a scene) which includes all instances that the target was viewed. For example, in reading research, a shift in visual attention occurs between eye fixations on a word in the text. As the word increases in complexity, longer fixations (gaze duration) occur. In turn, gaze duration is interpreted as an indication of the amount of time to process and comprehend the word (Inhoff & Radach, 1998; Rayner, 1998).

Many additional measures can be used in eye-tracking and include measures that emphasize movements, position, numerosity, distance, and latencies (see Holmqvist et al., 2011 for introduction to these measures). For example, pupillary responses such as the pupil dilation across time from onset of task to response demonstrates cognitive load and effort associated with information processing over time (e.g., Attar, Schneps, & Pomplun, 2016; Beatty, 1982; Heitz, Schrock, Payne, & Engle, 2008). The basic finding is that as the task demands increase, so does the amplitude of the pupil dilation, and early work on eye-tracking (Beatty & Wagoner, 1978; Hess & Polt, 1964; Kahneman, Beatty, & Pollack, 1967) as well as recent work applied to decision making (Franco-Watkins & Johnson, 2011b; see also Chapter 3) demonstrate this phenomenon. The downside of using pupillary measures is that changes in amplitude can be difficult to discern with a smaller number of observations or very brief tasks. Furthermore, specific metrics are also used to predict choice and model the decision process. For example, the first fixation can predict a consumer's final choice (Reutskaja, Nagel, Camerer, & Rangel, 2011), gaze bias predicts preferences (Shimojo, Simion, Shimojo, & Scheier, 2003), the last fixation predicts choosing a sooner or later option in an intertemporal task (Franco-Watkins, Mattson, & Jackson, 2016), and fixation durations (Krajbich & Rangel, 2011) provide a mechanism to model different decision parameters. Thus, information processing can be examined utilizing different measures to predict behavior. In sum, the advances in technology coupled with the abundance of high-resolution data from eye-tracking measures allows researchers to address complex cognitive processing during decision making, and allows stricter tests of theoretical assumptions of attention (e.g., "weights") as well as the ability to model decision processes as they evolve.

Mouse and Eye Movement Paradigms in Decision Research

The early work of Payne, Bettman, and Johnson (e.g., 1988, 1993) pioneered a process tracing paradigm using mouse movements to investigate information acquisition processes leading to choices and judgment. In this paradigm, an information matrix is displayed on a computer screen, but all individual cell information is hidden until the decision maker places the mouse cursor over a specific cell. The information corresponding to that cell is then revealed, and all other cell information remains hidden (see Chapter 6). In the lab version of recording mouse movements, the opening of a cell and duration within a cell are recorded over time to provide a measure of how the information was accessed. The resulting process data can be rich and complex, but for the most part it has been presented as summary information, such as the total number of acquisitions (cells accessed) and the average amount of time spent looking at each piece of information. To examine the search process, Payne et al. (1988) developed a pattern variable that indicates whether search proceeds primarily across columns or across rows, and others improved and expanded similar measures (Böckenholt & Hynan, 1994; Ball, 1997).

Initially, process tracing research with eye-tracking methods focused on addressing more applied questions such as consumer choice, marketing, and advertising (e.g., Pieters & Wedel, 2004; Pieters, Warlop, & Wedel, 2002; Russo & Dosher, 1983; Russo & Leclerc, 1994; Russo & Rosen, 1975; Wedel & Pieters, 2000). In the last decade, decision science has relied on eye movements and technology to capture attentional processing across a variety of different decision tasks including risky choice (Fiedler & Glöckner, 2012; Franco-Watkins & Johnson, 2011b; Stewart, Hermens, & Matthews, 2016), intertemporal choice (Franco-Watkins et al., 2016), probabilistic inference tasks (Franco-Watkins & Johnson, 2011a), and multiattribute choice (Franco-Watkins, Davis, & Johnson, 2016; Krajbich & Rangel, 2011). Recently, a special issue in the *Journal of Behavioral Decision Making* focused on applications and innovations of eye movement in decision research (Ashby, Johnson, Krajbich, & Wedel, 2016).

We present a process tracing method that we developed that is a hybrid of using mouse and eye movements. More specifically, interactive eye-tracking such as the *decision moving window* paradigm combines the cell by cell revelation used in mouse movement methods with eye-tracking. All cells (also known as areas of interest: AOIs in eye-tracking studies) are occluded until the individual directs their attention using their eyes to a specific cell on the screen, cell information within the foveal region of the eye when the eye remains relatively still (i.e., fixation) will be opened. Typically, the researcher determines how long a fixation must last to be able to reveal cell information (e.g., we used 20 msec in our design). Thus, this is an interactive fixation-contingent approach that relies on fixations rather than mouse cursor to reveal information cell by cell. Similar to mouse movements, the cell information needs to be sufficiently spaced apart such that a fixation only to one cell will reveal information and participants cannot use peripheral information to open adjacent cells. The AOI size and spacing between AOIs will depend on the eye-tracking apparatus's spatial resolution and the screen size of the study. For example, in our prior studies we have used a variety of different AOI sizes (or cells). AOI size depends on the question of interest and number of cells needed in the study design, and additional AOI were identified for task information (e.g., labels, choice options) presented on the screen. The important aspect is depending on the screen size to generate enough spacing between AOIs such that the individual can only direct their eyes to one cell at a time to reveal information. In standard eye-tracking where there is no occlusion the researcher can designate AOIs after the fact, however, it is good practice to establish similar AOI sizes and spacing between AOIs regardless of eye-tracking method used. Additionally, because of the novelty of explicitly revealing information with one's eyes, we recommend a few practice trials to allow the individual to acclimate to this method.

Comparisons between Methodologies

Theoretical Assumptions

In relation to attention theories, eye movements provide a distinct advantage over mouse movement in terms of measuring attention, assumed by relating overt (visual) and covert (cognitive) attention. Not only is the precedent better established in decades of eye-tracking research in reading and scene perception, but strong evidence suggests attentional shifts and eye movements are coupled for complex information processing (Hoffman, 1998; Rayner, 1998). It should be noted that mouse movements can provide correlations between visual attention measured via cell access and the weight given to the information (e.g., Norman & Schulte-Mecklenbeck, 2010; Wedell & Senter, 1997), however, it may be more of a theoretical leap to assume cell revelation is synonymous with cognitive attention in mouse movement paradigms. For instance, one can rely on working memory when making comparisons between several adjacent cell values in the table. The cell information can readily be held and processed in working memory without the need to repeatedly move the mouse back and forth between cells, even though attention might be shifted to the other cell mentally. The cursor may remain in a cell when attention is directed internally to computational processes such as addition (revealed in contrast, perhaps, by "out of area" data in eye-tracking as one looks up to think). Thus, mouse movements provide an indirect measure of the attentional processing of information. However, there are trade-offs between methods of process tracing: while mouse movements may be coarser or less precise, eye-tracking can result in very fine-grained data, and the researcher will need to make sure the translation between the data and attention are theoretically appropriate.

One might argue that cognitive and attentional processes associated with uncovering small bits of information, as in typical Mouselab studies, and potentially, in the decision moving window, are quite different than when all the information is prominently displayed, as in eye-tracking. Specifically, when the information is concealed, one has to process and maintain the information (taxing working memory capacity) in addition to recalling which piece of information is associated with a specific alternative. In Mouselab, the tool is meant to serve as a memory device to offset some of these concerns, and in the decision moving window, cell acquisition is quicker and people tend to reacquire cell information (greater detail in subsequent section) thereby potentially placing less demands on working memory. When all the information is prominently displayed, working memory concerns are less obvious. In fact, Gray, Schoelles, and Sims (2005) showed that people acquire much less information and change their strategies due simply to how long it takes to reveal information in concealed mouse movement paradigms. Consequently, eye-tracking alone reduces this potential cognitive load of acquiring information. As such, researchers should consider the potential load on cognitive resources or working memory that may be associated with the complexity of the information to be acquired as well as the quantity of information that needs to be held in mind before making a choice or judgment.

Metrics and Measures

As previously introduced, eye-tracking offers a rich data source in addition to the fixation location and duration (akin to table cell acquisition used with mouse movements). There exists both more precise measures of these key variables (e.g., first fixations, number of regressions, and microsaccades; see Inhoff & Radach, 1998; Holmqvist et al., 2011; and Rayner, 1998 for overviews) but also wholly different types of data such as pupil dilation revealing cognitive effort (Kahneman & Beatty, 1966, Chapter 3) during the decision process. For example, changes in pupil diameter differed between eye-tracking alone vs interactive eye-tracking. We demonstrated an increasing cognitive load for complex decisions using interactive eye-tracking as indexed by greater changes in pupil diameter during the decision process until a choice was made (Franco-Watkins & Johnson, 2011b). Additionally, the last fixation in a decision task (Franco-Watkins et al., 2016; Stewart, Gächter, Noguchi, & Mullett, 2016) predicts a person's choice. As mentioned previously, eye-tracking also affords the ability to obtain finer-grain measurements of attention that may supersede the coarse measurements of mouse movements.

Furthermore, mouse movements do not always correspond with eye movements, in that mouse measurements can be used as a proxy for eye movements (i.e., eye–mouse coordination: Guo & Agichtein, 2010), but this effect is contextual and depends on individuals' mouse practices, such as reading, scrolling, and clicking. These nuances indicate that mouse movements should go beyond measuring cursor position when predicting eye fixation (Huang, White, & Buscher, 2012).

Reactance

It is readily apparent that using a computer mouse to collect information involves more than simply moving the eyes to do so. Based on our daily experiences with a mouse, it may also seem natural to dismiss the effort required to navigate the mouse as trivial and inconsequential. However, using the computer mouse can give rise to artifacts in data compared to that obtained with eye-tracking. For example, Glöckner and Betsch (2008) make the argument that mouse tracing impacts the information search process and leads to theoretical misattribution, such as presuming that use of simplifying strategies is due to cognitive limitations. Instead, they argue that these observations may be the result of methodological constraints associated with mouse movements. In particular, they demonstrated that individuals could make decisions in line with "complex" strategies such as maximizing expected utility, even with very little time, when search was not constrained (eye-tracking). However, they found shifts to "simpler" strategies under time pressure when mouse movements were used, in line with the previous literature.

A key difference between paradigms that use mouse and eye movements is that the former has a (greater) tendency to induce systematicity in the search process. Glöckner and Betsch (2008, p. 1071) also claim that the use of a mouse for process tracing "is likely to induce deliberate processes." Interestingly, a more specific comparison by Franco-Watkins and Johnson (2011a) suggests this may be due to the occlusion necessary to implement this process tracing paradigm. When they compared eye-tracking, Mouselab, and the decision moving window, they found that both occlusion paradigms (Mouselab and the decision moving window) showed more systematic search processes compared to standard eye-tracking (no occlusion). Researchers should use caution and determine whether or not inducing systematicity is irrelevant, detrimental, or beneficial based on the research questions at hand. There may be situations where one would like to promote deliberate thought, but certainly not when trying to determine the "natural" behavior on any given task.

Other research has shown that simply the "cost" of moving the mouse can affect information search behavior. Franco-Watkins and Johnson (2011a) found that participants acquire much less information—less than half as many acquisitions—when using a mouse rather than eye-tracking, regardless of whether information is occluded (no differences were found between decision moving window and eye-tracking). Furthermore, Gray et al. (2005) found that as the time required to reveal information using a mouse increases, the degree of search decreases. This causes a tension between more reliable measurement—not revealing information until the mouse rests long enough to avoid misattributing "passing over" information cells as acquisitions—and less reactance. In general, people may suffer from simple (albeit mild) laziness in moving the mouse. Regardless, the greater number of acquisitions that characterizes eye-tracking data can also result in better application of the appropriate analytic techniques, especially those such as chi-square and other frequency analyses that rely on some minimum acquisition frequencies for proper application.

In sum, mouse movements have provided an initial step towards capturing and understanding the deliberation process and acquisition of information in decision making. However, because mouse movements are used as a proxy for attentional processing, a better direct measure of attention (via eye movements) provides an improvement in both the method and measurement of attentional processing within a decision-making framework. In addition, eye movements provide an extremely rich data source in that several different measures can be collected. However, methods such as Mouselab can capture data in situations where eye-tracking cannot, such as remotely online. Moreover, Mouselab appears to be most cost effective and easier to collect simultaneous data from many individuals (see later). Considered independently, each type of data provides information into the cognitive processes of attention and deliberation; however, combining multiple sources of data is a useful tool to provide convergence in understanding the dynamic processes associated with the acquisition and use of information in decision making.

Explicit Process Comparisons Across Tasks

Earlier work comparing eye and mouse movements demonstrated that as the task complexity increased based on number of attributes and alternatives, differences emerged in terms of processing time and reacquisitions (i.e., going back to a previously acquired cell; Lohse & Johnson, 1996). As noted previously, these comparisons are not as direct because eye-tracking alone (without occlusion) does not place the cognitive demands on the decision maker that are in place when all information is occluded and revealed piece by piece. As such, it is not surprising that the complexity of the task structure exacerbated the differences between standard eye-tracking and mouse movements. Since this time, several researchers have also made comparisons between these two paradigms (e.g., Arroyo, Selker, & Wei, 2006; Chen et al., 2001).

The different process tracing methods (eye tracking, mouse movement, and decision moving window: DMW) were examined in two separate decision tasks: a probabilistic inference task (Franco-Watkins & Johnson, 2011a) and a risky decision task (Franco-Watkins & Johnson, 2011b). A consistent pattern of processing results emerged regardless of task. Namely, in terms of information processing, we noted that both eye-tracking paradigms resulted in shorter processing times in terms of average time to acquire information which enabled participants to view more information.

In addition to basic summary measures depicted in Table 7.1, the eye-tracking pattern of results can be observed by plotting all fixations in a decision task to reveal which information is attended more, and how attention to different aspects of the task may predict choice. As an illustrative example, we present Figure 7.1 which represents Participant A who chose option C and attended more or less equally to all information whereas Participant B chose option B and attended more often to the information for the top two predictive cues in this task. As noted earlier, researchers have also used fixation patterns as well as first and last fixations to predict choices successfully (Russo & Leclerc, 1994).

Additionally, sometimes differences in decision strategies used by people emerge based on type of process tracing paradigm. Specifically, we focused on two often used strategies in decision research. One strategy is a simple lexicographic (LEX) strategy that involves searching across attributes (cues) in order of their importance (validity) and selecting an option based on the first attribute to discriminate between choice options (i.e., alternatives). A second more complex strategy, weighted additive (WADD) requires some calculation, namely, for each alternative, a weighted sum of attribute values is computed and then the decision maker selects the option with the highest sum. The strategies were applied to the probabilistic inference task shown in Figure 7.1 where we created each trial in the task to be diagnostic between WADD and LEX decision strategies. Using a WADD strategy in this task involves taking a cumulative predictive validity for each movie and selecting the movie with the highest sum, whereas a LEX strategy is characterized by choosing a movie based on the first attribute to discriminate from the other movies (greater task details are provided in Franco-Watkins & Johnson, 2011a; Franco-Watkins, Davis, & Johnson,

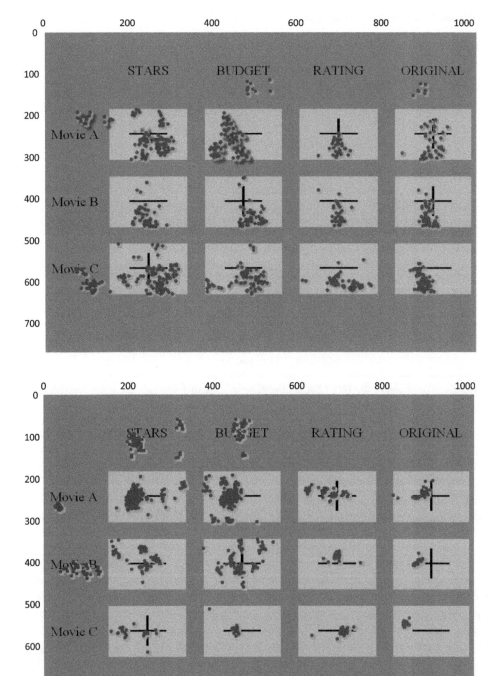

FIGURE 7.1 An illustrative example of eye fixation data patterns for two participants: Participant A (top panel) chose Movie C, and Participant B (bottom panel) chose Movie B. Axes represent actual screen resolution 768 x 1024 used in the probabilistic inference task from Franco-Watkins and Johnson, 2011a. Each dot represents a single fixation to a specific AOI. Although information cues are revealed, these cells represent the DMW paradigm where all cell information was occluded until the participant fixated in a specific area of interest denoted as a light gray box. Labels were presented openly and not occluded.

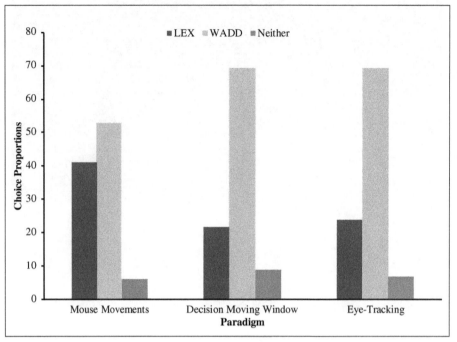

FIGURE 7.2 Proportion of WADD, LEX, and neither strategy in a probabilistic inference task across three process tracing paradigms (data based on Franco-Watkins & Johnson, 2011a).

2016). As can be noted in Figure 7.2, the mouse movement paradigm resulted in slightly less use of the more complex WADD strategy and increase in simpler LEX strategies as compared to both eye-tracking paradigms, replicating other previous work (e.g., Glöckner & Betsch, 2008).

Methodological Considerations and Applications

The three process tracing methodologies have advantages and disadvantages, and which one might be better suited to address a specific question may be contextual. As such, when one wishes to collect data via process tracing, the decision of which technology to utilize is best made after considering sample size necessity, availability of resources, and research environment. Despite the evolution of eye-tracking, recording mouse movements is still widely used today. Some of the benefits of recording mouse movements include location flexibility, as mouse movement technologies do not require participants to be present in the laboratory, as is currently the case with eye-tracking methodologies. Albeit there is some use of eye-tracking glasses and eye-tracker devices in naturalistic or simulated environments (e.g., driving: McCarley et al., 2004, and consumer choice: Gidlöf, Wallen, Dewhurst, & Holmqvist, 2013; see also Chapter 2), however, this approach is less often used than laboratory studies for eye-tracking, and the individual would need to return to the lab to have the data downloaded for processing and evaluation. Greater flexibility and use of natural environments increases usability and ensures the user's activity is generalizable across various domains.

Another advantage of mouse movements is when data is collected remotely, there could be fewer demand characteristics than could potentially occur in a laboratory setting. In addition to these benefits, perhaps the most pertinent advantages of mouse movements are their low cost, as no additional hardware (e.g., infrared cameras) is necessary, and many individuals can participate at the same time in different locations. As such, many researchers choose to use the mouse movement methodology, especially MouselabWEB (see Chapter 6) which is internet-based, over eye-tracking to sample a larger number of participants in a shorter amount of time.

The disadvantages associated with tracing mouse movements are perhaps best explained by analyzing the benefits of eye-tracking technologies. Eye-tracking, inarguably, gives the researcher richer data, although there are concerns about denoting the cognitive processes from these fine-grained data (e.g., calculating a fixation). With eye-tracking, there is no uncertainty of the location of an actual fixation because a direct eye measurement provides information about the person's attention. Additionally, eye-tracking cameras are able to detect the slightest saccade such that researchers have a finer-grain data of orientation and saccades between AOIs and information displayed to the individual. Although eye-tracking may mandate being restricted to the laboratory for the most part, this hindrance also provides a controlled environment by which studies may be more thoroughly conducted. Part of this restriction includes a limited ability to sample many populations as the location control can reduce sample size and access to individuals who may not be able to come to a laboratory to participate in the study. However, the data provided by the eye-tracking methodology is inherently more reliable due to experimental control, participants are less susceptible to distraction and random error by real-world influence that may occur when they participate remotely from their own home or business.

The decision moving window is very similar to regular eye-tracking in regard to advantages over mouse movement tracking, as well as the disadvantages of being restricted to laboratory studies. What the DMW offers above the capabilities of eye-tracking is the interactive mechanism of occluding AOIs which are not being fixated. By increasing latency between initial fixation and removal of occlusion, researchers can ensure that a fixation/saccade is truly indicative of attentional processing, rather than a simple sweeping of eyes en route to other areas of interest. However, the limitation of deliberate attention in the DMW (as well as Mouselab) is that one cannot investigate automatic processes (e.g., as in Glöckner & Betsch, 2008). Albeit, one has to adhere to the notion that processing time as an index of intuition and effortful attention may not be required in order to process information. The idea of using eye-tracking to denote dual processes of thinking is one that is still relatively unexplored in decision research with a few exceptions (e.g., Horstmann, Ahlgrimm, & Glöckner, 2009; Rubaltelli, Dickert, & Slovic, 2012). As such, each process tracing method has a lot to offer researchers both interested in theoretical and applied questions, and the practical limitations of each should guide researchers to determine if the benefits outweigh the limitations as to which approach is best for a given research question. Table 7.1 contains a summary of the pros and cons associated with each paradigm.

Summary

We compared three process tracing methodologies to illustrate how each method can enable researchers to address their question of interest. One concern is that comparison between methodologies is less common, and the apparatus used may affect how people process and attend to information, which may lead to different strategies being used by the individual. One future approach may include training participants to use specific efficacious strategies by having a prompt whereby individuals are prompted to acquire and consider information in a specific manner. This approach obviously reduces the natural movements of the user, however, in designs where it is important to train similarly, this approach may allow users to acquire information more readily and thereby reduce variability. For example, the DMW allows the ability to highlight AOIs and the individual must deliberately look at the AOI in order to reveal information while the program prevents the

TABLE 7.1 Summary of advantages and disadvantages of three process tracing paradigms

Summary of advantages and disadvantages of three process tracing paradigms

Mouselab

Pros

- Location flexibility: data may be collected remotely and in natural environments
- Low cost: no additional hardware necessary
- Location flexibility and low cost may increase sample size

Cons

- Theoretical oversimplification: assumes mouse movement is a sufficient proxy for visual attention in all circumstances
- Cell acquisition measurement is less specific than determining actual fixation location
- Cannot account for effects of working memory or information recall during the decision process

Standard Eye-Tracking

Pros

- Richer and more accurate data: complex information processing indicated by actual eye fixations
- Stronger theoretical soundness: direct relation of visual and cognitive attention
- Ability to measure pupil dilation
- Reduces potential cognitive load of moving mouse to acquire information
- Requires less time to acquire information than mouse-tracking

Cons

- In most research, participants required to be present in laboratory to collect data
- Expensive: additional hardware required that many researchers may not be able to afford
- Data must be collected from participants one at a time
- Potential for laboratory demand characteristics to decrease data generalization (e.g., lower sample size)

Decision Moving Window

Pros

- Same as eye-tracking
- Requires even less time to acquire information than eye-tracking alone
- Interactive mechanism: occludes areas of interest which are not being fixated

Cons

- Same as eye-tracking
- Similar to mouse-tracking, cannot investigate automatic processes

other AOIs from being revealed irrespective of the individual's gaze. This approach may be more applicable in human factor designs or applied contexts where an organization requires the same training and skills from its employees to master a task. Another facet of these three methodologies is that often the researcher determines the level of analysis and makes decisions about data (e.g., how much time must pass before fixation is calculated), and there lacks standardization across methodologies as well as across researchers and paradigms which may make comparisons between methodologies more difficult, thereby muddling the ability of researchers to evaluate consistently across studies and methods (see Chapter 5). Although more complex, it would be ideal to combine different process tracing approaches such as verbal protocols and/or neuroscience (e.g., EEG), with mouse or eye movements so that research questions are addressed with multiple converging evidence that allows for better test of process tracing theories. Much like MouselabWEB and its flexible use beyond the laboratory, the future of eye-tracking research should enable individuals to make decisions in a natural environment such as use of eye-tracking glasses where individuals are not confined to a laboratory. As such, we see the future of process tracing methods as improving the ability of researchers and practitioners in addressing both theoretical and applied questions.

As we continue to make advances in technology, we are excited about the additional avenues for capturing processes as our measurements will dove-tail with finer-grain and richer data from improved technologies that will become more accessible to researchers to address their questions of interest. The future of process tracing is strong and allows for converging approaches to better understand human decision makers.

Note

1 Note that we differentiate the recording of mouse movements, i.e., the opening and closing of covered information, most often in a matrix setup (done with e.g., MouselabWeb, see Chapter 6) from the continuous recording of the mouse position in mouse-tracking (see Chapters 8–10).

Recommended Reading List

- Holmqvist et al. (2011): an excellent compendium and general resource book regarding the basic methods and measures of eye-tracking.
- Hoffman (1998): a general chapter that provides an empirically based approach to understand visual attention to eye movements.

References

Arroyo, E., Selker, T., & Wei, W. (2006). Usability tool for analysis of web designs using mouse tracks. *CHI'06 extended abstracts on human factors in computing systems* (pp. 484–489). ACM.

Ashby, N. J., Johnson, J. G., Krajbich, I., & Wedel, M. (2016). Applications and innovations of eye-movement research in judgment and decision making. *Journal of Behavioral Decision Making, 29* (2–3), 96–102.

Attar, N., Schneps, M. H., & Pomplun, M. (2016). Working memory load predicts visual search efficiency: Evidence from a novel pupillary response paradigm. *Memory & Cognition, 44*(7), 1038–1049.

Baddeley, A. D. (2003). Working memory: Looking back and looking forward. *Nature Reviews Neuroscience, 4*(10), 829–839.

Baddeley, A. D., & Hitch, G. (1974). Working memory. In G. A. Bower (Ed.), *Recent advances in learning and motivation* (Vol. 8, pp. 47–90). New York: Academic Press.

Ball, C. (1997). A comparison of single-step and multiple-step transition analyses of multiattribute decision strategies. *Organizational Behavior and Human Decision Processes, 69*(3), 195–204.

Beatty, J. (1982). Task-evoked pupillary responses, processing load, and the structure of processing resources. *Psychological Bulletin, 91*(2), 276–292.

Beatty, J., & Wagoner, B. (1978). Pupillometric signs of brain activation vary with level of cognitive processing. *Science, 199*(4334), 1216–1218.

Böckenholt, U., & Hynan, L. S. (1994). Caveats on a process-tracing measure and a remedy. *Journal of Behavioral Decision Making, 7*(2), 103–117.

Busemeyer, J. R., & Johnson, J. G. (2004). Computational models of decision making. In D. Koehler & N. Harvey (Eds.), *Blackwell handbook of judgment and decision making* (pp. 133–154). Oxford, UK: Blackwell.

Buswell, G. T. (1935). *How people look at pictures.* Chicago: University of Chicago Press.

Chen, M. C., Anderson, J. R., & Sohn, M. H. (2001). What can a mouse cursor tell us more? Correlation of eye/mouse movements on web browsing. *CHI'01 extended abstracts on human factors in computing systems* (pp. 281–282). ACM.

Cowan, N. (2012). *Working memory capacity.* Hove, UK: Psychology press.

Edwards, W. (1962). Dynamic decision theory and probabilistic information processing. *Human Factors, 4*(2), 59–73.

Fiedler, S., & Glöckner, A. (2012). The dynamics of decision making in risky choice: An eye-tracking analysis. *Frontiers in Psychology, 3*, 1–18.

Franco-Watkins, A. M., Davis, M. E., & Johnson, J. G. (2016). The ticking time bomb: Using eye-tracking methodology to capture attentional processing under multiple time pressures. *Attention, Perception, and Psychophysics, 78*(8), 2363–2372.

Franco-Watkins, A. M., & Johnson, J. G. (2011a). Decision moving window: Using eye tracking to examine decision processes. *Behavior Research Methods, 43*(3), 853–863.

Franco-Watkins, A. M., & Johnson, J. G. (2011b). Applying the decision moving window to risky choice: Comparison of eye-tracking and mouse-tracing methods. *Judgment and Decision Making, 6*(8), 740–748.

Franco-Watkins, A. M., Mattson, R. E., & Jackson, M. D. (2016). Now or later? Attentional processing and intertemporal choice. *Journal of Behavioral Decision Making, 29*(2–3), 206–217.

Gidlöf, K., Wallen, A., Dewhurst, R., & Holmqvist, K. (2013). Using eye tracking to trace a cognitive process: Gaze behaviour during decision making in a natural environment. *Journal of Eye Movement Research, 6*(1), 1–14.

Glöckner, A., & Betsch, T. (2008). Multiple reason decision making based on automatic processes. *Journal of Experimental Psychology: Learning, Memory, and Cognition, 34*(5), 1055–1075.

Glöckner, A., & Herbold, A. (2011). An eye-tracking study on information processing in risky decisions: Evidence for compensatory strategies based on automatic processes. *Journal of Behavioral Decision Making, 24*(1), 71–98.

Gray, W. D., Schoelles, M. J., & Sims, C. R. (2005). Adapting to the task environment: Explorations in expected value. *Cognitive Systems Research, 6*(1), 27–40.

Guo, Q., & Agichtein, E. (2010). Towards predicting web searcher gaze position from mouse movements. *CHI'10 extended abstracts on human factors in computing systems* (pp. 3601–3606). ACM.

Heitz, R. P., Schrock, J. C., Payne, T. W., & Engle, R. W. (2008). Effects of incentive on working memory capacity: Behavioral and pupillometric data. *Psychophysiology, 45*(1), 119–129.

Hess, E. H., & Polt, J. M. (1964). Pupil size in relation to mental activity during simple problem solving. *Science, 143*(3611), 1190–1192.

Hoffman, J. E. (1998). Visual attention and eye movements. In H. Pashler (Ed.), *Attention* (pp. 119–153). Hove, UK: Psychology Press.

Holmqvist, K., Dewhurst, R., Jarodzka, H., Nyström, M., Andersson, R., & Weijer, J. C. (2011). *Eye tracking: A comprehensive guide to methods and measures.* Oxford, UK: Oxford University Press.

Horstmann, N., Ahlgrimm, A., & Glöckner, A. (2009). How distinct are intuition and deliberation? An eye-tracking analysis of instruction-induced decision modes. *Judgment and Decision Making, 4*(5), 335–354.

Huang, J., White, R., & Buscher, G. (2012). User see, user point. Proceedings of the 2012 ACM annual conference on human factors in computing systems – CHI '12.

Huey, E. B. (1908). *The psychology and pedagogy of reading.* New York, NY: Macmillan.

Inhoff, A. W., & Radach, R. (1998). Definition and computation of oculomotor measures in the study of cognitive processes. In G. Underwood (Ed.), *Eye guidance in reading and scene perception* (pp. 29–54). Oxford, UK: Elsevier.

Jacob, R. J. K. (1991). The use of eye movements in human-computer interaction techniques: What you look at is what you get. *ACM Transactions on Information Systems, 9*(3), 152–169.

Javal, É. (1878). Essai sur la physiologie de la lecture. *Annales d'Oculistique, 80*, 61–73.

Johnson, J. G., & Busemeyer, J. R. (2005). A dynamic, stochastic, computational model of preference reversal phenomena. *Psychological Review, 112*(4), 841–861.

Just, M. A., & Carpenter, P. A. (1980). A theory of reading: From eye fixations to comprehension. *Psychological Review, 87*(4), 329–354.

Kahneman, D. (1973). *Attention and effort.* Englewood Cliffs, NJ: Prentice-Hall.

Kahneman, D., & Beatty, J. (1966). Pupil diameter and load on memory. *Science, 154*(3756), 1583–1585.

Kahneman, D., Beatty, J., & Pollack, I. (1967). Perceptual deficit during a mental task. *Science, 157*(3785), 218–219.

Krajbich, I., & Rangel, A. (2011). Multialternative drift-diffusion model predicts the relationship between visual fixations and choice in value-based decisions. *Proceedings of the National Academy of Sciences, 108*(33), 13852–13857.

Lohse, G. L., & Johnson, E. J. (1996). A comparison of two process tracing methods for choice tasks. *Organizational Behavior and Human Decision Processes, 68*(1), 28–43.

McCarley, J. S., Vais, M. J., Pringle, H., Kramer, A. F., Irwin, D. E., & Strayer, D. L. (2004). Conversation disrupts change detection in complex traffic scenes. *Human Factors, 46*(3), 424–436.

McConkie, G. W., & Rayner, K. (1975). The span of the effective stimulus during a fixation in reading. *Attention, Perception, & Psychophysics, 17*(6), 578–586.

Norman, E., & Schulte-Mecklenbeck, M. (2010). Take a quick click at that! Mouselab and eye-tracking as tools to measure intuition. In A. Glöckner & C. L. M. Witteman (Eds.), *Foundations for tracing intuition: Challenges and methods* (pp. 24–44). Hove, UK: Psychology Press.

Orquin, J. L., & Loose, S. M. (2013). Attention and choice: A review on eye movements in decision making. *Acta Psychologica, 144*(1), 190–206.

Pashler, H. E. (1998). *The psychology of attention.* Cambridge, UK: MIT Press.

Payne, J. W., Bettman, J. R., & Johnson, E. J. (1988). Adaptive strategy selection in decision making. *Journal of Experimental Psychology: Learning, Memory, and Cognition, 14*(3), 534–552.

Payne, J. W., Bettman, J. R., & Johnson, E. J. (1993). *The adaptive decision maker.* Cambridge, UK: Cambridge University Press.

Pieters, R., & Wedel, M. (2004). Attention capture and transfer in advertising: Brand, pictorial, and text-size effects. *Journal of Marketing, 68*(2), 36–50.

Pieters, R., Warlop, L., & Wedel, M. (2002). Breaking through the clutter: Benefits of advertisement originality and familiarity for brand attention and memory. *Management Science, 48*(6), 765–781.

Pillalamarri, R. S., Barnette, B. D., Birkmire, D., & Karsh, R. (1993). Cluster: A program for the identification of eye-fixation-cluster characteristics. *Behavior Research Methods, Instruments, & Computers, 25*(1), 9–15.

Rayner, K. (1978). Eye movements in reading and information processing. *Psychological Bulletin, 85*(3), 618–660.

Rayner, K. (1998). Eye movements in reading and information processing: 20 years of research. *Psychological Bulletin, 124*(3), 372–422.

Reutskaja, E., Nagel, R., Camerer, C. F., & Rangel, A. (2011). Search dynamics in consumer choice under time pressure: An eye-tracking study. *American Economic Review, 101*(2), 900–926.

Rubaltelli, E., Dickert, S., & Slovic, P. (2012). Response mode, compatability, and dual-processes in the evaluation of simple gambles: An eye-tracking investigation. *Judgment and Decision Making, 7*(4), 427–440.

Russo, J. E., & Dosher, B. A. (1983). Strategies for multiattribute binary choice. *Journal of Experimental Psychology: Learning, Memory, and Cognition, 9*(4), 676–696.

Russo, J. E., & Leclerc, F. (1994). An eye-fixation analysis of choice processes for consumer nondurables. *Journal of Consumer Research, 21*(2), 274–290.

Russo, J. E., & Rosen, L. D. (1975). An eye fixation analysis of multialternative choice. *Memory & Cognition, 3*(3), 267–276.

Savage, L. J. (1954). *The foundations of statistics.* New York, NY: Wiley.

Schulte-Mecklenbeck, M., Johnson, J. G., Böckenholt, U., Goldstein, D. G., Russo, J. E., Sullivan, N. J., & Willemsen, M. C. (2017). Process-tracing methods in decision making: On growing up in the 70ties. *Current Directions in Psychological Science, 26*(5), 442–450.

Schulte-Mecklenbeck, M., Kühberger, A., Gagl, B., & Hutzler, F. (2017). Inducing thought processes: Bringing process measures and cognitive processes closer together. *Journal of Behavioral Decision Making, 30*(5), 1001–1013.

Shimojo, S., Simion, C., Shimojo, E., & Scheier, C. (2003). Gaze bias both reflects and influences preference. *Nature Neuroscience, 6*(12), 1317.

Stewart, N., Gächter, S., Noguchi, T., & Mullett, T. L. (2016). Eye movements in strategic choice. *Journal of Behavioral Decision Making, 29*(2–3), 137–156.

Stewart, N., Hermens, F., & Matthews, W. J. (2016). Eye movements in risky choice. *Journal of Behavioral Decision Making, 29*(2–3), 116–136.

Thagaseen, A., Dharani, K., Soundharya, M. G., Venkat, I., & Radha, N. (2016). Eye-movement tracking for physically challenged people using human computer interaction. *International Journal of Innovative Research in Computer and Communication Engineering, 4*(3), 3379–3384.

Tinker, M. A. (1946). The study of eye movements in reading. *Psychological Bulletin, 43*, 93–120.

Wästlund, E., Shams, P., & Otterbring, T. (2018). Unsold is unseen… or is it? Examining the role of peripheral vision in the consumer choice process using eye-tracking methodology. *Appetite, 120*, 49–56.

Weber, E. U., Johnson, E. J., Milch, K. F., Chang, H., Brodscholl, J. C., & Goldstein, D. G. (2007). Asymmetrical discounting in intertemporal choice. *Psychological Science, 18*(6), 516–523.

Wedel, M., & Pieters, R. (2000). Eye fixations on advertisements and memory for brands: A model and findings. *Marketing Science, 19*(4), 297–312.

Wedell, D. H., & Senter, S. M. (1997). Looking and weighting in judgment and choice. *Organizational Behavior and Human Decision Processes, 70*(1), 41–64.

8

MOUSE-TRACKING

A Practical Guide to Implementation and Analysis[1]

Pascal J. Kieslich, Felix Henninger, Dirk U. Wulff, Jonas M. B. Haslbeck, and Michael Schulte-Mecklenbeck

The motivation behind process tracing is to go beyond the mere observation of a choice as the behavioral outcome and more directly observe the psychological process by collecting additional variables. A central unobserved quantity in choice tasks is the degree to which each alternative received consideration during the choice process, and how commitment to and conflict between options developed over time. Mouse-tracking is based on the assumption that motor movements in a given time interval contain a signal of the cognitive processes during that period (Spivey & Dale, 2006). Specifically, it is assumed that the direction of movement towards or away from alternatives reflects their relative attraction at a given time point during the decision process. To gain access to this information, mouse-tracking records hand movements indirectly by sampling the cursor position of a computer mouse with a high frequency while participants decide between (and move towards) options presented at different locations on the computer screen. Mouse-tracking is an increasingly popular process tracing technique that has been applied to a wide range of questions throughout many fields of psychology (see Chapters 9–10; see also Freeman, Dale, & Farmer, 2011, Freeman, 2018, Stillman, Shen, & Ferguson, 2018).

This chapter provides an introduction to the collection, analysis, and visualization of mouse-tracking data using free, open-source software. We show how to create mouse-tracking experiments using the graphical experiment builder OpenSesame (Mathôt, Schreij, & Theeuwes, 2012) in combination with the mousetrap plugin (Kieslich & Henninger, 2017). Analysis and visualization rely on the mousetrap package (Kieslich, Wulff, Henninger, Haslbeck, & Schulte-Mecklenbeck, 2019) for the statistical programming language R (R Core Team, 2016).[2]

To illustrate the method and its implementation in mousetrap, we replicate a mouse-tracking experiment by Dale, Kehoe, and Spivey (2007). In this study, participants classified exemplars (animals) into one of two categories (e.g., mammal or bird) by clicking on the corresponding buttons located at the top-left and top-right of the screen. The independent variable was the typicality of each exemplar for its category. The experiment included typical exemplars (e.g., dog for mammal) as well as atypical ones that shared features both with the correct and the competing category (e.g., a bat, sharing both features with the correct category mammal and the incorrect category bird). Dale et al. (2007) hypothesized that for atypical exemplars, both response options would receive some degree of activation, whereas for the typical exemplars, activation would largely be limited to the correct category. Consequently, for atypical exemplars, the incorrect category should exert a stronger attraction, and mouse movements should deviate more in its direction even if participants finally choose the correct option.[3]

Creating Mouse-Tracking Experiments

In this section we demonstrate how a mouse-tracking experiment can be created in OpenSesame (Mathôt et al., 2012). OpenSesame is a free, open-source software for creating experiments via a graphical user interface which additionally allows for full customization of studies using Python code.[4] To simplify the creation of mouse-tracking experiments inside this framework, we developed the mousetrap plugin (Kieslich & Henninger, 2017) for OpenSesame. Installation instructions and additional documentation for the plugin are available in its GitHub repository at https://github.com/pascalkieslich/mousetrap-os.

Creating an Experiment

The first step is to start OpenSesame and create a new experiment by clicking on File/New and selecting the default template. Experiments in OpenSesame are assembled from a set of items, for example, a *sketchpad* item for presenting graphical content on the screen, a *keyboard_response* item for collecting key presses, and a *logger* item for writing data into log files. Figure 8.1 shows the OpenSesame interface with the item toolbar on the left-hand side. To its right, the overview area represents the study's structure, in that the items therein are run sequentially from top to bottom. An experiment is built by dragging and dropping items from the toolbar into the overview area. *Sequences* can be used to run a number of items in succession. In addition, *loop* items can be used to repeatedly run sequences with some degree of variation, for example trials with varying stimuli (Figure 8.1, right panel).

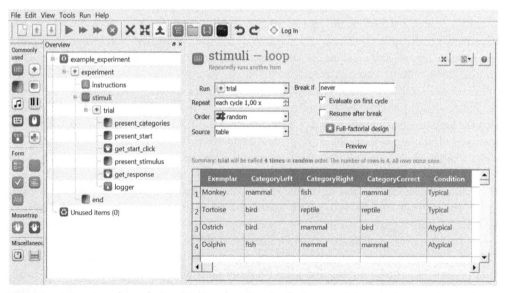

FIGURE 8.1 User interface of OpenSesame, showing the final state of the tutorial experiment. In the leftmost panel, the item toolbar contains the available items, including the mousetrap plugin items visible towards the bottom. The overview area represents the study's structure. The right panel shows the user interface of the stimulus loop containing four exemplary stimuli.

Setting Up the Screen

Mouse-tracking experiments are typically run in fullscreen mode. Therefore, before adding content to a new experiment, the screen resolution should be adjusted to match that of the computers used for data collection. This is done in the overall experiment settings, which are accessible by clicking on the topmost item in the study overview area ("example_experiment" in Figure 8.1).

Creating the Study Structure

The first item in the experiment provides the instructions. For this, we use a *form_text_display* item that presents text and a button to continue the study. It can be added to the study by dragging it from the item toolbar into the overview area (cf., Figure 8.1).

In the central part of our study, participants will make categorization decisions for different animal exemplars and pairs of response categories. To accommodate this recurring structure, we include a loop item that varies the information presented on each iteration. In the loop options, the stimulus material is represented as a table where rows reflect the different stimuli and columns contain the variables that differ for each stimulus (Figure 8.1, right panel). In our case, the vital pieces of information are the name of the exemplar and the response categories, which are contained in in the columns *Exemplar*, *CategoryLeft*, and *CategoryRight*. The additional columns specify the correct response and typicality of each combination; though not presented to participants, they are stored in the data set and facilitate later analysis. Using the default settings shown in Figure 8.1, the order of stimuli is randomized, and each stimulus is presented once.

Nested inside the loop, a *sequence* item is used to build each trial. It combines several screen pages as well as the collection of responses and logging of the stimulus and response information.

Building a Mouse-Tracking Screen

The central part of a mouse-tracking experiment is the stimulus display that presents the name of the exemplar and the two response buttons (located in the upper screen corners). We create this display by placing a *sketchpad* item into the trial sequence. In our example, it is named "present_stimulus" (Figure 8.2).[5] The content of the sketchpad item is added using a visual editor. The available types of elements for creating content are shown in the toolbar to the left of the preview. After selecting an element type, the contents can be drawn inside the preview (to move or edit them afterwards they can be selected using the topmost option in the toolbar). In our example, rectangles (*rect elements*) of equal size represent the response buttons, placed in the top-left and right screen corners. Button labels are added in the center of each button using *textline elements*. An additional *textline element* is used to present the name of the to-be-categorized exemplar in the lower part of the screen. By default, the inserted text is presented verbatim. However, one can easily vary content across trials by replacing static text with the appropriate variable names in square brackets (i.e., "[CategoryLeft]" and "[CategoryRight]" for the button labels and "[Exemplar]" for the exemplar name). In every iteration of the loop, OpenSesame will replace the variable name with the variable's current value. To make sure that the button borders are identifiable in the subsequent *mousetrap_response* item (cf., next section), we must furthermore label the two *rect elements* using the *Name* field (cf., Figure 8.2 top row). Each button border is labeled using the corresponding variable name ("[CategoryLeft]" and "[CategoryRight]").

FIGURE 8.2 Sketchpad item used to create the main stimulus display. The exemplar is displayed using a textline element that contains the name of the corresponding variable from the stimulus loop (cf. Figure 8.1). The two button borders are created using rect elements. Each button border is labeled using the Name field (see top row) and the corresponding values from the stimuli loop. The button labels are displayed using textline elements that are placed in the center of each button.

Tracking Mouse Movements

After creating the stimulus presentation, we specify the collection of mouse-tracking data and button clicks using the *mousetrap_response* item, which is inserted directly after the sketchpad item and called "get_response".[6] To start recording cursor positions immediately following stimulus presentation, the duration of the sketchpad is set to 0.

The *mousetrap_response* item records the cursor position at a constant sampling rate (10 msec by default) until the participant clicks on one of the buttons. To register responses, the corresponding buttons need to be defined (Figure 8.3, upper part): first, the number of buttons is specified. Then, the name of the sketchpad that presents the buttons is entered ("present_stimulus"). Finally, the buttons are specified via the labels of the button borders used on the sketchpad ("[CategoryLeft]" and "[CategoryRight]"). As a result, if the participant selects the left button, the value of the variable *CategoryLeft* is recorded as their response.

The *mousetrap_response* item also provides additional options (cf., lower part of Figure 8.3). For example, if the name of the correct button is specified, OpenSesame will automatically create a variable *correct* that is set to 1 or 0 for correct and incorrect answers, respectively (this is useful for

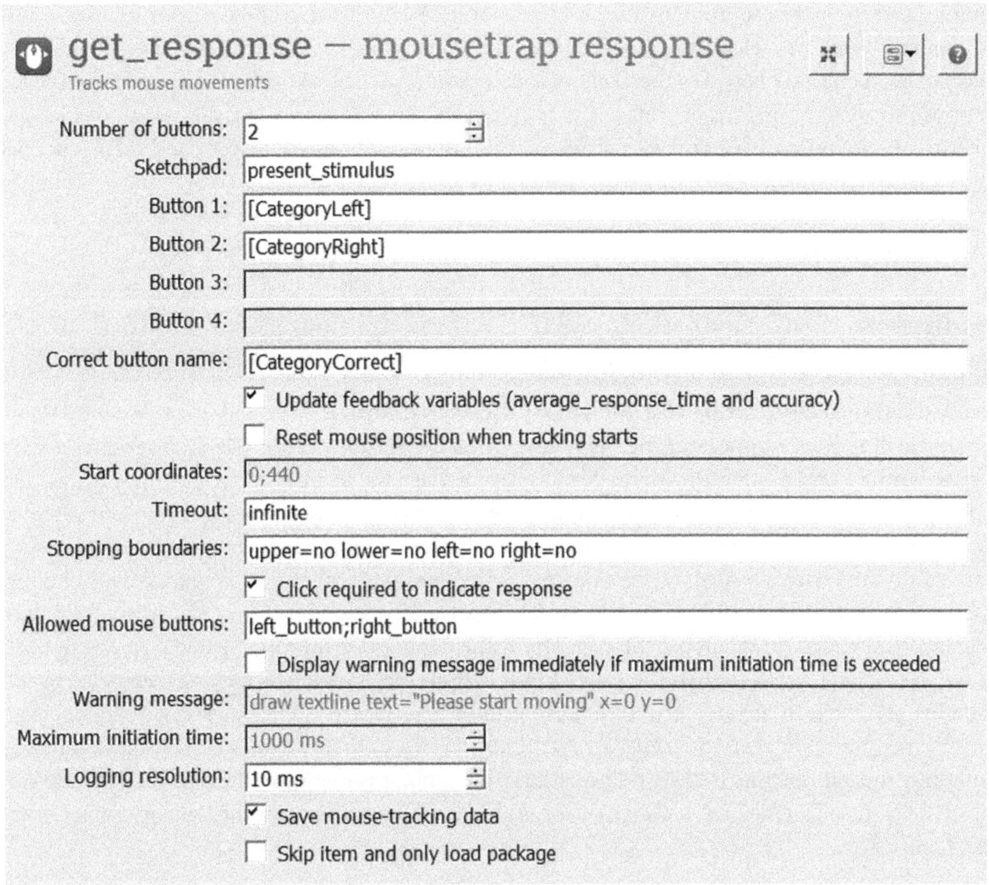

get_response — mousetrap response

Tracks mouse movements

Number of buttons:	2
Sketchpad:	present_stimulus
Button 1:	[CategoryLeft]
Button 2:	[CategoryRight]
Button 3:	
Button 4:	
Correct button name:	[CategoryCorrect]

☑ Update feedback variables (average_response_time and accuracy)

☐ Reset mouse position when tracking starts

Start coordinates:	0;440
Timeout:	infinite
Stopping boundaries:	upper=no lower=no left=no right=no

☑ Click required to indicate response

Allowed mouse buttons:	left_button;right_button

☐ Display warning message immediately if maximum initiation time is exceeded

Warning message:	draw textline text="Please start moving" x=0 y=0
Maximum initiation time:	1000 ms
Logging resolution:	10 ms

☑ Save mouse-tracking data

☐ Skip item and only load package

FIGURE 8.3   Settings of the mousetrap_response item.

analysis, as well as for providing feedback during the study). Additional design options are discussed in the section *Design Considerations*.

Storing Data

As the final part of the trial sequence, a logger item writes the data from the current trial into a log file. This includes variables pertaining to the study as a whole (e.g., the *subject_nr*), the current values of all variables in the stimuli loop (cf., Figure 8.1), and the response variables. OpenSesame stores participants' responses in two places—global variables (*response, response_time* etc.) that always store the last recorded response and response time in the experiment, and item-specific variables named after the item that collected the response (e.g., *response_get_response* in the current example). The recorded mouse positions and associated timestamps are stored in item-specific variables only, in order to save memory (*xpos_get_response, ypos_get_response*, and *timestamps_get_response*).

Design Considerations

When setting up mouse-tracking experiments, researchers are faced with a number of design choices. These include decisions about the starting procedure, the cursor speed and acceleration settings, and the response mode (click or mouse-over). Each of these choices aims to ensure that all cognitive processes relevant to the decision take place while the tracking is active (which is, in many cases, the period between the click on a start button and the selection of one of the response options), so that the process of interest is captured in the trajectories. In the remainder of this section, we discuss available options for a number of important design choices, and their potential impact on the recorded mouse trajectories (see also Fischer & Hartmann, 2014; Hehman, Stolier, & Freeman, 2015; Kieslich, Schoemann, Grage, Hepp, & Scherbaum, in press; Scherbaum & Kieslich, 2018; for additional discussions about design choices).

Start Button

Virtually all mouse-tracking experiments try to enforce a comparable start position of the cursor across trials, thereby ensuring that the cursor is centered horizontally and approximately equidistant to all response options at the beginning of each trial. To achieve this, another screen with a start button can be added prior to the display of the task stimulus. The button ensures that participants have to return to a common area before subsequently initiating mouse movements for a new choice. In the current experiment, this is implemented using a *sketchpad* called "present_start" combined with a *mousetrap_response* item called "get_start_click" (cf., Figure 8.1). As before, the screen content is assembled in the visual editor and a start button is placed in the lower center of the screen (and labeled "Start"). The name of the start button is entered in the options of the *mousetrap_response* item as the single possible response. As mouse-tracking data prior to the stimulus presentation are not of interest, the option *Save mouse-tracking data* can be unchecked for the "get_start_click" item. While the start button ensures that the cursor position at tracking onset is comparable across trials, it does not guarantee that it is identical. If this is desired, one can select *Reset mouse position when tracking starts* and specify coordinates in the "get_response" item (cf., Figure 8.3).

Information Presentation

Another key challenge in designing mouse-tracking studies is the temporal order in which task-relevant information is presented to the participant. On the one hand, the amount of information presented after the onset of tracking should be minimized to ensure that the collected mouse-tracking data reflects the decision processes. On the other hand, the decision-critical information needs to be withheld until tracking begins, to prevent participants from making their decision beforehand. In the current example, these considerations are accommodated by presenting the information about the two response categories for 2000 msec prior to tracking onset, but presenting the to-be-categorized exemplar only after the click on the start button (following the original procedure of Dale et al., 2007). We implemented this procedure by including another *sketchpad* item called "present_categories" at the beginning of the trial that presents only the two response categories, before the start button is made available to participants (cf., Figure 8.1).

Counterbalancing

Another design factor concerns the assignment of response options to the button positions on the screen. Specifically, in the current study we would like to ensure that the correct answer is not always presented on the same side. One solution for this is counterbalancing the position of the correct answer between stimuli, while keeping their position fixed for all participants (cf., Figure 8.1). Ideally, however, the position of both response options is drawn anew for each participant and stimulus (this can be achieved in OpenSesame through the advanced randomization operation shuffle horizontal).

Starting Procedure

For mouse-tracking to reflect the cognitive processes underlying the choice, movement must occur while the cognitive process is ongoing. It has been shown that the starting procedure has a considerable influence on the obtained trajectories (Scherbaum & Kieslich, 2018).

Many mouse-tracking studies have used a so-called *static starting procedure*, in which the stimulus is shown immediately after participants have clicked on the start button and without any specific measures taken to ensure movement during processing (our tutorial experiment following Dale et al., 2007, is an example for such a setup). While many mouse-tracking studies that use a static starting procedure find theoretically relevant effects in mouse trajectories, this procedure does not exclude the possibility that (in some trials) decision-relevant processes take place before the mouse movement is initiated and therefore are not captured by mouse trajectories.

To ensure that the cognitive processes under investigation do not take place before mouse movement initialization, some studies have modified the starting procedure. One option is the *static starting procedure with delay*, in which a brief lag of, for example, 500 msec, is inserted between clicking the start button and stimulus presentation. Previous studies reported that this often successfully led participants to initialize movement before the stimulus appeared (e.g., Spivey, Grosjean, & Knoblich, 2005). Other studies employ a static starting procedure with immediate stimulus presentation, but explicitly instruct participants to initiate their mouse movement within a certain time limit and display a warning to participants after the trial if the *initiation time* exceeds the threshold. The exact time limit depends on the task (a typical value is 400 msec; see Hehman et al., 2015, pp. 388–389, for a discussion).

A more rigorous option, however, is to implement a *dynamic starting* procedure that presents the stimulus only after the participant has moved the mouse upwards for a minimum distance (e.g., Scherbaum, Dshemuchadse, Fischer, & Goschke, 2010). The dynamic procedure forces participants to initiate their movement in order to receive the critical information needed to make the choice. It can be implemented by placing an invisible horizontal boundary slightly above the start button that triggers the presentation of the stimulus once it is crossed (cf., Frisch, Dshemuchadse, Görner, Goschke, & Scherbaum, 2015). This procedure has been shown to lead to more consistent movements and larger effects in within-trial temporal analyses (Scherbaum & Kieslich, 2018).[7]

Mouse Sensitivity

Another design choice is the computer's mouse sensitivity, in particular the cursor speed and acceleration. One option is to leave these settings to the operating system defaults (under Windows 7 and 10, medium speed with acceleration). However, it is often preferable to reduce mouse speed and switch off mouse acceleration (Fischer & Hartmann, 2014). This is particularly relevant when using a dynamic starting procedure to ensure that participants can read the dynamically presented stimulus information while continuously moving upwards. The mouse sensitivity settings cannot be adjusted directly within OpenSesame, but need to be set in the computer's system preferences.

Response Mode

The two main response modes in mouse-tracking studies are clicking on and moving over the response buttons. In the mousetrap plugin, users can switch between the two response modes by

118 Kieslich et al.

checking or unchecking the option *Click required to indicate response*, which is enabled by default (cf., Figure 8.3).

Data Collection and Testing

After creating the experiment, it can be run from within OpenSesame for testing or using *OpenSesame Run* for data collection in the laboratory (see Kieslich & Henninger, 2017, for more information on running mouse-tracking experiments). Mouse-tracking studies also usually assess the handedness of participants and the hand participants use for moving the mouse (with some authors recommending only to include right-handed participants, cf., Hehman et al., 2015).

Analyzing Mouse-Tracking Data

We will now demonstrate the typical steps of a basic mouse-tracking analysis using the data from the replication experiment described earlier (Kieslich & Henninger, 2017). For this analysis, we will use the *mousetrap* package (Kieslich et al., 2019) in the statistical programming language R (R Core Team, 2016), which facilitates preprocessing, analysis, and visualization of mouse-tracking data.[8] Once installed, mousetrap functions can then be made available within an R session by loading the package via `library(mousetrap)`. A detailed overview of its functionality is provided online at http://pascalkieslich.github.io/mousetrap/ or within R using the command `package?mousetrap`. In the following, we discuss the most important analysis steps, starting with data import and preprocessing operations, followed by the computation and analysis of common indices, temporal analyses, and visualizations.

Import

First, the raw data need to be read into R's workspace. OpenSesame stores the data for each participant in a separate csv file. To load all csv files from a directory and combine them into a single data set, we use the *read_opensesame* function from the *readbulk* package (Kieslich & Henninger, 2016). The following command assumes that all data files can be found in the folder "raw_data" in the working directory and stores the imported data in the data set "KH2017_raw" (this data set is available once the mousetrap package has been loaded, so no raw data have to be imported to follow this tutorial):

```
library(readbulk)
KH2017_raw <- read_opensesame('raw_data')
```

Next, the data need to be transformed into a *mousetrap data object* to perform analyses using the mousetrap R package.[9] This results in a mousetrap data object (called "mt_data" in the current analysis), which is described in detail in Box 8.1:

```
mt_data <- mt_import_mousetrap(KH2017_raw)
```

Using this two-step procedure of reading and importing the mouse-tracking data, the mousetrap R package can also be used for data collected in other software. An example for reading and importing raw data collected with MouseTracker (Freeman & Ambady, 2010) is given in the documentation of the *read_mt* function, which can be accessed by entering `?read_mt`.

Preprocessing

Spatial Transformations

In a typical two-alternative choice design (as implemented in the example experiment, see Figure 8.2), trajectories end either at the left or the right response option. As the overall spatial direction is irrelevant for most analyses (as opposed to the substantive meaning of the response button, which varies across trials if the position of alternatives is counterbalanced), all trajectories are remapped so that they end on the same side. By default, mousetrap maps the trajectories to the left, implying that trajectories that end on the right-hand side are flipped from right to left:

```
mt_data <- mt_remap_symmetric(mt_data)
```

Similarly, differences in the trajectories' starting points are often not of substantive interest. If the cursor's starting position was not reset to exact coordinates during the experiment (as is the case for the example data set), it can be aligned by shifting the trajectories in preprocessing:

```
mt_data <- mt_align_start(mt_data, start=c(0,0))
```

BOX 8.1 WORKING WITH MOUSETRAP DATA OBJECTS

The mousetrap R package represents mouse-tracking data in a specialized data structure, a mousetrap data object. This allows the package to store and process mouse trajectories efficiently, and to link them to other information collected during the study. All mousetrap analysis functions use mousetrap data objects as input; therefore, the collected data must be imported before processing and analysis. A newly imported mousetrap data object consists of a `data.frame` called `data` containing the trial information (without mouse trajectories) and an `array` called `trajectories` containing the recorded mouse-tracking data.

The mousetrap data object can hold multiple sets of trajectories (e.g., `mt_time_normalize` adds the time-normalized trajectories as `tn_trajectories`). In subsequent analyses, the user can specify via the `use` argument whether an analysis (or visualization) should be performed based on the raw trajectories (`use='trajectories'`, which is used by default in most functions) or another trajectory array (e.g., `use='tn_trajectories'`). Other functions add new `data.frames` to the mousetrap object (e.g., `mt_measures` adds a `data.frame` called `measures` that contains trial-level indices).

The mousetrap package is designed for processing and visualizing trajectories and the computation of indices. For statistical analyses of the computed indices, they can be merged with the other trial data via `results <- merge(mt_data$data, mt_data$measures, by='mt_id')`. Similarly, mouse trajectories can be transformed into a format required for the statistical analysis using the `mt_export_long` or `mt_export_wide` functions. The resulting data can then be analyzed outside of the mousetrap package using any standard analysis method.

Resampling

The cursor position is typically recorded at a constant sampling rate. The mousetrap plugin in OpenSesame records the mouse position every 10 msec by default (corresponding to a sampling rate of 100 Hz). Due to variation in trial durations, the number of recorded cursor positions may vary considerably across trials. To be able to aggregate trajectories or compare them statistically, one

120 Kieslich et al.

often requires an equal number of coordinates for all trajectories. To achieve this, studies commonly apply time-normalization.

Time-normalization interpolates trajectories so that each is represented by the same number of positions (101 by default, following Spivey et al., 2005) separated by a (within-trial) constant time interval. Mousetrap stores the time-normalized data as a new set of trajectories within the mousetrap data object (see Box 8.1):

```
mt_data <- mt_time_normalize(mt_data)
```

Another possibility is to interpolate trajectories so that each is represented by the same number of spatially equidistant positions (using *mt_spatialize*). This processing step facilitates the comparison of trajectory shapes and is instrumental in type-based analyses of trajectories (see Chapter 9).

Data Inspection and Filtering

As a final step prior to analysis, trials are typically screened and filtered based on one or more criteria. If choices can be graded as correct, studies often exclude trials with incorrect responses to ensure a consistent interpretation of curvature across all trials (i.e., that increased curvature always reflects attraction towards the distractor category). The *mt_subset* function can be used to select only correctly answered trials for further analysis (or to apply other filters):

```
mt_data <- mt_subset(mt_data, correct==1)
```

An additional concern in mouse-tracking analysis is whether the data contain movements that are presumably not related to the preference development but to other processes, such as information acquisition or slips of the hand. Information acquisition might, for example, be reflected by directed movements towards a point where information was presented on the screen. Slips of the hand, resulting for example from participants placing the mouse device somewhere else in order to avoid a physical obstacle (or in order to more comfortably move it), would lead to erratic movements and result in movements untypical for this context, for example comparatively large amounts of up and down movements. The challenge is finding precise criteria to differentiate between relevant and irrelevant movements. One possibility is an exploratory approach, for example visually inspecting all trials by plotting them either in a single figure (using *mt_plot* or *mt_heatmap*, see also top panel of Figure 8.5 in the section *Trajectory Types*) or separately (using *mt_plot_per_trajectory*). If to-be-excluded movement patterns have been specified, separate plots per trajectory might also be provided to human raters who can code whether these are present in a trial. Another possibility is to exclude trials based on a numeric criterion, such as trials exceeding an absolute or relative reaction time or trials containing several flips along the y-axis (which probably indicate large amounts of task-irrelevant tracking data). A more detailed discussion is provided in Kieslich et al. (2019). Especially if exclusion criteria were not defined *a priori*, the impact of the criterion applied should be reported; additional pre-registered studies might be conducted to validate the chosen criteria and to replicate the results under strictly confirmatory conditions.

Analysis

To analyze effects of the experimental manipulation, a common first step is the visual inspection of aggregate time-normalized mouse trajectories. Mousetrap provides the *mt_plot_aggregate* function, which, if used as follows, aggregates the time-normalized trajectories for each condition first within and then across participants and plots the result:

```
mt_plot_aggregate(mt_data,
  use='tn_trajectories',
  x='xpos',
  y='ypos',
  color='Condition',
  subject_id='subject_nr')
```

As can be seen in Figure 8.4, the aggregate mouse trajectory in the current study is more curved towards the non-chosen option for atypical than for typical exemplars—consistent with the hypothesis by Dale et al. (2007). Whether the aggregate trajectories are an adequate summary of the trial-level trajectories is discussed in the section *Trajectory Types*.

A wide range of analysis methods are available for mouse-tracking data (for overviews, see Hehman et al., 2015; Kieslich et al., 2019). They can roughly be categorized into analyses that focus on the temporal development of a certain characteristic over the course of a trial (such as x-position, velocity, or movement direction, see section *Temporal Analyses*) and those that summarize a particular characteristic of each trajectory by computing one index value per trial.

Many common indices can be computed using the *mt_measures* function:

```
mt_data <- mt_measures(mt_data)
```

An overview of the different indices is given in Table 8.1 and further information about working with the computed indices is provided in Box 8.1. Different types of indices and their interpretation will be discussed in the following.

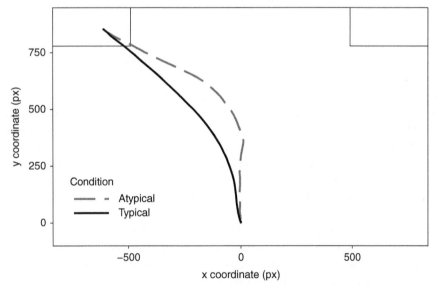

FIGURE 8.4 Aggregate time-normalized trajectories per typicality condition. Trajectories were first aligned to a common start position, remapped to the left, and finally aggregated first within and then across participants. Boxes representing the response buttons were added for clarity.

122 Kieslich et al.

TABLE 8.1 Selected mouse-tracking measures, their variable name (in brackets, as used by the *mt_measures* function of the mousetrap R package), and definition

Type	Measure	Definition
Curvature	Maximum absolute deviation (MAD)	Signed maximum absolute deviation of observed trajectory from direct path
	Maximum deviation above (MD_above)	Maximum deviation above direct path
	Average deviation (AD)	Average deviation of observed trajectory from direct path
	Area under curve (AUC)	Geometric area between observed trajectory and direct path
Complexity	x-flips (xpos_flips)	Number of directional changes along x-axis
	x-reversals (xpos_reversals)	Number of crossings of y-axis
	Sample entropy (sample_entropy)	Degree of unpredictability of movement along x-axis
Time	Response time (RT)	Time until response is given
	Initiation time (initiation_time)	Time until first movement is initiated
	Idle time (idle_time)	Total time without movement across trial
Derivatives	Total distance (total_dist)	Euclidean distance traveled by trajectory
	Max velocity (vel_max)	Maximum movement velocity
	Max acceleration (acc_max)	Maximum movement acceleration

Note: The direct path refers to the straight line connecting the start and end point of the observed trajectory. Deviations/ areas above the direct path receive a positive sign and deviations/areas below receive a negative sign. For all derivative measures, it is assumed that movements across both x and y dimensions are taken into account (derivatives have to be calculated using *mt_calculate_derivatives* before calling *mt_measures*). Sample entropy is computed using *mt_sample_entropy* (based on the time-normalized x-positions by default).

Curvature

The curvature of the response trajectory is used to assess the degree of its attraction towards the non-chosen option. It is assumed to be driven by the difference in activation between the non-chosen and the chosen option—in that a smaller difference in activations leads to a stronger curvature (Spivey, Dale, Knoblich, & Grosjean, 2010). A number of different indices have been suggested to quantify curvature (cf. Table 8.1). Their exact computation differs, but they are often highly correlated in practice (see Kieslich et al., 2019; Stillman et al., 2018).

In the following, we focus on a frequently used index known as the *(signed) maximum absolute deviation* (MAD). To compute the MAD, imagine an idealized, direct line between the start and end point of the trajectory, and that lines perpendicular to this idealized line are drawn to connect it with every point on the original trajectory. The value of the MAD is defined as the length of the longest of these lines. The sign of the MAD is positive if the deviation is largest above the direct path (in the direction of the non-chosen alternative) and negative if the point of strongest deviation occurs below.

To assess whether the MAD differs between experimental conditions, mouse-tracking studies often aggregate the MAD values across trials per participant and condition, and then compare the aggregate MAD values between conditions using a paired *t*-test.[10] These operations can be performed using *mt_aggregate_per_subject* and R's standard *t.test* function:

```
agg_mad <- mt_aggregate_per_subject(mt_data,
  use_variables='MAD',
```

```
use2_variables='Condition',
subject_id='subject_nr')

t.test(MAD~Condition,
  data=agg_mad,
  paired=TRUE)
```

In line with the hypothesis by Dale et al. (2007), the MAD values indicate larger curvature in the atypical (M = 343.8 px, SD = 218.6 px) than in the typical condition (M = 172.2 px, SD = 110.8 px), $t(59)$ = 6.73, p < .001. A replication of the original analyses by Dale et al. using the current data set can be found online at https://github.com/pascalkieslich/mousetrap-resources.

Trajectory Types

While aggregate response trajectories (cf., Figure 8.4) and curvature indices provide a first indication of the average curvature of the trajectories in each condition, they do not necessarily represent the shape of the individual trajectories well. Specifically, an aggregate curved trajectory might result from different types of trajectories, for example, a mixture of straight lines and triangular "change of mind" trajectories which first head directly to the non-chosen and then to the chosen option (cf., Chapter 9). If this is the case, the average trajectory might not be representative of the movement patterns observed in the study, but purely an artefact of aggregation. Under these circumstances, the shape of the aggregate trajectory would provide only limited (and potentially misleading) information about the underlying cognitive processes.

Several methods have been suggested to assess the degree of heterogeneity of the individual trajectories on the trial level. Previous approaches have focused on the distribution of trial-level curvature indices (such as area under curve or MAD, cf., Table 8.1) and tested them for indications of bimodality. The assumption behind these approaches is that gradually curved trajectories on the trial level should result in a unimodal distribution, while a combination of straight and extremely curved trajectories should result in a bimodal distribution (Hehman et al., 2015). The bimodality of the distribution is frequently assessed by computing the bimodality coefficient (BC; Pfister, Schwarz, Janczyk, Dale, & Freeman, 2013) which is interpreted as bimodal for values > .555 (Freeman & Ambady, 2010). Alternative methods for identifying bimodality have been discussed, especially the Hartigan's dip statistic (Freeman & Dale, 2013). Both methods are implemented in the *mt_check_bimodality* function.

Instead of attempting to detect mixtures of distinct trajectory types based on the distribution of curvature indices (which condense each trajectory to a single numeric value), more recent analysis methods take into account the complete shape of each trajectory by using every point of the trajectory. The shape of individual trajectories can be assessed visually by plotting raw or smoothed heatmaps with the *mt_heatmap* function and by comparing heatmaps between conditions using the *mt_diffmap* function (code examples are provided at https://github.com/pascalkieslich/mousetrap-resources).

As can be seen in Figure 8.5 (middle panel), there appear to be different types of trajectories on the trial level in the current study, with a large proportion of straight and mildly curved trajectories and a small proportion of extremely curved, "change of mind" trajectories. More importantly, a difference heatmap reveals that the relative occurrence of these types differs between conditions, with a higher proportion of extremely curved trajectories in the atypical condition (Figure 8.5, bottom panel). Analyses that go beyond a visual inspection to identify trajectory types and instead

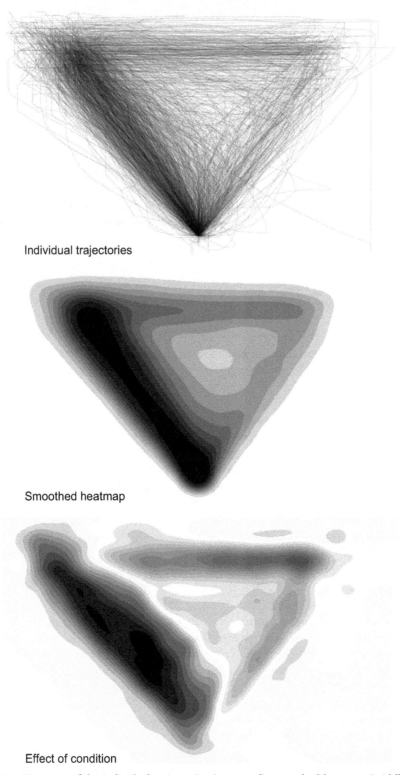

FIGURE 8.5 Heatmap of the individual trajectories (top panel), smoothed heatmap (middle panel), and difference of smoothed heatmaps between conditions (bottom panel), where darker areas indicate higher density in the typical and lighter areas higher density in the atypical condition (white indicates comparable density).

use a clustering approach based on spatial similarity (or the assignment of trajectories to different prototypes) are also implemented in the mousetrap R package and described in Chapter 9 (see also Wulff, Haslbeck, & Schulte-Mecklenbeck, 2019).

The different trajectory types and their frequency have also been used to distinguish between different theoretical models (see Chapters 9–10 for more information). When used to this end, it is important to keep in mind that the setup of mouse-tracking studies can influence the shape of individual trajectories (see section *Design Considerations*). In the current study, the occurrence of rather "extreme" trajectory types (straight and "change of mind") may have been caused by the relatively simplistic setup of the study with a static starting procedure, default mouse sensitivity settings, and the use of a click instead of a mouse-over response.

Complexity

In addition to curvature, mouse-tracking studies have also used the complexity of the movement as an indicator of response competition. If multiple response options simultaneously attract the cursor, this should result in more complex, less smooth trajectories compared to cases where only one option exerts an influence (Dale et al., 2007).

In two-alternative tasks, complexity is typically assessed with regard to movements along the horizontal axis, since this is the dimension that separates the options. The most common measure of complexity is x-flips, the number of directional changes along the x-axis (Freeman & Ambady, 2010), which is calculated by the *mt_measures* function (Table 8.1). As response competition might not always lead to directional changes, other mouse-tracking studies have used sample entropy (Dale et al., 2007; McKinstry, Dale, & Spivey, 2008) which quantifies the degree of unpredictability of movement along the x-axis. Sample entropy can be computed using *mt_sample_entropy*, which uses time-normalized trajectories by default, following the recommendation that each trajectory be represented by the same number of positions (Hehman et al., 2015):

```
mt_data <- mt_sample_entropy(mt_data, use='tn_trajectories')
```

Koop and Johnson (2013) propose a substantive interpretation of complexity-related measures in preferential choice tasks, based on the assumption that the x-position at a specific point during the trial is a proxy for the current absolute preference. They suggest that x-flips reflect changes in the momentary valence whereas x-reversals (i.e., the number of times the cursor crosses the vertical axis at the midpoint between the two options) indicate changes of absolute preference. Recently, the sequence in which certain areas of interest (one for each choice option) are visited with the mouse cursor has also been used to identify how often participants changed their mind during the decision-making process (Szaszi, Palfi, Szollosi, Kieslich, & Aczel, 2018; see also Travers, Rolison, & Feeney, 2016).

As with curvature indices, complexity indices can be analyzed either by aggregating values per participant and condition (using *mt_aggregate_per_subject*) and comparing the result across conditions, or on the trial level using mixed-effects models.

Temporal Analyses

Although many studies use it in this sense, mouse-tracking is not limited to the analysis of aggregate indices that collapse each trajectory to a single value. Analyses of trajectories' temporal development can shed light on the time course of response option activations across the trial and, in particular, how and when different cognitive processes influence the trajectory (Hehman et al., 2015). In the following, we will briefly illustrate some simple use cases.

One purpose of temporal analyses is to supplement aggregate analyses of trajectory curvature by showing at which point and for how long aggregate trajectories diverge between conditions. Previous studies (e.g., Dale et al., 2007) have examined this by comparing the horizontal positions of the time-normalized trajectories at each time step using a series of t-tests between conditions (code examples can be found at https://github.com/pascalkieslich/mousetrap-resources). Using this approach reveals that for time steps from 54 to 95 (of 101 steps) the aver-age x coordinates differed between conditions (Figure 8.6). If a theory provides specific predictions with regard to the temporal development, for example, whether the divergence between conditions should occur early or late in the decision-making process, this can be used to test them. Note that the comparison of trajectories between conditions can be problematic if response time differences between conditions are large, and that temporal analyses can also be conducted based on raw instead of time-normalized trajectories (see also Hehman et al., 2015).

As with aggregated trial-level indices, aggregated x-positions may not necessarily represent the underlying trial-level trajectories well. To inspect whether this is the case it is useful to illustrate the full distribution of trial-level x-positions across normalized time using the *mt_plot_riverbed* function (following an approach by Scherbaum et al., 2010). As can be seen in Figure 8.7, the aggregate x-positions displayed in Figure 8.6 are a rather poor representation of the individual trajectories, which vary greatly. Specifically, while the majority of trajectories go directly to the eventually chosen option, a substantial number of trajectories first moves to the non-chosen option (crossing the midline). This means that the data may be better analyzed on the trial level using, for instance, mixed-effects models or type-based analyses (Wulff et al., 2019; see also Chapter 9). Moreover, Figure 8.7 reveals that in most trials of both conditions the cursor remained in a neutral position

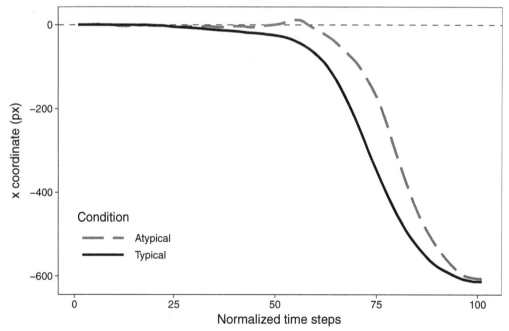

FIGURE 8.6 Plot of the average time-normalized x-position over time. For each time step, x-positions were first averaged within participants and condition.

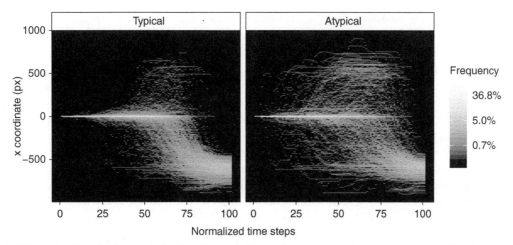

FIGURE 8.7 Riverbed plot of the distribution of x-positions across time for time-normalized trajectories separately for the two experimental conditions. For each time step, the shading indicates the relative frequency with which each bin of x-positions was observed.

(in many cases it stayed on the start button) for more than half of the trial, a behavior that is probably related to the use of a static starting condition that did not enforce early movement initiation (cf., Scherbaum & Kieslich, 2018).

In addition to analyzing the temporal development of the cursor position, previous mouse-tracking studies have also focused on other variables derived from it, especially velocity, acceleration, and movement angle. The analysis of velocity and acceleration has been used to investigate response activation and competition (Hehman et al., 2015). In mousetrap, velocity and acceleration can be computed using *mt_calculate_derivatives* which attaches velocity and acceleration values to each of the recorded cursor positions.[11] Subsequent analyses can be performed, as sketched earlier, using the velocity values instead of x-positions as the dimension of interest.

Finally, an emerging class of analyses has focused on the movement angle, which quantifies the direction of movement over time indicating, for example, whether participants move towards or away from a specific response alternative. Previous studies have used movement angles to disentangle when and to which extent different factors influence the movement direction (e.g., Dshemuchadse, Scherbaum, & Goschke, 2013; Scherbaum et al., 2010; Sullivan, Hutcherson, Harris, & Rangel, 2015). For details on these approaches, see Scherbaum and Dshemuchadse (2018).

Summary and Conclusion

In mouse-tracking studies, participants' cursor movements are recorded as they choose between different options represented as buttons on a computer screen. Thereby, mouse-tracking aims to measure the degree of conflict between the alternatives and the temporal development of its resolution. While Chapter 9 provides a detailed look at the types of trajectories revealed in this paradigm, and Chapter 10 provides an introduction to this method and its use in the literature, this chapter has shown how to construct a mouse-tracking study using the mousetrap plugin for the graphical experiment builder OpenSesame, and how to analyze the resulting data in the mousetrap R package. We have covered technical issues surrounding the application of this method, and highlighted design considerations and their influence on the collected data.

The strength of mouse-tracking lies in the ease with which it can be applied. Using only standard laboratory hardware, cognitive processes can be tracked at high temporal resolution. It is also a flexible tool that can be adapted to many different tasks, and which is even more powerful in combination with other process tracing methods (e.g., eye-tracking, cf., Koop & Johnson, 2013; Quétard et al., 2016). Data collection and processing as described in this chapter are handled entirely by free, open-source software (Kieslich & Henninger, 2017; Kieslich et al., 2019), making mouse-tracking easily accessible to interested researchers and transparent to those looking to replicate findings or adapt and extend the methods described herein.

As a fairly recent addition to the family of process tracing methods, many aspects of the method are not yet fully standardized. Therefore, the degrees of freedom with regard to data collection, processing, and analysis are substantial. Where available, we have pointed to the current state of knowledge regarding best practices, which is bound to grow over time. We advise users of mouse-tracking to seek convergence between analyses and indices where no standard has been established so far. In doing so, they should also consider the effects of aggregation by inspecting the distribution of trajectories and indices on the trial level (cf., Chapter 9). While researchers may often explore different experimental setups and analyses if they apply mouse-tracking in a new domain, (additional) pre-registered studies should be conducted to perform strictly confirmatory hypothesis testing (Wagenmakers, Wetzels, Borsboom, van der Maas, & Kievit, 2012).

In sum, we have demonstrated the potential mouse-tracking has as a process tracing method for various areas of decision research. Given the limits of an introductory tutorial, we have only covered the most frequently used analyses. Similarly, the current chapter has limited itself to the frequently investigated two-option design, but mouse-tracking can easily be extended to situations with more than two alternatives (e.g., Koop & Johnson, 2011). Lastly, more sophisticated analysis methods are being developed to more fully harvest the rich potential of mouse-tracking data, such as time-continuous multiple regression (Scherbaum & Dshemuchadse, 2018), entropy approaches (Calcagnì, Lombardi, & Sulpizio, 2017), generalized processing tree models (Heck, Erdfelder, & Kieslich, 2018), and decision landscapes (Zgonnikov, Aleni, Piiroinen, O'Hora, & di Bernardo, 2017). Thus, we are confident that mouse-tracking will continue to offer researchers novel insights into how decision processes unfold over time.

Notes

1 This work was supported by the University of Mannheim's Graduate School of Economic and Social Sciences funded by the German Research Foundation.
2 Note that other options for creating mouse-tracking experiments and analyzing mouse-tracking data are available (e.g., MouseTracker, cf., Freeman & Ambady, 2010) and a discussion of the different software packages is provided elsewhere (Kieslich & Henninger, 2017; Kieslich et al., 2019).
3 The data for this replication were collected by Kieslich and Henninger (2017); the corresponding material, data, analyses, and results are available at https://github.com/pascalkieslich/mousetrap-resources.
4 OpenSesame can be obtained free of charge from http://osdoc.cogsci.nl/, where a general introduction to the program and detailed documentation are also available.
5 The additional screens that are presented beforehand ("present_categories" and "present_start") will be described in the section *Design considerations*.
6 The mousetrap plugin includes two items for tracking mouse movements. As an alternative to the *mousetrap_response* item, a *mousetrap_form* item combines stimulus presentation and response collection; its contents are defined using a basic syntax instead of a visual editor. More information is provided in Kieslich and Henninger (2017).
7 An example experiment implementing this procedure can be found at https://github.com/pascalkieslich/mousetrap-os#examples.

8 R is open-source and freely available from www.r-project.org/. We recommend using R in combination with RStudio (available from www.rstudio.com/), which greatly facilitates code development and analysis by providing many useful features such as code highlighting, debugging, and tools for data inspection.

9 In case that only one mousetrap item in the experiment collected mouse-tracking data, the *mt_import_mousetrap* function automatically detects the mouse-tracking variables in the raw data. If more than one item stored mouse-tracking data, the variable names have to be set explicitly once using the *xpos_label*, *ypos_label*, and *timestamps_label* arguments when importing data via the *mt_import_mousetrap* function.

10 Analyses can also be performed on the trial level using mixed-effects models that can account for individual differences between participants as well as trial-level predictors (see https://github.com/pascalkieslich/mousetrap-resources).

11 Velocity and acceleration can be calculated for raw trajectories (by default) as well as for time-normalized trajectories. In addition, both can be computed based on the Euclidean distance traveled along the x- and y-dimension (by default) or for a single dimension only.

Recommended Reading List

- https://github.com/pascalkieslich/mousetrap-resources: resources for creating mouse-tracking experiments and analyzing mouse-tracking data (including the examples from the current chapter).
- Kieslich and Henninger (2017): an introduction into and validation of the mousetrap plugin for OpenSesame, which also provides detailed information about the example study used in the current chapter.
- Hehman et al. (2015): a description of several analytic approaches for mouse-tracking data.

References

Calcagnì, A., Lombardi, L., & Sulpizio, S. (2017). Analyzing spatial data from mouse tracker methodology: An entropic approach. *Behavior Research Methods*, *49*(6), 2012–2030.

Dale, R., Kehoe, C., & Spivey, M. J. (2007). Graded motor responses in the time course of categorizing atypical exemplars. *Memory & Cognition*, *35*(1), 15–28.

Dshemuchadse, M., Scherbaum, S., & Goschke, T. (2013). How decisions emerge: Action dynamics in intertemporal decision making. *Journal of Experimental Psychology: General*, *142*(1), 93–100.

Fischer, M. H., & Hartmann, M. (2014). Pushing forward in embodied cognition: May we mouse the mathematical mind? *Frontiers in Psychology*, *5*, 1315.

Freeman, J.B. (2018). Doing psychological science by hand. *Current Directions in Psychological Science*, *27*(5), 315–323.

Freeman, J. B., & Ambady, N. (2010). MouseTracker: Software for studying real-time mental processing using a computer mouse-tracking method. *Behavior Research Methods*, *42*(1), 226–241.

Freeman, J. B., & Dale, R. (2013). Assessing bimodality to detect the presence of a dual cognitive process. *Behavior Research Methods*, *45*(1), 83–97.

Freeman, J. B., Dale, R., & Farmer, T. A. (2011). Hand in motion reveals mind in motion. *Frontiers in Psychology*, *2*, 59.

Frisch, S., Dshemuchadse, M., Görner, M., Goschke, T., & Scherbaum, S. (2015). Unraveling the sub-processes of selective attention: Insights from dynamic modeling and continuous behavior. *Cognitive Processing*, *16*(4), 377–388.

Heck, D. W., Erdfelder, E., & Kieslich, P. J. (2018). Generalized processing tree models: Jointly modeling discrete and continuous variables. *Psychometrika*, *83*(4), 893–918.

Hehman, E., Stolier, R. M., & Freeman, J. B. (2015). Advanced mouse-tracking analytic techniques for enhancing psychological science. *Group Processes & Intergroup Relations*, *18*(3), 384–401.

Kieslich, P. J., & Henninger, F. (2016). Readbulk: An R package for reading and combining multiple data files. DOI: 10.5281/zenodo.596649

Kieslich, P. J., & Henninger, F. (2017). Mousetrap: An integrated, open-source mouse-tracking package. *Behavior Research Methods, 49*(5), 1652–1667.

Kieslich, P.J., Schoemann, M., Grage, T., Hepp, J., & Scherbaum, S. (in press). Design factors in mouse-tracking: What makes a difference? *Behavior Research Methods.*

Kieslich, P. J., Wulff, D. U., Henninger, F., Haslbeck, J. M. B., & Schulte-Mecklenbeck, M. (2019). *Mouse- and hand-tracking as a window to cognition: A tutorial on implementation, analysis, and visualization.* Manuscript in preparation.

Koop, G. J., & Johnson, J. G. (2011). Response dynamics: A new window on the decision process. *Judgment and Decision Making, 6*(8), 750–758.

Koop, G. J., & Johnson, J. G. (2013). The response dynamics of preferential choice. *Cognitive Psychology, 67*(4), 151–185.

Mathôt, S., Schreij, D., & Theeuwes, J. (2012). OpenSesame: An open-source, graphical experiment builder for the social sciences. *Behavior Research Methods, 44*(2), 314–324.

McKinstry, C., Dale, R., & Spivey, M. J. (2008). Action dynamics reveal parallel competition in decision making. *Psychological Science, 19*(1), 22–24.

Pfister, R., Schwarz, K. A., Janczyk, M., Dale, R., & Freeman, J. B. (2013). Good things peak in pairs: A note on the bimodality coefficient. *Frontiers in Psychology, 4*, 700.

Quétard, B., Quinton, J. C., Mermillod, M., Barca, L., Pezzulo, G., Colomb, M., & Izaute, M. (2016). Differential effects of visual uncertainty and contextual guidance on perceptual decisions: Evidence from eye and mouse tracking in visual search. *Journal of Vision, 16*(11), 28.

R Core Team. (2016). *R: A language and environment for statistical computing.* Vienna, Austria: R Foundation for Statistical Computing. Retrieved from www.R-project.org/

Scherbaum, S., & Dshemuchadse, M. (2018). *Psychometrics based on continuous measures: Exploiting the dynamics of computer mouse movements with time continuous multiple regression.* Manuscript in preparation.

Scherbaum, S., Dshemuchadse, M., Fischer, R., & Goschke, T. (2010). How decisions evolve: The temporal dynamics of action selection. *Cognition, 115*(3), 407–416.

Scherbaum, S., & Kieslich, P. J. (2017). Stuck at the starting line: How the starting procedure influences mouse-tracking data. *Behavior Research Methods, 1–14.*

Spivey, M. J., & Dale, R. (2006). Continuous dynamics in real-time cognition. *Current Directions in Psychological Science, 15*(5), 207–211.

Spivey, M. J., Dale, R., Knoblich, G., & Grosjean, M. (2010). Do curved reaching movements emerge from competing perceptions? A reply to van der Wel et al. (2009). *Journal of Experimental Psychology: Human Perception and Performance, 36*(1), 251–254.

Spivey, M. J., Grosjean, M., & Knoblich, G. (2005). Continuous attraction toward phonological competitors. *Proceedings of the National Academy of Sciences of the United States of America, 102*(29), 10393–10398.

Stillman, P. E., Shen, X., & Ferguson, M. J. (2018). How mouse-tracking can advance social cognitive theory. *Trends in Cognitive Sciences, 22*(6), 531–543

Sullivan, N., Hutcherson, C., Harris, A., & Rangel, A. (2015). Dietary self-control is related to the speed with which attributes of healthfulness and tastiness are processed. *Psychological Science, 26*(2), 122–134.

Szaszi, B., Palfi, B., Szollosi, A., Kieslich, P. J., & Aczel, B. (2018). Thinking dynamics and individual differences: Mouse-tracking analysis of the denominator neglect task. *Judgment and Decision Making, 13*(1), 23–32.

Travers, E., Rolison, J. J., & Feeney, A. (2016). The time course of conflict on the Cognitive Reflection Test. *Cognition, 150*, 109–118.

Wagenmakers, E.-J., Wetzels, R., Borsboom, D., van der Maas, H. L. J., & Kievit, R. A. (2012). An agenda for purely confirmatory research. *Perspectives on Psychological Science, 7*(6), 632–638.

Wulff, D. U., Haslbeck, J. M. B., & Schulte-Mecklenbeck, M. (2019). *Measuring the (dis-) continuous mind.* Manuscript in preparation.

Zgonnikov, A., Aleni, A., Piiroinen, P. T., O'Hora, D., & di Bernardo, M. (2017). Decision landscapes: Visualizing mouse-tracking data. *Royal Society Open Science, 4*(11), 170482.

9

MOUSE-TRACKING

Detecting Types in Movement Trajectories

Dirk U. Wulff, Jonas M. B. Haslbeck, Pascal J. Kieslich,
Felix Henninger, and Michael Schulte-Mecklenbeck

In recent years, mouse and hand tracking has become a popular method for studying the cognitive processes involved in various domains of research, including language processing (Spivey, Grosjean, & Knoblich, 2005; Tomlinson, Bailey, & Bott, 2013), memory functions (Papesh & Goldinger, 2012; Xiao & Yamauchi, 2014), social cognition (Freeman & Ambady, 2009, 2011; Yu, Wang, Wang, & Bastin, 2012), and preferential and moral decision making (Dshemuchadse, Scherbaum, & Goschke, 2013, Koop, 2013; Koop & Johnson, 2013; Kieslich & Hilbig, 2014), to name just a few. The popularity of mouse and hand tracking derives from its promise to provide a window into the evolution of cognitive processes with an unrivaled temporal resolution. This promise is based on a proposed link between the characteristics of the movement, such as the shape of its trajectory, and the characteristics of the underlying cognitive process. In present research, mouse and hand tracking is employed, more often than not, to infer the response competition created by different conditions or stimuli based on the curvature of aggregate movement trajectories (see Chapters 8, 10). However, we will argue that the aggregate-level analysis underlying this approach risks obscuring important trial-level variability in movement trajectories that can paint a different picture of the underlying cognitive process than the aggregate-level results do. Fortunately, mouse-tracking can do much more. In this chapter, we present a new approach to analyzing mouse trajectories based on trajectory clustering that overcomes the limitations of aggregation-based analyses of movement trajectories.

Henceforth, we will focus mainly on movement trajectories recorded using the computer mouse. However, the issues associated with aggregation-based analyses of movement trajectories and the usefulness of our new approach apply equally to data generated with other hand-tracking devices, such as camera-based motion tracking (e.g., Friedman, Brown, & Finkbeiner, 2013), Wii-motes (O'Hora, Tyndall, McMorrow, & Dale, 2013), touch- and track-pads (e.g., Wirth, Pfister, & Kunde, 2016), and robotic handles (e.g., Burk, Ingram, Franklin, Shadlen, & Wolpert, 2014).

Why Not Aggregate Mouse and Hand Trajectories?

Mouse-tracking methodologies seek to reveal the cognitive process by continuously recording the position of the computer mouse (or hand) while the subject reaches from a neutral start point to one of several, spatially separated choice options. An early and very influential study that used this approach was conducted by Spivey et al. (2005). In their study, individuals were asked to use the mouse to select one of two pictures presented in the top-right and top-left corners of the screen matching a word they heard over headphones. For example, participants would see images of a "candle" and a "candy" and, after a short delay, be instructed to click on the image depicting the word candle (see Figure 9.1). To uncover how phonological competition between words is resolved in the mind, Spivey et al. (2005) implemented two conditions that varied in the degree of phonological overlap between the words: In one condition, individuals chose between images depicting phonologically similar words (e.g., candle and candy; cohort condition) while in another condition they chose between images depicting phonologically dissimilar words (e.g., candle and jacket; control condition). Using this setup, Spivey et al. (2005) observed that images of phonologically similar words led to an average movement trajectory that was drawn further towards the unchosen alternative than images of phonologically dissimilar words (see Figure 9.1). Moreover, they found that average trajectories were continuously curved. Spivey et al. interpreted these results as evidence for continuous partial co-activation of the non-chosen option that drew the movement towards the corresponding picture, expressing what Spivey later coined the *continuity of mind hypothesis* (Spivey, 2008).

Spivey et al.'s investigation built on the assumption of a close link between cognitive and motor processes on a neuronal level (Song & Nakayama, 2009). In support of this idea, Cisek and Kalaska (2005) showed that regions of the primate brain involved in planning and execution of limb movements simultaneously encode multiple targets for selective reaching prior to choice, suggesting that "motor systems do not passively reflect the result of completed cognitive processes; rather, it is crucially linked to the dynamic decision-making process itself" (Song & Nakayama, 2009, p. 361). Movement trajectories, thus, appear to reflect the underlying cognitive process.

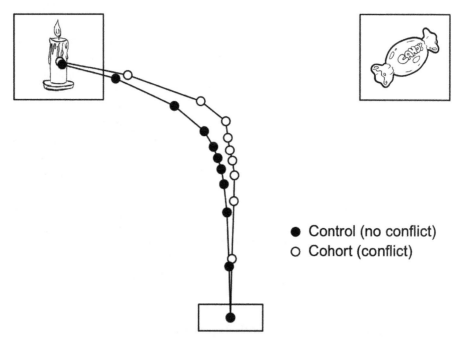

FIGURE 9.1 Design and results of Spivey et al. (2005). Lines represent the mean trajectories for the control and cohort conditions when the target was on the left side. Points mark 10 equidistant time points in the trajectory represent the average cursor position after every tenth percentile of the movement duration. Adapted from Spivey et al. (2005).

But in what way? What exactly is the mapping between the underlying cognitive process and the movement trajectory?

Spivey et al. (2005) assumed that the underlying response competition would map directly onto the degree of deflection. However, the mapping could also be of a different kind, as the authors themselves anticipated:

> In principle, it could be the case that, as with saccadic eye movements, there are some trials in which the competitor object does not attract the motor output and other trials in which it does. […] When averaged, this hypothetical data pattern would produce mean movement trajectories that could falsely suggest simultaneous partial activation and competition […]
>
> *p. 10395*

In this case, the observed average trajectories might not necessarily represent trial-level trajectories. Instead, the curved average trajectories could have been the result of a mixture of trajectory types, comprising both straight trajectories that immediately head to the chosen option and discrete trajectories that pass through the non-chosen option before moving to the chosen option. As a consequence, the average trajectories would drastically misrepresent the trial-level trajectories in terms of both shape (no trajectory matching the continuous curve of the aggregate trajectory) and location (no trajectory spatially close to the average trajectory's location). Moreover, the differences in average trajectories could have resulted from small changes in the proportion of trajectory types. This means that effects among aggregate trajectories could be driven by a very small number of trajectories, e.g., 5% vs 10% discrete revision trajectories.

Recent evidence has shown that such an indirect mapping might represent the rule rather than the exception. Specifically, a recent reanalysis of 40 published mouse- and hand-tracking studies revealed that the majority of data sets consist of multiple types of trajectories, including the two types described in Spivey et al.'s quote (Wulff, Haslbeck, & Schulte-Mecklenbeck, 2019). This finding has theoretical implications for what mouse-tracking can reveal about the underlying process and commands caution for the interpretation of smooth aggregate trajectories. It also implies that movement trajectories should be analyzed on the trial level rather than on the aggregate level to avoid obscuring variability in trajectory types. To achieve this, we will next present a novel procedure for the analysis of mouse and hand tracking data based on cluster analysis.

Detecting Trajectory Mixtures Using Cluster Analysis

In statistics, a common approach to identifying types in a set of objects is cluster analysis (Friedman, Hastie, & Tibshirani, 2001). Cluster analysis is a class of statistical techniques that sorts objects (in our case trajectories) into a predefined number of clusters, choosing clusters such that the similarity of objects within each cluster is maximized while the similarity between clusters is minimized. Using cluster analysis typically requires three steps: a) determining the distances between all pairs of objects, b) selecting a suitable clustering algorithm, and c) choosing an appropriate number of clusters to extract. In this section, we discuss each of these steps in the context of identifying types in movement trajectories and demonstrate the usefulness of the approach using the data of Spivey et al. (2005).

How to Determine Distances between Trajectories

A fundamental challenge in using cluster analysis for mouse and hand trajectories is that trajectories are recorded with different numbers of points. This is because movements are typically recorded at a fixed frequency, e.g., 100 Hz (100 samples per second). Trials of different duration, therefore, produce trajectories of different length, making it difficult to determine the distance between trajectories. As this problem affects many types of mouse-tracking analyses, it is common to use *time-normalized trajectories* (trajectories are interpolated such that they are represented by the same number—usually 101—of temporally equidistant points, Spivey et al., 2005; see also Chapter 8). However, time-normalization is not the ideal choice for identifying types of trajectories on the basis of their shape: Movements are typically slow at the beginning and end of the trajectory (due to movement initiation and target approach) and fast in-between, resulting in an uneven distribution of points over the path of the trajectory. The use of time-normalized trajectories would therefore place excessive weight on the relatively uninformative end and start phases of trajectories, where movement is slow and rarely differs in direction, and too little weight on the path in-between, where most of the movement happens and trajectories differ most from one another. A better solution is a spatial analogue of time-normalization, which represents trajectories using a fixed number of points equidistant in terms of their x- and y-positions on the screen, rather than in terms of time. Figures 9.2a and 9.2b illustrate this *spatial normalization*. The trajectory in Figure 9.2a represents a typical raw (or time-normalized) trajectory that has most points in the beginning and the end of the trajectory. By contrast, the points of the spatially normalized trajectory in Figure 9.2b are more uniformly distributed. As a result, the spatially normalized trajectories are represented with uniform precision, giving every part of the trajectories' shapes equal weight.

A key parameter of space-normalization is the number of points used to represent the trajectory. Traditional analyses normalize trajectories to 100 or 101 points. For identifying types, however, it is practical to space-normalize trajectories to a substantially smaller number of points, e.g., 20. The first reason for this is that the clustering procedure calculates the distance for every pair of trajectories, which can become computationally expensive if both the number of trajectories and the number of points per trajectory is large. Second, choosing a relatively small number of points to represent trajectories places the focus on the overall shape of the trajectory rather than its details, which aids the detection of commonalities between trajectories and, thus, the identification of basic types.

Once trajectories are represented by the same number of points, calculating distances between trajectories is straightforward using, for instance, the Euclidean distance (see Figure 9.2c). The Euclidian distance d_{ij} between two trajectories i, j is given by:

$$d_{ij}(x_i, y_i, x_j, y_j) = \sqrt{\sum_k (x_{ik} - x_{jk})^2 + (y_{ik} - y_{jk})^2} \tag{1}$$

where x and y are the x- and y-coordinates of trajectories i and j. However, other distance metrics are possible (e.g., city block) and justifiable. Having decided on a distance metric, the next step is to determine the full distance matrix by computing the distance between every pair of trajectories in the data set (Figure 9.2d). This step can be very computationally expensive, as the necessary amount of computation grows quadratically with the number of trajectories. This problem can be alleviated by using the high-performance tools implemented in the mousetrap R package (see Chapter 8).

How to Cluster Trajectories

Having obtained the distance matrix, the trajectory data is ready for further analysis using one of the many off-the-shelf cluster analysis algorithms, which commonly take a distance matrix as input. Two of the most popular clustering algorithms are hierarchical clustering and k-means clustering

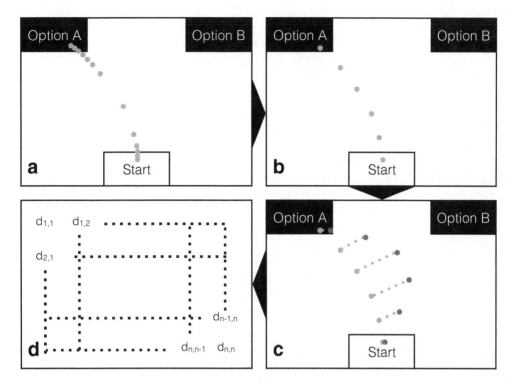

FIGURE 9.2 Computation of pairwise trajectory distances. Panel (a) illustrates the distribution of trajectory points in an exemplary raw (or time-normalized) trajectory. Panel (b) illustrates how the spatial normalization approach distributes trajectory points equally across the 2D-plane to give relatively more weight to the trajectories' body. Panel (c) illustrates the difference between two exemplary spatially normalized trajectories that give rise to one element in the distance matrix illustrated in panel (d).

(Friedman et al., 2001): Hierarchical clustering builds a hierarchy of clusters by either joining objects from the bottom up (agglomerative clustering) or splitting clusters from the top down (divisive clustering) using one of many available linkage criteria.[1] The single-linkage, agglomerative clustering criterion, for instance, will begin with each object occupying its own cluster and then proceed by repeatedly combining the two clusters that contain the closest pair of elements. K-means clustering, on the other hand, partitions the objects into k clusters by iteratively assigning an object to the cluster with the nearest cluster centroid, as measured by their Euclidian distance. The main difference between these two algorithms is the criterion used to form clusters. Whereas k-means is based on Euclidian distance and minimizing within-cluster variance, hierarchical clustering offers more flexibility. However, we have found that, in the case of movement trajectories, hierarchical clustering also performs best using criterions that minimize within-cluster variance (e.g., Ward's d).

How Many Clusters to Extract

A final consideration in extracting clusters is to choose the number of clusters k. There are several methods to estimate the number of clusters each based on a different criterion of a good clustering (see Hennig, Meila, Murtagh, & Rocci, 2015, for a discussion). One such method is k-selection

136 Wulff et al.

based on cluster stability (see e.g., Ben-Hur, Elisseeff, & Guyon, 2001; Haslbeck & Wulff, 2016; Tibshirani & Walther, 2005). This method seeks to identify the k that leads to most stable clustering in terms of its robustness against perturbations of the data. Other popular k-selection methods are the Gap statistic (Tibshirani, Walther, & Hastie, 2001), the Jump statistic (Sugar & James, 2003), and the Slope statistic (Fujita, Takahashi, & Patriota, 2014). As these methods rest on different definitions of a good clustering they often lead to different k estimates. In fact, when implementing the four methods mentioned earlier using the *cstab* package[2] (Haslbeck & Wulff, 2016) for the data sets contained in our meta-analysis the k-estimates varied widely (between two and 20 clusters, with 20 being the maximum number of clusters considered) and the correlations between k-estimates based on the four methods were negative across data sets. This low level of consistency between the methods illustrates the fundamental problem associated with identifying the true number of clusters. There is no principled way to evaluate the quality of a cluster solution given a certain k. This would only be possible if one knew the data generating process.

However, for the analysis of mouse and hand tracking this situation is actually not that problematic. If the data is composed of clearly distinguishable types, then 2D-plots of the extracted clusters will show qualitatively distinct trajectory shapes. Moreover, it is in fact not strictly necessary to have identified the true set of types underlying a data set or to know their exact number. Indeed, we argue that in the presence of some clearly identifiable types it always will be better to analyze the data using a type-based approach than to resort to averaging trajectories.

Clustering the Data of Spivey et al. (2005)

To demonstrate our approach, we reanalyzed the data of the experiment of Spivey et al. (2005)[3] presented earlier. To do this, we first aligned the start points of all trajectories and flipped all trajectories that ended on the right option to the left side. Next, we space-normalized trajectories to 20 points each. Finally, we extracted four clusters[4] using the k-means algorithm separately for the cohort and control condition. These and all other analyses in this chapter were run using the mousetrap R package (see Chapter 8; Kieslich, Wulff, Henninger, Haslbeck, & Schulte-Mecklenbeck, 2019).

This analysis revealed four important insights. First, the four clusters extracted for the cohort condition (Figure 9.3, top row) were remarkably similar to the four clusters extracted for the control condition (Figure 9.3, bottom row), speaking to the reliability of behavior and the analysis approach. Second, the analysis produced clusters of high homogeneity for both conditions, suggesting the presence of distinct types: A first cluster of trajectories that go straight up to the level of the two options and then directly to the chosen option, a second cluster of trajectories that head straight to the chosen option, a third cluster of trajectories that go from the start to the chosen option in a mild curve, and the fourth and final cluster whose trajectories visit the non-chosen option before going to the chosen option. Third, the trajectories were assigned to clusters in different proportions between conditions. In particular, the conditions differed mainly in terms of trajectories that go straight to the chosen option (23% vs 33%) and trajectories that visit the non-chosen option first (20% vs 8%). Fourth, the majority of trajectories (all but the third cluster) showed a shape that does not match the average trajectories presented in Figure 9.1.

The previously mentioned results strongly suggest the presence of distinct trajectory types. These types are, in three out of four cases, not well represented by the aggregate trajectory, and their relative proportions appear to produce the effect visible in Figure 9.1. This pattern of results

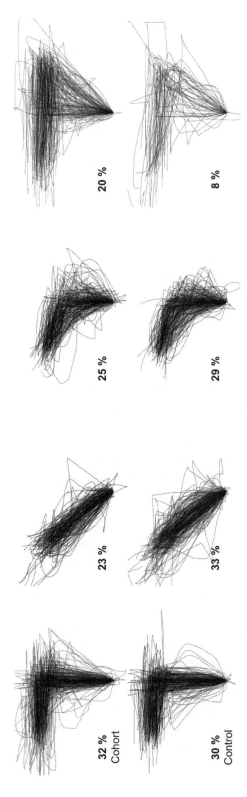

FIGURE 9.3 Trajectory clusters extracted from the data of Spivey et al. (2005). The figure shows in descending order of size (determined based on both conditions) the trajectory clusters extracted for the cohort (top-row) and control (bottom-row) conditions. Percentages indicate the proportion of trajectories within a condition assigned to the respective cluster.

has important consequences for how movement trajectories should be analyzed and interpreted. However, before we turn to these issues, let us address two important caveats.

First, to reiterate a point made earlier, clusters need not indicate types. That is, cluster analysis algorithms always produce as many clusters as they are instructed to produce. Furthermore, the extracted clusters will always contain non-overlapping sets of objects. It is, thus, possible that the clusters originate from a single type of trajectories that was arbitrarily divided. In fact, as mentioned above earlier, there is no way of knowing for sure whether the data is truthfully composed of different types or not. Still, we can interpret the data with regard to the presence or absence and the number of clusters. Consider a situation in which data originally came from a single type. In that case, trajectories should come in highly similar shapes, which for the present analysis is clearly not the case (Figure 9.3): For instance, the trajectories of two clusters show a clear kink, either at the midpoint between the options or at the location of the non-chosen option, whereas the other two clusters do not. Thus, in lieu of a principled statistical technique to decide upon the number of clusters, the visual inspection of clusters reveals clear qualitative differences between movement trajectories speaking in favor of trajectory types.

The second caveat is that, despite the high similarity across conditions, the clusters are not identical for both conditions. It is, therefore, difficult to compare cluster sizes across conditions and to characterize the effect of, e.g., an experimental manipulation in terms of trajectory types. To compare cluster frequencies across levels of an experimental design, it would be necessary to keep clusters constant across conditions. The next section describes such an approach based on prototype matching.

Detecting Trajectory Mixtures Using Prototype Matching

Cluster algorithms practically never produce the exact same partitioning of trajectories for different data sets. This makes it difficult to compare cluster solutions across different data sets or different experimental conditions. One way to address this issue is to define prototypical trajectories, and then to assign each trajectory to the closest prototypes based on some distance metric.[5] This is equivalent to creating a fixed set of clusters. As a result, clusters belonging to a given prototype will always contain the same kinds of trajectories, rendering the clustering of the data sets immediately comparable.

Another benefit of this approach is that one can tease apart qualitatively distinct trajectories that statistical algorithms may have difficulty separating. For instance, one might argue that the fourth cluster in Figure 9.3 is actually composed of two distinct types: those that go straight up to the level of the options and then visit the non-chosen before moving to the chosen option and those that go straight to the non-chosen option before going to the chosen option. Using a prototype-matching approach, this can easily be dealt with by defining separate prototypes for these sets of trajectories. In the case of Spivey et al., it might, thus, be reasonable to map trajectories onto five prototypes, three matching the first three cluster types in Figure 9.3 and two for the final cluster. For other data sets obtained using different experimental designs, however, different sets of prototypes might be more appropriate.

Figure 9.4 shows the five prototypes (Figure 9.4a), as well as the trajectories of the cohort (Figure 9.4b) and control groups (Figure 9.4c) that have been mapped to the closest prototype using Euclidian distance as defined in (1).[6] It can be seen that the extracted trajectory clusters represent much cleaner types than the clusters extracted using k-means. As expected, this is particularly the case for the fourth cluster of the k-means solution (Figure 9.3), which is now separated into two

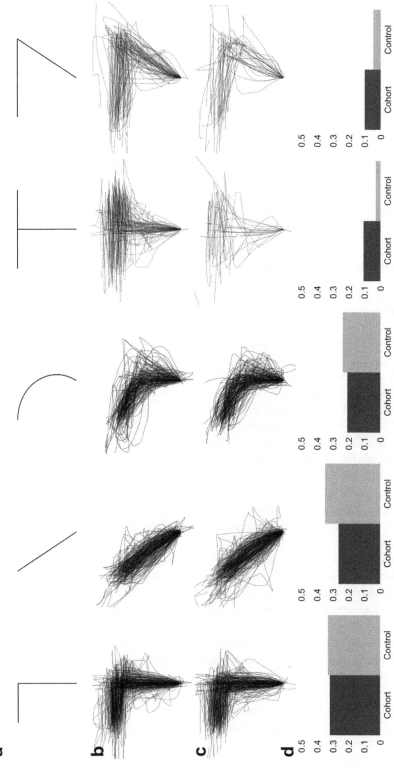

FIGURE 9.4 Prototype-matching for the data of Spivey et al. (2005). Panel (a) shows the five prototype trajectories. Panels (b) and (c) show the trajectories of the cohort and control conditions, respectively, for each of the prototypes they have been matched to. Panel (d) shows the proportions of trajectories in the cohort (dark grey) and control (light grey) conditions matched to each of the prototypes.

clusters that clearly represent the corresponding prototype. However, an improved differentiation of types can also be observed for the other three clusters.

Based on the prototype mapping, we can now characterize the effect of the manipulation of Spivey et al. (2005) by comparing the proportions of trajectories mapped to each prototype. This reveals a pattern similar to that obtained using the k-means clustering: The cohort condition includes more trajectories of types four and five, and thus of trajectories that visit the non-chosen option, whereas the control condition containes more straight trajectories of type two. Thus, the difference in aggregate curvature between the conditions arises mainly from trajectories that are either extremely deflected or not deflected at all.

Implications for Mouse and Hand Tracking as a Window to Cognition

The reanalysis of the data of Spivey et al. (2005) has produced a set of at least five qualitatively distinct types of trajectories. This finding raises several questions regarding the analysis of movement trajectories and what can be inferred about the underlying cognitive process from trajectory shapes.

How Prevalent are Trajectory Types?

One fundamental question is whether the types obtained from the data of Spivey et al. (2005) generalize to other data sets using mouse and hand tracking. Based on our meta-analysis of 40 data sets the answer is: it depends (Wulff et al., 2019). The majority of data sets, in particular those collected using the computer mouse as input device, exhibited trajectories similar to those found in the data of Spivey et al. (2005). However, several data sets, particularly those collected with cameras (e.g., Friedman et al., 2013) or a robotic handle (e.g., Burk et al., 2014), showed relatively homogenous sets of smoothly curved trajectories that might, indeed, be best described by a single cluster. Other important moderators are characteristics of the study design (for discussions, see Kieslich & Henninger, 2017; Kieslich, Schoemann, Grage, Hepp, & Scherbaum, in press; Scherbaum & Kieslich, 2018; Wulff et al., 2019). Figure 9.5 gives an illustration of the trajectories produced by four hand-picked studies, including the study by Spivey et al. (2005; Figure 9.5a), a mouse-tracking study using methodological setup similar to Spivey et al. (Koop & Johnson, 2013; Figure 9.5b), a mouse-tracking study using a different methodological setup than Spivey et al. (Scherbaum et al., 2010; Figure 9.5c), and a hand-tracking study using a robotic handle (Burk et al., 2014; Figure 9.5d). As can be seen, not all studies produced the types found in the data of Spivey et al. (2005) and some may not contain qualitatively different types at all. This implies that mouse-tracking researchers need a better understanding of how the methodological setup influences trajectory shapes and that they should investigate the nature of trajectories in each individual study before choosing a particular path of analysis.

One way the literature has previously attempted to test for the presence of trajectory types is via bimodality tests. Bimodality tests rest on the assumption that trajectories come in two types, deflected and not-deflected, as outlined in the quote by Spivey et al. (2005) cited earlier. Presence of these two types should result in a bimodal distribution of curvature measures. Under such circumstances, measures and tests of bimodality, such as the bimodality coefficient (SAS Institute Inc., 1989) and Hartigan's dip-statistic (Hartigan & Hartigan, 1985), would be able to identify the presence of (two) trajectory types. There are, however, two important problems with this approach. First, bimodality tests require that each trajectory is condensed to a single curvature value, rendering indistinguishable types with identical curvature values (e.g., in terms of MAD; see Chapter 8), such as, for instance, the fourth and fifth prototype in Figure 9.4. Second, bimodality tests are designed

Mouse-Tracking: Trajectory Types   **141**

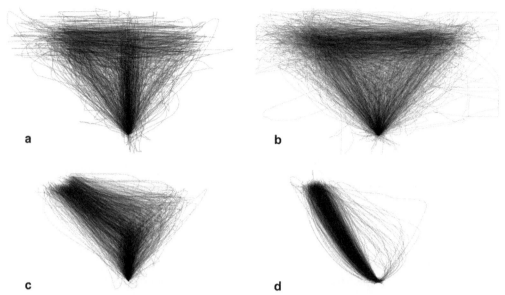

FIGURE 9.5 Overview of trajectories produced by different studies. Panel (a) shows the trajectories of the cohort condition of Spivey et al. (2005). Panel (b) shows the trajectories of choice of the risky option in experiment 2 of Koop and Johnson (2013), who used a similar design as Spivey et al. (2005). Panel (c) shows the trajectories of incongruent trials in Scherbaum, Dshemuchadse, Fischer, and Goschke (2010), who used a different design, in which participants had initiated their movement first in order to trigger stimulus presentation. Panel (d) shows the trajectories of trials with narrow option separation in Burk et al. (2014), who tracked the movement of the hand using a robotic handle.

to detect the presence of two modes. As soon as more trajectory types are involved, bimodality tests cannot be expected to reliably identify the presence of different types. As the number of types is usually not known in advance, bimodality tests do not provide a reliable indication of the presence or absence of different trajectory types. In our eyes, a generally more suitable approach to check for the presence of types is to employ a bottom-up clustering approach and to visually inspect plots of raw trajectories by cluster.

How to Conduct Statistical Analyses using Trajectory Types

Another question is how one should conduct group comparisons or statistical analyses, in general, when the trajectory data comes in types. Typically, analyses of mouse and hand trajectories are based on continuous trial-level statistics. That is, trajectories are condensed into single values representing, for instance, the trajectories' curvature, their complexity, or their velocity (see Chapter 8). Such analyses are sensible when the data stems from a homogenous distribution of trajectories that vary with respect to the statistic of choice. However, when trajectories occur in different types, several problems may ensue. For instance, the presence of types may imply a multi-modal distribution of, e.g., curvature, which cannot reliably be summarized by means of a central tendency, and which risk violating normality assumptions made by many statistical tests. More importantly, condensing trajectories to a single value may obscure important variability in trajectories such as between clusters four and five in Figure 9.4 that may offer valuable insight into the underlying cognitive process.

A more appropriate statistical approach seems to be the analysis of trajectory types as a categorical variable. For instance, researchers can test the equality of trajectory type distributions

142 Wulff et al.

TABLE 9.1 Prototype Frequencies, Proportions, and Standardized Residuals for the Data of Spivey et al. (2005)

Condition	Types				
	1	*2*	*3*	*4*	*5*
Frequencies					
Cohort	215 (32%)	178 (26%)	141 (21%)	71 (11%)	67 (10%)
Control	207 (33%)	218 (35%)	149 (24%)	19 (3%)	29 (5%)
Residuals					
Cohort	-0.28	-1.93	-0.78	3.55	2.43
Control	0.29	2.00	0.81	-3.69	-2.52

Note. Standardized residuals are based on a test of stochastic independence between the type-frequency distributions of the cohort and control conditions in Spivey et al. (2005).

across different conditions using chi-square tests of independence. For the data of Spivey et al. (2005), this approach revealed a systematic difference between the trajectories produced by the two conditions. Analyzing the residuals furthermore revealed that this difference arises mainly from the types two, five, and, in particular, four (see Table 9.1). Analyzing the data on the nominal scale delivered insights not readily available otherwise, such as which trajectory types were most affected by experimental manipulations, opening new angles on the underlying cognitive process.

Another possibility for analyzing trajectory types is to order types with regard to a dimension of interest to then run analyses using the resulting ordinal variable. For instance, many mouse tracking studies are interested in evaluating differences in curvature as a signal of the degree of competition between the response options. Such an analysis can also be carried out using trajectory types, by ordering the clusters (based on, e.g., k-means or prototype mapping) with regard to the degree of response competition that they embody, and using statistical tools suited for ordinal data, such as ordinal logistic regression. In the case of the types extracted from the data collected by Spivey et al. (2005; Figure 9.4), one may argue that an appropriate ordering of the types from low to high competition is cluster 2 < cluster 3 < cluster 1 < cluster 4 < cluster 5. Using this ordering, we again found that the manipulation of phonological similarity had an effect on the distribution of trajectories, this time confirming directly that the cohort condition produced trajectories consistent with higher degrees of competition.

How to Interpret Trajectory Types

Trajectory types offer the researcher interesting new possibilities for the analysis of movement trajectories. What we have not addressed sufficiently, so far, is how to interpret results of type-based analyses on the level of cognitive processes. That is, which conclusions regarding the underlying process can be drawn from, for instance, the finding that Spivey et al.'s (2005) manipulation affected only specific kinds of trajectories. For Spivey et al. (2005) and large parts of the mouse and hand tracking literature, (curved) trajectories are thought to arise from a continuous, partial co-activation of the available options, expressed continuously in the movement. However, this interpretation is not easy to reconcile with the fact that the trajectories impacted by Spivey et al.'s (2005) manipulation, i.e., those assigned to prototypes two, four, and five, either are perfectly straight or exhibit characteristic kinks in the trajectory shape. Such trajectories suggest either a) that the cognitive process is inherently discrete or b) that the underlying process expresses itself on a much coarser time-scale than typically assumed.

Currently, too little is known about the link between the cognitive process, the movement trajectory, and the design that elicits the movements to discern whether a), b), or potentially both are the case. It may seem plausible that the kinks in the trajectories result from a non-continuous mapping of the underlying process onto the movement, considering that cognitive processes reside in the near-continuous communication of neurons in the brain (Cisek & Kalaska, 2005; Song & Nakayama, 2009). However, decision scientists have also long been discussing lexicographic decision processes that consider pieces of information in sequence and thus could account for preference shifts as embodied by trajectory types four and five (e.g., Payne, Bettman, & Johnson, 1993). With respect to the usefulness of mouse-tracking as a window into the underlying cognitive process, the latter scenario would clearly be more desirable. That is, if kinks in trajectories arise because of a low-resolution mapping of the movement to the underlying cognitive process, then movements provide only a very narrow window into the development of the underlying cognitive processes. However, if those trajectories arise because of inherently discrete cognitive processes, then movements may reveal much more than the degree of competition between choice options, namely the discrete cognitive steps that led up to the decision.

Future research is needed to shed light on the link between movement trajectories and cognitive processes and to build theories capturing this link. Promising efforts in this direction have been made based on sequential sampling models (e.g., Resulaj, Kiani, Wolpert, & Shadlen, 2009; Wong, Haith, & Krakauer, 2015), accumulation models (e.g., Frisch, Dshemuchadse, Görner, Goschke, & Scherbaum, 2015), and decision landscapes (e.g., Zgonnikov, Aleni, Piiroinen, O'Hora, & di Bernardo, 2017). However, the empirical results regarding the validity of these models are still outstanding, in particular, the question of whether these models can account for the trajectory types presented here and the existence of trajectory types in general.

Conclusion

Mouse-tracking is a promising new tool for the study of cognitive processes. This tool is not and, as we have argued, should not be limited to aggregate-level analyses of movement trajectories. Instead researchers should consider analyzing trajectories on the trial level using, for instance, the clustering approaches presented here and made available through the mousetrap R package. Frequently, this will reveal that movement trajectories occur in distinct trajectory types, challenging the common conception of movement trajectories as a direct result of continuous co-activation of choice options. Further research is needed to better understand the link between the cognitive processes and movement trajectories, and how it is best utilized to reveal the underlying cognitive processes. To that end, the analysis of trajectory types presents an exciting new avenue offering rich data ready to be explored.

Notes

1 Agglomerative clustering is usually preferred as it shows much lower computational complexity than divisive clustering.
2 The *cstab* package can also be accessed via the mousetrap wrapper function *mt_cluster_k*.
3 We are grateful to Michael J. Spivey for providing us with the raw data.
4 We arbitrarily chose to extract four clusters, as this number appeared large enough to tease apart substantive clusters and small enough to not fraction. Clusters were extracted using the *mt_cluster* function of the mousetrap R package.
5 In the case of a Euclidian distance (defined in (1)), this essentially means to define in advance the cluster centroids that k-means would otherwise have to learn from the data.
6 Prototype-mapping was carried out using the *mt_map* function of the mousetrap R package.

Recommended Reading List

- Spivey et al. (2005): Early and highly influential study demonstrating a link between response competition and trajectory curvature.
- Haslbeck & Wulff (2016): Formal study discussing different methods to estimate the number of clusters in empirical data sets.

References

Ben-Hur, A., Elisseeff, A., & Guyon, I. (2001). A stability based method for discovering structure in clustered data. *Pacific Symposium on Biocomputing, 7*, 6–17.

Burk, D., Ingram, J. N., Franklin, D. W., Shadlen, M. N., & Wolpert, D. M. (2014). Motor effort alters changes of mind in sensorimotor decision making. *PLoS ONE, 9*(3), 92681.

Cisek, P., & Kalaska, J. F. (2005). Neural correlates of reaching decisions in dorsal premotor cortex: Specification of multiple direction choices and final selection of action. *Neuron, 45*(5), 801–814.

Dshemuchadse, M., Scherbaum, S., & Goschke, T. (2013). How decisions emerge: Action dynamics in intertemporal decision making. *Journal of Experimental Psychology: General, 142*(1), 93–100.

Freeman, J. B., & Ambady, N. (2009). Motions of the hand expose the partial and parallel activation of stereotypes. *Psychological Science, 20*(10), 1183–1188.

Freeman, J. B., & Ambady, N. (2011). A dynamic interactive theory of person construal. *Psychological Review, 118*(2), 247–279.

Friedman, J., Brown, S., & Finkbeiner, M. (2013). Linking cognitive and reaching trajectories via intermittent movement control. *Journal of Mathematical Psychology, 57*(3–4), 140–151.

Friedman, J. H., Hastie, T., & Tibshirani, R. (2001). *The elements of statistical learning.* New York, NY: Springer.

Frisch, S., Dshemuchadse, M., Görner, M., Goschke, T., & Scherbaum, S. (2015). Unraveling the sub-processes of selective attention: Insights from dynamic modeling and continuous behavior. *Cognitive Processing, 16*(4), 377–388.

Fujita, A., Takahashi, D. Y., & Patriota, A. G. (2014). A non-parametric method to estimate the number of clusters. *Computational Statistics & Data Analysis, 73*, 27–39.

Hartigan, J. A., & Hartigan, P. M. (1985). The dip test of unimodality. *The Annals of Statistics, 13*(1), 70–84.

Haslbeck, J. M. B., & Wulff, D. U. (2016). Estimating the number of clusters via normalized cluster Instability. *arXiv*:1608.07494.

Hennig, C., Meila, M., Murtagh, F., & Rocci, R. (Eds.). (2015). *Handbook of cluster analysis.* CRC Press.

Kieslich, P. J., & Henninger, F. (2017). Mousetrap: An integrated, open-source mouse-tracking package. *Behavior Research Methods, 49*(5), 1652–1667.

Kieslich, P. J., & Hilbig, B. E. (2014). Cognitive conflict in social dilemmas: An analysis of response dynamics. *Judgment and Decision Making, 9*(6), 510–522.

Kieslich, P. J., Schoemann, M., Grage, T., Hepp, J., & Scherbaum, S. (in press). Design factors in mouse-tracking: *What makes a difference? Behavior Research Methods.*

Kieslich, P. J., Wulff, D. U., Henninger, F., Haslbeck, J. M. B., & Schulte-Mecklenbeck, M. (2019). *Mouse- and hand-tracking as a window to cognition: A tutorial on implementation, analysis, and visualization.* Manuscript in preparation.

Koop, G. J., & Johnson, J. G. (2013). The response dynamics of preferential choice. *Cognitive Psychology, 67*(4), 151–185.

O'Hora, D. P., Tyndall, I. T., McMorrow, M., & Dale, R. A. (2013). Using action dynamics to assess competing stimulus control during stimulus equivalence testing. *Learning & Behavior, 41*(3), 256–270.

Papesh, M. H., & Goldinger, S. D. (2012). Memory in motion: Movement dynamics reveal memory strength. *Psychonomic Bulletin & Review, 19*(5), 906–913.

Payne, J. W., Bettman, J. R., & Johnson, E. J. (1993). *The adaptive decision maker.* Cambridge, UK: Cambridge University Press.

Resulaj, A., Kiani, R., Wolpert, D. M., & Shadlen, M. N., (2009). Changes of mind in decision-making. *Nature, 461*(7261), 263–266.

SAS Institute Inc. (1989). *User's guide*. Cary, NC: Statistical Analysis System Institute.

Scherbaum, S., Dshemuchadse, M., Fischer, R., & Goschke, T. (2010). How decisions evolve: The temporal dynamics of action selection. *Cognition, 115*(3), 407–416.

Scherbaum, S., & Kieslich, P. J. (2018). Stuck at the starting line: How the starting procedure influences mouse-tracking data. *Behavior Research Methods, 50*(5), 2097–2110.

Song, J. H., & Nakayama, K. (2009). Hidden cognitive states revealed in choice reaching tasks. *Trends in Cognitive Sciences, 13*(8), 360–366.

Spivey, M. (2008). *The continuity of mind*. Oxford, UK: Oxford University Press.

Spivey, M. J., Grosjean, M., & Knoblich, G. (2005). Continuous attraction toward phonological competitors. *Proceedings of the National Academy of Sciences of the United States of America, 102*(29), 10393–10398.

Sugar, C. A., & James, G. M. (2003). Finding the number of clusters in a dataset: An information-theoretic approach. *Journal of the American Statistical Association, 98*(463), 750–763.

Tibshirani, R., & Walther, G. (2005). Cluster validation by prediction strength. *Journal of Computational and Graphical Statistics, 14*(3), 511–528.

Tibshirani, R., Walther, G., & Hastie, T. (2001). Estimating the number of clusters in a data set via the gap statistic. *Journal of the Royal Statistical Society: Series B (Statistical Methodology), 63*(2), 411–423.

Tomlinson Jr, J. M., Bailey, T. M., & Bott, L. (2013). Possibly all of that and then some: Scalar implicatures are understood in two steps. *Journal of Memory and Language, 69*(1), 18–35.

Wirth, R., Pfister, R., & Kunde, W. (2016). Asymmetric transfer effects between cognitive and affective task disturbances. *Cognition and Emotion, 30*(3), 399–416.

Wong, A. L., Haith, A. M., & Krakauer, J. W. (2015). Motor planning. *The Neuroscientist, 21*(4), 385–398.

Wulff, D. U., Haslbeck, J. M. B., & Schulte-Mecklenbeck, M. (2019). *Measuring the (dis-)continuous mind: What movement trajectories reveal about cognition*. Manuscript in preparation.

Xiao, K., & Yamauchi, T. (2014). Semantic priming revealed by mouse movement trajectories. *Consciousness and Cognition, 27*, 42–52.

Yu, Z., Wang, F., Wang, D., & Bastin, M. (2012). Beyond reaction times: Incorporating mouse-tracking measures into the implicit association test to examine its underlying process. *Social Cognition, 30*(3), 289–306.

Zgonnikov, A., Aleni, A., Piiroinen, P. T., O'Hora, D., & di Bernardo, M. (2017). Decision landscapes: Visualizing mouse-tracking data. *Royal Society Open Science, 4*(11), 170482.

10

MOUSE-TRACKING TO UNDERSTAND REAL-TIME DYNAMICS OF SOCIAL COGNITION[1]

Benjamin S. Stillerman and Jonathan B. Freeman

In the early days of mouse-tracking, the method was deployed mainly for architectural debates centered on adjudicating between discrete-stage based, modular explanations of cognitive processing versus a more continuous and integrated view of the mind. This chapter traces the history and how it evolved into contemporary mouse-tracking research that features a diversity of theoretical perspectives seeking to answer novel questions across a range of topics, rather than focused squarely on architectural debates.

A typical computer mouse-tracking paradigm presents a rectangular screen and has participants click a start button at the bottom-center of the screen, revealing a stimulus. There are usually two response options at the top-left and top-right of the screen, although more than two response options may be present (see, e.g., Freeman, Nakayama, & Ambady, 2013). Participants usually have initiation deadlines (to start a mouse movement) and response deadlines (to choose a response) to impose pressure to begin their responses before they have finalized their choice, so that the decision process can be reflected in their unfolding mouse movements. The most popular dependent variable is attraction to an unchosen distractor response, operationalized as either maximum deviation (MD) away from the chosen response, as compared to an idealized direct path to the chosen response, or area-under-the-curve (AUC) of the trajectory. More sophisticated measures of the temporal dynamics of the mouse trajectory (like acceleration profiles—which is derived from changes in mouse position between time points—or the time of maximum deviation) can provide insights into the different stages of the cognitive processes underlying decisions. Similarly, taking a close look at the spatial dynamics of trajectories (such as the number of x-flips, or moments where trajectories switched their horizontal direction) can reveal cognitive processes in more detail.

For more detailed help to implement mouse-tracking studies—designing, collecting data, running analyses—see Freeman and Ambady (2010), Hehman, Stolier, and Freeman (2015), and Chapter 8. Free software for creating mouse-tracking experiments is available, for example, from www.mousetracker.org.

History and Rise of Mouse-Tracking

The first computer mouse-tracking experiments (e.g., Spivey, Grosjean, & Knoblich 2005) followed the tradition of research supporting continuous, dynamic, and parallel processing, which can be traced back to the influential connectionist models of the early 1980s (McClelland & Rumelhart, 1981; Rumelhart, Hinton, & McClelland, 1986). Connectionism challenged long-standing notions of modularity of mind and provided a key insight that formed the basis of mouse-tracking: if a stimulus's onset could initiate a cascade of neural events before each successive processing stage was complete, then motor responses could observably reflect ongoing processing (Cisek & Kalaska, 2005; Goodale, Pelisson, & Prablanc, 1986; Spivey & Dale, 2004). With this development, researchers could use continuous motor output to measure the nature of these overlapping stages, harnessing mouse-tracking to capture nuances in stimulus processing, for which the resolution of other methods was typically too coarse (e.g., reaction times, see Chapter 12 or eye-tracking see Chapters 1–5).

An early application of mouse-tracking was in the domain of spoken language processing, where Spivey et al. (2005) tracked participants' mouse trajectories towards images of objects as the names of those objects were being spoken. Researchers found that when the two candidate words shared the first syllable (e.g., "candle" and "candy"), mouse trajectories were partially attracted to the incorrect word, demonstrating that speech was being processed even before the word was pronounced in full. This threatened the dominant discrete stage-based models, which posited a strict separation between the perception and cognitive processing of the spoken stimuli. Whereas eye-tracking had previously yielded some evidence against an information encapsulation account of language comprehension, this approach was limited because of the discrete and ballistic nature of saccades, only allowing inferences as to whether processing conflict occurred in the midst of language comprehension (e.g., Tanenhaus, Spivey-Knowlton, Eberhard, & Sedivy, 1995). With mouse-tracking serving as a continuous output of response competition, one could observe graded partial activation of competing representations, or the extent of such conflicting activation within a single decision.

Discrete-stage, dual process models were directly tested against a continuous Dynamic Interactive (DI) model of social categorization and person perception (Freeman, Ambady, Rule, & Johnson, 2008; Freeman & Ambady, 2011a; Freeman & Johnson, 2016) with mouse-tracking by examining the distributional characteristic trajectories of every trial (Hehman et al., 2015). Although average mouse trajectories over an entire experimental block might exhibit a smooth path veering to unchosen distractor responses before the ultimate choice, if dual process accounts were correct, these averages would consist of two categorically distinct trial types: a) direct linear trajectories to the chosen response and b) two disjointed linear paths, one to the distractor response, reflecting an automatic response tendency, followed by a sudden correction towards the chosen response, reflecting a secondary control process coming online. Researchers can dissociate between these two accounts by examining the bimodality of the distribution of MDs, with a peak of small MDs corresponding to the direct paths to the correct response and a peak of large MDs corresponding to the disjointed paths (see Figure 10.1).

Therefore, simply ruling out a bimodal distribution can provide support for continuous and dynamic processing accounts (Freeman & Dale, 2013; for an alternative approach to identify trajectory types see Chapter 9).

However, some researchers proposed that a unimodal pattern of results could reflect two discrete cognitive mechanisms that are smoothly manifested by a continuous motor system (van der Wel, Eder, Mitchel, Walsh, & Rosenbaum, 2009). This explanation is less parsimonious because it presumes the presence of an encapsulated module for motor output, implying that motor executions receive a single (albeit changeable) response to execute. This contradicts evidence that motor neurons do in fact encode multiple directional signals (Cisek & Kalaska, 2005). Moreover, eye-tracking research has shown that incorrect candidate responses manifest in eye movements before response execution (Allopenna, Magnuson, & Tanenhaus, 1998; Dale, Kehoe, & Spivey,

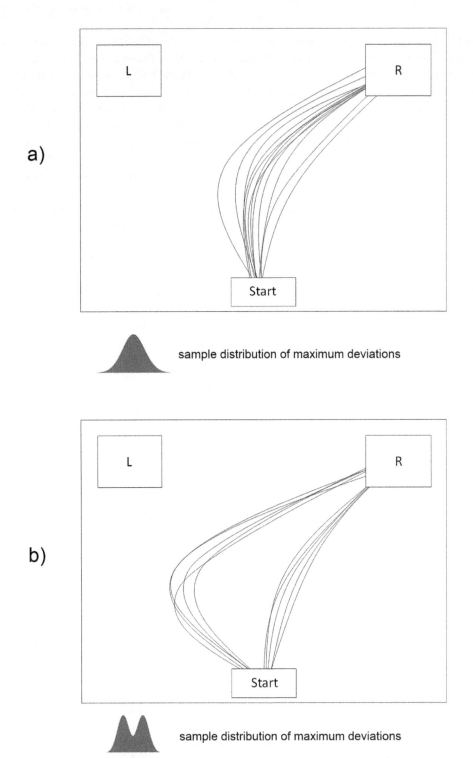

FIGURE 10.1 An example of unimodal and bimodal distributions of MD that would result in the same mean MD. In (a), each individual trajectory is smoothly attracted to the unchosen option in a graded fashion. In (b), some trajectories are direct towards the chosen option while some show an initial direct path to the unchosen option, followed by an abrupt shift towards the chosen option.

2007), raising questions about the plausibility of fully separate perceptual and motor modules. A closer examination of the timing of events, discussed in more detail later, also calls into question the plausibility of the van der Wel et al. (2009) account (Spivey, Dale, Knoblich, & Grosjean, 2010). Finally, mouse-tracking data, synchronized with fMRI, have been shown to mediate the relationship between neural indices of conflict processing and visual representations of to-be-categorized faces in a graded fashion (Stolier & Freeman, 2017; discussed later), consistent with a continuous and dynamic account of social categorization. It is therefore unlikely that uniformly smooth trajectories reflect discrete underlying cognitive processes. In light of this, recent years have seen an increased focus on continuous and dynamic frameworks (for a review focusing primarily on the domain of language comprehension, see Song & Nakayama, 2009).

Hidden, Competitive, and Parallel Activation

Beyond the debates between discrete and continuous processing, a major theoretical application of mouse-tracking has been testing the partial activation of multiple response options during a decision process. For example, within the framework of the DI model (Freeman & Ambady, 2011a; Freeman & Johnson, 2016), the act of slotting faces and other stimuli into social categories has been shown to involve dynamically unfolding competition between multiple possible categories that are activated at the same time. For instance, a gender-atypical male face (with some feminine cues) might temporarily activate representations of both gender categories, even if the face is ultimately resolved as male (see Figure 10.2; Freeman et al., 2008). Because no single face is a perfect exemplar of any category's prototype, faces will always evoke some degree of competition between categories, which then stabilizes over time into social categorical percepts.

Dynamic competition between activated response options has also been implicated in many domains other than face perception. In one experiment, researchers assessed the competition of evaluative categories (i.e., good and bad) of attitude objects, finding increased MDs for objects of more ambivalent evaluations (Schneider et al., 2015). An incomplete list of topics of inquiry in which experiments applied similar logic and task structure includes the categorization of animals (Dale et al., 2007), phonological competition during spoken word recognition (discussed earlier; Spivey et al., 2005), risky decision making (Koop & Johnson, 2013), semantic priming in written word comprehension (Finkbeiner, Song, Nakayama, & Caramazza, 2008), ambiguity resolution of discourse elements during sentence comprehension (Tomlinson, Bailey, & Bott, 2013), numerical cognition (Faulkenberry, 2014, 2016), moral decision making regarding distributive justice (Palmer, Paton, Barclay, & Hohwy, 2013), and truth judgments (McKinstry, Dale, & Spivey, 2008). Although some of these paradigms could be designed to elicit similar effects with reaction time differences, mouse-tracking is a more sensitive measure (Scherbaum, Gottschalk, Dshemuchadse, & Fischer, 2015).

While most of the previously mentioned work elicited category competition with the stimuli themselves, one important line of inquiry in our work with mouse-tracking and person perception is that perceptions do not occur inside a vacuum and may be subject to additional top-down influences of the environment, current goals, and prior knowledge and expectations (Freeman & Johnson, 2016). These top-down effects can alter the degree of activation of candidate social categories, which mouse-tracking can pick up on in ways similar to those just described. An example from the intergroup literature uses mouse-tracking to show that ingroup favoritism biases emotion category competition during emotion recognition of fearful and happy faces (Lazerus, Ingbretsen, Stolier, Freeman, & Cikara, 2016).

One study demonstrating such a top-down influence manipulated visual content surrounding faces to portray American or Chinese scene environments where perceivers would have a greater

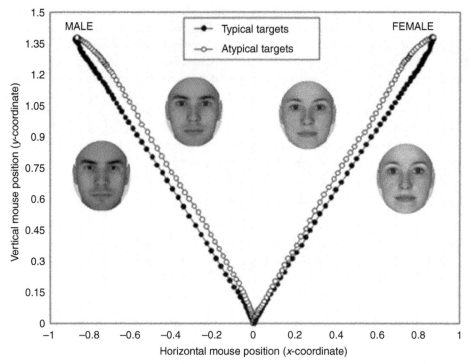

FIGURE 10.2 In a sex categorization task, participants' mouse trajectories deviated significantly more towards the unchosen response when the face was gender-atypical (e.g., man with feminine features), suggesting a stronger partial activation of the opponent category.

likelihood to expect a White or Asian face, respectively (Freeman, Ma, Han, & Ambady, 2013). Indeed, the scene influenced the competition between race categories such that an Asian face paired with an American scene would evoke trajectories exhibiting a partial attraction to the White response, indicating a biasing effect of the context on the evolving categorization of a face's race. In another study, faces along a continuum of Black to White were paired with attire indicating a high- or low-status occupation (see Figure 10.3; Freeman, Penner, Saperstein, Scheutz, & Ambady, 2011). A White face surrounded by low-status attire elicited trajectories that were initially attracted to the "Black" response, and a Black face surrounded by high-status attire elicited trajectories initially attracted to the "White" response, due to stereotypical associations in the U.S. associating Black Americans with low status and White Americans with high status. Both of these experiments exemplify the manner in which extra-facial cues of stimuli bear on social categorization by shifting the degree of parallel activation. Thus, parallel activation of multiple response categories may be driven by bottom-up factors, such as variability in facial features, as well as top-down factors, such as expectations from the environment in which a target is encountered or one's stereotypes.

An alternative to the parallel activation explanation is that, rather than a competition between multiple partially activated options, the relatively weaker activation of a single category option (due to, for example, ambiguity, noise, or non-prototypicality of the stimulus) results in more uncertainty leading up to the decision. Thus, this explanation favors the notion of a slower accumulation of evidence in favor of the selected response, rather than any competition among

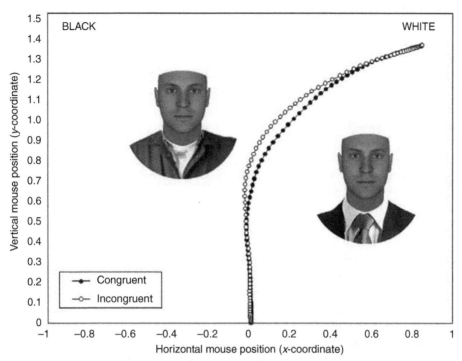

FIGURE 10.3 In a race categorization task, participants' mouse trajectories deviated significantly more towards the unchosen response when the faces were paired with attire stereotypically linked to that distractor response (e.g., a White face paired with low-status attire), suggesting a stronger partial activation of the opponent category, activated by a top-down influence of stereotypes.

response alternatives. This single category activation account is consistent with previous empirical work (e.g., Locke, Macrae, & Eaton, 2005) and could plausibly manifest similar attraction effects. However, if this were the case, the specific distractor category label would not influence mouse trajectories to the same stimuli. To return to the example of classifying a White face with Black-related features, an individual's mouse trajectories that ultimately end in the "White" category would exhibit the same maximum deviation to a category label of "Black" as to an irrelevant label, such as "Asian" (features of which are not present in the stimulus) because the ambiguity present in that face would be equal in both instances. Stolier and Freeman (2017) tested this very idea and ruled out a single activation account, finding that irrelevant distractor responses did not attract mouse trajectories when the stimuli did not depict any features of that response. The partial activation of multiple response option categories—rather than a graded amount of activation of a single category—has also been shown in the formation of explicit attitudes (Wojnowicz, Ferguson, Dale, & Spivey, 2009) and in the integration of auditory and visual gender cues (Freeman & Ambady, 2011c).

Temporal and Spatial Dynamics of Trajectories

One advantage mouse-tracking has over other implicit behavioral measures is its temporal resolution (Freeman & Ambady, 2010). By continuously streaming the coordinates of the hand's position over time, cascading mental events that manifest in motor output can be observed as they come online. Thus, research questions concerned with the order of rapidly unfolding cognitive processes can be tested using mouse-tracking. The temporal mouse-tracking is also well-suited to complement computational modeling approaches, particularly to behaviors that have already been extensively modeled (e.g., delay discounting in intertemporal choice). Similarly, by analyzing the spatial characteristics of trajectories, researchers can probe the discreteness versus continuity of cognitive processing outside of the traditional architectural debate. This is achieved by using more sophisticated measures such as acceleration profiles and x-flips, which are thought to reflect uncertainty and cognitive conflict (Cheng & González-Vallejo, 2017). As an example of an inquiry into the temporal sequence of psychological events, Freeman and Ambady (2011b) showed that the texture and pigmentation of faces exerts an influence 50 msec earlier that shapes information in classifying their gender, but not their age.

The temporal resolution of mouse-tracking allows for researchers to test hypotheses relating to how accessible different information is and at what time. For example, in the experiment discussed earlier, in which participants categorized faces as White or Asian that appeared in front of American or Asian background scenes, researchers were interested in how integrating the background information into the category judgment differed among American and Chinese participants, specifically in regards to timing. East Asian participants tend to process visual stimuli more holistically, gleaning information both from the focal and peripheral components of a stimulus, compared to participants from western cultures, who attend more analytically to the focal point (Masuda & Nisbett, 2001). Supporting this, Freeman et al. (2013) found that Chinese participants' mouse trajectories were biased by background scene earlier on in categorization than American participants, reflecting habitual or more automatic integration of peripheral information—indicative of holistic processing.

Another study leveraging the temporal precision of mouse-tracking investigated different factors contributing to intertemporal choices (Dshemuchadse, Scherbaum, & Goschke, 2013). Participants chose between smaller/sooner and larger/later monetary rewards, with the delay of the reward conveyed either as number of days in the future (e.g., "in seven days") or a calendar date (e.g., on November 13th). Researchers examined the angle of mouse movement (derived from the difference between current and previous mouse position) at every time point to establish the time intervals during which various sources of information were significant predictors of mouse angle. This method revealed that information about the magnitude and delay of monetary rewards were integrated into the decision process at different times, and that the timing of this integration depended on how the delay information was conveyed. When the delay was conveyed by a calendar date, the value of the reward more strongly influenced decisions mid-trajectory than the length of delay. Thus, careful examination of the temporal dynamics of trajectories ruled out competing explanations, like a general increase in deliberation when the delay information was conveyed by calendar date.

Other work has similarly focused on the timing of different sources of information related to self-control in a dieting context (Sullivan, Hutcherson, Harris, & Rangel, 2015). In deciding between food options, not only was tastiness information of the food integrated into the decision about 200 msec earlier than healthfulness information, but successfully inhibiting cravings for unhealthy food also depended on when tastiness information relative to healthfulness information was accessible.

In addition to the mere timing of processing, several cognitive abilities manifest in the spatial nature of trajectories, with smooth and abrupt changes to motor output and the underlying decision processes. If early certainty in an incorrect response nearly leads people to misinterpret the percepts they encounter, abrupt corrective measures might be required. The distinction between discrete and dynamic cognitive processes (manifested as abrupt and smooth motor trajectories, respectively) is important, as the two modes operate complementarily and have consequences for the outcomes of decisions. Investigations of this question often focus on the bimodality of the distribution of MDs (Freeman & Dale, 2013), as discussed earlier.

For example, successful exertion of self-control has been linked with more dynamic processing, with low self-control participants exhibiting abrupt shifts in trajectories more often in the domains of dieting and intertemporal choice (Stillman, Medvedev, & Ferguson, 2017). This may be due to a strong early activation of unhealthy choices or immediate rewards, which require a sudden correction late in the decision process. Additionally, the discreteness of processing has been investigated using mouse-tracking in the context of sentence comprehension, where past theories have described interpreting negation as a late-stage process that "flips" the meaning of a sentence (Wason, 1959). Consistent with this, participants evaluating the truth or sensibility of negated sentences demonstrated abrupt shifts in their trajectories, but this effect was erased by context that strongly predicted negations (Dale & Duran, 2011). Finally, during sex categorization of faces, both abrupt and smooth trajectories underlay decision processes and were sensitive to experimental context, reflecting, in some cases, a rapid reversal of early commitment to the incorrect category due to immediately salient sex-atypical features (e.g., long hair on a male; Freeman, 2014). These examples demonstrate the temporal and spatial characteristics of continuous motor paths (and their contextual sensitivity) and can bolster understanding provided by reaction time data on questions of when certain stimulus information is processed and how the dynamics of decisions evolve over time, influencing final outcomes.

Integrating Multiple Domains

Mouse-tracking is especially suited for measuring the real-time integration of multiple dimensions or attributes during a decision process. An example from the domain of social perception is the integration of information about race, gender, age, emotional state, and more all being rapidly gleaned from a quick glance at a face. These categories become conceptually entangled across dimensions, such that membership in a certain group biases categorization of another, due (at least in part) to overlapping stereotypes (Freeman & Ambady, 2011a). The DI Model, introduced earlier, theorizes that categories along one dimension (e.g., race) automatically activate stereotypes (as supported by traditional stereotyping theories, e.g., Blair & Banaji, 1996; Devine, 1989) and that these stereotypes can in turn initiate a cascading activation of categories along different dimensions (e.g., gender)—importantly, over and above whatever features of this category are present in the stimuli. The interaction of multiple dimensions of identity can be investigated using mouse-tracking, revealing the ways ostensibly unrelated aspects of a stimulus subtly interact and taint our perceptions.

For example, in the U.S., many stereotypes are shared by Black people and men (e.g., aggressive) and by Asian people and women (e.g., docile), leading to an overlap in mental representations of these groups. One study investigated this intersection of gender and race; when the gender and race of faces was systematically manipulated, mouse-tracking showed that gender categorization judgments of faces were biased by their race (Johnson, Freeman, & Pauker, 2012). That is, faces belonging to categories with incongruent or non-overlapping race and gender stereotypes (e.g., Black women or Asian men) induced more competition, such that trajectories showed greater MD to the incorrect gender category. This task was replicated using a slightly different paradigm (Freeman et al., 2013) and the same task structure was used by Hehman, Ingbretsen, and Freeman

(2014) to probe the intersection of race and emotion categories, specifically showing that stereotypes of Blacks as angry biased the category competition of both race and emotion judgments.

Aside from extracting information from faces, information can be inferred from body shape and movement, as well as voice quality providing cues to membership in various social groups. For example, Freeman and Ambady (2011c) presented participants with faces paired with voices that either reflected the same or opposing gender category. In making gender judgments, participants who viewed faces paired with sex-atypical vocal information (e.g., feminine male voice paired with male face) showed larger MDs to the opposing response option, suggesting that both audio and visual information jointly contributed to the activation of candidate gender categories.

Neural Correlates

Neuroscience can corroborate claims about cognitive processing that are commonly made on the basis of mouse-tracking (see also Chapters 8–9). Much research (including many mouse-tracking studies) on understanding decision processes has concentrated on the response conflict and resolution inherent to any process involving competition between candidate responses (Bartholow, 2010). Due to the anterior cingulate cortex's (ACC) well-established role in conflict processing (Botvinick, Braver, Barch, Carter, & Cohen, 2001), it is no surprise that it has been of great interest to those researchers working at the intersection of social cognition, vision sciences, decision science, and neuroscience. For example, faces that are less prototypical of their groups evoke more ACC activity, ostensibly in reaction to the higher conflict detection and resolution needs in categorizing these more difficult faces (Cassidy, Sprout, Freeman, & Krendl, 2017).

Further evidence of the ACC's importance in person perception and social categorization comes from a mouse-tracking study by Stolier and Freeman (2017), who linked data from synchronized fMRI trials to mouse-tracking from the same trials. Participants in this experiment classified faces either by gender or by race. The researchers observed an increased activation of the ACC to target faces belonging to race and gender categories with incongruent stereotypes associated with them (e.g., Asian men: Asian—docile; man—aggressive). Additionally, participants' neural patterns in the fusiform gyrus (FG; an important region for visual processing of faces, especially at a categorical level; Kanwisher & Yovel, 2006; Rotshtein, Henson, Treves, Driver, & Dolan, 2005) in response to atypical target faces were systematically skewed towards the opposing category (e.g., an atypical male target's neural pattern exhibited a similarity towards the average female pattern). Furthermore, mouse-tracking data revealed that on a trial-by-trial basis, mouse-trajectory deviation mediated the effect of multi-voxel pattern similarity in the FG on the increased engagement of the ACC. Thus, when categorizing a face, the extent to which the FG's pattern was closer towards the opposing category predicted greater mouse-trajectory deviation on that trial, which in turn predicted greater engagement of the ACC; and the trajectory deviation effect mediated the relationship between the FG and ACC. Researchers have also linked mouse trajectories to activity in the dlPFC, which is thought to inhibit automatically activated response tendencies (Chee, Sriram, Soon, & Lee, 2000), to provide further support both for this conflict-resolution model of social categorization and for the validity of interpretations of mouse-tracking data (Hehman et al., 2014). Together, these results suggest that visual representations involved in categorization judgments (in the FG) reflect multiple partially active categories, and that the ACC and dlPFC are recruited to resolve competition between them.

Apart from the conflict inherent to competitive categorization processes, one important network identified as central to social sorting is comprised of the anterior temporal lobe (ATL), the orbitofrontal cortex (OFC), and the FG (Freeman & Johnson, 2016). A key insight of this work posits that conceptual stereotype information may project to visual regions to bias the perceptual representations of stimuli, as predicted by the DI Model. Work pairing brain imaging and mouse-tracking has begun fruitful investigations into the interplay of these three regions.

Recent social neuroscience research on the OFC has suggested its role in imposing higher-order expectations on "early" visual processing brain regions, consistent with neuroscientific models in non-social domains (see, e.g., Bar et al., 2006; Summerfield & Egner, 2009). Indeed, the OFC has been shown to pattern with FG face representations, falling in line with social category dimensions that have become entwined due to shared stereotypes (as discussed earlier). Specifically, Stolier and Freeman (2016) collected participants' ratings of how stereotypical various traits were to different race, gender, and emotion categories, providing an assessment of conceptual stereotype similarity or overlap of these categories. They then tracked mouse trajectories during race, gender, and emotion face judgments to assess participants' idiosyncratic perceptual biases (e.g., bias to perceive Black faces as angry or female faces as happy; see Freeman, Johnson, Adams, & Ambady, 2012). Finally, participants passively viewed faces manipulated along these three dimensions (e.g., a happy Asian male face) in an fMRI scanner (see Chapter 15). Each participant's degree of biased conceptual similarity between any pair of social categories (as indexed by stereotype ratings) predicted the degree of biased perceptual similarity of those categories (as indexed by MD), which predicted biased neural-pattern similarity in the OFC and FG, over and above any bottom-up visual similarity of the faces. For example, the extent to which a participant stereotypically linked Black and anger categories together predicted the extent to which their mouse trajectories revealed a bias to perceive those faces similarly (i.e., deviation towards "angry" for a happy Black face). This in turn predicted greater similarity in OFC and FG patterns associated with those categories in response to faces. By showing such biasing effects in the FG, these findings add to the growing view that conceptual knowledge of stereotypes may impinge on face representations in visual representation.

Neuroscientific inquiries into cognition have recently begun to include mouse-tracking to answers outside the domain of social cognition, for example, in the domain of intertemporal choice (Calluso, Tosoni, Pezzulo, Spadone, & Committeri, 2015). However, these approaches could be adapted to the study of many other kinds of psychological processes.

Connecting to the Real World

Being able to predict behavior or real-world outcomes opens up the possibility to ask novel questions about how rapid and effortless categorization dynamics relate to more complex psychological phenomena. A small number of experiments have used mouse-tracking to predict large-scale social behaviors, but there are many possible facets of individual behaviors that may be explained by early categorization processes, given the extent to which quickly ascertained social information can be predictive of later impressions and outcomes (Ambady, Koo, Rosenthal, & Winograd, 2002).

Across a pair of studies, Hehman, Carpinella, Johnson, Leitner, and Freeman (2014) demonstrated that the gendered facial features of U.S. political candidates predicted their ultimate electoral success exclusively for female candidates, and that this was more pronounced among more politically conservative perceivers. The researchers found that a greater activation of the male category when perceiving female candidates' faces (i.e., greater gender-category competition), as indexed by mouse trajectory attraction to the opposite gender response, was associated with negative outcomes for those candidates. Women whose faces elicited less gender-category competition enjoyed higher chances at electoral success and higher margins of victory, even when controlling for other factors known to influence electoral success such as perceived attractiveness and competence. Subsequent work (e.g., Carpinella, Chen, Hamilton, & Johnson, 2015; Carpinella, Hehman,

Freeman, & Johnson, 2015) has replicated and extended this work to clarify the interacting role of political orientation and candidate gender and the timing with which these processes occur.

Such studies exemplify the importance of real-time perceptual and cognitive dynamics in shaping decisions and explaining substantial and consequential facets of behavior. Future research could further investigate when and how rapid categorization dynamics predict downstream behavioral outcomes, as well as how small changes in early person perception may potentially reduce pervasive expressions of bias. Moreover, such links between real-time and real-world dynamics are hardly limited to the domain of social perception.

The Future of Mouse-Tracking

As is evident from this review of current theoretical and methodological advancements, mouse-tracking is being increasingly used across the psychological sciences. Although the use of this method is becoming more widespread, there remains a potential for methodological refinement, as well as many unexplored avenues for future research.

One study (Stolier & Freeman, 2017, discussed earlier) has synchronized mouse-tracking and fMRI data to elucidate the nature of mouse-tracking effects on a trial-by-trial basis. This allows greater insight into the psychological mechanisms at play because more data is available to describe the same event. That is, rather than simply linking experiment-wide mouse-tracking and fMRI data, every single trial has both neural indices and behavioral markers of decision processes. Further, pairing mouse-tracking with other methodologies, including EEG (electroencephalography) and eye-tracking (e.g., Koop & Johnson, 2013; Quétard et al., 2016; Norman & Schulte-Mecklenbeck, 2010), unanswered questions may be addressed in enlightening ways. As mouse-tracking is a relatively noninvasive behavioral measure, the practical considerations for incorporating it into other research paradigms are minimal.

Additional new analysis techniques of mouse-tracking data have provided measures that can assess aspects of cognitive processes that have not previously been examined. The Entropic Mouse Tracker (EMOT) approach (Calcagnì, Lombardi, & Sulpizio, 2017) represents one such methodological innovation. The EMOT approach transforms the spatial information of mouse-tracking data to extract fast movements and momentary pauses, manifestations of uncertainty in the decision process. In a lexical decision task this analysis method was shown to differentiate levels of uncertainty in responding to frequent words, infrequent words, pseudowords, and nonsense strings. In recent years, computational approaches have been applied to mouse-tracking data in the context of well-modeled behavior, like intertemporal choice (Calluso, Committeri, Pezzulo, Lepora, & Tosoni, 2015; O'Hora, Carey, Kervick, Crowley, & Dabrowski, 2016; Scherbaum et al., 2016). In this domain, researchers have used principal components analysis to isolate aspects of mouse trajectories and link them to similar constructs like conflict and uncertainty (Cheng & González-Vallejo, 2017). Additional computational modeling techniques may allow for yet more nuanced questions and novel hypothesis testing.

Besides mouse-tracking's methodological advancements, many more empirical tests of theories can leverage the method. Investigations of self-control processes lend themselves naturally to mouse-tracking paradigms because how certain response tendencies are inhibited and overridden is a central phenomenon of interest. In the context of face processing and categorization, this has been explored extensively. However, self-control's role has traditionally been studied in a wider variety of behaviors and psychological processes, including goal pursuit, self-regulatory failures, and clinical disorders such as social anxiety that have been associated with control deficits. Such programs of research can benefit from the application of mouse-tracking.

That said, future research could also better address what aspects of mouse-tracking effects reflect automatic and controlled processing, including their interplay. Mouse-tracking is frequently described as an implicit measure, which is sensible in some respects, but many may take issue with overt manual behavior being described as implicit. Moreover, far more research could be undertaken to explore whether certain mouse-tracking effects (e.g., deviation effects) meet formal definitions of automaticity in certain tasks (Bargh, Schwader, Hailey, Dyer, & Boothby, 2012) or alternatively whether they reflect more deliberate control processes in certain tasks. These issues would have important theoretical relevance across a variety of domains, but also from a methodological perspective, it would be helpful to determine the particular task contexts, stimulus timing, response deadlines, and other experimental details (e.g., starting parameters, Scherbaum & Kieslich, 2017) to allow the paradigm to best reflect more automatic and implicit processes (or alternatively controlled or explicit processes).

Future mouse-tracking research should also expand its emphasis to predict behavior in a wider range of contexts. As covered in this chapter, a select few studies have predicted large-scale social behavior on the basis of subtle inflections in response trajectories. By contrast, a somewhat simpler extension would be to predict individual or smaller-scale behavior on this basis. Across multiple fields, there are countless precedents for predicting behavior in intergroup dyadic settings, long-term dieting and health success, and clinical prognoses. Mouse-tracking has the potential to improve researchers' ability to accurately forecast these real-world consequences and, possibly, bring about more desirable outcomes.

Note

1   This work was supposed in part by research grant NSF BCS-1423708 to JBF.

References

Allopenna, P. D., Magnuson, J. S., & Tanenhaus, M. K. (1998). Tracking the time course of spoken word recognition using eye movements: Evidence for continuous mapping models. *Journal of Memory and Language, 38*(4), 419–439.

Ambady, N., Koo, J., Rosenthal, R., & Winograd, C. H. (2002). Physical therapists' nonverbal communication predicts geriatric patients' health outcomes. *Psychology and Aging, 17*(3), 443–452.

Bar, M., Kassam, K. S., Ghuman, A. S., Boshyan, J., Schmid, A. M., Dale, A. M., … Rosen, B. R. (2006). Top-down facilitation of visual recognition. *Proceedings of the National Academy of Sciences of the United States of America, 103*(2), 449–454.

Bargh, J. A., Schwader, K. L., Hailey, S. E., Dyer, R. L., & Boothby, E. J. (2012). Automaticity in social-cognitive processes. *Trends in Cognitive Sciences, 16*(12), 593–605.

Bartholow, B. D. (2010). On the role of conflict and control in social cognition: Event-related brain potential investigations. *Psychophysiology, 47*(2), 201–212.

Blair, I. V., & Banaji, M. R. (1996). Automatic and controlled processes in stereotype priming. *Journal of Personality and Social Psychology, 70*(6), 1142–1163.

Botvinick, M. M., Braver, T. S., Barch, D. M., Carter, C. S., & Cohen, J. D. (2001). Conflict monitoring and cognitive control. *Psychological Review, 108*(3), 624–652.

Calcagnì, A., Lombardi, L., & Sulpizio, S. (2017). Analyzing spatial data from mouse tracker methodology: An entropic approach. *Behavior Research Methods, 49*(6), 2012–2030.

Calluso, C., Committeri, G., Pezzulo, G., Lepora, N., & Tosoni, A. (2015). Analysis of hand kinematics reveals inter-individual differences in intertemporal decision dynamics. *Experimental Brain Research, 233*(12), 3597–3611.

Calluso, C., Tosoni, A., Pezzulo, G., Spadone, S., & Committeri, G. (2015). Interindividual variability in functional connectivity as long-term correlate of temporal discounting. *PLOS ONE, 10*(3), e0119710.

Carpinella, C. M., Chen, J. M., Hamilton, D. L., & Johnson, K. L. (2015). Gendered facial cues influence race categorizations. *Personality and Social Psychology Bulletin, 41*(3), 405–419.

Carpinella, C. M., Hehman, E., Freeman, J. B., & Johnson, K. L. (2015). The Gendered face of partisan politics: Consequences of facial sex typicality for vote choice. *Political Communication, 33*(1), 21–38.

Cassidy, B. S., Sprout, G. T., Freeman, J. B., & Krendl, A. C. (2017). Looking the part (to me): Effects of racial prototypicality on race perception vary by prejudice. *Social Cognitive and Affective Neuroscience, 12*(4), 685–694.

Chee, M. W., Sriram, N., Soon, C. S., & Lee, K. M. (2000). Dorsolateral prefrontal cortex and the implicit association of concepts and attributes. *Neuroreport, 11*(1), 135–140.

Cheng, J., & González-Vallejo, C. (2017). Action dynamics in intertemporal choice reveal different facets of decision process. *Journal of Behavioral Decision Making, 30*(1), 107–122.

Cisek, P., & Kalaska, J. F. (2005). Neural correlates of reaching decisions in dorsal premotor cortex: Specification of multiple direction choices and final selection of action. *Neuron, 45*(5), 801–814.

Dale, R., & Duran, N. D. (2011). The cognitive dynamics of negated sentence verification. *Cognitive Science, 35*(5), 983–996.

Dale, R., Kehoe, C., & Spivey, M. J. (2007). Graded motor responses in the time course of categorizing atypical exemplars. *Memory & Cognition, 35*(1), 15–28.

Devine, P. (1989). Stereotypes and prejudice: Their automatic and controlled components. *Journal of Personality and Social Psychology, 56*(1), 5–18.

Dshemuchadse, M., Scherbaum, S., & Goschke, T. (2013). How decisions emerge: Action dynamics in intertemporal decision making. *Journal of Experimental Psychology: General, 142*(1), 93–100.

Faulkenberry, T. J. (2014). Hand movements reflect competitive processing in numerical cognition. *Canadian Journal Experimental Psychology, 68*(3), 147–151.

Faulkenberry, T. J. (2016). Testing a direct mapping versus competition account of response dynamics in number comparison. *Journal of Cognitive Psychology, 28*(7), 825–842.

Finkbeiner, M., Song, J. H., Nakayama, K., & Caramazza, A. (2008). Engaging the motor system with masked orthographic primes: A kinematic analysis. *Visual Cognition, 16*(1), 11–22.

Freeman, J. B. (2014). Abrupt category shifts during real-time person perception. *Psychonomic Bulletin & Review, 21*(1), 85–92.

Freeman, J. B., Ambady, N., Rule, N. O., & Johnson, K. L. (2008). Will a category cue attract you? Motor output reveals dynamic competition across person construal. *Journal of Experimental Psychology: General, 137*(4), 673–690.

Freeman, J. B., & Ambady, N. (2010). MouseTracker: Software for studying real-time mental processing using a computer mouse-tracking method. *Behavior Research Methods, 42*(1), 226–241.

Freeman, J. B., & Ambady, N. (2011a). A dynamic interactive theory of person construal. *Psychological Review, 118*(2), 247–279.

Freeman, J. B., & Ambady, N. (2011b). Hand movements reveal the time-course of shape and pigmentation processing in social categorization. *Psychonomic Bulletin & Review, 18*(4), 705–712.

Freeman, J. B., & Ambady, N. (2011c). When two become one: Temporally dynamic integration of the face and voice. *Journal of Experimental Social Psychology, 47*(1), 259–263.

Freeman, J. B., & Dale, R. (2013). Assessing bimodality to detect the presence of a dual cognitive process. *Behavior Research Methods, 45*(1), 83–97.

Freeman, J. B., & Johnson, K. L. (2016). More than meets the eye: Split-second social perception. *Trends in Cognitive Sciences, 20*(5), 362–374.

Freeman, J. B., Johnson, K. L., Adams, R. B., Jr., & Ambady, N. (2012). The social-sensory interface: Category interactions in person perception. *Frontiers in Integrative Neuroscience, 8*(81), 1–13.

Freeman, J. B., Ma, Y., Han, S., & Ambady, N. (2013). Influences of culture and visual context on real-time social categorization. *Journal of Experimental Social Psychology, 49*(2), 206–210.

Freeman, J. B., Nakayama, K., & Ambady, N. (2013). Finger in flight reveals parallel categorization across multiple social dimensions. *Social Cognition, 31*(6), 792–805.

Freeman, J. B., Penner, A. M., Saperstein, A., Scheutz, M., & Ambady, N. (2011). Looking the part: Social status cues shape race perception. *PLOS ONE, 6*(9), e25107.

Goodale, M. A., Pelisson, D., & Prablanc, C. (1986). Large adjustments in visually guided reaching do not depend on vision of the hand or perception of target displacement. *Nature, 320*(6064), 748–750.

Hehman, E., Carpinella, C. M., Johnson, K. L., Leitner, J. B., & Freeman, J. B. (2014). Early processing of gendered facial cues predicts the electoral success of female politicians. *Social Psychological and Personality Science*, *5*(7), 815–824.

Hehman, E., Ingbretsen, Z. A., & Freeman, J. B. (2014). The neural basis of stereotypic impact on multiple social categorization. *Neuroimage*, *101*, 704–711.

Hehman, E., Stolier, R. M., & Freeman, J. B. (2015). Advanced mouse-tracking analytic techniques for enhancing psychological science. *Group Processes & Intergroup Relations*, *18*(3), 384–401.

Johnson, K. L., Freeman, J. B., & Pauker, K. (2012). Race is gendered: How covarying phenotypes and stereotypes bias sex categorization. *Journal of Personality and Social Psychology*, *102*(1), 116–131.

Kanwisher, N., & Yovel, G. (2006). The fusiform face area: a cortical region specialized for the perception of faces. *Philosophical Transactions of the Royal Society of London. Series B: Biological Sciences*, *361*(1476), 2109–2128.

Koop, G. J., & Johnson, J. G. (2013). The response dynamics of preferential choice. *Cognitive Psychology*, *67*(4), 151–185.

Lazerus, T., Ingbretsen, Z. A., Stolier, R. M., Freeman, J. B., & Cikara, M. (2016). Positivity bias in judging ingroup members' emotional expressions. *Emotion*, *16*(8), 1117–1125.

Locke, V., Macrae, C. N., & Eaton, J. L. (2005). Is person categorization modulated by exemplar typicality? *Social Cognition*, *23*(5), 417–428.

Masuda, T., & Nisbett, R. E. (2001). Attending holistically versus analytically: Comparing the context sensitivity of Japanese and Americans. *Journal of Personality and Social Psychology*, *81*(5), 922–934.

McClelland, J. L., & Rumelhart, D. E. (1981). An interactive activation model of context effects in letter perception: Part 1. An account of basic findings. *Psychological Review*, *88*, 375–407.

McKinstry, C., Dale, R., & Spivey, M. J. (2008). Action dynamics reveal parallel competition in decision making. *Psychological Science*, *19*(1), 22–24.

Norman, E., & Schulte-Mecklenbeck, M. (2010). Take a quick click at that! Mouselab and eye-tracking as tools to measure intuition. In A. Glöckner & C. L. M. Witteman (Eds.), *Foundations for tracing intuition: Challenges and methods* (pp. 24–44). New York, NY: Psychology Press.

O'Hora, D., Carey, R., Kervick, A., Crowley, D., & Dabrowski, M. (2016). Decisions in motion: Decision dynamics during intertemporal choice reflect subjective evaluation of delayed rewards. *Scientific Reports*, *6*, 1–17.

Palmer, C. J., Paton, B., Barclay, L., & Hohwy, J. (2013). Equality, efficiency, and sufficiency: Responding to multiple parameters of distributive justice during charitable distribution. *Review of Philosophy and Psychology*, *4*(4), 659–674.

Quétard, B., Quinton, J. C., Mermillod, M., Barca, L., Pezzulo, G., Colomb, M., & Izaute, M. (2016). Differential effects of visual uncertainty and contextual guidance on perceptual decisions: Evidence from eye and mouse tracking in visual search. *Journal of Vision*, *16*(11), 28.

Rotshtein, P., Henson, R. N. A., Treves, A., Driver, J., & Dolan, R. J. (2005). Morphing Marilyn into Maggie dissociates physical and identity face representations in the brain. *Nature Neuroscience*, *8*(1), 107–113.

Rumelhart, D. E., Hinton, G. E., & McClelland, J. L. (1986). *A general framework for parallel distributed processing*. Cambridge, MA: MIT Press.

Scherbaum, S., Frisch, S., Leiberg, S., Lade, S. J., Goschke, T., & Dshemuchadse, M. (2016). Process dynamics in delay discounting decisions: An attractor dynamics approach. *Judgment and Decision Making*, *11*(5), 472–495.

Scherbaum, S., Gottschalk, C., Dshemuchadse, M., & Fischer, R. (2015). Action dynamics in multitasking: The impact of additional task factors on the execution of the prioritized motor movement. *Frontiers in Psychology*, *6*, 934.

Scherbaum, S., & Kieslich, P. J. (2017). Stuck at the starting line: How the starting procedure influences mouse-tracking data. *Behavior Research Methods*, 1–14.

Schneider, I. K., van Harreveld, F., Rotteveel, M., Topolinski, S., van der Pligt, J., Schwarz, N., & Koole, S. L. (2015). The path of ambivalence: tracing the pull of opposing evaluations using mouse trajectories. *Frontiers in Psychology*, *6*, 1–12.

Song, J. H., & Nakayama, K. (2009). Hidden cognitive states revealed in choice reaching tasks. *Trends in Cognitive Sciences*, *13*(8), 360–366.

Spivey, M. J., & Dale, R. (2004). The continuity of mind: Toward a dynamical account of cognition. In B. H. Ross (Ed.), *Psychology of learning and motivation: Advances in research and theory* (Vol. 45, pp. 87–142). San Diego, CA: Elsevier.

Spivey, M. J., Dale, R., Knoblich, G., & Grosjean, M. (2010). Do curved reaching movements emerge from competing perceptions? A reply to van der Wel et al. (2009). *Journal of Experimental Psychology: Human Perception and Performance, 36*(1), 251–254.

Spivey, M. J., Grosjean, M., & Knoblich, G. (2005). Continuous attraction toward phonological competitors. *Proceedings of the National Academy of Sciences of the United States of America, 102*(29), 10393–10398.

Stillman, P. E., Medvedev, D., & Ferguson, M. J. (2017). Resisting temptation: Tracking how self-control conflicts are successfully resolved in real time. *Psychological Science, 28*(9), 1240–1258.

Stolier, R. M., & Freeman, J. B. (2016). Neural pattern similarity reveals the inherent intersection of social categories. *Nature Neuroscience, 19*(6), 795–797.

Stolier, R. M., & Freeman, J. B. (2017). A neural mechanism of social categorization. *Journal of Neuroscience, 37*(23), 5711–5721.

Sullivan, N., Hutcherson, C., Harris, A., & Rangel, A. (2015). Dietary self-control is related to the speed with which attributes of healthfulness and tastiness are processed. *Psychological Science, 26*(2), 122–134.

Summerfield, C., & Egner, T. (2009). Expectation (and attention) in visual cognition. *Trends in Cognitive Sciences, 13*(9), 403–409.

Tanenhaus, M. K., Spivey-Knowlton, M. J., Eberhard, K. M., & Sedivy, J. C. (1995). Integration of visual and linguistic information in spoken language comprehension. *Science, 268*(5217), 1632–1634.

Tomlinson, J. M., Bailey, T. M., & Bott, L. (2013). Possibly all of that and then some: Scalar implicatures are understood in two steps. *Journal of Memory and Language, 69*(1), 18–35.

van der Wel, R. P. R. D., Eder, J. R., Mitchel, A. D., Walsh, M. W., & Rosenbaum, D. A. (2009). Trajectories emerging from discrete versus continuous processing models in phonological competitor tasks: A commentary on Spivey, Grosjean, and Knoblich (2005). *Journal of Experimental Psychology: Human Perception and Performance, 35*(2), 588–594.

Wason, P. C. (1959). The processing of positive and negative information. *Quarterly Journal of Experimental Psychology, 11*(2), 92–107.

Wojnowicz, M. T., Ferguson, M. J., Dale, R., & Spivey, M. J. (2009). The self-organization of explicit attitudes. *Psychological Science, 20*(11), 1428–1435.

11

MEASURING ELECTRODERMAL ACTIVITY AND ITS APPLICATIONS IN JUDGMENT AND DECISION-MAKING RESEARCH

Bernd Figner, Ryan O. Murphy, and Paul Siegel

The skin has electric properties that change on the relatively short time-scale of seconds and are closely related to psychological processes. These characteristics of skin, known for more than 100 years, have been widely used in research (see also Chapter 13). Changes in electrodermal activity (EDA) and skin conductance are related to changes in eccrine sweating which are, in turn, related to activity in the sympathetic branch of the autonomic nervous system (ANS). Accordingly, EDA measures have been used to study psychological processes related to sympathetic arousal. For example, skin conductance has become an important tool in studying affective processes because the ANS plays a significant role in emotion and motivation. While increasingly direct methods of assessing neural activity have been developed recently (e.g., fMRI and PET), skin conductance is still often used as a proxy for neural and brain activity because it is relatively cheap and can be measured unobtrusively, reliably, and accurately.

It is important to note that skin conductance is a multifaceted phenomenon and does not reflect a single psychological process. Thus, EDA and skin conductance have been used in a wide array of behavioral and neuroscientific research, serving as an indicator of attention, habituation, arousal, and cognitive effort in many different subdomains of psychology and related disciplines. In judgment and decision-making (JDM) research, skin conductance is often used as an indicator of affective processes and emotional arousal. Therefore the renewed interest in skin conductance in JDM is most likely related to the renaissance of affect and emotion in JDM in general, as part of what has been termed the emotions revolution (Weber & Johnson, 2009).

Skin conductance is well suited as a process tracing method. It can be measured virtually continuously and relatively unobtrusively. Further it provides information about otherwise hidden cognitive and affective processes that reflect the ways in which people make decisions and form judgments. It follows that skin conductance is a viable method in process tracing studies as it can serve, for example, as an indicator of the involvement of affective and emotional processes in judgment and choice. However, there are several peculiarities about the nature of skin conductance that one has to be familiar with and take into account in order to measure and interpret it successfully. The main goal of this chapter is to give an introduction to the use of skin conductance in JDM research with a focus on providing concrete and hands-on advice for the researchers who are unfamiliar with this psychophysiological measure but are interested in using it in their own research.

In this chapter, we focus on the type of EDA measurement and indicator most commonly used in JDM research—the skin conductance response (SCR). Concentrating primarily on advice regarding the practical steps involved in using skin conductance, we give only a brief overview of the physiological background of EDA, and then delve into pragmatic issues concerning its assessment. Our discussion of practical concerns starts with a description of the needed equipment, the setup of the skin conductance acquisition, and electrode placement, followed by considerations regarding task and study design, and ends with explanations of approaches for the preprocessing and statistical analysis of skin conductance data. We give most attention to more traditional and standard ways of study design and data analysis. However, we also briefly outline more recent—sometimes called model-based—data analysis approaches and we give some pointers towards the relevant literature and toolboxes so that researchers interested in using these more advanced methods have some starting points to delve into these approaches. It is important to mention that there is compelling evidence that some of these more recent methods may outperform more conventional analysis in terms of their sensitivity (see, e.g., Bach, 2014). Furthermore, these newer approaches are likely to be appropriate for a wider range of experimental designs (such as rapid-event designs). We hope that our chapter can help the reader make an informed decision about how to approach their analysis. Thus, while we focus here on the more conventional analysis approach (see also the 2012 recommendations by the Society for Psychophysiological Research, published in Boucsein et al., 2012), we strongly recommend that readers also look into the more recent analysis approaches. In the last section of our chapter, we list some recommended literature, including the excellent volume by Boucsein (2012) which gives detailed information about virtually all aspects of EDA.

Electrodermal Activity and Skin Conductance: Terminology and Background

Different terms have been used in the literature to refer to aspects of electrodermal activity and skin conductance, sometimes interchangeably. Thus, some clarification is in order. In 1967, the Society of Psychophysiological Research (Brown, 1967; see also Boucsein, 2012; Boucsein et al., 2012) published a proposal for a standardized terminology that has been widely accepted. The term electrodermal activity (EDA) was introduced by Johnson and Lubin (1966) and refers most generally to all (passive and active) electrical phenomena in the skin, while skin conductance is one form of EDA. Specifically, the term skin conductance refers to how well the skin conducts electricity when an external direct current of constant voltage is applied. Skin conductance is measured in microsiemens (μS).[1] Other measures of EDA are distinguished based on technical aspects of the assessment: EDA recordings that do not use an external current are called endosomatic, while recordings that do use an external current (such as skin conductance) are called exosomatic. Exosomatic techniques are further distinguished by whether a direct current (DC) or an alternating current (AC) is used. DC measurement that keeps the voltage constant is called skin conductance, as it reflects how well the skin conducts a current. DC measurement that keeps the current constant is called skin resistance, as it reflects the electrical resistance of the skin. For the case of AC, keeping effective *voltage* constant results in the measure of skin admittance, while keeping effective *current* constant results in skin impedance.

As previously mentioned, skin conductance is the most commonly used measure in JDM and thus we focus on it here. Skin conductance can be divided into tonic and phasic phenomena. The main differences between these phenomena are related to their time-scale and their relationship to the evoking stimuli.

Figure 11.1 shows a raw skin conductance signal from one participant in a risky decision making experiment using the "hot" Columbia Card Task (CCT; Figner et al., 2009; Figner &

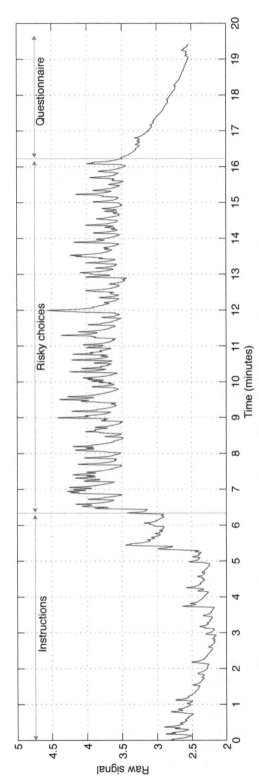

FIGURE 11.1 Raw skin conductance signal from one participant over the course of an experiment using the hot version of the Columbia Card Task (see Figner, Mackinlay, Wilkening, & Weber, 2009; Figner & Weber, 2011).

Weber, 2011).[2] The first 6 minutes of the session were used for administrative tasks, instructions, and practice trials. Then, starting at minute 6.2 and ending at minute 16.2 (see the area between the left and right vertical gray lines in Figure 11.1), the participant made incentivized risky choices in the computer-based hot CCT, which gave the participant real-time feedback regarding the outcomes of their choices. From minute 16.5 on, the participant filled out a questionnaire. In these 20 minutes of skin conductance data, one can see an overall and relatively slow drifting of the signal on which there are superimposed short (i.e., over the span of a few seconds) changes in skin conductance (seen as sharp peaks in Figure 11.1).

The longer-term manifestations are tonic, seen in the relatively low overall level in the "Instructions" and the "Questionnaire" phases versus the relatively elevated level during the "Risky choices" phase. The most common measure of this aspect of the data is the skin conductance level (SCL). This measure describes the overall conductivity of the skin over longer time intervals, typically ranging from tens of seconds to tens of minutes.

Within (and largely independent of) these different SCL levels, many sharp peaks in skin conductance can be seen. These short modulations in the signal are phasic phenomena and each peak represents an individual skin conductance response (SCR).[3] An SCR is a discrete and short fluctuation in skin conductance that lasts several seconds and usually follows a characteristic pattern of an initial, relatively steep rise, a short peak, and then a relatively slower return to baseline (see Figure 11.2). SCRs reflect the higher-frequency variability of the signal that is modulated on top of the slower changes in SCL.

In traditional analyses, SCL is typically operationalized by taking the average of several discrete measurement points distributed across the time window of interest (Boucsein, 2012). These measurement points should not be taken during an SCR (as this would lead to an overestimation of SCL), complicating automated approaches to quantify SCL.[4] In contrast to the SCRs, it is assumed that the SCL is *not* directly related to particular stimuli, but indicative of a more general level of arousal. Accordingly, since not all observable SCRs are directly related to an observable stimulus, a second, though less common, measure of *tonic* skin conductance has been suggested—the frequency of sometimes called non-specific (also called spontaneous) SCRs per time unit (usually per minute; typically, 1–3 per minute of these non-specific SCRs are observed during rest, Dawson, Schell, & Filion, 2007). As pragmatic criterion whether a SCR is specific (i.e., related to a stimulus) or non-specific, Boucsein (2012) suggests that SCRs that start more than 5 seconds after the end of a stimulus should be categorized as non-specific. We focus on SCR, the main indicator of *phasic* changes, because it is more commonly used in JDM research and typically will be better suited for process tracing studies due to its relatedness to specific events. SCR can also be operationalized across shorter time intervals than SCL (for a study using both SCL and SCR, see Nagai, Critchley, Featherstone, Trimble, & Dolan, 2004). SCRs have been quantified using various characteristics and measures (see Figure 11.2, and Boucsein, 2012). The onset latency (lat.) is the time between the onset of the stimulus and the start of an SCR, typically 1 to 3 sec. The rise time (ris.t.) is the time between the onset of the SCR and its peak amplitude, typically also 1 to 3 sec. The amplitude (amp.) is the difference between the conductivity at the onset (the baseline) and the peak. The recovery half time (rec.t/2) is also sometimes used but it is highly correlated with rise time and therefore somewhat redundant (Venables & Christie, 1980). Frequency (freq.) of SCRs per time unit is another measure to quantify skin conductance responses. We will focus on the measures most commonly used in JDM research, which are amplitude (particularly in older research) as well as the more recent indicator *area bounded by a curve* (see Figure 11.6 and explanations later). This latter measure is better suited for automated data analysis as it captures both the amplitude and

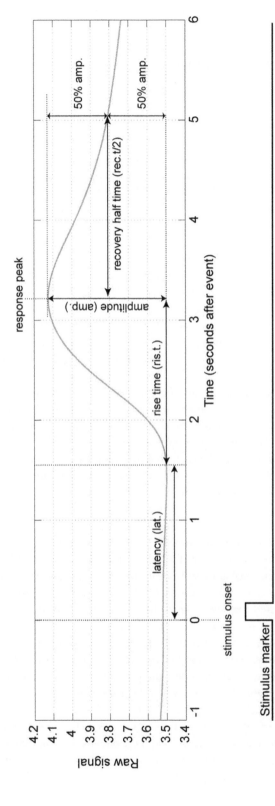

FIGURE 11.2 Raw unfiltered skin conductance signal, showing components of an SCR that can be used to quantitatively characterize SCRs. A stimulus marker corresponding to the participant turning over a loss card is also shown as part of the time course.

Physiological and Psychological Processes

Changes in skin conductance are related to the activity of eccrine sweat glands, innervated by sympathetic nerves. Changes in skin conductance reflect secretion of sweat from these glands. As sweat is an electrolyte solution, the more the skin's sweat ducts and pores are filled with sweat, the more conductive the skin becomes. The sympathetic branch of the ANS controls eccrine sweating, and thus skin conductance reflects the arousal of the sympathetic ANS that accompanies various psychological processes. The mechanisms and pathways involved in the central nervous control of eccrine sweating are relatively complex (Boucsein, 2012; Critchley, 2010). A recent fMRI study suggested that SCL and SCR are related to activity in different brain areas (Nagai et al., 2004).

While the central origins of the ANS are within the hypothalamus and the brainstem, other parts of the brain such as the amygdala, the hippocampus, the basal ganglia, and the prefrontal cortex have been found to be involved in the control of eccrine sweating. These "higher" areas are part of the limbic and paralimbic networks, which are crucially involved in affective processes. Thus it is not surprising that skin conductance is often used as an indicator of emotional arousal and other affective processes. Interestingly, it has been shown that these higher brain areas are not necessary for reflex SCRs to non-emotional stimuli such as deep breaths and orienting stimuli such as a loud noise, but they are necessary for SCRs in response to stimuli that have acquired emotional value through experience, e.g., in classical conditioning (Naqvi & Bechara, 2006; Tranel & Damasio, 1989, 1994).

Typically, skin conductance is measured from the volar[6] surfaces of the fingers or the palms of the hand. For example, two electrodes are attached to the index and middle finger of the non-dominant hand (thus allowing the participants to use their dominant hand to handle a computer mouse, fill out a questionnaire, etc.) and a small constant voltage is applied. The current is imperceptible to the participant. Differences in skin conductivity are revealed by the amount of current that passes between the electrodes. As an alternative to measurement on the palms of the hands, skin conductance can also be recorded from the soles and inner sides of the feet; this method is called *plantar* skin conductance, in contrast to *palmar* skin conductance recorded from the inner surface of the hands. Plantar skin conductance is used, for example, when the participant needs both hands for the experiment or sometimes in fMRI studies when the electrodes or their leads might interfere with the scanner environment. The palms of hands and soles of the feet are best suited for measuring skin conductance as they are easily accessible and also have a high density of eccrine sweat glands. Importantly, eccrine sweating on the volar surfaces is different from other locations, as it has been suggested that sweating in these skin parts is strongly related to mental processes (*emotional sweating*, e.g., in response to both positive and negative events as well as for anticipated and experienced outcomes; Boucsein, 2012), rather than thermoregulation.

In the psychological literature, EDA measures have been used in both normal and clinical populations as indicators of a wide range of underlying psychological processes, such as orienting responses (e.g., Uno & Grings, 1965; Williams et al., 2000), habituation (e.g., Sokolov, 1963), classical and operant conditioning (e.g., Delgado, Gillis, & Phelps, 2008), and as indicators of information processing and cognitive effort (e.g., Dawson, Filion, & Schell, 1989; Nikula, 1991). In JDM research and related work, it appears that SCR is most often used as an indicator of affective processes, and in the following section we will present some of the more recent work, including our own. Here, it is important to note what can and cannot be assessed with skin conductance. It is well established that SCR covaries with the arousal dimension of affect, indexing its *intensity* and changes thereof. In contrast to this quantitative aspect, the qualitative aspects of affect, such as its *valence* (positive/negative, approach/avoidance) or *which* emotion is present (e.g., fear versus anger versus joy versus disgust, etc.) are not reflected in EDA and have to be inferred from other sources. Often these qualitative aspects of affect, e.g., whether an affective response is negative or positive, might be clear and do not need additional measures, for example, when the participant experiences a gain versus a loss. In more ambiguous situations, or if finer-grained distinctions are of interest, it is necessary to assess these qualitative aspects either via the use of other physiological measures (e.g., electromyogram of facial muscles involved in smiling or frowning responses; Cacioppo, Berntson, Larsen, Poehlmann, & Ito, 2000; Rainville, Bechara, Naqvi, & Damasio, 2006) or—perhaps more reliable but obtrusive—a self-report measure such as an affect valence rating scale.

The studies by the Iowa group were pioneering in their use of skin conductance to investigate questions related to decision making. Damasio, Bechara, and colleagues have used SCR measures as tracers for otherwise unobservable implicit processes, both with healthy and brain-lesioned participants. Research with the Iowa Gambling Task (IGT; Bechara, Damasio, Damasio, & Anderson, 1994; Bechara, Damasio, Damasio, & Lee, 1999) has shown that participants not only exhibit SCRs to the outcomes of their choices (gains versus losses, reflecting experienced utility) but, over the course of repeated trials, healthy participants also develop *anticipatory* SCRs, assumed to index emotional arousal before and while they make their choices (reflecting anticipated and decision utility). These anticipatory SCRs were predictive of whether the participant would make an advantageous versus a disadvantageous choice. According to the Somatic Marker Hypothesis (SMH; Bechara, Damasio, Tranel, & Damasio, 2005), these anticipatory SCRs seem to develop *before* participants have explicit knowledge of the advantageousness of the different choice options. Thus, such autonomic arousal has been interpreted as guiding and influencing the participants' choice behavior. The SMH is the object of a lively debate and, together with the IGT, continues inspiring research with healthy normals as well as developmental and clinical populations, typically measuring anticipatory and outcome-related SCRs (e.g., Crone, Somsen, van Beek, & van der Molen, 2004; Jenkinson, Baker, Edelstyn, & Ellis, 2008; Luman, Oosterlaan, Knol, & Sergeant, 2008; Wright, Rakow, & Russo, 2017; for a review see Dunn, Dalgleish, & Lawrence, 2006). In summary, work by the Iowa group has demonstrated how SCRs can be used as a process indicator of affective processes before, during, and after making decisions that would otherwise be difficult to observe in an equally unobtrusive manner.

Other, more recent JDM work using SCR includes Reid and Gonzalez-Vallejo (2009) who used SCR in an innovative way as an indicator of affective processes, showing that decision weights derived from SCR magnitudes can improve choice models that try to capture how participants integrate symbolic and affective information during decision making. Holper, Wolf, and Tobler (2014), and Holper and Murphy (2014), have used EDA recordings to show that skin conductance appears to reflect objective (i.e., preference-independent) risk processing while lateral prefrontal cortex activity (assessed using functional near-infrared spectroscopy) appears to reflect subjective (i.e., preference-dependent) risk processing. In our own research, we use measures of skin conductance in combination with the CCT (Figner et al., 2009) as well as with a task involving morally challenging and ethical dilemma decisions (Krosch, Figner, & Weber, 2012). By using SCR, we were able to show that our two versions of the CCT—the affect-charged hot and the deliberative cold—indeed differed in the involvement of affective processes, explaining their differential developmental patterns in risk taking across childhood, adolescence, and adulthood. In the study on morally challenging choices, we found that increased affective arousal indexed by SCR during the dilemma-like choices predicted participants' reported decision difficulty as well as their projected future worry about their decision.

168 Figner, Murphy, and Siegel

In more clinically oriented work, Siegel and colleagues (Siegel & Gallagher, 2015; Siegel & Weinberger, 2012; Siegel, Warren, Jacobson, & Merritt, 2017) recently have shown that repeated exposures to masked phobic stimuli (e.g., pictures of spiders) can reduce avoidance behavior of phobic persons when the stimuli were presented briefly enough not to increase SCLs. This is important because earlier work (Öhman & Soares, 1994) had shown that even subliminal presentation of phobic stimuli can elicit SCRs and negative affect ratings. Thus, Siegel and colleagues' findings that very brief exposures to phobic stimuli can reduce fear (and thus arguably affect evaluations) suggests the existence of a non-conscious pathway that appears to operate independently of physiological affective systems, as indicated by the absence of SCRs.

In the following part of the chapter, we describe the steps necessary to conduct research with skin conductance. We provide descriptions of equipment, laboratory setup, task structure, and data analysis techniques, and discuss important considerations for planning and conducting research with skin conductance measures.

Equipment

There are several commercially available systems to measure skin conductance. For our own studies reported earlier, we used a Biopac system, consisting of a base module in combination with modules for skin conductance and cardiovascular activity. A desktop or laptop computer is needed to run the AcqKnowledge software that comes with the Biopac system. The AcqKnowledge software is used to set up the acquisition parameters, allows for real-time monitoring of the measurements, records the data to a hard drive, and can be used for data filtering and analysis. A second, separate desktop or laptop computer is typically used to administer the computer-controlled experimental task.

Parameters and Filters

To illustrate how a recording might look in one of our own studies, Figure 11.3 shows a screenshot of the AcqKnowledge software processing six channels of data: Channel A represents raw cardiovascular activity (with channel F being heart rate, estimated beats per minute, derived from the signal of channel A). Channel B records and displays the raw skin conductance signal, i.e., no filtering is applied.[7] This channel is similar to traditional skin conductance measurements and reflects both slow tonic and fast phasic changes (i.e., SCL and SCR). A second skin conductance channel is set up in AcqKnowledge to record the skin conductance signal, but this time with a software-based 0.5 Hz high-pass filter applied (shown on channel E). The high-pass filter effectively removes the tonic component of the raw skin conductance signal and shows only phasic changes, in effect isolating SCRs. Notice the strong phasic change on the right part of the figure—this corresponds to the participant turning over a loss card in the CCT and realizing a loss of money. Other ways to isolate the phasic changes and reduce or eliminate the slow drift present in the SCL signal are by using a difference function (see Naqvi & Bechara, 2006) or by computing a derivative of the raw signal (Nagai et al., 2004). Finally, channels C and D in our setup correspond to task markers in our experimental tasks.

Sampling Rate

When data storage capacity of several hundreds of megabytes is not a problem, we suggest that the sampling rate should not be lower than 100–200 Hz.[8] While such high sampling rates are not imperative to veridically represent a relatively slow signal like skin conductance, more complex analysis approaches and smoothing procedures can benefit from higher sampling rates; if a lower sampling rate is required, the signal can easily and quickly be downsampled during the

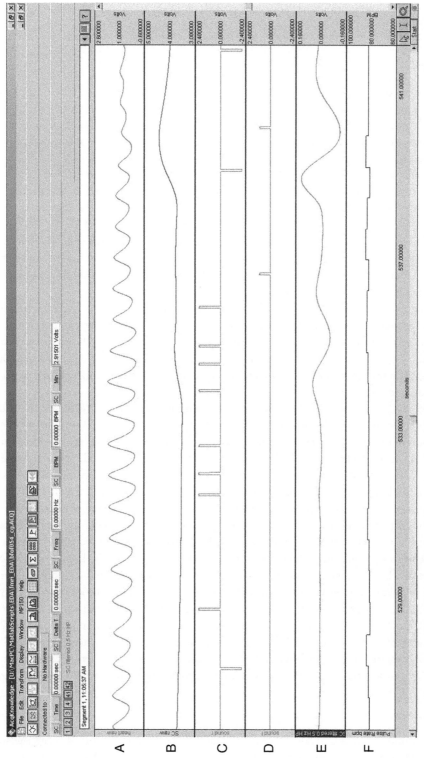

FIGURE 11.3 Screenshot of the AcqKnowledge software. Six channels of data are recorded and displayed here (see explanations in the main text).

data-processing stage. Since sampling rates can easily be set as high as 1 or 2 kHz without running into problems of computing resources or data recording speeds in modern computers, we usually sample at 1 kHz.[9]

Electrodes

Two main types of electrodes are available to be used for skin conductance measurement. Reusable electrodes must be cleaned after each use and are used in combination with an electrode gel for EDA use. Disposable electrodes are pre-gelled and do not require preparation or cleaning and disinfection after each use. This is particularly practical when doing research outside of the laboratory (e.g., at a school or workplace).

After participants provide informed consent, we first attach the electrodes to give the electrode gel enough time to soak into the skin and thereby result in a good and stable electrical connection. The electrodes are placed on the non-dominant hand, so the participants can still write or handle a computer. Before attaching the electrodes, we first clean the locations of electrode placement with small disposable alcohol pads as we observed that, if a participant applied hand cream shortly before coming to the laboratory or has otherwise very oily skin, the oil can prevent the electrodes from sticking to the skin[10] as well as prevent the electrolyte gel from establishing an electrical connection, which might result in a poor skin conductance signal.

However, there are various and contradicting recommendations in the literature regarding pretreatment, including no pretreatment at all, only water, water and soap, or alcohol (e.g., Naqvi & Bechara, 2006; Venables & Christie, 1980). As far as we know, no research has investigated the effects of these pretreatment methods on EDA signal quality. Regardless of which pretreatment is chosen, the same procedure should be used within an experiment and ideally reported as part of a corresponding methods section.

After briefly letting the alcohol dry, we put the electrodes on the distal (first) phalanges of the index and middle finger (see Figure 11.4).[11] Others have used the medial (second) phalanges or the palm of the hand (usually the thenar and hypothenar eminence). There is no agreed upon standard placement. It is again highly advisable that, within an experiment, the same electrode placement be used across all participants. It has been reported that SCR amplitudes from the distal phalanges were about 3.5 times larger than those from medial phalanges and SCLs were about twice as large from distal phalanges, compared to medial phalanges; in addition, SCRs from distal phalanges were more sensitive to habituation (Scerbo, Freedman, Raine, Dawson, & Venables, 1992; as cited in Boucsein, 2012). Some have argued that placement on the distal phalanges might increase the chances of movement artifacts, compared to the medial phalanges (Venables & Christie, 1980). Independent of actual electrode location, the experimenter should make sure that the participant can comfortably rest their hand either in their lap or on the desk using a pillow or a blanket to support the arm and hand to avoid signal artifacts, which may arise from movement of the hand to which the electrodes are attached. Finally, as temperature and humidity can influence skin conductance (Boucsein, 2012), we record the temperature and humidity at the start and end of each participant's session using an inexpensive combined hygrometer/thermometer (to determine whether there is a systematic relationship, and if so, to be able to statistically control for this potential influence on the EDA signal).

Event Markers

To enable a meaningful analysis of the skin conductance data and to be able to relate the stimuli and the participant's behavioral responses to the skin conductance signal, the physiological data

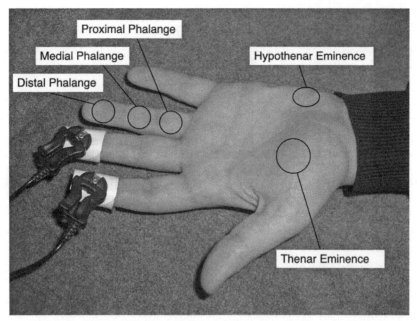

FIGURE 11.4 Electrode setup and terminology for common electrode placement locations.

recording, the stimulus display, and the participant's behavior all have to be synchronized somehow, preferably by recording these events on a common timeline. AcqKnowledge and Biopac allow for a direct interface with various commercial task-administration software packages (such as Direct RT, E-Prime, MediaLab, Presentation) so that task markers are recorded along with the physiological data. In our own studies, we opted for a customized solution that gives us maximal flexibility in the software we use to program experimental tasks. For example, the CCT version we used in Figner et al. (2009) was programmed using Microsoft's Visual Basic and plays custom-made sound files every time a participant makes a decision or a new round starts. These sound signals are not audible to the participant but are fed directly from the analog sound output of the stimulus computer into the analog inputs of the Biopac base module. The event markers are visible in Figure 11.3 as channels C and D.

Experimental Procedure

The electrodes should be attached at least 5 minutes prior to recording the physiological data to ensure that a good and stable electrical connection is achieved. We check whether everything is working by having the participant take a couple of deep sharp breaths, as this reliably results in very clear SCRs.[12] If there are no clear SCRs observed, it is possible that the gel needs more time to soak into the skin. Therefore, we would continue giving instructions and check a second time immediately before the critical part of the study is to begin. One could use the recording up to this point as a baseline. However, because the electrical connection might not yet have reached a steady state, it is more advisable to have a (second) baseline period towards the end of the experiment, e.g., while participants fill out some questionnaires. Naqvi and Bechara (2006) recommend the recording of—in addition to a resting baseline—an active baseline (the responses to a series of quick, sharp, deep breaths), which can be used to exclude non-responders or as covariate to account for individual differences in SCR magnitude.

Before the critical part of the experiment starts, we again check whether the skin conductance is recorded properly, having the participant take a deep breath. If there is a problem, one can try to remove the electrodes, clean the skin again, and start over. If participants have very cold hands, this can also reduce electrodermal activity (Boucsein, 2012).[13] If the second try fails again, it is likely that this participant is a non-responder[14] and the experimenter has to decide whether it is worth collecting the data (most probably resulting only in a meaningful behavioral but not a meaningful physiological data set) or to abort participation.

Experimental Design and Task Structure

As described earlier, skin conductance is a relatively slow signal. Not only does it change in the range of seconds but it is also *time-lagged*, i.e., between the occurrence of a stimulus and the resulting SCR, there is a latency of about 0.5 to 5 sec (most often, the latency of SCRs is between 1 and 2 sec; Boucsein, 2012). This makes the signal similar to the blood oxygenation level dependent (BOLD) response in fMRI research, which is also slow and time-lagged. While there are several differences between SCR and BOLD, similar considerations have to be taken into account when planning the study and the task. For example, a one-shot design, i.e., one single SCR measurement per participant per experimental condition, might result in data too noisy to yield any reliably discernable effects. In addition to other factors, the number of repetitions needed depends crucially on the stimuli (namely how reliably they trigger SCRs and how strong those SCRs are). Strongly aversive stimuli, such as an electrical shock in a conditioning experiment or a loss of a substantial amount of money in a risky choice task, can be expected to more reliably trigger strong SCRs compared to more subtle stimuli. To address the time-lag problem, SCR studies often use relatively long interstimulus intervals (ISI) of 6 to 12 sec or more between trials to make sure skin conductance has returned to baseline before a new trial starts (e.g., Bechara, Tranel, Damasio, & Damasio, 1996; Breska, Maoz, & Ben-Shakar, 2011; Reid & Gonzalez-Vallejo, 2009).

fMRI researchers came up with different ways to optimize their task designs in response to methodical challenges, which can be applied to skin conductance studies (for basics in fMRI research see Huettel, Song, & McCarthy, 2004). In *blocked designs*, longer periods of a specific task are counted as one period of interest (*block*), assuming that during the block relatively constant processes are engaged. We used this approach in Figner et al. (2009) to compare SCRs during a longer time period across the hot and the cold CCT, and to a baseline measure. Here, the whole risky choice phase of the (hot or cold) CCT counted as one block. Sufficient for the purpose of our manipulation check (that the hot CCT involved stronger affective processes than the cold CCT), we used a simple between-subject design in which each participant had only one block of interest, plus a baseline measure. More elaborate designs can be used to increase statistical power, e.g., repeatedly administering the blocks of interest within-subject, in random or counterbalanced order, with blocks of rest between the active blocks.

However, in many studies, investigating shorter time intervals (such as single trials) might be more appropriate. For such questions where the unit of analysis has to be shorter, we are confronted again with the problems regarding the slowness and time-lag of the skin conductance signal. Potential improvements from such designs can be found again in fMRI paradigms. While designs looking at relatively short time periods are generally called *event-related designs* (as the physiological data are analyzed with respect to single events, not blocks containing multiple events), so-called *rapid event-related designs*, wherein a train of stimuli follow each other in a tight sequence, are most interesting for our purpose. Such designs are likely to generate superimposed SCRs, i.e., overlapping SCRs in the sense that a new SCR starts before the previous SCR has ended; this has the effect that the two

Measuring Electrodermal Activity **173**

(or more) SCRs add up to what might look similar to one single larger and/or longer SCR, making it difficult to clearly say where each individual SCR starts and/or ends. Traditionally, this has been handled by measuring a superimposed SCR starting from its minimum value on the recovery limb of the prior SCR (Edelberg, 1967). More recently, mathematical deconvolution models have been proposed (i.e., methods to analytically disentangle the superimposed SCRs; see Alexander et al., 2005; Bach, Flandin, Friston, & Dolan, 2009; Benedek & Kaernbach, 2010a, 2010b; Lim et al., 1997). Two common toolboxes that provide such model-based analysis methods are the MATLAB toolbox *PsPM* (Psychophysiological Modelling; previous versions were known as SCRalyze) by Dominik Bach and colleagues (for more information, see http://pspm.sourceforge.net/reference/), and the MATLAB toolbox *Ledalab* by Kaernbach and Benedek (for more information, see www. ledalab.de/). For an excellent brief outline of the general approach and an empirical comparison of these two model-based analysis approaches and a traditional method, see Bach (2014). Importantly, such designs and the corresponding analysis approaches are based on the assumption that such repeated and overlapping and thus superimposed physiological responses aggregate linearly (in our case several SCRs; in fMRI, several BOLD responses).[15] If this assumption holds, separate events of interest do not have to be divided by long ISIs (the assumption of linearly additive SCRs seems to hold for ISIs that are approximately 2 sec or longer: Bach et al., 2010; shorter intervals are likely to induce non-linearities, which would require somewhat different modeling approaches, which are currently not implemented, e.g., in PsPM). Instead, responses can be allowed to overlap, as they can be deconvoluted statistically. In such an analysis, the dependent variable would be the continuous SCR data. Several independent regressors can be built for different types of events of interest, such as, in the CCT, a regressor coding each time the participant turns over a loss card; a second regressor codes each instant of turning over a gain card; a third regressor represents the decision to end a trial voluntarily, etc. Some regressors may have only two different values (0 and 1), coding whether the event is present or not. Other regressors can be parametrically varied (e.g., coding different loss magnitudes). As in fMRI analysis, these regressors are simple delta (i.e., stick) functions, being 0 for all time points without the event of interest and being some number greater than 0 for the events. Before they are used in the following GLM analysis, the delta functions are convoluted with a "canonical" SCR that can be taken from, for example, an averaged SCR (the mentioned toolboxes contain such canonical SCRs). Just as in fMRI analysis, the estimated weights and error indicators of the regressors from the individual-level analysis can then be transferred to the group analysis.[16]

Importantly, the intervals between events do not need to be long but they should be jittered (i.e., of unequal length). This can be achieved by programming randomly jittered ISIs as part of the computer task, or by using the self-pacing of the participants, an approach that we adopted in our CCT studies (although one has to keep in mind that subsequent events that are separated by less than 2 sec in time likely lead to non-linear aggregation and thus pose a problem for the currently available analysis approaches). These more recent model-based approaches allow stimuli to be presented closer in time, compared to more traditional analysis approaches, thus giving more freedom in task design. Accordingly, these approaches support more natural task designs that cannot be realized pragmatically with long ISIs. A second advantage of these model-based approaches that is at least as important is that they promise increased statistical power and greater sensitivity, without increasing the Type I error rate. While there appear to be differences across different modeling approaches (for a comparison, see Bach, 2014), the new methods clearly have the potential to outperform traditional analysis approaches. Therefore, we recommend considering using these more advanced analysis methods. That being said, there may be trade-offs for the user,

174 Figner, Murphy, and Siegel

for example, the conventional analysis approach is likely more intuitive and easier to understand for non-experts, is relatively model-free (though no analysis approach is completely model-free), and may require less time investment in terms of becoming familiar with a new toolbox. Since these model-based approaches are not the focus of our chapter and since there is a growing literature with excellent papers discussing them in more detail,[17] for the remainder of the chapter, we will focus on the traditional analysis method, assuming sufficiently long ISIs.

Data Management and Analysis

The data that result from skin conductance measurement are substantial. Assuming a sampling rate of 1 kHz, one participant taking part in a 20-minute experiment yields over 1 million (20 minutes × 60 seconds × 1000 observations per second = 1,200,000) numbers corresponding to the conductivity of their skin over time. This ordered vector of numbers is from just one channel and forms the raw signal that can be processed and analyzed on its own or in conjunction with other variables recorded along the same time course on different channels. We use MATLAB for the analysis, a powerful and flexible software package capable of dealing with large data sets (some possible alternatives are R or Octave). The proprietary AcqKnowledge files (.acq) can be exported into a generic tab delimited format compatible with MATLAB (.mat) where each row corresponds to one of the samples, and each column corresponds to a separate channel.[18]

Preprocessing

We first verify that the data were recorded properly during the experimental session by generating and examining plots of each of the channels over time. For example, the raw skin conductance signal should yield a plot that looks something like Figure 11.1. Examining the plots of each channel can reveal serious problems with a data set that would invalidate later results from the experimental session, e.g., if an electrode fell off a person's finger during the experiment or a wire becomes disconnected. For the remainder of the analysis, we focus on the high-pass filtered SCR data channel (channel E in Figure 11.3).

As high-frequency noise is likely to be present in the skin conductance signal, steps are often used to eliminate this source of error variance. For example, in the laboratory we used for Figner et al. (2009) and Krosch, Figner, and Weber (2012), the Biopac picked up electromagnetic disturbances (from sources such as the overhead florescent lights) and hence recorded a persistent low amplitude 60 Hz sub-signal. Such noise can be eliminated by administering a low-pass filter or a smoothing function (for our data collected with a sampling rate of 1 kHz, we use a simple moving average across 500 msec). By treating the raw signal with both a high-pass filter (thus removing tonic changes and slow drifts), and then a low-pass filter (to remove high-frequency noise), the result is a band-pass filtered signal.[19] This signal is the basis of subsequent analyses as it isolates the phasic SCRs that are of interest to us in our research. In Figure 11.5, we show the effects of high-pass and low-pass filters on a raw skin conductance signal.

In addition to processing the skin conductance signals, the task marker channels are processed. The channels are smoothed with the same moving average function to mitigate noise, and then a peak detect function is run on the channels. The result is a series of several binary markers that indicate when in the time course the participant performed a particular action or there was a particular event or outcome in the task. These markers are used to isolate portions of the SCR signal that are of particular interest (i.e., to define the measurement windows, see later).

Main Analysis

There are a variety of different ways to quantify SCRs and score the response as a single number. Traditionally, the most common indicator (using the unfiltered raw skin conductance signal) has been the SCR *magnitude*, reflecting the peak amplitude of the SCR. In order to quantify this variable, a latency onset window has to be defined. A typical criterion is that the onset of an SCR has to be between 1 and 3 sec after stimulus onset.[20] Then, the peak amplitude of this SCR is quantified by computing the difference between skin conductivity before the SCR onset and the skin conductivity at the peak of the SCR (Boucsein, 2012; Boucsein et al., 2012). In the literature, the variable SCR *magnitude* includes SCRs with 0 amplitude, whereas SCR *amplitude* only includes cases in which an actual SCR was observed (i.e., excluding cases in which no discernable SCR occurred in the time window).

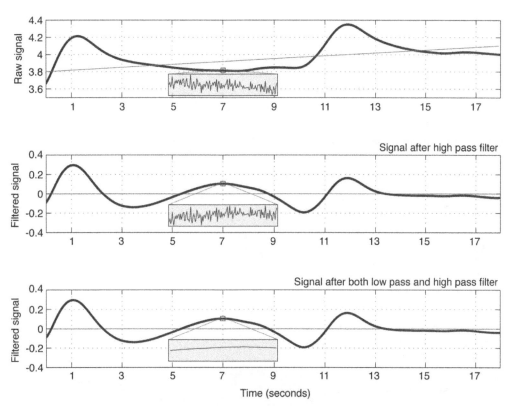

FIGURE 11.5 The effects of filters on signal data. Top panel, raw skin conductance signal, reflecting both SCL and SCR (equivalent to channel B in Figure 11.3). Middle panel, filtered signal after application of a 0.5 Hz high-pass filter (equivalent to channel E in Figure 11.3). The slow drift in the signal (representing the SCL) has been removed such that the filtered signal reflects only phasic changes, i.e., SCRs (note the difference in the slope of the straight gray line in the top panel compared to the middle and bottom panels). Bottom panel, signal after application of 2 Hz low-pass filter to remove high-frequency noise present in the data (see insets zooming in on a small time window of about 200 msec), the general shape of the signal remains unchanged by the third step but eliminates unwanted noise in the data. The last step is done after data collection, during data preprocessing, by applying a moving average smoothing function.

A more recent indicator, which lends itself more readily to automated analysis, is the *area bounded by the SCR curve*. Here, instead of an onset latency window, a window of interest is defined (the *measurement window*; see Figure 11.6). The measurement window has to be long enough to capture most of the SCR-related fluctuations, but short enough to avoid catching variance related to non-specific SCRs or SCRs to following stimuli. In general, longer ISIs allow longer measurement windows. Assuming sufficiently long ISIs, a common window of interest might start 1 sec after stimulus onset and end 6 sec after stimulus onset, making sure that most of the SCR-related activity will be captured in the 5 sec of interest. In the next step, the SCR-related variance in the data is quantified within this measurement window.

There are different approaches for this quantification. Naqvi and Bechara (2006), for example, use the area defined by the SCR curve and a sloped line delineated by the intersection of the measurement window and the SCR curve. We use the area bounded between the SCR curve and the abscissa within the window of interest (see Figure 11.6). As our filtering of the raw skin conductance signal has the effect that the resulting SCR data are centered around 0, the area bounded by the curve can be simply calculated by summing up the absolute values that lie within the time window.[21] Usually, the area bounded by the curve measure is standardized per time unit (typically per second) by dividing it by the length of the time window of interest in seconds such that the resulting measurement is in μS/sec.

The determination of the size of the measurement window is obviously somewhat arbitrary, specifically the endpoint. Conversely, the starting point cannot vary so much because it has to be between the stimulus onset and the SCR onset. We find it useful to plot the SCRs in relation to

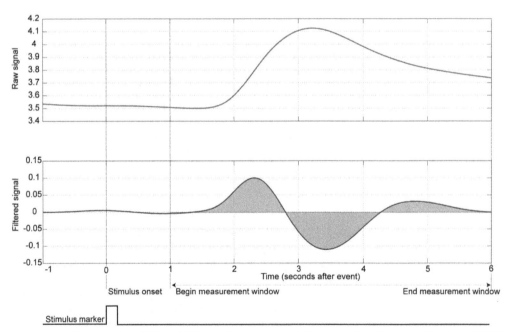

FIGURE 11.6 Raw (top) and filtered skin conductance signal (bottom), showing quantification of SCR within a time of interest window (measurement window) as the area bounded by the filtered SCR signal and the abscissa.

the stimulus onset: One plot represents each SCR by an individual curve in the same graph and one plot shows only one curve, representing the average of all SCRs. These graphs are very helpful in defining a sensible measurement window. Obviously, the time window of interest has to be the same for all participants and conditions within an experiment for this type of analysis, as results might otherwise be difficult to interpret. One caveat is regarding the selection of window size (as with any arbitrary parameter). Some researchers may be tempted to analyze their data using a wide range of different windows and then "cherry pick" results that correspond to a particular window size, reporting only those results and not disclosing their data-dredging activities. This is a kind of *p*-hacking as it capitalizes on error variance to yield particular results. Researchers are strongly discouraged from this practice as data-dredging is a kind of scientific misconduct and it undermines the accumulation of knowledge. Thus, the decision about the window of interest is ideally independent of the data of interest. For example, one solution would be to first conduct a pilot study and use these data to determine the window of interest.

Data Transformations: Normalizations and Standardizations

Normalization and standardization of skin conductance data do not refer to the same thing. In normalization, data transformations are conducted to make sure the relevant requirements for the used statistical method (such as regression, ANOVA, etc.) are met. For example, regression approaches (including ANOVA) require approximately normal distribution of the residuals. Accordingly, data transformation methods traditionally have been used to reduce, for example, skew or kurtosis so that the data are amenable to parametric statistical analysis (to avoid confusion, the typical statistical models require that the *residuals* follow a normal distribution, not the dependent variable; however, the transformation is applied to the dependent variable when the residuals violate the model assumptions). It is worth checking distributions of SCR magnitudes because they are typically positively skewed and leptokurtotic (Boucsein et al., 2012; Dawson et al., 2007). The most common normalization of SCR magnitudes is a logarithmic transformation. A log transformation should be applied after SCR magnitudes have been determined; a log should not be applied to the raw scores. If zero responses are included, it is often recommended that the log of (SCR + 1.0) should be used because the log of zero is undefined. Square root transformation can also be used to normalize SCR magnitudes, which unlike logarithmic transformation does not necessarily require the addition of a constant (Edelberg, 1972). Logarithmic or square-root transformation can also be used to normalize SCL data.

The transformations should be evaluated in terms of their capacity to reduce and mitigate skew, kurtosis of the residuals, and, if relevant for the used statistical model, heterogeneity of variance across groups (Ferguson & Takane, 1989). Log and square-root transformations tend to generate similar results. If distributional problems are not initially evident, then it is likely not necessary to apply these data transformations. A recommended alternative to transformations (and also an option if transformations are insufficient to mitigate distributional problems) is the use of robust or non-parametric statistical techniques.

Normalization does not address the considerable individual differences that characterize skin conductance data, which complicates inter-individual comparisons. An SCR of 1.0 μS may be relatively high for one participant and relatively low for another, depending on their idiosyncratic SCR ranges. EDA ranges can vary widely due to physiological variables (e.g., thickness of the corneum) that are unrelated to the psychological processes of interest. Standardization procedures can be used to correct for such individual differences so that SCRs or SCLs of different participants can be meaningfully compared (Boucsein, 2012; Dawson et al., 2007). This means that the skin conductance data is standardized *within each participant* prior to conducting between-group analyses.

Lykken, Rose, Luther, and Maley (1966) proposed the standardization method of EDA data known as *range correction*. A participant's maximum SCR is measured in response to an arousing and startling stimulus (e.g., the participant blows up a balloon until it bursts). Each SCR is then standardized by calculating the proportion of maximal response (i.e., dividing it by the participant's maximum SCR). To standardize SCL data, a participant's potential SCL range is first calculated, and individual SCLs are then transformed in terms of this range. The minimum value is typically measured during a rest period, and the maximum SCL during the most aroused period. SCL during any particular time period is than calculated as a proportion of his/her particular range according to the formula: (SCL − SCLmin)/(SCLmax − SCLmin).

The advantages of range correction are the reduction of error variance, and thus increased statistical power in analyses involving group comparisons. However, range correction should not be used if groups have quite different skin conductance ranges (Ben-Shakhar, 1985; Dawson et al., 2007). Further, it can be difficult to establish a participant's range (maximum and minimum responses) with adequate reliability. To address these limitations, Ben-Shakhar (1985) proposed using within-subject standardized (z-) scores to correct for individual differences because such scores are based on the mean, a more robust statistic than the maximum or minimum value. There is evidence that standard scores provide greater statistical power, e.g., compared to range correction or no standardization (Boucsein et al., 2012; Bach, 2014), and for example might mitigate the effect of SCR habituation within blocks of stimuli, thereby better highlighting relevant effects (Ben-Shakhar & Dolev, 1996).

Conclusions

There are several advantages and disadvantages to be taken into account when considering using EDA measures in JDM research. Some advantages are that skin conductance is a comparatively robust physiological measure that can be measured relatively cheaply, easily, and unobtrusively. It yields a continuous measure that is related to activity in the sympathetic branch of the ANS. Accordingly, it does not reflect one single psychological process, which can be seen either as an advantage or a disadvantage. Irrespective of this, skin conductance measurement requires that the setup of the experiment and/or additional measures such as self-reports constrain the possible interpretations of the changes in skin conductance by constraining the psychological processes that such changes reflect. A clear disadvantage of skin conductance is the slowness and time-lag of its signal, typically requiring long ISIs. Newer analysis approaches, however, mitigate this issue, while at the same time increasing sensitivity and statistical power.

Notes

1 Particularly in older literature—and sometimes on hardware used to measure skin conductance—the outdated unit micromho ($\mu\mho$) can still be found. Mho is derived from spelling ohm backwards. This unit should not be used anymore as it has been replaced by the unit siemens (S) in the International System of Units.

2 The CCT is a dynamic risky decision-making task that assesses levels of risk taking and information use. Two different versions of CCT exist—a relatively affect-charged *hot* version and a more deliberative *cold* version (Figner et al., 2009; Figner & Weber, 2011). In both versions, participants turn over cards from a deck, which consists of a known number of gain and loss cards. Gain and loss amounts and probability to win or lose vary between trials to assess their influence on participants' risk taking.

3 The older term galvanic skin reaction or galvanic skin reflex (GSR) can still be found in the literature. It should be avoided as it is technically incorrect and it is not always clear to what aspect of EDA it refers (Boucsein, 2012).

4 More simply, a measure of the central tendency, e.g., the mean or median, over the whole time interval of interest could be taken. However, this is likely to lead to an overestimation of the true SCL, as such a measure includes the data points forming the SCRs.

5 This measure has been suggested to index *quantity of affect* by Traxel (1957; see also Boucsein, 2012; Naqvi & Bechara, 2006). Sometimes it is also referred to as *area under the curve*, which can be misleading as the measure includes areas both *under* and *above* the SCR curve.

6 *Volar* refers to the underside of hands and feet, i.e., the palm of the hand and the sole of the foot (including the underside of fingers and toes).

7 For our studies, we set up the EDA acquisition parameters as follows: On the Biopac hardware, amplification is set to 5 μSiemens/V, the low-pass filter is set to 1 Hz, and no hardware high-pass filters are activated (i.e., the switches are set to DC).

8 While lower sampling rates are still sometimes used in the literature and are often sufficient for many types of analysis, the computing speed of regular computers today and the relatively low cost of data storage media allow use of much higher sampling rates than was common several years ago.

9 In the more recent JDM literature, sampling rates most commonly are in the range between 100 Hz and 2 kHz.

10 We found it useful to additionally secure the electrodes by applying a short piece of scotch tape to connect the ends of the electrodes to make sure that they do not fall off.

11 We also have used placement of skin conductance electrodes on the middle and third finger in a study in which we used a transducer for cardiovascular activity on the index finger. We did not observe any systematic changes; again, it seems to be more important to be consistent within an experiment.

12 Participants are typically curious about what we are recording with the electrodes. Therefore, we show them the AcqKnowledge monitor at this time. Afterwards, we make sure that the participant cannot see the monitor since it might distract them. The experimenter also avoids watching the monitor as this might make participants feel overly scrutinized.

13 In general, we and others (e.g., Venables & Christie, 1980) have found that higher room temperatures work better than low room temperatures.

14 About 5 to 10% or even up to 25% of the population have been found to be non-responders (Dawson et al., 2007), with some clinical groups exhibiting even higher rates of non-responders (e.g., in schizophrenia; Boucsein, 2012).

15 For work on the linearity of overlapping SCRs see Bach, Flandin, Friston, and Dolan, 2009, 2010; Freedman et al., 1994; Lim et al., 1997; Lykken and Venables, 1971.

16 If the dependent variable is the area bounded by the SCR curve, Bach, Friston, and Dolan (2010) proposed a solution for obtaining area measures from overlapping SCRs based on a convolution model of the SCL-corrected time integral.

17 For an introduction and methods comparison, see Bach (2014). For work related to the PsPM toolbox and its foundations, see Bach et al. (2009, 2010); Bach and Friston (2013). For work related to the ledalab toolbox and its foundations, see Benedek and Kaernbach (2010a, 2010b). For decision-making papers using these approaches, see, e.g., Nicolle, Fleming, Bach, Driver, and Dolan (2011); Talmi, Dayan, Kiebel, Frith, and Dolan (2009).

18 There are also free MATLAB functions that allow the direct import of.acq files, available at MATLAB Central.

19 Alternatively, a low-pass filter with a cutoff of 2 Hz can be applied, leading to the identical result of removing high-frequency noise without altering the shape of the curve. As sympathetic neural activity operates at low frequencies (below 0.15 Hz; Nagai et al., 2004), even relatively low-frequency low-pass filters do not remove substantial information.

20 SCRs with an onset time outside this onset latency window would be counted as non-specific. Only the onset of the SCR has to lie within this window, usually there is no criterion when the SCR has to be finished as SCR recovery time can be very long.

180 Figner, Murphy, and Siegel

21 Usually, the two methods will lead to very similar results. However, it appears that our method provides a more consistent index of the SCR compared to the previous approach, as it is less sensitive to variations in the defined location of the time window: If either the start or the end of the measurement window falls onto an SCR, our approach leads to a more reliable SCR quantification due to not relying on a sloped bounding line but using the abscissa instead.

Author Note

This work was supported by grants from the Swiss National Science Foundation (PA001–115327 and PBZH1–110268) and a grant by the US National Science Foundation (SES—0720932), awarded to the first author; and a grant by the US National Science Foundation (SES-0637151), awarded to the second author.

Acknowledgments

Thanks to Amy Krosch for her assistance with experiment administration, data organization, and analysis, and to both Amy Krosch and Annie Ma for their help with manuscript preparation.

Recommended Reading

- Boucsein (2012), Dawson et al. (2007) and Venables and Christie (1980) provide excellent and thorough overviews on measuring EDA.
- Critchley, Dolan and colleagues (an overview can be found in Critchley, 2010) focus on the neural substrates involved in EDA.
- See Alexander et al., 2005; Bach, 2014; Bach et al., 2009, 2010; Bach and Friston, 2013; Benedek and Kaernbach, 2010a, 2010b; de Clercq, Verschuere, de Vlieger, & Crombez, 2006; Lim et al., 1997 for more novel analysis approaches using short ISIs.
- For model-based analysis approaches, we recommend the PsPM toolbox, which also includes a very helpful manual (http://pspm.sourceforge.net/).

References

Alexander, D. M., Trengove, C., Johnston, P., Cooper, T., August, J. P., & Gordon, E. (2005). Separating individual skin conductance responses in a short interstimulus-interval paradigm. *Journal of Neuroscience Methods, 146*(1), 116–123.

Bach, D. R. (2014). A head-to-head comparison of SCRalyze and Ledalab, two model-based methods for skin conductance analysis. *Biological Psychology, 103*(1), 63–68.

Bach, D. R., Flandin, G., Friston, K., & Dolan, R. J. (2009). Time-series analysis for rapid event-related skin conductance responses. *Journal of Neuroscience Methods, 184*(2), 224–234.

Bach, D. R., Flandin, G., Friston, K. J., & Dolan, R. J. (2010). Modelling event-related skin conductance responses. *International Journal of Psychophysiology, 75*(3), 349–356.

Bach, D. R., & Friston, K. J. (2013). Model-based analysis of skin conductance responses: Towards causal models in psychophysiology. *Psychophysiology, 50*(1), 15–22.

Bach, D. R., Friston, K. J., & Dolan, R. J. (2010). Analytic measures for quantification of arousal from spontaneous skin conductance fluctuations. *International Journal of Psychophysiology, 76*(1), 52–55.

Bechara, A., Damasio, A. R., Damasio, H., & Anderson, S. W. (1994). Insensitivity to future consequences following damage to human prefrontal cortex. *Cognition, 50*(1–3), 7–15.

Bechara, A., Damasio, H., Damasio, A. R., & Lee, G. P. (1999). Different contributions of the human amygdala and ventromedial prefrontal cortex to decision-making. *Journal of Neuroscience, 19*(13), 5473–5481.

Bechara, A., Damasio, H., Tranel, D., & Damasio, A. R. (2005). The Iowa Gambling Task and the somatic marker hypothesis: Some questions and answers. *Trends in Cognitive Sciences*, *9*(4), 159–162.

Bechara, A., Tranel, D., Damasio, H., & Damasio, A. R. (1996). Failure to respond autonomically to anticipated future outcomes following damage to prefrontal cortex. *Cerebral Cortex*, *6*(2), 215–225.

Benedek, M., & Kaernbach, C. (2010a). A continuous measure of phasic electrodermal activity. *Journal of Neuroscience Methods*, *190*(1), 80–91.

Benedek, M., & Kaernbach, C. (2010b). Decomposition of skin conductance data by means of nonnegative deconvolution. *Psychophysiology*, *47*(4), 647–658.

Ben-Shakhar, G. (1985). Standardization within individuals: A simple method to neutralize individual differences in psychophysiological responsivity. *Psychophysiology*, *22*(3), 292–299.

Ben-Shakhar, G., & Dolev, K. (1996). Psychophysiological detection through the guilty knowledge technique: Effects of mental countermeasures. *Journal of Applied Psychology*, *81*(3), 273–281.

Boucsein, W. (2012). *Electrodermal activity* (2nd ed.). New York, NY: Plenum Press.

Boucsein, W., Fowles, D. C., Grimnes, S., Ben-Shakhar, G., Roth, W. T., Dawson, M. E., & Filion, D. L. (2012). Publication recommendations for electrodermal measurements. *Psychophysiology*, *49*(8), 1017–1034.

Breska, A., Maoz, K., & Ben-Shakhar, G. (2011). Inter-stimulus intervals for skin conductance response measurement. *Psychophysiology*, *48*(4), 437–440.

Brown, C. C. (1967). A proposed standard nomenclature for psychophysiologic measures. *Psychophysiology*, *4*(2), 260–264.

Cacioppo, J. T., Berntson, G. G., Larsen, J. T., Poehlmann, K. M., & Ito, T. A. (2000). The psychophysiology of emotion. In M. Lewis & J. M. Haviland-Jones (Eds.), *The handbook of emotion* (2nd ed., pp. 173–191). New York, NY: Guilford Press.

Critchley, H. D. (2010). Electrodermal responses: What happens in the brain. *Neuroscientist*, *8*(2), 132–142.

Crone, E. A., Somsen, R. J., van Beek, B., & van der Molen, M. W. (2004). Heart rate and skin conductance analysis of antecendents and consequences of decision making. *Psychophysiology*, *41*(4), 531–540.

Dawson, M. E., Filion, D. L., & Schell, A. M. (1989). Is elicitation of the autonomic orienting response associated with allocation of processing resources? *Psychophysiology*, *26*(5), 560–572.

Dawson, M. E., Schell, A. M., & Filion, D. L. (2007). The electrodermal system. In J. T. Cacioppo, L. G. Tassinary, & G. G. Berntson (Eds.), *Handbook of psychophysiology* (3rd ed., pp. 159–181). Cambridge, UK: Cambridge University Press.

de Clercq, A., Verschuere, B., de Vlieger, P., & Crombez, G. (2006). Psychophysiological Analysis (PSPHA): A modular script-based program for analyzing psychophysiological data. *Behavior Research Methods*, *38*(3), 504–510.

Delgado, M. R., Gillis, M. M., & Phelps, E. A. (2008). Regulating the expectation of reward via cognitive strategies. *Nature Neuroscience*, *11*(8), 880–881.

Dunn, B. D., Dalgleish, T., & Lawrence, A. D. (2006). The somatic marker hypothesis: a critical evaluation. *Neuroscience and Biobehavioral Reviews*, *30*(2), 239–271.

Edelberg, R. (1967). Electrical properties of the skin. In C. C. Brown (Ed.), *Methods in psychophysiology* (pp. 1–53). Baltimore, MD: Williams & Wilkins.

Edelberg. R. (1972). Electrical activity of the skin: Its measurement and uses in psychophysiology. In N. S. Greenfield & R. A. Sternbach (Eds.), *Handbook of psychophysiology* (pp. 367–418). New York, NY: Holt.

Ferguson, G. A., & Takane, Y. (1989). *Statistical analysis in psychology and education* (6th ed.). New York, NY: McGraw-Hill.

Figner, B., Mackinlay, R. J., Wilkening, F., & Weber, E. U. (2009). Affective and deliberative processes in risky choice: Age differences in risk taking in the Columbia Card Task. *Journal of Experimental Psychology: Learning, Memory, and Cognition*, *35*(3), 709–730.

Figner, B., & Weber, E. U. (2011). Who takes risk when and why? Determinants of risk-taking. *Current Directions in Psychological Science*, *20*(4), 211–216.

Freedman, L. W., Scerbo, A. S., Dawson, M. E., Raine, A., McClure, W. O., & Venables, P. H. (1994). The relationship of sweat gland count to electrodermal activity. *Psychophysiology*, *31*(2), 196–200.

Holper, L., & Murphy, R. O. (2014). Hemodynamic and affective correlates assessed during performance on the Columbia Card Task (CCT). *Brain Imaging and Behavior*, *8*(4), 517–530.

Holper, L., Wolf, M., & Tobler, P. N. (2014). Comparison of functional nearl-infrared and electrodermal activity in assessing objective versus subjective risk during risky financial decisions. *NeuroImage, 84*(1), 833–842.

Huettel, S. A., Song, A. W., & McCarthy, G. (2004). *Functional magnetic resonance imaging.* Sunderland, MA: Sinauer.

Jenkinson, P. M., Baker, S. R., Edelstyn, N. M.-J., & Ellis, S. J. (2008). Does autonomic arousal distinguish good and bad decisions? Healthy individuals' skin conductance reactivity during the Iowa gambling task. *Journal of Psychophysiology, 22*(3), 141–149.

Johnson, L. C., & Lubin, A. (1966). Spontaneous electrodermal activity during waking and sleeping. *Psychophysiology, 3*(1), 8–17.

Krosch, A. R., Figner, B., & Weber, E. U. (2012). Choice processes and their consequences in morally conflicting military decisions. *Judgment and Decision Making, 7*(3), 224–234.

Lim, C. L., Rennie, C., Barry, R. J., Bahramali, H., Lazzaro, I., Manor, B., & Gordon, E. (1997). Decomposing skin conductance into tonic and phasic components. *International Journal of Psychophysiology, 25*(2), 97–109.

Luman, M., Oosterlaan, J., Knol, D. L., & Sergeant, J. A. (2008). Decision-making in ADHD: Sensitive to frequency but blind to the magnitude of penalty? *Journal of Child Psychology and Psychiatry, 49*(7), 712–722.

Lykken, D. T., Rose, R., Luther, B., & Maley, M. (1966). Correcting psychophysiological measures for individual differences in range. *Psychological Bulletin, 66*(6), 481–484.

Lykken, D. T., & Venables, P. H. (1971). Direct measurement of skin conductance: A proposal for standardization. *Psychophysiology, 8*(5), 656–672.

Nagai, Y., Critchley, H. D., Featherstone, E., Trimble, M. R., & Dolan, R. J. (2004). Activity in ventromedial prefrontal cortex covaries with sympathetic skin conductance level: a physiological account of a "default mode" of brain function. *Neuroimage, 22*(1), 243–251.

Naqvi, N. H., & Bechara, A. (2006). Skin conductance: A psychophysiological approach to the study of decision making. In C. Senior, T. Russell, & M. S. Gazzaniga (Eds.), *Methods in mind* (pp. 103–122). New York, NY: MIT Press.

Nicolle, A., Fleming, S. M., Bach, D. R., Driver, J., & Dolan, R. J. (2011). A regret-induced status quo bias. *Journal of Neuroscience, 31*(9), 3320–3327.

Nikula, R. (1991). Psychological correlates of nonspecific skin conductance responses. *Psychophysiology, 28*(1), 86–90.

Öhman, A., & Soares, J. (1994). "Unconscious anxiety": Phobic responses to masked stimuli. *Journal of Abnormal Psychology, 103*(2), 231–240.

Rainville, P., Bechara, A., Naqvi, N., & Damasio, A. R. (2006). Basic emotions are associated with distinct patterns of cardiorespiratory activity. *International Journal of Psychophysiology, 61*(1), 5–18.

Reid, A. A., & Gonzalez-Vallejo, C. (2009). Emotion as a tradeable quantity. *Journal of Behavioral Decision Making, 22*(1), 62–90.

Scerbo, A. S., Freedman, L. W., Raine, A., Dawson, M. E., & Venables, P. H. (1992). A major effect of recording site on measurement of electrodermal activity. *Psychophysiology, 29*(2), 241–246.

Siegel, P., & Gallagher, K. A. (2015). Delaying in vivo exposure to a tarantula with very brief exposure to phobic stimuli. *Journal of Behavior Therapy and Experimental Psychiatry, 46*, 182–188.

Siegel, P., Warren, R., Jacobson, G., & Merritt, E. (2017). Masking exposure to phobic stimuli reduces fear without inducing electrodermal activity. *Psychophysiology, 55*(5), 13045.

Siegel, P., & Weinberger, J. (2012). Less is more: The effects of very brief versus clearly visible exposure. *Emotion, 12*(2), 394–402.

Sokolov, E. N. (1963). *Perception and the conditioned reflex.* Oxford, UK: Pergamon Press.

Talmi, D., Dayan, P., Kiebel, S. J., Frith, C. D., & Dolan, R. J. (2009). How humans integrate the prospects of pain and reward during choice. *Journal of Neuroscience, 29*(46), 14617–14626.

Tranel, D., & Damasio, H. (1989). Intact electrodermal skin-conductance responses after bilateral amygdala damage. *Neuropsychologia, 27*(4), 381–390.

Tranel, D., & Damasio, H. (1994). Neuroanatomical correlates of electrodermal skin-conductance responses. *Psychophysiology, 31*(5), 427–438.

Traxel, W. (1957). Über das Zeitmass der psychogalvanischen Reaktion. *Zeitschrift für Psychologie, 161*, 282–291.

Uno, T., & Grings, W. W. (1965). Autonomic components of orienting behavior. *Psychophysiology, 1*(4), 311–321.

Venables, P. H., & Christie, M. J. (1980). Electrodermal activity. In I. Martin & P. H.Venables (Eds.), *Techniques in psychophysiology* (pp. 3–67). Chichester, UK: John Wiley & Sons.

Weber, E. U., & Johnson, E. J. (2009). Mindful judgment and decision-making. *Annual Review of Psychology, 60*(1), 53–85.

Williams, L. M., Brammer, M. J., Skerrett, D., Lagopolous, J., Rennie, C., Kozek, K., ... & Gordon, E (2000). The neural correlates of orienting: An integration of fMRI and skin conductance orienting. *Neuroreport, 11*(13), 3011–3015.

Wright, R. J., Rakow, T., & Russo, R. (2017). Go for broke: The role of somatic states when asked to lose in the Iowa Gambling Task. *Biological Psychology, 123,* 286–293.

12

RESPONSE TIMES AS IDENTIFICATION TOOLS FOR COGNITIVE PROCESSES UNDERLYING DECISIONS

Mario Fifić, Joseph W. Houpt, and Jörg Rieskamp

One central aim of contemporary research in cognitive psychology is the identification of the cognitive mechanisms engaged in judgment and decision making. In contrast, standard economic approaches to decision making have followed an axiomatic approach, according to which people's choice can be described by expected utility models if their choice obeys various choice axioms, without aiming for understanding the cognitive process that leads to decisions (cf., Rieskamp, Busemeyer, & Mellers, 2006). Although the former approach can be quite successful in describing people's choices in various domains it could be limited when making predictions for future and independent behavior not used for fitting a model, because it lacks the understanding of the causal mechanisms of people's behavior. In contrast, recent approaches in cognitive psychology, behavioral economics, and decision neuroscience of studying judgment and decision making have led to advances towards unpacking the black box. Understanding the underlying cognitive processes of human decision making allows to explain when and why people violate important choice axioms and should ultimately lead to better independent, out of sample predictions.

Current Approaches to Identification of Processes Involved in Decision Making

Perhaps one of the most effective approaches to discovering how decision makers use information is the process tracing approach, which includes both overt and covert methods. Overt process tracing methods rely on directly observable behavior during the decision-making process. Interactive information displays (Chapters 6–7), eye-tracking (Chapters 1–5), and verbal protocols (Chapters 17–18) are all types of overt process tracing methods used to investigate information search during decision making. These methods can indicate what information people search for, the order in which they search, and the amount of time they devote to each information source. These data can indicate whether assumptions about the fundamental cognitive processes hold and provide strong constraints on models of the decision process (e.g., Bröder, 2000; Newell & Shanks, 2003; Payne, Bettman, & Johnson, 1988, 1993; Rieskamp & Hoffrage, 1999, 2008). Despite the clear value of these overt methods, it is possible that they provide less constraint on how the decision is made once the decision maker has collected information. Furthermore, some researchers have suggested that these overt methods are particularly vulnerable to participants being aware of the manipulations and adapting their performance accordingly (Reisen, Hoffrage, & Mast, 2008).

Covert process tracing methods, in contrast, rely on indirect inferences from the observed behaviors about the cognitive processes. Examples of covert methods are those that rely on collected choice responses, scaled choice preferences, and/or response times (e.g., Busemeyer & Townsend, 1993; Nosofsky & Palmeri, 1997; Ashby, 2000; Glöckner, 2009). Normally, any of these observations could not be directly connected to underlying cognitive process. However, by using specific experimental designs (input), researchers can collect the appropriate response data (output) to constrain the possible models of the decision-making process. The input-output analysis is achieved by the means of model testing. The best model of underlying cognitive processes is inferred from likelihoods of the observed input-output relationship across the candidate models, or within the Bayesian approaches, the posterior probability of a decision-making model given the input-output patterns.

Covert and overt methods are in many ways complementary. The main limitation of the covert input-output methods is that they provide minimal information about the pre-decision stage where the overt methods are strongest. However, covert methods can be informative about the final decision stage in which overt methods are the least informative. This final decision stage is considered inaccessible to introspection. Importantly at this stage, many cognitive factors could significantly affect the decision, particularly memory storage and retrieval, perceptual context, attention, and others.

Many researchers have applied the input-output model analyses of choices to examine this final decision stage. Although there have been notable successes, progress has been stymied by the problems with model identifiability: several classes of different models predict the exact same choice patterns. The strategic plan to avoid such choice model mimicking has been considered in several publications (e.g., Rieskamp & Hoffrage, 1999, 2008; Bröder, 2000; Lee & Cummins, 2004).

In addition to choice patterns, response time analysis is another covert approach that can offer insight into the cognitive processes underlying decision making. Sophisticated modeling based on response times dates back to the early days of experimental psychology in the latter half of the 19th century starting with the work of Donders (1868) and Wundt (1880), and flourished with the development of the information-processing approach (e.g., Sternberg, 1966, 1969). When combined with choice patterns, response times have led to a number of important advances in cognitive psychology (e.g., Ashby, 2000; Ashby & Maddox, 1994; Heath, 1992; Lamberts, 1998, 2000; Link, 1992; Nosofsky & Palmeri, 1997; Ratcliff, 1978; Smith, 1995; Donkin, Nosofsky, Gold, & Shiffrin, 2013; Little, Nosofsky, Donkin, & Denton, 2013).

In the present chapter, we will not discuss the response time predictions that can be derived from all the models mentioned earlier. Instead, for illustration purposes we will only focus on how response times can be used to test two prototypical inference strategies suggested by the strategy approach (Gigerenzer, Todd, & The ABC Research Group, 1999; Payne et al., 1993). This illustration, however, can be generalized to a variety of decision-making models. The strategy approach assumes that people are equipped with a repertoire of different strategies to make inferences.

Response Time Analysis for Testing Process Model of Probabilistic Inferences

Several research publications used the analysis of response times in examining probabilistic inferences. Bergert and Nosofsky (2007) tested a generalized, lexicographic take-the-best (TTB) and a generalized weighted additive (WADD) model. They demonstrated that the resulting generalized model was able to make identical choice predictions, so that choice behavior alone does not allow to differentiate between the two models. However, response time data provided an additional source of information for testing the models; indeed, results of response time analysis largely supported TTB over WADD.

Bröder and Gaissmaier (2007) re-examined five of Bröder and Schiffer's (2003) experiments. They split the participants into four groups with identical strategy classifications on the basis of their observed inferences. Bröder and Gaissmaier computed the median response time[1] and found that the response times followed the predicted pattern and supported the assumption of sequential search: Participants classified as using TTB showed an increase in response time depending on the position of the best discriminating cue, while this increase was much less pronounced for participants who were classified as using WADD or Tally. In sum, the response time analysis results converged to the previous conclusions of the previous choice behavior analyses, and strongly supported the main results.

Persson and Rieskamp (2009) performed a response time analysis to confirm the results of their strategy classification analysis, similar to Bröder and Gaissmaier (2007). Overall their results supported the strategy-based approach in decision making, in which a decision maker adapts to the constraints in the environment, including factors such as time pressure, information search costs, the nature of feedback, and presentation format of information.

One of the main questions posed by this research was whether the prevalence of TTB in Bröder and Schiffer (2003) was induced by the experimental requirements. For instance, participants were given the rank order of cue validities, which may have fostered the selection of TTB. In contrast, if participants had to learn the validities of the cues, this might lead them to use other inference strategies, such as Tally, which does not require any cue validities. This issue was addressed in the later study (Persson & Rieskamp, 2009) using response time analysis: the results indicated that the noncompensatory TTB strategy and compensatory (WADD) strategy are dependent on the type of decision feedback provided.

The reported studies illustrate how a response time analysis can be used to validate the inference that had been made on a pure analysis of people's choices. The goal of the reported response time analyses was to find convergent evidence for the processes assumed to underlie memory-based probabilistic inferences. For memory-based decisions monitoring external information search processes cannot be applied. Therefore, response times were analyzed to validate the idea of sequential cue search in inference processes and as an independent source of support for the outcome-based strategy classification method. In this manner, Bergert and Nosofsky (2007), Bröder and Gaissmaier (2007), and Persson and Rieskamp (2009) tried to achieve the goal that models should be testable with different kinds of data.

Potential Limitations of the Traditional Response Time Analysis and the Solution

Although response time analysis improves inferences over the analysis of choice responses alone, there can still be significant model identifiability problems, even with simple decision-making systems. For example, one fundamental question in understanding the decision stage is whether individuals consider each piece of evidence one-at-a-time (in series) or all at once (in parallel). Despite a clear conceptual distinction between serial and parallel processing, serial and parallel systems can exactly mimic each other across a wide range of empirical settings (Townsend & Ashby, 1983). One reason this mimicking can occur is that slow-downs or speed-ups across conditions can be explained equally well by differences in temporal structure (i.e., parallel versus serial) as by differences in processing efficiency (e.g., Townsend, 1972; Townsend & Ashby, 1983).

In sum, several approaches have been created to answer the questions about the organization of cognitive processes in decision making. One of the most challenging issues faced was model mimicking. Different models are able to predict the same outcomes either at the choice levels or at the response time levels. This poses a serious challenge to discriminating among candidate descriptions of the decision-making process. To overcome the model mimicking, and to unlock more powerful ways of decision-making model identification, we propose a synthesis between the *systems factorial technology* (SFT) with the traditional decision-making analysis.

As a preview, to show how SFT deals with the response time mimicking, a simulations study was conducted using two different decision strategies. First we simulated a response time output of TTB in a situation where stopping can occur on the first discriminating cue. Second, we simulated the coactive model—one of the possible candidate variants for the cognitive model underlying a WADD decision strategy. In the coactive model information from all cue attributes is processed in parallel fashion. The two simulated models differ critically on three fundamental cognitive properties (search, stopping, integration). However, the simulation results showed that the two models can perfectly mimic each other's response times (Figure 12.1 A). Nonetheless, we see that data from the same models with the same parameterization reveals quite distinct diagnostic patterns of response times when analyzed using SFT (Figure 12.1 B). The response time data function for the TTB model is almost flat (randomly hovering around zero), while the coactive WADD model shows an S-shaped function. The SFT approach thus avoids the response time mimicking problem and provides sufficient model discriminability power to distinguish between the two different decision-making strategies.

The Systems Factorial Technology Methodology

Systems factorial technology (SFT) is a suite of methodological tools aimed at discovering the fundamental properties of cognitive operations by the decomposition of output response time (Townsend & Ashby, 1983; Townsend & Nozawa, 1995; also see the related approach Schweickert, Fisher, & Sung, 2012). The SFT analysis provides rigorous tests and mathematical tools for discerning the fundamental properties of the cognitive processes underlying many decision-making models:

1. Type of information search (serial, parallel, or coactive),
2. Scope of information search (limited/self-terminating versus total/exhaustive),
3. Type of information integration (whether cognitive processes are independent or dependent of each other),
4. Capacity of the system under investigation; that is, amount of work done by the decision-making system, when information load increases (limited, unlimited, or supercapacity).

We include a necessarily brief overview of the approach later. For additional details, there are several tutorials on SFT (Fifić & Little, 2017; Altieri, Fifić, Little, & Yang, 2017; Harding et al., 2016; Houpt, Blaha, McIntire, Havig, & Townsend, 2014). In a nutshell, SFT requires the factorial manipulation of the time spent considering each of the sources of information available. We refer to the manipulations that slow down or speed up the processing of each source as "stretching factors". Critically, each stretching factor should influence the processing of a specific target source of information and not others (selective influence).

Consider a generic study in which a choice must be made between two options based on two attributes. One stretching factor should influence the speed with which an individual evaluates attribute 1, with the two levels: Fast (F) for faster evaluation and Slow (S) for slower evaluation. The second stretching factor operates similarly for attribute 2. Stretching factor 1 should not affect the processing of attribute 2 and stretching factor 2 should not affect the processing of attribute 1. A factorial combination of the levels of each stretching factor yields four experimental

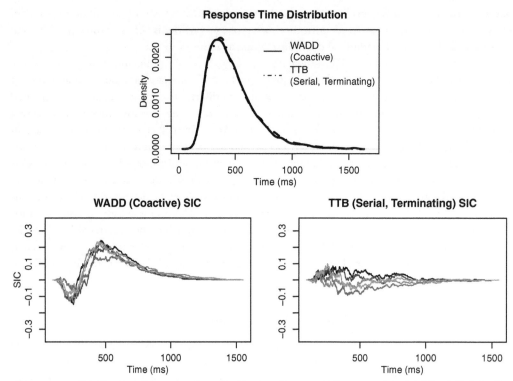

FIGURE 12.1 (A) Simulated response time distributions for two different models WADD and TTB. The two distributions almost perfectly overlap, implying that at this level two models can't be differentiated in the output. Both models' choice accuracies were also equal ($p = .999$) meaning that both models achieved high decision accuracy. (B) When the SFT analyses were applied on the same data from A, we can see that the two models generated clearly distinct SIC signatures, thus implying that the models can now differentiate in the output.

conditions: SS, SF, FS, and FF. Here, each letter indicates whether the evaluation process was stretched in time or not. For example, SF means that the first attribute evaluation was stretched (slow), and the second attribute evaluation was not stretched (fast). We denote the collection of response times in each factorial condition with RT_{SS}, RT_{SF}, RT_{FS}, and RT_{FF}.

The factorial design uses the stretching effects that are conducted on at least two (decision) processes of interest, to investigate the interaction of the stretching effects. In the SFT approach the interaction analysis provides the most diagnostic information about the organization of underlying processes.

Double Factor Manipulation: Stretching Two Processes

The orthogonal factors can be used to calculate the interaction contrast, much like in factorial ANOVA. The first interaction test can be expressed as the difference between stretching effects on response times. Using the M.. to indicate the mean time across the collection RT.., the mean interaction contrast (MIC) is given by:

$$MIC = (M_{SS} - M_{SF}) - (M_{FS} - M_{FF}).$$

Additional diagnostic information can be gleaned using survivor functions. Completely analogous to deriving the MIC, one can compute the survivor interaction contrast (SIC). The survivor function describes the probability that a response time will occur after a given time and is one minus the more familiar cumulative distribution function. By replacing the mean RTs for each condition by the survivor function S, at each value of t, one computes:

$$SIC(t) = [S_{SS}(t) - S_{SF}(t)] - [S_{FS}(t) - S_{FF}(t)].$$

Both the MIC and SIC provide powerful information for exploring the fundamental properties of the decision-making process. Figure 12.2 shows the correspondence between MIC and SIC signatures (middle), and cognitive processes that could be used to make a decision model (left-hand side), and the interpretation of the signatures in terms of decision-making model properties (right-hand side).

SFT has been used in the context of various cognitive tasks and domains: perceptual processes, visual and memory search tasks, face perception tasks, and classification and categorization (see Little, Altieri, Fifić, & Yang, 2017 for a comprehensive literature overview). The SFT tools were recognized as potentially the most important and promising methodology in understanding cognitive processes (Greenwald, 2012), and also invited to the domain of decision making as a promising new direction in model testing (Busemeyer, 2017; Gaissmaier, Fifić, & Rieskamp, 2011).

Applying Systems Factorial Technology to the Probabilistic Inference Task

In order to apply SFT we follow the three-step instructions described by Fifić and Little (2017):

1. Identify a processing model(s) of interest that will be tested in terms of its fundamental cognitive processes: processing order, stopping rule, and process interdependency.
2. Determine the task structure, particularly the stretching manipulations.
3. Collect RT data, analyze the corresponding response distributions using MIC and SIC, and interpret.

STEP 1: Identify Processing Models of Interest, and the SFT Model Predictions

A first prototypical strategy that we consider is a noncompensatory lexicographic one, of which the TTB heuristic (Gigerenzer & Goldstein, 1996) is an example. The strategy predicts limited and serial processing of information. TTB assumes that people compare cues across objects, starting with the most valid cue with regard to predicting the criterion, and stop as soon as one cue is found that discriminates between the two objects. That is, a person using TTB first searches for the most valid cue, which is the best discriminating cue between two objects on a criterion. If this cue discriminates, the person does not search further and makes a decision. Otherwise, searching for cues continues until a discriminating cue is found. Therefore, when TTB finds the first (i.e., most valid) discriminating cue, it stops searching and makes a decision based on that cue alone, while all the remaining cues are ignored. If TTB stops on processing of the first discriminating cue then one can expect to observe MIC=0 and flat SIC, as shown in Figure 12.2A (serial self-terminating model). If TTB stops on the second discriminating cue, after processing the first non-discriminative cue, then one can expect MIC=0 and S-shaped SIC, as shown in Figure 12.2B (serial exhaustive model). In contrast, compensatory strategies, such as the WADD strategy, assume that all available information is processed in series (e.g., Gigerenzer & Goldstein, 1996; Payne et al., 1988). WADD assumes that each cue is weighted (usually by the validity of the cue), and that a decision maker calculates the sum of all weighted cue values when choosing

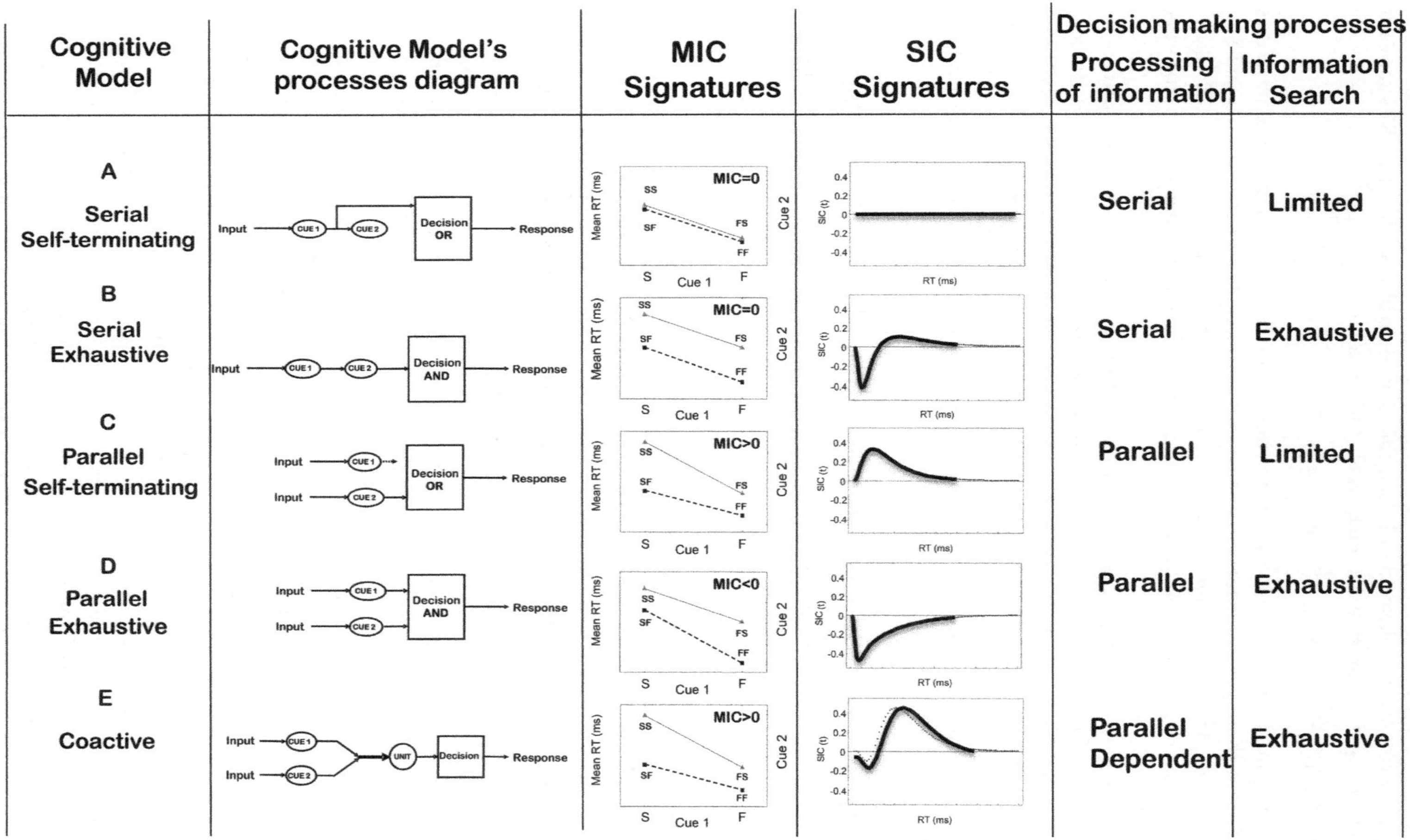

FIGURE 12.2 The correspondence among cognitive models (left), SFT signatures (middle), and the inferred decision process structure (right).

between two alternatives. A decision maker chooses the alternative with the largest weighted sum. WADD needs to process all cues, so it could be expected that MIC=0 and SIC function should be the form of Figure 12.2B (serial exhaustive model), regardless of the position of the discriminating cue. Other variants of compensatory strategies are Bayesian inference models (Naïve Bayes or NB). A Bayesian inference that is built into a connectionist processing model assumes that all available cues are processed in parallel (cf., Glöckner, Hilbig, & Jekel, 2014). In these cases one can expect to observe MIC<0 and negative SIC function, as shown in Figure 12.2D. However, if the processing of cues are dependent of each other, then one can expect to observe the coactive signature that is MIC>0 and SIC has a mainly positive shape with a small negative initial blip, Figure 12.2E (the exemplar model, e.g., Fifić, Little, & Nosofsky, 2010; Fifić & Townsend, 2010). The cue dependencies can be formed either by creating a learning environment in which a decision maker learns statistical dependencies between the options' cues; and/or could be created in the parallel network systems which assigns conjoint weights to the cue representations. Finally, some decision-making systems can benefit from parallel self-terminating processing, so called horse-race models (Marley & Colonius, 1992; Pike, 1973; Townsend & Ashby, 1983), in which the first discriminating attribute can terminate the parallel information search and lead to final decision, as shown in Figure 12.2C. Taken together, we could see that among several dominant decision-making models the critical distinguishing cognitive properties are the processing order, the extent of processing, and processing integration structure, all of which could be diagnosed using SFT.

STEP 2: Task Selection and Stretching Manipulation

In a probabilistic inference task, participants have to compare objects and decide which objects score higher based on several attributes (cues) of the objects. For example, assume that participants must decide which of two bugs is more poisonous based on their legs and body texture (Bergert & Nosofsky, 2007). Researchers have modeled this choice process using connectionist models (Glöckner, et al., 2014), exemplar models (Juslin & Persson, 2002), sequential sampling models (Lee & Cummins, 2004; Wallsten & Barton, 1982), and procedural strategies (Gigerenzer et al., 1999; Payne et al., 1993). Furthermore, people may use different strategies based on whether both attributes are necessary for decision making (compensatory environment) or a single attribute is sufficient (noncompensatory environment).

Generally speaking, when viewers approach this task they could check the attributes in series (e.g., legs, then bodies) or examine all attributes of a bug before moving on to the other. At this point, we focus our description on testing the former attribute-wise search, although the design and analysis also apply to the latter option-wise search. Hence, our question can be framed as how a decision maker processes the attributes and combines them to make a decision? To answer the question we can design a learning phase with two environments (compensatory and noncompensatory) and three cues (legs, antenna, and body). On each trial two randomly selected bugs are displayed simultaneously next to each other, separated by a fixation point. The task is to decide which bug was more poisonous as quickly as possible without making errors. Probabilistic feedback is provided and participants are informed that the feedback would help them to learn to recognize poison levels of bugs.

In a subsequent test phase, the SFT methodology was applied. The stretching manipulation, that is speeding up or slowing down the processes of interest (S=slow, F=fast), was achieved by visually masking attributes: In this case, we used semi-transparent leaves to occlude attributes

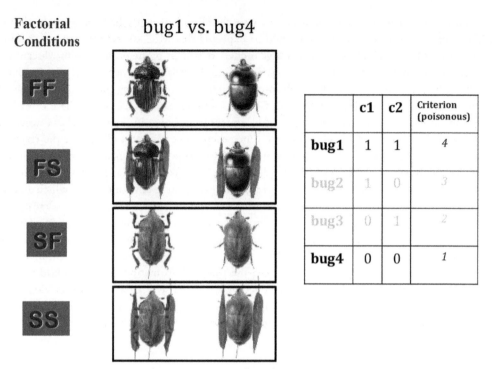

FIGURE 12.3 Demonstration of SFT stretching when the most poisonous bug1 is compared to the least poisonous bug4. The left column processing: F stands for "fast" and S stands for "slow". The mask is used to slow processing.

(see Figure 12.3). Cue stretching (S, F) was factorially combined across the factor cues (factor cue 1 body and factor cue 2 legs), leading to the four conditions: SS, SF, FS, and FF (Figure 12.3). The indices on the left indicate saliency level of cue 1 (body) and the indices on the right indicate saliency of cue 2 (legs). Thus, "SF" indicates a condition in which two simultaneously displayed bugs had their cue 1 (body) semi-transparently masked, and the cue 2 (legs) unmasked. No feedback is provided in the test phase. Otherwise, the task instructions are the same as the learning phase: decide which bug is more poisonous as rapidly as possible without making errors.

STEP 3: Face Validity of the SFT in Testing Probabilistic Inference Task: Simulation Study

We use results from two subjects in a probabilistic inference task to demonstrate the application of SFT. One subject is tested in a noncompensatory condition and another one in a compensatory condition. Recall that the Naïve Bayes and WADD predict that participants will use an exhaustive strategy, with Naïve Bayes normally being not so strongly associated with parallel or coactive processing and WADD associated with serial processing, in both environments. In contrast, the TTB strategy predicts a serial first-terminating process in the noncompensatory environment and a serial exhaustive process in the compensatory condition. A non-zero MIC would rule out serial processing, hence a non-zero MIC in either environment would rule out TTB. A change in MIC sign between the compensatory and noncompensatory conditions, indicating a switch between

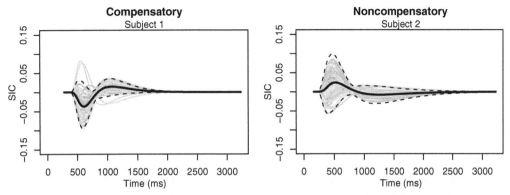

FIGURE 12.4 The two selected SIC functions. The left compensatory SIC function indicates serial exhaustive processing across attributes (for comparison see Figure 12.2B); the right noncompensatory SIC function indicates serial self-terminating processing, and is statistically "flat" (for comparison see Figure 12.2A).

exhaustive and first-terminating decision making, would rule out standard versions of Naïve Bayes and WADD models.

For subjects in both the compensatory and noncompensatory conditions the posterior probabilities favored an MIC equal to zero ($p > .75$). We applied follow-up SIC analysis at the individual level: In the compensatory condition the subject had a significantly negative SIC value, which along with the MIC result indicates serial-exhaustive processing (Figure 12.4). In the noncompensatory condition the subject had no significant deviations from zero in the SIC, indicating serial first-terminating processing (Figure 12.4). The pattern of results is exactly that predicted by TTB and the zero MIC with a lack of SIC deviations from zero rule out WADD and Naïve Bayes models. Thus, this approach has allowed us to conclude that these participants were using a one-at-a-time (serial) strategy and stopped assessing information once they had enough to make a decision (self-terminating).

Collecting more subjects' data would allow for making inference about decision-making strategies both at the group and individual levels.

Conclusions

In this chapter, we argued that response times are a valuable resource for testing process models of judgment and decision making. Cognitive models of decision making imply different types of information processing that can lead to a decision. One can differentiate three very general aspects of information processing: the scope of information search (self-terminating versus exhaustive) the type of information processing (serial versus parallel), and the type of information integration. These three aspects can be found in different combinations in a variety of models. Despite different processing assumptions, however, these models often cannot be distinguished by the decisions they predict, leading to an identification problem.

Bergert and Nosofsky (2007) were able to distinguish between two different models based on mean response time analyses. These models were identical in their choice predictions but very different in the spirit of the underlying process assumptions. Moreover, the response time analyses of both Bröder and Gaissmaier (2007) and Persson and Rieskamp (2009) supported the assumption of self-terminating, serial cue search in memory-based decision making, for a substantial proportion of their participants. The results demonstrate the usefulness of response time analyses as a method for tracing processes that are not directly observable. The analysis of response times can therefore provide valuable information on whether the interpretations drawn from an analysis of participants' decisions alone appear valid.

Unfortunately, even response time analysis is prone to model mimicking. We showed that two very distinct decision-making models could predict identical response time distributions (Figure 12.1A). This illustrates that under certain conditions, models under investigation cannot be clearly identified even using both choice accuracy and response time analyses. To address these limitations we demonstrated the SFT methodology which provides an assessment of the type of information processing (serial versus parallel), the scope of information search (self-terminating versus exhaustive), and type of information integration (process dependency). SFT could be used to identify different decision-making strategies, such as noncompensatory strategies and compensatory strategies. The SFT approach requires adding more experimental conditions to the original decision task (such as in the example earlier in a probabilistic inference task) so that researchers can selectively influence a processing time of each decision attribute. This SFT stretching manipulation allows output analysis in terms of patterns of either mean response times (MIC) or survivor function (SIC), so that a distinct decision-making model would leave different output patterns of both MICs and SICs. These diagnostic patterns could provide needed diagnostic edge to distinguishing between the models of interest. Thus the SFT approach can be seen as a methodological extension to standard task (Greenwald, 2012).

The key to SFT is the selective influence of the different information sources. Other traditional approaches to decision model testing might also benefit from these manipulations and be combined with the stretching manipulations. For example, one typical approach to examining decision-making processes is to manipulate the distribution of attribute validities for options that are considered in decision making. Researchers typically create two different environments, hoping to encourage different decision strategies. In a compensatory environment, compensatory strategies would be appropriate, in which a low value of an attribute of an option can be compensated by a high value on a different attribute. A typical representative would be weighted additive strategy (WADD). In a noncompensatory environment, strategies that do not allow attribute values on one attribute to compensate for low values on another attribute could be sufficient. Take-the-best strategy (TTB) is a typical example of noncompensatory strategy. In practice, to identify TTB and WADD decision-making models, one has to compare the response outcomes between the two environments. So in the traditional approach analyzing response data from only one environment doesn't provide sufficient and necessary conditions for decision model comparison.

The required SFT application can be done orthogonal to the manipulation of attributes validities. Selective stretching of the cognitive processes are all that is required for SFT. The time stretching manipulation (Fifić & Little, 2017) could be defined completely independent from the attribute validities, which in turn gives more degrees of freedom for SFT application.

Response time analysis is a fruitful endeavor that can increase understanding of cognitive processes underlying peoples' judgments and decisions. Researchers are encouraged to take advantage of the converging principle in process tracing, by employing not only different analyses but also complementary approaches to analysis underlying cognitive process in decision making. One such approach could be SFT that could add to the informativeness of other process tracing methods such as eye-tracking (Chapters 1–5), and/or interactive information displays methods (Chapters 6–7).

Note

1 Analysis of median RT rather than mean RT can offer more robust results because RTs are often skewed. Extreme outliers may also be an issue for RT analysis, which is to some degree mitigated by the use of medians. For distributional analyses, such at the SIC described later, outliers are even less of an issue than for median-based approaches. When mean RT is the statistic of interest, we recommend a contaminant model such as that presented in Craigmile, Peruggia, and van Zandt (2010).

Recommended Reading List

- Bröder and Gaissmaier (2007): showed how response time analyses can provide convergent evidence for assumptions about information search in memory-based decision making.
- Persson and Rieskamp (2009): tested an exemplar-based approach to predicting people's inferences from memory against the strategy-based approach and used response time analyses to confirm strategy classifications.
- Houpt and Fifić (2017): defined the mathematical tools for combining SFT technology with the hierarchical Bayesian inference.
- Fifić and Little (2017): provided a tutorial of how SFT methodology can be applied to different experimental paradigms and research domains.

References

Altieri, N., Fifić, M., Little, D. R., & Yang, C.-T. (2017). Historical foundations and a tutorial introduction to systems factorial technology. In D. R. Little, N. Altieri, M. Fifić, & C.-T. Yang (Eds.), *Systems factorial technology: A theory driven methodology for the identification of perceptual and cognitive mechanisms* (pp. 3–25). London, UK: Academic Press.

Ashby, F. G. (2000). A stochastic version of general recognition theory. *Journal of Mathematical Psychology*, *44*(2), 310–329.

Ashby, F. G., & Maddox, W. T. (1994). A response time theory of separability and integrality in speeded classification. *Journal of Mathematical Psychology*, *38*(4), 423–466.

Bergert, F. B., & Nosofsky, R. M. (2007). A response-time approach to comparing generalized rational and take-the-best models of decision making. *Journal of Experimental Psychology: Learning, Memory, and Cognition*, *33*(1), 107–129.

Bröder, A. (2000). Assessing the empirical validity of the "take-the-best" heuristic as a model of human probabilistic inference. *Journal of Experimental Psychology: Learning, Memory, and Cognition*, *26*(5), 1332–1346.

Bröder, A., & Gaissmaier, W. (2007). Sequential processing of cues in memory-based multi-attribute decisions. *Psychonomic Bulletin and Review*, *14*(5), 895–900.

Bröder, A., & Schiffer, S. (2003). Take the best versus simultaneous feature matching: Probabilistic inferences from memory and effects of representation format. *Journal of Experimental Psychology: General*, *132*(2), 277–293.

Busemeyer, J. R. (2017). Old and new directions in strategy selection. *Journal of Behavioral Decision Making*, *31*(2), 199–202.

Busemeyer, J. R., & Townsend, J. T. (1993). Decision field theory: A dynamic-cognitive approach to decision making in an uncertain environment. *Psychological Review*, *100*(3), 432–459.

Craigmile, P. F., Peruggia, M., & van Zandt, T. (2010). Hierarchical bayes models for response time data. *Psychometrika*, *75*(4), 613–632.

Donders, F. C. (1868). Over de snelheid van psychische processen. Onderzoekingen gedaan in het physiologisch laboratorium der Utrechtsche Hoogeschool, 1868–1869. *Tweede Reeks*, *2*, 92–120.

Donkin, C., Nosofsky, R. M., Gold, J. M., & Shiffrin, R. M. (2013). Discrete-slots models of visual working-memory response times. *Psychological Review*, *120*(4), 873–902.

Fifić, M., & Little, D. R. (2017). Stretching mental processes: An overview of and guide for SFT applications. In D. R. Little, N. Altieri, M. Fifić, & C-T. Yang (Eds.), *Systems factorial technology: A theory driven methodology for the identification of perceptual and cognitive mechanisms* (pp. 27–51). London, UK: Academic Press.

Fifić, M., Little, D. R., & Nosofsky, R. M. (2010). Logical-rule models of classification response times: A synthesis of mental-architecture, random-walk, and decision-bound approaches. *Psychological Review, 117*(2), 309–348.

Fifić, M., & Townsend, J. T. (2010). Information-processing alternatives to holistic perception: Identifying the mechanisms of secondary-level holism within a categorization paradigm. *Journal of Experimental Psychology: Learning, Memory, and Cognition, 36*(5), 1290–1313.

Gaissmaier, W., Fifić, M., & Rieskamp, J. (2011). Analyzing response times to understand decision processes. In M. Schulte-Mecklenbeck, A. Kühberger, & R. Ranyard (Eds.), *A handbook of process tracing methods for decision making* (pp. 141–163) New York, NY: Taylor & Francis.

Gigerenzer, G., & Goldstein, D. (1996). Reasoning the fast and frugal way: Models of bounded rationality. *Psychological Review, 103*(4), 650–669.

Gigerenzer, G., Todd, P. M., & The ABC Research Group. (1999). *Simple heuristics that make us smart.* New York, NY: Oxford University Press.

Glöckner, A. (2009). Investigating intuitive and deliberate processes statistically. *Judgment and Decision Making, 4*(3), 186–199.

Glöckner, A., Hilbig, B. E., & Jekel, M. (2014). What is adaptive about adaptive decision making? A parallel constraint satisfaction account. *Cognition, 133*(3), 641–666.

Greenwald, A. G. (2012). There is nothing so theoretical as a good method. *Perspectives on Psychological Science, 7*(2), 99–108.

Harding, B., Goulet, M., Jolin, S., Tremblay, C., Villeneuve, S., & Durand, G. (2016). Systems factorial technology explained to humans. *Tutorials in Quantitative Methods for Psychology, 12*(1), 39–56.

Heath, R. A. (1992). A general nonstationary diffusion model for two choice decision making. *Mathematical Social Sciences, 23*(3), 283–309.

Houpt, J. W., Blaha, L. M., McIntire, J. P., Havig, P. R., & Townsend, J. T. (2014). Systems factorial technology with R. *Behavior Research Methods, 46*(2), 307–330.

Houpt, J. W., & Fifić, M. (2017). A hierarchical Bayesian approach to distinguishing serial and parallel processing. *Journal of Mathematical Psychology, 79*, 13–22.

Juslin, P., & Persson, M. (2002). PROBabilities from EXemplars (PROBEX): A "lazy" algorithm for probabilistic inference from generic knowledge. *Cognitive Science, 26*(5), 563–607.

Lamberts, K. (1998). The time course of categorization. *Journal of Experimental Psychology: Learning, Memory, and Cognition, 24*(3), 695–711.

Lamberts, K. (2000). Information–accumulation theory of speeded categorization. *Psychological Review, 107*(2), 227–260.

Lee, M. D., & Cummins, T. D. R. (2004). Evidence accumulation in decision making: Unifying the "take the best" and "rational" models. *Psychonomic Bulletin and Review, 11*(2), 343–352.

Link, S. W. (1992). *The wave theory of difference and similarity.* Hillsdale, NJ: Lawrence Erlbaum Associates.

Little, D., Altieri, N., Fifić, M., & Yang, C. T. (Eds.). (2017). *Systems factorial technology: A theory driven methodology for the identification of perceptual and cognitive mechanisms.* London: Academic Press.

Little, D. R., Nosofsky, R. M., Donkin, C., & Denton, S. E. (2013). Logical rules and the classification of integral-dimension stimuli. *Journal of Experimental Psychology: Learning, Memory, and Cognition, 39*(3), 801.

Marley, A. A. J., & Colonius, H. (1992). The "horse race" random utility model for choice probabilities and reaction times, and its competing risks interpretation. *Journal of Mathematical Psychology, 36*(1), 1–20.

Newell, B. R., & Shanks, D. R. (2003). Take the best or look at the rest? Factors influencing "one-reason" decision making. *Journal of Experimental Psychology: Learning, Memory, and Cognition, 29*(1), 53–65.

Nosofsky, R. M., & Palmeri, T. J. (1997). An exemplar-based random walk model of speeded classification. *Psychological Review, 104*(2), 266–300.

Payne, J. W., Bettman, J. R., & Johnson, E. J. (1988). Adaptive strategy selection in decision making. *Journal of Experimental Psychology: Learning, Memory, and Cognition, 14*(3), 534–552.

Payne, J. W., Bettman, J. R., & Johnson, E. J. (1993). *The adaptive decision maker.* Cambridge, UK: Cambridge University Press.

Persson, M., & Rieskamp, J. (2009). Inferences from memory: Strategy- and exemplar-based judgment models compared. *Acta Psychologica, 130*(1), 25–37.

Pike, A. R. (1973). Response latency models for signal detection. *Psychological Review, 80*(1), 53–68.

Ratcliff, R. (1978). A theory of memory retrieval. *Psychological Review, 85*(2), 59–108.

Reisen, N., Hoffrage, U., & Mast, F. W. (2008). Identifying decision strategies in a consumer choice situation. *Judgment Decision Making, 3*(8), 641–658.

Rieskamp, J., Busemeyer, J. R., & Mellers, B. A. (2006). Extending the bounds of rationality: Evidence and theories of preferential choice. *Journal of Economic Literature, 44*(3), 631–661.

Rieskamp, J., & Hoffrage, U. (1999). When do people use simple heuristics, and how can we tell? In G. Gigerenzer, P. M. Todd, & The ABC Research Group (Eds.), *Simple heuristics that make us smart* (pp. 141–167). New York, NY: Oxford University Press.

Rieskamp, J., & Hoffrage, U. (2008). Inferences under time pressure: How opportunity costs affect strategy selection. *Acta Psychologica, 127*(2), 258–276.

Schweickert, R., Fisher, D. L., & Sung, K. (2012). *Discovering cognitive architecture by selectively influencing mental processes* (Vol. 4). Hackensack, NJ: World Scientific.

Smith, P. L. (1995). Psychophysically principled models of visual simple reaction time. *Psychological Review, 102*(3), 567–591.

Sternberg, S. (1966). High speed scanning in human memory. *Science, 153*(3736), 652–654.

Sternberg, S. (1969). The discovery of processing stages: Extensions of Donder's method. In W. G. Koster (Ed.), *Attention and performance II* (pp. 276–315). Amsterdam, NL: North Holland.

Townsend, J. T. (1972). Some results concerning the identifiability of parallel and serial processes. *British Journal of Mathematical and Statistical Psychology, 25*(2), 168–199.

Townsend, J. T., & Ashby, F. G. (1983). *The stochastic modeling of elementary psychological processes*. Cambridge, UK: Cambridge University Press.

Townsend, J. T., & Nozawa, G. (1995). Spatio-temporal properties of elementary perception: An investigation of parallel, serial, and coactive theories. *Journal of Mathematical Psychology, 39*(4), 321–359.

Wallsten, T. S., & Barton, C. (1982). Processing probabilistic multidimensional information for decisions. *Journal of Experimental Psychology: Learning, Memory, and Cognition, 8*(5), 361–384.

Wundt, W. (1880). *Grundzüge der physiologischen Psychologie* [Foundations of physiological psychology] (2nd ed.). Leipzig: Engelmann.

13

A PRACTICAL GUIDE FOR AUTOMATED FACIAL EMOTION CLASSIFICATION[1]

Sabrina Stöckli, Michael Schulte-Mecklenbeck, Stefan Borer, and Andrea C. Samson

Faces are the most complex, nonverbal sources of information about peoples' emotions (Ekman & Friesen, 1982; Hwang & Matsumoto, 2016). Facial expressions signal emotions such as anger, disgust, fear, happiness, sadness, and surprise—voluntarily or involuntarily produced by facial muscle contractions (Ekman & Friesen, 1976; Hwang & Matsumoto, 2016). Measuring facial expressions allows inferences about decision makers' emotional states and can thus provide insight into an important component of human judgment and decision making (JDM).

Researchers apply different approaches to assess emotions. In general, researchers differentiate between five emotional response systems (and typical corresponding measures): a) subjective experience (e.g., self-report measures), b) peripheral physiology (e.g., autonomic nervous system measures such as electrodermal activity), c) affect-modulated startle (e.g., startle response measure such as Electromyogram (EMG) measure of eye blink amplitude), d) central physiology (e.g., brain state measures such as Electroencephalography (EEG)), and e) behavior. When considering the behavioral response system, facial expressions are the most commonly used measure (Mauss & Robinson, 2009). One of the most prominent approaches to assess emotions expressed in the face is the anatomically based Facial Action Coding System (FACS) (Ekman & Friesen, 1976); it allows trained human coders to categorize and infer emotions based on visible facial cues, often with the help of video recordings. Yet, certified human FACS coders require training that lasts up to 100 hours (e.g., at workshops by the Paul Ekman Group). The coding process itself is also time- and labor-intensive: video material of people's faces is often recorded with a frequency of 24 frames per second, meaning that for each second of recording the coder has to categorize the facial cues, defined in FACS, 24 times. Scaling this calculation, one minute of video requires 1440 individual ratings; assuming that a human coder rates one picture per second, approximately 24 minutes are required to code one minute of material (Ekman & Oster, 1979). Given this time- and labor-intensive process, there have been attempts to streamline and automatize the classification process through computer software. As a consequence, the market for automated FACS-based facial expression analysis has been steadily growing (Lewinski, den Uyl, & Butler, 2014; Swinton & El Kaliouby, 2012; Valstar, Jiang, Mehu, Pantic, & Scherer, 2011).

So far, facial expression analysis has hardly been used as a process tracing method in JDM research (for exceptions see Rasch, Louviere, & Teichert, 2015; Ross, Fasel, & Sanfey, 2011). Of course the JDM field recognizes that emotions influence how people judge and decide, that emotions interact and influence cognitions and, in turn, that people's emotions provide information about underlying mechanisms of decision making (Bechara, 2004; Brosch & Sander, 2013; Dolan, 2002; Loewenstein, Weber, Hsee, & Welch, 2001; Luce, Bettman, & Payne, 1997; Schwarz, 2000). Automated facial expression analysis seems to be a promising process tracing method for JDM research because facial expressions are an indicator for emotions (Chentsova-Dutton, & Tsai, 2010; Ekman & Friesen, 2003; Mauss & Robinson, 2009; Scherer & Ceschi, 2000; Wolf, 2015) and allow for inferences on underlying decision-making mechanisms. The purpose of this chapter is to give a user-oriented introduction of automated facial expression analysis.

Measuring Emotions in the Face

There is a vast literature on methods to assess emotions by means of facial expressions, including their advantages and disadvantages (Mauss & Robinson, 2009). These methods can be divided in two major groups: *indirect* and *direct* approaches. Indirect approaches require holistic observer judgments of facial expressions that are used to infer emotions. Specifically, observer judgments are obtained by letting (non-expert) human judges rate facial expressions by means of emotion scales, or by letting them classify facial expressions into emotion categories (Hwang & Matsumoto, 2016). In contrast, direct approaches utilize single facial muscle movements and their categorization within FACS to infer the displayed emotions. These muscle movements can be recorded and classified through different means: a) human FACS (expert) coders, b) *facial Electromyography* (fEMG), or c) automated video analysis.

Human FACS coding is non-intrusive and acknowledged as the most established, comprehensive, objective, and reliable system to describe facial expressions (Meiselman, 2016; Wolf, 2015). The origins of FACS lie in *Discrete Emotion Theory* (DET; Ekman, 1992a, 1992c; Ekman et al., 1987) that focuses on universally recognized facial expressions of six basic emotions: anger, disgust, fear, happiness, sadness, and surprise. The DET assumes that basic facial expressions reflect holistic emotion programs that cannot be broken down into smaller emotion units. The FACS provides an objective framework to describe facial *Action Units* (AUs) that reflect distinct facial movements emerging from the activation of different facial muscles (Ekman et al., 1987; Ekman & Friesen, 1976). Within FACS, there are 46 AUs that can be described in regard of their activity, timing, and intensity. These descriptions allow inferences on emotions, because combinations of specific AUs are assumed to represent specific basic emotions. For example, an activated AU 4 (i.e., brow lowerer; corrugator supercilii muscle) reflects a lowering of the eyebrows. This typically occurs when expressing emotions such as anger, disgust, or sadness (Du, Tao, & Martinez, 2014; Ekman & Friesen, 2003). In general, the introduction of FACS has significantly contributed to the dominance of the DET's *basic emotion perspective*. Nevertheless, the wide acceptance of FACS cannot make up for the earlier illustrated limitation of time and labor expenditure (see introduction of this chapter).

Facial Electromyography Activity (fEMG) directly measures electrical changes in facial muscles and thus can record even subtle, and to the human eye invisible, facial muscle activities. However, this measurement approach requires biosensors placed on the face, is sensitive to motion artifacts, and can be intrusive, i.e., the electrodes can raise awareness about the measurement (see Schulte-Mecklenbeck et al., 2017 for a discussion on the intrusiveness of process tracing methods). Moreover, the number of muscles fEMG can capture is limited by how many electrodes can be applied. Other disadvantages of fEMG are crosstalk signals that originate from surrounding muscles. Therefore, the measured activity cannot be attributed distinctly to specific muscles alone. Thus, it is often not possible to clearly classify a distinct emotion. For instance, fEMG is not able to identify which emotion is shown when capturing brows moving, because this muscle activity (i.e., corrugator supercilii) is associated with different emotions such as anger and sadness (iMotions, 2016; Stets & Turner, 2014; Wolf, 2015). In order to overcome the limitations of human FACS coding and fEMG, automated facial expression analysis, based on video material, seems to be a promising alternative.

Automated Facial Expression Analysis

In the last decade, most advancements in the area of automated, video-based facial expression analysis were on describing specific facial AUs and their link to distinct basic emotions (El Kaliouby & Robinson, 2005; Lewinski et al., 2014; Valstar et al., 2011; Zeng, Pantic, Roisman, & Huang, 2009). In what follows, we will focus on computer-based systems that allow the automated classification of distinct basic emotions.

To date, there exist multiple algorithms for automated facial expression analysis (for an overview see Calvo, Gutiérrez-García, Fernández-Martín, & Nummenmaa, 2014): The *Computer Expression Recognition Toolbox* (CERT; Littlewort et al., 2011) and Noldus's FaceReader (den Uyl & van Kuilenburg, 2005) were the first software tools developed to automatically classify static (i.e., still pictures) and dynamic (i.e., videos) facial expressions. Since the development of these software tools, the market for automated facial expression analysis changed rapidly. At present, there are three major tools for automated AU description and emotion classification: Noldus's FaceReader (den Uyl & van Kuilenburg, 2005), iMotions's AFFDEX module (El Kaliouby & Robinson, 2005; McDuff, El Kaliouby, Cohn, & Picard, 2015; Zeng et al., 2009) and iMotions's FACET module (Littlewort et al., 2011).

Initially, iMotions implemented automated facial expression analysis based on the FACET algorithm developed by Emotient. In 2016, iMotions switched to AFFDEX, an algorithm developed by Affectiva.[2] FACET and AFFDEX are both machine learning, neural network algorithms that learn to recognize and classify emotional facial expressions based on databases of face pictures.

Since the implementation of automated facial expression analysis tools, commercial applications of this technology have increased. This becomes evident when considering that companies such as Google, Microsoft, Kairos, or Emovu[3] invest considerable resources in the development of interfaces that allow third party applications to integrate and use facial analysis technology including the classification of emotions.

Technical Background

The algorithms that underlie automated facial expression analysis apply a set of rules that are based on psychological theories and statistical procedures. In general, facial expression analysis algorithms work in three steps: a) detecting faces, b) detecting facial landmarks, and c) inferring emotions.

In the first step, a face in a video frame is detected, e.g., by means of a Viola-Jones cascaded classifier algorithm (Viola & Jones, 2001). This algorithm is based on a machine learning approach that uses different features to identify faces in an image and discard background regions. This step of facial detection applies to each video frame. Only frames with a positive detection rate, i.e., an identified face, are used in the subsequent analysis.

In the second step, significant facial landmarks (i.e., AUs) such as eye corners, eye centers, nose tip, mouth corner, and mouth center are detected. Technically speaking, a number of Regions of Interest (ROI) that represent significant facial landmarks are identified and a likelihood value for its presence at a given (x,y) location is estimated. There are diverse methods to detect facial landmarks (see Cootes, Edwards, & Taylor, 2001; McDuff, El Kaliouby, Kassam, & Picard, 2010). Based on detected facial landmarks, an artificial reticular face model that represents a simplified version of the actual face is developed. Another machine learning approach, a Support Vector Machine (SVM), typically does this. Such SVMs estimate intensities for facial landmarks using diverse facial databases (with FACS coding). With the SVM, the position, size, and scale of the actual face are adjusted instantly when the face moves (for more details see, e.g., Littlewort et al., 2011; McDuff et al., 2010).

In the third step, a classification algorithm is used to translate estimates for facial landmarks into a likelihood for an emotion. While AFFDEX uses estimates for 34 facial landmarks, FACET uses estimates for only six facial landmarks. In general, facial expression analysis algorithms implement a set of basic emotion detectors by feeding their facial landmarks estimates into a multivariate logistic regression classifier. This classifier is trained on facial databases and generates posterior probabilities for each emotion. Thus, the classification expresses how likely it is that the detected face expresses a certain basic emotion.

In order to train AFFDEX and FACET, deep learning methods are used. AFFDEX and FACET automatically build up a training database of various (real-world) expressions. To improve the quality of the training data set, i.e., the ground truth for the classification, human FACS coders additionally label the generated expressions. Given that facial expression analysis algorithms are trained on different facial databases, it is possible that they provide different results for a certain facial expression image (iMotions, 2016). Details on the characteristics and interpretation of iMotions's likelihood values can be found later in this chapter.

Validity of Automated Facial Expression Analysis

To date, scientific effort on testing whether automated facial expression analysis is as valid and reliable as other methods to measure emotions in the face such as human FACS coding or fEMG is limited. There is only a surprisingly small number of peer-reviewed publications validating these algorithms (except for several conference presentations on this topic, e.g., Baltrusaitis, Robinson, & Morency, 2016; Littlewort et al., 2011; McDuff et al., 2010). It is notable that the lack of validation for emotion classification is more pronounced than the lack of validation for detection and description of distinct AUs (Lewinski et al., 2014; Littlewort et al., 2011; Terzis, Moridis, & Economides, 2010).

Noldus's FaceReader is the only tool, we are aware of, with published validation work (see den Uyl & van Kuilenburg, 2005; Lewinski et al., 2014; van Kuilenburg, Wiering, & den Uyl, 2005). Lewinski et al. (2014) validated FaceReader (version 6) by examining how accurately it measures AUs and how accurately it classifies basic emotions for two data sets of prototypical facial expressions of basic emotions: the Warsaw Set of Emotional Facial Expression Pictures (WSEFEP) (Olszanowski et al., 2015) and the Amsterdam Dynamic Facial Expression Set (ADFES) (van der Schalk, Hawk, Fischer, & Doosje, 2011). In line with the approach of Lewinski et al. (2014), the authors of this chapter validated iMotions's AFFDEX and FACET on the WSEFEP and ADFES (see Stöckli, Schulte-Mecklenbeck, Borer, & Samson, 2017).

Figure 13.1 shows classification accuracies for all emotions for WSEFEP and ADFES for FaceReader, iMotions's AFFDEX, and iMotions's FACET. Overall, all algorithms show variance in accuracy across distinct emotions. The overall classification accuracy of FaceReader was 88%. While FaceReader performed best for happiness (classification accuracy of 96%), it performed worst for anger (classification accuracy of 76%). The overall classification accuracy for iMotions's AFFDEX was 68%. AFFDEX performed best for happiness (classification accuracy of 100%) and worst for fear (classification accuracy of 3%). The overall classification accuracy for iMotions's FACET was

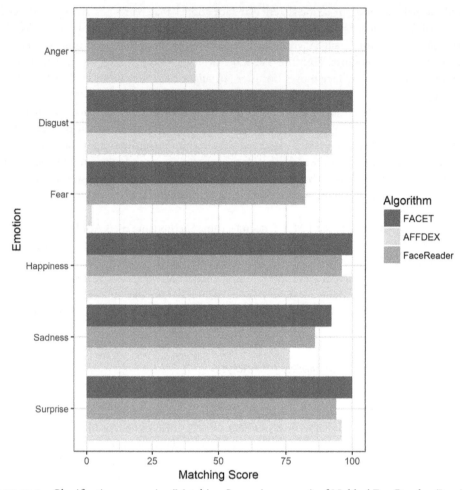

FIGURE 13.1 Classification accuracies (Matching Scores in percent) of Noldus' FaceReader (Lewinski et al., 2014) and iMotions's AFFDEX and FACET (Stöckli et al., 2017) for basic emotions for the WSEFEP and ADFES databases. Classification accuracy was defined as the percentage of pictures that the software/modules classified correctly. A classification was recorded as "correct" when the highest likelihood out of all values for all basic emotions matched with the database's emotion label.

96%. FACET performed best for happiness, disgust, and surprise (classification accuracy of 100%) and worst for fear (classification accuracy of 84%).

In order to validate iMotions for more natural, i.e., less standardized and less prototypical, emotional facial expressions, Stöckli et al. (2017) conducted a laboratory study: Based on the idea that the respondents would portray emotionally congruent facial expressions towards positive or negative emotional pictures taken from the International Affective Picture System (IAPS) (Lang, Bradley, & Cuthbert, 1999) and Geneva Affective Picture Database (GAPED) (Dan-Glauser & Scherer, 2011), 110 respondents were exposed to some of these emotionally evocative pictures while recording their facial responses. The video material of respondents' facial expressions was then automatically analyzed by AFFDEX and FACET and used to assess classification accuracy for positive and negative facial expressions in response to positive and negative emotional pictures, respectively.[4] Results revealed that iMotions's AFFDEX had

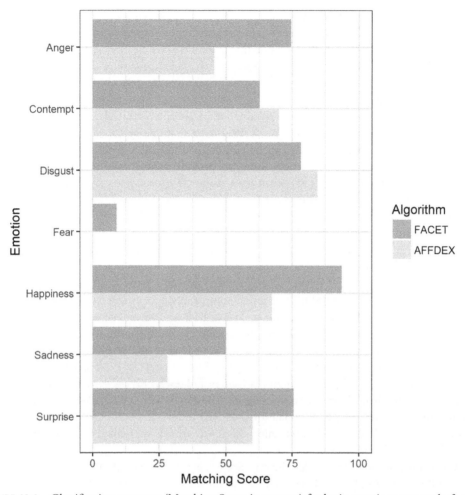

FIGURE 13.2 Classification accuracy (Matching Score in percent) for basic emotions separately for the iMotions modules AFFDEX and FACET. A classification was recorded as "correct" when the highest likelihood out of all values for all basic emotions matched with the instructed emotion, i.e., emotion label of the RaFD picture (see Stöckli et al., 2017).

a classification accuracy of 17% for positive pictures and a classification accuracy of 97% for negative pictures.[5] iMotions's FACET showed a classification accuracy of 63% for positive pictures and a classification accuracy of 71% for negative pictures. Overall, iMotions's AFFDEX module had a classification accuracy of 57% and iMotions's FACET had a classification accuracy of 67%.

In addition, Stöckli et al. (2017) validated how accurate iMotions classified the 110 respondents' facial expressions when instructed to imitate basic facial expressions from pictures of the *Radboud Faces Database* (RaFD) (Langner et al., 2010). This database contains prototypical facial expressions of basic emotions. Figure 13.2 provides an overview of the classification accuracies for respondents' facial responses to the RaFD pictures of all emotions for iMotions's AFFDEX and FACET. Overall, AFFDEX classified 55% and FACET 63% of all facial imitations with the correct emotion. Accuracy differed considerably across emotions. While AFFDEX and FACET were relatively accurate in recognizing expressions of happiness (AFFDEX: 91%; FACET: 98%), they were relatively inaccurate for expressions of fear (AFFDEX: 1%; FACET: 10%; frequent confusion with surprise) or sadness (AFFDEX: 35%; FACET: 40%; frequent confusion with anger/surprise/contempt).

Taken together, Stöckli et al. (2017) found that iMotions's classification accuracy differs for distinct emotions and valence. iMotions was more accurate for prototypical than for more natural, subtle facial expressions. Overall, iMotions's FACET more accurately classified emotional facial expressions than AFFDEX.

It is important to understand the performance of automated facial expression analysis in relation to other approaches such as human (non-expert) judgment or human (expert) FACS coding. Accuracy measures for FaceReader, iMotions's AFFDEX, and iMotions's FACET indicate that automated facial expression analysis can provide data as valid as when produced by human (non-expert) judges. In fact, human (non-expert) performance in recognizing emotions in prototypical facial expressions in database pictures is often situated between 60% and 80% and normally does not attain 90% accuracy (Nelson & Russell, 2013). Human judges are usually better at selecting the correct emotion label for *happy* than for other emotional facial expressions. When discriminating between non-happy expressions (i.e., anger, disgust, fear, sadness, surprise), human judges' accuracy in recognizing emotions is particularly weak for fearful faces (Calvo et al., 2014; Nelson & Russell, 2013). Testing FaceReader's and iMotions's accuracy on the WSEFEP and ADFES revealed comparable performance to human judges. For the WSEFEP and ADFES databases, human judges had a performance of 85% (see Lewinski et al., 2014; Olszanowski et al., 2015; van der Schalk et al., 2011). Similarly, FaceReader had a classification accuracy of 88%, AFFDEX had a classification accuracy of 70%, and FACET had a classification accuracy of 96% (see Study 1 in Stöckli et al., 2017). Hence, while FACET clearly and FaceReader slightly outperform human judges, AFFDEX's accuracy is the lowest and lies in the middle of the range of the accuracy of human judges (i.e., 60–80%). Moreover, it becomes apparent that similar to human (non-expert) judges, the accuracy of automated facial expression analysis differs for distinct emotions and performs particularly well for happy and poorly for fearful faces.

Overall, it has become evident that the classification accuracy is best for iMotions's FACET and worst for iMotions's AFFDEX. These results can be due to various characteristics of the algorithms such as the different number of facial landmarks: 20 (FaceReader) versus 6 (FACET) versus 34 (AFFDEX). It is important to consider that the present comparison of the performance of Noldus's FaceReader and iMotions's AFFDEX and FACET could also be biased because developers do not use the same face databases in the algorithm's training set. If one facial expression analysis engine, but not the others, includes WSEFEP or ADFES in the machine learning process, this will result in an overestimated relative classification accuracy. More comprehensive specifications of the different training sets would help to solve this issue.

Overall, contextualizing the accuracy of FaceReader and iMotions with the accuracy of other approaches to measure emotional facial expressions such as human (non-expert) judgment and human FACS coding reveals that automated facial expression analysis can produce data with an acceptable degree of classification accuracy for prototypical facial expressions. Regarding a direct comparison of the validity of automated facial expression analysis with human (expert) FACS coders, two problems are noteworthy. First, automated facial expression analysis is based on FACS and uses FACS classified pictures as training database. Second, FACS coders primarily describe AUs and do not directly measure emotions. Looking into the literature reveals that many studies on FACS coder accuracy focus on performance on certain AUs rather than on emotion classification (cf., Lewinski et al., 2014). Clearly, certain AU configurations are associated with certain basic emotions. Such predictions of emotions, however, involve comprehensive definitions of AU configurations and consistent decisions on which (variants of prototypical) AU configurations account for a certain basic emotion. This makes direct comparisons unreliable.

It is important to note that classification accuracy for more natural facial expressions is considerably lower than that of prototypical facial expressions. Previous studies on the accuracy of traditional (not automated) methods to measure facial expressions focused on intense prototypical emotional facial expressions, i.e., facial expressions that are posed or exaggerated. Since expression intensity is a strong predictor of rating accuracy (Hess, Blairy, & Kleck, 1997; Matsumoto, Olide, Schug, Willingham, & Callan, 2009; Naab & Russell, 2007) many studies may overestimate the accuracy of classifying emotions in facial expressions. The fact that accuracy of recognizing emotions decreases when facial expressions are low in intensity is particularly crucial when considering that real-life facial expressions are often subtle, i.e., low in intensity (Matsumoto & Hwang, 2014). Hence, automated facial expression analysis is less accurate in measuring subtle, natural facial expressions compared to prototypical facial expressions; however, this accuracy loss is also evident for other methods.

A Critical View on the Theory Behind Automated Facial Expression Analysis

There is an ongoing debate for appropriate theory integration of (automated) facial emotion classification (see, e.g., Mortillaro, Meuleman, & Scherer, 2015). This debate roots in the paradigm shift from a basic emotion perspective to an appraisal perspective. Initially, discrete emotion theorists have understood emotions as a limited repertoire of basic categories. Later, appraisal theorists have called for the existence of a broader range of emotions. According to appraisal theory, emotions are shaped by a series of different cognitive evaluations (i.e., appraisals) on different levels of processing. As situations can be evaluated differently by different individuals, the same context can elicit different emotions. While DET emphasizes expressive consequences of few basic emotions, appraisal theory emphasizes the variety of emotions and their cognitive antecedents (Ellsworth & Scherer, 2003; Roseman & Smith, 2001; Scherer, Schorr, & Johnstone, 2001).

With this in mind, it becomes clear that the criticism of automated facial expression analysis lies in the nature of its theoretical foundation, i.e., its strong basic emotion perspective. In addition, the assumption that emotions expressed in the face are the exact mirror of a felt emotional state, i.e., that emotional response components are synchronized or in coherence (i.e., emotional coherence between subjective feeling states and emotional facial expressions, see Bonanno & Keltner, 2004; Reisenzein, Studtmann, & Horstmann, 2013), limits the interpretation of data generated by automated facial expression analysis and questions the generalizability of automated emotion classification (Wolf, 2015). In what follows, we elaborate on three key issues that arise due to the criticized theoretical background of automated facial expression analysis and refer to the potential of adopting an appraisal perspective to address these issues. In fact, automated facial expression analysis: a) assumes that facial expressions are prototypical in their nature; b) expects emotional coherence, i.e., that facial expressions can be directly translated into emotions, and c) ignores the decisive role of the context when using facial expressions to make inferences on psychological states and processes.

The first issue roots in the fact that automated facial expression analysis identifies and describes AUs to predict a limited number of basic emotions. Automated facial expression analysis ignores emotions that are not in this set of prototypical basic emotions (for example, for the domain of positive emotions, there is not only "happiness", but many other positive emotional states such as amusement, awe, wonder, excitement, pride, etc.). This is particularly problematic as most facial expressions are not prototypical. Characteristically, prototypical facial expressions have a high degree of expression intensity and are distinct (versus mixed). Moreover, research has relatively often addressed prototypical facial expressions of basic emotions (Ekman, Freisen, & Ancoli, 1980; Hess, Banse, & Kappas, 1995) without considering that real-life facial expressions often reflect mixed and not distinct basic emotion categories (Kreibig & Gross, 2017). Although the paradigm of distinct basic emotions (Ekman, 1992a, 1992b) holds a predominant position in research related to emotion and facial expressions (e.g., Du et al., 2014; Jordi, 2014; Scherer et al., 2001), it has become subject to diverse criticism (see Du et al., 2014; Scherer & Ellgring, 2007). There is considerable empirical support that there are facial expressions of mixed emotions, i.e., combinations of single components of basic emotions (Du et al., 2014; Kreibig, Samson, & Gross, 2013, 2015). Given that spontaneous facial expressions are rather subtle, at times mixed, but rarely prototypical (Naab & Russell, 2007; Scherer & Ellgring, 2007), automated facial expression analysis frequently fails. It is therefore not surprising that automated facial expression analysis is successful with prototypical facial expressions but runs into trouble for subtle and mixed facial expressions (see Stöckli et al., 2017).

The second issue concerns the assumption of a simple coherence between emotional experiences and facial expressions (Bonanno & Keltner, 2004; Reisenzein et al., 2013). Indeed, research often implicitly assumes that there is a one-to-one translation from facial expressions to underlying emotional experiences, although the link between the two is often not clear and it may be myopic to directly infer underlying emotional experiences from facial expressions (Barrett & Wager, 2006; Ortony & Turner, 1990; Scherer & Ellgring, 2007). For instance, people frequently alter outward facial expressions to regulate their own emotional states, which is known as response modulation (Gross, 1998). That is, people may hide, suppress, or even exaggerate their facial expressions with the aim to regulate their emotions (Gross, 2002). A further aspect that contradicts a strong link between facial expressions and emotional experiences is that people often use facial expressions for communication purposes. In social interactions, facial expressions do not primarily reflect actual emotional states, but are often used to communicate and reflect display rules, that is, norms about when, where, and how certain emotions should (not) be expressed (Jordi, 2014; Keltner, Ekman, Gonzaga, & Beer, 2003). Apparently, these examples may lead to emotional incoherence, which underlines the limits of the generalizability of the results of automated facial expression analysis on emotional experiences (Wolf, 2015). The need for a critical view on the relation between experience and expression of emotions becomes even more pronounced when considering the recent unsuccessful attempt to replicate findings supporting the facial feedback hypothesis (Wagenmakers et al., 2016). This hypothesis postulates that due to the close link between emotional experiences and facial expressions, altering facial expressions would impact emotional feeling states.

The third issue relates to the lacking inclusion of contextual factors when making inferences on emotions with automated facial expression analysis. Automated facial expression analysis ignores contextual factors such as the environment, the subject(s), or other situational aspects such as culture. Yet, such factors are decisive for the interpretation of both expressed emotions and actual underlying emotions (Aviezer, Trope, & Todorov, 2012; Barrett, Mesquita, & Gendron, 2011; Elfenbein & Ambady, 2002). To infer causes of expressed emotions and underlying processes, it is not enough to assume a one-to-one relationship between expression and emotion and it seems necessary to include contextual factors. Appraisals may potentially help to render facial expression analysis more sensitive, since inferring appraisals from facial AUs (and linking them to emotional states) may be more context sensitive.

Taken together, these issues (prototypical emotions, emotional coherence, and context) have their roots in the shortcomings of DET. It has been suggested to build upon appraisal theory that allows more flexibility. Here, "flexibility" means that automated facial expression analysis could include expressions that go beyond prototypical basic emotions as well as underlying appraisals and the influence of contextual factors. In this vein, appraisals would allow taking contextual and cultural factors into account, as well as inter-individual differences about how such factors are evaluated and in turn influence the expressions of emotions. Interestingly, several studies showed that appraisals were linked to distinct facial expressions (see, for an overview, Mortillaro, Meuleman, & Scherer, 2012) and could therefore represent the missing link not only between experience and expression, but also between emotion production and emotion recognition. Moreover, a recent empirical study showed that participants can infer appraisals and emotions from facial expressions (Scherer, Mortillaro, Rotondi, Sergi, & Trznadel, 2018). Therefore, the integration of an algorithm is needed that considers subjective appraisals that underlie emotional states. Such algorithms should model people's subjective evaluations of the emotional situation as well as the emotional state by linking models of emotion recognition and production. Ideally, such algorithms would include contextual factors (e.g., whether other people are present or not) and social norms (facial display rules) and allow the detection not only of prototypical but also of subtle and mixed emotional states. Yet, to the best of our knowledge, there is no algorithm that is sufficiently able to implement this complex appraisal perspective.

An Applied Perspective Using iMotions's Automated Facial Expression Analysis

We will now give a step-by-step overview of applying iMotions Biometric Research Platform for automated facial expression analysis. Specifically, we provide descriptions and advice on equipment, experimental setting, and aspects of the study design and procedure such as task structure, timing, and respondent instructions. Finally, we discuss several key considerations for data handling and data analysis.

Note that although some of the following descriptions specifically refer to iMotions software (version 6.2), much information and advice is applicable for automated facial expression analysis in general and for other software and hardware platforms.

Equipment and Settings

iMotions Software

Conducting facial expression analysis with iMotions requires the installation of multiple software modules. We recommend the minimal installation of the following modules: iMotions core, iMotions API (Application Programming Interface), iMotions Facet and/or Affectiva, and iMotions survey module (see https://imotions.com).

iMotions core module is a prerequisite module to integrate any other iMotions modules. It allows the actual study execution including setting up a study and data collection. iMotions API module allows connections and stream from and to third party software and hardware. Thus, this module is required when a study needs data input into iMotions or if iMotions is thought to export events, markers, and triggers into third party software. iMotions Affectiva module and Facet module allow automated facial expression analysis based on the AFFDEX or FACET algorithm, respectively. For both modules, there are base and advanced versions available. While the base version detects basic emotions and valence, the advanced version additionally provides the possibility of detecting and describing single AUs. iMotions survey module enables to setup and collect questionnaire data (e.g., multiple choice, text answers). In addition to these previously described modules, there are other modules available for other biosensors such as eye-tracking (see Chapters 1–5), GSR (see Chapter 11), and EMG (iMotions, 2016).

Hardware

To run iMotions's facial expression analysis modules, a desktop or laptop computer is required. In line with iMotions's recommendations (see iMotions, 2016), we use a Laptop with Windows 8.1 to run experiments with iMotions's facial expression analysis. The laptop in our laboratory is attached to a 24" (60 cm) screen to display stimuli to respondents.

To record videos, we use a consumer webcam. Importantly, the webcam should use a standard lens (avoid wide-angle or fisheye lenses), provide a resolution of the video that is at least 640 × 480 pixels, offer stable framerates (60 fps or more), auto-focus, and allow access to aperture, brightness, and white balance settings.

Experimental Setup

Automated facial expression analysis requires the visibility of the face. When setting up the environment for a study, there are three aspects concerning the experimental setting that need to be considered: a) hardware placement, b) respondent positioning, and c) adjusting surrounding influences (lighting). These aspects are decisive for the successful detection of faces and relevant facial landmarks and have a direct impact on data quality.

If respondents use a keyboard, it is recommended to place the camera below the monitor as often head movements and orientation towards the keyboard are necessary. If head movements are too pronounced, facial detection can fail (see https://imotions.com).

Inappropriate positioning of respondents can largely impair the detection of facial landmarks. Particularly, it must be considered that respondents change their positions. It is thus recommended that respondents are seated comfortably and instructed to remain in a stable and straight position. Given that respondents vary in their body height, it might be required to adapt the positioning of the chair. In addition, iMotions requires a minimum size of the face on the video (i.e., minimal pixel distance from ear-to-ear) for the analysis.

In terms of lighting, facial expression analysis works best with uniform and diffuse indoor light. Strong or varying lights should be avoided (e.g., direct sunlight from a window).

Note that iMotions can either use a webcam to generate video material online that is subsequently analyzed or analyze existing video material offline. For the latter case the video files have to be compatible to the Windows Media Player (i.e., use codecs such as MP4 and WMV). To analyze static facial expressions from pictures, an intermediate step of converting a picture file into a video file is required (MP4 or WMV). One way to do this is using the ffmpeg video encoding program to read all pictures from a folder and produce a video, which displays every image (see Stöckli et al., 2017)

Study Procedure

A meaningful analysis of facial expression data requires that respondents' facial expressions can be related to displayed stimuli or survey elements. This synchronization of facial expression measurement, stimuli presentation, and survey elements is enabled by the API module. As facial expressions are responsive, one should consider the sequence and duration of stimuli and/or other survey elements. Between target stimuli, neutral baseline stimuli are suggested to be displayed to respondents; we suggest to display static, gray slides with a centrally displayed fixation cross (and the instruction to the respondents to look at these crosses). Baseline stimuli are useful for two aspects: first, they allow that facial expressions can rest or cool-off, i.e., that respondents start again from a neutral state

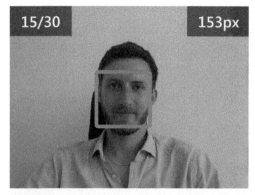 

FIGURE 13.3 Illustration of how iMotions indicates successful or unsuccessful facial detection. The rectangle (facial detection) is a prerequisite to detect facial landmarks required by facial expression analysis algorithms.

with the next stimulus. Allowing facial expressions to return to a neutral baseline state is particularly important for study designs with multiple consecutive stimuli.

Second, baseline stimuli are useful to record data that reflect respondents' individual baseline expression before the presentation of an experimental stimulus (with emotional content). Recording respondents' individual baseline values for separate experimental stimuli is a prerequisite for stimuli-wise baseline correction. Later in this chapter, we will delve into the procedure and advantages of the stimuli-wise baseline correction.

At the beginning of the experiment, it is important to inform respondents about the procedure of the experiment. This can help to attenuate the effect that respondents express emotions due to their surprise of unexpected stimuli or questions. Initial instructions should ask respondents to omit superfluous facial movements (e.g., talking, eating, chewing gum, drinking) and to avoid or remove other disturbing sources (e.g., hands in the face, large or tinted glasses, facial jewelry and piercings, hats and caps, hair styling that covers the face). Figure 13.3 shows how iMotions interface notifies whether facial detection has succeeded or failed.

Data Analysis

Data Output

There are two ways to gain insight into iMotions's facial expression data: first, iMotions interface transfers respondent-wise raw data into live graphs showing the probability of the presence of all basic emotions and valence.

Second, iMotions allows the export of comprehensive raw data. The live graphs allow online data monitoring. This is a useful tool for error correction during the experiment. Data analysis should solely be conducted on comprehensive raw data.

Note that step-by-step instructions on how to export raw data in iMotions can be found online (see https://imotions.com). iMotions only allows respondent-wise export of raw data (in the form of txt files). Survey data, that is, data stemming from a questionnaire, must be exported separately. The authors of this chapter provide R-code for merging respondent-wise raw data into one data frame.[6]

We recommend using the comprehensive data export legends for both iMotions's AFFDEX and FACET module that can be found online (see https://imotions.com). Most importantly, the raw data includes variables for respondents, stimulus name (i.e., stimuli displayed to respondents), frame number, frame time (frame number translated in msec; iMotions provides measures for approximately every 32 msec), X and Y coordinates of the rectangle that frames the face (in pixels), width and height of rectangle that frames the face, measures for AUs and likelihoods for basic emotions and valence.

Baseline Correction

Before computing descriptive and inferential statistics, it is important to decide whether raw or baseline corrected data is used. Raw data reflect likelihoods for basic emotions of the analyzed face and relate the analyzed facial expression to facial expressions in the global training database. Analyzing raw data can be appropriate when aggregating data of several individuals, for instance, to compare data of two or more groups of individuals (see https://imotions.com).

In most cases it is better to analyze baseline corrected data. Given that a certain individual has a high baseline for happiness, this individual's raw data would misestimate the actual expression of happiness or the actual change of happiness expression. To prevent such misestimating, raw data should be corrected by individual expression baselines. In contrast to raw data, baseline corrected data consider that people differ in their "neutral" expression and allow to detect changes in emotional expression relative to their neutral expression. Hence, baseline corrected data allow more accurate emotion estimates and comparison (see https://imotions.com).

Given that individuals' initial baseline expressions can vary within a trial of diverse experimental stimuli with emotional content or change over the course of an experiment, stimuli-wise correction of individual baseline expressions is most appropriate. We highly recommend conducting stimuli-wise baseline corrections instead of correcting raw data with only an overall

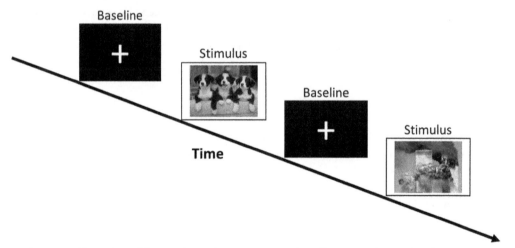

FIGURE 13.4 Illustration of the timeline of an experiment that allows stimuli-wise baseline correction. This figure shows the experimental setup of Stöckli et al. (2017; see Study 2) with emotionally evocative IAPS pictures (experimental stimuli) and preceding black slides with a white, centrally displayed fixation cross (neutral baseline slide).

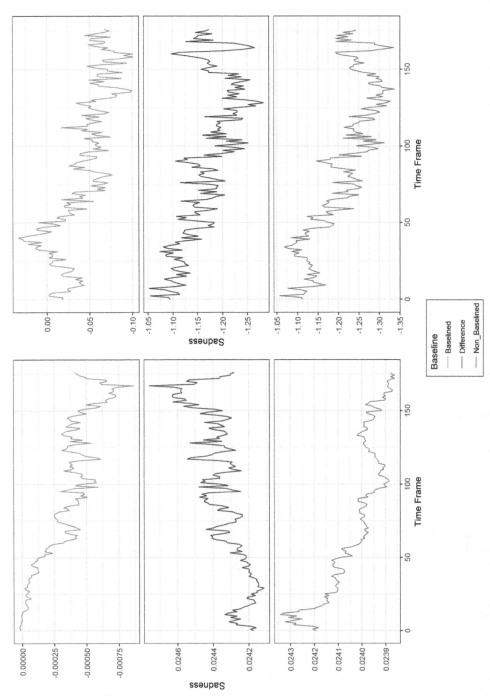

FIGURE 13.5 Illustration of how baseline corrected data differ from non-baseline corrected data (raw data) for iMotions's AFFDEX and FACET. Data stem from 110 respondents who were exposed to one emotionally evocative picture (IAPS nr. 1750, positive valence) for approximately 6400 msec (i.e., 200 time frames; one time frame is generated every 32 msec). Expectedly, AFFDEX (left) and FACET (right) show decreasing likelihood for expressed sadness over time irrespective of whether or not data was baseline corrected (see Study 2 in Stöckli et al., 2017). Baseline corrected data have a red color code, non-baseline corrected data have a blue color code.

212 Stöckli et al.

baseline value. In practice, stimuli-wise baseline correction requires to subtract baseline probability values, recorded during the presentation of a baseline slide, from the probability measures of the following experimental stimuli (see Figure 13.4).

For the baseline values it is recommended to compute the median of the likelihoods from the baseline slides. Figure 13.5 depicts how non-baseline corrected data and baseline corrected data can differ. The authors of this chapter provide exemplary R-code for stimuli-wise baseline correction[7].

Data Interpretation

We pointed out that iMotions provides likelihoods (evidence values for FACET, probabilities for AFFDEX) for all basic emotions. The evidence from FACET represents odds in the form of a logarithmic scale (base 10) for the presence of a certain basic emotion. That is, positive (negative) values indicate evidence that a certain emotion is expressed (absent). While values larger than three indicate strong evidence for the presence of a certain emotion, negative values smaller than three indicate strong evidence for the absence of an emotion. A value of zero indicates that there is no evidence either way. An evidence value of 10 means that the expression is 100 times more likely and an evidence value of 1 means that the expression is 10 times more likely to be present than not to be present.

AFFDEX provides probabilities for the presence of all basic emotions in the form of a numeric value between zero and 100. Here, zero indicates that the target emotion was not expressed, 100 indicates that the target emotion was expressed, and 50 indicates even odds for the target emotion to be present.

Conclusion

In this chapter, we introduced the idea that facial expressions allow drawing inferences about emotional states. We see a potential for facial expression analysis as a process tracing method for JDM research. Although the approach of automated facial expression analysis promises many advantages over more conventional approaches (e.g., human FACS coding, fEMG), there is only a small number of studies that apply automated facial expression analysis. We have outlined that this may be due to the limited validity of automated facial expression analysis in classifying emotions and inferring emotional experiences. To overcome these limitations, we have particularly referred to the appraisal theorists' call to implement a paradigm shift from basic emotion perspective to an appraisal perspective in automated facial expression analysis systems.

The main aim of this chapter was to equip the reader to run automated facial expression analysis studies. It contains a user-oriented introduction of automated facial expression analysis, provides guidance in applying automated facial expression analysis by introducing iMotions's facial expression analysis, and gives recommendations for equipment, study setup, study design, procedure, and data analysis.

Notes

1   We would like to thank Ben Meuleman for his useful comments on an earlier version of the manuscript.
2   This switch is linked to the acquisition of Emotient by Apple Inc. While new customers of iMotions are only able to purchase AFFDEX, existing users of iMotions's FACET are still able to apply FACET until 2020.

3 See: https://cloud.google.com/vision/; www.microsoft.com/cognitive-services/en-us/emotion-api; www.kairos.com/docs/api/; http://emovu.com/e/developers/api/
4 Classification accuracy was defined as the percentage of pictures that the module classified correctly. A classification was recorded as "correct" when the highest valence likelihood (positive valence, negative valence) matched with the database's valence label (see Stöckli et al., 2017).
5 Note that this bias (i.e., better recognition of negative versus positive facial expressions) is due to the valence classification with only one emotion for positive valence (happiness) and five emotions for negative valence (anger, contempt, disgust, fear, and sadness).
6 https://github.com/michaelschulte/FacialExpressionAnalysis
7 https://github.com/michaelschulte/FacialExpressionAnalysis

Recommended Reading List

- Meiselman (2016): for a comprehensive overview of diverse methods to measure emotions.
- Hwang and Matsumoto (2016; Chapter 6 in Meiselman, 2016): for different methods to measure emotions in the face with a sound and brief outline on FACS and its derivatives.
- Mortillaro et al. (2015): for a critical view on the theoretical background of automated facial expression analysis by pointing out theoretical and practical limitations of inferring emotions based on the distinct emotion perspective.
- iMotions (2016): for compact product information (AFFDEX and FACET module) and guidance for automated facial expression analysis studies with iMotions software.

References

Aviezer, H., Trope, Y., & Todorov, A. (2012). Holistic person processing: Faces with bodies tell the whole story. *Journal of Personality and Social Psychology, 103*(1), 20–37.

Baltrusaitis, T., Robinson, P., & Morency, L.-P. (2016). OpenFace: An open source facial behavior analysis toolkit. *Proceedings from 2016 IEEE Winter Conference on Applications of Computer Vision (WACV)* (pp. 1–10).

Barrett, L. F., Mesquita, B., & Gendron, M. (2011). Context in emotion perception. *Current Directions in Psychological Science, 20*(5), 286–290.

Barrett, L. F., & Wager, T. D. (2006). The structure of emotion: Evidence from neuroimaging studies. *Current Directions in Psychological Science, 15*(2), 79–83.

Bechara, A. (2004). The role of emotion in decision-making: Evidence from neurological patients with orbitofrontal damage. *Brain and Cognition, 55*(1), 30–40.

Bonanno, G., & Keltner, D. (2004). Brief report: The coherence of emotion systems: Comparing "on-line" measures of appraisal and facial expressions, and self-report. *Cognition and Emotion, 18*(3), 431–444.

Brosch, T., & Sander, D. (2013). Neurocognitive mechanisms underlying value-based decision-making: From core values to economic value. *Frontiers in Human Neuroscience, 7*, 398–398.

Calvo, M. G., Gutiérrez-García, A., Fernández-Martín, A., & Nummenmaa, L. (2014). Recognition of facial expressions of emotion is related to their frequency in everyday life. *Journal of Nonverbal Behavior, 38*(4), 549–567.

Chentsova-Dutton, Y. E., & Tsai, J. L. (2010). Self-focused attention and emotional reactivity: The role of culture. *Journal of Personality and Social Psychology, 98*(3), 507–519.

Cootes, T. F., Edwards, G. J., & Taylor, C. J. (2001). Active appearance models. *IEEE Transactions on Pattern Analysis & Machine Intelligence*, (6), 681–685.

Dan-Glauser, E. S., & Scherer, K. R. (2011). The Geneva affective picture database (GAPED): A new 730-picture database focusing on valence and normative significance. *Behavior Research Methods, 43*(2), 468–477.

den Uyl, M. J., & van Kuilenburg, H. (2005). The FaceReader: Online facial expression recognition. *Proceedings of Measuring Behavior, 30*, 589–590.

Dolan, R. J. (2002). Emotion, cognition, and behavior. *Science, 298*(5596), 1191–1194.

Du, S., Tao, Y., & Martinez, A. M. (2014). Compound facial expressions of emotion. *Proceedings of the National Academy of Sciences, 111*(15), 1454–1462.

Ekman, P. (1992a). An argument for basic emotions. *Cognition & Emotion, 6*(3–4), 169–200.

Ekman, P. (1992b). Are there basic emotions? *Psychological Review, 99*(3), 550–553.

Ekman, P. (1992c). Facial expressions of emotion: New findings, new questions. *Psychological Science, 3*(1), 34–38.

Ekman, P., & Friesen, W.V. (1976). Measuring facial movement. *Environmental Psychology and Nonverbal Behavior, 1*(1), 56–75.

Ekman, P., & Friesen, W.V. (1982). Felt, false, and miserable smiles. *Journal of Nonverbal Behavior, 6*(4), 238–252.

Ekman, P., & Friesen, W.V. (2003). *Unmasking the face: A guide to recognizing emotions from facial clues.* Cambridge, MA: Malor Books.

Ekman, P., Freisen, W. V., & Ancoli, S. (1980). Facial signs of emotional experience. *Journal of Personality and Social Psychology, 39*(6), 1125–1134.

Ekman, P., Friesen, W. V., O'Sullivan, M., Chan, A., Diacoyanni-Tarlatzis, I., Heider, K., … others. (1987). Universals and cultural differences in the judgments of facial expressions of emotion. *Journal of Personality and Social Psychology, 53*(4), 712–717.

Ekman, P., & Oster, H. (1979). Facial expressions of emotion. *Annual Review of Psychology, 30*(1), 527–554.

El Kaliouby, R., & Robinson, P. (2005). Real-time inference of complex mental states from facial expressions and head gestures. In B. Kisacanin, V. Pavlovic, & T. S. Huang (Eds.), *Real-time vision for human-computer interaction* (pp. 181–200). New York, NY: Springer.

Elfenbein, H. A., & Ambady, N. (2002). On the universality and cultural specificity of emotion recognition: A meta-analysis. *Psychological Bulletin, 128*(2), 203–235.

Ellsworth, P. C., & Scherer, K. R. (2003). Appraisal processes in emotion. In R. J. Davidson, K. R. Scherer, & H. H. Goldsmith (Eds.), *Handbook of affective sciences* (pp. 572–595). New York, NY: Oxford University Press.

Gross, J. J. (1998). Antecedent- and response-focused emotion regulation: Divergent consequences for experience, expression, and physiology. *Journal of Personality and Social Psychology, 74*(1), 224–237.

Gross, J. J. (2002). Emotion regulation: Affective, cognitive, and social consequences. *Psychophysiology, 39*(3), 281–291.

Hess, U., Banse, R., & Kappas, A. (1995). The intensity of facial expression is determined by underlying affective state and social situation. *Journal of Personality and Social Psychology, 69*(2), 280–288.

Hess, U., Blairy, S., & Kleck, R. E. (1997). The intensity of emotional facial expressions and decoding accuracy. *Journal of Nonverbal Behavior, 21*(4), 241–257.

Hwang, H. C., & Matsumoto, D. (2016). Facial expressions. In D. Matsumoto, H. C. Hwang, & M. G. Frank (Eds.), *APA handbook of nonverbal communication* (pp. 257–287). Washington, DC: American Psychological Association.

iMotions. (2016). Facial expression analysis: The definitive guide. Retrieved from https://imotions.com/facialexpression-guide-ebook/

Jordi, V. (2014). *Handbook of research on synthesizing human emotion in intelligent systems and robotics.* Hershey, PA: IGI Global.

Keltner, D., Ekman, P., Gonzaga, G. C., & Beer, J. (2003). Facial expression of emotion. In R. J. Davidson, K. R. Scherer, & H. H. Goldsmith (Eds.), *Series in affective science. Handbook of affective sciences* (pp. 415–432). Oxford, UK: Oxford University Press.

Kreibig, S. D., & Gross, J. J. (2017). Understanding mixed emotions: Paradigms and measures. *Current Opinion in Behavioral Sciences, 15*, 62–71.

Kreibig, S. D., Samson, A. C., & Gross, J. J. (2013). The psychophysiology of mixed emotional states. *Psychophysiology, 50*(8), 799–811.

Kreibig, S. D., Samson, A. C., & Gross, J. J. (2015). The psychophysiology of mixed emotional states: Internal and external replicability analysis of a direct replication study. *Psychophysiology, 52*(7), 873–876.

Lang, P. J., Bradley, M. M., & Cuthbert, B. N. (1999). *International affective picture system (IAPS): Instruction manual and affective ratings.* The Center for Research in Psychophysiology, University of Florida.

Langner, O., Dotsch, R., Bijlstra, G., Wigboldus, D. H., Hawk, S.T., & van Knippenberg, A. (2010). Presentation and validation of the Radboud Faces Database. *Cognition and Emotion, 24*(8), 1377–1388.

Lewinski, P., den Uyl, T. M., & Butler, C. (2014). Automated facial coding: Validation of basic emotions and FACS AUs in FaceReader. *Journal of Neuroscience, Psychology, and Economics, 7*(4), 227–236.

Littlewort, G., Whitehill, J., Wu, T., Fasel, I., Frank, M., Movellan, J., & Bartlett, M. (2011). The computer expression recognition toolbox (CERT). *Proceedings from 2011 IEEE International Conference on Automatic Face & Gesture Recognition and Workshops (FG 2011)* (pp. 298–305).

Loewenstein, G. F., Weber, E. U., Hsee, C. K., & Welch, N. (2001). Risk as feelings. *Psychological Bulletin, 127*(2), 267–286.

Luce, M. F., Bettman, J. R., & Payne, J. W. (1997). Choice processing in emotionally difficult decisions. *Journal of Experimental Psychology: Learning, Memory, and Cognition, 23*(2), 384–405.

Matsumoto, D., & Hwang, H. C. (2014). Judgments of subtle facial expressions of emotion. *Emotion, 14*(2), 349–357.

Matsumoto, D., Olide, A., Schug, J., Willingham, B., & Callan, M. (2009). Cross-cultural judgments of spontaneous facial expressions of emotion. *Journal of Nonverbal Behavior, 33*(4), 213–238.

Mauss, I. B., & Robinson, M. D. (2009). Measures of emotion: A review. *Cognition and Emotion, 23*(2), 209–237.

McDuff, D., El Kaliouby, R., Cohn, J. F., & Picard, R. W. (2015). Predicting ad liking and purchase intent: Large-scale analysis of facial responses to ads. *Affective Computing, IEEE Transactions, 6*(3), 223–235.

McDuff, D., El Kaliouby, R., Kassam, K., & Picard, R. (2010). Affect valence inference from facial action unit spectrograms. In *Proceedings from 2010 IEEE Computer Society Conference on Computer Vision and Pattern Recognition — Workshops* (pp. 17–24).

Meiselman, H. L. (2016). *Emotion measurement.* Cambridge, UK: Woodhead Publishing.

Mortillaro, M., Meuleman, B., & Scherer, K. R. (2012). Advocating a componential appraisal model to guide emotion recognition. *International Journal of Synthetic Emotions, 3*(1), 18–32.

Mortillaro, M., Meuleman, B., & Scherer, K. R. (2015). Automated recognition of emotion appraisals. In J. Vallverdu (Ed.), *Handbook of research on synthesizing human emotion in intelligent systems and robotics* (pp. 338–351). Hershey, PA: IGI Global.

Naab, P. J., & Russell, J. A. (2007). Judgments of emotion from spontaneous facial expressions of new guineans. *Emotion, 7*(4), 736–744.

Nelson, N. L., & Russell, J. A. (2013). Universality revisited. *Emotion Review, 5*(1), 8–15.

Olszanowski, M., Pochwatko, G., Kuklinski, K., Scibor-Rylski, M., Lewinski, P., & Ohme, R. K. (2015). Warsaw set of emotional facial expression pictures: A validation study of facial display photographs. *Frontiers in Psychology, 5*, 1–8.

Ortony, A., & Turner, T. J. (1990). What's basic about basic emotions? *Psychological Review, 97*(3), 315–331.

Rasch, C., Louviere, J. J., & Teichert, T. (2015). Using facial EMG and eye tracking to study integral affect in discrete choice experiments. *Journal of Choice Modelling, 14*, 32–47.

Reisenzein, R., Studtmann, M., & Horstmann, G. (2013). Coherence between emotion and facial expression: Evidence from laboratory experiments. *Emotion Review, 5*(1), 16–23.

Roseman, I. J., & Smith, C. A. (2001). Appraisal theory. *Appraisal Processes in Emotion: Theory, Methods, Research*, 3–19.

Rossi, F., Fasel, I., & Sanfey, A. G. (2011). Inscrutable games? Facial expressions predict economic behavior. *BMC Neuroscience, 12*(1), 281.

Scherer, K. R., & Ceschi, G. (2000). Criteria for emotion recognition from verbal and nonverbal expression: Studying baggage loss in the airport. *Personality and Social Psychology Bulletin, 26*(3), 327–339.

Scherer, K. R., & Ellgring, H. (2007). Are facial expressions of emotion produced by categorical affect programs or dynamically driven by appraisal? *Emotion, 7*(1), 113–130.

Scherer, K. R., Mortillaro, M., Rotondi, I., Sergi, I., & Trznadel, S. (2018). Appraisal-driven facial actions as building blocks for emotion inference. *Journal of Personality and Social Psychology, 114*(3), 358.

Scherer, K. R., Schorr, A., & Johnstone, T. (2001). *Appraisal processes in emotion: Theory, methods, research.* Oxford, UK: Oxford University Press.

Schulte-Mecklenbeck, M., Johnson, J. G., Böckenholt, U., Goldstein, D., Russo, J., Sullivan, N., & Willemsen, M. (2017). Process tracing methods in decision making: On growing up in the 70ties. *Current Directions in Psychological Science, 26*(5), 442–450.

Schwarz, N. (2000). Emotion, cognition, and decision making. *Cognition & Emotion, 14*(4), 433–440.

Stets, J. E., & Turner, J. H. (2014). *Handbook of the sociology of emotions* (Vol. 2). Heidelberg: Springer.

Stöckli, S., Schulte-Mecklenbeck, M., Borer, S., & Samson, A. C. (2018). Facial expression analysis with AFFDEX and FACET: A validation study. *Behavior Research Methods, 50*(4), 1446–1460.

Swinton, R., & El Kaliouby, R. (2012). Measuring emotions through a mobile device across borders, ages, genders and more. In *Proceedings of the ESOMAR Congress* (pp. 1–12).

Terzis, V., Moridis, C. N., & Economides, A. A. (2010). Measuring instant emotions during a self-assessment test: The use of FaceReader. In A. J. Spink, F. Grieco, O. E. Krips, L. W. S. Loijens, L. P. J. J. Noldus, & P. H. Zimmerman (Eds.), *Proceedings of measuring behavior 2010* (pp. 192–195). Eindhoven, NL: ACM.

Valstar, M. F., Jiang, B., Mehu, M., Pantic, M., & Scherer, K. (2011). The first facial expression recognition and analysis challenge. In *Proceedings from 2011 IEEE International Conference on Automatic Face & Gesture Recognition and Workshops (FG 2011)* (pp. 921–926).

van der Schalk, J., Hawk, S. T., Fischer, A. H., & Doosje, B. (2011). Moving faces, looking places: Validation of the Amsterdam Dynamic Facial Expression Set (ADFES). *Emotion, 11*(4), 907–920.

van Kuilenburg, H., Wiering, M., & den Uyl, M. (2005). A model based method for automatic facial expression recognition. *Proceedings of the 16th European Conference on Machine Learning, Porto, Portugal, 2005* (pp. 194–205). Heidelberg: Springer.

Viola, P., & Jones, M. (2001). Rapid object detection using a boosted cascade of simple features. In *Proceedings of the 2001 IEEE Computer Society Conference on Computer Vision and Pattern Recognition, 2001. CVPR 2001*, p. 511.

Wagenmakers, E. J., Beek, T., Dijkhoff, L., Gronau, Q. F., Acosta, A., Adams Jr, R. B., ... & Bulnes, L. C. (2016). Registered replication report: Strack, Martin, & Stepper (1988). *Perspectives on Psychological Science, 11*(6), 917–928.

Wolf, K. (2015). Measuring facial expression of emotion. *Dialogues in Clinical Neuroscience, 17*(4), 457–462.

Zeng, Z., Pantic, M., Roisman, G. I., & Huang, T. S. (2009). A survey of affect recognition methods: Audio, visual, and spontaneous expressions. *IEEE Transactions on Pattern Analysis and Machine Intelligence, 31*(1), 39–58.

14

EEG AND ERPS AS NEURAL PROCESS TRACING METHODOLOGIES IN DECISION-MAKING RESEARCH[1]

Mary E. Frame

EEG as a Process Tracing Method

The goal of any process tracing method is to observe cognition in action, given technological constraints. There has also been increased appreciation for the usefulness of understanding human biology and brain activity as it relates to all cognitive activity, including decision making. As researchers pursue this goal, it is important to implement methods that are safe and noninvasive while still providing a rich source of data to measure information acquisition, fluctuations in preference, and implementation of action in a temporally precise manner. Temporal precision and noninvasiveness are two of the strengths of utilizing electroencephalography (EEG) in the study of the neural and biological bases of decision making. Although there are many ways of studying EEG activity, two particular approaches have become popular for studying the neural correlates of the decision-making process: 1) spectral analysis, which attempts to decompose EEG signals into their component sine waves and examine particular bands of activity that are correlated with cognitive processes, and 2) Event Related Potentials (ERPs), which are averaged series of EEG activity time locked to a particular event, such as the onset of a stimulus or the execution of a response. This chapter will provide a broad description of the value added by examining both of these process tracing methods, contributions that have been made to the field of decision making, and a brief future outlook for additional process tracing techniques using EEG and ERPs.

Value Added by Studying Brain Activity

Although other process tracing metrics such as eye-tracking (see Chapters 1–5) and mouse-tracking (see Chapters 9–10) are capable of elucidating the decision-making process online, there is added benefit to examining dynamic brain activity. One of the strongest added benefits is that understanding brain activity during decision-making can increase the neural plausibility of current models of decision making. Understanding brain activity has improved our comprehension of numerous cognitive processes and has been examined using a variety of methods, many of which are outlined in other chapters (see Chapter 16 for fMRI and Chapter 17 for rTMS and tDCS). Although examining brain activity does not provide a full picture of all small-scale and large-scale processes, it provides an important foundation for improving the assumptions of cognitive models (Palm, 2016). In this case the benefit between models of decision-making and results of EEG/ERP analyses are bidirectional, with models improving our understanding of brain activity, and brain activity improving the construction and conceptualization of cognitive models.

Models of decision-making can be improved via an understanding of the neural processes that relate to decision-making. In particular, cognitive architectures that attempt to model the complex array of higher-order cognitive processes are often improved by understanding brain activity. As an example outside of decision making, studies of neural correlates of mental workload have been effectively used to modify tasks in real time to optimize performance by adjusting task difficulty according to objective neural indicators of boredom and overwork (Berka et al., 2007).

Within the framework of decision making, there has been substantial progress tying neural correlates to mathematical models such as the drift diffusion model (DDM; Ratcliff, 1978; van Vugt, Simen, Nystrom, Holmes, & Cohen, 2014). Utilizing EEG as a process tracing method is still relatively new in the field of decision making, however, in large part due to the complexity of the decision-making process. Compared to basic perceptual processes, higher-level cognition such as decision-making consists of numerous co-occurring and overlapping processes as well as complex neural feedback processes prior to execution of a response. This makes it difficult to directly analyze and model each of these complex processes using any individual neuroimaging method. However, with the high temporal precision and the improved spatial resolution of dense-array EEG systems, there is the potential for tremendous added value from collecting and analyzing EEG data alongside other process tracing methodologies. Despite the listed potential limitations from using EEG in isolation, a few important findings have still been made regarding the neural correlates of certain subclasses of the decision-making processes. These findings include neural correlates of decisional processes such as evidence accumulation, response competition, and preference reversals.

Another valuable contribution to studying EEG activity is that it is possible to model most of or the entire decision process, from information acquisition to execution of response. This is due to the temporal precision and capacity to examine electrical activity on most of the cortex, particularly when collecting data with dense-array EEG. The value added in modeling neural processes is in the richness of neural data. Depending on how the data is processed, which channels are examined, whether it is focused on the time or frequency domain, etc., it may be possible to eventually model most or all of the decision process with multiple dynamics using EEG alone. There is even more power to understand decisional processes when combining the rich data obtained from EEG with other process tracing methods (see Chapters 22–24).

Finally, an important added value of examining neural data is that it can be collected concurrently with other methods such as eye-tracking and movement tracking, provided that movement does not cause excessive artifacts. It also can provide insight into some of the assumptions of other process tracing methods. For example, mouse-tracking assumes that the value of examining movement over time is that it reflects continuously cascading neural processes that unfold online during the decision process (see Chapters 8–10; Spivey & Dale, 2006; Freeman, Pauker, Apfelbaum, & Ambady, 2010; Freeman, Dale, & Farmer, 2011; Koop & Johnson, 2013, for a few examples in different decision-making applications). As such, deflections in the trajectory can indicate higher level cognition of unfolding preference, even though the person moving the mouse is not explicitly trying to make their movements reflect this evidence/preference accumulation (Koop & Johnson, 2013; Freeman et al., 2011). Although some studies have successfully found patterns of EEG activation that provide convergent validity for these assumptions (see Frame, Johnson, & Thomas, 2017 for one example), there is still additional work to be done to fully settle the ongoing debate in the neural literature regarding continuous, overlapping neural activity versus discrete steps of activation (Miller, 1988).

Specific EEG Activity and ERPs Examined in Decision-Making Research

Spectral Analysis

Spectral analysis of EEG activity involves decomposing the EEG signal into component sine waves. Unlike with Event Related Potentials (ERPs; see later) that require averaging across many trials to be interpreted, examining periodicity or oscillations (component sine waves) in EEG signals can be done on an individual or aggregated trial level. Typically these types of analysis involve examining the total induced power in a particular spectral band during different periods of cognitive activity, separated from any evoked components or background noise (David, Kilner, & Friston, 2006). Evoked oscillations or evoked potentials are classified as being phase-locked to a particular event such as the appearance of a stimulus. By contrast, induced potentials are oscillations that are not phase-locked to the stimulus. Both of these measures of oscillatory activity are relevant neural measures of cognitive activity, but are typically computed using differing analyses. Higher-order cognitive activity such as decision-making consists of multiple neural activities that may not all be temporally precise. Some activation pertinent to decision-making may be evoked by given stimuli while other activity may not be precisely phase-locked. This indicates the need for studying both types of activation to get a more nuanced and complete understanding of the decision-making process. For the purposes of this discussion of spectral analysis, the focus will be primarily on induced oscillations, while the following section on ERPs will be focused on evoked potentials as they pertain to the study of decision-making.

Increased power in a particular frequency band is known as synchronization and a decrease of power in a given frequency band is called desynchronization. Power in the context of EEG refers to the squared magnitude of the signal, where magnitude is the integral average of the amplitude of the EEG signal within an epoch. The term synchronization is used since increased power in a frequency band indicates that multiple neurons in an area of cortex are synchronized in activity (Wang, 2010). These oscillations are classified as induced because their emergence is self-organized through autonomous neural mechanisms that pertain to cognitive activity, rather than evoked by a particular stimulus (David et al., 2006). Although various methods of spectral decomposition can be used and visually represent the component sine waves (e.g., Fast Fourier Transform, Discrete Fourier Transform, Joint Time-Frequency Analysis, etc. for a few examples), regardless of method, generally when linking spectral information to cognitive activity, focus is given to increases and decreases in power in a particular frequency band rather than a single sine wave frequency. These bands are typically: delta (1–3 Hz), theta (4–7 Hz), alpha (8–13 Hz), beta (14–30 Hz), and gamma (31–90 Hz), with a very small variability in band width depending on analysis and publication. Rounding to whole numbers is somewhat arbitrary for these spectral bands and is rooted in convenience when EEG signals were recorded on paper and interpreted by eye. However, the cutoff points between bands are distinguished today based on correlations with cognitive activity and pathology. See Figure 14.1 for an illustration of these bands of frequencies. Although ERPs are more commonly examined in the study of decision-making, a handful of studies have been done examining the relationship between theta band activity (4–9 Hz) and decision making as well as between beta band activity (13–25 Hz) and decision making. Although other bands of spectral activity have not been as thoroughly examined in the study of

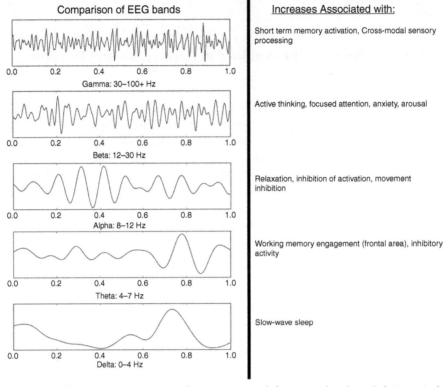

FIGURE 14.1 An illustrative comparison of various spectral frequency bands and their typical ranges in human electroencephalography. Note that certain frequencies may go by a different name when localized to a particular area of cortex, such as the alpha band being referred to as "Mu" when isolated over motor cortex. Original left figure taken from (Nacy, Kbah, Jafer, & Al-Shaalan, 2016).

decision-making, they have been used in broader applications such as in studying sleep disorders, concussions and other head trauma, and speech disorders.

Theta Activity

Frontal theta activity is commonly associated with higher order cognitive processes and increased theta has been found to be a sign of cognitive organization and coordinative processes such as working memory, attention, action selection, decision making, and feedback processing (Cohen, Elger, & Fell, 2009; Cohen, Elger, & Ranganath, 2007; Isomura et al., 2006; Klimesch, 1999; Kubota et al., 2001, among many other studies). Evidence accumulation and combination in perceptual decision making has been linked to increases in theta band activity (van Vugt, Sekuler, Wilson, & Kahana, 2013), and oscillations in the 4–7 Hz band has also been found to co-vary with decisional uncertainty (Jacobs, Hwang, Curran, & Kahana, 2006). In a simple decision-making game which included feedback after each trial, Cohen and his colleagues (2009) found that different stages of the decision-making process are associated with fluctuations in theta as well as delta activity in the medial frontal cortex. During the decision and feedback periods of the task, there was enhanced theta and delta power. In addition there was increased cross-trial phase coherence, which is an increase in the probability of oscillation phases taking specific values at a given time point.

However, during feedback anticipation there was a shift from delta and theta dominance to alpha and beta band activity dominating (Cohen et al., 2009). A later study by van Vugt, Simen, Nystrom, Holmes, and Cohen (2012) helped to further differentiate the relationship of delta activity and decision-making from the relationship between theta activity and decision making, and provided stronger ties between theta band fluctuations and mathematical models of decision making.

Important progress has also been made in tying fluctuations in theta activity to models of decision-making, in particular the drift diffusion model (DDM; Ratcliff, 1978). In a perceptual decision-making task in which participants would judge the direction of motion for a group of randomly moving dots, van Vugt and colleagues (2012) were able to demonstrate that there was an increase in theta band activity prior to response in the integrated condition requiring deliberation and evidence accumulation, and that this increase of activity was not present in a control condition which required no evidence accumulation. Although other EEG bands showed an increase in power prior to response in the integrated condition, such as the delta band, these increases were also seen in the non-integrated condition, indicating that the theta band only was associated with a condition requiring evidence accumulation. The dynamics of evidence accumulation were best associated with theta band activity in superior parietal channels. In addition to this overall trend, when represented as theta activity over time, the slope of this theta accumulation process for individual participants significantly covaried with individual differences in the drift rate with associated behavioral data in the same decision-making task.

Beta Band Activity

Brain activity associated with motor preparation has been widely studied in decision-making, as these neural signatures tend to be fairly robust and can provide a link between brain and behavior. The beta band has been studied somewhat in perceptual decision making but is less established in preferential choice paradigms. The relationship between beta band activity and motor preparation is long established, with beta activity (14–30 Hz typically) decreasing during motor preparation (Jasper & Penfield, 1949). Although fluctuations in beta have been heavily studied in regard to motor inhibition and preparation, the functional role of beta in higher-order cognition and decision making is less well-explored, but given the role of beta in studying cognitive engagement and attention, not necessarily unimportant. Haegens and colleagues (2011) examined beta band oscillations as they pertain to perceptual decision-making in primates and found that differences in beta band fluctuations were able to distinguish between correct and incorrect responses and were not present in a control condition. The specific role of beta band activity in human decision making, however, has been less thoroughly studied.

Additional Spectral Analyses

Although not featured heavily in published studies of decision making, preliminary work has been conducted examining other spectral frequency bands. Cohen et al. (2009) conducted an analysis of cross-trial phase coherence of delta, theta, alpha, beta, and gamma spatially localized in the medial frontal cortex during a decision-making game. There were no significant findings pertaining to distinguishing wins and losses in regard to gamma fluctuations. However, spectral power and cross-trial phase coherence were greater in the theta, alpha, and beta frequency bands after a participant experienced a loss compared to a win. Furthermore, Cohen et al. (2009) were able to distinguish various periods of the decision-making process based on patterns of oscillatory activity. Prior to the button press, while participants are accumulating information, there were moderate increases in the delta and theta bands and strong increases in cross-trial phase coherence. Following their decisions, when subjects would anticipate feedback, there was a shift in power from the predominantly lower frequencies of the theta and delta bands to the higher alpha and beta frequencies. Finally, when receiving feedback, there was a strong but brief increase of power in the delta and theta bands of activity and an across-the-board increase of cross-trial phase coherence in all frequency bands.

Event Related Potentials

Under the larger umbrella of EEG research, Event Related Potentials (ERPs) have been widely used across fields to uncover the process dynamics of important sensory, cognitive, and motoric processes (Kappenman & Luck, 2011). The study of ERPs has particularly dominated in the study of cognition. ERPs represent analysis of EEG in the time domain due to the preservation of detailed temporal dynamics in ERP waveforms, which can be observed down to the millisecond. Much of raw EEG activity recorded is considered to be noise that is randomly distributed across trials (Bastiaansen, Mazaheri, & Jensen, 2012) and unrelated to cognition. To separate the signal of interest from this noise, raw EEG data is segmented into equal time epochs with each segment locked to a common anchor point, such as the onset of a stimulus or execution of a response. These segments are all then averaged to create an ERP waveform. It is assumed that since the noise is randomly distributed across trials, the signal buried in the noise will gradually be uncovered as more segments of data are averaged (Luck & Kappenman, 2011).

The Lateralized Readiness Potential (LRP) has been the most widely studied ERP in decision making thus far and there is a rich, building body of research applying the LRP to both perceptual and preferential choices. As such, the bulk of this section will be devoted to how the LRP has been examined as a neural correlate of decision-making processes and has been tied to well-respected and established process models of decision-making that lend themselves to the high temporal resolution of EEG/ERPs, such as the drift diffusion model (DDM; Ratcliff, 1978). However, the general logic of studying the LRP could be applied to other potentially interesting ERP signatures such as error related negativity (ERN).

The Lateralized Readiness Potential

Although EEG data is extremely rich and can be analyzed a multitude of ways, certain ERPs have proven to be particularly useful in the study of decision-making. Many studies over the past decade examining EEG and decision-making have successfully used the Lateralized Readiness Potential (LRP), a particular type of ERP that elucidates movement preparation by measuring activity over the motor cortex. Often this is used as a means of examining the transition from a state of evidence accumulation to reaching a threshold and making a decision (Smulders & Miller, 2012). For example, when preparing for a voluntary selection of a left- versus right-hand response, an increase of activation occurs in primary and secondary motor cortex, with stronger activation occurring in the hemisphere contralateral to the hand of response (Luck, 2014). In tasks involving the LRP, both hands of response are used, so not all responses are made with the left or the right hand. To determine the degree of unilateral motor activation irrespective of hand of response, researchers implement a double subtraction procedure. In addition to canceling out the asymmetric activation differences based on hand of response, this procedure also isolates lateralized motoric activity other than lateralized asymmetries (de Jong, Coles, Logan, & Gratton, 1990; Gratton, Coles, Sirevaag, Eriksen, & Donchin, 1988; Smulders & Miller, 2012). Typically, the segmentation of the LRP is either stimulus-locked or response-locked. Stimulus-locked LRPs elucidate stimulus processing prior to response activation and response-locked LRPs can be used to ascertain activity between the LRP onset (preparation of a unimanual movement) and overt response (Smulders & Miller, 2012).

Generally, specific features of the LRP are examined in decision-making research. The first, most commonly studied feature of the LRP is the *average LRP amplitude*. As a difference wave, the amplitude of the LRP is inversely related to the degree of competition between two choice alternatives, with higher amplitudes indicating a strong priming of one hand of response but not the other, and conversely, lower amplitudes indicating a similar degree of priming for both hands (Smulders & Miller, 2012; Frame et al., 2017).

Another feature examined is the *Gratton dip*, which is not always present in the LRP but may occur prior to the onset of the LRP. The Gratton dip is most likely to occur when, robustly across trials, an incorrect or unchosen response is strongly primed and almost executed before being inhibited for the ultimately selected hand of response to be moved (Gratton et al., 1988). The magnitude and timing of the Gratton dip have been interpreted as indicators of the strength of response competition. Although there are no strictly defined rules for determining the presence of a Gratton dip, the feature typically is denoted as a significant deviation from baseline during the time it occurs compared to other baseline samples, which tend to average to zero when adjusted properly during ERP computation. Figure 14.2 illustrates an idealized LRP which includes a Gratton dip for illustrative purposes.

Finally, *response onset latency* can be conceptualized as the time when LRP amplitude can be distinguished from EEG noise by exceeding a threshold for a minimum length of time (so as not

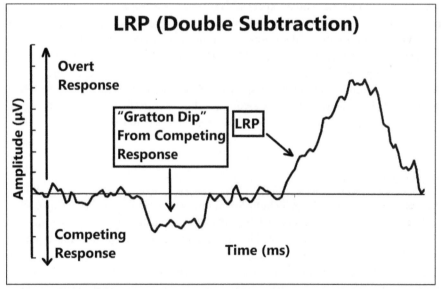

FIGURE 14.2 An idealized Lateralized Readiness Potential (LRP) waveform that has been heavily smoothed for ease of interpretation. The significant negative deflection, the Gratton dip, precedes the LRP and represents activation of the hand that did not ultimately respond. In the context of decision making, this represents preparation to choose the alternative option. The LRP represents the lateralized difference of unimanual response preparation. When the amplitude of the LRP is attenuated, this represents both hands of response being strongly primed and a weaker degree of choice preference of one over the other. By contrast, higher amplitudes reflect a greater difference between activation of the chosen and unchosen hand of response.

to mischaracterize high amplitude noise as the onset of the LRP), and essentially serves to designate the beginning of the LRP (Coles, Gratton, Bashore, Eriksen, & Donchin, 1985). Typically, the amplitude threshold for the onset of the LRP is much higher than the standard for the Gratton dip. Some researchers have argued for fixed amplitude thresholds (e.g., .5 µV), relative criteria (e.g., 25% of the peak amplitude), thresholds based on consistent deviation from baseline activity (e.g., 2*SD of baseline for at least 100 msec), or the "break point" of a regression equation (Mordkoff & Gianaros, 2000). Any of these criteria can be applied separately to single subjects or calculated to subsample grand-averages using a jackknife procedure. An onset latency occurring closer to the response in a response-locked LRP indicates greater competition between the stimuli due to the mutual inhibition of activated responses and is diagnostic of a longer information extraction period prior to response activation (Miller, 1988).

As a motoric potential, the LRP has a couple of specific advantages for examining decision-making, and has an interesting potential relationship with other process tracing methodologies. One advantage of the LRP is that the channels that are used to generate the LRP are located over the motor preparatory cortex. This can provide a potential neural correlate with other motion-based process tracing methods and a window into the step before motoric activation that is captured in mouse or movement tracking. The LRP can be generated even if a response is ultimately withheld, albeit with a lower amplitude than if a response is given, provided that motoric preparation has occurred (Smulders & Miller, 2012). This is useful in decision-making to study fluctuations in preference and can elucidate a preferred option, even if a participant does not make a response. In addition, due to the relationship with activation in motor areas, this ERP has an opportunity to provide either convergent or divergent validity with other process tracing metrics such as mouse-tracking. One would expect if the assumptions of mouse-tracking hold true that measuring continuous hand movement reflects continuously updating cognition and preference, this same accumulation might be demonstrated in the slow buildup of the LRP (Spivey & Dale, 2006; Koop & Johnson, 2013; Frame et al., 2017). Due to the location of the LRP and the nature of its slow building potential, it has been widely studied in the field of decision-making.

The following sections will detail the specific valuable contributions the study of LRPs has enhanced to the field's understanding of decision making, specifically looking at the cognitive and neural processes that precede an actual response: evidence accumulation, response competition, and preference reversals.

Evidence Accumulation

Various models of decision-making, including drift diffusion models (Ratcliff, 1978), decision field theory (DFT; Busemeyer & Townsend, 1993), and race accumulator models such as the linear ballistic accumulator model (LBA; Brown & Heathcote, 2008) represent the decision-making process as an accumulation of evidence that eventually reaches a threshold where a sufficient degree of evidence has been collected to commit to one decision alternative over the other(s). When discussed in these models, it is not specifically delineated what neural processes occur when a person's decision state transitions from indecision to a decisive action (Shadlen & Kiani, 2013).

When mapping the decision accumulation and threshold crossing processes to EEG data, the Lateralized Readiness Potential has been widely studied. Although previous research has presumed that the slow building potential of the LRP corresponds to the process of evidence accumulation (Spencer & Coles, 1999) or to a response (Rinkenauer, Osman, Ulrich, Müller-Gethmann, & Mattes, 2004), van Vugt and colleagues (2014, 2015) specifically sought to determine the specific subcomponents of the LRP that correspond to the process of evidence accumulation and crossing a decision threshold. They conceptualized the LRP as having two major phases: 1) an earlier, smoothly rising phase that would correspond to evidence accumulation during stimulus evaluation, and 2) a later occurring ballistic phase that would correspond to finalizing a decision and executing a response. If the conceptualization holds, the first phase should display correlations with the drift parameter of the drift diffusion model (DDM), indicating evidence accumulation en route to a decision. Changes in drift estimated based on behavioral metrics (accuracy and response time) should further correlate with differences in the LRP curves when the high-drift LRP is subtracted from the low-drift LRP curve. Differences in LRP peak amplitude across bias conditions should further be correlated with variation in the starting point parameter of the DDM.

The primary task used in van Vugt and colleagues' (2014) study was a dot motion task. This is a common perceptual decision-making task that involves an array of moving dots with some proportion moving in one direction with the remainder moving in the other direction. Participants must decide which direction the majority of the dots are moving. Difficulty on this task can be varied via manipulating the proportion of coherently moving dots. In a high-coherence condition, one can clearly see the majority of the dots moving in a particular direction and responses on these trials tend to be much faster and more accurate. On low-coherence trials, only a small majority of the dots move in a coherent direction, making it more challenging to distinguish the correct response. In addition to this primary task, an initial control task was used to determine signal detection reaction times by requesting that participants press either a left or right key when a predefined stimulus would appear. Using the data from this task, a second control task called the arrow task was designed to be virtually identical to the dot-motion task. Although both tasks demand similar perceptual and motor processing, the cognitive difference between the dot-motion task and arrow task is that the former requires longer, noisier evidence accumulation.

Van Vugt and colleagues (2014) found that response-locked LRPs were modulated with changes in the drift rate in the corresponding behavioral model of the data. As the arrow task required less evidence accumulation, the LRP was found to ramp up to a peak much more quickly than the LRP for the dot-motion task. This indicates that a response was reached much more rapidly and decisively. The increased drift rate of the dot-motion condition also caused the peak of the LRP to occur closer temporally to the behavioral response. Figure 14.3 illustrates the difference in LRPs for the three tasks (signal detection control task, arrow task, and dot-motion task) as well as the relationship between high- and low-coherence LRPs of the dot-motion task. Predictably, on the more difficult low-coherence trials, LRP onset was shifted later and the peak amplitude was attenuated.

Response Competition

Another study that implicated the value of the response-locked LRP was a series of studies of preferential choice by Frame et al. (2017), which examined the LRP amplitude and onset latencies in the context of binary choices. Choice options were affectively valenced images from the International Affective Picture System (IAPS; Lang, Bradley, & Cuthbert, 2005) in the first experiment and monetary gambles in the second and third experiments. Participants were told to simply choose which image or gamble they preferred. Stimuli were either highly dissimilar or highly similar to one another in regard to affective valence (Experiment 1) or degree of risk as measured by coefficient of variation (Experiments 2 and 3). The effect of similarity of options in decision making has been studied using both behavioral methods (Smith & Osherson, 1989; Hastie, 2001) and other process tracing methods such as response dynamics (Spivey & Dale, 2006; Koop & Johnson, 2013).

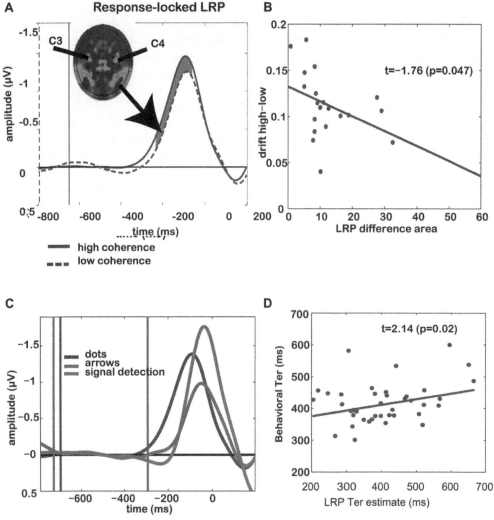

FIGURE 14.3 Results from Experiment 1 of van Vugt et al. (2014). Panel (A) illustrates the delay of response-locked LRP onset as well as attenuation of the LRP in the more behaviorally difficult low-coherence condition of the dot-motion task. Shaded area indicates time points where this difference is significant. Panel (B) plots the significant correlation of this shaded area with the drift rate of the DDM. Panel (C) illustrates LRP differences between the three tasks, and Panel (D) provides a plot of the significant correlation between LRP threshold estimate and the behavioral threshold.

The stimuli used in Frame et al. (2017) were similarly constructed to images and gambles used in Koop and Johnson (2013). An important aspect of the Frame et al. (2017) findings is that they provide convergent validity to the response dynamics method as reported by Koop and Johnson (2013). The theory underlying response dynamics as a methodology presumes that continuous cascading cognition occurs in the brain and this is what can be captured using the response dynamics methodology. However, there is tremendous difficulty in linking neural updating to response dynamics, so Frame and colleagues (2017) hypothesized that observations of response competition observable in the brain prior to execution of a response, could provide

EEG and ERPs **227**

plausibility to the notion that fluctuations in mouse movements reflect meaningful cognitive updating processes. Although not the primary purpose of conducting studies of decision making using process tracing methods, an important side effect of utilizing methodologies to examine cognitive processes is that they can bolster or contradict assumptions carried by other process tracing methods.

As with van Vugt and colleagues' (2014) study mapping the response-locked LRP to evidence accumulation, Frame and colleagues (2017) were able to use features of the response-locked LRP to capture response competition between decision alternatives. Figure 14.4 contains the paneled response-locked LRPs for each of the three studies conducted. Regardless of stimulus type (images or gambles) the same overall pattern was observed, with choices between similar stimuli generating an LRP with attenuated amplitude—less asymmetry in response preparation—compared to the dissimilar condition. In the similar condition, by contrast, there is relatively equal preparation for both hands of response at the time of a response occurring. This robust pattern directly mirrors the findings of Koop and Johnson (2013) and other response dynamics studies in decision making (Kieslich & Hilbig, 2014; Koop, 2013; Scherbaum et al., 2016), where increased response competition was embodied as increased curvature towards the unchosen alternative en route to clicking on a choice option. Although the Frame et al. (2017) study was not designed to collect both mouse-tracking and EEG data, the dynamics of the LRP prior to making a decision illustrate the plausibility of the embodiment in response dynamics.

Preference Reversals

Preference reversals are often studied alongside response competition in preferential choice paradigms, particularly those involving process tracing methods. These are similar concepts that represent what might both be thought of colloquially as "indecisiveness", or "changing one's mind", but they are conceptually distinct from one another. Although response competition can be thought of as a gradual pull towards an alternative (or multiple) option(s) that occurs throughout a trial, a preference reversal is a much more discrete switch in preference. The second experiment of Koop and Johnson (2013) shows how this discrete change is manifest in mouse-tracking, and can be seen in the averaged trajectory of trials involving risky gains. Even in the averaged trajectories, it is clear that participants initially moved towards the unchosen option, in this case the safe gamble, before abruptly switching and choosing the risky gamble. Corresponding velocity profiles also showed that the speed of hand movement following the change in direction was substantially faster than the initial movement within trial and the overall movement when the safe gamble was chosen instead.

In addition to examining the LRP for neural correlates of response competition, Frame et al. (2017) examined the LRP to determine if there is a neural correlate of preference reversals in preferential choice tasks. Since the Gratton dip represents what is essentially an inhibited LRP in the opposite direction, this feature seemed to be the strongest candidate for a neural signature of preference reversals. It was hypothesized that when making decisions between affectively valenced pictures or gambles, in cases where the similarity between the stimuli was high, in addition to having an attenuated LRP, there might also be a Gratton dip in the averaged waveform that would not be present in the dissimilar condition. In other words, when making a hypothetical decision between two attractive images such as between a picture of a laughing child and a baby, people may prefer the child initially, which will activate the start of an LRP, but will inhibit this response in favor of selecting the image of a baby, causing an LRP to fully activate in the other direction, making the earlier initialized LRP appear as a Gratton dip in the final waveform. However,

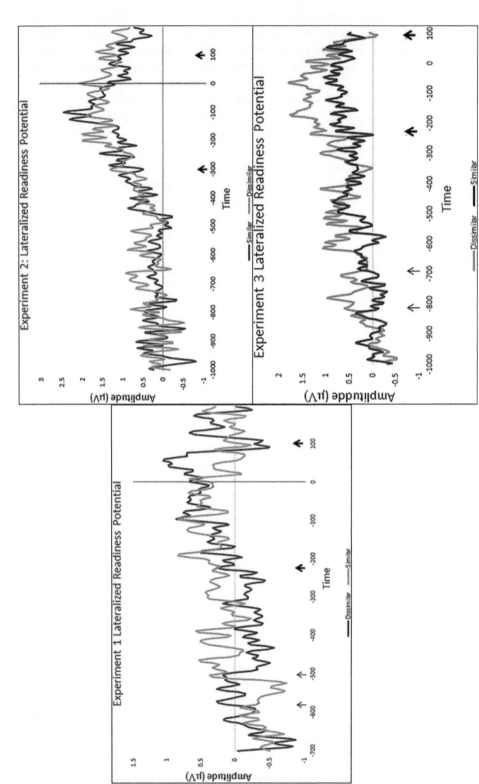

FIGURE 14.4 Paneled graph of the three LRP waveforms from Frame et al. (2017). The left panel (Experiment 1) contains a significantly attenuated LRP when participants evaluated similarly valenced images as well as a Gratton dip. The top-right panel (Experiment 2) and bottom-right panel (Experiment 3) contain a significantly attenuated LRP when participants evaluated similarly risky gambles, but only Experiment 3 contained a Gratton dip. Arrows indicate the timing of the LRP (bolded) and Gratton dip (unbolded).

this would only appear if preference reversals were robust across trials in the similar condition. Inconsistent effects could be washed out in the averaging process.

In two out of their three experiments, Frame and colleagues (2017) found that there was a Gratton dip present across decisions involving similar alternatives. This pattern was not present in selections between dissimilar decision options. The Gratton dip could robustly capture strong preference reversals in two out of the three studies. This finding echoes the results from the second study of Koop and Johnson (2013), where trajectories proceeded towards a safer alternative before changing direction and selecting the riskier option in a manner that overtly crossed the y-axis, which was not seen in other conditions. Just as crossing over the y-axis represents a more discrete switching behavior above and beyond increased average absolute deviation in mouse-tracking, the Gratton dip neutrally represents a discrete switching between preparing for one hand of response for another above and beyond an attenuated LRP. Figure 14.5 illustrates the linkage of these patterns of results by providing an illustration of these concepts.

Conclusions/Summary

EEG and ERPs have demonstrated their usefulness as a process tracing method across a variety of decision domains, ranging from simple perceptual decision-making tasks to higher order preferential choices. However, as a young methodology applied to the realm of decision making, there is still much to be explored. Due to the richness of data, it is possible to spend years parsing a single data set and still obtain meaningful results. As can be seen by the literature surveyed here, there are numerous applications of EEG to decision-making and if one takes the time to thumb through a book on Event Related Potentials or spectral analysis, decision-making studies have only begun to scratch the surface of all possible high temporal resolution analysis possibilities (see Recommended Reading section for excellent starting resources that explain EEG and ERP methods broadly).

In addition to providing valuable insights as methods used in isolation, EEG and ERPs have the potential to be paired with other process tracing methods such as eye-tracking or response dynamics. Utilizing multiple methods in concert can help provide insight into many of the assumptions made by other methodologies concerning the underlying brain dynamics. Understanding how these dynamics actually occur, whether assumptions are correct or incorrect, is crucial for modifying current models and developing new models of decision making and provides an important opportunity to update some of the current assumptions of other methods based on empirical findings.

All of the studies focused on in this review have centralized on human decision making. Naturally, a great deal of additional work has been done in non-human studies that has been instrumental in incorporating EEG as a process tracing method and tying EEG to models of decision making. An excellent example is Ratcliff and Smith's (2004) work with single channel spikes in the middle temporal area, lateral parietal area in extrastriate cortex, and the frontal eye field, successfully linked patterns of neural firing to eye movement decisions. Neural firing rates increased in cells coding selected decision alternatives which did not occur nearly as strongly in nonselected stimulus alternatives. Another important contribution of this work was that the findings were consistent with multiple sequential sampling models of decision making, including the leaky competing accumulator model and the drift diffusion model. Additionally, work has been done with primates tying local field potentials and beta band spectral activity to somatosensory decision making (Haegens et al., 2011). In particular, Haegens and colleagues (2011) found that differential beta activity fluctuated throughout perceptual decision processes and there were distinct fluctuation differences between correct and incorrect responses. Generally, beta power increased along with gamma power and alpha power decreased as a response to the task. Differential activity was

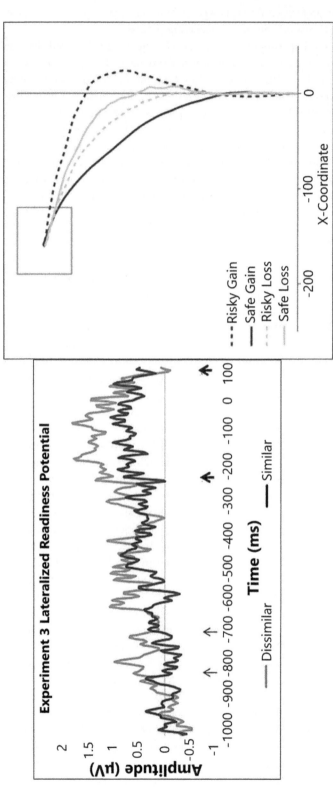

FIGURE 14.5 This illustrates the similar conceptual interpretation between the results of Koop and Johnson (2013). Experiment 2 involving gambles (right panel, gain gambles only) and the LRP findings of Frame et al. (2017). Differences in LRP amplitude seem to roughly correspond to differences with Average Absolute Deviation in mouse trajectories and the Gratton dip roughly corresponds to the discrete response switching seen in the right panel's risky gain trajectory. Not only is there an increased area under the curve, but the line overtly seems to proceed towards the unchosen right gamble before switching directions and choosing the left gamble. In the same vein, the Gratton dip indicates a nearly initiated LRP for the unchosen option.

not present in a control condition that involved movement without requiring decision-making. This distinction is crucial since previous research has focused nearly exclusively on alpha activity as reflecting motor inhibition or the "status quo" in the brain and little has been explored regarding how to model the functional role of alpha or beta in higher order cognition.

Although the findings from EEG and ERPs and decision-making have thus far been rich and fascinating, there is still a great deal more work that needs to be done, particularly in connecting and bolstering mathematical and computational models of decision making. Also, to more directly test connections between multiple process tracing methods, such as EEG and response dynamics, will require simultaneous collection of these metrics. Chapters 23 and 24 will delve further into the connection between process tracing methods: mathematical models and collecting multiple process tracing metrics, respectively. The temporal precision of EEG has made it a popular choice in studies of decision making, but future studies will also require more precise spatial resolution than what even dense arrays currently provide. Future studies of decision-making will likely pull in even more new technologies that have been thus far largely unexplored in the study of cognition and decision making, such as functional near-infrared spectroscopy (fNIRS).

Note

1   This research was funded in part by National Science Foundation grant #1260882. 4035 Colonel Glenn Hwy, Beavercreek, OH 45431.

Recommended Reading List

*   Cohen, M. X., 2014: An excellent tutorial introduction to analyzing EEG as time series data, with emphasis on analyzing EEG data in both the time and frequency domains. This book includes both comprehensive theoretical information on electroencephalography as well as Matlab programming and tutorials.
*   Luck, S. J., 2014: Fundamental text for conducting Event Related Potential (ERP) research. Provides information to readers regarding design of ERP research from the ground up and is considered by many ERP researchers to be a fundamental reference in both the laboratory and in the classroom.
*   Luck, S. J., & Kappenman, E. S., 2011: Provides more detail into specific components that can be generated using ERP techniques, including sensory ERP components, error related negativity, the lateralized readiness potential and other movement potentials, and fundamental components such as the P300. This book condenses information about numerous components into a single comprehensive guide and serves as an excellent reference resource to researchers starting out in ERP research.

References

Bastiaansen, M., Mazaheri, A., & Jensen, O. (2012). Beyond ERPs: oscillatory neuronal dynamics. In S. J. Luck & E. S. Kappenman (Eds.), *The Oxford handbook of event-related potential components* (pp. 31–50). Oxford, UK: Oxford University Press.

Berka, C., Levendowski, D. J., Lumicao, M. N., Yau, A., Davis, G., Zivkovic, V. T., ... & Craven, P. L. (2007). EEG correlates of task engagement and mental workload in vigilance, learning, and memory tasks. *Aviation, Space, and Environmental Medicine, 78*(5), 231–244.

Brown, S. D., & Heathcote, A. (2008). The simplest complete model of choice response time: Linear ballistic accumulation. *Cognitive Psychology, 57*(3), 153–178.

232 Frame

Busemeyer, J. R., & Townsend, J. T. (1993). Decision field theory: A dynamic-cognitive approach to decision making in an uncertain environment. *Psychological Review, 100*(3), 432–459.

Cohen, M. X. (2014). *Analyzing neural time series data: theory and practice*. MIT Press.

Cohen, M. X., Elger, C. E., & Fell, J. (2009). Oscillatory activity and phase–amplitude coupling in the human medial frontal cortex during decision making. *Journal of Cognitive Neuroscience, 21*(2), 390–402.

Cohen, M. X., Elger, C. E., & Ranganath, C. (2007). Reward expectation modulates feedback-related negativity and EEG spectra. *Neuroimage, 35*(2), 968–978.

Coles, M. G., Gratton, G., Bashore, T. R., Eriksen, C. W., & Donchin, E. (1985). A psychophysiological investigation of the continuous flow model of human information processing. *Journal of Experimental Psychology: Human Perception and Performance, 11*(5), 529–553.

David, O., Kilner, J. M., & Friston, K. J. (2006). Mechanisms of evoked and induced responses in MEG/EEG. *Neuroimage, 31*(4), 1580–1591.

de Jong, R., Coles, M. G., Logan, G. D., & Gratton, G. (1990). In search of the point of no return: The control of response processes. *Journal of Experimental Psychology: Human Perception and Performance, 16*(1), 164–182.

Frame, M. E., Johnson, J. G., & Thomas, R. D. (2017). A neural indicator of response competition in preferential choice. *Decision*. Advance online publication.

Freeman, J. B., Dale, R., & Farmer, T. A. (2011). Hand in motion reveals mind in motion. *Frontiers in Psychology, 2*, 59.

Freeman, J. B., Pauker, K., Apfelbaum, E. P., & Ambady, N. (2010). Continuous dynamics in the real-time perception of race. *Journal of Experimental Social Psychology, 46*(1), 179–185.

Gratton, G., Coles, M. G., Sirevaag, E. J., Eriksen, C. W., & Donchin, E. (1988). Pre-and poststimulus activation of response channels: A psychophysiological analysis. *Journal of Experimental Psychology: Human Perception and Performance, 14*(3), 331–344.

Haegens, S., Nácher, V., Hernández, A., Luna, R., Jensen, O., & Romo, R. (2011). Beta oscillations in the monkey sensorimotor network reflect somatosensory decision making. *Proceedings of the National Academy of Sciences, 108*(26), 10708–10713.

Hastie, R. (2001). Problems for judgment and decision making. *Annual Review of Psychology, 52*(1), 653–683.

Isomura, Y., Sirota, A., Ozen, S., Montgomery, S., Mizuseki, K., Henze, D. A., & Buzsáki, G. (2006). Integration and segregation of activity in entorhinal–hippocampal subregions by neocortical slow oscillations. *Neuron, 52*(5), 871–882.

Jacobs, J., Hwang, G., Curran, T., & Kahana, M. J. (2006). EEG oscillations and recognition memory: Theta correlates of memory retrieval and decision making. *Neuroimage, 32*(2), 978–987

Jasper, H., & Penfield, W. (1949). Electrocorticograms in man: Effect of voluntary movement upon the electrical activity of the precentral gyrus. *Archiv für Psychiatrie und Nervenkrankheiten, 183*(1–2), 163–174.

Kappenman, E. S., & Luck, S. J. (2011). ERP components: The ups and downs of brainwave recordings. In S. J. Luck & E. S. Kappenman (Eds.), *The Oxford handbook of event-related potential components* (pp. 3–30). Oxford, UK: Oxford University Press.

Kieslich, P. J., & Hilbig, B. E. (2014). Cognitive conflict in social dilemmas: An analysis of response dynamics. *Judgment and Decision Making, 9*(6), 510–522.

Klimesch, W. (1999). EEG alpha and theta oscillations reflect cognitive and memory performance: A review and analysis. *Brain Research Reviews, 29*(2), 169–195.

Koop, G. J. (2013). An assessment of the temporal dynamics of moral decisions. *Judgment and Decision Making, 8*(5), 527–539.

Koop, G. J., & Johnson, J. G. (2013). The response dynamics of preferential choice. *Cognitive Psychology, 67*(4), 151–185.

Kubota, Y., Sato, W., Toichi, M., Murai, T., Okada, T., Hayashi, A., & Sengoku, A. (2001). Frontal midline theta rhythm is correlated with cardiac autonomic activities during the performance of an attention demanding meditation procedure. *Cognitive Brain Research, 11*(2), 281–287.

Lang, P. J., Bradley, M. M., & Cuthbert, B. N. (2005). *International affective picture system (IAPS): Affective ratings of pictures and instruction manual*. Gainesville, FL: National Institute of Mental Health, Center for the Study of Emotion and Attention, University of Florida.

Luck, S. J. (2014). *An introduction to the event-related potential technique*. Cambridge, MA: MIT Press.

Luck, S. J., & Kappenman, E. S. (2011). *The Oxford handbook of event-related potential components.* Oxford, UK: Oxford University Press.

Miller, J. (1988). Discrete and continuous models of human information processing: Theoretical distinctions and empirical results. *Acta Psychologica, 67*(3), 191–257.

Mordkoff, J. T., & Gianaros, P. J. (2000). Detecting the onset of the lateralized readiness potential: A comparison of available methods and procedures. *Psychophysiology, 37*(3), 347–360.

Nacy, S. M., Kbah, S. N., Jafer, H. A., & Al-Shaalan, I. (2016). Controlling a servo motor using EEG signals from the primary motor cortex. *American Journal of Biomedical Engineering, 6*(5), 139–146.

Palm, G. (2016). Neural information processing in cognition: We start to understand the orchestra, but where is the conductor? *Frontiers in Computational Neuroscience, 10*(3), 1–6.

Ratcliff, R. (1978). A theory of memory retrieval. *Psychological Review, 85*(2), 59–108.

Ratcliff, R., & Smith, P. L. (2004). A comparison of sequential sampling models for two-choice reaction time. *Psychological Review, 111*(2), 333–367.

Rinkenauer, G., Osman, A., Ulrich, R., Müller-Gethmann, H., & Mattes, S. (2004). On the locus of speed-accuracy trade-off in reaction time: Inferences from the lateralized readiness potential. *Journal of Experimental Psychology: General, 133*(2), 261–282.

Scherbaum, S., Frisch, S., Leiberg, S., Lade, S. J., Goschke, T., & Dshemuchadse, M. (2016). Process dynamics in delay discounting decisions: An attractor dynamics approach. *Judgment and Decision Making, 11*(5), 472–495.

Shadlen, M. N., & Kiani, R. (2013). Decision making as a window on cognition. *Neuron, 80*(3), 791–806.

Smith, E. E., & Osherson, D. N. (1989). Similarity and decision making. In S. Vosniadou & A. Ortony (Eds.), *Similarity and analogical reasoning* (pp. 60–75). Cambridge, UK: Cambridge University Press.

Smulders, F. T., & Miller, J. O. (2012). The lateralized readiness potential. In S. J. Luck & E. S. Kappenman (Eds.), *The Oxford handbook of event-related potential components* (pp. 209–229). Oxford, UK: Oxford University Press.

Spencer, K. M., & Coles, M. G. (1999). The lateralized readiness potential: Relationship between human data and response activation in a connectionist model. *Psychophysiology, 36*(3), 364–370.

Spivey, M. J., & Dale, R. (2006). Continuous dynamics in real-time cognition. *Current Directions in Psychological Science, 15*(5), 207–211.

van Vugt, M. K., Sekuler, R., Wilson, H. R., & Kahana, M. J. (2013). An electrophysiological signature summed similarity in visual working memory. *Journal of Experimental Psychology: General, 142*(2), 412.

van Vugt, M. K., Simen, P., Nystrom, L. E., Holmes, P., & Cohen, J. D. (2012). EEG oscillations reveal neural correlates of evidence accumulation. *Frontiers in Neuroscience, 6*(106), 1–13.

van Vugt, M. K., Simen, P., Nystrom, L., Holmes, P., & Cohen, J. D. (2014). Lateralized readiness potentials reveal properties of a neural mechanism for implementing a decision threshold. *PloS ONE, 9*(3), 90943.

van Vugt, M. K., Simen, P., Nystrom, L., Holmes, P., & Cohen, J. D. (2015). Correction: Lateralized readiness potentials reveal properties of a neural mechanism for implementing a decision threshold. *PloS ONE, 10*(6), e0132197.

Wang, X. J. (2010). Neurophysiological and computational principles of cortical rhythms in cognition. *Physiological Reviews, 90*(3), 1195–1268.

15

DECISION NEUROSCIENCE

fMRI Insights into Choice Processes[1]

Vinod Venkatraman and Crystal Reeck

The human brain sits at the center of all decision making: inputs from the environment are perceived and evaluated, options are weighed, and action is chosen. Over the past 15 years, the field of decision neuroscience has made enormous strides in understanding how the brain supports these (decision) processes. Decision neuroscience is a relatively young field, but it is rapidly growing (Figure 15.1). Up to the end of the year 2000, only 16 articles had been published using neuroscience to understand decision making. Those numbers have since increased exponentially, with 264 such articles published in 2018 alone. Importantly, during that time the field has also matured. Early studies in this area focused on trying to map relevant decision processes to brain regions, such as loss aversion (Tom, Fox, Trepel, & Poldrack, 2007), impatience (Kable & Glimcher, 2007), or risk (Huettel, Stowe, Gordon, Warner, & Platt, 2006). The field has since evolved considerably, and now data from neuroimaging experiments have been used to predict market-level outcomes in diverse areas, including advertising effectiveness (Venkatraman et al., 2015), project crowdfunding (Genevsky & Knutson, 2015), and music popularity (Berns & Moore, 2012). In the present chapter, we provide an orientation to the use of neuroimaging in decision-making research with a focus specifically on functional magnetic resonance imaging (fMRI).

Understanding fMRI Signal and Experimental Design

fMRI is a noninvasive technique that has been used for measuring brain activity during cognitive tasks (Ogawa, Lee, Kay, & Tank, 1990). The most common mechanism for measuring neural activity uses blood oxygenation level dependent (BOLD) contrast. When performing a specific cognitive task, the corresponding regions of the brain involved in the task utilize oxygen. The brain vasculature responds to this demand for oxygen by increasing the flow of oxygen-rich blood, through a process known as hemodynamic response. This leads to changes in the relative levels of oxygenated and deoxygenated blood in the corresponding brain regions. Critically, hemoglobin in the blood has different magnetic properties, depending on its oxygenation state. This allows the ensuing changes to be captured using high-field magnetic resonance scanners (Huettel, Song, & McCarthy, 2008). Thus, the BOLD fMRI signal represents an indirect and correlative measure of local neuronal activity. In this section, we introduce some fundamental

Decision Neuroscience **235**

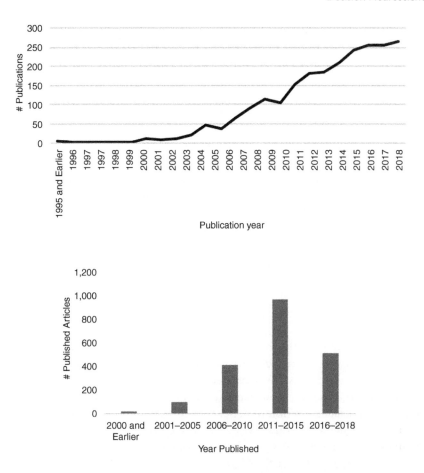

FIGURE 15.1 Evolution of research in decision neuroscience. The field of decision neuroscience has grown exponentially, as seen from the number of articles examining decision making using neuroscience published in academic journals.[2]

aspects of fMRI experimental design that may be relevant for a behavioral researcher interested in the technique.

A typical fMRI response to a single trial or event, known as the hemodynamic response function, begins after a delay of 1–2 sec, peaks at about 5–6 sec following event onset and returns to baseline (default activation prior to onset of the event) after about 14–16 sec. Although this seems extremely slow for any task, the hemodynamic responses to multiple subsequent events sum in a roughly linear manner (Dale & Buckner, 1997; Huettel & McCarthy, 2000). Therefore, using careful experimental designs outlined later in this chapter, one can estimate neural responses to multiple events that are presented in close temporal proximity.

The simplest form of fMRI experiments involves a block design where neural activity is integrated over multiple trials of the same task type grouped together (a block typically consists of a set of six–eight trials lasting about 20–30 sec) and compared against activity when a subject is not doing any task (rest) or performing a different task (control). For example, imagine a researcher is interested in elucidating the neural response to sadness. Participants may be presented with a series of sad faces in one block and a series of neutral faces in a different block (control). By computing the differences in aggregate brain activity between these blocks, one could identify the areas of the brain involved with processing sadness. However, such designs do not help isolate responses to each individual face within the block, even if the faces are associated with different levels of emotion for each participant. Therefore, block designs are excellent for detecting the presence of a difference in response across conditions, but limited in their ability to estimate the size of that response to specific events.

Most recent designs involve event-related experiments, where the response to each trial can be modeled separately. Here, the events of interest are randomly interspersed (e.g., sad and neutral faces). Since the response to each event sums in a linear manner, one can use statistical techniques to tease out the contributions of each individual event of interest to the overall neural response. Event-related designs also allow the incorporation of subjective responses into the estimates of brain activity. For example, one could use subjective ratings about the emotionality of each face to identify brain regions where the response scales to experienced emotions at the individual level. Similarly, one could also use post-hoc responses (e.g., Do you remember seeing this face before?) as a way of classifying brain responses subsequently. Such event-related designs are much more common in decision-making research, as the approach allows estimation of responses based on participants' choices during individual trials.

This discussion highlights three critical aspects of fMRI design for behavioral researchers. First, fMRI studies involve repeated designs and are often aggregated across multiple repetitions of the stimuli. These repetitions are often necessary to reliably isolate activations related to the process of interest, given the slow nature of hemodynamic response, and other sources of system noise during data acquisition (Huettel & McCarthy, 2001). A critical limitation, therefore, lies with not being able to use fMRI when questions cannot be repeatedly presented. However, unlike the one-shot designs that are commonly used in behavioral studies, the repeated-measures designs used in fMRI are much more powerful statistically for detecting differences between different conditions. Second, fMRI designs also rely heavily on contrasts, making it important to carefully design control conditions. In the earlier example, if one just presented sad faces to understand the neural correlates of sadness, the brain responses cannot be isolated to sadness, as it would also include processing of faces, visual attention, and other relevant processes. However, by also using neutral faces (which controls for these confounds), one could isolate brain regions that are specifically related to sadness (by subtracting brain responses to neutral faces from sad faces). Lastly, the rigidity of the scanning environment itself poses certain constraints in terms of studies that can be answered using fMRI. Participants are often lying down in a supine position and are instructed to be as still as possible (so that data is recorded from exactly the same region in the brain in every trial). This prevents researchers from conducting certain types of experiments that require the use of physical materials or interactions when in the scanner.

Neural Correlates of Decision Making

As research in decision neuroscience has matured, several key neural regions have emerged as central to many different aspects of decision making. In this section, we introduce some of the key brain regions that have been commonly implicated in decision making and discuss their specific roles (Figure 15.2).

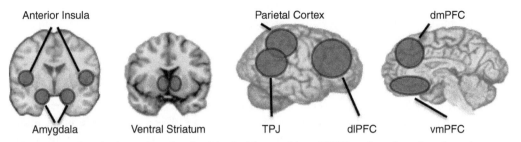

FIGURE 15.2 Key brain regions involved in decision making. dlPFC = dorsolateral prefrontal cortex. dmPFC = dorsomedial prefrontal cortex. TPJ = temporoparietal junction. vmPFC = ventromedial prefrontal cortex.

Ventromedial Prefrontal Cortex

Spend the day at any decision neuroscience conference, and you will see plenty of presentations discussing the ventromedial prefrontal cortex (vmPFC). A series of fMRI studies demonstrate converging evidence supporting the role of the vmPFC specifically for the computation of value (Bechara, Tranel, Damasio, & Damasio, 1996; Hare, O'Doherty, Camerer, Schultz, & Rangel, 2008; Padoa-Schioppa & Assad, 2006; Plassmann, O'Doherty, & Rangel, 2007). Estimating the value and costs associated with available options is a key component of decision making. Not surprisingly, there has been increased focus in decision neuroscience research on brain systems that are responsible for these evaluative processes (Rangel, Camerer, & Montague, 2008; Sugrue, Corrado, & Newsome, 2005). According to most theories, the input signal (which is usually some form of sensory or reward signal) is transformed into a higher-order representation of value. This value representation is then linked to the available courses of action and finally to the selection of a discrete choice among alternatives (Sugrue et al., 2005). Lesions in vmPFC have also been shown to impair choice behavior in domains such as eating, learning about options, and social decision making (Fellows & Farah, 2007; Izquierdo, Suda, & Murray, 2004; Koenigs & Tranel, 2007).

Ventral Striatum

The neurotransmitter dopamine plays an important role in motivation and reward processing, making it a key component in the neurobiology of decision making (Wise, 2004). These dopamine neurons originate in the ventral tegmental area (VTA) and connect primarily to the ventral striatum and the medial prefrontal regions like the vmPFC (Schultz, Dayan, & Montague, 1997). In humans, midbrain dopamine neurons are activated by unexpected rewards (Schultz et al., 1997). However, when these rewards become predictable, the neurons begin to respond to the cues that predict the reward rather than the actual delivery of the reward. Additionally, when the actual reward is omitted, the firing of dopamine neurons is inhibited. These findings suggest that dopamine might be involved with predicting rewards following conditioned stimuli as well as the subsequent errors in reward prediction. While several fMRI studies have also found support for the role of the ventral striatum in reward prediction error (Hare et al., 2008; Seymour, Daw, Dayan, Singer, & Dolan, 2007), considerable controversy still exists, with others arguing for the role of this region in computing values (Kable & Glimcher, 2007; Knutson, Taylor, Kaufman,

Peterson, & Glover, 2005; Yacubian et al., 2006). Ventral striatum has also been shown to play an important role in motivation and reward-related learning (O'Doherty, Dayan, Friston, Critchley, & Dolan, 2003).

Anterior Insula

The anterior insula is involved in several processes, including detecting internal bodily sensations (e.g., heartbeat), emotion, and awareness (Craig, 2009). It also plays a critical role in attention and decision making. For instance, several studies have shown activation in the anterior insula to be associated with anticipation and experience of emotionally negative events, anticipation of threat, disgust and distrust (Paulus, Rogalsky, Simmons, Feinstein, & Stein, 2003; Phillips et al., 1997). Activation in this region has also been shown to predict risk-averse choices in decision-making tasks (Kuhnen & Knutson, 2005; Venkatraman, Payne, Bettman, Luce, & Huettel, 2009a) and plays a key role in assessing uncertainty and integrating risk prediction errors in decision making (Preuschoff, Quartz, & Bossaerts, 2008).

Amygdala

The amygdala has been a focus of research on affect and emotions because it is a key part of the limbic system and connects to subcortical structures that process autonomic functions (Pessoa & Adolphs, 2010; Phelps, 2006). The amygdala has been associated with learning about emotional information, most notably in supporting fear conditioning and arousing negative events (LaBar, Gatenby, Gore, LeDoux, & Phelps, 1998; Phelps, 2006). It is also widely accepted that the amygdala plays an important role in the recognition of negative, unpleasant emotions (LaBar et al., 1998; Phelps, 2006; Phelps & LeDoux, 2005) and may be critical for loss aversion (de Martino, Camerer, & Adolphs, 2010). However, lesion studies indicate that the amygdala may play a more important role in emotional arousal than in valence (Glascher & Adolphs, 2003). Imaging studies have also demonstrated that the amygdala plays a key role in mediating the framing effect (de Martino, Kumaran, Seymour, & Dolan, 2006) as well as the attraction effect (Hedgcock & Rao, 2009). These studies argue for a more general role for the amygdala in mediating decision biases and learning emotional information.

Parietal Cortex

The parietal cortex or the lateral intraparietal sulcus (LIP) is another region that has often been associated with value computations. While vmPFC has been associated with context-independent computation of value, the parietal cortex plays a central role in integrating value signals based on context. The LIP is anatomically positioned in between the sensory-motor chain, with inputs from sensory regions such as visual cortex, and outputs to motor response regions (Gold & Shadlen, 2007). Studies in non-human primates using perceptual decision-making paradigms demonstrate linear increase in firing rates of LIP neurons with increasing task difficulty (Shadlen & Newsome, 2001). More importantly, for the purposes of decision making, Platt and Glimcher show that activity in the LIP neurons is modulated by expected magnitude as well as probability of rewards, consistent with a role for this region in integrating value information (Platt & Glimcher, 1999). Human studies using imaging have also found consistent activation in the parietal regions for tasks involving risk and uncertainty (Huettel et al., 2006; Paulus et al., 2001).

Dorsolateral Prefrontal Cortex

The frontal lobe is typically referred to as the executive processing center of the brain (Miller & Cohen, 2001) and largely consists of the dorsolateral prefrontal cortex and anterior cingulate cortex (the dorsal aspect is more commonly associated with control processes in decision making). The dorsolateral prefrontal cortex (dlPFC) plays an important role in goal maintenance, task switching, inhibition of prepotent responses, action selection, attention, and working memory—all processes that are central to decision making (Miller & Cohen, 2001). Of particular interest for decision making is the role of prefrontal cortex in inhibition, particularly in overriding impulses, temptations, and desires (Knoch, Pascual-Leone, Meyer, Treyer, & Fehr, 2006b). For example, Sanfey and colleagues found that increased activation in the dlPFC in the ultimatum game could help override the emotional response from anterior insula towards accepting unfair offers (Sanfey, Rilling, Aronson, Nystrom, & Cohen, 2003). This was further validated in an independent study using repetitive transcranial magnetic stimulation, where right dlPFC was temporarily disrupted, resulting in increased risk taking (Knoch et al., 2006a).

Dorsomedial Prefrontal Cortex

The dorsomedial prefrontal cortex (dmPFC), which includes the anterior cingulate cortex, was traditionally associated with resolving response conflict as well as error monitoring (Botvinick, Braver, Barch, Carter, & Cohen, 2001; Carter et al., 1998). However, studies have extended its role to decision making (de Martino et al., 2006; Pochon, Riis, Sanfey, Nystrom, & Cohen, 2008) and emotional processing (Etkin, Egner, & Kalisch, 2011; Walton, Devlin, & Rushworth, 2004). Additional studies also suggest that the dmPFC could facilitate the integration of signals between the cognitive and emotional systems (Meriau et al., 2006), potentially helping individuals to strike a balance between different strategies during decision making based on decision context and individual capabilities (de Martino et al., 2006; Taren, Venkatraman, & Huettel, 2011; Venkatraman & Huettel, 2012; Venkatraman, Rosati, Taren, & Huettel, 2009b).

Neuroscience in Decision Making: Common Concerns and Criticisms

Despite the increasing number of studies that bridge the methods of neuroscience with behavioral studies of decision-making phenomena, we wish to highlight some important notes of caution. First, it is highly unlikely that a subset of individual brain regions described earlier can independently facilitate complex decision preferences. Therefore, one must be careful not to overgeneralize from one set of brain imaging results to conclude that the sole cause of a phenomenon has been found. For example, though the vmPFC plays a key role in valuation as discussed earlier, activation in this region has also been attributed to other functions like emotion regulation and social cognition (Delgado et al., 2016). One also needs to guard against making "reverse inferences", wherein a researcher observes activation in a particular brain region and assumes a particular psychological function is involved (Poldrack, 2006; see also Chapter 6 for a similar issue). For instance, observing activation in the amygdala during a particular task does not imply people are engaging in emotional processing or experiencing fear, as the amygdala might also be involved with other cognitive functions and decision biases as discussed earlier. However, if the amygdala is reliably activated as part of a network of other regions associated with emotional processing, then it provides valuable insights into the underlying processes which can then be tested in subsequent follow-up behavioral studies.

A common criticism of decision neuroscience often pertains to the incremental value that neuroscience data can provide regarding decision processes above and beyond behavioral experiments. Huettel and Payne (2009) argue that one attitude—frequently seen in popular accounts of the latest neuroscience studies—is that measurements of brain function provide access to previously hidden mechanisms. Measuring the brain, in lay terms, is like opening the hood of a car, with previously inferred components now laid bare to the viewer. This attitude has been labeled *neuroessentialism* (Racine, Bar-Ilan, & Illes, 2005). An alternative perspective, as adopted by commentators decrying the expansion of neuroscience methods into the social sciences, is that neuroscience data are unnecessary for understanding behavior (Clithero, Tankersley, & Huettel, 2008). This is often referred to as the *behavioral sufficiency* argument: knowing the brain regions activated during performance of some task might be of interest to neuroscientists, but that knowledge has no consequences for our behavioral research. Instead, one should just manipulate the context in which that phenomenon occurs and then measure changes in the associated behavior. We believe that these two perspectives are equally misguided. Behavioral researchers should not dismiss neuroscience data as irrelevant to their goals, particularly since an increasing number of studies are beginning to demonstrate that neural activation predicts real-world outcomes better than behavioral measures alone (Berns & Moore, 2012; Genevsky & Knutson, 2015; Knutson, Rick, Wimmer, Prelec, & Loewenstein, 2007; Venkatraman et al., 2015). However, neuroscience data cannot simply replace behavioral research, despite the breathless descriptions in the popular press.

As illustrated in the example later, we, like several other researchers, are particularly excited about using converging neuroscience and behavioral data to understand variability in decision making (see also relevant discussion in Chapter 24). Even the most robust decision phenomena are subject to individual and task variability. Within any fMRI experiment there is a welter of data specific to each individual, as reflected in the magnitude of activation within and across regions of interest. One obvious analysis is to show differences in brain activation as a function of differences in task or context variables. One can also examine whether the subjects who are more influenced by the presence of a particular task or context variable show more or less neural activation relative to others. Huettel and Payne (2009) argue that such analysis could be extended by using neural data (e.g., activation in regions of interest), alongside behavioral data, to predict trial-to-trial choices within a logistic regression model, as has been done previously (Chiu, Lohrenz, & Montague, 2008; Kuhnen & Knutson, 2005). To the extent that neuroscience can illuminate the mechanisms underlying individual choice biases and strategic preferences, it may become critical for creating robust and flexible models of real-world decision behavior.

Huettel and Payne (2009) suggest guidelines for integrating neuroscience and behavioral data. First, they argue that neuroscience experiments should be designed so that they test specific hypotheses about brain function; those hypotheses must be made as precise as possible. Subsequently, researchers should attempt to use neuroscience data to identify constraints for behavioral models, so that we can identify those models that are biologically implausible (and thus are candidates for revision). Last, the results of the neuroscience experiments should motivate new studies of behavior, to confirm the revised models. As illustrated in the following section, this iterative approach—moving from behavior to brain and back to behavior—recognizes the converging value of both forms of data without privileging either.

Neural Insights into Decision Strategies

Many choice tasks, including early studies in decision neuroscience, involve paradigms where individuals choose between two options: a safe option with lower-magnitude outcome and a riskier option with higher outcomes (Coricelli et al., 2005; de Martino et al., 2006; Huettel, 2006; Tom et al., 2007). Across these studies, it was found that activation in distinct regions of the brain reliably predicted choices. For example, the anterior insula was consistently associated with risk-averse choices (Paulus et al., 2003; Preuschoff et al., 2008), while activation in the ventromedial PFC and striatum predicted risk-seeking choices (Kuhnen & Knutson, 2005; Tobler, O'Doherty, Dolan, & Schultz, 2007). Similarly, in most of these studies, the prefrontal and parietal regions supported executive control processes associated with risky decisions, including the estimation of risk and judgments about probability and value (Barraclough, Conroy, & Lee, 2004; Huettel, Song, & McCarthy, 2005; Paulus et al., 2001; Sanfey et al., 2003).

A popular and common framework for understanding the neuroscience of decision making was a dual-systems framework, where competition between executive control regions and emotional regions pushed choices towards one option or the other (Kuhnen & Knutson, 2005; Loewenstein, Rick, & Cohen, 2008; Sanfey et al., 2003). This framework in neuroscience also fits nicely with the dual-systems framework in behavioral decision making, which argues for a System 1 that is associated with an intuitive and fast response to most decisions, and a System 2 that is deliberative and slow and is often invoked to override System 1 when necessary (Kahneman & Frederick, 2005). Initial evidence argued for a direct mapping between these two frameworks. For example, using a framing task, de Martino and colleagues demonstrated that choices consistent with the framing effect were associated with increased activation in the amygdala while choices that ran counter to the framing effect were associated with increased activation in the dmPFC (de Martino et al., 2006). These results demonstrated that framing-consistent choices were mediated by a rapid intuitive brain response in the amygdala (System 1). However, this rapid System 1 response could be overridden by more effortful processing in the dmPFC (System 2) for choices that run counter to the framing effect.

Despite the intuitive ease of understanding the dual-systems framework, it has become increasingly apparent that people employ a variety of strategies to simplify the representations of decision problems and reduce computational demands (Camerer, 2003; Gigerenzer & Goldstein, 1996; Kahneman & Frederick, 2002; Payne, Bettman, & Johnson, 1988; Tversky & Kahneman, 1974). Across several studies, there is now considerable evidence for adaptive decision making involving multiple strategies that each may be adopted based on the context and computational demands of the task (Gigerenzer & Goldstein, 1996; Payne, Bettman, & Johnson, 1993). In a series of studies, Venkatraman and colleagues sought to understand the neural correlates underlying the adaptive use of decision strategies (Venkatraman & Huettel, 2012; Venkatraman et al., 2009a, 2009b). In the first study, they used a variant of the value allocation task (Payne, 2005). In this task, subjects choose between adding money to (i.e., improving) specific outcomes within mixed gambles (that feature potential wins and losses). They are first presented with a five-outcome gamble $G = (x1, p1; x2, p2; x3, p3; x4, p4; x5, p5)$, where pi indicates the probability of monetary outcome xi (Figure 15.3). The outcomes are rank-ordered $x1 > x2 > x3 > x4 > x5$, where at least two outcomes are strict gains ($x1 > x2 > \$0$) and two are strict losses ($x5 < x4 < \$0$). The value of the middle, reference outcome ($x3$) varies across trials, but is typically $\$0$ or slightly negative. When faced with this complex decision scenario, some individuals can adopt a simplifying strategy that de-emphasizes the relative magnitudes of the outcomes but maximizes the overall probability of winning (Pmax choice). Other individuals can emphasize the minimization of potential losses (Loss minimizing or Lmin choice) or the maximization of potential gains (Gain maximizing or Gmax choice) in ways consistent with more compensatory models of risky choice such as cumulative prospect theory (Tversky & Kahneman, 1992). Payne found that participants systematically violated the predictions of models like expected utility and cumulative prospect theory, and chose options that maximized the overall probability of winning (Payne, 2005). In a follow-up study, Venkatraman and colleagues

$75	p=0.20
$35	p=0.20
$0 + $15 = $15	p=0.20
-$25	p=0.20
-$75 + $15 = -$60	p=0.20

FIGURE 15.3 Schematic of the value-allocation task. Subjects initially viewed a multiattribute mixed gamble consisting of five different outcomes, each associated with a probability of occurrence. Then, they were asked to choose between two alternatives for improving the gamble: by adding $15 to the intermediate outcome which changes the overall probability of winning (Pmax), or adding $15 to the largest loss outcome to minimize its effect (Loss minimizing, Lmin). In other trials, they may be asked to choose between Pmax and adding money to the largest gain outcome (Gail maximizing, Gmax). The amounts and probabilities varied across trials.

sought to dissociate the neural mechanisms that underlie choices from those that shape strategic preferences using a variant of this task (Venkatraman et al., 2009a). To this end, they characterized participants' strategic preferences according to their relative proportion of simplifying (Pmax) versus compensatory (Gmax and Lmin) choices.

Consistent with previous behavioral studies (Payne, 2005), participants in the scanner made Pmax choices on approximately 70% of the trials. These Pmax choices were associated with increased activation in dlPFC and parietal cortices, regions that are typically associated with executive processing. On the other hand, choices to allocate value in order to maximize the largest gains and minimize the worst losses were predicted by activation in vmPFC and anterior insula respectively, regions typically associated with more emotional processing. At the outset, these findings seem counterintuitive and inconsistent with a dual-system framework: compensatory choices were predicted by emotional systems, and heuristic/simplifying choices were predicted by executive control regions. One conjecture from these findings is that the Pmax choices represent a deliberative heuristic, with participants using explicit cognitive strategies like counting the number of positive outcomes or the combined probabilities of any positive outcome. Alternatively, Gmax and Lmin choices may also represent heuristic strategies, driven by differences in the attention paid to the different attributes. Subsequent eye-tracking studies (see Chapters 1 and 4) using a similar paradigm confirmed that the choices were driven by differences in relative attention to the various attributes, rather than consistency with specific models (Venkatraman, Payne, & Huettel, 2014). Therefore, it is important to highlight that no one brain region, nor any set of regions, can be unambiguously claimed to implement a decision-making process. Instead, it is likely that specific brain regions contribute to particular computations, which may or may not be consistent with models for rational behavior. Some regions may even exert context-dependent influences, like that shown for dmPFC in the earlier experiment, making it impossible to categorize them within a traditional dual-systems framework (Frank, Cohen, & Sanfey, 2009).

Critically, activation in dmPFC predicted strategic variability across subjects (Venkatraman et al., 2014). Specifically, activation in this region increased when subjects made choices that were inconsistent with their preferred strategy (i.e., greater activation when people with a preference for Pmax choices made Gmax/Lmin choices, and vice versa). A similar role for this region was also demonstrated in an independent follow-up study, using a different task that involved very different strategies (Venkatraman et al., 2009b). Therefore, this region facilitates strategic control such that it is not associated with any specific choice preferences, but instead codes for deviations from an individual's preferred strategy.

Using a commonly used analysis (psychophysiological interaction or PPI) for discerning functional connectivity between brain regions, they also found that the dmPFC showed differential functional connectivity to regions associated with different types of choices. For the Pmax choices, there was increased connectivity between dmPFC and dlPFC, while for value-focused choices (Lmin or Gmax), there was increased functional connectivity between dmPFC and anterior insula. These findings suggest that control signals from dmPFC modulate the activation of choice-related brain regions, with the strength and directionality of this influence dependent on an individual's preferred strategy.

Lastly, given a potentially large repertoire of strategies, it remains unclear how individuals determine which strategy to employ for a given choice. The traditional view of strategy selection is that it presents a cost/benefit analysis (Payne et al., 1988). Like other aspects of decision making, strategic preferences can also vary both as a function of the decision context and the decision maker itself. Alternatively, strategy selection may also represent a learned response that is based on past experiences with different strategies (Rieskamp & Hoffrage, 2008; Rieskamp & Otto, 2006), such that the decision maker merely chooses the most efficient strategy for each situation based on prior experience (e.g., reward history). We contend that decision neuroscience can help answer the question of how people decide how to decide, through advances in methodology described next.

Emerging Trends in Decision Neuroscience Methodologies

Methodologies in neuroimaging continue to evolve and improve. There are two emerging trends in technical methodologies that are highly relevant to decision neuroscience. The first involves a shift in focus from the roles of individual brain regions to thinking about how networks—constellations of these regions—support function. Techniques like diffusion tensor imaging have provided valuable insights into connectivity between brain regions, and their relationship to decision processes and temporal discounting (Hampton, Alm, Venkatraman, Nugiel, & Olson, 2017). Recently, researchers have also started using meta-analysis software packages like Neurosynth (Yarkoni, Poldrack, Nichols, van Essen, & Wager, 2011) to identify a network of regions commonly associated with specific decision processes. Then, using neural similarity analyses, one can estimate the correspondence between activations in specific tasks and a series of pre-selected brain maps to identify the underlying processes. For example, in a framing task, Li and colleagues found that activations during choices consistent with the framing effect were most correlated with activation associated with resting brain, while activation during choices inconsistent with the framing effect were most correlated with task engaged brain (Li et al., 2017). Therefore, contrary to the popular view that framing effects represent a trade-off between cognition and emotion, the authors contend that framing effects result from differential cognitive engagement across frames and individuals.

The second emerging trend is the adoption of pattern classification algorithms to decode representations in the brain. These algorithms rely on support vector machines—classifiers that infer boundaries between categories—to estimate the presence of specific representations in different brain areas at particular points in time (Norman, Polyn, Detre, & Haxby, 2006). As with machine learning approaches in other fields, these multi-voxel pattern analyses (MVPA) are typically trained on a subset of the data, then tested to make predictions on a holdout sample. These attempts to decode neural information aspire to generate greater insight into the representations and processes underlying decisions. For example, one experiment used MVPA to decode activation while participants played a simplified Poker game against either another person or a computer that chose randomly (Carter, Bowling, Reeck, & Huettel, 2012). These analyses revealed that one specific brain region—the temporoparietal junction—was uniquely able to predict whether participants would bluff or fold while participants played against another human but not against a computer, especially when they judged that the human was a good poker player. Such techniques are gaining popularity in decision neuroscience as a means to elucidate decision processes.

Conclusion

Neuroscience holds excellent promise for advancing our understanding of decision-making processes (see also Chapters 14 and 16). However, it is expensive and provides only an indirect and correlative measure of neuronal activity. Though it is not possible to attribute causality—the activated regions may be associated with but not essential to the task—using fMRI, the use of other complementary techniques that disrupt brain function, such as transcranial magnetic stimulation and transcranial direct-current stimulation (Chapter 16), can help establish the causality of the different brain systems in altering decision-making processes. The field has matured greatly in the past 15 years, and we look forward to the new discoveries awaiting the field in the future.

Notes

1 The authors wish to thank Dr. John W. Payne for his contributions to the previous version of this chapter.
2 Data for the figure was generated from Web of Science (last accessed date: April 10, 2019) by searching for published articles on both "decision making" and "neuroscience."

References

Barraclough, D. J., Conroy, M. L., & Lee, D. (2004). Prefrontal cortex and decision making in a mixed-strategy game. *Nature Neuroscience, 7*(4), 404–410.

Bechara, A., Tranel, D., Damasio, H., & Damasio, A. R. (1996). Failure to respond autonomically to anticipated future outcomes following damage to prefrontal cortex. *Cerebral Cortex, 6*(2), 215–225.

Berns, G. S., & Moore, S. E. (2012). A neural predictor of cultural popularity. *Journal of Consumer Psychology, 22*(1), 154–160.

Botvinick, M. M., Braver, T. S., Barch, D. M., Carter, C. S., & Cohen, J. D. (2001). Conflict monitoring and cognitive control. *Psychological Review, 108*(3), 624–652.

Camerer, C. F. (2003). Behavioural studies of strategic thinking in games. *Trends in Cognitive Sciences, 7*(5), 225–231.

Carter, C. S., Braver, T. S., Barch, D. M., Botvinick, M., Noll, D., & Cohen, J. D. (1998). Anterior cingulate cortex, error detection, and the online monitoring of performance. *Science, 280*(5364), 747–749.

Carter, R. M., Bowling, D. L., Reeck, C., & Huettel, S. A. (2012). A distinct role of the temporal-parietal junction in predicting socially guided decisions. *Science, 337*(6090), 109–111.

Chiu, P. H., Lohrenz, T. M., & Montague, P. R. (2008). Smokers' brains compute, but ignore, a fictive error signal in a sequential investment task. *Nature Neuroscience, 11*(4), 514–520.

Clithero, J. A., Tankersley, D. T., & Huettel, S. A. (2008). Foundation of neuroeconomics: From philosophy to practice. *PLoS Biology, 6*(11), 2348–2353.

Coricelli, G., Critchley, H. D., Joffily, M., O'Doherty, J. P., Sirigu, A., & Dolan, R. J. (2005). Regret and its avoidance: A neuroimaging study of choice behavior. *Nature Neuroscience, 8*(9), 1255–1262.

Craig, A. D. (2009). How do you feel – now? The anterior insula and human awareness. *Nature Reviews Neuroscience, 10*(1), 59–70.

Dale, A. M., & Buckner, R. L. (1997). Selective averaging of rapidly presented individual trials using fMRI. *Human Brain Mapping, 5*(5), 329–340.

Delgado, M. R., Beer, J. S., Fellows, L. K., Huettel, S. A., Platt, M. L., Quirk, G. J., & Schiller, D. (2016). Viewpoints: Dialogues on the functional role of the ventromedial prefrontal cortex. *Nature Neuroscience, 19*(12), 1545–1552.

de Martino, B., Camerer, C. F., & Adolphs, R. (2010). Amygdala damage eliminates monetary loss aversion. *Proceedings of the National Academy of Sciences, 107*(8), 3788–3792.

de Martino, B., Kumaran, D., Seymour, B., & Dolan, R. J. (2006). Frames, biases, and rational decision-making in the human brain. *Science, 313*(5787), 684–687.

Etkin, A., Egner, T., & Kalisch, R. (2011). Emotional processing in anterior cingulate and medial prefrontal cortex. *Trends in Cognitive Sciences, 15*(2), 85–93.

Fellows, L. K., & Farah, M. J. (2007). The role of ventromedial prefrontal cortex in decision making: judgment under uncertainty or judgment per se? *Cerebral Cortex, 17*(11), 2669–2674.

Frank, M. J., Cohen, M. X., & Sanfey, A. G. (2009). Multiple systems in decision making: A neurocomputational perspective. *Current Directions in Psychological Sciences, 18*(2), 73–77.

Genevsky, A., & Knutson, B. (2015). Neural affective mechanisms predict market-level microlending. *Psychological Science, 26*(9), 1411–1422.

Gigerenzer, G., & Goldstein, D. G. (1996). Reasoning the fast and frugal way: Models of bounded rationality. *Psychological Review, 103*(4), 650–669.

Glascher, J., & Adolphs, R. (2003). Processing of the arousal of subliminal and supraliminal emotional stimuli by the human amygdala. *Journal of Neuroscience, 23*(32), 10274–10282.

Gold, J. I., & Shadlen, M. N. (2007). The neural basis of decision making. *Annual Review pf Neuroscience, 30*(1), 535–574.

Hampton, W. H., Alm, K. H., Venkatraman, V., Nugiel, T., & Olson, I. R. (2017). Dissociable frontostriatal white matter connectivity underlies reward and motor impulsivity. *Neuroimage, 150*, 336–343.

Hare, T. A., O'Doherty, J., Camerer, C. F., Schultz, W., & Rangel, A. (2008). Dissociating the role of the orbitofrontal cortex and the striatum in the computation of goal values and prediction errors. *Journal of Neuroscience, 28*(22), 5623–5630.

Hedgcock, W., & Rao, A. R. (2009). Trade-off aversion as an explanation for the attraction effect: A functional magnetic resonance imaging study. *Journal of Marketing Research, 46*(1), 1–13.

Huettel, S. A. (2006). Behavioral, but not reward, risk modulates activation of prefrontal, parietal, and insular cortices. *Cognitive, Affective, and Behavioral Neuroscience, 6*(2), 141–151.

Huettel, S. A., & McCarthy, G. (2000). Evidence for a refractory period in the hemodynamic response to visual stimuli as measured by MRI. *Neuroimage, 11*(5), 547–553.

Huettel, S. A., & McCarthy, G. (2001). Regional differences in the refractory period of the hemodynamic response: an event-related fMRI study. *Neuroimage, 14*(5), 967–976.

Huettel, S. A., & Payne, J. W. (2009). Integrating neural and decision sciences: Convergence and constraints. *Journal of Marketing Research, 46*(1), 14–17.

Huettel, S. A., Song, A. W., & McCarthy, G. (2005). Decisions under uncertainty: Probabilistic context influences activity of prefrontal and parietal cortices. *Journal of Neuroscience, 25*(13), 3304–3311.

Huettel, S. A., Song, A. W., & McCarthy, G. (2008). *Functional magnetic resonance imaging* (2nd ed.). Sunderland, MA: Sinauer Associates.

Huettel, S. A., Stowe, C. J., Gordon, E. M., Warner, B. T., & Platt, M. L. (2006). Neural signatures of economic preferences for risk and ambiguity. *Neuron, 49*(5), 765–775.

Izquierdo, A., Suda, R. K., & Murray, E. A. (2004). Bilateral orbital prefrontal cortex lesions in rhesus monkeys disrupt choices guided by both reward value and reward contingency. *Journal of Neuroscience, 24*(34), 7540–7548.

Kable, J. W., & Glimcher, P. W. (2007). The neural correlates of subjective value during intertemporal choice. *Nature Neuroscience, 10*(12), 1625–1633.

Kahneman, D., & Frederick, S. (2002). Representativeness revisited: Attribute substitution in intuitive judgement. In T. Gilovich, D. Griffin, & D. Kahneman (Eds.), *Heuristics and biases: The psychology of intuitive thought* (pp. 49–81). New York, NY: Cambridge University Press.

Kahneman, D., & Frederick, S. (2005). A model of heuristic judgment. In K. J. Holyoak, & M. R. G. (Eds.), *The Cambridge handbook of thinking and reasoning* (pp. 267–293). New York, NY: Cambridge University Press.

Knoch, D., Gianotti, L. R., Pascual-Leone, A., Treyer, V., Regard, M., Hohmann, M., & Brugger, P. (2006a). Disruption of right prefrontal cortex by low-frequency repetitive transcranial magnetic stimulation induces risk-taking behavior. *Journal of Neuroscience, 26*(24), 6469–6472.

Knoch, D., Pascual-Leone, A., Meyer, K., Treyer, V., & Fehr, E. (2006b). Diminishing reciprocal fairness by disrupting the right prefrontal cortex. *Science, 314*(5800), 829–832.

Knutson, B., Rick, S., Wimmer, G. E., Prelec, D., & Loewenstein, G. (2007). Neural predictors of purchases. *Neuron, 53*(1), 147–156.

Knutson, B., Taylor, J., Kaufman, M., Peterson, R., & Glover, G. (2005). Distributed neural representation of expected value. *Journal of Neuroscience, 25*(19), 4806–4812.

Koenigs, M., & Tranel, D. (2007). Irrational economic decision-making after ventromedial prefrontal damage: Evidence from the Ultimatum Game. *Journal of Neuroscience, 27*(4), 951–956.

Kuhnen, C. M., & Knutson, B. (2005). The neural basis of financial risk taking. *Neuron, 47*(5), 763–770.

LaBar, K. S., Gatenby, J. C., Gore, J. C., LeDoux, J. E., & Phelps, E. A. (1998). Human amygdala activation during conditioned fear acquisition and extinction: A mixed-trial fMRI study. *Neuron, 20*(5), 937–945.

Li, R., Smith, D. V., Clithero, J. A., Venkatraman, V., Carter, R. M., & Huettel, S. A. (2017). Reason's enemy is not emotion: Engagement of cognitive control networks explains biases in gain/loss framing. *The Journal of Neuroscience, 37*(13), 3588–3598.

Loewenstein, G. F., Rick, S., & Cohen, J. D. (2008). Neuroeconomics. *Annual Review of Psychology, 59*, 647–672.

Meriau, K., Wartenburger, I., Kazzer, P., Prehn, K., Lammers, C. H., van der Meer, E., … Heekeren, H. R. (2006). A neural network reflecting individual differences in cognitive processing of emotions during perceptual decision making. *Neuroimage, 33*(3), 1016–1027.

Miller, E. K., & Cohen, J. D. (2001). An integrative theory of prefrontal cortex function. *Annual Review of Neuroscience, 24*(1), 167–202.

Norman, K. A., Polyn, S. M., Detre, G. J., & Haxby, J. V. (2006). Beyond mind-reading: Multi-voxel pattern analysis of fMRI data. *Trends in Cognitive Sciences, 10*(9), 424–430.

O'Doherty, J. P., Dayan, P., Friston, K., Critchley, H., & Dolan, R. J. (2003). Temporal difference models and reward-related learning in the human brain. *Neuron, 38*(2), 329–337.

Ogawa, S., Lee, T. M., Kay, A. R., & Tank, D. W. (1990). Brain magnetic resonance imaging with contrast dependent on blood oxygenation. *Proceedings of the National Academy of Sciences, 87*(24), 9868–9872.

Padoa-Schioppa, C., & Assad, J. A. (2006). Neurons in the orbitofrontal cortex encode economic value. *Nature, 441*(7090), 223–226.

Paulus, M. P., Hozack, N., Zauscher, B., McDowell, J. E., Frank, L., Brown, G. G., & Braff, D. L. (2001). Prefrontal, parietal, and temporal cortex networks underlie decision-making in the presence of uncertainty. *Neuroimage, 13*(1), 91–100.

Paulus, M. P., Rogalsky, C., Simmons, A., Feinstein, J. S., & Stein, M. B. (2003). Increased activation in the right insula during risk-taking decision making is related to harm avoidance and neuroticism. *Neuroimage, 19*(4), 1439–1448.

Payne, J. W. (2005). It is whether you win or lose: The importance of the overall probabilities of winning or losing in risky choice. *Journal of Risk and Uncertainty, 30*(1), 5–19.

Payne, J. W., Bettman, J. R., & Johnson, E. J. (1988). Adaptive strategy selection in decision-making. *Journal of Experimental Psychology: Learning Memory and Cognition, 14*(3), 534–552.

Payne, J. W., Bettman, J. R., & Johnson, E. J. (1993). *The adaptive decision maker.* New York, NY: Cambridge University Press.

Pessoa, L., & Adolphs, R. (2010). Emotion processing and the amygdala: from a 'low road' to 'many roads' of evaluating biological significance. *Nature Reviews Neuroscience, 11*(11), 773–783.

Phelps, E. A. (2006). Emotion and cognition: Insights from studies of the human amygdala. *Annual Review of Psychology, 57*, 27–53.

Phelps, E. A., & LeDoux, J. E. (2005). Contributions of the amygdala to emotion processing: From animal models to human behavior. *Neuron, 48*(2), 175–187.

Phillips, M. L., Young, A. W., Senior, C., Brammer, M., Andrew, C., Calder, A. J., ... David, A. S. (1997). A specific neural substrate for perceiving facial expressions of disgust. *Nature, 389*(6650), 495–498.

Plassmann, H., O'Doherty, J., & Rangel, A. (2007). Orbitofrontal cortex encodes willingness to pay in everyday economic transactions. *Journal of Neuroscience, 27*(37), 9984–9988.

Platt, M. L., & Glimcher, P. W. (1999). Neural correlates of decision variables in parietal cortex. *Nature, 400*(6741), 233–238.

Pochon, J. B., Riis, J., Sanfey, A. G., Nystrom, L. E., & Cohen, J. D. (2008). Functional imaging of decision conflict. *Journal of Neuroscience, 28*(13), 3468–3473.

Poldrack, R. A. (2006). Can cognitive processes be inferred from neuroimaging data? *Trends in Cognitive Sciences, 10*(2), 59–63.

Preuschoff, K., Quartz, S. R., & Bossaerts, P. (2008). Human insula activation reflects risk prediction errors as well as risk. *Journal of Neuroscience, 28*(11), 2745–2752.

Racine, E., Bar-Ilan, O., & Illes, J. (2005). fMRI in the public eye. *Nature Reviews Neuroscience, 6*(2), 159–164.

Rangel, A., Camerer, C., & Montague, P. R. (2008). A framework for studying the neurobiology of value-based decision making. *Nature Reviews Neuroscience, 9*(7), 545–556.

Rieskamp, J., & Hoffrage, U. (2008). Inferences under time pressure: How opportunity costs affect strategy selection. *Acta Psychologica, 127*(2), 258–276.

Rieskamp, J., & Otto, P. E. (2006). SSL: A theory of how people learn to select strategies. *Journal of Experimental Psychology: General, 135*(2), 207–236.

Sanfey, A. G., Rilling, J. K., Aronson, J. A., Nystrom, L. E., & Cohen, J. D. (2003). The neural basis of economic decision-making in the Ultimatum Game. *Science, 300*(5626), 1755–1758.

Schultz, W., Dayan, P., & Montague, P. R. (1997). A neural substrate of prediction and reward. *Science, 275*(5306), 1593–1599.

Seymour, B., Daw, N., Dayan, P., Singer, T., & Dolan, R. (2007). Differential encoding of losses and gains in the human striatum. *Journal of Neuroscience, 27*(18), 4826–4831.

Shadlen, M. N., & Newsome, W. T. (2001). Neural basis of a perceptual decision in the parietal cortex (area LIP) of the rhesus monkey. *Journal of Neurophysiology, 86*(4), 1916–1936.

Sugrue, L. P., Corrado, G. S., & Newsome, W. T. (2005). Choosing the greater of two goods: Neural currencies for valuation and decision making. *Nature Reviews Neuroscience, 6*(5), 363–375.

Taren, A. A., Venkatraman, V., & Huettel, S. A. (2011). A parallel functional topography between medial and lateral prefrontal cortex: Evidence and implications for cognitive control. *Journal of Neuroscience, 31*(13), 5026–5031.

Tobler, P. N., O'Doherty, J. P., Dolan, R. J., & Schultz, W. (2007). Reward value coding distinct from risk attitude-related uncertainty coding in human reward systems. *Journal of Neurophysiology, 97*(2), 1621–1632.

Tom, S. M., Fox, C. R., Trepel, C., & Poldrack, R. A. (2007). The neural basis of loss aversion in decision-making under risk. *Science, 315*(5811), 515–518.

Tversky, A., & Kahneman, D. (1974). Judgment under uncertainty: Heuristics and biases. *Science, 185*(4157), 1124–1131.

Tversky, A., & Kahneman, D. (1992). Advances in prospect theory: Cumulative representation of uncertainty. *Journal of Risk and Uncertainty, 5*(4), 297–323.

Venkatraman, V., Dimoka, A., Pavlou, P. A., Vo, K. D., Hampton, W., Bollinger, B., ... Winer, R. S. (2015). Predicting advertising success beyond traditional measures: New insights from neurophysiological methods and market response modeling. *Journal of Marketing Research, 52*(4), 436–452.

Venkatraman, V., & Huettel, S. A. (2012). Strategic control in decision-making under uncertainty. *European Journal of Neuroscience, 35*(7), 1075–1082.

Venkatraman, V., Payne, J. W., Bettman, J. R., Luce, M. F., & Huettel, S. A. (2009a). Separate neural mechanisms underlie choices and strategic preferences in risky decision making. *Neuron, 62*(4), 593–602.

Venkatraman, V., Payne, J. W., & Huettel, S. A. (2014). An overall probability of winning heuristic for complex risky decisions: Choice and eye fixation evidence. *Organizational Behavior and Human Decision Processes, 125*(2), 73–87.

Venkatraman, V., Rosati, A. G., Taren, A. A., & Huettel, S. A. (2009b). Resolving response, decision, and strategic control: evidence for a functional topography in dorsomedial prefrontal cortex. *Journal of Neuroscience*, *29*(42), 13158–13164.

Walton, M. E., Devlin, J. T., & Rushworth, M. F. (2004). Interactions between decision making and performance monitoring within prefrontal cortex. *Nature Neuroscience*, 7(11), 1259–1265.

Wise, R. A. (2004). Dopamine, learning and motivation. *Nature Reviews Neuroscience*, *5*(6), 483–494.

Yacubian, J., Glascher, J., Schroeder, K., Sommer, T., Braus, D. F., & Buchel, C. (2006). Dissociable systems for gain- and loss-related value predictions and errors of prediction in the human brain. *Journal of Neuroscience*, *26*(37), 9530–9537.

Yarkoni, T., Poldrack, R. A., Nichols, T. E., van Essen, D. C., & Wager, T. D. (2011). Large-scale automated synthesis of human functional neuroimaging data. *Nature Methods*, *8*(8), 665–670.

16

PROBING THE DECISIONAL BRAIN WITH NONINVASIVE BRAIN STIMULATION[1]

Nadège Bault, Elena Rusconi, and Giorgio Coricelli

Noninvasive Brain Stimulation

Probing brain function and its relation with behavior is one of the most intriguing challenges of our era. Until about 25 years ago the most reliable way to investigate human brain function via its altered states was limited to occurrences of lesions, intra-operatory stimulation, neurosurgical resections (i.e., removal of parts of the brain due to a tumor or epilepsy), and congenital malformations (i.e., brain defects present at birth or manifesting during development). In other words, it was not possible to independently manipulate the state of healthy brains in a targeted, reversible, and noninvasive manner as it is today. In the past quasi-experiments were the gold standard (i.e., experiments in which the independent variable had been manipulated by nature itself or based on primarily clinical considerations). It has become possible, instead, to experimentally modulate the state of neural circuits in the healthy human brain for basic research purposes. With noninvasive brain stimulation, e.g., transcranial magnetic stimulation (TMS) or transcranial direct current stimulation (tDCS), the healthy brain is not structurally disrupted and its function is modulated only locally and for a limited amount of time. This new experimental approach, made possible by recent technical developments, can provide more accurate information about the intact system, upon which theoretical models of mental processes are based. It allows causal links to be drawn between neural states and behavior, where techniques such as functional magnetic resonance imaging (fMRI, see Chapter 15), event related potentials (ERPs, see Chapter 14), and magnetoencephalography (MEG) can only report covariations between brain activity and behavior and cannot tell whether a given neural substrate is necessary or not for a specific behavior (Walsh & Cowey, 2000). With noninvasive brain stimulation, the same participants—or a group of participants from the very same sample as the experimental participants—can serve as their own control. Control and experimental measures can be made within minutes and in the same session in within-subject designs, thus gaining in statistical power. Functional reorganization, compensatory changes, and deficit attenuation do not have time to settle because the alteration in brain function is relatively short-lived (unless stimulation is regularly performed for rehabilitation or therapeutic purposes), thus these methods are reversible and safe when used within established parameters (e.g., Rossi, Hallett, Rossini, & Pascual-Leone, 2009; Bikson et al., 2016). Moreover, given the relatively weak (and not necessarily disruptive) impact of noninvasive stimulation on cognitive resources, there is no need to create ad hoc, easier versions of already existing experimental protocols, unlike with many neuropsychological patients.

The use of electricity to alter neural function has a long history, and noninvasive stimulation with electrodes applied on the surface of the scalp has remained the main stimulation device in medical and experimental settings for centuries, in spite of being associated with painful sensations. However, the discovery of the principle of electromagnetic induction by Faraday in the 19th century paved the way for the advent of a new noninvasive brain stimulation technique (Barker, Jalinous, & Freeston, 1985). The principle that a changing magnetic field can induce an electric current in a neighbor electric material is at the basis of TMS, where a stimulation coil serves as an electromagnet that generates a rapidly changing magnetic field. When the coil is placed on the scalp and the magnetic field is directed to the brain, an electric current is induced in the underlying neural tissues with reasonable spatial (about 1–2 cm^2, varying with coil/brain geometry and stimulation parameters) and temporal resolution (on the order of a few tens of milliseconds).

TMS (Figure 16.1) is thought to actively initiate action potentials in neurons and/or alter their level of excitability during and after stimulation, although its precise mechanisms of action are still far from clear (see Wagner, Rushmore, Eden, & Valero-Cabre (2009) for hypotheses on the mechanisms of action of TMS, and Miniussi, Ruzzoli, & Walsh (2010); Rusconi & Bestmann (2009); Siebner, Hartwigsen, Kassuba, & Rothwell (2009); Ziemann (2010) for more general discussions on the interpretation of TMS effects in neurocognitive studies). A prolonged slow sequence of pulses (e.g., 1 Hz repetitive transcranial magnetic stimulation (rTMS) over an area for 10 min) produces modification in cortex excitability that can last for a few minutes after stimulation. A fast sequence of pulses (e.g., 10 Hz rTMS over an area for 500 msec) produces a short-term modification that only persists during the time of the stimulation (Robertson, Théoret, & Pascual-Leone, 2003). The more recent theta-burst protocol, with triple-pulse stimulation at 50 Hz delivered every 200 msec (i.e., in the theta band, 5 Hz) for less than 1 min, has both rapidity and long-term efficacy (e.g., Huang, Edwards, Rounis, Bhatia, & Rothwell, 2005). rTMS can be applied online (i.e., during task performance) or offline (i.e., before-hand). The advantage of the offline approach is that the participant can perform a task without any extraneous additional sensation or discomfort produced by active stimulation, and the difference between active and sham stimulation is less obvious to the participant. Its disadvantage consists of the necessity for resting periods, to wash out the effects of stimulation at any one site, thus lengthening experimental sessions. Moreover, temporal specificity is lost, since any kind of effect cannot be directly related to specific time windows during task execution, a drawback it shares with tDCS.

Transcranial direct current stimulation (tDCS) is a technique for modulating cortical excitability, which involves the application of two surface electrodes: an anode and a cathode. A weak (e.g., 1 mA or 2 mA) direct current is applied for up to 30 min between moistened sponge electrodes (usually having a surface of 35 cm^2) placed on the head. The current flows from the anode to the cathode, leading to increases or decreases of cortical excitability, dependent on the direction and intensity of the current, with an effect lasting for up to 1 hour post-stimulation (Miranda, Lomarev, & Hallett, 2006; Nitsche & Paulus, 2001). Typically, anodal tDCS exerts an excitatory effect on the underlying cerebral cortex via subthreshold depolarization of neurons, whereas cathodal stimulation has a hyperpolarizing effect that results in neural inhibition. In general tDCS can be conceptualized as a method to change the likelihood that an incoming action potential will result in post-synaptic firing in the cortical areas underneath electrodes (Nitsche et al., 2003). tDCS produces a tingling sensation under the electrodes that is most noticeable at the beginning of a session, while the current is ramping up. It has limited temporal and spatial resolution and might be efficient only when stimulation regions are already activated by the current task (Fertonani &

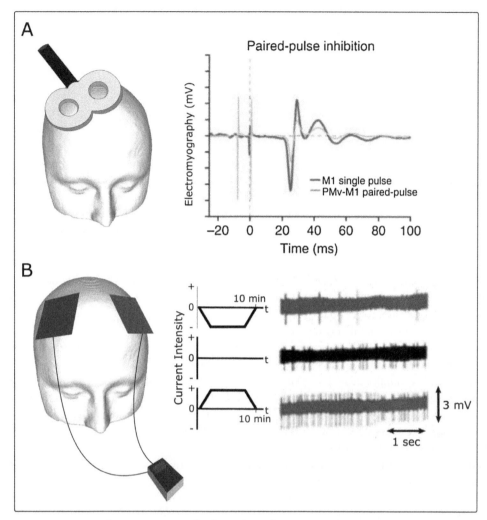

FIGURE 16.1 TMS and tDCS setups and effects. **A. Left.** Figure-eight TMS coil placed on the scalp, over the motor cortex. **Right.** Motor evoked potentials recorded from the first dorsal interosseous (FDI) muscle using surface electromyography after single pulse TMS to M1 (dark gray line) and paired-pulse TMS to the ventral premotor cortex and M1 (light gray line). **B. Left**. Bipolar tDCS electrode configuration, with the anodal electrode over the right dorsolateral prefrontal cortex and the cathodal electrode over the left dorsolateral prefrontal cortex. **Right.** Cathodal and Anodal stimulations with fade-in and fade-out periods. Negative polarization (cathodal, left hemisphere electrode) decreases the firing-rate of neurons, compared to baseline (black), whereas positive polarization (anodal, right hemisphere) increases neural activity. Adapted with permission from Dayan, Censor, Buch, Sandrini, & Cohen (2013), and Fertonani & Miniussi (2016).

Miniussi, 2016). However, it is safe, inexpensive, wearable, can be compared to a sham condition that produces sensations on the scalp similar to that of real stimulation such as subjects cannot usually distinguish sham from real stimulation. This technique has already provided useful evidence in the neuroscientific study of both single-subject decision making and simultaneous social interactions with large experimental groups (see later). In sum, TMS is well established as a research and potential clinical tool, and direct electrical stimulation is now undergoing renewed interest due to technical improvements, which have enormously reduced painful sensations to the scalp.

How to Do It

Selecting stimulation parameters (intensity, frequency, and duration) and a paradigm is difficult and often arbitrary (for discussions of related issues, see Paulus, 2003; Wassermann et al., 2008). Beyond the physical parameters, which require expert guidance, the stimulation site should be carefully chosen, especially with tDCS as this technique will only modulate the activity of neurons putatively recruited by the current task; it will affect the neuronal excitability but it will not induce firing in inactive cells. A sound approach consists of using a task for which fMRI data are available and stimulating a region showing reliable activity. The position of the reference electrode may be chosen in order to optimize the current trajectory through the area of interest (and away from other areas potentially involved in the task) by running a simulation of the electric field induced by the stimulation. TMS is more focal than tDCS and can induce firing in inactive neurons. Therefore, the use of a neuronavigation system is recommended to ensure accurate targeting during stimulation. A neuronavigation system locates, in real-time, the position of the stimulating device relative to the head of the participant. Then, using a high resolution image of the participant brain, it projects the stimulation target on the cortex, thus allowing the experimenter to adjust the position and orientation of the stimulating device.

The choice of control conditions is key. An alternative stimulation area may serve as a control, but "sham" stimulation on the target area should always be included. The stimulation procedure is associated with a number of sensory perceptions that can nonspecifically interfere with task performance. For instance, with TMS, the discharging coil produces a click sound that may induce arousal, thereby modulating task performance, irrespective of the exact demands of the experimental design (i.e., via intersensory facilitation). Sham rTMS stimulation is generally carried out by tilting the coil away from the scalp (Sandrini, Umiltà, & Rusconi, 2011), so that the sound and the scalp contact are roughly similar to the active stimulation but the magnetic field does not reach the cortical neurons, cutaneous receptors, or superficial muscles. Commercially available sham-coils produce the same sound during stimulation, but no magnetic field is generated, so they can rest tangential to the scalp surface exactly as active stimulation coils. With tDCS, sham stimulation is achieved with a 10–30 sec current ramping up and down at the beginning of the session and sometimes at the end as well. The current intensity is null the rest of the time. Most subjects report sensations at the beginning of the stimulation, and then due to habituation, the tingling sensation disappears. Therefore real and sham tDCS are nearly indistinguishable. Notably though, some studies reported differences in sensation, such as a small difference between anodal and sham stimulation (Fertonani, Ferrari, & Miniussi, 2015). The authors advise asking participants, at the end of the experiment, which type of stimulation (real or sham) they believe they have received.

Safety Guidelines

Methodological issues cannot be entirely separated from safety and ethical considerations. The last decade has seen a rapid increase in the use of TMS to study cognitive functions: the brain–behavior relationship (see Sandrini et al., 2011, for a synthesis). Transient side-effects of TMS and rTMS may include headache, neck ache, and mild discomfort, but they are secondary effects not directly related to the cortical stimulation itself. Cortical stimulation can induce seizures. Based on the available empirical data, the use of TMS and rTMS is safe, with concern only for stimulation protocols outside currently available safety guidelines. Considerations regarding the following main points should be kept in mind when designing a TMS or rTMS study (Rossi et al., 2009):

1. Research application must be governed by three fundamental ethical and legal requirements: informed consent, risk–benefit ratio, and equal distribution of the burdens and benefits of research.
2. Based on their demands for protection of the subjects and expected benefits, studies with normal subjects are classified as providing indirect benefit at low risk.
3. With regard to protocol safety, any "novel paradigm" (i.e., one that is not a conventional method of high- or low-frequency rTMS performed with a flat butterfly coil and biphasic stimulation) or any TMS applied on more than a single brain region, or any conventional high-frequency protocol with parameters (intensity, frequency, train length, or intertrial interval) exceeding the safety limits (see tables 4–6 in Rossi et al., 2009), increases the risk of inducing epileptic seizures.
4. It is a requirement to know the stimulation site, who should do the TMS, and how to manage emergencies (syncope and seizures; Rossi et al., 2009).
5. TMS candidates should undergo medical screening via a standard questionnaire.
6. Additional safety issues should be considered when performing TMS in the MRI area and/or in the MRI scanner.

The same general rules apply for tDCS. Although no case of tDCS-induced seizure has been reported, epileptic subjects should not be stimulated. Very few reports found injuries (e.g., acute skin irritation under the sponges) and the technique is considered safe as long as experimenters conform to the parameters described in the literature. Skin damage can occur in cases of dried-out contact media under the electrodes (Woods et al., 2016). Fertonani et al. (2015) recommend maintaining low impedance at the stimulation site, by using an electro-conductive gel spread on sponges soaked with saline solution, and by improving the adherence of the electrodes on the scalp with a tubular net-shaped elastic bandage around the head.

Noninvasive Brain Stimulation in Value-Based Decision Making: Empirical Reports

Decision making is a complex mental function recruiting a distributed cortico-subcortical network (e.g., Ernst & Paulus, 2005; Mobbs, Lau, Jones, & Frith, 2007). Decisions are performed by comparing the values of stimuli or courses of action. Evidence from fMRI, lesion, and intra-cortical recording converge in attributing a role in valuation to two interconnected structures, the striatum and ventromedial prefrontal cortex (vmPFC). Unfortunately, these two regions are difficult to target with stimulation techniques since they do not lie near the surface of the brain. There is hope, though, to reach the vmPFC using a double-coil approach (see recent developments and future directions).

Another important node in this network is the dorsolateral prefrontal cortex (DLPFC). The DLPFC is commonly considered to be involved in cognitive control and inhibition of impulsive responses (Koechlin, Ody, & Kouneiher, 2003; Miller & Cohen, 2001). This region has been the target of several transcranial brain stimulation studies investigating intertemporal choice, decisions between risky prospects, and the enforcement of social norms during inter-individual decision making.

In social settings, the causal role of the temporo-parietal junction is increasingly subject to investigation using brain stimulation. fMRI studies have identified this region as tracking socially relevant information such as the beliefs, abilities, or trustworthiness of other individuals, in order to modulate decisions. Table 16.1 summarizes the methodology and main results of the brain stimulation studies described in the following section.

TABLE 16.1 Short summary table of the studies discussed in this chapter

Study	Method	Task	Sites	Main results
Knoch et al. (2006a)	1 Hz rTMS (100% individual resting motor threshold) for 15 min	**Risk Task** (offline)	Left/right DLPFC	Compared to sham and left DLPFC stimulation, subjects receiving right DLPFC stimulation select the high-risk option more often
Fecteau et al. (2007a)	Anodal/cathodal bilateral tDCS	**Risk Task**	F3–F4 (left/right DLPFC)	The right anodal/left cathodal group showed more safe-prospect choices, responded faster, and earned more than the left anodal/right cathodal and sham groups
Fecteau et al. (2007b)	Anodal/cathodal bilateral tDCS; anodal unilateral tDCS	**Balloon Analog Risk Task**	F3–F4 (left/right DLPFC)	Reduced risk taking with bilateral DLPFC stimulation. No effect of unilateral stimulation.
Figner et al. (2010)	1 Hz rTMS (54% max stimulator output) for 15 min	**Intertemporal choice task** (offline)	F3–F4 (left/right DLPFC)	Proportion of impulsive choices (smaller immediate rewards over larger delayed rewards) increased with disruption of the left DLPFC
Beharelle et al. (2015)	Anodal/cathodal tDCS (1.5mA)	**Bandit Task**	Right fronto-polar cortex (MNI 27, 57, 6)	Enhancing rFPC neural excitability through anodal stimulation increased exploration, whereas decreasing excitability with cathodal stimulation increased the number of exploitative decisions
van't Wout et al. (2005)	6 Hz rTMS (25% max stimulator output) for 5 min + 1 Hz rTMS (45% max) for 12 min	**Ultimatum Game** (offline)	F4 (right DLPFC)	Compared to sham, right DLPFC slows down rejection times to unfair offers + tendency to accept more unfair offers
Knoch et al. (2006a)	1 Hz rTMS (100% individual resting motor threshold) for 15 min	**Ultimatum Game** (offline)	Left/right DLPFC	Compared to sham and left DLPFC stimulation, subjects receiving right DLPFC stimulation accept the unfair offer more often and faster, whereas fairness judgments remain unaffected
Knoch et al. (2008)	Cathodal tDCS	**Ultimatum Game** (social setting)	Right PFC	Fair behavior is reduced when suppressing right PFC activity

Baumgartner et al. (2011)	1 Hz rTMS (54% of max stimulator output) for 15 min Followed by fMRI	**Ultimatum Game** (offline)	F3–F4 (left/right DLPFC)	Disrupting the activity of the DLPC reduced the rejection rate through a down-regulation of the VMPFC
Ruff et al. (2013)	Anodal/cathodal tDCS (1mA)	**Dictator Game with costly punishment**	rLPFC region (MNI 52, 28, 14)	Without punishment, mean voluntary transfer decreased with the excitability of the DLPFC whereas it increased when punishment threat was present
Soutschek et al. (2015)	1Hz rTMS (110% of resting motor threshold) for 8 min	**Prisoner dilemma**	Left/right DLPFC (MNI 44, 25, 48 and -43, 22, 49)	Less cooperation after left and right stimulation compared to control, especially after an opponent defection.
Maréchal et al. (2017)	Anodal/cathodal tDCS (1.5mA) for 30 min	**Die-rolling task**	Right DLPFC	The amount of self-interested lies decreased with anodal stimulation of the DLPFC, compared to sham and cathodal stimulation
Young et al. (2010)	1 Hz rTMS (70% of max stimulator output) for 25 min	**Moral Judgment Task** (offline)	rTPJ	rTMS to the rTPJ decreased the role of mentalizing in moral judgements
Hill et al. (2017)	TBS—Bursts of 3 pulses at 50 Hz repeated at 5 Hz during 40 sec Followed by fMRI	**Inspection Game**	rTPJ	Stimulation reduced the role of mentalizing-related computation during strategic choices

Source: Author generated

Studying Behavior with Noninvasive Brain Stimulation

Given its involvement in cognitive control and self-control, the DLPFC could be expected to play an important role in decision making, particularly when there is a conflict between emotional impulses and long-term goals, such as when resisting choosing a smaller immediate reward over a delayed larger reward. Indeed, participants chose more often immediately available small rewards over delayed larger rewards when the left DLPFC was disrupted compared to sham stimulation (Figner et al., 2010). In contrast, attractiveness ratings of the options were not affected by the stimulation. This impulsive preference reversal effect (choosing the immediate reward despite higher valuation of the delayed reward) confirmed that the DLPFC exerts self-control in intertemporal choice.

Self-control is important as well when making risky decisions. Several studies described later have unraveled the role of DLPFC in modulating the temptation for rewarding but highly risky prospects.

The Role of DLPFC in Risky Decisions

Risk tasks provide a measure of self-control in individual decision making (Knoch & Fehr, 2007). That right PFC may exert a control role on risk-taking behavior has already been suggested by neuro-psychological observations (e.g., Clark, Manes, Antoun, Sahakian, & Robbins, 2003), however, only in recent years has the hypothesis undergone direct testing in the normal brain. Two studies, one with rTMS (Knoch et al., 2006a) and one with tDCS (Fecteau et al., 2007b), employed a risk task in which participants have to decide between a relatively safe choice providing either a low reward with high probability or a small loss with low probability and a risky choice providing either a high reward with low probability or a high loss with high probability (see Figure 16.2).

Participants whom right DLPFC activity was disrupted became more risk prone and more sensitive to reward (Knoch et al., 2006a). They chose the high-risk prospect more often than the control groups, except when it was associated with smaller rewards. Those results point to a crucial role for right DLPFC in suppressing superficially seductive but risky options. Interestingly, this interpretation was supported by the finding that individuals with higher baseline activity in the right PFC were more risk-averse (Gianotti et al., 2009).

Fecteau et al.'s (2007a) results, obtained with a different technique, tDCS, provided converging evidence. By upregulating right DLPFC activity while down-regulating left DLPFC activity using concomitant right anodal/left cathodal tDCS, they were able to decrease risk-taking behavior in a group of participants performing the previously mentioned Risk task. Compared to sham and left anodal/right cathodal tDCS groups, right anodal/left cathodal participants chose the safe option more often and earned many more points. In other words, Fecteau et al. (2007b) were able to reverse the behavioral effect that Knoch et al. (2006a) found with low-frequency rTMS over right DLPFC. However, their right cathodal/left anodal condition did not increase risk-taking behavior, which might be due to a difference in the neurophysiological impact of the two techniques. This suggests that it is not possible to draw simple inferences about the underlying mechanisms of action in different techniques based only on the direction of their net behavioral effect. Moreover, tDCS was applied to both right and left DLPFCs at the same time in Fecteau et al.'s (2007a) study, whereas Knoch et al. (2006a) applied rTMS unilaterally.

A tDCS study tackling similar issues but with a different task was conducted by Fecteau et al. (2007b). They measured risk-taking behavior with the Balloon Analog Risk Task (BART). In BART, participants have to make a choice in a context of increasing risk. A computerized balloon,

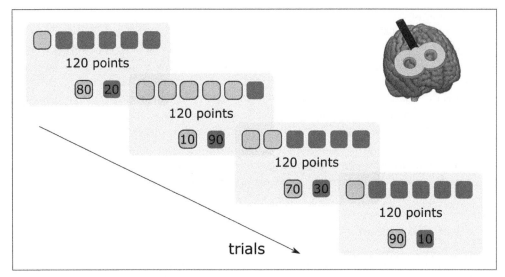

FIGURE 16.2 Experimental protocol employed by Knoch et al. (2006a). rTMS (1 Hz) was applied before the last over left or right DLPFC. The task consisted in accurately guessing the color of the box that contained a winning token. The ratio of light and dark gray boxes (i.e., the level of risk) was thus directly related to the probability of winning by picking the corresponding color. This ratio changed from trial to trial, and the numbers inside the two bottom boxes show the reward and punishment sizes associated with each color. The larger reward and penalty were associated with choice of the high-risk prospect, and vice versa for the low-risk prospect (a typical conflict in risk-taking situations).

which can explode at any moment, is inflated by pushing a pump. Participants can decide at any moment to stop pumping. Each push is associated with the same monetary reward, but if the balloon explodes all of the money accumulated is lost. In other words, both the probability of losing money and the potential loss increase with each push of the pump. Each balloon has a different exploding point making prediction difficult. Quite surprisingly, both groups receiving bilateral stimulation, not only the right anodal/left cathodal group, showed more cautious behavior compared to the sham group. Besides, unlike the sham group, they did not show the normal increase in the number of risky choices that is usually observed over the course of a session. Finally, all participants receiving bilateral stimulation earned less money than participants receiving sham stimulation. No tDCS effects were found when unilateral anodal stimulation was applied to either the left or the right DLPFC.

Overall, the findings from both TMS and tDCS techniques consistently showed that decisions under risk are regulated by the DLPFC. However, the conclusion that higher activity of the right DLPC decreases risk taking might be too simplistic. It might be more accurate to consider that cognitive control in risky choices results from a fine balance of activity between the left and right DLPFC.

The Role of the Fronto-Polar Cortex in Exploration–Exploitation Trade-Offs

Survival in a changing environment requires keeping track of the potential return of several courses of actions to facilitate efficient adaptation. Exploring options previously associated with lower reward is costly; therefore, optimal decision making requires finding the right balance between exploration and exploitation. In fMRI studies, the activity of the frontopolar cortex increased when switching from exploitative to explorative choices (Daw, O'Doherty, Dayan, Seymour, & Dolan, 2006). In order to test for a causal effect of the frontopolar cortex (rFPC) in triggering exploration, Beharelle et al. (2015) applied cathodal, anodal, and sham tDCS stimulation over that region of the brain. Compared to sham stimulation, the frequency of exploratory choices increased when enhancing rFPC neural excitability through anodal stimulation and decreased when depressing excitability with cathodal stimulation. This effect was mediated by a modified sensitivity to specific aspects of the decision problem. tDCS stimulation affected the threshold at which participants decided to abandon the currently exploited option and start exploring alternatives. Participants receiving anodal stimulation were more willing to forego immediate rewards to explore potentially less profitable options whereas participants receiving cathodal stimulation adhered to the pay-off of the current option. Moreover, the change in exploration decisions was mediated by a change in sensitivity to recent unpredicted bad outcomes (negative prediction error). The use of brain stimulation thus allowed better characterization of the type of computations performed by the frontopolar neurons. Even though the set of regions involved in balancing exploration and exploitation has already been identified with imaging techniques, this study sheds light on the causal role of the frontopolar cortex in integrating signals about current reward, negative prediction error, and the cost of information about options potentially more rewarding in the long term.

Studying Social Decision Making with Noninvasive Brain Stimulation

The Role of DLPFC in Enforcing Social Norms

Models based on social preferences propose to describe the mechanisms underlying fairness, trust, and reciprocity observed during social interactions. Cooperative behavior with genetically unrelated individuals occurs in all human societies (even though there are variations in threshold settings between fair and unfair in different cultures), but it is much less frequently observed in other species, from invertebrates up to and including nonhuman primates. The question thus arises whether possessing a specific cognitive ability or set of abilities is a prerequisite for cooperation and reciprocity to emerge in a social group.

Studying cooperation and reciprocity is, to a large extent, about studying the mechanisms for enforcing or reinforcing pro-social behavior, which includes both positive (reward of pro-social behavior) and negative (punishment of social norms violations) drives. In social settings, violating the norm affects members of a group in terms of status, reputation, and exclusion. Punishment of "free-riders" in a society where cooperative behavior is expected is believed to be the main way through which norms are maintained, since the fear of punishment can deter selfish behavior. The Ultimatum Game (Güth, Schmittberger, & Schwarze, 1982) provides a measure of the ability to implement social norms in the context of social interactions. In that game, punishment is costly and is inherently linked to the degree to which norms are internalized. The Ultimatum Game involves splitting a sum of money: a "proposer" is endowed with a sum and then offers a share to a "responder", who can accept or refuse the offer. If the offer is accepted, they split the money accordingly; if refused, both players leave empty-handed. This and other such games have been used to highlight the fact that humans do not always act as purely rational decision makers. According to game theory (von Neumann & Morgenstern, 1944), recipients should accept anything above zero offered by the proposer. Anticipating recipients' reasoning, proposers should give only a minimal fraction of the total sum.

Results obtained from the Ultimatum Game, however, show a clear deviation from this standard theoretical solution. In fact, in general, most proposers often make much larger offers than predicted, thus acting in a suboptimal and irrational way. On the other hand, recipients reject very small offers that may seem insulting relative to some standard of fairness (e.g., Fehr & Schmidt, 1999; Rabin, 1993; Sanfey, Rilling, Aronson, Nystrom, & Cohen, 2003). These results are usually interpreted as evidence that behavior is often driven by social emotions and not just by the need to maximize personal gain (e.g., Sanfey et al., 2003; van't Wout et al., 2005). Other-regarding preferences, which are guided by fairness and equality motives, play as big a role as self-regarding preferences (Bowles, 2006; de Quervain et al., 2004; Fehr & Gächter, 2002). Thus, players' acceptance of social norms (e.g., fairness) and their enforcement as driven by emotional responses to others' behavior induce a divergence between the players' actual behavior and the rational behavior.

In the Ultimatum Game, the DLPFC of responders is more activated after receiving an unfair offer than after a fair offer (Sanfey et al., 2003). Given the known role of the DLPFC in overriding immediate urges, two alternative hypotheses can be considered: the DLPFC implements fair behavior by exerting a down regulation on 1) the emotional impulse to reject an unfair offer or on 2) the selfish, economic motive to accept the money.

To disentangle these potential mechanisms, rTMS was applied in an offline protocol over the right DLPFC (area F4), with participants receiving both real and sham (using a placebo coil over F4) stimulation in the same session separated by a 30 min interval (van't Wout et al., 2005). Immediately after stimulation, participants performed a version of the Ultimatum Game, always playing the responder role (see Figure 16.3). After receiving rTMS, participants were slower to reject unfair offers and showed a trend towards higher acceptance than without stimulation. The study showed that rTMS affected only the unfair condition, as predicted, and not the fair one.

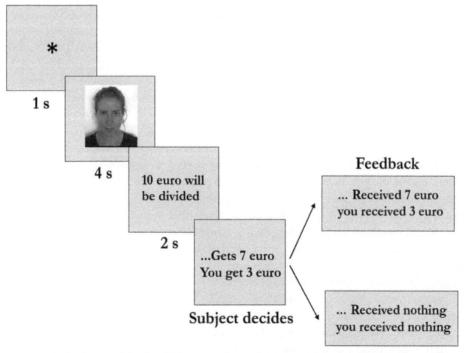

FIGURE 16.3 A single round in the Ultimatum Game. A picture of the proposer is shown, then their offer. The participant has to decide whether to accept the offer, in which case the money will be shared as proposed, or to reject it, in which case both players get nothing. Adapted with permission from van't Wout et al., 2005.

Results from two studies showed a significant increase in the acceptance rate of unfair offers after right rTMS in comparison to left rTMS or sham (placebo stimulation) treatment groups (Knoch, Pascual-Leone, Meyer, Treyer, & Fehr 2006b) or with cathodal tDCS applied to the right DLPFC (Knoch et al., 2008). Interestingly, disrupting the right DLPFC with rTMS disrupted reciprocal fairness behavior but it did not alter how participants rated the fairness of the offers. With stimulation on the right DLPFC, no difference in response times was found between accepting fair offers versus unfair ones; by contrast, participants in the control condition took longer to accept unfair offers than fair ones. This suggested that a disruption of the right DLPFC reduces the conflict between self-interest and fairness and increases the automatic nature of the behavioral response. Additionally, when the unfair offer was made by a computer rather than a human counterpart, the acceptance rate substantially increased in all groups, with no more difference between real and sham stimulation. Thus, the right rTMS group behaved normally when reciprocity motives were not present. Therefore, according to Knoch et al. (2006a) the main function of the DLPFC is to implement behavior based on fairness considerations overriding selfish motives and impulses.

To further characterize the mechanisms by which the right DLPFC influence decisions to accept or reject unfair offers, Baumgartner et al. (2011) measured the effect of TMS on the left and right DLPFC on brain activity. Participants received stimulation before they were placed in an MRI scanner where they played the game. Several hypotheses were tested: whether the DLPFC regulated decisions to reject unfair offers 1) by downregulating the activity of the insula, thought to be involved in processing emotional aspects of receiving an unfair offer, 2) by downregulating the anterior cingulate cortex (ACC) which activity reflects the conflictive motives of rejecting an unfair offer or accepting the money, or 3) by modulating the activity of the VMPFC which encodes the values of the available options. In the absence of stimulation, subjects exhibited increased connectivity between the right DLPFC and posterior VMPFC when facing unfair offers compared to fair offers. This was not the case for participants who received TMS to the right DLPFC. Besides, disrupting the activity of the right DLPFC reduced activity of the pVMPFC. No effect of DLPFC stimulation was found on the activity of the ACC and insula. These results suggest that the DLPFC and pVMPFC interact with one another to commit to the costly normative alternatives in case of conflict between self-interest and fairness.

The studies described so far have focused on the role of the offer recipient and the neural mechanisms involved in punishing norm violation. Understanding how social pressure (i.e., punishment threat) influences fairness and honesty is important to describe how social norms are implemented. Has the human brain developed neural processes that generate behavioral changes to punishment threats? This question was answered by stimulating the right DLPFC while volunteers decided how much of their endowment to transfer to another person in two different contexts: in the punishment condition, the responder could use their earning to destroy some of the first player's pay-off; while in the baseline condition, the second player had to take the offer (Figure 16.4; Ruff et al., 2013). The norm-enforcement procedure worked since significantly more money was transferred in the punishment than in the baseline condition. The amount of money voluntarily transferred decreased with heightened excitability of the DLPFC (Cathodal > Sham > Anodal) in the baseline condition. In the punishment condition, the effect was reversed; participants transferred more money with increased excitability of the DLPFC (Cathodal < Sham < Anodal). Neither participants' beliefs about the angry feelings of the receiver, nor their beliefs about the fairness of their offers, were affected by tDCS, showing that the DLPFC is not involved in the knowledge of fairness norms but rather in its implementation. The direction of the effect is puzzling if we consider that the DLPFC is suppressing first impulses in that context as well. However, it should

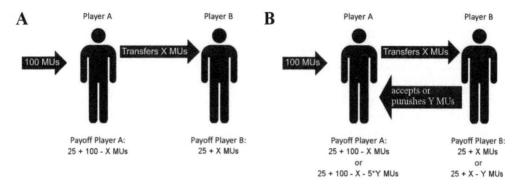

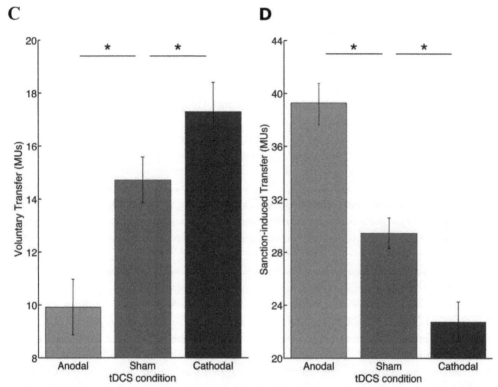

FIGURE 16.4 Design and results from Ruff et al.'s (2013) study. A. Dictator game in baseline condition. B. Dictator game in punishment condition. C. Voluntary transfer in the three types of stimulation in the baseline condition. D. Sanction-induced transfer in the three types of stimulation in the punishment condition. Adapted with permission from Ruff et al. (2013).

be noted that the stimulation site was less dorsal than in previous studies. Nonetheless, the study clearly shows that norm compliance depends causally on neural activity in the right LPFC.

The DLPFC was also found to modulate cooperative behavior with others (Soutschek et al., 2015). Indeed, TMS of the left and right DLPFC reduced the level of cooperation in a repeated game compared to no stimulation. More precisely, stimulated participants stopped cooperating after their partner had defected while non-stimulated participants did not. Mutual cooperation can only be maintained if players overlook occasional defection from their partner. The results of this study suggest that the DLPFC could have a causal role in suppressing the impulse to reciprocate defection in order to restore a cooperative interaction.

The transcranial brain stimulation studies described here confirm the causal role of the DLPFC norm reinforcement in cases of conflicting motives. The role of the DLPFC is not mediated by changing participants' declarative knowledge or beliefs about fairness and social norms. Besides, most of the effects following DLPFC stimulation described earlier disappeared when participants were told they were interacting with a computer, demonstrating that the DLPFC implements aspects of behavioral control that are specifically social. Similarly to intertemporal or risky decision-making domains, it remains to be understood whether modulation of behavior by the DLPFC is mediated by an influence on the valuation system, perhaps through connectivity with the VMPFC.

The Role of TPJ in Integrating Socially Relevant Information in the Decision Process

If the DLPFC is responsible for implementing social norms without modifying agents' beliefs about those norms or how their behavior is affecting others, a different region, the temporo-parietal junction (TPJ) might support this latter function. The primary function ascribed to TPJ is attributing mental states, such as beliefs, intentions, and desires, to others (Gallagher et al., 2000). Disrupting the activity of the right TPJ with rTMS has an effect on belief attribution and moral judgment (Young et al., 2010). Generally, we judge harmful actions towards others as very reprehensible when the harm was intentional, then slightly less reprehensible in the case of a failed attempt to harm someone, and quite acceptable when effective harm was not intentional. rTPJ disruption significantly increased the perceived acceptability of failed attempts to harm, but had not effect on moral judgment of the other two cases. Only the consequence of the action mattered, the intentions of the person doing harm were disregarded. This result shows that rTPJ has a role in considering the mental states of others during moral judgment.

Decision neuroscientists have recently started to investigate which computations are executed by the TPJ and the adjacent posterior superior temporal sulcus during cooperative and competitive decisions (Bault, Pelloux, Fahrenfort, Ridderinkhof, & van Winden, 2015; Hampton, Bossaerts, & O'Doherty, 2008; Hare, Camerer, Knoepfle, & Rangel, 2010). Connectivity analyses in fMRI revealed a functional link between activity of the TPJ that tracks socially relevant information, and activity of the vmPFC involved in valuation. Thus it has been proposed that TPJ modulates the activity of the vmPFC to integrate information about social context into the valuation process (Bault et al., 2015), although the directionality of the effect had not been established.

By combining brain stimulation with fMRI, Hill et al. (2017) could directly address this question. They applied theta-burst stimulation to the right TPJ of participants before they entered the MRI scanner (Figure 16.5). Disrupting the activity of rTPJ reduced participants' ability to consider the influence of their past choices on their opponent (second-order beliefs) in a repeated competitive game. fMRI results confirmed a reduction of mentalizing-related activity in rTPJ. More interestingly, the functional connectivity between rTPJ and two other regions was disturbed as well: the dmPFC, also involved in mentalizing, and the vmPFC. The authors conclude that the change of connectivity reflects a perturbation of the integration of second-order beliefs into choice value. This interpretation should be considered with caution, though, since no significant difference between the TMS and control groups was reported, BOLD signals supposedly encoding

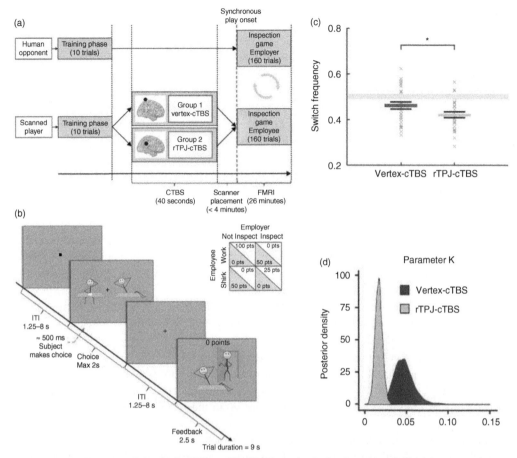

FIGURE 16.5 Design and results in Hill et al.'s (2017) study. A. Study protocol. Participants underwent TBS on rTPJ or on the vertex before entering the MRI scanner where they played the Inspection game in the employee role with an opponent outside the scanner. B. Inspector game and pay-off matrix. The task was an inspector game, in which two protagonists have opposite motives: employers need to make sure their employees are working and can inspect them at a cost, while employees are better off not working but only if they are not inspected. Good performance in this coordination game requires anticipating the other player's next move (first-order belief), and keeping track of how one's behavior is influencing the opponent (influence: second-order belief). The employer was earning 50 points if he could correctly predict the action of the employers, zero otherwise. C. Difference in frequency of switching strategy between conditions. Subjects in the rTPJ-cTBS group were less likely to switch than those in the vertex-cTBS group. D. The authors fitted a model on participants' choices to estimate how these two components guided behavior. The estimate of the second order-beliefs parameter was lower for the group receiving rTPJ stimulation than for the control group. Adapted with permission from Hill et al. (2017).

value or one's own influence on others, in those two regions. Disrupting the activity of a brain area necessarily changes its functional connectivity with the rest of the network. Thus it is important to characterize the computational changes occurring in other areas. Combining rTMS and fMRI allows not only to ensure that the activity of the targeted region is disrupted but also to investigate how this disruption affects the activity of functionally connected regions.

Unravelling the Process of Choice with Noninvasive Brain Stimulation

A large body of research investigating decision processes with noninvasive brain stimulation has focused on the DLPFC. Interfering with the neural activity of this region modifies behavior in situations where the drive to blindly commit to options associated with highest rewards has to be repressed in order to fulfill long-term goals, avoid risky options, or punish those who violate social norms. Although fMRI studies had conferred a prominent role to the right DLPFC in overriding impulsive urges, results from brain stimulation studies suggest otherwise. The inter-hemispheric balance of activity between the right and left DLPFC is more likely to mediate cognitive control mechanisms rather than the right DLPFC alone (Fecteau, et al., 2007b).

Recent Developments and Future Directions

One important challenge of transcranial stimulation is to reach deep structures beyond superficial cortical regions. Due to the rapid decay of the magnetic field and dissipation of electrical currents, standard TMS coils cannot successfully stimulate subcortical structures. It would require unsafe levels of current intensity and would result in also stimulating all the neural tissue that lies between the stimulator and the target region. New types of coils, called H-coils, are being developed to overcome those obstacles (Roth, Zangen, & Hallett, 2002). The underlying principle of deep TMS is the convergence of several electric fields in the desired region. The fields from different coil elements placed around the skull accumulate in the targeted region. Although most of the research with deep TMS has focused on treating psychiatric disorders, some studies reported an effect of deep TMS on the insula, DLPFC, or mPFC on tobacco or alcohol addiction and on obsessive compulsive disorder (Dinur-Klein et al., 2014). Decision-making research could potentially bene-ficiate from deep TMS by disturbing valuation processes in the vmPFC or even attempt to reach the ventral striatum.

A different way of modulating the activity of subcortical structures is by indirect stimulation. Approaching the study of decision processes from a network perspective rather than investigating the role of different regions separately seems promising. Such an approach is facilitated by com-bining brain stimulation with neuroimaging techniques. tDCS applied on the prefrontal cortex may modulate BOLD response in the vmPFC and in the ventral midbrain (Chib, Yun, Takahashi, & Shimojo, 2013). In resting-state fMRI studies, tDCS impacted cortico-striatal and thalamo-cortical connectivity (Polanía, Paulus, & Nitsche, 2012) as well as the default mode network frontal-parietal networks (Keeser et al., 2011). Studies of regional cerebral blood flow changes induced by brain stimulation (e.g., Eisenegger, Treyer, Fehr, & Knoch, 2008) can certainly com-plement behavioral studies and provide useful clues to an appropriate interpretation of behavioral effects. Combining fMRI with brain stimulation while participants are making decisions (e.g., Chib et al., 2013; Hill et al., 2017) seems an even more promising approach. It allows monitoring the effect of brain stimulation on the BOLD signal in the stimulated brain region, as well as in interconnected remote regions. In addition, variations in BOLD signal in regions of the entire network can be related to behavioral changes, on an individual basis. Combining stimulation and imaging also allows assessing long-term effects of repetitive TMS and tDCS on cortical reorgan-ization, which can provide valuable information in the study of learning processes and in the context of rehabilitation.

An additional interesting development in the field of brain stimulation consists of targeting a specific brain-oscillation band by applying a sinusoidal current to the surface of the scalp. Transcranial alternating current stimulation (tACS) can enhance the amplitude of an electroencephalographic oscillation. Entraining brain rhythms in sensorimotor cortices has been found to alter resting state fMRI connectivity (Bächinger et al., 2017). With tACS comes the possibility to probe a cognitive process that is characterized by a specific brain oscillation which has potentially interesting application in the field of decision making (Sela, Kilim, & Lavidor, 2012).

Limitations

Of course there are limits to the application of noninvasive brain stimulation techniques to the study of decision making. As already mentioned, decision making is likely supported by a complex network of interacting areas. Some of them are close to the cortical surface, whereas others are deeper and subcortical. On the other hand, if it is reasonable to assume that the effect is maximum at the stimulation site, it might well be that concomitant behavioral effects are induced by upregulation or downregulation of distant areas that are synaptically connected with the neuronal populations under the stimulation site. Therefore, results of stimulation studies should be interpreted considering that entire neuronal networks are being disrupted. Regarding tDCS, we can benefit from the observation that stimulation will primarily affect the neurons of a network engaged by the current task (Fertonani & Miniussi, 2016). If two networks overlap in neuroanatomical space and only the network involved in the task benefits from the stimulation, then it should possible, in principle, to distinguish between the functions of those two networks.

Another problem concerns the high variability between individuals in their neural responses to stimulation. While cortical excitability is thought to increase with stimulation frequency, the relationship can be inverted in some individuals (Maeda, Keenan, Tormos, Topka, & Pascual-Leone, 2000). A study showed that only half of the sample showed a reliable response to tDCS (Wiethoff, Hamada, & Rothwell, 2014). One possible explanation is the difference in initial skills, strategies, and task engagement of the participants (Fertonani & Miniussi, 2016). If tDCS modulates the activity of near-threshold neurons, it will affect differently the brain activity of participants with different cognitive styles who might engage different brain regions to solve the same task. Therefore, measures of cognitive skills, as well as task engagement, are needed for a sound interpretation of the stimulation results. Besides, combining brain stimulation with neuroimaging to monitor the effective changes in brain regional activity might become the standard approach to overcome those limitations.

Conclusion

In summary, noninvasive stimulation techniques are a powerful tool that can provide strong but complementary evidence with respect to neuroimaging methods, and their potential may be best exploited when they are used in combination with other techniques. When observing a stimulation-induced change in choice behavior, it is important to consider how this behavioral shift operates. Taking into account the effect of brain stimulation on diverse variables, such as response times, rating scales, and choices in control conditions can shed light on the sub-processes being targeted by the stimulation. It provides an important insight in the mechanistic level of explanation that may facilitate a finer understanding of the whole system.

The limitations of the technique, mainly the lack of spatial specificity and stimulation of connected areas, can be overcome by taking precaution in choosing control stimulation sites and adopting a system approach in the interpretation of the results.

Finally, it should not be neglected that, irrespective of their theoretical basis and interpretation, behavioral effects obtained with noninvasive stimulation that shift impulsive behavior towards safer prospects can be desirable in clinical settings too. In turn, the long-term effects of such applications can inform theoretical models of decision making in both the healthy and pathological brain, and elicit additional research hypotheses.

Note

1 This work was supported by a European Research Council (ERC-2013-CoG) grant to G. C. and a CIMeC Research Fellowship to E. R.

Recommended Reading List

For a general introduction to the use of noninvasive stimulation in cognitive neuroscience and more technical details, see:

- Miniussi et al. (2010): the mechanism of transcranial magnetic stimulation in cognition.
- Rusconi & Bestmann (2009): the contribution of TMS to structure–function mapping in the human brain; action, perception, and higher functions.
- Sandrini et al. (2011): the use of transcranial magnetic stimulation in cognitive neuroscience: A new synthesis of methodological issues.
- Woods et al. (2016): a technical guide to tDCS, and related noninvasive brain stimulation tools.

References

Bächinger, M., Zerbi, V., Moisa, M., Polania, R., Liu, Q., Mantini, D., … Wenderoth, N. (2017). Concurrent tACS-fMRI reveals causal influence of power synchronized neural activity on resting state fMRI connectivity. *Journal of Neuroscience, 37*(18), 4766–4777.

Barker, A. T., Jalinous, R., & Freeston, I. L. (1985). Non-invasive magnetic stimulation of human motor cortex. *The Lancet, 325*(8437), 1106–1107.

Bault, N., Pelloux, B., Fahrenfort, J. J., Ridderinkhof, K. R., & van Winden, F. (2015). Neural dynamics of social tie formation in economic decision-making. *Social Cognitive and Affective Neuroscience, 10*(6), 877–884.

Baumgartner, T., Knoch, D., Hotz, P., Eisenegger, C., & Fehr, E. (2011). Dorsolateral and ventromedial prefrontal cortex orchestrate normative choice. *Nature Neuroscience, 14*(11), 1468–1474.

Beharelle, A. R., Polanía, R., Hare, T. A., & Ruff, C. C. (2015). Transcranial stimulation over frontopolar cortex elucidates the choice attributes and neural mechanisms used to resolve exploration–exploitation trade-offs. *The Journal of Neuroscience, 35*(43), 14544–14556.

Bikson, M., Grossman, P., Thomas, C., Zannou, A. L., Jiang, J., Adnan, T., … Woods, A. J. (2016). Safety of transcranial direct current stimulation: evidence based update 2016. *Brain Stimulation, 9*(5), 641–661.

Bowles, S. (2006). Group competition, reproductive leveling, and the evolution of human altruism. *Science, 314*(5805), 1569–1572.

Chib, V. S., Yun, K., Takahashi, H., & Shimojo, S. (2013). Noninvasive remote activation of the ventral midbrain by transcranial direct current stimulation of prefrontal cortex. *Translational Psychiatry, 3*(6), 268.

Clark, L., Manes, F., Antoun, N., Sahakian, B. J., & Robbins, T. W. (2003). The contributions of lesion laterality and lesion volume to decision-making impairment following frontal lobe damage. *Neuropsychologia, 41*(11), 1474–1483.

Daw, N. D., O'Doherty, J. P., Dayan, P., Seymour, B., & Dolan, R. J. (2006). Cortical substrates for exploratory decisions in humans. *Nature, 441*(7095), 876–879.

Dayan, E., Censor, N., Buch, E. R., Sandrini, M., & Cohen, L. G. (2013). Noninvasive brain stimulation: From physiology to network dynamics and back. *Nature Neuroscience, 16*(7), 838–844.

de Quervain, D. J. F., Fischbacher, U., Treyer, V., Schellhammer, M., Schnyder, U., Buck, A., & Fehr, E. (2004). The neural basis of altruistic punishment. *Science, 305*(5688), 1254–1258.

Dinur-Klein, L., Dannon, P., Hadar, A., Rosenberg, O., Roth, Y., Kotler, M., & Zangen, A. (2014). Smoking cessation induced by deep repetitive transcranial magnetic stimulation of the prefrontal and insular cortices: a prospective, randomized controlled trial. *Biological Psychiatry, 76*(9), 742–749.

Eisenegger, C., Treyer, V., Fehr, E., & Knoch, D. (2008). Time-course of "off-line" prefrontal rTMS effects — a PET study. *NeuroImage, 42*(1), 379–384.

Ernst, M., & Paulus, M. P. (2005). Neurobiology of decision making: A selective review from a neurocognitive and clinical perspective. *Biological Psychiatry, 58*(8), 597–604.

Fecteau, S., Knoch, D., Fregni, F., Sultani, N., Boggio, P., & Pascual-Leone, A. (2007a). Diminishing risk-taking behavior by modulating activity in the prefrontal cortex: a direct current stimulation study. *The Journal of Neuroscience, 27*(46), 12500–12505.

Fecteau, S., Pascual-Leone, A., Zald, D. H., Liguori, P., Théoret, H., Boggio, P. S., & Fregni, F. (2007b). Activation of prefrontal cortex by transcranial direct current stimulation reduces appetite for risk during ambiguous decision making. *The Journal of Neuroscience, 27*(23), 6212–6218.

Fehr, E., & Gächter, S. (2002). Altruistic punishment in humans. *Nature, 415*(6868), 137–140.

Fehr, E., & Schmidt, K. M. (1999). A theory of fairness, competition, and cooperation. *Quarterly Journal of Economics, 114*(3), 817–868.

Fertonani, A., Ferrari, C., & Miniussi, C. (2015). What do you feel if I apply transcranial electric stimulation? Safety, sensations and secondary induced effects. *Clinical Neurophysiology, 126*(11), 2181–2188.

Fertonani, A., & Miniussi, C. (2016). Transcranial electrical stimulation: What we know and do not know about mechanisms. *The Neuroscientist, 23*(2), 109–123.

Figner, B., Knoch, D., Johnson, E. J., Krosch, A. R., Lisanby, S. H., Fehr, E., & Weber, E. U. (2010). Lateral prefrontal cortex and self-control in intertemporal choice. *Nature Neuroscience, 13*(5), 538–539.

Gallagher, H. L., Happé, F., Brunswick, N., Fletcher, P. C., Frith, U., & Frith, C. D. (2000). Reading the mind in cartoons and stories: An fMRI study of 'theory of mind' in verbal and nonverbal tasks. *Neuropsychologia, 38*(1), 11–21.

Gianotti, L. R. R., Knoch, D., Faber, P. L., Lehmann, D., Pascual-Marqui, R. D., Diezi, C., … Fehr, E. (2009). Tonic activity level in the right prefrontal cortex predicts individuals' risk taking. *Psychological Science, 20*(1), 33–38.

Güth, W., Schmittberger, R., & Schwarze, B. (1982). An experimental analysis of ultimatum bargaining. *Journal of Economic Behavior & Organization, 3*(4), 367–388.

Hampton, A. N., Bossaerts, P., & O'Doherty, J. P. (2008). Neural correlates of mentalizing-related computations during strategic interactions in humans. *Proceedings of the National Academy of Sciences, 105*(18), 6741–6746.

Hare, T. A., Camerer, C. F., Knoepfle, D. T., & Rangel, A. (2010). Value computations in ventral medial prefrontal cortex during charitable decision making incorporate input from regions involved in social cognition. *Journal of Neuroscience, 30*(2), 583–590.

Hill, C. A., Suzuki, S., Polania, R., Moisa, M., O'Doherty, J. P., & Ruff, C. C. (2017). A causal account of the brain network computations underlying strategic social behavior. *Nature Neuroscience, 20*(8), 1142–1149.

Huang, Y.-Z., Edwards, M. J., Rounis, E., Bhatia, K. P., & Rothwell, J. C. (2005). Theta burst stimulation of the human motor cortex. *Neuron, 45*(2), 201–206.

Keeser, D., Meindl, T., Bor, J., Palm, U., Pogarell, O., Mulert, C., … Padberg, F. (2011). Prefrontal transcranial direct current stimulation changes connectivity of resting-state networks during fMRI. *Journal of Neuroscience, 31*(43), 15284–15293.

Knoch, D., & Fehr, E. (2007). Resisting the power of temptations. The right prefrontal cortex and self-control. *Annals of the New York Academy of Sciences, 1104*(1), 123–134.

Knoch, D., Gianotti, L. R., Pascual-Leone, A., Treyer, V., Regard, M., Hohmann, M., & Brugger, P. (2006a). Disruption of right prefrontal cortex by low-frequency repetitive transcranial magnetic stimulation induces risk-taking behavior. *Journal of Neuroscience, 26*(24), 6469–6472.

Knoch, D., Nitsche, M. A., Fischbacher, U., Eisenegger, C., Pascual-Leone, A., & Fehr, E. (2008). Studying the neurobiology of social interaction with transcranial direct current stimulation — the example of punishing unfairness. *Cerebral Cortex, 18*(9), 1987–1990.

Knoch, D., Pascual-Leone, A., Meyer, K., Treyer, V., & Fehr, E. (2006b). Diminishing reciprocal fairness by disrupting the right prefrontal cortex. *Science, 314*(5800), 829–832.

Koechlin, E., Ody, C., & Kouneiher, F. (2003). The architecture of cognitive control in the human prefrontal cortex. *Science*, 302(5648), 1181–1185.

Maeda, F., Keenan, J. P., Tormos, J. M., Topka, H., & Pascual-Leone, A. (2000). Interindividual variability of the modulatory effects of repetitive transcranial magnetic stimulation on cortical excitability. *Experimental Brain Research*, 133(4), 425–430.

Maréchal, M. A., Cohn, A., Ugazio, G., & Ruff, C. C. (2017). Increasing honesty in humans with noninvasive brain stimulation. *Proceedings of the National Academy of Sciences*, 114(17), 4360–4364.

Miller, E. K., & Cohen, J. D. (2001). An integrative theory of prefrontal cortex function. *Annual Review of Neuroscience*, 24(1), 167–202.

Miniussi, C., Ruzzoli, M., & Walsh, V. (2010). The mechanism of transcranial magnetic stimulation in cognition. *Cortex*, 46(1), 128–130.

Miranda, P. C., Lomarev, M., & Hallett, M. (2006). Modeling the current distribution during transcranial direct current stimulation. *Clinical Neurophysiology*, 117(7), 1623–1629.

Mobbs, D., Lau, H. C., Jones, O. D., & Frith, C. D. (2007). Law, responsibility, and the brain. *PLoS Biology*, 5(4), 693–700.

Nitsche, M. A., Fricke, K., Henschke, U., Schlitterlau, A., Liebetanz, D., Lang, N., … Paulus, W. (2003). Pharmacological modulation of cortical excitability shifts induced by transcranial direct current stimulation in humans. *The Journal of Physiology*, 553(1), 293–301.

Nitsche, M. A., & Paulus, W. (2001). Sustained excitability elevations induced by transcranial DC motor cortex stimulation in humans. *Neurology*, 57(10), 1899–1901.

Paulus, W. (2003). Transcranial direct current stimulation (tDCS). In W. Paulus, F. Tergau, M. A. Nitsche, J. G. Rothwell, U. Ziemann, & M. Hallett (Eds.), *Supplements to clinical neurophysiology, transcranial magnetic stimulation and transcranial direct current stimulation: Proceedings of the 2nd International Transcranial Magnetic Stimulation (TMS) and Transcranial Direct Current Stimulation (tDCS) Symposium* (Vol. 56, pp. 249–254). Amsterdam, NL: Elsevier.

Polanía, R., Paulus, W., & Nitsche, M. A. (2012). Modulating cortico-striatal and thalamo-cortical functional connectivity with transcranial direct current stimulation. *Human Brain Mapping*, 33(10), 2499–2508.

Rabin, M. (1993). Incorporating fairness into game theory and economics. *The American Economic Review*, 83(5), 1281–1302.

Robertson, E. M., Théoret, H., & Pascual-leone, A. (2003). Studies in cognition: The problems solved and created by transcranial magnetic stimulation. *Journal of Cognitive Neuroscience*, 15(7), 948–960.

Rossi, S., Hallett, M., Rossini, P. M., & Pascual-Leone, A. (2009). Safety, ethical considerations, and application guidelines for the use of transcranial magnetic stimulation in clinical practice and research. *Clinical Neurophysiology*, 120(12), 2008–2039.

Roth, Y., Zangen, A., & Hallett, M. (2002). A coil design for transcranial magnetic stimulation of deep brain regions. *Journal of Clinical Neurophysiology*, 19(4), 361–370.

Ruff, C. C., Ugazio, G., & Fehr, E. (2013). Changing social norm compliance with noninvasive brain stimulation. *Science*, 342(6157), 482–484.

Rusconi, E., & Bestmann, S. (2009). On tickling brains to investigate minds. *Cortex*, 45(9), 1021–1024.

Sandrini, M., Umiltà, C., & Rusconi, E. (2011). The use of transcranial magnetic stimulation in cognitive neuroscience: A new synthesis of methodological issues. *Neuroscience & Biobehavioral Reviews*, 35(3), 516–536.

Sanfey, A. G., Rilling, J. K., Aronson, J. A., Nystrom, L. E., & Cohen, J. D. (2003). The neural basis of economic decision-making in the ultimatum game. *Science*, 300(5626), 1755–1758.

Sela, T., Kilim, A., & Lavidor, M. (2012). Transcranial alternating current stimulation increases risk-taking behavior in the balloon analog risk task. *Frontiers in Neuroscience*, 6, 22.

Siebner, H. R., Hartwigsen, G., Kassuba, T., & Rothwell, J. C. (2009). How does transcranial magnetic stimulation modify neuronal activity in the brain? Implications for studies of cognition. *Cortex*, 45(9), 1035–1042.

Soutschek, A., Sauter, M., & Schubert, T. (2015). The importance of the lateral prefrontal cortex for strategic decision making in the prisoner's dilemma. *Cognitive, Affective, & Behavioral Neuroscience*, 15(4), 854–860.

van't Wout, M., Kahn, R. S., Sanfey, A. G., & Aleman, A. (2005). Repetitive transcranial magnetic stimulation over the right dorsolateral prefrontal cortex affects strategic decision-making. *Neuroreport*, 16(16), 1849–1852.

von Neumann, J., & Morgenstern, O. (1944). *Theory of games and economic behavior*. New Jersey, NJ: Princeton University Press.

Wagner, T., Rushmore, J., Eden, U., & Valero-Cabre, A. (2009). Biophysical foundations underlying TMS: Setting the stage for an effective use of neurostimulation in the cognitive neurosciences. *Cortex, 45*(9), 1025–1034.

Walsh, V., & Cowey, A. (2000). Transcranial magnetic stimulation and cognitive neuroscience. *Nature Reviews Neuroscience, 1*(1), 73–80.

Wassermann, E. M., Epstein, C. M., Ziemann, U., Walsh, V., Paus, T., & Lisanby, S. (2008). *Oxford handbook of transcranial stimulation*. Oxford, UK: Oxford University Press.

Wiethoff, S., Hamada, M., & Rothwell, J. C. (2014). Variability in response to transcranial direct current stimulation of the motor cortex. *Brain Stimulation, 7*(3), 468–475.

Woods, A. J., Antal, A., Bikson, M., Boggio, P. S., Brunoni, A. R., Celnik, P., … Nitsche, M. A. (2016). A technical guide to tDCS, and related non-invasive brain stimulation tools. *Clinical Neurophysiology, 127*(2), 1031–1048.

Young, L., Camprodon, J. A., Hauser, M., Pascual-Leone, A., & Saxe, R. (2010). Disruption of the right temporoparietal junction with transcranial magnetic stimulation reduces the role of beliefs in moral judgments. *Proceedings of the National Academy of Sciences, 107*(15), 6753–6758.

Ziemann, U. (2010). TMS in cognitive neuroscience: virtual lesion and beyond. *Cortex, 46*(1), 124–127.

17

VERBAL REPORTS AND DECISION PROCESS ANALYSIS

Rob Ranyard and Ola Svenson

This chapter takes a broader look at the use of verbal data in contemporary decision process research. We examine a range of approaches to the elicitation and analysis of verbal reports with the purposes of both describing decision processes and testing theories about them. We aim to recommend and illustrate good practice, thereby providing researchers with the means to make good research design decisions.

We define a decision process as a transformation of a structure over time. A decision maker's mental representation of a decision problem is such a structure, one that includes both cognitive and affective components. Decision problems can be represented in many different ways. For example, decision alternatives can be represented either holistically, or by the attractiveness of different cues, or by arguments for or against the alternatives (Pennington & Hastie, 1992; Shafir, Simonson, & Tversky, 1993; Svenson & Jakobsson, 2010). Fundamental to process theories is the notion that mental representations can change from the beginning of a decision process until the decision is made (Janis & Mann, 1977; Payne, Bettman, & Johnson, 1992; Russo, Medvec, & Meloy, 1996; Svenson, 1979), and can continue to change after the decision (Festinger, 1957; Simon, Krawczyk, Bleicher, & Holyoak, 2008; Svenson, 1996, 2003). These transformations of decision representations are brought about by processes, or operations, defined by a process model or theory, such as the elementary information processes (EIPs) described by Huber (1989) and by Payne et al. (1992).

Without postulating a structure no process can be measured. Hence, in a process study of decision making it is necessary to measure the mental structure of a decision problem at different points in time. Studies that do this by eliciting verbal reports vary in several ways, notably: 1) verbal evidence may be the sole means of measuring processes, or alternatively, it may be combined with nonverbal process tracing methods; 2) report elicitation may be either concurrent with the decision process, or post-decision; and 3) verbal responses may be either structured or unstructured.

An important method that elicits and analyzes concurrent, unstructured verbal reports is protocol analysis, based on the think-aloud procedure (Newell & Simon, 1972). It was introduced into decision research in the 1970s by Svenson and Montgomery (Montgomery & Svenson, 1976; Svenson, 1974, 1979) and by Payne, Braunstein, and Carroll (1978). The status of the think-aloud method was enhanced by the exposition of rigorous procedures for protocol analysis by Ericsson and Simon (1980, 1993) and by Svenson (1989a, 1989b). These were, and continue to serve as, the gold standard for protocol analysis in decision research.

Since the 1980s the use of verbal reports in decision process analysis has continued to develop and has made valuable contributions to knowledge and theory in different ways. For example, many studies have shown how unstructured verbal reports can provide information of great value in the construction of detailed decision process models for a given context and category of decision or judgment (Lundgrén-Laine & Salanterä, 2010; Montgomery, 1983; Montgomery & Svenson, 1983; Pennington & Hastie, 1992; Ranyard & Charlton, 2006). However, the role of verbal data is not limited to the creation of process theories: the analysis of both unstructured and structured verbal reports can provide crucial tests of hypotheses concerning central aspects of process models (Harte, Westenberg, & van Someren, 1994; Weber & Johnson, 2009).

Prerequisites and Key Design Decisions

There are two fundamental prerequisites to consider before designing a study to elicit and analyze measures of human decision processes, whether these are based on verbal or nonverbal responses. First, as indicated earlier, a general theory must be assumed with a psychological structure that can be measured at different points in time, in this way describing a decision process. Second, the ecology of the decision context must be specified; that is, the physical and social structures and processes into which the decision problem is embedded. This involves specifying the decision makers to whom the theory applies (experts, non-experts, students, the public in general), along with task demands such as time pressure and stress, as well as the particular context, e.g., personal, social, health, financial, or professional.

Some of the key design decisions for studies eliciting verbal reports were indicated earlier, i.e., concurrent versus post-decision; verbal process evidence alone versus verbal combined with non-verbal measures; structured versus unstructured responses. In addition at least the following must be decided: a) how to communicate to the decision maker the type of responses required; b) how to structure parameters of the decision task so that the information elicited is relevant to the theory; and c) how to elicit and record relevant information concerning at least two points during the modeled sequence of pre-decision, decision, and post-decision phases. Note that a study with two or more consecutive measuring points must refer to a process model or theory to qualify as a process study.

In addition, the possible distortion effects of introducing a process tracing method on the normally occurring decision processes have to be modeled and estimated, and a framework for the analysis of the elicited data must be devised based on the specified decision process theory. Finally, researchers must think in advance about the level of detail she or he wants to use for describing a decision representation and process (e.g., holistic, cue) and from what perspective (value, argument, etc.).

Figure 17.1 gives an overview of components and steps in designing a process tracing study eliciting verbal reports. To the left there are the researcher's theory and the problem ecology. Next, there is a box indicating how the researcher uses the theory and specifies the research problem, the context, the instructions, and response formats. As illustrated, these determine the coding scheme for analyzing verbal reports and models for the analysis of other data. They also inform the participant about the decision to make and how to respond. The first stage of data analysis involves coding the verbal responses and summarizing the other process or outcome data, and the second involves interpreting these data in relation to the researcher's theory. Finally, the analyses of verbal

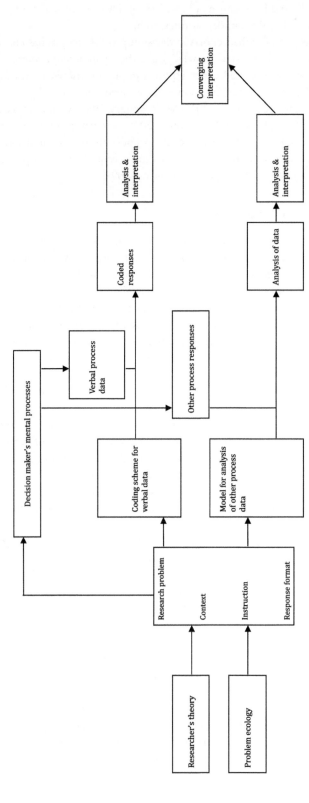

FIGURE 17.1 Stages in process studies from a researcher's theory to the interpretation of results. The upper path shows a design with verbal reports described in this chapter and the lower path outlines control studies involving other process methods.

and other process or outcome data are combined to give a unified description of the decision maker's decision processes.

Combining Verbal Reports and Nonverbal Measures

Although a process tracing study may elicit only verbal reports along with decision behavior, combining these with nonverbal process measures (bottom path in Figure 17.1) is more informative and provides opportunities for cross-validation. Whether, and if so, how, to combine verbal reports is an important question for process studies that focus on monitoring information search (Walsh & Gluck, 2016) or measuring physiological or neural correlates of decision processes (McClure, Laibson, Loewenstein, & Cohen, 2004, see Chapters 14–16). The main advantage of doing so is to obtain more direct information concerning the subjective meaning of the behavior recorded (Figure 17.1). For example, an information search monitoring study (e.g., using Mouselab, see Chapter 6) may find that an aspect of information was attended to by a decision maker. Alternatively, a study monitoring skin conductance (see Chapter 11) may record a physiological change associated with an emotional response. In the first case, eliciting a concurrent verbal report could indicate how the information attended to, and therefore apparently of interest, was interpreted and used by the decision maker. In the second case, a concurrent verbal report could indicate the nature of the emotional response experienced by the decision maker. These important benefits, however, bring with them potential hazards that must be minimized, as we will consider in later sections: incompleteness or omission (information that is important to the participant and/ or the researcher being omitted); reactivity (influences of the verbalization on the decision process); and other threats to the validity of responses, such as self-presentation or justification bias and the construction of responses by inference.

The following examples illustrate the need of multiple and converging methods in process studies. First, in a process study of multiple-cue probabilistic inference, Walsh and Gluck (2016) used both think-aloud protocols and the analysis of numerical responses. They found converging results that were used to test and verify that most participants used a take-the best heuristic process. Second, Aitken and collaborators (Aitken, Marshall, Elliott, & McKinley, 2011) compared behavioral observations and think-aloud methods in a study of intensive care nurses' sedation decisions. They found that assessment and management decisions were the most common kinds of decisions. In addition, more decisions in total, and more assessment decisions in particular, were identified by the think-aloud method than by observation, while observation identified more management decisions.

Concurrent Versus Retrospective Verbal Reports

In the previous examples researchers may be worried that eliciting a concurrent verbal report may be reactive, i.e., this secondary verbal process may interfere with and change the primary decision process under investigation. The recommended validity check for this is to introduce a control group to the design, whereby participants are randomly assigned either to a condition with a verbal elicitation procedure or to one without such a procedure. Various measures are then compared across groups to directly assess the extent to which the verbalization procedure changed either the decision process (e.g., made it slower) or outcome (e.g., changed judgments, decisions). In an extensive review of studies using concurrent verbal reports, Fox, Ericsson, and Best (2011) found that, in general, think-aloud studies are not reactive and do not change performance. This contrasts with the change of processes and performance found in studies of participants asked to explain or describe certain aspects of their thoughts or behavior. Schooler (2011) pointed out that thoughts that are non-conscious are not reported and that the non-reactivity of verbal protocols is only a necessary but not sufficient condition for the validity of such data.

The problem of reactivity could be avoided completely if verbal reports were elicited retrospectively. As long as participants are not warned in advance that a retrospective verbal report will be required the procedure would not be reactive. However, if advanced notice is given, a particular form of reactivity known as "justification bias" may change the pre-decision process (Lerner & Tetlock, 1999).

Although retrospective verbal elicitation procedures can be designed to eliminate reactivity, they are nevertheless prone to other threats to their validity, including memory distortion or failure, and the construction rather than recall of information (Nisbett & Wilson, 1977; Russo, Johnson, & Stephens, 1989). Kuusela and Paul (2000) compared unstructured concurrent and retrospective reports of decision processes and found important differences in the data obtained: concurrent reports contained more relevant information overall and more useful information about intermediate changes during the decision process. This indicates that unstructured retrospective elicitation is more prone to errors of omission. However, Kuusela and Paul also found that the structure of retrospective reports was different in that they contained many more and more relevant references to the chosen alternative than the concurrent reports. This suggests that both procedures may suffer from different omission problems, and that neither is clearly better in this respect. Nevertheless, if it is important to understand the subjective meaning of behavioral process measures, then concurrent or retrospective verbal reports should be elicited and the earlier threats to validity addressed.

The issue of whether to elicit concurrent or retrospective verbal reports has been informed by subjective well-being research using the experienced sampling method (Larson & Csikszentmihalyi, 1983) and the day reconstruction method (Kahneman, Krueger, Schkade, Schwarz, & Stone, 2004). In the former, participants are asked structured questions about their concurrent experiences at random points during the day, while in the latter they are asked to retrospectively describe their experiences during the previous day, again with a structured procedure. The experience sampling method has been found to have good reliability and validity (Csikszentmihalyi & Larson, 2014), as has the day reconstruction method (Anusic, Lucas, & Donnellan, 2017; Krueger & Schkade, 2008). They can be used in combination to elicit rich data of a person's experiences (Bylsma, Taylor-Clift, & Rottenberg, 2011), including those related to everyday decision making.

Structured Versus Unstructured Verbal Reports

Another basic design decision for process tracing studies eliciting verbal reports is whether responses should be structured or unstructured. This question is a standard one in social research. In an interview study, for example, one could pose the highly structured, closed question, "*Is your hair dark or fair?*" or the unstructured, open question, "*How would you describe the color of your hair?*" Obviously, the response to the former is expected to be either "dark" or "fair", which presupposes a simplified researcher's model of respondents' representations (Figure 17.1) of hair color that would not be challenged by the data. The open question, on the other hand, allows the respondents to clarify how they see themselves. This suggests the following basis for deciding whether to use structured or unstructured responses in a process tracing study. If a researcher's theory is well established and specific predictions have been derived, and the process tracing study is designed to test them, then structured verbal responses would be efficient and informative. However, in some such cases unstructured responses might still give important additional information. On the other hand, in a more exploratory phase of research, when the researcher's theory is under construction and the study aims to build the theory, unstructured responses would be much more informative.

A related procedural issue is whether *prompt* or *probe* questions should be used. Usually, unstructured think-aloud protocols are elicited by an initial prompt such as: *Please speak aloud all your thoughts.* Subsequently, every so often a prompt to keep speaking is given: *Remember to speak aloud your thoughts.* However, the reports of these thoughts are not probed, as by the question: *Why do you think that this aspect is good?* Some have argued that such probe questions can elicit useful decision process information in a think-aloud study (Williamson, Ranyard, & Cuthbert, 2000), although others argue that probes like this increase the risk of reactivity (Ericsson & Simon, 1993). Although the problem of the reactivity of probe questions has been extensively considered for unstructured procedures, it has been less discussed in the case of structured responses. In fact, most structured response procedures involve the presentation of a probe question. For example, a study of the role of emotion might use the structured probe question: *How angry do you feel at the moment?* Responses on, say, a seven point scale could be requested, 1 representing *not at all angry* and 7 *very angry.* Clearly, this kind of probe question may be reactive: respondents may not feel angry at all until someone asks them about it. To assess the reactivity of structured verbal reports, Backlund, Skånér, Montgomery, Bring, and Strender (2003) investigated doctors' drug prescribing decisions using a standard think-aloud procedure. Participants were allocated to one of two conditions at random, either with or without an additional rating procedure. The ratings were elicited at several points prior to the final decision. Participants rated their opinion on an analogue scale with end points *prescription unreasonable* (0%) and *prescription obvious* (100%). Overall, analysis of both structured and unstructured responses were similarly sensitive to changes in differentiation between the two alternatives (to prescribe or not to prescribe) as more information was received. However, when structured responses were required, participants spoke more about drug treatments and less about alternatives. This is evidence of a degree of reactivity of the rating procedure with decision processes being directed to actions related to the end-point labels. These findings suggest that studies using rating scales to measure aspects of the decision process need to acknowledge and minimize potential problems of reactivity. Generally speaking, good practice is to test for reactivity using the standard experimental design with control groups described earlier.

Eliciting Concurrent Verbal Reports

Characteristics of Decision Problems

The quality of concurrent verbal protocols depends on key characteristics of the decision problem, including complexity (e.g., number of alternatives, number of aspects, presentation of aspects), familiarity, importance, or whether singular or repeated. Generally speaking, it is easier to elicit concurrent verbal protocols if a problem does not require too much working memory capacity and yet does not trigger only automatic non-conscious processing. In the former case there is no capacity left for verbal reports, and in the latter there is no verbal report to give because the participant does not have access to her or his own thought processes. To illustrate the former, a decision maker who makes an emotionally and/or cognitively very difficult decision may become silent when making the decision. To illustrate the latter, in everyday routine decisions and laboratory settings with repeated decisions, the decisions may become so fast and automatized that the decision makers do not know what they are doing on a conscious level. Furthermore, with repeated decisions the participant may feel no need to repeat what was already reported a number of times and stops repeating the same words again and again. Greater numbers of alternatives and aspects tend to give richer protocols than decision problems with smaller numbers of alternatives, because if there are few aspects there is not so much to report.

Unfamiliar problems have the advantage of generating protocols that describe the structuring of a problem and the solution process. In contrast, familiar problems are associated with routines that may be automatic and not accessible to the participant. In the latter case there is a greater need for a theory of the decision process and, if possible, another data source to support protocol analysis. If a problem takes a few minutes or more to solve, the risk of automated routines being used is smaller, especially if the problem is unfamiliar.

Motivation plays an important role in any situation, and important decision problems are likely to affect both the way in which a decision is made and the verbal protocol given. If a problem is perceived as very important by the participant, there may be little capacity left for concurrent verbalization and a retrospective protocol may be needed. If a problem is perceived as artificial and/ or unimportant the participant may solve it in a simplistic way without much reflection so that the decision process differs from a corresponding problem in real life. Then, the results from the verbal protocols in the laboratory cannot be generalized to other situations.

Task Instructions

The first important issues to consider in devising a verbal elicitation procedure concern the instructions to participants. In particular, these must be understood in the way the researcher wants them to be understood. If a researcher fosters an erroneous mental model of the decision maker, she or he will not be able to correctly communicate the instructions and will elicit responses that have different meanings to the researcher and to the participant. Of course, the most common error is the assumption of a greater similarity of the mental models of the researcher and the participant than in reality. If participants interpret the instructions in a different way to the experimenter new problems could appear when the protocols are elicited and coded. In advance of a study, it is important to investigate how participants from the same population interpret the instructions before running a pilot of the experimental procedure as a whole. This could be done in interviews with the participants in a pretest.

Instructions given to participants with the aim of providing indicators of a decision process can be structured, semi-structured, or free. An example of the first is when a decision maker is given a response format with predefined attributes on which the alternatives should be judged in degree of attractiveness from 0 (no attractiveness) to 100 (maximum attractiveness) at different points in time. An example of the second is when a participant is asked to give her or his reasons for and against the available decision alternatives (Shafir et al., 1993; Svenson & Jakobsson, 2010). Giving free associations to decision alternatives is another example of a semi-structured approach (Slovic, Flynn, & Layman, 1991; Svenson & Slovic, 2002). Finally, a free response is when a participant is asked to think aloud about anything that comes into her or his mind while making a decision. The decision maker can express any information while talking aloud and the only requirement is that she or he uses the verbal information channel given in the instruction (Russo, Johnson, & Stephens, 1986; Svenson, 1989a, 1989b).

Think-Aloud Instructions

The following is an example of a think aloud, free instruction for eliciting a concurrent verbal protocol given by Russo et al. (1986). The experiment and the results were also described without the complete instruction in Russo et al. (1989):

As soon as you begin working on the problem, please start thinking aloud. The best way to do so is to be as spontaneous as possible. Tell me everything you are thinking as you are thinking it, even if details or sidetracks that seem insignificant or embarrassing. If you think aloud spontaneously, you will soon forget that you are speaking at all. There is no need to explain to me why you are thinking what you are thinking. You do not have to interpret or justify your approach to a problem. Just tell me what you are thinking at the moment. If you are silent for more than a few seconds, I will remind you by saying: Please tell me what you are thinking.

Process Sampling Instructions

In general, process sampling invites the application of a longitudinal research design, i.e., one where the decision process of each participant on a decision problem is measured at different points. Although it is possible to apply a cross-sectional design, with a collection of responses from different participants at different phases of a decision process, longitudinal, repeated-measures designs are recommended. The latter designs require some control participants, each providing measures only once during the decision process, with different participants responding at different stages of the process. This enables tests of the effects of response elicitation at different stages on decision processes and behavior.

One example of a repeated measures approach is the study by Svenson and Jakobsson (2010) that used process-sampling at different stages of the decision process and a semi-structured approach which elicited reasons for and against alternatives. Participants were asked to write down reasons for and against each of two available alternatives. These were presented side by side at the top of a page, with an instruction to list reasons supporting each alternative in columns below them. In this way, participants indicated a number of different reasons for choosing both the preferred and the non-preferred alternative. On the next response sheet, the procedure was repeated for the same alternatives but now asking for reasons against choosing each alternative. Participants were also asked, in a structured response format, to indicate next to each reason how strong that reason was for or against the alternative under which it was listed (0 = no strength; 100 = maximum strength).

To summarize, free, semi-structured, and structured responses represent a continuum from minimum researcher monitoring to maximum researcher monitoring of a verbal protocol. Free responses run the least risk of reactivity, while structured responses are reactive in the sense that they are highly influenced by the instruction. On the other hand, free responses are open to errors of omission in relation to the researcher's theory (no information about important aspects of a theory), some of which can be avoided in well-designed structured response studies

One way to overcome the limitations of each type of response is to elicit them in combination. For example, in addition to making a decision under think-aloud instructions, a participant can also be asked to judge the difference in attractiveness between the two leading alternatives. Combining such free responses to a decision problem and structured judgment responses will give richer data than think-aloud protocols only. The judgment responses can shed light on decision processes and may also be used for more detailed quantitative analysis as Russo and collaborators have shown (Russo et al., 1996; Russo, Meloy, & Wilks, 2000). However, the addition of a judgment task after each decision may interfere with subsequent decisions so a control group is needed to check for this possible bias.

Practical Arrangements

There are unobtrusive verbal protocols, such as recordings of verbal communications on the flight deck. However, most concurrent verbal protocols are elicited in more obtrusive situations, such as a laboratory or an applied real-life context. Then, the instructions should be written and read by the participant first. After this, with the voice recorder on, the participants should be given the opportunity to discuss and clarify the task requirements. It is important that participants get used to talking aloud before a study begins and therefore some examples of decision problems should be solved in pre-tests before the main study starts. The experimenter should stay in the room without making eye contact with the decision maker and prompt the decision maker if and when s/he stops talking for more than 5 sec. The participant should not be able to stop the recording, which can happen in emotional, conflict, and other situations (Svenson, 1989b).

Eliciting Post-Decision Verbal Reports

As discussed earlier, the main advantage of eliciting verbal reports about a decision process retrospectively is that the threat of reactivity with respect to pre-decision processes can be eliminated completely. In order for this to be achieved, participants must not anticipate post-decision discussion. This should be born in mind in preparing the instructions to participants, who should not be warned about this procedure.[1] It is also important to make sure that participants who take part in an experiment do not convey the design to new participants from the same pool. Furthermore, a study involving a series of decisions should be designed so that all verbal reports are elicited after all decisions have been made. However, this introduces another problem: participants' recall of earlier decisions in the sequence may be impaired or distorted, in particular, when a decision process changes over time. This could clearly pose a threat to the validity of the verbal data elicited. Possible solutions to this dilemma that should be considered in designing and piloting the study are as follows. First, only a small number of decision tasks could be presented in order to minimize post-decision recall problems (the maximum number possible before recall problems become significant should be identified in a pilot study). Second, the method of stimulated recall (Lyle, 2003), as described later, could be used. Finally, the ideal procedure recommended earlier could be relaxed and verbal reports elicited after each decision at least for some subgroup of those investigated. Although problematic, there may be circumstances where the data would be useful, for example in exploratory or applied research, or where key dependent variables could be derived from post-decision reports. In such cases the risk of justification bias should be acknowledged.

Stimulated recall procedures involve re-presenting decision tasks to participants after they have made their decisions as an aide memoire for their retrospective reports. For "static" decisions, in which complete information is presented and decisions require a simple act of choice, the procedure is straightforward: Each decision task is re-presented, participants are reminded of their choice, and the post-decision report is elicited. On the other hand, decision tasks may be sequential or dynamic, or may otherwise involve more than one step. For example, a number of alternatives may be explicitly eliminated in a screening phase prior to a final decision, or items of information may be gathered sequentially in an information search monitoring study. In such cases the participant would be reminded of her or his action and its outcome at each step, in a kind of "action replay" procedure, and retrospective reports elicited at each point. If a computer trace, video recording, or a visual scan or Mouselab path of a person's decision process is available it can be used in a replay session. Sometimes preparing action replays for complex tasks may take some time and effort, and there may be a delay between the initial decision and post-decision report phases of the study. In such cases the researchers' challenge is to minimize such delays.

Two Types of Information From Post-Decision Verbal Reports

It is useful at this point to distinguish two broad categories of information that can be elicited from post-decision verbal reports: 1) retrospective information concerning pre-decision experiences, as discussed earlier; and 2) current post-decision information. The latter is that concerning current thoughts and feelings about the decision just made, and the chosen and non-chosen alternatives. Such reports can be very important for process tracing studies because they provide evidence of the mental representation of the decision task immediately following the moment of decision. They cannot be described as being "concurrent" with pre-decision processes at this point, since the primary decision task has already been completed. Examples of theories for which current post-decision information has been particularly useful include coherence theories of decision making, e.g., Differentiation and Consolidation theory (Svenson, 2003), Constraint Satisfaction theory (Holyoak & Simon, 1999), and those specifying roles of anticipated emotions, such as, anticipated regret theory (Zeelenberg & Pieters, 2007).

As described later, the instructions for eliciting post-decision reports can vary depending on whether retrospective or current information is most relevant for the research questions under investigation.

Specific Instructions

"How" and "Why" Questions

As for concurrent reports, post-decision verbal reports can be free, semi-structured, or structured. For all types of decision problems, a simple prompt for a free or unstructured response can elicit valuable information. For example, Williamson et al. (2000) recommend a simple instruction such as: "*Could you tell me how you came to choose A?*" For a series of decision tasks, such requests could be made for each task using the stimulated recall procedure. An alternative simple instruction to this can also be useful: "*Could you explain why you chose A?*" This can be regarded as a semi-structured instruction since it probes for a particular type of information, reasons for a decision. In practice the responses to either instruction may be rather similar, since many decision problems are approached as a search for a good reason for choosing one course of action or another (Montgomery, 1983; Shafir et al., 1993). However, they can elicit different information, and the choice of instruction depends on the researcher's goals. The "how" instruction is intended to focus participants on retrospective information such as the decision process they went through, the decision rule or strategy, or changes in representation they may have been aware of as they made their choice, whereas the "why" instruction is intended to focus participants on information relevant to their motives and reasons for a decision. Reasons given for choice often reveal key aspects of such representations such as evaluations of chosen and non-chosen alternatives. Note that asking for reasons post-decision cannot be reactive if the procedural recommendations made earlier are followed. Nevertheless, the risks of omission and other threats to validity remain, and must be carefully considered.

Other Semi-Structured and Structured Instructions

Eliciting structured retrospective responses can avoid the variability that inevitably accompanies free response data and can be more efficient with respect to obtaining information crucial for testing specific predictions of process theories. Some examples of retrospective structured and semi-structured responses that have been used include: ratings of the diagnostic value of information in medical diagnosis studies (Kostopoulou, Devereaux-Walsh, & Delaney, 2009); ratings of the importance of an attribute in multiattribute decision tasks (Salo & Svenson, 2001; Svenson, 2003); and evaluations of aspects on specific attributes (Svenson, 1983).

Stimulated Recall Procedures for Complex Tasks

Two examples illustrate the value of stimulated recall procedures in relatively complex decision and judgment tasks: Australian researchers have pioneered the use of video-cued recall in dynamic decision making (Omodei, Wearing, & McLennan, 1997); and Kostopoulou and colleagues (2009) have used stimulated recall to obtain evidence of how general practitioners interpreted information elicited in a diagnostic reasoning simulation.

McLennon, Pavlou, and Omodei (2005) investigated the cognitive control processes of commanders engaged in fire fighter training simulations involving four, three-person fire crews. Trainees taking the role of fire ground commanders (FGCs) were fitted with head-mounted cameras that video and audio recorded events from the FGC's viewpoint. Afterwards they participated in a video-cued debriefing session preceded by the following instructions:

> We are going to watch a replay of footage of the exercise taken from the helmet camera. As you watch, I want you to take yourself back to being in the role of the FGC. I want you to recall as much as you can of what was going on in your mind when you were managing the incident. I want you to speak these recollections out loud – just begin talking and I will pause the tape so you have plenty of time to recall as much as you can …
>
> *McLennon et al., 2005, pp. 212–213*

When the video playback was about to start, participants were asked: "Now, as you watch this picture of the start of the exercise take yourself back – what do you recall thinking just as the exercise was about to begin?" (McLennon et al., 2005, p. 213). The video tape was started when the participant finished this initial recollection, and he or she continued to think aloud as the video was played. The researcher encouraged participants to recall as much as possible, using non-directive prompts if necessary.

Turning to the second example, Kostopoulou et al. (2009) used stimulated recall to investigate the cognitive processes underlying family physicians' misdiagnosis of celiac disease in a realistic patient scenario. In the first part of the study, physicians were presented with initial information about the patient, and sought further information in the context of the active information search procedure (Chapter 19). After diagnosing the patient, the scenario was re-presented to a sample of those who had misdiagnosed it (but were unaware of this). Using the stimulated recall procedure, the participants' information search was played back to them and their diagnostic reasoning was probed. Specifically, at each step, they were asked why they had elicited the specific item of information (cue). After the cue value was re-presented on the screen, they were asked how they had interpreted it. This enabled researchers to identify components of the reasoning process underlying misdiagnosis, such as whether they failed to consider the correct hypothesis, or whether they under-interpreted critical cues.

In conclusion, stimulated recall procedures provide non-intrusive measures of pre-decision and decision processes. The provision of recordings of what really happened protects from memory distortions of overt decisions and action. However, covert decision processes, such as reasons for a decision, may still be distorted in a participant's memory.

Verbal Data and Decision Process Analysis

Process Components, Sequences, and Descriptions

A useful framework for analyzing verbal reports of decision processes was presented in an early literature review of think-aloud studies (Harte et al., 1994). The authors considered whether the purpose of an analysis was to seek evidence of either a single component (structural or process), a sequence of processes, or a complete description of the process leading to a decision. Component processes are processes that produce a specific change in representation, also called EIPs.[2]

A componential analysis seeks evidence of the presence, absence, or prevalence of specific component processes. A sequential analysis considers, e.g., the relative position of a component process in the sequence of processes, or the sequential order of two types of operation. Specifying the purpose of the analysis is an important decision in designing the coding scheme. Carefully conducted pilot studies should be used to inform this important design decision.

Units of Analysis

Harte at al. (1994) also classified think-aloud studies according to the main unit of analysis adopted, either the whole protocol (e.g., Ranyard & Abdel-Nabi, 1993) or statements within the protocol. The whole protocol is a useful unit of analysis for establishing the presence, absence, or prevalence of a component process or sequence. Alternatively, the division of protocols into statements allows a much more detailed and complex analysis. Then, protocols are divided into statement units each consisting of a group of words characterized by one main idea. In some cases this follows from the design, as in the case of studies using associations and reasons. If in doubt about the delineation of a statement, a smaller group of words in the protocol should be preferred to a larger group. It is good practice to have two independent coders dividing the protocols into statements initially, to make sure that the segmentation rules are clear and reliable.

Coding

Each unit of analysis is usually classified into one of a set of mutually exclusive and exhaustive categories.[3] Sometimes, it is difficult to classify a statement or protocol unit into a category because more than one category seems applicable (e.g., collection of information and/or evaluation of information). In such cases, it is recommended that a hierarchy order is employed, so that when in doubt, the category higher up in the hierarchy is preferred (e.g., collection of information). Increased reliability is gained at the price of a less precise higher level categorization that could have been more precise. This may lead to a systematic bias that should be controlled so that the higher level coding works against the hypothesis tested (e.g., a predicted increase of statements of a category over time). Later, it is always possible to go back and refine the coding of the higher level coding categories. It is recommended to have at least two independent coders, and work towards an acceptable level of coder agreement with inter-coder reliability described by, e.g., Cohen's kappa (Siegel & Castellan, 1988). In reporting the coding scheme, it is helpful if, in addition to defining the categories, protocol extracts illustrating them are presented.

Analysis of Coded Data and Presentation of Results

The analysis of coded data depends on whether the purpose of the study is to seek evidence of process components, sequences, or complete models. A componential analysis usually begins by quantifying the prevalence of components across different decision tasks.[4]

A sequential analysis can be carried out at the statement level and requires that each coded statement's ordinal position in time was recorded; a qualitative description of a sequence can then be presented. A range of quantitative analyses are possible, for example: 1) comparison of statement categories early and late in the protocol, e.g., first half compared to second half (Montgomery & Svenson, 1983); 2) identification of sequences of statements corresponding to "macro" processing units such as structuring plans (Huber, 1989); and 3) comparisons of components at different points in the decision process (Svenson, 1983). In addition, transitional analyses, such as those carried out in information board studies, can be carried out on sequences of statements.

Finally, Harte et al. (1994) describe procedures for constructing complete process models using concurrent verbal protocols using the example of multiattribute choice. Following the classic approach of Newell and Simon (1972) they begin with a task analysis of the decision problem to generate alternative preliminary models that take into account the principles of bounded rationality. For each of these, alternative predictions of complete process sequences that could lead to observed choices are specified, which are tested against elicited protocols coded at the statement unit of analysis. This approach provides a rigorous basis for constructing and testing models based on sequential processing and may be able to handle missing information to a certain extent.

Concluding Remarks

This chapter has described and discussed alternative techniques for using verbal reports of decision processes whose primary function is to provide evidence of decision processes not readily available from other sources. An extensive range of information can be elicited, including: information recalled or constructed; evaluations of information presented; interpretations of information heeded; conscious contents of mental representations such as goals and plans; processes consciously applied such as decision rules; and feelings of specific emotions. However, although potentially of great value, verbal data are open to important criticisms that must be addressed, in particular issues of incompleteness, reactivity, and other threats to validity such as justification bias and the construction of responses by inference. In this chapter we have considered these issues with respect to four main designs for eliciting verbal reports, the combinations of concurrent or post-decision elicitation, and structured or unstructured responses. We have not concluded that one of these designs is necessarily better for a given research question and decision task. Rather, we have sought to elucidate the advantages and disadvantages of each, and to explain different ways that the problems that need to be addressed should be dealt with in practice. It should be stressed that for all designs it is important that the cross-validation of findings from verbal data is obtained where possible. As a minimum, findings from verbal data concerning decision processes should be checked for consistency with decision behavior and cross-validated with other verbal or nonverbal process measures such as information search, physiological or neural correlates, and reaction times (Reisen, Hoffrage, & Mast, 2008). A researcher who is well aware of, and able to control, the methodological problems associated with the collection and analysis of verbal data as covered in the present chapter will be able to make more significant and insightful contributions to the advancement of decision science.

Notes

1 As this inevitably involves an element of deception by omission, ethical considerations require that it is explained to participants at the end of the session that it was necessary to withhold information about post-decision verbal reports in order to avoid justification bias.

Verbal Reports **283**

2 Elementary information processes, EIPs, can include mental operations like reading the distance of a journey into short-term memory, judging which of two journeys is longer, or calculating travel time (Newell & Simon, 1972).
3 For example, a statement can be categorized as an evaluation of an aspect (e.g., this chair has a nice color), or a causal relation (e.g., this color of the chair would lead me to paint it again in another color).
4 To illustrate, Ranyard and Charlton, (2006) showed that knowledge-based statements were more prevalent in football gambles compared to lotteries and tested differences using conventional statistical techniques. A quantitative analysis like this can be enriched by a qualitative analysis exploring the contexts in which decision process components occur.

Recommended Reading List

• Ericsson and Simon (1993): for procedures and analysis of unstructured verbal reports the classic sources referred to earlier are recommended.
• Harte et al. (1994): for procedures and analysis of unstructured verbal reports the classic sources referred to earlier are recommended together with this important paper and others referred to in the chapter.
• Svenson (1989a, 1989b): for procedures and analysis of unstructured verbal reports the classic sources referred to earlier are recommended.

References

Aitken, L. M., Marshall, A., Elliott, R., & McKinley, S. (2011). Comparison of 'think aloud' and observation as data collection methods in the study of decision making regarding sedation in intensive care patients. *International Journal of Nursing Studies*, *48*(3), 318–325.

Anusic, I., Lucas, R. E., & Donnellan, M. B. (2017). The validity of the day reconstruction method in the German socio-economic panel study. *Social Indicators Research*, *130*(1), 213–232.

Backlund, L., Skånér, Y., Montgomery, H., Bring, J., & Strender, L. (2003). Doctors' decision processes in a drug-prescription task: The validity of rating scales and think-aloud reports. *Organizational Behavior and Human Decision Processes*, *91*(1), 108–117.

Bylsma, L. M., Taylor-Clift, A., & Rottenberg, J. (2011). Emotional reactivity to daily events in major and minor depression. *Journal of Abnormal Psychology*, *120*(1), 155–167.

Csikszentmihalyi, M., & Larson, R. (2014). Validity and reliability of the experience-sampling method. In M. Csikszentmihalyi, & R. Larson (Eds.), *Flow and the foundations of positive psychology* (pp. 35–54). New York, NY: Springer.

Ericsson, K. A., & Simon, H. A. (1980). Verbal reports as data. *Psychological Review*, *87*(3), 215–251.

Ericsson, K. A., & Simon, H. A. (1993). *Protocol analysis: Verbal reports as data* (2nd ed.). London, UK: MIT Press.

Festinger, L. (1957). *A theory of cognitive dissonance*. Stanford, CA: Stanford University Press.

Fox, M. C., Ericsson, K. A., & Best, R. (2011). Do procedures for verbal reporting of thinking have to be reactive? A meta-analysis and recommendations for best reporting methods. *Psychological Bulletin*, *137*(2), 316–344.

Harte, J. M., Westenberg, M. R. M., & van Someren, M. (1994). Process models of decision making. *Acta Psychologica*, *87*(2–3), 95–120.

Holyoak, K. J., & Simon, D. (1999). Bidirectional reasoning in decision making by constraint satisfaction. *Journal of Experimental Psychology: General*, *128*(1), 3–31.

Huber, O. (1989). Information-processing operators in decision making. In H. Montgomery, & O. Svenson (Eds.), *Process and structure in human decision making* (pp. 3–21). Chichester, UK: Wiley.

Janis, I. L., & Mann, L. (1977). *Decision making: A psychological analysis of conflict, choice, and commitment*. New York, NY: Free Press.

Kahneman, D., Krueger, A. B., Schkade, D. A., Schwarz, N., & Stone, A. A. (2004). A survey method for characterizing daily life experience: The day reconstruction method. *Science*, *306*(5702), 1776–1780.

Kostopoulou, O., Devereaux-Walsh, C., & Delaney, B. C. (2009). Missing celiac disease in family medicine: The importance of hypothesis generation. *Medical Decision Making, 29*(3), 282–290.

Krueger, A. B., & Schkade, D. A. (2008). The reliability of subjective well-being measures. *Journal of Public Economics, 92*(8), 1833–1845.

Kuusela, H., & Paul, P. (2000). A comparison of concurrent and retrospective verbal protocol analysis. *The American Journal of Psychology, 113*(3), 387–404.

Larson, R., & Csikszentmihalyi, M. (1983). The experience sampling method. *New Directions for Methodology of Social and Behavioral Science, 15*, 41–56.

Lerner, J. S., & Tetlock, P. E. (1999). Accounting for the effects of accountability. *Psychological Bulletin, 125*(2), 255–275.

Lundgrén-Laine, H., & Salanterä, S. (2010). Think-aloud technique and protocol analysis in clinical decision-making research. *Qualitative Health Research, 20*(4), 565–575.

Lyle, J. (2003). Stimulated recall: A report on its use in naturalistic research. *British Educational Research Journal, 29*(6), 861–878.

McClure, S. M., Laibson, D. I., Loewenstein, G., & Cohen, J. D. (2004). Separate neural systems value immediate and delayed monetary rewards. *Science, 306*(5695), 503–507.

McLennon, J., Pavlou, O., & Omodei, M. M. (2005). Cognitive control processes discriminate between better versus poorer performance by fire ground commanders. In H. Montgomery, R. Lipshitz, & B. Brehmer (Eds.) *How professionals make decisions* (pp. 209–222). Mahwah, NJ: Erlbaum.

Montgomery, H. (1983). Decision rules and the search for a dominance structure: Towards a process model of decision-making. In P. C. Humphreys, O. Svenson, & A. Vari (Eds.), *Analyzing and aiding decision processes* (pp. 343–369). Amsterdam, NL: North-Holland.

Montgomery, H., & Svenson, O. (1976). On decision rules and information processing strategies for choices among multiattribute alternatives. *Scandinavian Journal of Psychology, 17*(4), 283–291.

Montgomery, H., & Svenson, O. (1983). A think aloud study of dominance structuring in decision processes. In R. Tietz (Ed.), *Aspiration levels in bargaining and economic decision making* (pp. 166–183). Berlin: Springer.

Newell, A., & Simon, H. A. (1972). Human problem solving (Vol. 104, No. 9). Englewood Cliffs, NJ: Prentice-Hall.

Nisbett, R. E., & Wilson, T. D. (1977). Telling more than we can know: Verbal reports on mental processes. *Psychological Review, 84*(3), 231–259.

Omodei, M. M., Wearing, A. J., & McLennan, J. (1997). Head-mounted video recording: A methodology for studying naturalistic decision making. In R. Flin, M. Strub, E. Salas, & L. Martin (Eds.), *Decision making under stress: Emerging themes and applications* (pp. 137–146). Aldershot, UK: Ashgate.

Payne, J. W., Bettman, J. R., & Johnson, E. J. (1992). Behavioral decision research: A constructive processing perspective. *Annual Review of Psychology, 43*(1), 87–131.

Payne, J. W., Braunstein, M. L., & Carroll, J. S. (1978). Exploring predecisional behavior: An alternative approach to decision research. *Organizational Behavior and Human Performance, 22*(1), 17–44.

Pennington, N., & Hastie, R. (1992). Explaining the evidence: Tests of the story model for juror decision making. *Journal of Personality and Social Psychology, 62*(2), 189–206.

Ranyard, R., & Abdel-Nabi, D. (1993). Mental accounting and the process of multiattribute choice. *Acta Psychologica, 84*(2), 161–177.

Ranyard, R., & Charlton, J. (2006). Cognitive processes underlying lottery and sports gambling decisions: The role of stated probabilities and background knowledge. *European Journal of Cognitive Psychology, 18*(2), 234–254.

Reisen, N., Hoffrage, U., & Mast, F. W. (2008). Identifying decision strategies in a consumer choice situation. *Judgment and Decision Making, 3*(8), 641–658.

Russo, J. E., Johnson, E. J., & Stephens, D. L. (1986). The validity of verbal protocols (Unpublished manuscript).

Russo, J. E., Johnson, E. J., & Stephens, D. L. (1989). The validity of verbal protocols. *Memory & Cognition, 17*(6), 759–769.

Russo, J. E., Medvec, V. H., & Meloy, M. G. (1996). The distortion of information during decisions. *Organizational Behavior and Human Decision Processes, 66*(1), 102–110.

Russo, J. E., Meloy, M. G., & Wilks, T. J. (2000). Predecisional distortion of information by auditors and salespersons. *Management Science, 46*(1), 13–27.

Salo, I., & Svenson, O. (2001). Constructive psychological processes before and after a real-life decision. In C. M. Allwood, & M. Selart (Eds.), *Decision making: Social and creative dimensions* (pp. 137–151). Dordrecht, NL: Kluwer.

Schooler, J. W. (2011). Introspecting in the spirit of William James: Comment on Fox, Ericsson, and Best (2011). *Psychological Bulletin, 137*(2), 345–350.

Shafir, E., Simonson, I., & Tversky, A. (1993). Reason-based choice. Cognition, *49*(1–2), 11–36.

Siegel, S., & Castellan Jr, N. J. (1988). Nonparametric statistics for the behavioral sciences. Nonparametri~ Statistics for the Behavioral Sciences (pp. 190–222). New York: McGraw-Hill.

Simon, D., Krawczyk, D. C, Bleicher, A., & Holyoak, K. J. (2008). The transience of constructed preferences. *Journal of Behavioral Decision Making, 21*(1), 1–14.

Slovic, P., Flynn, J. H., & Layman, M. (1991). Perceived risk, trust, and the politics of nuclear waste. *Science, 254*(5038), 1603–1607.

Svenson, O. (1974). A note on think aloud protocols obtained during the choice of a home. *Reports from the Psychological Laboratory, University of Stockholm, No. 421.*

Svenson, O. (1979). Process descriptions of decision-making. *Organizational Behavior and Human Performance, 23*(1), 86–112.

Svenson, O. (1983). Scaling evaluative statements in verbal protocols from decision processes. In P. Humphreys, O. Svenson, & A. Vári, (Eds.), *Analyzing and aiding decision processes* (pp. 371–382). Amsterdam, NL: North-Holland.

Svenson, O. (1989a). Eliciting and analyzing verbal protocols in process studies of judgment and decision making. In H. Montgomery, & O. Svenson (Eds.), *Process and structure in human decision making* (pp. 65–81). Chichester, UK: Wiley.

Svenson, O. (1989b). Illustrating verbal protocol analysis: Individual decision processes and dialogues preceding a joint decision. In H. Montgomery, & O. Svenson (Eds.), *Process and structure in human decision making* (pp. 83–98). Chichester, UK: Wiley.

Svenson, O. (1996). Decision-making and the search for psychological regularities: What can be learned from a process perspective? *Organizational Behavior and Human Decision Processes, 65*(3), 252–267.

Svenson, O. (2003). Values, affect and processes in human decision making: A Differentiation and Consolidation Theory Perspective. In S. L. Schneider, & J. Shanteau (Eds.), *Emerging perspectives on judgment and decision making* (pp. 287–326). Cambridge, UK: Cambridge University Press.

Svenson, O., & Jakobsson, M. (2010). Creating coherence in real-life decision processes: Reasons, differentiation and consolidation. *Scandinavian Journal of Psychology, 51*(2), 93–102.

Svenson, O., & Slovic, P. (2002). *Can word associations and affect be used as indicators of differentiation and consolidation in decision making?* Report N0. 02–04 Eugene, OR: Decision Research www.decisionresearch.org

Walsh, M. M., & Gluck, K. A. (2016). Verbalization of decision strategies in multiple-cue probabilistic inference. *Journal of Behavioral Decision Making, 29*(1), 78–91.

Weber, E. U., & Johnson, E. J. (2009). Mindful judgment and decision making. *Annual Review of Psychology, 60*(1), 53–85.

Williamson, J., Ranyard, R., & Cuthbert, L. (2000). Conversation-based process tracing methods for the study of naturalistic decisions: An evaluation study. *British Journal of Psychology, 91*(2), 203–221.

Zeelenberg, M., & Pieters, R. (2007). A theory of regret regulation 1.0. *Journal of Consumer Psychology, 17*(1), 3–18.

18

THINKING ALOUD DURING SUPERIOR PERFORMANCE ON TASKS INVOLVING DECISION MAKING[1]

K. Anders Ericsson and Jerad H. Moxley

Any time someone makes an important decision, such as taking another job, buying an expensive boat, or beginning to train for a marathon, they engage in decision making. Even going to a restaurant requires a person to make an order, which involves a decision among the available alternatives unless the decision is made implicitly because they always order the same dish in that particular restaurant. If we ask someone why they chose their dinner order, they can give many reasons, such as that they like this dish, that they find that it is the best value among the alternatives. How can we assess the validity of such verbal reports?

Over 30 years ago Nisbett and Wilson (1977) showed that the reasons given by participants in many experiments did not reflect each person's thought processes. Nisbett and Wilson (1977) presented convincing evidence that when participants are asked why they made certain judgments or actions they often infer the reason from their actions rather than retrieve any memories of their actual thought processes. In fact, the participants report the same reasons as those given by an observer who is asked to guess the reason for the participants' action. This paper led Simon and the first author of this chapter to explore under what conditions participants generated valid reports of thoughts that mediated their production of actions. In their paper on "Verbal reports as data" they found that concurrent direct verbalization of thoughts (without descriptions and explanations) during the generation of the actions in the context of a well-defined task provided the best evidence on their participants' thought processes (Ericsson & Simon, 1980). In contrast, they found that explanations and verbal comments generated after the completed action become increasingly prone to errors of recall, inferences, and reconstructions. When participants are able to verbalize thoughts as they generate their responses without changing the accuracy of their final responses, Ericsson and Simon (1980, 1993) proposed that one could analyze the verbalized thoughts as stepping stones towards the generation of the final response. It is possible to conduct a task analysis of decision-making tasks and specify many possible series of calculations and judgments that would lead to selecting the correct answer. These sequences can then be compared to a sequence of verbalized thoughts recorded from participants' thinking-aloud protocols.

In this chapter we describe a general rigorous methodology for collecting, transcribing, and encoding verbalizations of thoughts as reliable and valid data (see also Chapter 17). This methodology has been developed over the last several decades and differs fundamentally from a wide range of verbal descriptions and introspections regarding people's decision-making and judgment processes. In a brief review we discuss the methodological problems of collecting and analyzing verbal reports in the more recent history of psychology and how many of these problems are addressed by our methodological approach. In particular we show how our recommended approach minimizes (eliminates significant) reactive effects of verbalization on performance. Our approach relies on a theoretical model which specifies the hypothesized relation between the cognitive processes and the verbalizations associated with the thoughts mediating the superior performance. From that model we derive practical recommendations for how to instruct participants and how to remind them to keep verbalizing without reactive effects on the thought processes.

A Brief Introduction to Methodological Problems with Verbal Reports on Thinking

The emergence of psychology in the 19th century was motivated as an empirical method to study philosophical questions and issues and naturally focused on introspective analyses of thinking and memory (Boring, 1929). Introspective reports were severely criticized as unscientific in the beginning of the 20th century (Watson, 1913). In response experimental psychologists developed standardized tasks, such as problem solving and recall of presented lists, where successful performance on the task assured the participants' engagement in predictable types of cognitive processes. The fact that only observable behavior could be collected as data led researchers to move away from complex mental processes, such as thinking.

In the 1950s and 1960s the cognitive revolution renewed interest in higher-level cognitive processes. Investigators began to study how mediating thought processes could explain such psychological activities as problem solving and could be used to form theories based upon strategies, concepts, and rules (Miller, Galanter, & Pribram, 1960). Information processing theories (Newell & Simon, 1972) attempted to build computational models of behavior by programming computers to replicate the procedures traced by observation of human participants' behavior during problem solving and their reported thoughts during and after the task.

Almost immediately some investigators raised concerns about the validity of the information derived from verbal protocols (for a review, see Ericsson & Simon, 1993). A particularly important development for establishing the validity for some types of verbal reports emerged when researchers assessed the validity and reactivity of elicited verbalized thoughts and explanations by an analysis of objective task performance. For example, evidence was produced that having a participant explain why they made each move on the tower of Hanoi improved subsequent performance compared to a silent control condition (Gagné & Smith, 1962). If these instructions changed the performance then by inference the cognitive processes in the verbalizing condition must differ from the cognitive processes in the silent control condition. Consequently, insights from the verbalizing condition could not be generalized to explain cognitive processes in the silent condition.

Towards Valid and Non-Reactive Verbal Reports of Thinking

A convincing account of how participants can, under some circumstances, give valid and non-reactive verbal reports requires at least two parts. First, a theoretical account is needed that outlines how participants can generate overt verbalizations of thoughts without changing the content and structure of cognitive processes. Second, suitable tasks need to be identified where performance can be repeatedly reproduced to allow a comparison of performance during verbalization of thinking to the performance in a silent (control) condition.

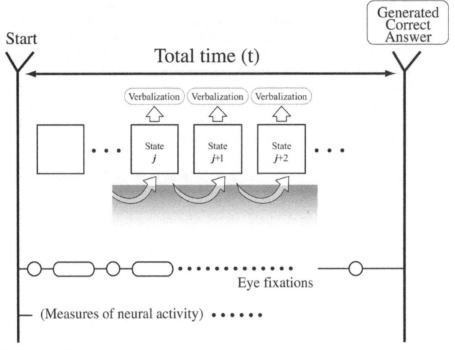

FIGURE 18.1 An illustration of the time interval between the presentation of a task and the generation of a given participant's response. Within that time interval a covert sequence of thoughts (center) generated in response to a presented task concurrently with other types of observable nonverbal indicators of cognitive processes. (From Ericsson, 2003, Figure 2, copyright Imprint Academic).

A Theoretical Framework for Minimally Reactive Verbalization of Thoughts

In laboratory studies of thinking, participants are first given instructions about the type of tasks studied in the experiment. The participants are then presented with a specific task and work on this task until the answer or response is overtly generated (right side of Figure 18.1). The famous behaviorist, John Watson (1920), was the first to publish a study where he had a friend "think aloud" while solving a problem. Watson theorized a person's thoughts were accompanied by a sequence of covert bursts of "inner speech" (see sequence of states between beginning and end of trial in Figure 18.1) and these covert verbalizations could be given overt expression by vocalizing them aloud without any need for intermediate "observation" or introspection. Ericsson and Simon (1993) similarly have argued that concurrent verbalizations of thoughts during the completion of a task provide the closest and most reliable connection to actual thinking (see Figure 18.1). In the Ericsson and Simon framework, just as for Watson, thinking aloud is merely overtly verbalizing inner speech that would have otherwise remained inaudible. An example can be seen for a participant who was asked to multiply 36★24 in his head on two test-occasions one week apart giving the following concurrent verbal report:

> OK, 36 times 24, um, 4 times 6 is 24, 4, carry the 2, 4 times 3 is 12, 14, 144, 0, 2 times 6 is 12, 2, carry the 1, 2 times 3 is 6, 7, 720, 720, 144 plus 720, so it would be 4, 6, 864.
>
> 36 times 24, 4, carry the – no wait, 4, carry the 2, 14, 144, 0, 36 times 2 is, 12, 6, 72, 720 plus 144, 4, uh, uh, 6, 8, uh, 864

These two examples do not include any introspective analysis but instead verbally expressed and referenced products such as "carry the 1", "36", and "144 plus 720". The participant is never asked to stand outside the problem-solving process and explain it, but just to solve the problem and say out loud the thoughts that have entered conscious awareness while they generate the solution.

The Requirement for Performance-Based Tasks

Cognitive researchers have attempted to develop tasks that would require a specific thought process to arrive at the correct answer. For instance, it would be improbable to consistently guess the answer to a math problem like "258+893=?", and only a skilled mental calculator could possibly have memorized the correct answer allowing them to directly access it from memory. Because many tasks require specific knowledge for their solution, researchers can conduct task analyses where they can *a priori* identify various procedures people could possibly have used given their prior knowledge and skills. This task analysis provides a theoretical analysis of possible thought sequences for the successful task performance, where the application of alternative procedures is associated with different sequences of thoughts (intermediate steps).

Multiplying two 2-digit numbers "in one's head" provides a good illustration. Most people can directly access some basic mathematical knowledge such as the standard times table and then can supplement that with the "paper and pencil" method taught in school. Therefore, when solving a problem such as 36★24 they will usually first solve 4★36 and then 20★36 and add the products to solve the problem. However, someone with more advanced math knowledge might recognize that 36★24 equals (30–6)★(30+6) and use the formula (a+b)★(a-b) = a²-b², thus calculating 36★24 as $30^2-6^2 = 900-36 = 864$. Other participants may recognize even more advanced shortcuts, such as 36★24 = (3★12) ★ (2★12) = 6★12^2 = 6★144 = 864. When conducting a task analysis it is possible to generate a relatively small number of solution sequences for each task and their associated correct response. To conduct a task analysis requires that the participant is assigned some task with a description of the type of response that satisfies the criteria for an answer or solution. If a participant is asked to merely think aloud while answering a question, such as "What is one interesting empirical phenomena in psychology?", there is no correct answer. In such cases there is no way for investigators to conduct a task analysis of sequences of thoughts leading to the correct answer because the number of acceptable answers and the processes that generated them cannot be meaningfully constrained. Even more problematic is the fact that there might be no comparable observable behavior or performance that can be observed in both the silent and verbalizing conditions. Without a clear task given to participants in the silent control condition it is not possible to establish a baseline to which performance with verbal reporting instructions can be compared to assess significant evidence of reactivity.

Verbalization of Cognitive Processes that Mediate Successful Task Performance

When participants generate their answers to tasks under normal silent conditions their sequence of thoughts generated during the performance of a task is not directly observable. However, some aspects of their performance are associated with observable indicators. The total time required to generate an answer (response latency) can be viewed as the difference between the time at presentation and the time of generating the response. By comparing the verbalized thoughts against sequences of intermediate steps generated in the task analysis we can infer which method best fits the observed latencies. Similarly, task analysis permits the generation of hypotheses for patterns of eye movements required by certain cognitive strategies which we can test against actual data collected with eye-tracking technology (see Chapters 1–2 and 4). Performance in silent and verbal conditions can be compared using either of these methods to validate that the same process is occurring in both conditions and that the process is one that is possible based on a task analysis.

In a very similar manner it is possible to externalize thoughts by having participants "think aloud" and thus give verbal expression to their thoughts as they enter. Other methods (Chapter 17) include having the participant give a retrospective report of their thoughts immediately after completion of a task, or give a general description of her strategies throughout many tasks during a session. All these alternative methods to thinking aloud to some degree have the problems of introspection because they require an extra cognitive process not generated from the natural performance of the task.

If the thought sequence is unchanged by verbalization then there should be no change in performance between a think-aloud group and a silent control group. In a meta-analysis of more than 3500 participants across more than 70 studies with objective task performance, Fox, Ericsson, and Best (2011) compared across these conditions and showed that the effect size on accuracy of performance from "think aloud" is indistinguishable from zero. These findings of non-reactivity are consistent with the facts that participants can give overt expression to their covert speech easily, such as the regulatory private speech during childhood (Diaz & Berk, 1992) as well as spontaneous overt vocalization of inner speech by adults in noisy environments (Ericsson & Simon, 1993). However, Fox et al. (2011) found some evidence that thinking aloud could slow down participants, presumably due to extra time needed to overtly state their thoughts.

The Ericsson and Simon theoretical framework can also explain why other forms of verbalization do change performance. Fox et al. (2011) found that when participants were asked to concurrently explain their performance this type of instruction changed the accuracy of performance. If participants are forced to explain their actions they cannot simply focus primarily on completing the task and verbalize only the thoughts as they pass through attention while generating the answer or solution. With explanation instructions they must initiate goals, such as generating explanations, which changes their thought processes and leads to the generation of additional thoughts. These additional steps change the mediating thoughts and hence when the participant attempts to resume the task their sequence of thoughts will be different and as a consequence so will their performance on the task.

In conclusion, with proper instructions (see Ericsson & Simon, 1993 for detailed instructions as well as warm-up tasks recommended for laboratory research) participants can think aloud without systematic change to their sequence of thoughts.

Reproducibility of Performance, and Associated Process Data

When participants are given instructions to think aloud for a task they often want to explore different ways to perform it. To eliminate this variability for the first few trials experimenters provide opportunities for "warm-up" and familiarization with the task before they collect the experimental data on performance (Ericsson & Oliver, 1988). Under these constrained performance conditions, participants are assumed to find the maximal stable performance. Similarly, under these maximal performance conditions devious participants should not be able to generate false verbal reports consistent with one cognitive strategy while using another at the same time. As with any method of data collection, there will never be perfect test-retest reliability for think-aloud protocols even with the same participant completing the same task at a later time (Ericsson & Simon, 1993). This is due in large part to lack of verbalization of all attended thoughts. However, there are often many different methods for obtaining the correct answer, especially for non-routine problems. In this regard verbal reports will reflect variability from trial to trial in the same way that eye-movement (see Chapters 1–2 and 4) or latency data (see Chapter 12) show variability when the same participants complete the same problems on different test-occasions.

Using Concurrent Verbal Reports to Identify Mediating Cognitive Mechanisms

It is possible to infer hypothesized mechanisms mediating thinking and superior performance based on the recorded verbalizations of thoughts (Ericsson & Simon, 1993). In particular, experts with reproducibly superior performance offer unique opportunities to study the mental representations for individual participants that support complex skill. It is then possible to design experimental tests that are capable of distinguishing theoretical alternative hypotheses from the cognitive mechanisms inferred from experts as they think aloud. For instance, Chase and Ericsson (1981, 1982) designed several experiments where the collected verbal reports after each trial were analyzed to identify the encoding strategies used to memorize groups of digits in the digit span task. Based on these, Chase and Ericsson (1981) altered the task in a manner that was predicted to disrupt use of the identified encoding mechanisms and thus cause decrements in performance.

Other Types of Verbal Reports of Thinking and Cognition that might be Reactive

The main goal for Simon and the first author (Ericsson & Simon, 1980, 1993) was to identify the optimal conditions and to develop a verbal-report procedure that would elicit valid and verifiable verbalizations of thinking. It is, however, possible to use this model to examine other types of verbal reporting procedures that deviate from the recommended procedures for eliciting non-reactive concurrent reports.

When retrospective verbal reports are given immediately after the completion of a task the content of these reports should closely relate to "think-aloud" verbalizations. When the latency to generate the response is brief (1–5 sec), it is likely that the participant can recall their sequence of thoughts reasonably accurately. In a review, Ericsson and Simon (1993) showed that when participants are asked merely to recall their thoughts, the reported information is consistent with other observations of the same processes, such as latencies. This method is particularly useful in real-time environments with high time pressure, such as sports. In sport situations, where delays of responses by a dozen milliseconds could disrupt the success of motor responses, the delay induced by concurrently generating verbal reports can be disruptive and retrospective reports are the best available option.

However, most other methods of collecting verbal reports require participants to go beyond immediate recall of previously generated thoughts. Ericsson and Simon (1980, 1993) demonstrated that two such methods give reactive reports. The first is to ask the participant to give more information than their thought process can provide by asking "why" the participant acted as they did (see Chapter 22). Sometimes the participant can recall, but other times they must go beyond retrieval of a memory. Often the participants will not know what caused some thoughts to come to mind and hence will feel the need to speculate. Many factors that influence speed of access to information, such as priming, do not have corresponding processes that leave intermediate thoughts and thus do not leave reportable processes in conscious memory (Ericsson & Kintsch, 1995). This is likely why explanations of behavior by the participant is sometimes no different than that given by an observer (Nisbett & Wilson, 1977). Requiring a participant to explain their decisions or actions has been found to lead to significant changes in the accuracy of performance (Fox et al., 2011). When participants anticipate having to give such an explanation their processes are likely to change, which in turn changes the accuracy of performance.

A second questionable method for collecting verbal reports involves asking participants about their problem-solving methods after performance of a long series of tasks (Ericsson & Simon, 1993). Only the participants using the same strategy across the whole experiment would be able to recall thought sequences consistent with their average behavior by recalling their thoughts for a single recent trial. In most cases participants learn how to perform better during the experiment and thus change their strategies. Under these circumstances no single strategy could accurately describe their cognitive processes. It is therefore not surprising that typical participants' descriptions are imperfectly related to their average performance during the entire experiment.

Studies of Verbal Reports on Decision Making

Research on decision making during the first half of the 20th century was led by economists using formal mathematical analyses of human decision making that were based on subjective representations of probability and utility (Edwards, 1953). However, Simon (1955) argued that even if human decision making could be described by mathematical models, the complex mathematical calculations in these models did not describe the cognitive processes of humans making decisions. A completely different approach was needed, where investigators tried to describe the sequence of verbalized thoughts that humans reported mediated their decision making. Just as information processing models of cognition (Newell & Simon, 1972) simulated human problem solving within the limits of human memory and processing capacities, pioneering decision-making researchers followed suit. Consequently, researchers developed tasks, such as selecting an apartment to rent, where all dimensions were perceptually available with their attributes, such as rent, noise level, distance to shopping, and distance to public transportation. These tasks relieved participants from having to look up apartments in newspapers, from contacting the landlords for information about each relevant attribute, and visiting each apartment to discover important attributes, such as nearness to parks and noise levels. When the pioneering researchers (cf. Montgomery & Svenson, 1976; Payne, 1976) had participants think aloud while making these decisions they found that difficulties with these types of tasks involved the integration of information about each choice option in order to find the alternative with the highest overall appeal. More specifically, as shown by their verbal reports, participants in these tasks had problems comparing unfamiliar alternatives with many aspects within the constraints of the limited capacity of their short-term memory. These studies uncovered decision-making strategies where participants first reduced the number of alternatives by rejecting alternatives based on unacceptable values on one or more significant dimensions, such as expense. Only after the set of alternatives had been reduced to a couple of alternatives would participants engage in trade-offs, such as willingness to pay a little more for a better location.

Verbal Protocols in Everyday Activities

Verbal protocols have also lent support to the use of heuristics in everyday situations. For example, think-aloud protocols collected from recently diagnosed cancer patients showed that people access the information that comes most easily to mind (the availability heuristic) by focusing on salient information such as what friends or family had done in similar situations and how that had turned out (Steginga, Occhipinti, Gardiner, Yaxley, & Heathcote, 2002). Furthermore, when midwives were asked to diagnose two simulated cases of birth complications while thinking aloud, they recalled similar cases from memory (representativeness heuristic) and reported thoughts consistent with the use of other heuristics (Cioffi & Markham, 1997). Think-aloud protocols have been shown to give more information on the types of decisions nurses make when evaluating if sedation is needed than can be given by observation alone (Aitken, Marshall, Elliot, & McKinley, 2011). Recently a think-aloud study showed a tight link between the family physician's initial impression of a patient's problems and their final diagnoses in cases designed to merit referral to an appropriate specialist (Kostopoulou, Sirota, Round, Samaranayaka, & Delaney, 2017).

It may be important to note that of these studies only Cioffi and Markham (1997) used cases with known best decisions but unfortunately suffered from a ceiling effect because all participants correctly diagnosed all cases. We believe that unless decision outcomes can be measured objectively it is not possible to compare decision-making performance while giving "think-aloud" protocols to decision making under silent control conditions. Without the ability to assess generalizable performance and potential reactivity, protocol studies become susceptible to the methodological problems of introspection such as an inability to scientifically resolve conflicting results as we discussed earlier. In order to avoid the classic issue of need for trusting the participants' reported preferences, attitudes, and reasons, we think it is necessary to study phenomena defined by objective task performance. Verbal protocols can still be collected with any type of decision-making behavior and will always offer suggestions for relevant concepts and processes, but if these ideas and supporting evidence ever become contested by other scientists then we don't know of any current experimental methods that are capable of demonstrating their validity and generalizability to decision making under silent control conditions.

Accuracy of Experts' Decisions and Judgments

It is a common assumption that experts (identified by extended experience or peer nomination) will make superior decisions, but there is a large body of evidence that has examined the accuracy of decisions made by experts challenging this belief (Camerer & Johnson, 1991; Ericsson & Lehmann, 1996). In many types of domains experts, as defined by longer professional experience and social nominations by their peers, do not make significantly more accurate decisions and forecasts than less experienced individuals or, even in some instances, chance alone. For instance, research on violent offenders has shown that expert clinicians are barely above chance in identifying male re-offenders and are at chance in identifying female re-offenders (Swets, Dawes, & Monahan, 2000). In domains with collections of objective outcomes of past decisions it is possible to compare experts' forecasts and decisions to those generated by mechanical statistical models. The statistical models have generally been shown to produce superior decisions (Dawes, Faust, & Meehl, 1989). While a meta-analysis shows that clinicians with any experience diagnose better than those with none there is no significant benefit of additional experience (Miller, Spengler, & Spengler, 2015). Other analyses of performance in medicine show that professional experience is not associated with superior performance (Choudhry, Fletcher, & Soumerai, 2005). In fact, in many cases performance for experienced physicians gets worse from the time they complete medical training. More generally, knowledge and experience alone are typically poor predictors of decision-making performance once an initial learning period has been completed (Ericsson, 2006b; Ericsson & Lehmann, 1996).

Considerations in Using Protocol Analysis to Study Decision-Making Processes

Protocol analysis is a very time and resource demanding methodology. Ericsson and Simon (1993) recommended that it be used to understand stable phenomena involving human performance. This methodology can be used to study other psychological activities, such as day-dreaming, food preferences, and personal judgments, however it is not possible to evaluate the accuracy of responses in these domains based on objective methods. Even for tasks with performance measures it will be essential to find participants who perform well above the chance level. Unless the accuracy of decision making is significantly better than chance it is not possible to discover the mechanisms that mediate that superior performance. The discovery of superior decision-making mechanisms might allow us to train and measure the development of decision making (Ericsson, 2005). It is also possible that we might identify characteristics that are correlated with development of superior decision making that will be useful for selection of individuals for costly extended training, such as fighter pilots and surgeons. The central challenge for any approach seeking to develop expert performance in judgment and decision making involves identifying individuals who display reproducibly superior decision-making performance for representative tasks in their domain.

Nursing over the past few decades has demonstrated the wisdom of these standards. Benner's theory of nursing expertise (Benner & Tanner, 1987) proposed that expert nurses relied mainly on intuitive judgments developed through extended experience in their work environment. Verbal protocols on experienced nurses performing representative tasks, where all participants solved all tasks, also lent support to these assumptions (Cioffi & Markham, 1997; Forsberg, Ziegert, Hult, & Fors, 2014). However, a comprehensive review of the literature has shown that experienced nurses, when asked to perform representative tasks, do not consistently perform better then less experienced nurses (Ericsson, Whyte, & Ward, 2007). Unfortunately, this suggests that while Benner and Tanner may well have accurately described the thought processes of experienced nurses compared to less experienced nurses, the differences related to experience have not been shown to improve outcomes of treated patients. In the absence of objective measures of reliably superior performance we are concerned that researchers settle for studying differences as a function of social status and accumulated experience, which may have a weak or absent relations to objectively superior outcomes.

Seeking Out Superior Decision Making among Expert Performers

Our interest in decision making as being the mechanism associated with the selection of superior actions leads us to look for individuals who display superior performance in domains where the essence of expertise involves selecting the correct actions. For example, doctors who diagnose patients in a superior manner (decide on the appropriate diagnosis among plausible alternative diagnoses) will be able to give their patients more appropriate treatments and thus their patients will have increased speed of recovery and less likelihood of re-admittance with the same symptoms. Similarly, a chess master who can beat less skilled chess players is able to select better moves during the chess match.

In order to apply and validate think-aloud protocols it is necessary to develop a series of standardized tasks that capture the generation of superior actions in representative situations from a given domain. Once individuals with superior reproducible performance have been identified the first step of uncovering the associated mechanisms with the expert-performance approach (Ericsson & Smith, 1991; Ericsson & Williams, 2007) is to identify such a collection of tasks and situations. The problem is that two chess games are never the same, and hence the chess players in two different games are unlikely to encounter the same chess position after the 10–15 opening moves have been made. Similarly, two doctors would rarely encounter and independently diagnose the same patients and thus their diagnoses and their accuracies cannot be directly compared. In his pioneering work on expertise de Groot (1978) solved this problem by selecting challenging middle-game positions that he presented to chess players differing in skill. This task is highly prototypical for what chess players do during playing a game of chess, the only difference being the players must familiarize themselves with the structure of an unfamiliar chess position before they can generate an appropriate move.

De Groot (1978) first validated that his search task, with think-aloud verbalizations, captured the superiority of the highly ranked players compared to club players. Based on an analysis of the chess players' think-aloud protocols de Groot (1978) found that all of the chess players first perceived, and then interpreted, the chess position in order to create candidate moves. Promising moves were checked by a forward search of potential moves and countermoves. During this evaluation the world class players generally found the best move, rarely did they start there, while the weaker players could not discover the best move even with the extra time. This demonstrated that the performance of experts is mediated by increasingly complex control processes. While there are situations whereby experts will simply retrieve the correct move (Calderwood, Klein, & Crandall, 1988; Klein, 1998), their move selections can often be improved by planning, reasoning, and evaluation, at least for positions where move selection is challenging for average and weaker chess players.

De Groot's (1978) analysis of think-aloud protocols showed that the grandmasters rapidly perceived the tactical structure of chess positions in manners that weaker players could not. Experts were able to detect weaknesses in their own and their opponent's positions that suggested the course of action and directed their systematic exploration of consequences of longer sequences of moves. In this process of perception and encoding of complex chess relationships only the end product is verbalized, much as we mentioned earlier with mental calculators. Impressively de Groot (1978) supported these conclusions using only three chess positions, demonstrating that the processes that discriminated experts from non-experts could be demonstrated within controlled experimental situations. Subsequent research collecting verbal protocols, starting with Charness (1981), has shown that experts search more moves, and explore consequences of those moves to a deeper level while selecting the best move. A few decades later, Connors, Burns, and Campitelli (2011) summarized the research and also showed that Master players choose better moves, and search faster as measured by how many board states are generated per minute, and again as with the previous studies found a trend for Masters to search deeper.

Chess research using think-aloud protocols has now gone beyond quantifying the search to attempting to measure the value of search. Some theories of skill development have speculated that experts make decisions intuitively and search is mostly a process of confirming that intuition, while weaker players must rely on search to attempt to solve problems they cannot intuitively grasp (Dreyfus & Dreyfus, 1986; Klein, 1998). Research using verbal protocols measured the strength of the first move players mentioned after seeing the position, the first move they searched, and the move they chose (Moxley, Ericsson, Charness, & Krampe, 2012). This research found experts did initially select a stronger move, but with additional search they often found even better moves as did weaker players. This effect was moderated by a significant interaction whereby on relatively easier problems weaker players did gain more from search but the opposite was the case for difficult problems. Recently this result from protocols was confirmed by experimentally manipulating time, finding again that better players gained an immediate advantage on average but also improved their move selection just as much on average as weaker players did with more time (Moxley, 2016).

Again this result was moderated by an interaction whereby weaker players benefited relatively more from extra time on easier problems and stronger players benefited relatively more from extra time on difficult problems.

Similar findings have been observed in other games. St. Germain and Tenenbaum (2011) had poker players of different skill levels (based on their success at poker tournaments) make decisions about how to play a fixed set of poker hands while thinking aloud. The more skilled players performed significantly better on this task than the less skilled. More interestingly, the more skilled players verbalized specific information relevant to each particular hand, whereas the less skilled tended to make more general comments.

The success of the application of protocol analysis methods in chess and other games has been extended to real-world domains, such as medicine, and highly time pressured domains, such as sports. In domains where reproducibly superior performance by experts is shown, think-aloud protocols show similar consistent cognitive mechanisms to those observed in chess. For example, studies of electrocardiogram interpretation (ECG; Simpson & Gilhooly, 1997) and microscopic pathology (Crowley, Naus, Stewart, & Friedman, 2003) have collected verbal protocols that identified rapid encoding of perceptual information leading to a more refined generation of options and alternatives (cf. de Groot's, 1978, similar findings in chess). Other research has minimized the types of perceptual cues experts may rely on and instead has used verbal descriptions of patients' symptoms and problems. These studies show that as a student progresses through medical school their information processing becomes more efficient and is mediated by increasingly higher levels of mental representations which can support more efficient clinical judgments (Boshuizen & Schmidt, 1992; Schmidt & Boshuizen, 1993). Specialists have been shown to be able to make more accurate diagnoses on difficult and complex problems than medical students (Norman, Trott, Brooks, & Smith, 1994). They also give more detailed and supported diagnoses reflecting higher order representations (Patel & Groen, 1991) that they can use to support their clinical reasoning (Ericsson & Kintsch, 1995).

Verbal protocols have also been successful in providing information on mediating cognitive processes even in sports, where collecting them is more challenging due to the various external constraints on the successful performance of their perceptual motor capacities. For example, when expert players in snooker (type of billiards) are instructed to prepare for making a shot for a given designed configuration of pool balls, they verbalize deeper plans and more far-reaching exploration of consequences of their shots than less skilled players (Abernethy, Neal, & Koning, 1994). Athletes at expert levels have given verbal reports about dynamic situations presented as videos in soccer (Ward, Hodges, Williams, & Starkes, 2004) and these reports consistently show that more skilled performers have a more accurate and detailed representation of the particular game situation. Roca, Ford, McRobert, and Williams (2013) went one step further and had soccer players stand in front of a life-size screen and think aloud as recorded game situations were presented on the screen. They found that more skilled players reported more information that was directly related to decisions about what to do next than less skilled players. A recent experiment on golfers showed a clear role for planning and strategic thinking while putting, particularly for long putts, finding most importantly that stronger golfers actually do more of this type of thinking then weaker golfers (Arsal, Eccles, & Ericsson, 2016). These studies demonstrate the robustness and flexibility of the Ericsson and Simon (1993) system of collecting verbal data and the generalizablility of cognitive mechanisms discovered in chess and other domains more easily accessed during the examination of expert performance (Ericsson and Smith, 1991).

There is also an emerging body of evidence coming from studies collecting verbal reports from athletes at different skill levels as they engage in playing matches or in training. Some of the first studies collected verbal reports while baseball players were asked to respond to different defensive situations (French et al., 1996) and another had tennis players record their thoughts about the match during the changes of sides (McPherson & Kernodle, 2007). These studies found that expert-level players used more dynamic and complex representations of the actions and make much more detailed tactical plans then non-experts.

In sum, when it is possible to find large differences in accuracy in decision making between expert performers and less accomplished individuals it is possible to analyze the associated verbal protocols to identify the mental representations that are the primary mechanisms that account for superior selection of actions (decision making). Evidence suggests these representations have a two-fold function (Ericsson, 1996, 2006a, 2006b). First, they provide experts with greater control of relevant aspects of performance, including the ability to anticipate, evaluate, plan, and reason about alternative courses of action. Second, they provide tools for experts to continue improving, or at least maintaining, their high level of performance. An extensive body of research has been developing on how expert performers acquire their complex representations through extended engagement in deliberate practice, but this goes beyond the scope of this chapter and the reader is directed to recent reviews of this work (e.g., Ericsson, 2015).

Conclusion

In the last decades there has been considerable progress made in the rigorous collection and analysis of verbal reports and we have shown how this emerging methodology differs from the early use of introspection at the beginning of the 20th century. In this chapter we have discussed how some of the methods to establish validity of verbally reported information on decision making have been compromised by the types of tasks selected for study. There are certain prerequisites for objective testing and evaluation of reactivity of the generation of verbal reports. The Ericsson and Simon (1980, 1993) framework was developed to describe rigorous collection of verbal reports in a way that minimized threats to validity. They additionally outlined empirical methods for testing if the proposed methods of eliciting verbal reports systematically altered the cognitive processes and the associated task performance compared to silent control conditions.

The problems with the verbal-report research on decision making appears to concern the general difficulty in designing tasks, which capture superior decision-making performance. Until reliable individual differences in objective decision-making performance can be reproduced and studied, we don't believe that the issue of reactivity can be addressed for concurrent and retrospective verbal reports or any other type of process measure, such as reaction time (Chapter 12), eye-movement recordings (Chapters 1–2 and 4) and brain imaging (Chapters 14–16). The tradition of defining correct decisions by asking experienced and highly regarded individuals, such as wine experts, has been shown to be equally flawed. For example, wine experts do not show consistent superiority in describing or identifying characteristics of wine under blind tasting conditions (Ericsson, Prietula, & Cokely, 2007). Unless researchers had insisted on objective measurement many experts' decisions and judgments might still be viewed as better than those of less experienced individuals (see Ericsson, Roring, & Nandagopal, 2007, for a review).

The expert-performance approach, while developed for research on expertise, offers a general procedure for identifying superior performance and the tools for analyzing its structure including think-aloud protocols. Once objective criteria for decision-making performance have been established, it will be possible to identify the mechanisms that mediate superior performance and to develop better theories to explain how decisions are made at all levels of performance. Once successful theories have been validated it will be possible to compare different types of data, such as elicited knowledge, interviews, and think-aloud protocols, in their ability to account for individual differences in judgment and decision-making performance. It will also be possible to compare different types of data and research methods for how well they can generate effective training procedures that would allow individuals to improve their decision-making performance in a given domain.

In this chapter we have described how verbal protocols have helped in both the development and testing of theoretical models. The ultimate criterion for types of data and research methods is their ability to predict objective performance and to lead to the design of effective training methods. One of the pioneers of the study of the brain, Lashley (1923, p. 352), said: "introspection may make the preliminary survey, but it must be followed by the chain and transit of objective measurement." We have argued in this chapter that it is possible to design methods for collecting verbal reports that are minimally reactive, such as think-aloud reports, and that meet all the criteria of objective recording and analysis as more traditional data, such as reaction times and eye fixations. However, it is essential that we design studies of decision making based on objective task performance so reactivity can be assessed to allow the tests to permit transit to reproducible objective measurement.

In conclusion, we argue that verbal protocols will be essential to increasing our understanding of expert decision making in various situations, decision making in general, and how decision making can be improved. The expert performance approach laid out here has already proven effective at increasing our understanding of expertise in diverse domains and we are optimistic about its effectiveness in exploring decision making.

Note

1 The first author is grateful for the financial support provided by the FSCW/Conradi Endowment Fund of Florida State University Foundation. We also want to thank Len Hill for his valuable comments on previous drafts.

Recommended Reading

- Ericsson, Hoffman, Kozbelt, and Williams (2018, pp. 192–212): General description of how protocol analysis has been used to uncover the cognitive processes of experts performing representative tasks.
- Ericsson et al. (2018, pp. 745–769): General description of how expert performance is related to engagement in purposeful and deliberate practice
- Ericsson & Pool (2016): General description of the expert-performance approach to the study of experts' reproducibly superior performance.

References

Abernethy, B., Neal, R. J., & Koning, P. (1994). Visual-perceptual and cognitive differences between expert, intermediate, and novice snooker players. *Applied Cognitive Psychology*, *8*(3), 185–211.

Aitken, L. M., Marshall, A., Elliot, R., & McKinley, S. (2011). Comparison of 'think-aloud' and observation as data collection methods in the study of decision making regarding sedation in intensive care patients. *International Journal of Nursing Studies*, *48*(3), 318–325.

Arsal, G., Eccles, D. W., & Ericsson, K. A. (2016). Cognitive mediation of putting: Use of a think-aloud measure and implications for studies of golf-putting in the laboratory. *Psychology of Sport and Exercise*, *27*(1), 18–27.

Benner, P., & Tanner, C. (1987). Clinical judgment: How expert nurses use intuition. *The American Journal of Nursing*, *87*(1), 23–34.

Boring E. (1929). *A history of experimental psychology*. New York, NY: Century.

Boshuizen, H. P. A., & Schmidt, H. G. (1992). On the role of biomedical knowledge in clinical reasoning by experts, intermediates and novices. *Cognitive Science, 16*(2), 153–184.

Calderwood, R., Klein, G. A., & Crandall, B. W. (1988). Time pressure, skill, and move quality in chess. *The American Journal of Psychology, 101*, 481–493.

Camerer, C. F., & Johnson, E. J. (1991). The process-performance paradox in expert judgment: How can the experts know so much and predict so badly? In K. A. Ericsson & J. Smith (Eds.), *Towards a general theory of expertise: Prospects and limits* (pp. 195–217). Cambridge, UK: Cambridge University Press.

Charness, N. (1981). Search in chess: Age and skill difference. *Journal of Experimental Psychology: Human Perception and Performance, 7*(2), 467–476.

Chase, W. G., & Ericsson, K. A. (1981). Skilled memory. In J. R. Anderson (Ed.), Cognitive skills and their acquisition (pp. 141–189). Lawrence Erlbaum Associates.

Chase, W. G., & Ericsson, K. A. (1982). Skill and working memory. In Psychology of learning and motivation (Vol. 16, pp. 1–58). Academic Press.

Choudhry, N. K, Fletcher, R. H., & Soumerai, S. B. (2005). Systematic review: The relationship between clinical experience and quality of health care. *Annals of Internal Medicine, 142*(4), 260–273.

Cioffi, J., & Markham, R. (1997). Clinical decision-making by midwives: Managing case complexity. *Journal of Advanced Nursing, 25*(2), 265–272.

Connors, M. H., Burns, B. D., & Campitelli, G. (2011). Expertise in complex decision making: The role of search in chess 70 years after de Groot. *Cognitive Science, 35*(8), 1567–1579.

Crowley, R. S., Naus, G. J., Stewart, J., & Friedman, C. P. (2003). Development of visual diagnostic expertise in pathology: An information processing study. *Journal of the American Medical Informatics Association, 10*(1), 39–51.

Dawes, R. M., Faust, D., & Meehl, P. E. (1989). Clinical versus actuarial judgment. *Science, 243*(4899), 1668–1674.

de Groot, A. D. (1978). *Thought and choice in chess*. The Hague, NL: Mouton.

Diaz, R., & Berk, L. (Eds.) (1992). *Private speech: From social interaction to selfregulation*. Hillsdale, NJ: Erlbaum.

Dreyfus, H. L., & Dreyfus, S. E. (1986). From Socrates to expert systems: The limits of calculative rationality. In Philosophy and Technology II (pp. 111–130). Dordrecht: Springer.

Edwards, W. (1953). Probability-preferences in gambling. *American Journal of Psychology, 66*(3), 349–364.

Ericsson, K. A. (1996). The acquisition of expert performance: An introduction to some of the issues. In K. A. Ericsson (Ed.), *The road to excellence: The acquisition of expert performance in the arts and sciences, sports, and games* (pp. 1–50). Mahwah, NJ: Erlbaum.

Ericsson, K. A. (2003). Valid and non-reactive verbalizations of thoughts during performance of tasks: Towards a solution to the central problems of introspection as a source of scientific data. *Journal of Consciousness Studies, 10*, 1–18.

Ericsson, K. A. (2005). Recent advances in expertise research: A commentary on the contributions to the special issue. *Applied Cognitive Psychology, 19*(2), 233–241.

Ericsson, K. A. (2006a). Protocol analysis and expert thought: Concurrent verbalization of thinking during experts' performance on representative task. In K. A. Ericsson, N. Charness, P. Feltovich, & R. R. Hoffman (Eds.), *Cambridge handbook of expertise and expert performance* (pp. 223–243). Cambridge, UK: Cambridge University Press.

Ericsson, K. A. (2006b). The influence of experience and deliberate practice on the development of superior performance. In K. A. Ericsson, N. Charness, P. Feltovich, & R. R. Hoffman (Eds.), *Cambridge handbook of expertise and expert performance* (pp. 683–704). Cambridge, UK: Cambridge University Press.

Ericsson, K. A. (2015). Acquisition and maintenance of medical expertise: A perspective from the expert-performance approach with deliberate practice. *Academic Medicine, 90*(11), 1471–1486.

Ericsson, K. A., Hoffman, R. R., Kozbelt, A., & Williams, A. M. (Eds.). (2018). The Cambridge handbook of expertise and expert performance. Cambridge Handbooks in Psychology. Cambridge: Cambridge University Press.

Ericsson, K. A., & Lehmann, A. C. (1996). Expert and exceptional performance: Evidence on maximal adaptations on task constraints. *Annual Review of Psychology, 47*(1), 273–305.

Ericsson, K. A., & Kintsch, W. (1995). Long-term working memory. *Psychological Review, 102*(2), 211–245.

Ericsson, K. A., & Oliver, W. (1988). Methodology for laboratory research on thinking: Task selection, collection of observation and data analysis. In R. J. Sternberg & E. E. Smith (Eds.), *The psychology of human thought* (pp. 392–428). Cambridge, UK: Cambridge University Press.

Ericsson, K. A., & Pool, R. (2016). *Peak: Secrets from the new science of expertise*. New York: Eamon Dolan Books/ Houghton Mifflin & Harcourt.

Ericsson, K. A., Prietula, M. J., & Cokely, E. T. (2007). The making of an expert. *Harvard Business Review, 85*(7/8), 114–121.

Ericsson, K. A., Roring, R. W., & Nandagopal, K. (2007). Giftedness and evidence for reproducibly superior performance: An account based on the expert-performance framework. *High Ability Studies, 18*(1), 3–56.

Ericsson, K. A., & Simon, H. A. (1980). Verbal reports as data. *Psychological Review, 87*(3), 215–251.

Ericsson, K. A., & Simon, H. A. (1993). *Protocol analysis: Verbal reports as data (revised edition)*. Cambridge, MA: MIT Press.

Ericsson, K. A., & Smith, J. (1991). Prospects and limits in the empirical study of expertise: An introduction. In K. A. Ericsson & J. Smith (Eds.), *Toward a general theory of expertise: Prospects and limits* (pp. 1–38). Cambridge, UK: Cambridge University Press.

Ericsson, K. A., Whyte IV, J., & Ward, P. (2007). Expert performance in nursing: Reviewing research on expertise in nursing within the framework of the expert-performance approach. Advances in Nursing Science, 30(1), E58–E71.

Ericsson, K. A., & Williams, A. M. (2007). Capturing naturally occurring superior performance in the laboratory: Translational research on expert performance. *Journal of Experimental Psychology: Applied, 13*(3), 115–123.

Forsberg, E., Ziegert, K., Hult, H., & Fors, U. (2014). Clinical reasoning in nursing, a think-aloud study using virtual patients – A base for an innovative assessment. *Nurse Education Today, 34*(4), 538–542.

Fox, M. C., Ericsson, K. A., & Best, R. (2011). Do procedures for verbal reporting of thinking have to be reactive? A meta-analysis and recommendations for best reporting methods. *Psychological Bulletin, 137*(2), 316–344.

French, K. E., Nevett, M. E., Spurgeon, J. H., Graham, K. C., Rink, J. E., & McPherson, S. L. (1996). Knowledge representation and problem solution in expert and novice youth baseball players. *Research Quarterly for Exercise and Sport, 67*(4), 386–395.

Gagné, R. M., & Smith Jr, E. C. (1962). A study of the effects of verbalization on problem solving. *Journal of Experimental Psychology, 63*(1), 12–18.

Klein, G. A. (1998). *Sources of power: How people make decisions*. Cambridge, MA: MIT Press.

Kostopoulou, O., Sirota, M., Round, T., Samaranayaka, S., & Delaney, B. C. (2017). The role of physicians' first impressions in the diagnosis of possible cancers without alarm symptoms. *Medical Decision Making, 37*(1), 9–16.

Lashley, K. S. (1923). The behavioristic interpretation of consciousness II. *Psychological Review, 30*(5), 329–353.

McPherson, S., & Kernodle, M. W. (2007). Mapping two new points on the tennis expertise continuum: Tactical skills of adult advanced beginners and entry-level professional during competition. *Journal of Sports Sciences, 25*(8), 945–959.

Miller, D. J., Spengler, E. S., & Spengler, P. M. (2015). A meta-analysis of confidence and judgment accuracy in clinical decision making. *Journal of Counseling Psychology, 62*(4), 553–567.

Miller, G. A., Galanter, E., & Pribram, K. H. (1960). *Plans and the structure of behavior*. New York, NY: Holt, Rinehart and Winston.

Montgomery, H., & Svenson, O. (1976). On decision rules and information processing strategies for choices among multiattribute alternatives. *Scandinavian Journal of Psychology, 17*(1), 283–291.

Moxley, J. H. (2016). *Knowledge structures and decision making in chess* (Unpublished doctoral dissertation). Florida State University, Tallahassee, FL.

Moxley, J. H., Ericsson, K. A., Charness, N., & Krampe, R. T. (2012). The role of intuition and deliberative thinking in experts' superior tactical decision-making. *Cognition, 124*(1), 72–78.

Newell, A., & Simon, H. A. (1972). *Human problem solving*. Englewood Cliffs, NJ: Prentice-Hall.

Nisbett, R. E., & Wilson, T. D. (1977). Telling more than we can know: Verbal reports on mental processes. *Psychological Review, 84*(3), 231–259.

Norman, G. R., Trott, A. D., Brooks, L. R., & Smith, E. K. M. (1994). Cognitive differences in clinical reasoning related to postgraduate training. *Teaching and Learning in Medicine: An International Journal, 6*(2), 114–120.

Patel, V. L., & Groen, G. J. (1991). The general and specific nature of medical expertise: A critical look. In K. A. Ericsson & J. Smith (Eds.), *Toward a general theory of expertise* (pp. 93–125). Cambridge, MA: Cambridge University Press.

Payne, J. W. (1976). Task complexity and contingent processing in decision making: An information search and protocol analysis. *Organizational Behavior and Human Performance, 16*(2), 366–387.

Roca, A., Ford, P. R., McRobert, A. P., & Williams, A. M. (2013). Perceptual-cognitive skills and their interaction as a function of task constraints in soccer. *Journal of Sport and Exercise Psychology, 35*(2), 144–155.

Schmidt, H. G., & Boshuizen, H. (1993). On acquiring expertise in medicine. *Educational Psychology Review, 5*(3), 205–221.

Simon, H. A. (1955). Behavioral model of rational choice. *Quarterly Journal of Economics, 69*(1), 99–118.

Simpson, S. A., & Gilhooly, K. J. (1997). Diagnostic thinking processes: Evidence from a constructive interaction study of electrocardiograph (ECG) interpretation. *Applied Cognitive Psychology, 11*(6), 543–554.

St. Germain, J., & Tenenbaum, G. (2011). Decision-making and thought processes among poker players. *High Ability Studies, 22*(1), 3–17.

Steginga, S. K., Occhipinti, S., Gardiner, R. A., Yaxley, J., & Heathcote, P. (2002). Making decisions about treatment for localized prostate cancer. *BJU International, 89*(3), 255–260.

Swets, J. A., Dawes, R. M., & Monahan, J. (2000). Psychological science can improve diagnostic decisions. *Psychological Science in the Public Interest, 1*(1), 1–26.

Ward, P., Hodges, N. J., Williams, A. M., & Starkes, J. L. (2004). Deliberate practice and expert performance: Defining the path to excellence. In A. M. Williams & N. J. Hodges (Eds.), *Skill acquisition in sport: Research, theory and practice* (pp. 231–258). London, UK: Routledge.

Watson, J. B. (1913). Psychology as the behaviorist views it. *Psychological Review, 20*(2), 158–177.

Watson, J. B. (1920). Is thinking merely the action of language mechanisms? *British Journal of Psychology, 11*, 87–104.

19

TRACKING FREE INFORMATION ACCESS

The Method of Active Information Search[1]

Oswald Huber, Anton Kühberger, and Michael Schulte-Mecklenbeck

What information do individuals seek when performing decision tasks? This question is relevant in different areas of Psychology (e.g., reasoning, decision making, judgement, or evaluating social situations) because accessing a specific item of information is often taken as indicating (albeit not perfectly) its use in the task at hand. Data about the information used—or not used—is the basis for descriptive model construction and theory development. Many theories explicitly predict information access: either qualitatively (e.g., that people access probabilities), or quantitatively (e.g., that they more frequently access information about outcomes than about probabilities), or by specific patterns of information acquisition (e.g., that information is accessed in an outcome-probability sequence). Examples of access-based decision models are Beach, 1990; Huber, Bär, and Huber, 2009; Montgomery and Willén, 1999; Johnson, Schulte-Mecklenbeck, and Willemsen, 2008; Ratcliff, Smith, Brown, and McKoon, 2016.

In general, model building based on information access follows a confirmatory strategy—it tracks whether decision makers actually access the information items predicted by the model. This can be done, e.g., through analysis of access to an information item; comparison of predicted and actual sequences and patterns; or time spent on different types of information (see Chapters 1, 2, 6, 7, 23, and 24 for examples). For instance, classical Subjective Expected Utility (SEU) requires that decision makers access outcomes and probabilities and integrate them, and nothing else. SEU makes no assumptions about sequence, which therefore can safely be ignored. The confirmatory strategy is useful in many situations, but tends to be self-assuring: process tracing cannot reveal alternatives to your model under investigation, if you do not look for model-irrelevant information. It thus is important to look for information items that are not envisioned by your model from the outset. The method of Active Information Search (AIS), as described in this chapter, is a structured method for doing exactly this.

Imagine a researcher who is investigating the role of probabilities in risky choice. The primary model is SEU, and thus gambles consisting of probabilities and outcomes are presented to participants and choices are collected. All the model-relevant information thus is readily presented to participants. This approach is often referred to as a *decision from description* (see Chapter 20). The confirmatory strategy with decision from description faces two issues: First, there is the possibility of demand effects: decision makers might not be interested in probability information at all, but only use this information because it is explicitly presented. Second is the issue of selectivity: whatever the decision maker is interested in other than outcomes and probabilities is ignored. To use an analogy, imagine a researcher who was interested in learning how people are crossing rivers. In order to understand their problem-solving behavior, she describes the problem in terms of canoes and paddles. When observing the problem-solving behavior she presumably would see people rowing. She then would conclude that rowing is the way people cross rivers. True, but this approach makes it impossible to learn about additional ways of crossing rivers, for instance, by swimming. To learn about the standard way of crossing rivers, the researcher is well advised to pre-structure the situation as little as possible, and see how behavior develops. If people began by sticking the finger into the water to see how cold it was, one could conclude that swimming was the standard way, even if people later were using a boat because the water was cold.

In the following we describe the method of AIS, whose goal is to investigate spontaneous information acquisition while avoiding the limitations that come with pre-structuring the decision task.

Active Information Search (AIS)

The method of AIS was developed to understand information needs in decision making with as little demand effects as possible. Engländer and Tyszka (1980) identified the problem of reactivity in decision making, and proposed a method where the researcher acts as an expert whom the participant could ask for any information he or she wanted. This basic approach was developed and extended by Huber, Wider, and Huber (1997), who used AIS mainly to investigate the role of risk in quasi-realistic decision tasks.

The main steps in running an AIS experiment are as follows:

1. Describing the scenario: Participants are presented in broad terms with a quasi-realistic decision scenario, and some general information about the available alternatives. This information is the same for all participants and, in the case of risky decision making, explicitly mentions risk, i.e., the possibility of a negative outcome.
2. Sampling questions: Participants ask questions to obtain information. We distinguish two AIS versions: In the basic version of AIS, participants are free to ask any question they want, and freely formulate questions. In the list version, participants get a list of questions to choose from.
3. Providing answers: Each question has a prepared answer (developed in extensive pilot testing), printed on a card or displayed on a computer monitor. Answers are printed instead of given verbally to enhance standardization. Usually, answer cards are removed before the next question can be asked. Therefore, answers have to be stored in memory. Participants can ask as many questions as they want.
4. Collecting choices: When they have collected whatever amount of information they need, participants choose their preferred option. No further explanation is required.

An Instructive Example

We provide one of the scenarios we have been working with in Box 19.1—the *Turtle Scenario*. After describing the scenario in general terms as a decision task, two alternatives to choose from are presented, both including potential negative consequences (this introduces the situation as a risky decision-making task). In our example, there is a non-risky alternative, and a risky alternative. It is useful to label the alternatives by descriptive terms (e.g., "beach") instead of letters because labels facilitate memorization. Of course, all alternatives in a scenario may be risky. The level of detail in the description of the alternatives may vary, depending on the research question.

BOX 19.1 TURTLE SCENARIO

The Hawsgeorge Turtle living in the southern pacific is acutely threatened by extinction. The last remaining turtles are held in a lab. Unfortunately, the turtles do not breed in the lab. You are the head of an international program to protect these turtles. Marine biologists have found two possible breeding places. You have to decide where the turtles shall be relocated.

Location Beach

A beach situated close to the lab would be suitable for breeding. There the turtles are not at risk, since there are no predators. However, the quality of the water is only moderate. Therefore, the reproduction rate of the turtles will be quite low.

Location Island

A little island provides a perfect environment for breeding. It is also free of predators. Unfortunately, from time to time a species of little mites can occur which live in the sea. If they occur, they attack the clutch and thus kill the offspring.

To successfully administer AIS scenarios, extensive pilot-testing is necessary for finding the optimal initial task description, and for the development of a standardized answer pool. The proper pre-testing of an AIS scenario is a prerequisite to achieve adequate reliability and validity.

Selection of the Topic

To successfully investigate the information needs of decision makers requires a topic that is interesting to participants so that they are motivated to make a good decision. In addition, it should not require too much domain specific knowledge. Otherwise, participants can retrieve information from memory rather than doing external search. For selecting an appropriate topic, it might be sufficient to test the topic by informally interviewing a few participants of the target population.

First Version: General Description and Preparation of Answers

The first version of the task should contain at least a description of the role of the participant, and the general decision situation. Based on this version of the task brainstorming by the researchers and a few participants can produce a first list of likely questions to be asked. For these questions, appropriate answers are generated. Each answer should be coded unambiguously into one answer category (see the section *Statistical Analysis*).

Optimization of the Task Description and of the Answers

Often the initial version of the task description will have to be modified. First, dominance of alternatives should be avoided. If one alternative is clearly superior, questions about the inferior alternative will hardly be asked. Second, (subjectively) implausible facts should be avoided, as they

Tracking Free Information Access **305**

TABLE 19.1 Overview of different Active Information Search versions used in the literature

Authors	AIS version used
Beer & Bender (2015)	Basic version, limited subsequent questions
Huber, Wider, R., & Huber, O.W. (1997)	Basic version
Huber, Beutter, Montoya, & Huber (2001)	Basic vs. list ("structured") version
Huber & Huber (2003, 2008)	Basic version
Huber, Huber, & Bär (2011)	Combination of basic and list version
Huber, Huber, & Bär (2014)	Basic version
Huber & Macho (2001)	Basic version
Michailova, Tyszka, & Pfeifer (2016)	Basic version
Ranyard, Williamson, & Cuthbert (1999)	Conversation-based version
Ranyard, Hinkley, & Williamson (2001)	Basic version
Schulte-Mecklenbeck & Huber (2003)	Computerized version
Tyszka & Zaleśkiewicz (2006)	Basic version
Wilke, Haug, & Funke (2008)	Conversation-based version
Williamson, Ranyard, & Cuthbert (2000a)	Conversation-based version

cause participants to question the whole task. Third, the description may be too rich, making information search partly unnecessary. Applying a concurrent thinking-aloud procedure in this phase is helpful (see e.g., Chapters 17–19; Ericsson & Simon, 1993). This procedure requires participants to verbalize all thoughts while deciding with the AIS method. The session is audio taped and later analyzed. However, the analysis of thinking-aloud protocols is very costly and time-consuming. Alternatively, post-experimental interviews can serve a similar purpose.

Versions of the Active Information Search Method

Several different versions of AIS have been used in the literature (see Table 19.1). As can be seen, the basic AIS version was most frequently used.

Basic AIS Version

In the basic AIS version participants are free to ask any question, as many as they want. Questions are coded for analysis. Coding is an iterative process of an initial coding round followed by discussion with other investigators to update the coding. Eventually, a generally agreed upon coding scheme is produced (see the section *Statistical Analysis* for details).

List AIS Version

In the list version of AIS participants are presented a list of questions. They can select one question at a time to be answered by the experimenter. Questions may be posed repeatedly. Table 19.2 contains a list of exemplary questions and respective coding that has been found useful for various scenarios.

In the list version, the sequence of questions should either be randomized, or kept constant. Participants can be given the opportunity to ask additional questions not on the list. It may be necessary to distinguish subcategories, for example, positive or negative outcomes, and questions about the existence or the characteristics of risk defusing operators (to be explained later).

306 Huber, Kühberger, and Schulte-Mecklenbeck

TABLE 19.2 List of question categories for Active Information Search

Question	Code
Can I learn more about the situation?	General situation
What are the positive consequences of doing X?	Outcome; positive
What is the probability for the positive consequences to occur with alternative X?[a]	Probability; positive
What are the negative consequences of alternative X?	Outcome; negative
What is the probability for the negative consequences to occur with alternative X?[a]	Probability; negative
Can I do something to prevent the negative consequences of alternative X?	Risk defusing
Are there other options besides these two?	Alternative; new

a Positive and negative consequences can be independent (e.g., a medicine may lead to healing with probability 0.7, but may entail negative side-effects with probability 0.1).

The main advantage of the list version is that the questions do not have to be coded by the researcher during the experimental session, easing the workload on the experimenter. On the other hand, the list of questions pre-structures the scenario and may alert participants to specific aspects of the problem. Using the list version sacrifices openness for control.

In the list version, the problem may occur that participants begin by simply asking all available questions (one after the other). To prevent such behavior small costs can be introduced for answers. Costs can be monetary, but can also be computational. For example, presenting the answer cards only until the next question is asked forces participants to consider answers immediately. It is also possible to limit the total number of questions allowed. We recommend the latter procedure if the goal of the study is to reveal the most important types of information.

If questions are very specific, the list can become very long, making it unwieldy to work with. A solution to this problem is the introduction of a hierarchy of questions: a specific question (or group of questions) is presented only if a participant has asked another question before.

In a face-to-face experiment with the list version, the hierarchical version may be too demanding for the experimenter. It is, on the other hand, particularly adequate for a computerized version. It should be noted that in the basic AIS version, participants usually pose questions in a hierarchical manner spontaneously, i.e., after having asked for a specific topic (e.g., a consequence), they often ask about properties or details of it.

Computerized Versions of AIS

The basic as well as the list version of AIS can be translated into a computer program. The experiment can be administered in the laboratory but also on the internet. For instance, basic AIS may be applied with only little programming effort via the internet with chat or messaging programs. In a setup utilizing a chat program, participants and experimenter do not have face-to-face contact (although video streams might easily be added). Participants send the questions and the experimenter responds by retrieving the appropriate answers from a set of prepared text blocks (Studer, 2007).

Another application is WebDiP (Web DecisIon Processes), a program implementing a variant of AIS. This can be downloaded free of charge from https://github.com/michaelschulte/webdip (a detailed description of the software can be found in Schulte-Mecklenbeck & Neun, 2005). One crucial difference between the classical AIS method and WebDiP is that in the web-based study, clicking on a link is used as the central dependent measure. Using server log timestamps enables the measurement of the time between clicks (e.g., the time between the pressing of the search button and the selection of a question), or the time needed for deciding on a scenario, or the whole experiment.

Statistical Analysis

Development of a Coding Scheme

As an example, we will present our coding scheme for risky decision making. In much of our research we distinguish among six categories: 1) general situational information; 2) outcomes; 3) probabilities; 4) risk defusing operators; 5) new alternatives; 6) miscellaneous.

"General situational information" refers to all questions concerning the decision situation in general. This includes questions about the background, the role of the decision maker, circumstances the decision is made in, and the situation itself (e.g., "How many turtles are held in the lab?"). "Consequences" refers to the outcomes of alternatives (e.g., "What happens if I put the turtles on the island and the mites invade?"). "Probabilities" refers to a probability of the occurrence of the consequences. Probability questions might contain the word "probability" or "probable", may involve a frequency format, but also may contain related expressions (e.g., "What is more likely…?"). "Risk defusing operators (RDOs)" refer to information concerning the control or prevention of negative consequences by actions that are executed in addition to choosing an existing alternative. Two subcategories can be distinguished: i) questions inquiring on the existence of an RDO (e.g., "Can the offspring be preserved if the mites occur?", "Is there an insurance?"), or suggesting a specific RDO (e.g., "Can I kill the mites by spraying insecticides onto the sand at the beach?"); and ii) questions inquiring a quality of an RDO (e.g., its cost, or effectiveness). "New alternatives" refers to questions about additional alternatives not included in the presented set (e.g., "Is there a possible breeding area with perfect water conditions but without the threat of mites?"). Thus, in contrast to an RDO question, a "New alternative" question does not aim at an action that is intended to be performed in addition to an existing alternative. Finally, "Miscellaneous" refers to questions that cannot be coded into one of the other categories.

This coding scheme contains, in addition to the traditional entries (outcomes, probabilities), two new entries: risk defusing operators, and new alternatives. This is because our research has shown (e.g., Huber, 2012) that in quasi-realistic decision situations, people are interested in these additional types of information, whereas they are irrelevant in the classic gambling paradigm. An RDO is an action anticipated by the decision maker to eliminate, or decrease, the risk associated with an alternative. For example, buying insurance is an RDO that reduces the risk of the negative outcome, without changing its basic probability. Risk and probability thus can dissociate if people bring RDOs to bear. RDOs can be evaluated for acceptability, and if an acceptable RDO is detected with a promising alternative, that alternative is usually chosen. RDOs can be of different varieties, either preventing a negative outcome (e.g., vaccination), or compensating for a negative outcome (e.g., insurance). There is also the possibility of a "positive" RDO, when somebody wants to increase the chances of a positive outcome (Huber et al., 2014). In addition, people may want to learn about existence, or the qualities of RDOs. Questions of the latter type are posed only after the existence of an RDO has been assured (for an overview see Huber, 2012).

Besides asking for possible RDOs, and evaluating alternatives after considering RDOs, people also do actively enrich the decision situation in quasi-realistic tasks. For instance, they frequently are seeking for possible additional options to choose from. This observation points to another shortcoming of classic risky choice research: it not only deals with the choice of a risky option, but in addition consists of active risk management. That is, people often search for additional possible actions, either with respect to choice options, or with respect to risk management.

Running an AIS experiment typically results in an ordered list of questions. Analysis includes: a) the quantity of information searched in total, or within a specific coding category; b) sequential order or patterns of information searched; and c) choices, as a function of information search.

The basic dependent variable in AIS is the sequential position of questions of the respective category measured on individual participants (e.g., first, third, and sixth). For analysis the mean (modal) sequential position of categories are computed for each participant. This variable also indicates which category is asked first, or last, or what the sequence or pattern of categories is. For instance, we often find that more questions are asked on the finally chosen alternative.

In some cases, the sequence of questions does not fulfill the scale and distribution requirements for parametric analysis. Two problems frequently occur: i) the number of questions is zero, or very small, for a fraction of participants; and ii) a subset of participants is asking the same type of questions repeatedly, whereas others are not asking for that type at all. Standard U or Wilcoxon-tests may be appropriate in such cases. We recommend also the computation of percentages of participants asking at least one probability question, or at least one RDO, in a specific task. Logit analysis allows for the concurrent analysis of several factors varied between subjects. A logit analysis performs statistical tests by fitting a hierarchy of logit models to the data (see e.g., DeMaris, 1992) thus enabling the identification of effective factors. For factors varied within subjects, standard Sign and Cochran's Q tests (see e.g., Agresti, 1990) may be appropriate.

Procedural Issues

We will now address procedural issues that can emerge during the data collection process.

First, some types of questions can be asked separately for each alternative (e.g., outcomes, probabilities, RDOs). It thus may be necessary to additionally code the alternative the question refers to. Some questions specifically pertain to RDOs (e.g., "Is there a vaccine against this disease?"). For such cases, it is necessary to be equipped with possible RDO proposals and to prepare answers indicating the existence or nonexistence of the proposed measure (e.g., "Your proposal to prevent the infection would work well."). Second, decision makers may ask identical questions repeatedly (e.g., "What are the consequences of alternative X?"). It should be determined in advance what to do with repetitions: they can either be included in the analysis or discarded altogether.

The precision of answers is important: for probability questions, questions about consequences, or questions referring to a property of an RDO, the experimenter can provide a precise answer (e.g., the probability is 80%), or an imprecise one (e.g., the probability is high). Evaluating the provided answers regarding the degree of precision might be important (see also Huber et al., 2001). The answer to a "New alternative" question usually is negative. Otherwise the decision maker may invent new attractive or even dominating alternatives.

Sometimes, the experimenter is confronted with unclear questions. We isolated the following cases for which the procedure should be standardized: i) Ambiguous question. In this case, the experimenter should ask for clarification, or reformulation. The experimenter should log this. (ii) More than one question asked at a time. Here, the experimenter can provide the answer randomly, or ask the participant to reformulate, or specify the question. (iii) New question. The list of questions and answers will never be exhaustive. Indeed, experimenters may face questions lacking a prepared answer. In our studies we either invented a plausible answer ad hoc (this is impractical when the answers have to be pre-recorded), or informed participants that this information was not available. It is also possible to invent a plausible answer in the first instance of a new question and then use this answer in all following instances. Typically, unexpected questions do not threaten the validity of the research, because they do not deal with central aspects of the scenario (which have been identified in the pilot studies). Nevertheless, logging these cases is important.

Reliability of the Coding System

The reliability of the coding of questions (and answers) is crucial for the administration of the method and the validity of the results. Therefore, the inter-rater reliability (e.g., Cohen's kappa) of the coding system should be calculated not only for the final version but also earlier during the development process.

In our research we were mainly interested in non-expert decision making. Indeed, like most other experimental research, research using the AIS method frequently uses psychology students as experimental participants. Note, however, that the AIS method can be easily adapted to be used with expert decision makers (see e.g., Kostopoulou et al., 2008, Chapter 12). Frequently experts are producing a richer set of questions, thus requiring a more thorough preparation of plausible answers than is necessary for students. The basic approach of AIS, however, remains identical.

Discussion

The AIS method helps to understand reasoning, judgment and decision making, or complex problem solving, by providing process measures of the type, quantity, and sequence of information people are interested in. As at least the basic AIS version leaves the formulation of questions completely to the participants, the method pushes only limited information onto them. Therefore, the genuine information need of participants is recorded. The method is especially useful for testing the predictions of models about information usage, and patterns of information acquisition. It has up to now mainly been used with quasi-realistic risky decision-making scenarios with a focus on revealing which information people do actually search for when arriving at a risky choice. The main finding is that the model of a gamble is inadequate for most realistic risky choice situations, since it fails to include the constructive aspect that people bring in: they do not simply choose among the given things but actively try to manage the risk (see Huber, 2017).

An important question is whether it is possible with the AIS method to identify all information a participant uses. The answer is: no. Information stored in the long-term memory, for instance, will not be asked for. Bär and Huber (2008) combined the AIS method (basic version) with a concurrent thinking-aloud procedure and found that about 30% of the participants who did not ask for an RDO nevertheless seemed to tacitly assume that an RDO existed. This underscores the necessity of using scenarios where participants have only little background knowledge. If, however, it is inevitable to use scenarios where background knowledge is prevalent—e.g., in expert decision making—the method should be tested in pilot studies with concurrent thinking aloud to identify if the measured information needs are suitable to answer the research question, or if the information central to it is generated from memory and does not leave traces in information search.

An equally important question is whether participants do actually use the information they search for in forming a preference. It seems that they usually do, provided the answer is informative to them. Bär and Huber (2008), for example, found that successful or unsuccessful RDO search (as revealed by the answer to the corresponding question) had a significant effect on the choices. Also, indirect support is available showing that actively searched information is remembered better than information presented in the scenario itself, two days after a decision with AIS (Huber, O.W, 2007).

Admittedly, as with other methods measuring information acquisition (e.g., Mouselab, Chapters 6–7), AIS cannot evaluate whether the searched information is used, over and beyond the relationship between search and choice.

Results of Huber and Huber (2008) corroborate the validity of the method, by demonstrating that the frequent finding of limited search for probability information in many realistic scenarios is not an artifact of the AIS method. These authors compared the search for probabilities and RDOs in scenarios and choices between gambles. With scenarios respondents were more interested in RDOs than in probabilities, while in gambles participants searched for probabilities and did not think of RDOs. Equally important, Shiloh, Gerad, and Goldman (2006) administered the AIS method during real counseling sessions regarding family planning for people with known genetic deficiencies. They also found little interest in probabilities and extensive search for RDOs. In sum, the amount of RDO search, and of search for probability information, is obviously task dependent (e.g., Huber & Huber, 2008; Michailova et al., 2016). RDOs are not searched in gambles because everyday wisdom has it that gambles do not provide means for avoiding risk (other than avoiding the gamble at all, or taking recourse to magic).

Can AIS be used to investigate specific groups, like clinical samples? To our knowledge, AIS has been employed with two specific groups of participants: patients with brain damage, and children. Eggen et al. (2015) successfully administered AIS to patients with ventromedial prefrontal brain damage. While she found no basic differences in information search between these and a matched control group of healthy people, the clinical participants displayed a higher tendency for perseverance than healthy individuals by asking identical questions repeatedly. Thus, AIS in general may be administered to clinical samples. In contrast, Belau's (2007) attempt to use AIS with children between 4 and 8 years did fail. Children failed in executive control, since they spontaneously produced comments as early as in the initial description of the situation and RDO proposals. They could not await the end of the story before beginning to ask questions. Thus, we do not recommend the AIS method with younger children.

The AIS method also helps to ease the problem of pre-structuring, although initially introducing some kind of structure is unavoidable. However, this structure can be rudimental, enabling the development and construction of the final representation by the participant. If pre-structuring is relevant for the research question, the structure of the short description can be varied as an independent variable and its effect thus be tested. Huber and Wicki (2004) varied the initial description in such a way that the specific causal structure of the alternatives could or could not be easily recognized. This manipulation had a predictable effect on type and pattern of questions asked.

Both the basic AIS version and the list version have been used in several experiments. Each has its advantages and disadvantages: in the basic version, little structure for the information search is presented to participants, because they are free to formulate any question in any way. On the other hand, the burden on the experimenter is quite high, since she has to categorize the questions immediately, and provide answers. She has also to decide critical cases (e.g., unclear questions) on the spot. In contrast, the list version has some practical advantages, since it eases the burden of the experimenter. In addition, coding is easier in the list version, because it is generally done before the experiment. In addition, the list version can be easily employed under time pressure (Huber & Kunz, 2007). The major disadvantage of the list version is its increased reactivity because it suggests questions to the participant.

Thus, in weighing the pros and cons of the different AIS versions, we conclude that the list AIS version (lab or computerized), due to its higher degree of pre-structuring, is more appropriate for comparing information needs in different experimental conditions. An example is a comparison of information search with and without justification (Huber et al., 2009). However, researchers interested in the absolute amount of search, and in its quality and pattern, should use the basic AIS version. An example is research on whether or not decision makers search for probability information in a specific type of decision tasks.

We believe that with the method of AIS, researchers are equipped with a tool to measure information needs of decision makers in problem solving and decision making and application of AIS in choice experiments will promote the enrichment of theories in the field.

Note

1 Odilo W. Huber co-authored the chapter on AIS for the 2011 edition of this handbook. Odilo died in January, 2014.

Recommended Reading

- Huber et al. (1997): provide a general introduction into the different AIS methods.
- Huber (2012): discussed the method in the framework of risk management.

References

Agresti, A., (1990). *Categorical data analysis*. New York, NY: Wiley.

Bär, A. S., & Huber, O. (2008). Successful or unsuccessful search for risk defusing operators: Effect on decision behaviour. *European Journal of Cognitive Psychology, 20*(4), 807–827.

Beach, L. R. (1990). *Image theory. Decision making in personal and organizational contexts*. Chichester, UK: Wiley.

Beer, B., & Bender, A. (2015). Causal inferences about others' behavior among the Wampar, Papua New Guinea – and why they are hard to elicit. *Frontiers in Psychology, 6*, 128.

Belau, C. (2007). *Das Entscheidungsverhalten von Kindern zwischen 4 und 8 Jahren in quasi-realistischen Risikoentscheidungssituationen. [Decision behavior of children between 4 and 8 years in quasi-realistic risky decision situations.]* (Unpublished master's thesis). University of Fribourg, Switzerland.

DeMaris, A., (1992). *Logit modeling: Practical applications*. Newbury Park, CA: Sage.

Eggen, C., Huber, O., Bär, A., Huber, O. W., Perrig, W. J., Müri, R., & Gutbrod, K. (2015). Impairments in an early stage of the decision-making process in patients with ventromedial prefrontal damage: Preliminary results. *Neurocase, 21*(4), 509–519.

Engländer, T., & Tyszka, T. (1980). Information seeking in open decision situations. *Acta Psychologica, 45*(1–3), 169–176.

Ericsson, K. A., & Simon, H. A. (1993). *Protocol analysis: Verbal reports as data*. Cambridge, MA: MIT Press.

Huber, O. (2007). Behavior in risky decisions: Focus on risk defusing. In M. Abdellaoui, R. D. Luce, M. Machina, & B. Munier (Eds.), *Uncertainty and risk* (pp. 291–306). Berlin: Springer.

Huber, O. (2012). Risky decisions: Active risk management. *Current Directions in Psychological Science, 21*(1), 26–30.

Huber, O. (2017). Evaluation-dependent representation in risk defusing. *Frontiers in Psychology, 8*, 836.

Huber, O., Bär, A. S, & Huber, O. W. (2009). Justification pressure in risky decision making: Search for risk defusing operators. *Acta Psychologica, 130*(1), 17–24.

Huber, O., Beutter, C., Montoya, J., & Huber, O. W. (2001). Risk defusing behavior: Towards an understanding of risky decision making. *European Journal of Cognitive Psychology, 13*(3), 409–426.

Huber, O., & Huber, O. W. (2003). Detectability of the negative event: Effect on the acceptance of pre- or post-event risk-defusing actions. *Acta Psychologica, 113*(1), 1–21.

Huber, O., & Huber, O. W. (2008). Gambles versus quasi-realistic scenarios: Expectations to find probability and risk defusing information. *Acta Psychologica, 127*(2), 222–236.

Huber, O., Huber, O. W., & Bär, A. S. (2011). Information search and mental representation in risky decision making: The advantages first principle. *Journal of Behavioral Decision Making, 24*(3), 223–248.

Huber, O., Huber, O. W., & Bär, A. S. (2014). Framing of decisions: Effect on active and passive risk avoidance. *Journal of Behavioral Decision Making, 27*(5), 444–453.

Huber, O., & Kunz, U. (2007). Time pressure in risky decision making: Effect on risk defusing. *Psychology Science, 49*(4), 415–426.

Huber, O., & Macho, S. (2001). Probabilistic set-up and the search for probability information in quasi-naturalistic decision tasks. *Risk, Decision and Policy, 6*(1), 1–16.

Huber, O., & Wicki, D. (2004). Risk defusing in decision making: Prevention or intervention? *Risk, Decision and Policy, 9*(4), 359–370.

Huber, O., Wider, R., & Huber, O.W. (1997). Active information search and complete information presentation in naturalistic risky decision tasks. *Acta Psychologica, 95*(1), 15–29.

Huber, O. W. (2007). Active search for probability information and recall performance: Is probability an outstanding element in the mental representation of risky decisions? In M. Abdellaoui, D. R. Luce, M. J. Machina, & B. Munier (Eds.) *Uncertainty and Risk, Mental, Formal, and Experimental Represenatations. Theory and Decision Library, Series C* (261–274). Berlin, Heidelberg: Springer.

Johnson, E. J., Schulte-Mecklenbeck, M., & Willemsen, M. C. (2008). Process models deserve process data: Comment on Brandstätter, Gigerenzer, and Hertwig (2006). *Psychological Review, 115*(1), 263–272.

Kostopoulou, O., Oudhoff, J., Nath, R., Delaney, B. C., Munro, C. W., Harries, C., & Holder, R. (2008). Predictors of diagnostic accuracy and safe management in difficult diagnostic problems in family medicine. *Medical Decision Making, 28*(5), 668–680.

Michailova, J, Tyszka, T., & Pfeifer, K. (2016). Are people interested in probabilities of natural disasters? *Risk Analysis, 37*(5), 1005–1017.

Montgomery, H., & Willén, H. (1999). Decision making and action: The search for a good structure. In P. Juslin & H. Montgomery (Eds.), *Judgment and decision making* (pp. 147–173). Mahwah, NJ: Erlbaum.

Ranyard, R., Hinkley, L., & Williamson, J. (2001). Risk management in consumers' credit decision making: A process tracing study of repayment insurance choices. *Zeitschrift für Sozialpsychologie, 32*(3), 152–161.

Ranyard, R., Williamson, J., & Cuthbert, L. (1999). The development of conversation-based process tracing methods for the study of naturalistic decision making. In B. Green (Ed.), *Risk behavior and risk management in business life.* Dordrecht, NL: Kluver.

Ratcliff, R., Smith, P. L., Brown, S. D., & McKoon, G. (2016). Diffusion decision model: Current issues and history. *Trends in Cognitive Sciences, 20*(4), 260–281.

Schulte-Mecklenbeck, M., & Huber, O. (2003). With or without the experimenter: Information search in the laboratory and on the Web. *Behavior Research Methods, Instruments, & Computers, 35*(2), 227–235.

Schulte-Mecklenbeck, M., & Neun, M. (2005). WebDiP: A tool for information search experiments on the World-Wide Web. *Behavior Research Methods, 37*(2), 293–300.

Shiloh, S., Gerad, L., & Goldman, B. (2006). Patients' information needs and decision-making processes: What can be learned from genetic counseling? *Health Psychology, 25*(2), 211–219.

Studer, R. (2007). *Der Einfluss von Framing auf den Informationsverarbeitungsprozess in Risikoentscheidungen [The effect of framing on information processing in risky decisions]* (Unpublished master's thesis). University of Fribourg, Switzerland.

Tyszka, T., & Zaleśkiewicz, T. (2006). When does information about probability count in choices under risk? *Risk Analysis, 26*(6), 1623–1636.

Wilke, M., Haug, H., & Funke, J. (2008). Risk-specific search for risk-defusing operators. *Swiss Journal of Psychology, 67*(1), 29–40.

Williamson, J., Ranyard, R., & Cuthbert, L., (2000a). A conversation-based process tracing method for use with naturalistic decisions: An evaluation study. *British Journal of Psychology, 91*(1), 203–221.

20

UNCOVERING THE ANATOMY OF SEARCH WITHOUT TECHNOLOGY[1]

Dirk U. Wulff and Ralph Hertwig

Admittedly, our chapter is a somewhat odd addition in a Handbook of Process Tracing Methods. We will not revel at the ever growing and ever more sophisticated methods to trace processes nor will we conceive of still another technology. Nevertheless, our concern will be with "information search prior to choice"—the object of desire of what Schulte-Mecklenbeck et al. (2017) called "movement-based (process tracing) such as computer-based information boards, eye-tracking, joy-stick and slider bar, mouse tracking or the tracking of reaching pointing" (p. 443). Our starting point is this observation: Process tracing methods often focus on cognitive tasks that in themselves are devoid of an explicit and extended episode of search, thus requiring sophisticated technologies and efforts to look through this dimly lit and small window of search. Our chapter will be concerned with a very different way, requiring much less engineering, of laying bare the anatomy of the search process, and in fact, giving search a leading role in behavioral experiments and theories of choice. The cognitive task that we focus on is risky choice, still one of the most important domains for studying the way humans make decisions. Since the early 2000s research on risky choice has (again) begun to study experiential-based paradigms (for reviews see Hertwig & Erev, 2009; Wulff, Mergenthaler-Canseco, & Hertwig, 2018)—often in parallel with description-based paradigms. In the experiential paradigms, the search process and its major defining properties—that is, for instance, amount of search and the search policy—unfolds for everyone to see. Experiential paradigms in risky choice and many other lines of research, according to our key argument, represent an alternative to the use of sophisticated process tracing technologies and auxiliary assumptions necessary to lift the veil and to understand the processes preceding choice.

Let us emphasize that our goal in this chapter is not to pit process tracing technologies against experiential paradigms. Barely any aspect of modern life—from technology, science, commerce, and literature to news media and the World Wide Web—is conceivable without symbolic descriptions. Therefore, it is important to understand how people search information in environments in which symbolic descriptions of information can be directly perused. Yet, research employing process tracing technologies may nevertheless benefit greatly from the consideration of experiential of paradigms, for instance in parallel to the description-based paradigms, thus enjoying a view on search that is less obscured and requires fewer assumptions.

Two Modes of Learning and the Description–Experience Gap

One of the most frequently studied "fruit flies" in cognitive psychology is choice between monetary lotteries. In theory, this Drosophila melanogaster can be studied from many angles. In practice, however, many researchers have grown accustomed to relying on a single one (see Pleskac & Hertwig, 2014; Weber, Shafir, & Blais, 2004): lotteries in which the outcomes and their probabilities are explicitly stated (either numerically or visually in terms of, e.g., pie charts), and respondents thus make decisions from description (Hertwig, Barron, Weber, & Erev, 2004). This fruit fly—fully described lotteries—has populated both economists' and psychologists' laboratories. For instance, one of the most famous violations of expected utility theory, the Allais paradox, involves choices between explicitly stated outcomes and probabilities (Allais, 1953, p. 514). Similarly, in his informal experiment designed to illustrate ambiguity aversion, another violation of expected utility theory, Ellsberg (1961, p. 650) relied on a setting with stated outcomes and probabilities (except in the ambiguous urn, in which probabilities were left unspecified). Hardly any learning was necessary. The same was true for Kahneman and Tversky's (1979) numerous demonstrations of violations of expected utility. Researchers have characterized such decisions based on full description as "static" (Edwards, 1962) and noted that:

> When a static decision task is used, the decision maker does not have to learn from past experience with the outcomes of previous decisions. ... This feature of the static decision task becomes a problem when generalizing results to the many day-to-day decisions that repeatedly confront individuals, since explicit information concerning outcome probabilities is frequently not available and must be learned from previous experience.
>
> *Busemeyer, 1982, p. 176*

Indeed, in everyday life, people are rarely able to consult explicit descriptions of probabilities and outcomes. Instead, they often cannot help but rely on past or online experience—if existent—with these options, thus making decisions from experience rather than decisions from description (Hertwig et al., 2004; Wulff et al., 2018). For instance, when crossing a street a person typically cannot rely on actuarial data; that is, there is no table of descriptions available that would inform her about the probabilities and outcomes. However, the individual will have made potentially relevant experiences in other traffic environments that she can bring to bear to the present situation and, in addition or alternatively, can explore the present situation hands-on. A similar case can be made for a plethora of situations involving real-world risks (e.g., postponing the back-up on one's hard drive, having unprotected sex, experimenting with drugs). The distinction between description- and experience-based choice has raised a number of new questions, the two most important ones being: First, to what extent do these two modes of learning about the world result in similar or systematically different choices? Second, if they do lead to different choices, can this be reflected in the existing models of choice or are new ones required? These questions have received much attention since a set of three articles in the early 2000s demonstrated a systematic discrepancy between description- and experience-based choices:[2] the description–experience gap (Barron & Erev, 2003; Hertwig et al., 2004; Weber et al., 2004).

To study decisions from experience researchers have commonly turned the monetary lotteries with their stated outcomes and probabilities into a kind of experience generator. One particular implementation of this generator is the *sampling paradigm*. Individuals initially know nothing about the options but are permitted to explore them (neither gaining nor losing any money in so doing) by sampling possible outcomes from the payoff distributions (the options) before making a choice

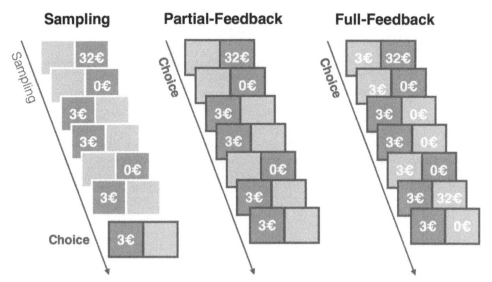

FIGURE 20.1 An illustration of how squares are divided into five equal sized bins according to the range principle and five equally used bins according to the frequency principle.

(typically with a press of a button; see Figure 20.1 for an example). Each sample usually produces a single outcome drawn (with replacement) from its respective distribution. Participants also typically determine the number of outcomes they sample (the sample size); specifically, they are instructed to sample until they feel confident enough to decide which option to choose in a final draw involving real monetary payoffs. Once they terminate sampling, they indicate their preferred option. Two related paradigms are the *partial-* and *full-feedback paradigms*. In contrast to the sampling paradigm, the feedback paradigm suspends free information search by rendering each selection of an option a consequential choice. The feedback paradigms thus require individuals to trade off between their exploration goal (i.e., learning about the options) and their exploitation goal (i.e., maximizing their returns). In the partial-feedback paradigm, feedback is provided in each trial only for the selected option (dark gray box) whereas the full-feedback paradigm provides feedback also concerning the foregone payoff (i.e., the payoff that the person would have received, had she selected the other option; light gray box). These paradigms fostered a simple but informative comparison between decisions made from experience and decisions made from description, revealing what has become known as the description–experience gap (D–E gap; Hertwig & Erev, 2009; Wulff et al., 2018).

It is now well established that decisions made from description and decisions from experience can result in systematically different choices. Recently, Wulff et al. (2018) conducted a meta-analysis of 33 data sets[3] using the sampling paradigm examining, among other analyses, the difference in the average proportion of choices consistent with Cumulative Prospect Theory[4] between description and experience. When the choice problems included a risky and a safe option—the type of problem frequently used in economics and psychology to infer individuals' risk preference—the average gap size in choice behavior was large, namely, about 20 percentage points. This gap in choice behavior is, however, not premised on any particular theory of choice (e.g., one that assumes probability weighting). That is, it occurs under different measurement approaches, including approaches that evaluate choices as a function of maximization, namely whether individuals choose the option that promises the higher expected return based on the available information (see Wulff et al., 2018), or risk, where they choose the option with objectively higher variance (e.g., Ludvig & Spetch, 2011). It also occurs across experimental paradigms, including the partial- and full-feedback paradigms (Figure 20.1; see also Hertwig & Erev, 2009; Wulff et al., 2018), and within individuals (e.g., Camilleri & Newell, 2009), and it represents a systematic difference from expected value maximization. Yet, the direction of this description–experience gap is typically summarized in terms of the (as-if) weighting of rare events (for a recent analysis see also Regenwetter & Robinson, 2017). In decisions from description, individuals tend to choose as if they *overweight* the impact of rare events, that is, as if rare events receive more weight than they deserve based on their objective probability. In decisions from experience, by contrast, they tend to choose as if they *underweight* rare events.

The Roles of Information Search in Decisions from Experience

Several explanations for the emergence of the description–experience gap have been proposed. In one way or another, information search is often invoked in those explanations. In the following, we address two of these explanations for the description–experience gap in the context of two different roles that information search takes in decision from experience: a) search as a driver of experience and b) search as a signal of preference. Henceforth, we focus on the sampling paradigm of decisions from experience, as it has been the focus of most experimental work on the description–experience gap and its cognitive underpinnings.

Search as a Driver of Experience

Research on the sampling paradigm has shown that people on average rely on about 20 samples per problem, implying a sample size of about 10 samples per option (see Table 1 in Wulff et al., 2018). Such frugal exploration has two important consequences for people's experiences. First, it will prevent many individuals from experiencing the unlikely event in the first place. For instance, when taking 10 samples from the option \$4 with probability .8 and \$0 otherwise versus \$3 guaranteed, 11% of individuals are expected to not see the unlikely event (0 with 20%) at all. Second, the majority of all individuals, including those who did experience the unlikely event, are expected to see it less often than expected from its objective probability. In this example, the expected number of times of experiencing the rare event with 10 samples is two. Based on the binomial distribution, which governs the sample distribution of two outcome lotteries, 30% of individuals are expected to see the rare event exactly twice and 32% of individuals are expected to see the rare event more than twice; however, more individuals, namely 38%, are expected to experience the rare event never or only once. The reason for this result is that the binomial sampling distribution is right-skewed for events with a probability smaller than .5, implying more mass below than above the expected value, and vice versa for events with probability larger than .5. Figure 20.2 illustrates this regularity for 40,246 empirical sampling trials analyzed by Wulff et al. (2018): The medians of experienced relative frequencies fall below the identity line for small probabilities, tend to be clustered around the identity line for medium probabilities, and fall above the identity line for large probabilities. Furthermore, the plots of the marginal distributions in Figure 20.2 show that, relative to the decision problems' objective probabilities, the experienced relative frequencies are systematically shifted towards the boundaries (0 and 1). Based on these statistical regularities, frugal search, ceteris paribus, can explain the as-if underweighting (conditioned on the objective probabilities) regularity in decisions from experience. That is, individuals make choices that appear

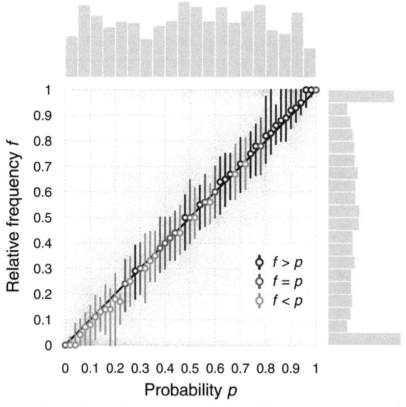

FIGURE 20.2 Small samples, sampling error, and rare events. This figure plots the true probability p versus the experienced relative frequency f for all sampling trials in our analysis (excluding options with $p = 1.0$). The points in the background represent the individual trials. The circles and lines in the foreground represent the median experienced probabilities for each unique true probability and the respective interquartile range. The bar graphs at the top and on the right show the marginal distribution of the objective probabilities and of the experienced relative frequencies, respectively. Adapted from Wulff et al. (2018).

to underweigh rare events because they tend to "underexperience" them. Thus information search has a substantial and systematic impact on the environments that individuals experience and the choices that they subsequently make.

Why do people curtail their search so soon and forego the opportunity to obtain an accurate representation of an option? Two factors are likely to contribute to frugal search. First, individuals usually do not know in advance the set of possible outcomes and hence cannot discern when their sample of experience offers a veridical reflection of the true state. Individuals thus cannot know for sure whether it is worth continuing to search or not. Second, the incremental value of search drastically diminishes over time. In a simulation involving risky lotteries, Hertwig and Pleskac (2010) demonstrated that although choices derived from small samples are not optimal, they are surprisingly good. With a sample as tiny as one draw, the chance of selecting the better lottery was approximately 60% in the simulated environment of 1,000 pairs of randomly generated lotteries (simulated person samples from two payoff distributions, each consisting of two outcomes of the type "a probability p to win amount x; otherwise win amount y"). Drawing as few as seven times from each deck offers an 81% chance of selecting the better lottery. Moreover, accuracy continues to increase at a diminishing rate. An individual can, for example, increase the likelihood of selecting the higher expected value lottery from 60% to 78% by increasing the sample size from one to five. By doubling the sample size from 10 to 20 draws, accuracy increases by merely 2 percentage points. This means that beyond a small sample of draws the further investment of search effort promises increasingly small returns. In light of this cost–benefit ratio, individuals' limited exploration may be anything but unreasonable.

Search as a Signal of Preference

Permitted to search for as long as they like, individuals usually take only a limited number of samples per payoff distribution with the consequence that the information acquired by individuals systematically misrepresents the true underlying properties and quality of the choice options. Yet, in light of the inherent uncertainty and the diminishing returns expected from continued sampling, the individual's explorative behavior represents an adaptive response to the choice environment they are in. And this is not the only indication that people adapt to internal and external characteristics of the choice environment. Wulff et al. (2018) summarized the known factors in how much people explore: Individuals have been found to *increase* their sample size, for instance, in the presence of potential losses (Lejarraga, Hertwig, & Gonzalez, 2012), in response to the affective state of fear (Frey, Hertwig, & Rieskamp, 2014), and when the number of options increases (Hills, Noguchi, & Gibbert, 2013; Noguchi & Hills, 2016). Sampling efforts are also boosted by increasing the monetary stakes (Hau, Pleskac, Kiefer, & Hertwig, 2008); similarly, Wulff, Hills, and Hertwig (2015a) showed that sample size can also be increased by incentivizing individuals to maximize the long-run rather than the short-run return. Taken together these and other results (e.g., the drastic effects of competitive versus noncompetitive search shown by Phillips, Hertwig, Kareev, & Avrahami, 2014) suggest that people are *adaptive explorers*. In their explorative behavior, they reveal their sensitivity to the costs and benefits of search and, more generally, their goals, aspirations, and the properties of their choice options and choice environment.

People's capacity for adaptive exploration suggests a link between search and preference, which can be utilized in order to better understand the underpinnings of choice in decisions from experience. The revealed preference approach assumes that a person's preference is laid bare through the explicit choices she makes. The work on experienced-based choice suggests a different or at least a complementary possibility. When searching sequentially (as in the sampling paradigm) each sample offers, and in fact requires, a choice to continue or to terminate search. This implies that the number of samples that individuals draw may be another reflection of a person's preferences and vice versa. This link between search and preference has recently been conceptualized in terms of an evidence accumulation framework (Markant, Pleskac, Diederich, Pachur, & Hertwig, 2015; Wulff, Markant, Pleskac, & Hertwig, in press; see also Ostwald, Starke, & Hertwig, 2015; Pleskac, Yu, Hopwood, & Liu, in press; Zeigenfuse, Pleskac, & Liu, 2014). Specifically, the *CHASE* model (Markant et al., 2015) is built on the idea that observed outcomes contribute to an accumulated preference in proportion to their subjective value. Over the course of a search, the subjective values accumulate to form a preference for one option over the other until, at some point, the preference strength reaches one of two thresholds, one for each alternative (see Figure 20.3). The final choice is then determined by the particular threshold that is reached and the sample size is determined by the time it takes (or, more precisely, the number of steps taken) to reach the threshold.

Using the computational framework of CHASE, sample size can help us recover characteristics of the decision process. For instance, a lack of a clear preference in terms of choices can be the result of low threshold separation, which may be interpreted as "trigger-happy," given that relatively little

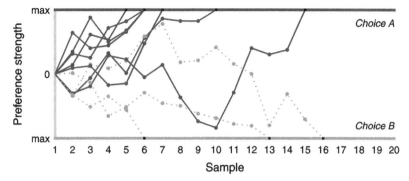

FIGURE 20.3 Model of preference accumulation. Figure illustrates for 10 hypothetical choices the accumulation of preference strength (y-axis) across samples (points) from a neutral start point (zero) towards one of the decision thresholds. Black squares mark the sample at which the decision threshold was reached. They thus also determine the number of samples at which point search is terminated.

evidence needs to be accumulated before a choice is made. However, the same choice behavior can also be the result of a low sensitivity to the magnitude of outcomes or probabilities, which results in only small changes of preference strengths associated with each sample.[5] Thus, in this case, two independent elements of the decision process can produce the same choice behavior. What holds for choice, however, does not hold for search; that is, low threshold separation will lead to relatively small sample sizes whereas low sensitivity will lead to large sample sizes. Therefore, based on a key property of information search—namely, sample size that precedes the supposed choice behavior—we can now characterize the decision process in ways we could not by considering choice alone. For the details on CHASE please see Markant et al. (2015; Wulff et al., in press).

Strong evidence for CHASE and the link between search and preference, in general, is provided by a sampling-cascade effect for exploration in the sampling paradigm analogue to the gaze-cascade effect for eye tracking (Wulff et al., 2018). The traditional gaze-cascade effect refers to the finding that gaze measured through eye-tracking gradually shifts to the eventually chosen option before making a choice, a behavioral pattern that has been taken as evidence that "gaze is actively involved in preference formation" (Shimojo, Simion, Shimojo, & Scheier, 2003, p. 1317). Similarly, individuals in the sampling paradigm have been found to also sample more often from the eventually chosen option towards the end of the sampling sequence, suggesting that sampling, and in particular the decision to terminate sampling, are closely related to the process of making a decision. Corroborating this interpretation, this sampling-cascade effect seems to only occur in self-terminated (i.e., autonomous) sampling, where the authority to stop search resides with the participant, and not in experimenter-terminated (regulated) environments, where sample size is predetermined by the experimenter (Figure 20.4). Notably, the gaze-cascade-like effect is a parameter-free prediction of CHASE and any evidence accumulation model.

An interesting consequence of the kind of optional stopping implied by CHASE and the sampling-cascade effect is that it gives rise to recency; that is, experiences sampled later in the sequence will be more correlated to the final choice than earlier ones. To see why, consider that the very last sample must necessarily be in favor of the eventually chosen option, as otherwise it would not have pushed the relative preference strength over the threshold. Similarly, the second to last sample must have likely been in favor of the eventually chosen option, as otherwise the relative preference strength would not have been close enough for the last sample to cross the threshold. And so on. This has an important consequence for the description–experience gap.

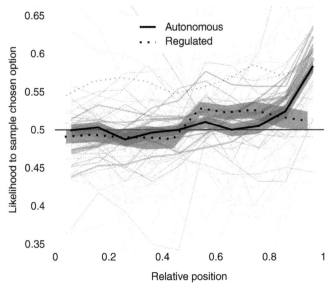

FIGURE 20.4 The sampling-cascade effect in decisions from experience. The figure shows, separately for autonomous and regulated sampling, the likelihood of sampling from the (ultimately) chosen option as a function of the draw's relative position in the sampling sequence. The lines in the background show the results separately for data sets with autonomous search termination, in which individuals self-terminate search, and data sets with regulated search termination, in which search is experimenter-terminated. The error bars represent the standard error of the mean. Reprint of Wulff et al. (2018).

Attempts to explain a description–experience gap have frequently recruited the notion of recency as the main factor leading to a gap beyond sampling error (Hertwig & Erev, 2009; Wulff et al., 2018). Specifically, these attempts assumed that recency was the result of a decision process that assigns more weight to recent samples than earlier samples due to, for instance, memory limitations. A demonstrable result of such differential weighting is that it reduces the effective samples size and thus amplifies, on a subjective level, the "underexperiencing" of rare events (see Wulff et al., 2018). However, the finding of optional stopping, as embodied in the sampling-cascade effect, implies that recency may not arise from differential weighting and, thus, may actually not contribute to the description–experience gap.

Optional stopping is only one way to terminate search. Evidence suggests that individuals also employ a planned stopping strategy. For instance, when analyzing the grammar of sample sizes, we have found that multiples of 10—for instance, 20—occur notably more frequently as sample sizes than would be expected by chance. This suggests that some individuals planned in advance to terminate search on specific prominent numbers (e.g., round numbers). Corroborating this conclusion, Markant et al. (2015) found that a planned-stopping model outperformed the online evidence-accumulation process as assumed in the CHASE model for a substantial proportion of individuals.

In sum, individuals appear to be adaptive explorers. They adjust their exploration to external and internal variables, within and across decision problems. This adaptive exploration implies that people engage implicitly or explicitly in some form of cost–benefit analysis that takes into account the characteristics of the environment as well as their preferences. One way of conceptualizing the underlying process is in terms of a process of evidence accumulation. Such a process explores the two options until the accumulated preference reaches a threshold. As a result, later samples will necessarily be more indicative of choice than earlier ones, rivaling the common interpretation that recency arises from differential weighting and suggesting that factors other than recency give rise to the description–experience gap beyond sampling error. Moreover, preference will be expressed not only in choice, as assumed by the revealed preference approach, but also in observable search. In other words, the dynamics of search offer a window on the decision maker's preference. The latter conclusion converges with a similar one drawn in eye-tracking studies; see Shimojo et al., 2003. Using a computational model such as CHASE, information search can thus be utilized to shed light on the underlying preference in ways that would not be possible based on choice alone.

Conclusions

Traditional process tracing techniques such as Mouselab (Chapters 6–7), eye-tracking (Chapters 1–5), or mouse tracking (Chapters 8–10) seek to shed light on the cognitive processes underlying behavior by making observable how individuals search for information. To achieve this, one of two paths is usually taken: One is to conceal the available information so that individuals' actions to uncover the pieces of information can be recorded, such as in the case of Mouselab and Flashlight (Schulte-Mecklenbeck, Murphy, & Hutzler, 2011). Another is to infer information acquisition from behavioral proxies such as ocular fixations or hand movements, such as in the case of eye and hand tracking. Here we have proposed a third path for studying information search. It rests on "experiential" paradigms that put search center stage and readily lay bare the information-search behavior for everyone to see (i.e., public rather than private search, external rather than internal search), without the use of technological crutches. In this sense, experiential paradigms represent an alternative or, at least, complement the arsenal of existing sophisticated process tracing method-ologies. In making our case for the utility of experiential paradigms that naturally disclose search processes, we have taken advantage of recent research on the description–experience gap. Although a still relatively young line of research, it has already offered interesting insights into how search and choice appear to be coupled when people face uncertainty and incomplete information and search is the strategy to reduce both.

The sampling paradigm in research on decisions from experience and the description–experience gap allowed us and other researchers to identify different ways in which search can foreshadow choice. In experiential paradigms, one can easily gauge the amount and content of people's encoded information. In addition, one can do so without worrying, or at least less so, about delicate distinctions such as that between the initial phase of reading, in which the experi-mental stimuli are encoded, and the subsequent phase of information acquisition that is taken to be indicative of specific choice strategies at work. Assumptions about this reading phase (e.g., all boxes in Mouselab are examined once) are critical for quantitative models of information acquisition and can make the tests of different choice models on this basis quite tricky (see the discussion in the Appendix B of Pachur, Hertwig, Gigerenzer, & Brandstätter, 2013). Of course, this does not mean that the experiential paradigms and the interpretation of the collected search data would be free of assumptions such as, for instance, about the relative memorability of events (also of relevance in process tracing technology)—but our conjecture is that the number is smaller.

We do not question that process tracing technologies represent valuable efforts to reveal processes of information acquisition and eventually move to model search and decision processes. Indeed, recent investigations have begun to entertain cell openings or eye fixations as inputs to compu-tational models of choice, such as the attentional drift–diffusion model (e.g., Krajbich, Armel, & Rangel, 2010; see also Chapters 22–24). Yet is it noteworthy—and here we take research on risk choice as rather representative of the use of process tracing technologies—that these technologies are often used in the context of decisions from description? Individuals in description-based studies can usually quite easily obtain complete information about the available options. In contrast, this is not possible—or is at least much more difficult—for individuals in experience-based studies. Consequently, in decisions from description the space for information search to profoundly shape experience and knowledge and interindividual differences therein is often limited to the rarer cases in which individuals fail to open or glance at a piece of information at all. This implies that the most important (but by no means only) role of information in experiential choice—namely how small samples interact with the environment to produce systematically "biased" experiences (relative to the "true" environment)—is by design excluded in traditional process tracing studies. Admittedly, employing process tracing in the context of decisions from description, with all information accessible, can sometimes help to boost sensitivity for detecting associations between search policy and strategy use. However, this focus comes at the price of passing over key properties of mortal decision makers, namely, uncertainty and incomplete knowledge.

Research on the description–experience gap in choice between monetary lotteries is of key importance because findings from the description-only paradigm "have formed the bedrock of contemporary decision theories, most notably prospect theory" (Fantino & Navarro, 2012, p. 303); however, the impact of the description–experience distinction is not limited to choices between monetary lotteries. Numerous other choice and judgment phenomena have, for several decades, been studied primarily with description-based paradigms, including base-rate neglect, sunk-cost effects, and social and strategic dilemmas (see Fantino & Navarro, 2012). Recently, researchers have begun to examine the possibility of description–experience gaps in other domains, such as temporal discounting (Dai, Pachur, Pleskac, & Hertwig, 2018; Kemel & Travers, 2016), strategic reasoning in social games (Fleischhut, Artinger, Olschewski, Volz, & Hertwig, 2014; Martin, Gonzalez, Juvina, & Lebiere, 2014), consumer choice (Wulff, Hills, & Hertwig, 2015b), medical decisions and reasoning (Armstrong & Spaniol, 2017; Fraenkel, Peters, Tyra, & Oelberg, 2016), and adolescent risk taking (Pollak et al., 2016; van den Bos & Hertwig, 2017). This means that turning to the process of exploration and learning with the help of experiential paradigms to understand the cognitive processes behind a wide range of important cognitive tasks has just begun.

Let us highlight again what we said at the outset. Our point is not to pit process tracing methodologies against experiential paradigms. The ability to search and explore and learn from experience as well as the ability to process symbolic descriptions are both hallmarks of human cognition. Yet, research harnessing process tracing methodologies has—to the best of our knowledge—exclusively focused on decisions from description. This requires sophisticated methodologies and auxiliary assumptions to interpret the data. Experiential paradigms render it easier, according to our conjecture, to study search and how it shapes choice. Let us conclude by inviting everyone to test this conjecture, for instance by employing simultaneously experiential paradigms and process tracing technologies, and, equally important, by conceiving of ways to utilize such technologies to study how the mind navigates uncertainty. Let us also find out to what extent the findings from both windows on the processes suggest converging or diverging inferences and interpretations. In the end, we believe it is not method fetishism that fosters progress but healthy competition.

Notes

1 We gratefully acknowledge editorial support from Susannah Goss and the editors' helpful comments.
2 The study of experience-based decision making is in fact much older and harks back to the beginnings of behavioral decisions science with Edwards (1956, 1961, 1962), Rapoport (1964), and Busemeyer (1982)

The Anatomy of Search **323**

to give but a few references. New in the early 2000s was that researchers began to systematically pit experience- and description-based decisions against each other and to characterize whether and why decisions based on these two modes of learning diverge.

3 For a description of the data set collection see also van den Bos, Jenny, and Wulff (2014).
4 Based on the parameters determined by Tversky and Kahneman (1992).
5 CHASE weights probabilities as a function of the associated outcomes rank in the empirical cumulative distribution mimicking in the limit rank-dependent utilities models used to describe decisions from description, such as Cumulative Prospect Theory (see Markant et al., 2015).

Recommended Reading List

- Wulff et al. (2018): Meta-analysis demonstrating a systematic discrepancy between choices based on description and experience and evaluating the various drivers involved in creating this description-experience gap.
- Wulff, Hills, and Hertwig, (2015a): Experimental study establishing a link between an individual's goals and information search in decisions from experience.
- Hertwig, Hogarth, and Lejarraga, (2018): Review working out the psychological implications associated with two distinct ways, experience and descriptions, to learn about choice options.

References

Allais, M. (1953). Le comportement de l'homme rationnel devant le risque, critique des postulats et axiomes de l'école americaine. *Econometrica, 21*, 503–546.

Armstrong, B., & Spaniol, J. (2017). Experienced probabilities increase understanding of diagnostic test results in younger and older adults. *Medical Decision Making, 37*(6), 670–679.

Barron, G., & Erev, I. (2003). Small feedback-based decisions and their limited correspondence to description-based decisions. *Journal of Behavioral Decision Making, 16*(3), 215–233.

Busemeyer, J. R. (1982). Choice behavior in a sequential decision-making task. *Organizational Behavior and Human Performance, 29*(2), 175–207.

Camilleri, A. R., & Newell, B. R. (2009). The role of representation in experience-based choice. *Judgment and Decision Making, 4*(7), 518–529.

Dai, J., Pachur, T., Pleskac, T., & Hertwig, R. (2018). *A description–experience gap in intertemporal choice.* Manuscript submitted for publication.

Edwards, W. (1956). Reward probability, amount, and information as determiners of sequential two-alternative decisions. *Journal of Experimental Psychology, 52*(3), 177–188.

Edwards, W. (1961). Behavioral decision theory. Annual Review of *Psychology, 12*(1), 473–498.

Edwards, W. (1962). Dynamic decision theory and probabilistic information processing. *Human Factors, 4*(2), 59–74.

Ellsberg, D. (1961). Risk, ambiguity, and the Savage axioms. *The Quarterly Journal of Economics, 75*(4), 643–669.

Fantino, E., & Navarro, A. (2012). Description–experience gaps: Assessments in other choice paradigms. *Journal of Behavioral Decision Making, 25*(3), 303–314.

Fleischhut, N., Artinger, F., Olschewski, S., Volz, K. G., & Hertwig, R. (2014). Sampling of social information: Decisions from experience in bargaining. In P. Bello, M. Guarini, M. McShane, & B. Scassellati (Eds.), *Program of the 36th annual conference of the cognitive science society* (pp. 1048–1053). Austin, TX: Cognitive Science Society.

Fraenkel, L., Peters, E., Tyra, S., & Oelberg, D. (2016). Shared medical decision making in lung cancer screening: Experienced versus descriptive risk formats. *Medical Decision Making, 36*(4), 518–525.

Frey, R., Hertwig, R., & Rieskamp, J. (2014). Fear shapes information acquisition in decisions from experience. *Cognition, 132*(1), 90–99.

Hau, R., Pleskac, T. J., Kiefer, J., & Hertwig, R. (2008). The description–experience gap in risky choice: The role of sample size and experienced probabilities. *Journal of Behavioral Decision Making, 21*(5), 493–518.

Hertwig, R., Barron, G., Weber, E. U., & Erev, I. (2004). Decisions from experience and the effect of rare events in risky choice. *Psychological Science, 15*(8), 534–539.

Hertwig, R., Hogarth, R. M., & Lejarraga, T. (2018). Experience and description: Exploring two paths to knowledge. *Current Directions in Psychological Science, 27*(2), 123–128.

Hertwig, R., & Erev, I. (2009). The description–experience gap in risky choice. *Trends in Cognitive Sciences, 13*(12), 517–523.

Hertwig, R., & Pleskac, T. J. (2010). Decisions from experience: Why small samples? *Cognition, 115*(2), 225–237.

Hills, T. T., Noguchi, T., & Gibbert, M. (2013). Information overload or search-amplified risk? Set size and order effects on decisions from experience. *Psychonomic Bulletin & Review, 20*(5), 1023–1031.

Kahneman, D., & Tversky, A. (1979). Prospect theory: An analysis of decision under risk. *Econometrica, 47*(2), 263–291.

Kemel, E., & Travers, M. (2016). Comparing attitudes toward time and toward money in experience-based decisions. *Theory and Decision, 80*(1), 71–100.

Krajbich, I., Armel, C., & Rangel, A. (2010). Visual fixations and the computation and comparison of value in simple choice. *Nature Neuroscience, 13*(10), 1292–1298.

Lejarraga, T., Hertwig, R., & Gonzalez, C. (2012). How choice ecology influences search in decisions from experience. *Cognition, 124*(3), 334–342.

Ludvig, E. A., & Spetch, M. L. (2011). Of black swans and tossed coins: Is the description-experience gap in risky choice limited to rare events? *PLoS ONE, 6*(6), e20262.

Markant, D. B., Pleskac, T. J., Diederich, A., Pachur, T., & Hertwig, R. (2015). Modeling choice and search in decisions from experience: A sequential sampling approach. In D. C. Noelle, R. Dale, A. S. Warlaumont, J. Yoshimi, T. Matlock, C. D. Jennings, & P. P. Maglio (Eds.), *Proceedings of the 37th annual meeting of the cognitive science society* (pp. 1512–1517). Austin, TX: Cognitive Science Society.

Martin, J. M., Gonzalez, C., Juvina, I., & Lebiere, C. (2014). A description–experience gap in social interactions: Information about interdependence and its effects on cooperation. *Journal of Behavioral Decision Making, 27*(4), 349–362.

Noguchi, T., & Hills, T. T. (2016). Experience-based decisions favor riskier alternatives in large sets. *Journal of Behavioral Decision Making, 29*(5), 489–498.

Ostwald, D., Starke, L., & Hertwig, R. (2015). A normative inference approach for optimal sample sizes in decisions from experience. *Frontiers in Psychology, 6*, 1342.

Pachur, T., Hertwig, R., Gigerenzer, G., & Brandstätter, E. (2013). Testing process predictions of models of risky choice: A quantitative model comparison approach. *Frontiers in Psychology, 4*, 646.

Phillips, N. D., Hertwig, R., Kareev, Y., & Avrahami, J. (2014). Rivals in the dark: How competition influences search in decisions under uncertainty. Cognition, 133(1), 104–119.

Pleskac, T. J., & Hertwig, R. (2014). Ecologically rational choice and the structure of the environment. *Journal of Experimental Psychology: General, 143*(5), 2000–2019.

Pleskac, T. J., Yu, S., Hopwood, C., & Liu, T. (in press). Characterizing deliberation during preferential choice. *Decision.*

Pollak, Y., Oz, A., Neventsal, O., Rabi, O., Kitrossky, L., & Maeir, A. (2016). Do adolescents with attention-deficit/hyperactivity disorder show risk seeking? Disentangling probabilistic decision making by equalizing the favorability of alternatives. *Journal of Abnormal Psychology, 125*(3), 387–398.

Rapoport, A. (1964). Sequential decision-making in a computer-controlled task. *Journal of Mathematical Psychology, 1*(2), 351–374.

Regenwetter, M., & Robinson, M. M. (2017). The construct–behavior gap in behavioral decision research: A challenge beyond replicability. *Psychological Review, 124*(5), 533–550.

Schulte-Mecklenbeck, M., Murphy, R. O., & Hutzler, F. (2011). Flashlight: Recording information acquisition online. *Computers in Human Behavior, 27*(5), 1771–1782.

Schulte-Mecklenbeck, M., Johnson, J. G., Böckenholt, U., Goldstein, D. G., Russo, J. E., Sullivan, N. J., & Willemsen, M. C. (2017). Process-tracing methods in decision making: On growing up in the 70s. *Current Directions in Psychological Science, 26*(5), 442–450.

Shimojo, S., Simion, C., Shimojo, E., & Scheier, C. (2003). Gaze bias both reflects and influences preference. *Nature Neuroscience, 6*(12), 1317–1322.

Tversky, A., & Kahneman, D. (1992). Advances in prospect theory: Cumulative representation of uncertainty. *Journal of Risk and Uncertainty, 5*(4), 297–323.

van den Bos, W., & Hertwig, R. (2017). Adolescents display distinctive tolerance to ambiguity and to uncertainty during risky decision making. *Scientific Reports, 7*, 40962.

van den Bos, W., Jenny, M. A., & Wulff, D. U. (2014). Open minded psychology. In S. A. Moore (Ed.), *Issues in open research data* (pp. 107–127). London, UK: Ubiquity Press.

Weber, E. U., Shafir, S., & Blais, A. R. (2004). Predicting risk sensitivity in humans and lower animals: Risk as variance or coefficient of variation. *Psychological Review, 111*(2), 430–445.

Wulff, D. U., Hills, T. T., & Hertwig, R. (2015a). How short- and long-run aspirations impact search and choice in decisions from experience. *Cognition, 144*, 29–37.

Wulff, D. U., Hills, T. T., & Hertwig, R. (2015b). Online product reviews and the description–experience gap. *Journal of Behavioral Decision Making, 28*(3), 214–223.

Wulff, D. U., Markant, D. B., Pleskac, & Hertwig, R. (in press). Adaptive exploration: What you see is up to you. In R. Hertwig, T. Pleskac, T. Pachur, & The ARC Research Group (in press). *Taming uncertainty*. Cambridge, MA: MIT Press.

Wulff, D. U., Mergenthaler-Canseco, M., & Hertwig, R. (2018). A meta-analytic review of two modes of learning and the description–experience gap. *Psychological Bulletin, 144*(2), 140–176.

Zeigenfuse, M. D., Pleskac, T. J., & Liu, T. (2014). Rapid decisions from experience. *Cognition, 131*(2), 181–194.

21

PROCESS TRACING, SAMPLING, AND DRIFT RATE CONSTRUCTION[1]

Neil Stewart and Timothy L. Mullett

What can process tracing tell us about the nature of evidence accumulation during choice? In this chapter, we review the idea from a model called decision by sampling (Stewart, Chater, & Brown, 2006; Stewart, Reimers, & Harris, 2015) and show how we have used process tracing data to constrain the development of this model into a process model of choice. In the decision by sampling model decisions are the result of a series of binary, ordinal comparisons between attribute values. That is, people make lots of comparisons between attribute values and use the number of wins each alternative achieves as the criteria for making a decision. In this chapter we explain how people counting wins will behave as if the subjective value for an attribute value is given by its rank position against other attribute values. We discuss how this sort of tally can be particularly robust and can be considered as optimal. We review evidence for the rank hypothesis in judgment and choice, and also evidence from neuroimaging studies including fMRI and single cell recording. We then consider the attentional drift diffusion model (Krajbich, Armel, & Rangel, 2010; Krajbich & Rangel, 2011). The attentional drift diffusion model integrates process tracing data from eye movements during choice and attribute values to produce accounts of the choice made, the time taken to make the choice, and the patterns of visual attention seen whilst the choice is made. We conclude with a discussion of how the rank hypothesis and drift diffusion can be combined and developed into a new mathematical model of multiattribute choice, with modeling assumptions constrained by process data.

Decision by Sampling and the Rank Hypothesis in Judgment and Choice

Parducci (1965, 1995) proposed range-frequency theory as an explanation of how people assign a set of categorical judgments to stimuli varying on a single perceptual dimension. For example, people might be assigning a set of category labels "very small"–"very large" to a series of squares varying in their size. Parducci assumes people make these assignments using two principles: the range principle and the frequency principle (see Figure 21.1). According to the range principle, the stimulus continuum, here square size, is divided into equal width bins. According to the frequency principle, the stimulus continuum is divided up such that each category label is used equally often (e.g., for three squares in Figure 21.1). For example, if people have five categories to use equally often they should put the smallest fifth of squares into the first category, the next smallest fifth into the next category, and so on, no matter what the actual sizes are.

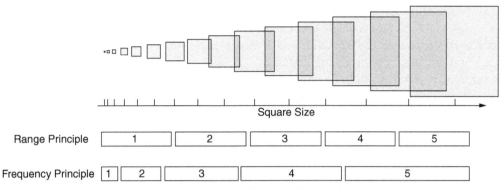

FIGURE 21.1 An illustration of how squares are divided into five equal sized bins according to the range principle and five equally used bins according to the frequency principle.

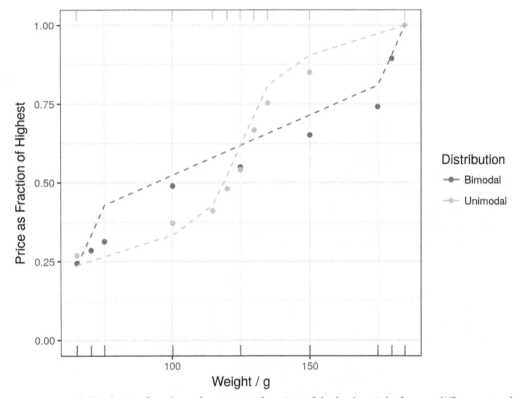

FIGURE 21.2 Judged price for a bag of sweets as a function of the bag's weight for two different sets of bags. Dashed lines are the predictions of the frequency principle.

One consequence of the frequency principle is that people will tend to evaluate magnitudes as a function of their ranks. An unpublished experiment from Brown and Saktreger illustrates this well for judgments of the price of bags of sweets varying in weight (though results are similar for perceptual magnitudes, e.g., Parducci & Wedell, 1986). Figure 21.2 plots the price elicited by an incentive compatible Becker, DeGroot, and Marschak (1964) auction for bags as a function of weight. To facilitate averaging over participants, prices for each participant were divided by the price they judged for the heaviest bag. Brown and Saktreger used two different sets of bags of sweets. In one set the prices of the bags followed a unimodal distribution, with many bags weighing between 100g and 150g (see the rug plot at the top of Figure 21.2). In the other set the bags followed a bimodal distribution, with many bags less than 100g and many bags more than 150g (see the rug at the bottom of Figure 21.2). Brown and Saktreger were careful to hold the range of weights fixed across the sets, and to include common weights of 100g, 125g, and 150g in both sets. Prices are very different for the 100g and 150g bags across the sets as this is where their respective rank positions within the sets differ most. The dashed lines are the predictions of the frequency principle, and match the qualitative pattern in the data well. Both predictions and observed judgments increase most quickly where the distribution is most dense, as this is where rank position changes most quickly.

Drawing upon Parducci's (1965, 1995) frequency principle, the original exposition of the decision by sampling model (Stewart et al., 2006) offers an account of the origin of the subjective values for economic quantities like money, risk, and time. Consider a person forming a subjective valuation for £100. The idea is that they compare the £100 against a series of sums of money sampled from their memories—perhaps other values presented in the choice context, or values that come to mind because they have been recently experienced or are evoked by the context. Suppose, in this example, people have in mind the sums £10, £17, £30, and £240; £100 compares favorably with £10, £17, and £30, and unfavorably with £240. Thus three of the four possible comparisons with the sample in memory would lead to a win for £100. The probability that each comparison leads to a win for £100 is 3/4, which means people would behave as if, in this context, £100 has a subjective value of 3/4.

Many chapters in this Handbook provide a discussion on the processes of external information search in decision making, which is one origin for the samples people might have in mind. Though information search is clearly critical, Stewart et al. (2006) sidestepped detailed assumptions about information search by assuming that the distributions people have in mind reflect the distributions of attribute values in the environment (cf., Anderson & Schooler, 1991). Stewart et al. used credits and debits into bank accounts as a proxy for the shapes of the distributions of gains and losses that people experience in the environment. Figure 21.3 shows the frequencies of different credits (left) and debits (middle) in a large sample of bank accounts. Both distributions have the property that there are more small transactions than large ones, and the (very approximate) straight line in log-log space indicates the distributions follow something resembling a power law. Figure 21.3 also shows the resulting decision by sampling value function (right). The top right quadrant plots the relative rank of a given gain as a function of the size of the gain. The function is steep just above zero, because that is where the distribution of credits is most dense—and thus where a given absolute increase in the size of a gain has the largest effect on rank position. But nearer £1000 the function is flat, because that is where the distribution of credits is less dense—and thus where a given absolute increment in the size of a gain has only a small effect on rank position. The bottom left quadrant plots the value function for losses. The function is plotted upside down because large losses are bad (whereas large gains are good). Like the function for gains, the function is steepest near 0 where the debits are most dense and flatter for higher magnitude losses where the debits are much less dense. The asymmetry in the function, with a steeper initial function for losses than gains results from the asymmetry in the distribution of gains and losses in the credits and debits, where there are more small debits than small credits. This decision by sampling value function bears a striking resemblance to the value function from prospect theory (Kahneman & Tversky, 1979). In prospect theory the shape of the value function is motivated by risky choice phenomena, including risk aversion for gambles involving gains and risk seeking for gambles involving losses. In decision

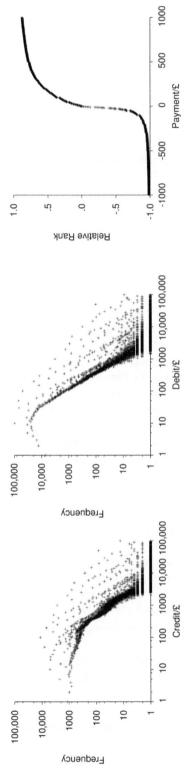

FIGURE 21.3 The frequencies of credits and debits in bank accounts (left and middle) and the value function that would result from sampling from these credits and debits (right) (after Stewart et al., 2006, Figures 1 and 2, based on a sample of 1,800,000 transactions).

by sampling, the shape emerges from the environmental distribution of gains and losses combined with the cognitive process of counting favorable binary comparisons. In other words, decision by sampling offers an explanation, in terms of the distribution of values in the environment, as to why people make the decisions they do, whereas prospect theory just describes the decisions.

Decision by sampling is able to offer an account of the risky choice phenomena that motivated prospect theory because it predicts that people will behave as if they have a prospect theory value function in worlds with positively skewed distributions of gains and losses. Stewart and Simpson (2008) and Stewart (2009) developed the model from judgments into choice. They proposed an explicit mechanism whereby wins for each alternative are accumulated until a threshold is reached, with the probability of a win for each attribute of each alternative defined just as earlier. The model is able, for example, to explain the patterns in risky choice seen in Kahneman and Tversky (1979) that were used to motivate prospect theory, like, for example, the Allais paradox. In the Allais paradox people prefer a sure $3000 over a 75% chance of $4000 otherwise nothing, but prefer a 20% chance of $4000 over a 25% chance of $3000. This is a violation of expected utility because people reverse their preferences for the $3000 option over the $4000 option across the pair of choices even though the first choice is related to the second choice simply by dividing the probabilities by four. In decision by sampling, the reversal occurs because the difference in the relative ranks of 75% and 100% is much larger than the difference in the relative ranks of 20% and 25% within the sample of probabilities people have in mind (Stewart & Simpson, 2008).

Ungemach, Stewart, and Reimers (2011) conducted a test of this model. According to decision by sampling, changes to the amount of money available in people's memory should change their subjective valuations of those amounts. Ungemach et al. (2011) used visits to the campus supermarket as a natural priming experiment. Upon leaving the store, people were asked to give up their receipt in return for a choice between two lotteries. One lottery offering an unlikely prize of £1.50 and the other offered a more likely prize of £0.50. Thus participants faced a choice between a higher risk but higher reward lottery and a lower risk but lower reward lottery. Ungemach et al. (2011) found that the fraction of item prices on the supermarket receipt between £0.50 and £1.50 predicted the lottery choice. Assuming that the prices of the supermarket receipts have some correspondence to the prices in memory, decision by sampling makes a clear prediction. When most of the items were between £0.50 and £1.50, £0.50 is one of the lowest ranking amounts in memory and £1.50 is one of the highest ranking amounts in memory. But when most of the items were lower than £0.50 or higher than £1.50, £0.50 and £1.50 will get very similar ranks. The proportion of prices on the bill between £0.50 and £1.50 did indeed predict preference for the high risk £1.50 lottery, while the total spend, and other economic variables, did not (see Matthews, 2012, for a failure to replicate in the intertemporal domain and Canic, 2016, for a meta-analysis of studies with the same logic in choices between simple lotteries).

The idea in decision by sampling, that values are judged against a small sample of comparison items, is related to ideas in norm theory (Kahneman & Miller, 1986) where the typicality or normality of a hypothesis is judged against a sample of counterfactual hypotheses evoked by the context, and support theory (Tversky & Koehler, 1994) where the likelihood of a hypothesis is based upon comparisons to a sample of alternative hypotheses. It is also related to the notion of the construction of preference (Bettman, Luce, & Payne, 1998; Payne, Bettman, & Johnson, 1992; Slovic, 1995), because the subjective value of attribute values is derived on the fly during the series of binary ordinal comparisons, rather than being static. Finally, the counting of favorable binary ordinal comparisons is tallying (Dawes, 1979), which is quite robust because less information needs to be estimated about how to combine information across dimensions (signs of coefficients are sufficient, rather than magnitudes).

Diffusion Models

One weakness of decision by sampling as a process model is that it makes only coarse predictions for reaction time. In cases where there are relatively few binary comparisons to be made, decision by sampling also predicts that the current estimate of value may undergo large changes during deliberation. This is because when there are few possible comparisons, any single one will be a large proportion of the underlying value information. This suggests that any process measure of the current value estimate should also show this coarse step change in the representation of value. This is important because neuroscience methods have provided insights into the moment-to-moment representation of value at a neural level, and how this information is combined to reach a decision. The findings suggest that rather than exhibiting dramatic changes during deliberation, the neural representation of value is noisy moment-to-moment, but on average it is relatively stable (Thorpe, Rolls, & Maddison, 1983; Tremblay & Schultz, 1999).

Some alternative models do much better at predicting both the neuroimaging patterns and reaction times, in particular those predicated upon evidence accumulation, such as drift diffusion. This family of models assumes that because the neural representation of value is so noisy moment-to-moment, the decision maker accumulates evidence. This is akin to drawing repeated samples from this noisy neural representation of value so that the average can be estimated. Within the drift diffusion framework this is thought of within the structure of a single number: the accumulator. The value of option A has a positive effect on this number, and the value of option B has a negative effect on this number. Multiple samples are taken from the noisy value representations meaning that, on average, if option A has a higher value, the accumulator will become more positive over time, and if option B is more valuable, the accumulator will become more negative over time. This is referred to as drift, because over time the accumulator number will drift higher or drift lower. This will continue until the accumulator value becomes so positive or so negative that it hits a positive or negative decision threshold and thus the relevant option is selected. Because this process is assumed to be noisy, these models do well at predicting reliable patterns in choices and response times, such as easier choices being quicker, and that response times will exhibit a positive skew.

There are several successful models that make use of the drift diffusion mechanism (Busemeyer & Townsend, 1993; Roe, Busemeyer, & Townsend, 2001; Ratcliff, 1978; Ratcliff & Rouder, 1998). In addition to having high accuracy when predicting choice error rates and reaction times, they have a degree of neural plausibility that few other approaches can match (Gold & Shadlen, 2007); a noisy accumulation system can be efficiently performed by neuronal firing patterns, and structures necessary for the implementation of choice have been identified in the brain. They can also predict the relative stability of average neural activity in reward regions by assuming this activity is a temporally smoothed representation of drift rate, and some degree of context dependency by assuming interactions and inhibitory links between attributes and options (Busemeyer, Jessup, Johnson, & Townsend, 2006). More recent developments of this class of models also incorporate findings from eye-tracking and attention research (Krajbich et al., 2010). By assuming that evidence accumulation is biased to accumulate evidence in favor of the option currently being looked at, the model is able to fit numerous aspects of visual attention during deliberation, as well as improving predictive accuracy in other measures by incorporating attention as a predictor.

Despite their success, there are some fundamental questions that evidence accumulation models struggle to answer. One of the most fundamental of these is: where does the initial representation of value come from? These accumulation models do very well at describing how this noisy signal is accumulated and turned into decisions and reaction times, but are silent on how the properties of the stimuli are turned into this noisy signal. The most common assumption is that the drift rate is simply a linear transformation of the objective stimulus value, sometimes with additional tweaks and biases that allow the model to capture non-linear patterns of comparison or biases to give some attributes more weight than others. However, even the more complex assumptions still fail to capture many contextual phenomena that are quite naturally explained by decision by sampling.

A question therefore becomes, could a sampling and comparison process play a role in the construction of these noisy representations of value? One way to answer this is to turn to evidence from neuroscience (see also Chapters 14–16). These techniques allow for a direct measurement of activity in regions known to represent option values, and the drift rate component of evidence accumulation models (for a review see Konovalov & Krajbich, 2016). One of the key areas for value representation is a frontal region called the vmPFC (ventro-medial Pre-Frontal Cortex; Plassmann, O'Doherty, & Rangel, 2007; Clithero & Rangel, 2014). Results from fMRI experiments show that there is greater activity here when an individual is considering a more valuable item. This activity is also relatively stable on average, rather than representing an increasing activity pattern as more evidence is accumulated, so we can be relatively confident that it is representing the value signal/drift rate (for discussion of which candidate regions may be encoding the decision or evidence accumulation see Mazurek, Roitman, Ditterich, & Shadlen, 2003; Katz, Yates, Pillow, & Huk, 2016).

By looking at activity in the vmPFC we can therefore test different assumptions of how this value signal is constructed. A simple way to do this is with money, as different amounts of money can be easily compared on the same scale. However, the numerical properties of money are difficult to represent neurally: financial reward can increase infinitely, but neural activity (neuron firing rates) has a finite range. This suggests that in a given task, there must be some mechanism that can rescale to the range of values on offer. The most common assumption is that neural firing linearly rescales based upon the range of values in the environment (Rangel & Clithero, 2012; cf., Parducci's, 1965, 1995 range principle) or upon the mean of the values in the environment (Knutson & Peterson, 2005; cf., Helson's 1964 adaptation level principle). However, this mechanism does not answer how value is perceived and constructed in the first place, before undergoing this transformation. In fact it assumes representation of additional absolute values—for the range or mean of values—which simply moves the problem of magnitude representation to a different part of the process. Furthermore, no neural regions have been identified that represent range or averages.

If drift rates are constructed by sampling, many of these issues are sidestepped. If decisions, and thus drift rates, are based upon some mechanism of sampling and comparison then such a mechanism would inherently normalize the encoding of value. This is because it is likely that the alternatives sampled will be relevant to the current choice and therefore on a similar scale to the currently attended item; though even if they are very different magnitudes, an ordinal comparison is still simple. Value can then be encoded entirely in terms of favorable/unfavorable comparisons. This is easy to test because it makes unique predictions that cannot be explained by other rescaling hypotheses. Specifically, the decision by sampling framework of ordinal comparisons predicts that the neural activity representing value will be based upon rank. This leads to unique predictions when the distribution of values in the environment is non-linear or unevenly distributed in some way. When Mullett and Tunney (2013) presented values to subjects that were drawn from a very non-linear environment, it was found that activity in dopaminergic regions of the ventral striatum, and the vmPFC, represented the reward's rank position within the distribution of values. The effect was sufficiently strong that the difference in fMRI neural signal (BOLD) between 10p and 30p stimuli was the same as the difference between £5 and £10 despite the difference in values being more than 16 times larger in the latter case.

A sampling-based mechanism would also explain the robust within-choice context effects showing that the neural activity in the vmPFC is encoded based on whether the current option compares relatively favorably or unfavorably with the alternative outcomes on a given trial. For example, when a monkey is told they will be awarded a piece of apple, neural firing rates are high if the other possible outcome was a piece of (less preferred) cereal, but low if the other possible outcome was a piece of (more preferred) raisin (Tremblay & Schultz, 1999). A similar effect is found in humans when receiving monetary rewards: neural firing for a win of 50p is high when the alternative possibility was 10p, and low when the alternative possibility was £1 (Elliott, Agnew, & Deakin, 2008). This is also true when individuals switch their attention during deliberation, with neural firing being higher whilst they are looking at a higher value reward (Lim, O'Doherty, & Rangel, 2011; McGinty, Rangel, & Newsome, 2016).

To this point, we have reviewed the decision by sampling model and some of the context effects in studies of economic judgment and choice that support the assumption that judgment and choice are sensitive to rank effects. We have also reviewed evidence from neuroeconomics suggesting that evidence is accumulated over time until a choice is made, a process well accounted for by drift diffusion models. These models, however, do not offer a natural account of where drift rates come from and how they might vary across different contexts. In the following we review how process tracing evidence has been used to constrain the integration of the decision by sampling model and the drift diffusion/evidence accumulation frameworks.

Using Process Tracing to Constrain Assumptions: Multialternative Decision by Sampling

In the following we review key evidence from process tracing studies which we have used to constrain ideas about how evidence is aggregated over time in the accumulator framework. Both sources of evidence involve eye movements (see Chapters 1–5)): The first explores the link between eye movements between attribute values in multialternative choice and the choice ultimately made. The second concerns changes in the pattern of eye movements in the run up to a choice.

Alternatives are Compared in Pairwise Comparisons on Single Dimensions

Noguchi and Stewart (2014) explored the link between eye movements and choice, testing in particular the idea that the accumulation of favorable binary, ordinal comparisons between pairs of attribute values might be driving choice. Participants made a series of choices, each between three alternatives on two dimensions. For example, one choice was between three cars, each with different safety ratings and fuel efficiency. Figure 21.4 shows two screenshots from the experiment for the car choice. Each choice involved a different consumer-good cover story.

The attribute values were chosen to create attraction, similarity, and compromise questions. The attraction, similarity, and compromise effects are important in multialternative choice because together they set a significant benchmark for modelling (see Roe et al., 2001). Figure 21.5 illustrates the choice sets used to demonstrate the attraction, similarity, and compromise effects. The alternatives vary on two attribute dimensions x and y, with more of each dimension being better. Each set starts with a pair of core alternatives, A and B, which are, roughly, equally likely to be chosen. Adding either D, S, or C to the choice set leads to a favoring of alternative A over alternative B. In particular, D is asymmetrically dominated by A, adding D to the choice set increases the choice share for A over B due to the attraction effect. Adding alternative S, which is similar to B, also leads to an increase preference for A over B—the similarity effect. Adding a competitive but

Imagine you are going to buy a car.	Safety 5.0
	Efficiency 31.05mpg
The safety rating will appear on the upper line, and the fuel efficiency (in miles per gallon) will be seen on the lower line.	
	Safety 4.9 Safety 4.0
The safety is rated on a scale from 0 to 5, where 0 is poor and 5 means excellent.	
Please press SPACEBAR to proceed.	Efficiency 32.91mpg Efficiency 49.65mpg

(a) Choice Description   (b) Choice Set

FIGURE 21.4 A screenshot from Noguchi and Stewart (2014, their Figure 3), depicting a choice between three cars.

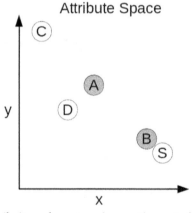

FIGURE 21.5 The attraction, similarity, and compromise questions sets. A and B are common alternatives. The addition of an asymmetrically dominated alternative D creates an attraction choice set favoring A, the addition of a similar alternative S creates a similarity choice set favoring A, and the addition of a distant alternative C creates a compromise choice set favoring A.

distant option C makes A a compromise between C and B and increases the relative preference for A over B. The attraction, similarity, and compromise effects represent a violation of regularity (the property that adding an alternative cannot increase the choice share for any existing alternative) and independence from irrelevant alternatives (the property that adding an alternative cannot reverse the ordering of choice shares for existing options). Both of these principles are properties of any model in which the value of an alternative remains stable across different choices and is invariant to the other alternatives in the choice set (see Rieskamp, Busemeyer, & Mellers, 2006, for a review). As such, the existence of the attraction, similarity, and compromise effects points towards a construction of preference, where people behave as if the values of the different alternatives are constructed during the choice process in a context-dependent way.

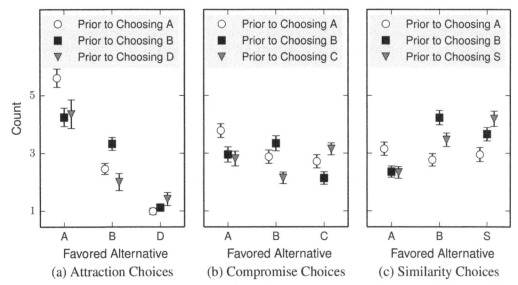

FIGURE 21.6 The number of transitions made during a choice favoring each alternative, separately for each choice outcome (from Noguchi & Stewart, 2014, Figure 11).

The models of these effects are all quite similar, in that they all embody the idea that microsamples of evidence are accumulated over time until a decision is reached (e.g., Bhatia, 2013; Roe et al., 2001; Trueblood, Brown, & Heathcote, 2014; Usher & McClelland, 2004; Wollschläger & Diederich, 2012). Where they differ is in how they define the evidence that is accumulated—and it is this question that Noguchi and Stewart were attempting to answer using process tracing data. Noguchi and Stewart recorded participants' eye movements while they made each choice. They considered transitions between attribute values—defined as moving gaze from one attribute to another. Each transition can be defined as favoring one alternative. For example, the transition between Alternatives A and B on Dimension X favors Alternative B (because Alternative B is better on Dimension X) and the transition between Alternatives A and B on Dimension Y favors Alternative A (because Alternative A is better on Dimension Y). For each choice, Noguchi and Stewart counted the number of transitions favoring each alternative. Figure 21.6 shows how the number of transitions favoring an option is higher on trials where that option was indeed chosen. That is, the trials where Alternative A is chosen are those where transitions that favor Alternative A happen to have been made more often and transitions favoring the other options were made less often. For example, for the attraction choices in Figure 21.6(a), prior to choosing A (○ symbols) the transitions which favor A are more frequent and the transitions favoring B and D are less frequent. Prior to choosing B (■ symbols) the pattern reverses, so that transitions favoring A are less frequent and transitions favoring B are more frequent. And thus these fluctuations over trials in the pattern of eye movements are associated with changes in the alternative finally chosen.

Noguchi and Stewart (2014) used these results to discriminate between different types of evidence accumulation. The previous finding is most consistent with *attribute-and-alternative-wise* models in which one pair of alternatives is compared on a single dimension at each point in the accumulation process. *Alternative-wise* models assume that all of the attributes of an alternative are integrated before comparisons. *Attribute-wise* models assume that one dimension is attended and all of the alternatives (not just the two in the attended pair) are simultaneously evaluated on that dimension. Neither attribute-wise models nor alternative-wise models can predict the interaction between the pair of alternatives and the dimension attended. So, because the process data implicate an attribute-and-alternative-wise model, multialternative decision by sampling was implemented as an attribute-and-alternative-wise model. The process data constrained the modeling assumption.

The Gaze Bias Effect Implicates a Relative Stopping Rule

One of the most robust findings in visual attention during choice is the late onset bias (also known as the gaze cascade). This describes the phenomenon that in the final moments before a choice is made, subjects become increasingly likely to attend the option they subsequently choose (Figure 21.7). In a series of model simulations Mullett and Stewart (2016) show that this pattern can be captured by an evidence accumulation model with a simple attentional bias assumption that is present in a number of existing models: evidence is accumulated more rapidly for the option that is currently attended (e.g., Krajbich et al., 2010). However, these models can only capture the effect if they also assume a relative decision threshold, that is, a decision is made once one of the options has accumulated a total amount of evidence that is X *more than* the evidence for the other alternative. This is in contrast to models which assume an absolute threshold, where a decision is made once any one option has accumulated an amount of evidence that surpasses a predefined amount of X, regardless of whether the amount accumulated for the alternative is very similar, or much lower. The underlying conceptual cause is that in a relative threshold model, whenever evidence is accumulated for one of the options, it changes the relative amount of evidence in that option's favor, i.e. closer towards that threshold. However, the relative nature means that it also moves further away from the decision threshold for the competitor. Because of this back and forth nature of a relative rule, it is necessary for there to be a run of evidence accumulated in favor of an item. Without this run, or series of samples in favor of the option, the relative evidence would not stray over the threshold before the bias changed to favor the alternative. This need for a run of samples prior to crossing a threshold means that the bias in sampling must onset prior to choice. Furthermore, the bias will appear to develop smoothly when averaged across choices because the random noise in evidence accumulation means that sometimes the accumulator will already be close to a threshold and only require a relatively short run, whereas other times it will be further away and require a longer run (which is less likely to occur due to the variable distribution of attention, and thus "run length").

This finding demonstrates the importance of process data in constraining models. In any model where there is an increasing bias towards accumulating evidence or sampling in favor of the attended item, the decision rule must be relative. Only a relative model involves a run of evidence for one alternative in the run up to a decision. In fact, the late onset bias cannot be captured in an absolute model even when assuming a feedback loop between evidence accumulated and attention. For this reason, the decision rule in multialternative decision by sampling is a relative decision rule. Again, the process data constrained the modeling assumption.

Multialternative Decision by Sampling

The process tracing evidence from Noguchi and Stewart (2014) suggests that alternatives are compared in pairs on single dimensions, at least in attraction, similarity, and compromise-like multialternative choice sets. The Mullett and Stewart (2016) simulations implicate a relative stopping rule. Noguchi and Stewart (2018) have used these two pieces of process tracing evidence to constrain a new accumulator model called multialternative decision by sampling. The

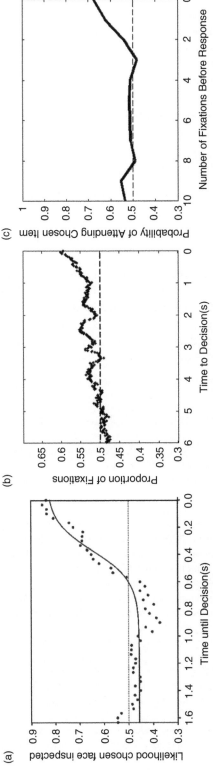

FIGURE 21.7 The late onset bias as measured in: (A) a face preference task (Shimojo, Simion, Shimojo, & Scheier, 2003); (B) a multiattribute choice task (Mullett & Tunney, 2015); (C) risky gamble choices (Stewart, Hermans, & Matthews, 2016). Adapted from Mullett and Stewart (2016).

models offer a quantitative account of the attraction, similarity, and compromise effects equal to that of competitor models like decision field theory (Roe et al., 2001) and multialternative linear ballistic accumulators (Trueblood et al., 2014), and, at the same time, provides the most broad account of the range of qualitative phenomena in the multialternative choice based on a review of the literature, including the location of decoys, time pressure effects, alignability effects, attribute range and spacing effects, background contrast effects, less is more effects, perceptual focus effects, and phantom decoy effects (Noguchi & Stewart, 2018). We think that constraining the modeling assumptions with process data has contributed to the success of the model in explaining the wide range of multialternative choice phenomena.

Note

1 This research was supported by Economic and Social Research Council grants ES/K002201/1, ES/P008976/1, and ES/N018192/1.

Recommended Reading

- Krajbich et al. (2010) extended the drift diffusion framework to include attention, and thus model choice, choice time, and eye movement fixations during choice all at once.
- Noguchi and Stewart (2014) use eye movements during choice to explore comparison processes and how they relate to the big-three choice anomalies.
- Mullett and Tunney (2013) find BOLD activation in fMRI is related to the rank of a reward against the other available rewards and not its actual magnitude.

References

Anderson, J. R., & Schooler, L. J. (1991). Reflections of the environment in memory. *Psychological Science*, *2*(6), 396–408.

Becker, G. M., DeGroot, M. H., & Marschak, J. (1964). Measuring utility by a single-response sequential method. *Behavioral Science*, *9*(3), 226–232.

Bettman, J. R., Luce, M. F., & Payne, J. W. (1998). Constructive consumer choice processes. *Journal of Consumer Research*, *25*(3), 187–217.

Bhatia, S. (2013). Associations and the accumulation of preference. *Psychological Review*, *120*(3), 522–543.

Busemeyer, J. R., & Townsend, J. T. (1993). Decision field theory: A dynamic-cognitive approach to decision making in an uncertain environment. *Psychological Review*, *100*(3), 432–459.

Busemeyer, J. R., Jessup, R. K., Johnson, J. G., & Townsend, J. T. (2006). Building bridges between neural models and complex decision making behaviour. *Neural Networks*, *19*(8), 1047–1058.

Canic, E. (2016). *Value is context dependent: On comparison processes and rank order in choice and judgment* (Unpublished doctoral dissertation). University of Warwick, Coventry, UK.

Clithero, J. A., & Rangel, A. (2014). Informatic parcellation of the network involved in the computation of subjective value. *Social Cognitive and Affective Neuroscience*, *9*(9), 1289–1302.

Dawes, R. M. (1979). The robust beauty of linear models of decision making. *American Psychologist*, *34*(7), 571–582.

Elliott, R., Agnew, Z., & Deakin, J. F. W. (2008). Medial orbitofrontal cortex codes relative rather than absolute value of financial rewards in humans. *European Journal of Neuroscience*, *27*(9), 2213–2218.

Gold, J. I., & Shadlen, M. N. (2007). The neural basis of decision making. *Annual Review of Neuroscience*, *30*(1), 535–574.

Helson, H. (1964). *Adaptation-level theory*. New York, NY: Harper & Row.

Kahneman, D., & Miller, D. T. (1986). Norm theory: Comparing reality to its alternatives. *Psychological Review*, *93*(2), 136–153.

Kahneman, D., & Tversky, A. (1979). Prospect theory: An analysis of decision under risk. *Econometrica*, *47*(2), 263–292.

Katz, L. N., Yates, J. L., Pillow, J. W., & Huk, A. C. (2016). Dissociated functional significance of decision-related activity in the primate dorsal stream. *Nature*, *535*(7611), 285–288.

Knutson, B., & Peterson, R. (2005). Neurally reconstructing expected utility. *Games and Economic Behavior*, *52*(2), 305–315.

Konovalov, A., & Krajbich, I. (2016). Over a decade of neuroeconomics: What have we learned? *Organizational Research Methods*, 10–26.

Krajbich, I., Armel, C., & Rangel, A. (2010). Visual fixations and the computation and comparison of value in simple choice. *Nature Neuroscience*, *13*(10), 1292–1298.

Krajbich, I., & Rangel, A. (2011). Multialternative drift-diffusion model predicts the relationship between visual fixations and choice in value-based decisions. *Proceedings of the National Academy of Sciences of the United States of America*, *108*(33), 13852–13857.

Lim, S. L., O'Doherty, J. P., & Rangel, A. (2011). The decision value computations in the vmPFC and striatum use a relative value code that is guided by visual attention. *Journal of Neuroscience*, 31(37), 13214–13223.

Matthews, W. J. (2012). How much do incidental values affect the judgment of time? *Psychological Science*, *23*(11), 1432–1434.

Mazurek, M. E., Roitman, J. D., Ditterich, J., & Shadlen, M. N. (2003). A role for neural integrators in perceptual decision making. *Cerebral Cortex*, *13*(11), 1257–1269.

McGinty, V. B., Rangel, A., & Newsome, W. T. (2016). Orbitofrontal cortex value signals depend on fixation location during free viewing. *Neuron*, *90*(6), 1299–1311.

Mullett, T. L., & Stewart, N. (2016). Implications of visual attention phenomena for models of preferential choice. *Decision*, *3*(4), 231–253.

Mullett, T. L., & Tunney, R. J. (2013). Value representations by rank order in a distributed network of varying context dependency. *Brain and Cognition*, *82*(1), 76–83.

Mullett, T. L., & Tunney, R. J. (2015). Attention in multi-attribute choice. *Working paper*.

Noguchi, T., & Stewart, N. (2014). In the attraction, compromise, and similarity effects, alternatives are repeatedly compared in pairs on single dimensions. *Cognition*, *132*(1), 44–56.

Noguchi, T., & Stewart, N. (2018). Multialternative decision by sampling: A model of decision making constrained by process data *Psychological Review*, *125*(4), 512–544.

Parducci, A. (1965). Category judgment: A range-frequency model. *Psychological Review*, *72*(6), 407–418.

Parducci, A. (1995). *Happiness, pleasure and judgment: The contextual theory and its applications*. Mahwah, NJ: Erlbaum.

Parducci, A., & Wedell, D. H. (1986). The category effect with rating-scales: Number of categories, number of stimuli, and method of presentation. *Journal of Experimental Psychology: Human Perception and Performance*, *12*(4), 496–516.

Payne, J. W., Bettman, J. R., & Johnson, E. J. (1992). Behavioral decision research: A constructive processing perspective. *Annual Review of Psychology*, *43*(1), 87–131.

Plassmann, H., O'Doherty, J., & Rangel, A. (2007). Orbitofrontal cortex encodes willingness to pay in everyday economic transactions. *Journal of Neuroscience*, 27(37), 9984–9988.

Rangel, A., & Clithero, J. A. (2012). Value normalization in decision making: Theory and evidence. *Current Opinion in Neurobiology*, *22*(6), 970–981.

Ratcliff, R. (1978). Theory of memory retrieval. *Psychological Review*, *85*(2), 59–108.

Ratcliff, R., & Rouder, J. N. (1998). Modeling response times for two-choice decisions. *Psychological Science*, *9*(5), 347–356.

Rieskamp, J., Busemeyer, J. R., & Mellers, B. (2006). Extending the bounds of rationality: A review of research on preferential choice. *Journal of Economic Literature*, *44*(3), 631–661.

Roe, R. M., Busemeyer, J. R., & Townsend, J. T. (2001). Multialternative decision field theory: A dynamic connectionist model of decision making. *Psychological Review*, *108*(2), 370–392.

Shimojo, S., Simion, C., Shimojo, E., & Scheier, C. (2003). Gaze bias both reflects and influences preference. *Nature Neuroscience*, *6*(12), 1317–1322.

Slovic, P. (1995). The construction of preference. *American Psychologist*, *50*(5), 364–371.

Stewart, N. (2009). Decision by sampling: The role of the decision environment in risky choice. *Quarterly Journal of Experimental Psychology, 62*(6), 1041–1062.

Stewart, N., Chater, N., & Brown, G. D. A. (2006). Decision by sampling. *Cognitive Psychology, 53*(1), 1–26.

Stewart, N., Hermens, F., & Matthews, W. J. (2016). Eye movements in risky choice. *Journal of Behavioral Decision Making, 29*(2–3), 116–136.

Stewart, N., Reimers, S., & Harris, A. J. L. (2015). On the origin of utility, weighting, and discounting functions: How they get their shapes and how to change their shapes. *Management Science, 61*(3), 687–705.

Stewart, N., & Simpson, K. (2008). A decision-by-sampling account of decision under risk. In N. Chater & M. Oaksford (Eds.), *The probabilistic mind: Prospects for Bayesian cognitive science* (pp. 261–276). Oxford, UK: Oxford University Press.

Thorpe, S. J., Rolls, E. T., & Maddison, S. (1983). The orbitofrontal cortex: Neuronal activity in the behaving monkey. *Experimental Brain Research, 49*(1), 93–115.

Tremblay, L., & Schultz, W. (1999). Relative reward preference in primate orbitofrontal cortex. *Nature, 398*(6729), 704–708.

Trueblood, J. S., Brown, S. D., & Heathcote, A. (2014). The multiattribute linear ballistic accumulator model of context effects in multialternative choice. *Psychological Review, 121*(2), 179–205.

Tversky, A., & Koehler, D. J. (1994). Support theory: A nonextensional representation of subjective probability. *Psychological Review, 101*(4), 547–567.

Ungemach, C., Stewart, N., & Reimers, S. (2011). How incidental values from our environment affect decisions about money, risk, and delay. *Psychological Science, 22*(2), 253–260.

Usher, M., & McClelland, J. L. (2004). Loss aversion and inhibition in dynamical models of multi-alternative choice. *Psychological Review, 111*(3), 757–769.

Wollschläger, L. M., & Diederich, A. (2012). The 2N-ary choice tree model for N-alternative preferential choice. *Frontiers in Psychology, 3*(189), 1–11.

22

USING MULTIPLE METHODS TO ELICIT CHOICES AND TO IDENTIFY STRATEGIES[1]

Ulrich Hoffrage and Nils Reisen

To identify the processes underlying judgment and decision making has been of great interest to researchers for several decades already. In this context, two major paradigms have been used: structural modeling and process tracing (Abelson & Levi, 1985; Billings & Marcus, 1983; Einhorn, Kleinmuntz, & Kleinmuntz, 1979; Ford, Schmitt, Schlechtman, Hults, & Doherty, 1989; Harte & Koele, 1995; Payne, 1976; Svenson, 1979). Structural modeling aims to uncover psychological processes by relating the provided information to the decisions or judgments, typically via multiple linear regression analysis. The parameters in these models are thought to represent important features of participants' decision strategies, for instance, if a particular attribute receives a high weight in a regression equation it is interpreted as being very important for the decision maker. Despite its popularity, this approach has been criticized for ignoring the pre-decisional phase, that is, the processes that take place between stimulus presentation and final decision. For example, Svenson (1979) concluded that it is "gradually becoming clear that human decision making cannot be understood simply by studying final decisions" (p. 86) and, similarly, Payne, Braunstein, and Carroll (1978) argued that the "input-output analyses that have been used in most decision research are not fully adequate to develop and test process models of decision behavior" (p. 19).

As a response to these and other objections against structural modeling (for an overview, see Bröder, 2000), Payne (1976) and others developed the process tracing approach further by adapting methods from research on human problem solving. As opposed to structural modeling, the aim of process tracing is to directly describe the processes taking place during the pre-decisional phase. To achieve this, the participants' information search is closely observed while they work on a decision task. Frequently used methods within this paradigm are information boards (Chapter 6), verbal protocols (Chapters 17–18), eye-tracking (Chapters 1–5), and the method of Active Information Search (AIS; Chapter 19).

In this chapter, we present a tool called InterActive Process Tracing (IAPT), which we (Reisen et al., 2008) developed to identify the decision processes underlying preferential choice. IAPT uses various elements of the process tracing measures mentioned earlier to combine their strengths and simultaneously overcome some of their weaknesses.

Process Tracing Techniques

What are the major process tracing methodologies and what are their strengths and weaknesses?

Information Search: Mouselab, Eye-Tracking, and the Method of Active Information Search

A range of techniques have been developed within the process tracing paradigm, each of them having both strengths and weaknesses (see Table 22.1). A popular method is Mouselab (Payne, Bettman, & Johnson, 1993), the computerized version of the information board (Payne, 1976; see also Chapters 6–7). In a typical Mouselab-based study, participants can acquire information about the choice alternatives by using the computer mouse to click on or move a pointer over the cells of an attributes-by-alternatives matrix. Mouselab provides data concerning the information acquisition phase, such as which cells are looked up, in which order, and how much time was spent looking at each cell. Besides being relatively easy to use for experimenters, this method is also quite convenient for participants because they are confronted with a relatively well-structured decision situation in which all the available information is clearly arranged.

TABLE 22.1 Strengths and weaknesses of four process tracing techniques

Strengths	*Weaknesses*
Mouselab	
+ Convenient to use.	− Overly structured: participant may be influenced as to what information to use or to consider important.
+ A large amount of data: which and how much information is retrieved and the sequence of the information acquisition.	− Only data concerning the search for information, but no data concerning information integration.
Eye-Tracking	
+ A large amount of data: which and how much information is retrieved and the sequence of the information acquisition.	− Expensive equipment.
+ Very fast and effortless information acquisition.	− A reliable calibration cannot be achieved for all participants.
+ Mostly nonreactive: behavior cannot easily be censored by the participants.	− Overly structured: participant may be influenced as to what information to use or to consider important.
+ Better suited than Mouselab to problems with more complex information displays.	− Only data concerning the search for information, but no data concerning information integration.
Active Information Search (AIS)	
+ Enhanced realism: participants are less affected by the experimental setup.	− Less exact monitoring of the information acquisition process than with Mouselab.
	− Only data concerning the search for information, but no data concerning information integration.
Retrospective Verbal Protocol	
+ Rich and detailed information: information search *and* integration.	− Doubts that people can introspectively access their cognitive processes.
+ No interference with decision making when participants work on the task.	− Reactivity: forgetting and fabrication.
	− Extremely time-consuming analysis.

Another way to trace participants' information search is to record their eye movements. Instead of using a computer mouse to obtain information, here participants simply look at a screen where the information is displayed. The eye-tracking equipment records which information is fixated and so produces data that are similar to Mouselab's. However, for eye-tracking (see Chapters 1–5), the process of information acquisition resembles a more natural situation (simple reading) as compared to Mouselab (opening cells).

Similar to Mouselab and eye-tracking, the method of AIS (Huber, Wider, & Huber, 1977, see Chapter 19) is aimed at discovering the information that is actually requested by the decision maker. In contrast to studies using Mouselab, the decision task in a typical AIS study is presented with as little structure as possible. In this manner, participants can build up a cognitive representation of the task that is virtually unaffected by the experimental setup (Brucks, 1988; Huber et al., 1977). Specifically, the participants receive a minimal description of the decision situation and have to query the experimenter for any further information.

A major weakness of these information search techniques is, however, that they provide no direct data about how participants integrate the obtained information (for other reactive effects of, e.g., information boards, see Arch, Bettman, & Pakkar, 1978). Although it is commonly assumed that characteristics of the evaluation process can be deduced from participants' information search (e.g., Harte & Koele, 2001), it is not entirely clear exactly how information search and information integration are related to each other (for a critical position, see Bröder, 2000; Rieskamp & Hoffrage, 2008; Schulte-Mecklenbeck, Kühberger, Gagl, & Hutzler, 2017).

Information Integration: Retrospective Verbal Protocol

One way to gain more explicit insight into the processing of the obtained information is to collect verbal protocols, which can be done in two different ways. Concurrent verbal protocols are collected while the participant works on the task, whereas retrospective verbal protocols are collected only after task completion. In both variants, the participants are asked to "think aloud", that is, to tell the experimenter everything that comes or came to their minds when working on the task. Typically, these verbalizations are recorded and subsequently coded by the experimenter (see Chapters 17–19).

Although intuitively appealing, serious concerns have been raised regarding the use of verbal protocols in general and retrospective protocols in particular. In a classic paper, Nisbett and Wilson (1977) questioned the assumption that people have introspective access to their cognitive processes and concluded that people often cannot observe and report upon higher order mental operations. Ericsson and Simon (1984; see also Chapter 18) challenged this conclusion and claimed that "better methods for probing for that awareness (concurrent or immediate retrospective reports) would yield considerable insight into the cognitive processes occurring in *most* of the studies discussed by Nisbett and Wilson" (p. 29, italics in the original). However, they point out that retrospective verbal protocols should be collected immediately after task completion and that the general instruction should be "to report everything you can remember about your thoughts during the last problem" (p. 19). When these conditions are met then retrospective verbal reports can be powerful means for studying cognitive processes. In contrast, Russo, Johnson, and Stephens (1989) have a more negative view on verbal protocols. They argue that in concurrent protocols the instruction to think aloud may interfere with the task the participant is working on, which can alter the accuracy of the response. Even worse, these authors found significant reactivity when collecting verbal protocols retrospectively. This reactivity was manifested in errors of omission (forgetting) and errors of commission (fabrication). Russo et al. (1989) conclude that retrospective protocols should be dismissed as nonveridical.

In our view, the position taken by Russo et al. (1989) is overly pessimistic, especially given that the problems associated with retrospective protocols are not without remedies. First, the problem of forgetting can be effectively diminished when cues are provided that facilitate the participants' recall during the collection of the retrospective protocol. Such a procedure has been shown to increase the completeness of the verbal protocol (van Gog, Paas, van Merriënboer, & Witte, 2005). Second, to verify whether fabrication really occurred and whether the verbal protocols do or do not accurately describe participants' decision processes, one can compare the protocols to some behavioral data. If, for example, the protocol data are used to formulate an algorithm that can replicate the decisions made by the participants then this provides considerable evidence for the validity of such protocols.

InterActive Process Tracing (IAPT)

Given that each of the four process tracing techniques described earlier has weaknesses and limitations, we developed a new method that uses and combines features of these methods, thereby overcoming some of their downsides. As pointed out by various authors, multimethod approaches are a particularly useful way to trace decision behavior (e.g., Einhorn et al., 1979; Harte & Koele, 2001; Payne, 1976; Payne et al., 1978; Riedl, Brandstätter, & Roithmayr, 2008; Russo, 1978).

A major feature of our method is that an attempt is made to detect the cognitive processes interactively with the participant, which is why we call it InterActive Process Tracing. In the experiments, participants first selected the attributes they considered important (AIS), then they made a series of choices (Mouselab in Experiments 1 and 2, eye-tracking in Experiment 2), and finally, they were interviewed about their choice strategies. Note, however, that the last phase of our method deviates from the conditions specified by Ericsson and Simon (1984) in that participants were not asked to report a stream of thought but rather to construct, in retrospect, a precise process model that resembles their own decision strategy as closely as possible. We are aware that these changes in the procedure might reduce the validity of the verbal protocols. However, the described strategies can be used to model the choices actually made by the participants. The degree of correspondence between the actual choices and the predictions of the described strategies can then be used as a measure of the validity of the described strategies.

In two experiments, we used our new method of IAPT to address the question of whether people are indeed able to gain introspective access to their cognitive processes, and ultimately, to what extent those verbal protocol data are instrumental in constructing process models that can accurately predict their choices. In addition, we were interested in the convergent validity of the information search techniques and the verbal protocol.

The Use of InterActive Process Tracing to Identify Strategies (Experiment 1)

Method

The experiment had three phases, focusing on 30 choice trials to select one of four mobile phones (for more details on methods and results, see Reisen et al., 2008). Even though the purchase was hypothetical, the phones were real and were drawn randomly from a pool of 50 in each trial, with the only restriction being that no phone appeared twice in the same trial. To avoid biases due to previously established preferences and to force participants to collect relevant information from the information board rather than from their own memory, phone brand and model name were not displayed.

Phase 1: Selection of Attributes

Participants (N=31) were first asked to freely state the attributes that interested them. Some participants randomly assigned to a *with-list* condition were then additionally given a list of all 33 available attributes from which they could select further attributes that had not occurred to them. After the participants in both conditions had completed their individual selection of the attributes—henceforth referred to as the *selected attributes*—they ranked these attributes with respect to their importance. They were informed that in the next phase, the attribute they considered most important would appear on the top and the one they considered least important on the bottom of the information board. Moreover, participants in both conditions were informed that once this ranking was complete, they could not access any information other than that concerning the selected attributes.

Phase 2: Information Acquisition and Choices

In this phase, the information on the selected attributes was presented in an attributes-by-alternatives matrix (see Figure 22.1), similar to the display used in typical Mouselab studies. Once a cell had been clicked on, the information contained within it remained visible throughout the remainder of the trial. A choice could be made at any time during a given trial and participants could only proceed to the next trial after having selected an option. It was not possible to go back to previous trials.

Phase 3: Strategy Identification

In Phase 3, participants were asked to explain and formalize their strategy in an exact enough manner so that it was possible to create an algorithm which could stand in for the decision maker in future choice situations. For instance, when participants wanted to eliminate "too expensive" alternatives the experimenter asked them to define precise cut-offs. Similarly, when the strategy required decisions based on subjective attributes such as design, the participants were asked to

FIGURE 22.1 Screenshot of the computer-based process tracing measure used in Experiment 1 (after 12 cells had been clicked on).

346 Hoffrage and Reisen

assign values to the alternatives for these attributes. Finally, when the strategy demanded the calculation of ratios or overall values, participants were asked to assign weights to the attributes. To reduce biases due to forgetting, we presented screenshots of the information board of five of the trials (a procedure known as cued retrospective reporting; van Gog et al., 2005). The experimenter was careful not to influence the participant in any way when assisting with the formulation of the strategy. This phase was completed once a strategy had been a) described by the participant, b) formalized and written down by the experimenter, and c) verified by the participant. The outcome of this procedure will henceforth be referred to as a participant's *described strategy*.

To enhance participants' motivation to carefully describe and formalize the strategies they used, they were informed that their remuneration depended on the number of times their strategies correctly predicted their choices. Note that while working on Phases 1 and 2, participants were not aware that they would be asked to formalize their strategy in Phase 3, and how their payment would be determined.

Results

Described Strategies

In general, two types of strategies could be identified: elimination strategies and additive strategies. Elimination strategies eliminate alternatives based on attribute values, for instance, when a particular attribute value does not reach the acceptance threshold specified by the participant. Such strategies follow a logic similar to that of lexicographic strategies like the elimination-by-aspects strategy (Tversky, 1972), or that of the take-the-best heuristic (TTB, Gigerenzer, & Goldstein, 1996). The number of attributes that were used for elimination varied between one and nine ($M = 3.03$, $Mdn = 3$). About a third of the participants (10 of 31) used *just-noticeable-differences* when eliminating alternatives. A just-noticeable-difference is the difference between the attribute values on two alternatives that is sufficiently small to treat the values as psychologically equal. Strategies of the second type—additive strategies—add up the values (either weighted or not) of all or some attributes for each alternative to determine an overall score for the alternatives.

Of the 31 participants, almost all (30) used elimination, 23 (74%) added up attribute values in a linear fashion, and 22 (71%) combined the two types of strategy. Of those 23 participants who used an additive strategy, 17 (74%) assigned weights to the attributes according to their subjective importance.

Prediction Accuracy

We counted how often the strategies described by the participants could predict their own choices. The averaged percentage of correct predictions across all 30 trials was 73% (Figure 22.2, second bar). Within the subset of the five cuing trials, the averaged prediction accuracy was virtually the same (75%, first bar). Note that these percentages are far greater than the 25% that would be obtained when choosing randomly.

Chance, however, may not be a good standard of comparison, because for a certain number of trials some alternatives (here, mobile phones) may be favored over others independently of the strategy used, especially when a phone dominated the others on that trial. Thus, a high number of correct predictions does not necessarily imply that participants were able to accurately describe their strategies. Therefore, we determined, as another benchmark, the percentage of correct predictions that resulted from using a certain participant's strategy to predict the choices of all other participants. Across all participants, this resulted in 34% correct predictions (Figure 22.2, third bar)—much closer to chance level than to the percentage of correct predictions that resulted when using the participants' own strategies to predict their choices. This result indicates the uniqueness of the participants' strategies and that they cannot be replaced easily by each other.

As a third benchmark, we determined the fit when modeling the observed choices with two established strategies from the literature. Specifically, we used six variants of the Weighted ADDitive (WADD) strategy. Each of these variants calculated a score for each alternative by adding up the weighted values of each attribute and then choosing the alternative with the highest overall score. In addition, we used five variants of TTB, a lexicographic strategy that applies one-reason decision making (e.g., Rieskamp & Hoffrage, 2008). For the preferential choice task used in the present experiment, this heuristic works as follows. It looks up the values on the most important attribute (as specified by the participant) and chooses the alternative with the best value. If two or more alternatives have this best value, then TTB eliminates all other alternatives from further consideration and compares the remaining alternatives on the second most important attribute, and so on.[2]

We predicted the 30 choices of each participant separately using each of these variants of WADD and TTB. The only difference in each strategy between participants was the ranking of the selected attributes, which was determined by the participants' responses in Phase 1. The fit of the six variants of WADD ranged between 55% and 57% correct predictions, suggesting that (consistent with Dawes, 1979) different weighting schemes did not make a big difference (Figure 22.2 displays only the two most extreme variants of WADD and TTB). The fit of the six variants of TTB (averaged across all participants) ranged between 47% and 51%. The most important result is that for each of these established strategies the fit is much lower than for the described strategies. Even when we selected the best fitting model for each participant predictive accuracy (66%) was still lower than the fit achieved when applying IAPT.

Information Search

Overall, participants included 5.7 (17%) of the 33 available attributes in the information board, with no significant difference between the two conditions (5.13 and 6.33). To see whether the way in which participants searched for information is in agreement with the strategies they described, we focused on three main questions.

First, are the described strategies reflected in the direction of the participants' search for information? To examine the direction of their search we used the *Payne Index* (PI, Payne, 1976), which indicates whether the information search tends to proceed within or across attributes (attribute-wise versus alternative-wise). An alternative-wise search pattern is typically associated with compensatory strategies (such as WADD) whereas attribute-wise search is indicative of noncompensatory strategies (such as TTB). Twenty-two (71%) participants had an observed PI that differed significantly from their chance PI and that indicated an attribute-wise search[3], and five (16%) of the participants had an observed PI that indicated an alternative-wise search (the remaining four participants could not be classified). This finding is in line with other process tracing studies where it has been found that attribute-wise search patterns prevail (Ford et al., 1989). Two other search measures also indicate the use of noncompensatory decision strategies: the depth and the variability of search (Ford et al., 1989). Specifically, participants accessed on average 76% of the information (range: 47% to 100%, SD = 17%) and accessed equal amounts of information on each alternative in only 35% of the trials.

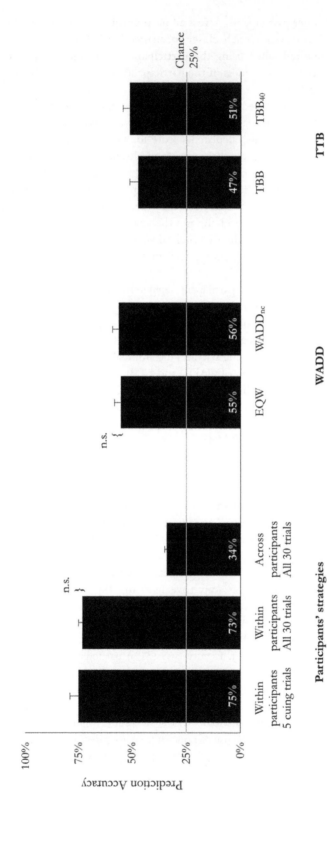

FIGURE 22.2 Percentage of choices correctly predicted by various decision strategies in Experiment 1: The vertical bars denote standard errors; EQW = EQual Weighting, WADD$_{nc}$ = Weighted ADDitive with a noncompensatory set of weights, TTB = take-the-best, TTB$_{40}$ = take-the-best with a just-noticeable-difference of 40%.

Second, did participants stop acquiring further information for a specific alternative once this alternative should be eliminated according to their described strategies? Indeed, participants stopped search on a particular alternative after its elimination in one-third (33%) of the trials. Conversely, in the remaining two-thirds (67%) at least one piece of information was acquired on an alternative even though it was already doomed to elimination.

Third, does the frequency with which they accessed information on the selected attributes reflect the attributes' ranking that they had established in the first phase of the experiment? Generally, we found that the more important an attribute was rated on average, the more often it was accessed by the participants. However, it should be noted that attribute importance was confounded with the vertical position on the screen, which may have artificially enhanced this effect.

Discussion

Our main finding is that people facing a consumer choice situation are able to verbally formalize the strategy they used to make their decisions. The strategies identified with our method correctly predicted the observed choices in 73% of the cases, which is far greater than chance. Moreover, the identified strategies were able to predict the actual choices much better than several variants of linear and lexicographic strategies. Thus, our findings do not lend support to Nisbett and Wilson's (1977) claim that people's ability to observe and report upon higher order mental operations is underdeveloped—if existent at all. On the other hand, in 27% of the cases the decisions made by the described strategies did not correspond to the actual choices.

Mismatches Between Observed and Predicted Choices

One simple reason for these prediction errors could be that at least some participants changed their strategy (including parameters of their strategy such as elimination thresholds) while proceeding through the choice phase. Such changes over time could not be considered in the analysis because the participants were asked to formalize only *one* strategy. Although this explanation might potentially account for some misclassifications, the interviews did not provide much evidence for such changes over time. Moreover, there was virtually no difference in the prediction accuracy between the first and the second half of the trials (72.5% and 73.6%).

Another reason for the wrong predictions could be execution errors and unreliable choices on the part of the participants. From the literature on bootstrapping, for instance, it is well known that laypeople and experts are often unable to execute a strategy reliably and without errors. This is also the major explanation why in almost all studies on this issue it was found that linear models outperformed the people on whom these models were based (for a review, see Dawes, Faust, & Meehl, 1989). Future research could both check for participants' re-test reliability (see Experiment 2 later) and also confront them with those cases in which the strategy they had formulated deviated from their own previous choices. Would they change the formulation of the strategy or would they prefer to choose differently?

Finally, the mismatch between described strategies and observed processes could be due to the fact that the participants' strategy description resulted from an attempt to characterize the conditions under which a specific alternative is chosen. This description should not be confused with the strategy the participants used when making the choices—maybe such strategies did not even exist in the first place and the descriptions were just constructed post-hoc, after the experimenter asked the participants to do so. Likewise, we cannot exclude the possibility that participants used complex strategies in Phase 2 but that they could not adequately describe them in Phase 3.

Information Search versus Described Strategies

Many of the described strategies are in line with previous research stating that people often start with a noncompensatory strategy to reduce the number of alternatives in the choice set, and then switch to a compensatory strategy to make a decision between the remaining options (Billings & Marcus, 1983; Ford et al., 1989; Payne, 1976; see, however, Glöckner & Betsch, 2008). Such two-step strategies pose a challenge for any attempt to contrast the described strategies and the choices they predict with the information acquisition data. And in fact, our findings are mixed.

First, the information search measures generally indicated that participants engaged in more noncompensatory search, which is consistent with the finding that most of the described strategies contained noncompensatory elements. However, beyond such indication for noncompensatory processing, no correspondence could be found between the described strategies and other information search measures (depth and variability of search). Second, participants' search for information reflects, by and large, their ranking of the attributes. Third, participants very frequently (in 66% of the trials) looked up information for alternatives that they should have already eliminated according to the strategy they described.

Given that the protocol and information search data converge only to a certain degree, the question arises as to what extent a given strategy actually directs the search for information, and, ultimately, how valid and specific the conclusions that can be drawn from information search data are (for a critique on information search techniques see Bröder, 2000). A possible explanation for the discrepancy between people's actual search behavior and the search behavior that is expected given their strategies is that the acquisition of information serves the purpose of giving a general overview of the choice options rather than providing only the information that is needed for the execution of a decision strategy. It may be that the particular strategy is generated and executed only after having obtained a certain amount of information. Considering that strategy choice is often adaptive (Payne et al., 1993), it is reasonable to assume that the decision maker first acquires a certain amount of information and then decides which strategy to use (or how to adjust certain parameters of it).

Overall, the first test of IAPT yielded reasonably satisfactory results. In Experiment 2, we sought to further develop and eventually improve it by integrating eye-tracking technology.

Mouselab versus Eye-Tracking (Experiment 2)

One of the fastest and most natural ways for humans and many other species to acquire information is to simply look at it. Eye movements are very fast, accurate, and, due to their spontaneity, they cannot easily be censored by the participants. Consequently, the recording of eye movements is expected to yield very reliable and complete data about a person's information search. The researchers' optimism concerning this technology is reflected in many studies that used eye-tracking in a large variety of disciplines, such as neuroscience, psychology, and marketing, to name just a few (see Chapters 1–4 of this book for reviews on eye-tracking; and see Lohse & Johnson, 1996; van Raaij, 1977; and Chapter 7 for comparisons between Mouselab and eye-tracking).

In Experiment 2 we used eye-tracking in addition to Mouselab within IAPT to test for possible influences of the research method on the participants' cognitive processes and behavior, and, ultimately, whether the use of eye-tracking increased the proportion of observed choices that were correctly predicted by the strategies revealed by our method. A further, minor point of interest in Experiment 2 was the phenomenon of choice deferral, that is, the decision not to select any of the presented options (White, Hoffrage, & Reisen, 2015)—for methodological details and results related to choice deferral, see Reisen et al. (2008).

Method

As in Experiment 1, participants' (N=27) task was to select a mobile phone for purchase out of a set of four. Each participant experienced, in Phase 2 of IAPT, both conditions, Mouselab (ML) and eye-tracking (ET), with the order counterbalanced. Each condition consisted of 12 trials. Half of the trials of the first condition were repeated in the second condition, but with a different random ordering of the alternatives. Except for the changes related to the new research questions and some minor modifications, the general procedure was identical to the one of our first experiments (for more details on methods and results, see Reisen et al., 2008).

Results and Discussion

In Experiment 2, we successfully replicated our finding that the idiosyncratic strategies identified with IAPT have good predictive power. In 66% of the cases (69% for ML, and 63% for ET), the described strategies correctly predicted the participants' choices, which is very similar to the 73% we observed in Experiment 1. Moreover, it appears that many of the incorrect predictions can be attributed to inconsistent choices rather than to unreliable strategy descriptions: participants made consistent choices in only 73% of the trials and the prediction accuracy was considerably higher in the consistent trials (78%) than in the inconsistent trials (40%).

Similar to what we found in the first experiment, the described strategies were only partly reflected in the information search data. Regardless of the condition, participants accessed significantly more information than their strategy required for execution (about 50% more than needed—though this number hinges on assumptions such as how long a fixation needs to be to allow for the extraction of information). However, they obtained almost all the necessary information for their strategy to work, which demonstrates at least some convergence between the information search measures and the verbal protocol.

The comparison between the two information search techniques suggests eye-tracking was generally faster, that is, even though participants had a higher number of accesses (i.e., more fixations in the ET condition than cell openings in the ML condition), they needed less time to complete a trial. Furthermore, the information search was more selective (i.e., there was a higher variability of search) in the eye-tracking condition. However, participants searched for virtually the

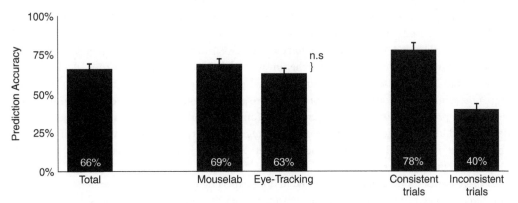

FIGURE 22.3 Percentage of choices correctly predicted by the participants' decision strategies in Experiment 2: The vertical bars denote standard errors.

same proportion of the total information in both conditions, and the difference in the number of accesses can almost completely be attributed to the fact that participants simply reacquired some cells several times. Many of these reacquisitions might have served the purpose of validating a tentative choice, which corresponds to the validation stage reported by Russo and Leclerc (1994). Moreover, the pattern of search and the relation of attribute rank and frequency of access did not differ between the ML and the ET condition. The search was generally more attribute-wise and selective (indicating noncompensatory processing), which was in line with the nature of the described strategies, and reflected, by and large, their ranking of the attributes according to their importance.

What can we now conclude about the use of eye-tracking with IAPT? It appears that this methodology improves neither the exactness of the description of the cognitive processes nor the quality of the results concerning the information search. Although this method allows for a more natural way of searching for information, it does not provide more informative data than does Mouselab. When using eye-tracking, there is considerable noise in the information search data, reflecting random fixations that occurred while the participant was thinking. When using Mouselab, the process of information acquisition seems to be more systematic, which could be a result of some reactivity of the method on the one hand (see Glöckner & Betsch, 2008), but which leads to data that is easier to interpret on the other hand. With Mouselab, many participants can be run at the same time and even over the internet with a ready-to-use program called MouselabWEB (Willemsen & Johnson, 2006; also see Chapter 6). Given that the advantages of eye-tracking were not very pronounced in our experiment, we conclude that Mouselab is the more convenient and efficient method for this kind of task.

General Discussion and Conclusions

In two experiments we have shown that our IAPT method, which combines multiple approaches to process tracing, is quite useful for identifying human decision processes. Procedures similar to IAPT have been used by other authors in various contexts. Bettman (1970), for example, obtained concurrent verbal protocols from five housewives who were encouraged to think aloud while shopping. Based on these protocols, he then developed a computational model and subsequently tested whether this model could replicate the decisions made by the participants reasonably well. He found that the predictions were highly accurate. In another study, Larcker and Lessig (1983) asked participants to evaluate the stocks of 50 actual companies with respect to possible purchase. Immediately after the evaluation, participants provided a verbal report of their procedure and developed diagrammatic representations of how they made their judgment. In addition, a linear model was estimated. The retrospective process tracing models predicted the participants' actual choices correctly in 84.4% of the cases (chance was 50%), which was even higher than the percentage of correct predictions made by the linear model (73%). Finally, Einhorn et al. (1979) and Li, Shue, and Shiue (2000) used concurrent verbal protocols to construct a model that was subsequently validated by comparing its predictions to the decisions made by the participants. Again, the models predicted the decisions quite well. Consistent with these studies, we found that the detailed and idiosyncratic descriptions of the strategies our participants used when making a purchase decision predicted their actual decisions far better than various general decision strategies proposed in the literature.

A more critical finding that we observed in both experiments is that people's search for information often deviated from what would be expected given the described strategy. It should be noted that this is certainly not the first study that revealed a mismatch between the process that is expected from the identified strategy and the process that is actually observed. Rieskamp and Hoffrage (2008), for instance, found that participants who were classified as selecting a weighted additive strategy did not search for information alternative-wise as one would expect from the description of their strategies but instead searched for information attribute-wise. Following Tversky (1969), these authors speculated that participants, when applying a WADD strategy, did not compute a score for each alternative sequentially, but instead computed several scores in parallel, one for each alternative, by looking up information attribute-wise and by using the information of each additional attribute to update the scores. This procedure appears cognitively more demanding, because all scores must be maintained in memory. However, it has the advantage that at any point during the evaluation, all alternatives are comparable on a subset of attributes, so that when making inferences under time pressure, a decision can be made on the basis of the preliminary scores.

Moreover, it appears that the data obtained with Mouselab and eye-tracking are on a rather general level and, consequently, are not specific enough to allow for discrimination among candidate decision strategies. This casts some doubt on the general usefulness of information search techniques, at least in this context (but see Chapters 4–5 on how to best use such techniques). It may even be that the link between information search and cognitive processes is less pronounced than commonly assumed. Thus, we believe that it is sensible to use verbal protocols in addition to the search measures to obtain data from two different sources that, it seems, highlight two qualitatively different aspects of the decision-making process. For IAPT this means that in particular Phases 1 and 3 are crucial for the detection of cognitive decision processes. However, we nevertheless think that the use of information search techniques is still worthwhile when integrated into a multimethod approach such as IAPT, where the data of one method can be validated with the data of the other.

In conclusion, our findings demonstrate that IAPT is a useful tool for the description of decision processes. Moreover, in addition to the purely descriptive use of IAPT, we can also imagine it being used for applied purposes. For instance, the IAPT technique could prove beneficial for the creation of purchase environments, especially regarding the presentation of product information (e.g., selection and positioning of attributes presented to consumers). Another possibility would be to use the obtained findings for the development of decision support systems, such as interactive choice aids that can be implemented in consumer websites (e.g., Edwards & Fasolo, 2001; Häubl & Trifts, 2000; Reisen & Hoffrage, 2010). These choice aids facilitate the process of choosing by directly assisting the consumers in the execution of typical decision strategies (e.g., by providing tools for quickly eliminating alternatives or calculating overall values). Thus, IAPT does not only provide valid descriptions of decision strategies, it also has rich potential for applications.

Notes

1 This chapter is an abridged and updated version of Reisen, Hoffrage, and Mast (2008). We would like to thank the editors for their helpful comments and the Schweizer Nationalfonds (Grant numbers 100011–116111/1 and 100014–140503/1) for its financial support.

2 The six variants of WADD differed with respect to the skewness of these weights. At one extreme, we used EQual Weights (EQW). At the other extreme, we used a set of noncompensatory weights (WADD$_{nc}$) in which the weight of the attribute that was ranked highest by a participant was bigger than the sum of the weights of all the lower-ranked attributes, the weight of the attribute that was ranked second highest was bigger than the sum of all following weights, and so on. Here we report only these two extremes. Moreover, we report only the two most extreme variants of TTB, namely the one without just-noticeable-differences (TTB) and the one with a just-noticeable-difference of 40% (TTB$_{40}$). For more details and for the predictive accuracy of all variants, see Reisen et al. (2008).

3 A score of 1.0 represents a fully alternative-based search whereas a score of −1.0 represents a fully attribute-based search. However, for asymmetrical matrices (i.e., when the number of attributes is not equal to the number of alternatives), the expected PI score for a random information search is not zero. Therefore, instead of taking zero as a reference point to distinguish alternative-wise from attribute-wise search, we used the expected value of a random search in a particular matrix. To obtain these chance PIs, we first simulated 10,000 random sequences of information search for each participant and each trial, with the number of boxes opened by the simulation being equal to the number of boxes opened by the participant in the respective trial. We then calculated the PI for each sequence and, finally, the mean of these PIs, which served as the values for our chance PIs. It turned out that participants' chance PIs ranged between −0.03 and 0.62.

References

Abelson, R., & Levi, A. (1985). Decision making and decision theory. In G. Lindzey & E. Aronson (Eds.), *Handbook of social psychology, 1. Theory and method* (pp. 231–309). New York, NY: Random House.

Arch, D. C., Bettman, J. R., & Pakkar, P. (1978). Subjects' information processing in information display board studies. In H. K. Hunt (Ed.), *Advances in consumer research* (Vol. 5, pp. 555–560). Ann Arbor, MI: Association for Consumer Research.

Bettman, J. R. (1970). Information processing models of consumer behavior. *Journal of Marketing Research, 7*(3), 370–376.

Billings, R. S., & Marcus, S. A. (1983). Measures of compensatory and noncompensatory models of decision behavior: Process tracing versus policy capturing. *Organizational Behavior and Human Performance, 31*(3), 331–352.

Bröder, A. (2000). A methodological comment on behavioral decision research. *Psychological Test and Assessment Modeling, 42*(4), 645–662.

Brucks, M. (1988). Search monitor: An approach for computer-controlled experiments involving consumer information search. *Journal of Consumer Research, 15*(1), 117–121.

Dawes, R. M. (1979). The robust beauty of improper linear models in decision making. *American Psychologist, 34*(7), 571–582.

Dawes, R. M., Faust, D., & Meehl, P. E. (1989). Clinical versus actuarial judgment. *Science, 243*(4899), 1668–1674.

Edwards, W., & Fasolo, B. (2001). Decision technology. *Annual Review of Psychology, 52*(1), 581–606.

Einhorn, H. J., Kleinmuntz, D. N., & Kleinmuntz, B. (1979). Linear regression and process-tracing models of judgment. *Psychological Review, 86*(5), 465–485.

Ericsson, K. A., & Simon, H. A. (1984). *Protocol analysis: Verbal reports as data*. Cambridge, MA: MIT Press.

Ford, J. K., Schmitt, N., Schlechtman, S. L., Hults, B. M., & Doherty, M. L. (1989). Process tracing methods: Contributions, problems, and neglected research questions. *Organizational Behavior and Human Decision Processes, 43*(1), 75–117.

Gigerenzer, G., & Goldstein, D. G. (1996). Reasoning the fast and frugal way: Models of bounded rationality. *Psychological Review, 103*(4), 650–669.

Glöckner, A., & Betsch, T. (2008). Multiple-reason decision making based on automatic processing. *Journal of Experimental Psychology: Learning, Memory, and Cognition, 34*(5), 1055–1075.

Harte, J. M., & Koele, P. (1995). A comparison of different methods for the elicitation of attribute weights: Structural modeling, process tracing, and self-reports. *Organizational Behavior and Human Decision Processes, 64*(1), 49–64.

Harte, J. M., & Koele, P. (2001). Modelling and describing human judgement processes: The multiattribute evaluation case. *Thinking and Reasoning, 7*(1), 29–49.

Häubl, G., & Trifts, V. (2000). Consumer decision making in online shopping environments: The effects of interactive decision aids. *Marketing Science, 19*(1), 4–21.

Huber, O., Wider, R., & Huber, O. W. (1997). Active information search and complete information presentation in naturalistic risky decision tasks. *Acta Psychologica, 95*(1), 15–29.

Larcker, D. F., & Lessig, V. P. (1983). An examination of the linear and retrospective process tracing approaches to judgment and modeling. *Accounting Review, 58*(1), 58–77.

Li, S., Shue, L., & Shiue, W. (2000). The development of a decision model for liquidity analysis. *Expert Systems with Applications, 19*(4), 271–278.

Lohse, G. L., & Johnson, E. J. (1996). A comparison of two process tracing methods for choice tasks. *Organizational Behavior and Human Decision Processes, 68*(1), 28–43.

Nisbett, R. E., & Wilson, T. D. (1977). Telling more than you can know: Verbal reports on mental processes. *Psychological Review, 84*(3), 231–259.

Payne, J. W. (1976). Task complexity and contingent processing in decision making: An information search and protocol analysis. *Organizational Behavior and Human Performance, 16*(2), 366–387.

Payne, J. W., Bettman, J. R., & Johnson, E. J. (1993). *The adaptive decision maker.* New York, NY: Cambridge University Press.

Payne, J. W., Braunstein, M. L., & Carroll, J. S. (1978). Exploring predecisional behavior: An alternative approach to decision research. *Organizational Behavior and Human Performance, 22*(1), 17–44.

Reisen, N., & Hoffrage, U. (2010). The interactive choice aid: A new approach to supporting online consumer decision making. *AIS Transactions on Human-Computer Interaction, 2*(4), 112–126.

Reisen, N., Hoffrage, U., & Mast, F. (2008). Identifying decision strategies in a consumer choice situation. *Judgment and Decision Making, 3*(8), 641–658.

Riedl, R., Brandstätter, E., & Roithmayr, F. (2008). Identifying decision strategies: A process- and outcome-based method. *Behavior Research Methods, 40*(3), 795–807.

Rieskamp, J., & Hoffrage, U. (2008). Inferences under time pressure: How opportunity costs affect strategy selection. *Acta Psychologica, 127*(2), 258–276.

Russo, J. E. (1978). Eye fixations can save the world: A critical evaluation and a comparison between eye fixations and other information processing methodologies. In H. K. Hunt (Ed.), *Advances in consumer research* (pp. 561–570). Ann Arbor, MI: Association for Consumer Research.

Russo, J. E., Johnson, E. J., & Stephens, D. L. (1989). The validity of verbal protocols. *Memory and Cognition, 17*(6), 759–769.

Russo, J. E., & Leclerc, F. (1994). An eye-fixation analysis of choice processes for consumer nondurables. *Journal of Consumer Research, 21*(2), 274–290.

Schulte-Mecklenbeck, M., Kühberger, A., Gagl, S., & Hutzler, F. (2017). Inducing thought processes: Bringing process measures and cognitive processes closer together. *Journal of Behavioral Decision Making, 30*(5), 1001–1013.

Svenson, O. (1979). Process descriptions of decision making. *Organizational Behavior and Human Performance, 23*(1), 86–112.

Tversky, A. (1969). Intransitivity of preferences. *Psychological Review, 76*(1), 31–48.

Tversky, A. (1972). Elimination by aspects: A theory of choice. *Psychological Review, 79*(4), 281–299.

van Gog, T., Paas, F., van Merriënboer, J. J. G., & Witte, P. (2005). Uncovering the problem-solving process: Cued retrospective reporting versus concurrent and retrospective reporting. *Journal of Experimental Psychology: Applied, 11*(4), 237–244.

van Raaij, F. W. (1977). Consumer information processing for different information structures and formats. In W. D. Perreault, Jr. (Ed.), *Advances in consumer research* (Vol. 4, pp. 176–184). Atlanta, GA: Association for Consumer Research.

White, C., Hoffrage, U., & Reisen, N. (2015). Choice deferral can arise from absolute evaluation or relative comparison. *Journal of Experimental Psychology: Applied, 21*(12), 140–157.

Willemsen, M. C., & Johnson, E. J. (2006). *Mouselabweb: Monitoring information acquisition processes on the web.* Retrieved July 21, 2017, from www.mouselabweb.org/designer.html

23

TESTING COGNITIVE MODELS BY A JOINT ANALYSIS OF MULTIPLE DEPENDENT MEASURES INCLUDING PROCESS DATA

Andreas Glöckner and Marc Jekel

One central aim of psychological research in the field of judgment and decision making is to identify properties of the underlying cognitive processes as well as to develop and critically test cognitive models. In previous chapters of this volume, various methods for process tracing were discussed. These allow generating multiple dependent measures potentially relevant for these aims. In many research projects, specific hypotheses concerning one of the dependent measures, for example distribution of attention, are tested. In computer-based studies, however, many different measures are available or it is possible to record multiple measures with minimal additional effort. In a typical eye-tracking study (see Chapters 1–5), for example, aside from data concerning the distribution of attention, a variety of other data may be simultaneously available, such as choice data, response times, information search data (fixations, transition), and measures for physiological arousal (pupil dilation).

The core question that arises is how these multiple dependent measures can be used to efficiently inform research about cognitive processes and to test cognitive models. There are at least three approaches:

1) The most relevant dependent measure is reported. Hypotheses tests for this critical measure are applied only.
2) All dependent measures are reported independently. The overall picture is discussed qualitatively: Do all measures lead to the same conclusions and therefore provide converging evidence? In the simplest case, a multivariate omnibus test can be applied to test for an overall effect of all measures.
3) A more elaborate procedure is applied to integrate all measures to conduct a simultaneous test for multiple dependent measures. This allows identifying the cognitive model that describes the entire set of measures best. Individual model parameters (e.g., learning rate) can be fitted on the aggregate level. In case individual differences for model parameters are expected (e.g., participants might differ how fast they learn associations), parameters can be fitted per participant.

Critical Property Testing

The first approach of testing and comparing models on one critical measure only can be used in various ways. A simple possibility is to determine the model that accounts best for the observations on the most important measure in quantitative terms. For example, a researcher can compare the proportion of choices that are correctly predicted by each model. Another way is to conduct a critical property testing on a single measure. This means that predictions of models are identified and tested that are unique to one group of models and cannot be accounted for by competitor models. Critical property testing has the advantage of being straightforward as well as easy to conduct and communicate. Critical property testing has, for example, been used in the domain of risky choice. Thereby, choice anomalies are tested that are predicted by one theory but cannot be accounted for by another for any combinations of free parameter values (e.g., Birnbaum, 1999, 2008) and set of preferences (e.g., Regenwetter, Dana, & Davis-Stober, 2011; Tversky, 1969).

Since any reasonable model for decision making should at least predict choices, the focus has often been on this outcome variable and entire classes of cognitive models could be ruled out by critical properties tests (e.g., violations of transitivity or the invariance principle of expected utility theory). Critical property testing also avoids the problem of alpha error accumulation due to multiple testing, if the hypotheses are specified *a priori* (and ideally pre-registered).

Still, researchers will be interested in learning more about whether other measures support and validate their conclusions concerning cognitive models. More generally, ignoring or not collecting part of the data that might allow for further testing of the model is inefficient, and can even be unethical due to the unnecessarily increased burden on participants (e.g., a group of persons with rare memory disorders). Therefore, exclusively focusing on one dependent measure only will mainly be recommendable if there is only one such critical measure that allows differentiating between the currently concurring hypotheses (cf., Platt, 1964).

Independent Tests on Multiple Dependent Measures and Aggregated Multivariate Analyses

The second approach to report multiple significance tests and potentially a multivariate omnibus test comes in various flavors. One common way is to report the effect of a manipulation, such as the effect of the change of an environment structure (e.g., many versus few options), on each of several dependent measures such as the number of information acquisitions, direction of information search, response time and choice accuracy as for example in Payne, Bettman, and Johnson (1988). Payne et al. additionally conducted a multivariate analysis of variance (MANOVA) to test the overall effect of their manipulation on the set of dependent measures. Furthermore, they discuss the best potential interpretation of their findings qualitatively.

This way of analyzing and discussing multiple dependent measures in the context of a clear manipulation is applicable in many contexts. One important limitation, however, is that it mainly can be used to identify effects on the aggregate level across all participants. Furthermore, a manipulation with unidirectional effects on all dependent measures is required. Complex interactions as well as gradual (interval scaled) effects on multiple measures are hard to test with such an approach. If, for example, complex mixtures of positive and negative effects of different magnitude and null effects on various measures are predicted by some of the models, standard analytical approaches (e.g., MANOVA) cannot be applied. As a further limitation, recent criticism also indicates potential problems of aggregated analyses for inferring individual decision strategies (e.g., Regenwetter & Robinson, 2017). It usually also precludes comparative testing of multiple cognitive models with free parameters for which no single clear predictions can be derived. Particularly due to the wealth of computational models being developed in recent years, the issue of comparing between multiple specified models becomes increasingly important. This requirement has motivated the development of a more complex method of simultaneously modelling multiple dependent measures. We will focus on this method in this chapter.

Simultaneous Modelling of Multiple Dependent Measures

This approach allows analyses on the level of individuals and therefore avoids aggregation problems. It also allows (at least in some versions) to comparatively test complex models with free parameters. According to this approach, the effect of, for example, a manipulation of the environment structure on information acquisition and response time can be simultaneously quantified and the fit of both measures with model predictions can be summarized in a single value. There is no need for unspecific qualitative summaries of model performance on various measures.

The approach, however, requires that quantitative predictions concerning all relevant dependent measures can be derived from all cognitive models under consideration. In the following, we will briefly summarize the core ideas of several methods that have been suggested and describe their commonalities as well as differences. Then, the general multiple measure maximum likelihood approach is described in more detail. This approach also provides the mathematical foundations for the other more complex methods presented—that is (non-) hierarchical Bayesian methods and multinomial processing trees. Finally, we conclude with limitations as well as future directions.

Methods for Strategy Classification based on Multiple Dependent Measures

Cognitive models in judgment and decision making predict "choice" (e.g., exercising or not?) or "judgment" (e.g., how likely will it increase health?). Some of them additionally allow predictions concerning process measures such as how quickly a choice should be made, which information is considered, in which order information is searched, how certain the person will be in his or her choices, etc. Given these multiple dependent measures, conclusions will often diverge depending on the measure used when comparing models. Individual choices, for example, could be more in line with predictions of one model while response times and information search might be better described by another one. Finding ways to identify which cognitive model describes individual behavior best when taking all measures into account is the core problem to be solved.

If the task is to identify the best predicting model per person, one solution would be to only identify models for persons for which all dependent measures are predicted best by a single model in comparison to all alternative models. Still, given the wealth of dependent measures, this will lead to a high number of persons for which no such model can be identified, which is problematic. Furthermore, unclassified participants might not be a random sample of all participants. They could systematically differ on some unobserved characteristics (e.g., low levels of numeracy or conscientiousness) so that excluding them can lead to systematic biases in the remaining sample, which can undermine the validity of the entire study. Also, it seems suboptimal to let a potentially small comparative disadvantage on one of ten measures compromise the entire model identification by overruling clear advantages of the model on all other nine variables.

Serial Stepwise Approaches

One of the early approaches to integrate multiple process measures used a serial stepwise process to identify the decision strategy that explains behavior best (Riedl, Brandstätter, & Roithmayr, 2008). The method suggested by Riedl et al. allows classifying participants' decisions strategies by applying an algorithm for sequentially checking three measures of information search and one for outcomes. Specifically, for multiattributive decisions one out of 13 pre-specified models could be classified by serially considering a set of four attributes. First, the authors determined whether search is mainly option-wise or alternative-wise. Second, they tested whether search is equally distributed over options or not. Third, they checked whether more important attributes are looked up more often than less important ones. Fourth, they checked which model predicts the rank order of choice preferences best (i.e., the rank correlation between predicted and observed choices).

One limitation of this and similar decision-tree-based approaches is that they can lead to severe misclassifications because even small errors on the first criterion can never be compensated by other criteria. Consider—for example—a person who perfectly applies a certain decision strategy but—perhaps due to random fluctuation—shows a small tendency for the wrong search direction. Since the algorithm suggested by Riedl et al. checks direction of information search first, this person will be misclassified as a user of some strategy. Hence, sequential algorithms have their limits.

Simultaneous Methods for Testing Cognitive Models

In recent years, more complex methods to comparatively test cognitive models have been developed. There have been three general approaches to test cognitive models by simultaneously considering multiple dependent measures. These approaches mainly focus on choices and add further dependent process measures (e.g., response times).

Multinomial Processing Trees

One approach is an extension of the prominent class of multinomial processing trees (MPTs) (Batchelder & Riefer, 1999; Erdfelder et al., 2009). MPTs are models for categorical data assuming that observed frequencies follow multinomial distributions. They thereby not merely reconstruct observed frequencies but postulate that different latent processes can result in identical observable responses. To formalize this assumption, MPTs assume a tree structure of (conditional) probabilities for the transitions between latent states. The transition probabilities are free parameters that are estimated and allow for conclusions concerning the underlying processes.

Assume, for example, a recognition task in which a list of items is learned. In a subsequent test phase, participants indicate for targets and lures whether they recognized the item or not. In a simple example of MPTs, a one-high threshold (1HT) model (Swets, 1961), one would postulate separate processing trees for targets and lures. In the processing tree for targets, it is assumed that individuals can enter two intermediary cognitive states of recollection certainty or recollection uncertainty with probabilities r and $1 - r$, respectively. For the state of recollection certainty, it is assumed that the state directly translates into the response "item recognized". For the recollection uncertainty state, it is assumed that participants guess and respond "item recognized" with probability g and "item unrecognized" with probability $1 - g$. Hence, for targets, the model predicts that the probability of correct responses is $r + (1 - r)*g$, whereas the probability for incorrect responses is $(1 - r) \star (1 - g)$. In the processing tree for lures, the 1HT model assumes that participants are always in the uncertainty state and generate the incorrect answer "item recognized" with the guessing probability g and the correct answer "item unrecognized" with probability $1 - g$. From the four response frequencies (i.e., "recognized" / "unrecognized" for lures / targets), the two parameters r and g can be estimated. Those parameters define the structure of the model and are defined to have a psychological meaning. Specifically, g captures a general response bias indicating whether a person tends to be conservative versus lenient in guessing "item recognized", whereas r captures good versus bad memory for the studied items.

MPTs have prominently been introduced to judgment and decision making for testing whether participants make choices in line with a recognition heuristic (Hilbig, Erdfelder, & Pohl, 2010).

As a limitation of MPTs, until recently, it was not possible to integrate continuous variables such as response times since MPTs are multinomial models for categorical responses by definition. This fundamental problem has recently been solved by categorizing continuous measures (e.g., decision time) into bins (e.g., 0 to 100 msec, 100 to 200 msec, ...) and including them as additional categories into the trees of the model (Heck & Erdfelder, 2016). Using this approach in a meta-analysis of prior studies, it was shown that only few participants consistently apply a recognition heuristic (Heck & Erdfelder, 2017). Instead, most participants used additional knowledge as indicated by response times. Importantly, without considering response times, many participants would have been misclassified as users of a simple heuristic. Thus, only by focusing on systematic effects on response times, it could be shown that information is integrated in a more complex manner, which in turn allowed settling a long and controversial debate. Importantly, the general procedure of including continuous variables into multinomial processing trees by categorizing them (Heck & Erdfelder, 2016) opens the door for strategy classification based on any number and any kind of multiple dependent measures. Given the power and the flexibility of this approach, the MPT framework seems to be a promising candidate for testing cognitive models using multiple outcome and process measures.

Three limitations of MPTs need to be considered: A first theoretical limitation is that MPTs are pure measurement tools. Predictions do not follow from the model but have to be built into the tree structure (e.g., differences in response times for various items do not follow from the model but can only be estimated and tested by free parameters). That is—in contrast to process models of cognition—MPTs do not allow deriving new and surprising predictions from model simulations. A second limitation is that categorizing continuous measures into bins is only an approximation to modelling continuous measures. Third, if the model is applied for individual model classifications using a large number of bins for the continuous measures, large samples of behavioral data are required for reliable estimation of the considerable number of free parameters that are necessary.

(Non-)Hierarchical Bayesian Frameworks

A second class of models that has been increasingly applied to judgment and decision making issues in recent years are hierarchical and non-hierarchical Bayesian models, including latent class models. The Bayesian framework is extremely flexible and models can capture any functional relation between variables (Kruschke, 2014; Lee & Wagenmakers, 2014). A typical application to judgment and decision-making research involves a) defining an (often graphical) model that describes the data generating process including priors concerning the (relative) usage of strategies and errors in these strategies and b) estimating the distribution of strategies that most likely produced the observed data (e.g., Lee, 2016). In its hierarchical form it also allows modelling inter-individual differences and it can integrate latent classes capturing subtypes of behavior (or different strategies). Notable models have been developed to test various versions of strategy selection models against each other by investigating how many strategies provide the best fit to the choice data (Scheibehenne, Rieskamp, & Wagenmakers, 2013). Furthermore, Bayesian models have been applied to estimate parameters for risky choice models (Kellen, Pachur, & Hertwig, 2016; Scheibehenne & Pachur, 2015). Interestingly, the application of Bayesian models for strategy classification including multiple dependent measures is, however, still rare.

One notable exception is described in the work by Lee and Newell (Lee & Newell, 2011; Ravenzwaaij, Moore, Lee, & Newell, 2014). These authors successfully apply a hierarchical Bayesian approach to simultaneously account for search, stopping, and choices in probabilistic inference tasks.

Applying hierarchical Bayesian models to both outcome and process measures seems to be a promising avenue for future research. Bayesian models benefit from their generality of application. This generality, however, comes with the price that their application and software implementations are not always easy. Hence, although (non-)hierarchical Bayesian models have the potential to be broadly applied to testing cognitive models with multiple dependent measures, there is not much experience yet with this generally promising approach. Future model development and validation is necessary.

Multiple Measure Maximum Likelihood Estimation

A simplified version of the Bayesian method that also shares central parts with the MPT approach is a maximum likelihood approach that takes into account multiple dependent measures simultaneously. Generally, this approach postulates data generating processes that describe how different dependent measures such as choices and response times are generated. This often includes a specification of a systematic component (e.g., which choice and response time is predicted) and an error component (e.g., constant choice errors over different items; normally distributed errors for confidence ratings) as well as further simplifying assumptions. One important difference to full Bayesian models is that model fitting does not involve sampling from prior distributions; the likelihood function (see Equation 23.1) used in both approaches can be, however, equivalent. Stated differently, in full Bayesian models, (often) equivalent likelihood functions are combined with priors in a more sophisticated but also computationally more demanding way. A second difference is that the simplified method analyzes each participant separately, while hierarchical Bayesian methods conduct a joint analysis for all participants.

Choice-Based Strategy Classification

The first application of this maximum likelihood approach to testing cognitive models in judgment and decision making was the choice-based strategy classification method by Bröder and Schiffer (2003), which focused on one dependent measure—namely choices—only. The simple assumption is that people apply a decision strategy k with a constant trembling hand error ε_k. The method estimates the error rate that maximizes the likelihood $L_{k(C)}$ of observing the specific pattern of choices. Stated differently, the assumption is that people apply a certain decision strategy and thereby make the same amount of errors for all kinds of choices. This assumption of constant errors has, for example, been applied in the domain of probabilistic inferences (in which people have to choose one out of several options based on the predictions of probabilistic cues) and risky choice (e.g., Bröder & Gaissmaier, 2007; Dummel, Rummel, & Voss, 2016; Garcia-Retamero, Hoffrage, Dieckmann, & Ramos, 2007; Glöckner & Betsch, 2008a; Kämmer, Gaissmaier, & Czienskowski, 2013; Pachur & Galesic, 2013).

The gist of applying the method is as follows (further details later): Assume a researcher has observed a sequence of choices from an individual and he or she is interested, which of two decision strategies (described by two models) is most likely to have produced this sequence? Further assume that the researcher is interested in choices between two options A and B based on probabilistic cues that make binary predictions concerning whether each option is good (+) or bad (-). To apply the choice-based strategy classification method, one would first need to generate a set of cue patterns that include a sufficient number for which the strategies make different predictions.[1] These cue patterns are repeatedly presented to a participant and for each cue pattern the number of choices in line with the strategy predictions is counted. Let us assume a simple example with two cue patterns and ten repetitions each (i.e., the individual makes 20 choices). For strategy S1, we observe

362 Glöckner and Jekel

seven out of ten and nine out of ten choices in line with its predictions. For strategy S2, we observe three of ten and nine of ten choices in line with its predictions, respectively. Note that due to the requirement of at least one cue pattern with different predictions, for this cue pattern probabilities are complementary (i.e., seven/ten versus three/ten for the first cue pattern). From mere eyeballing it is obvious that strategy S1 accounts better for the data than S2. It is, however, also important to quantify how much more likely the choices are produced by S1 than by S2. This provides important information concerning how certain the classification is. It is also crucial if one wants to take into account potentially conflicting multiple measures in which a better explanation of choices has to be combined with a worse explanation of other measures (e.g., confidence or response times). To be able to calculate these likelihoods, we define a likelihood function that describes how choices in line with the strategy as well as choices that are not in line with the strategy (errors) are generated. With the mentioned assumption of the same error probability for both cue patterns, this likelihood directly follows from the binomial equation (Equation 23.1), which is implemented in most statistical packages. For strategy S1, the error rate that most likely produced this choice pattern is .20, that is the average error over both cue patterns $((.30 + .10)/2)$. The likelihood of observing seven out of ten and nine out of ten in a binomial process with correct strategy application of .8 $(= 1 - .2)$ is: .201 $\star$ .268 = .054. For strategy S2, the respective best error rate is .4 and the likelihood of observing three out of ten and nine out of ten in a binomial process with .6 correct strategy application is: .042 $\star$ .040 = .0017. Hence, choices are 32 times more likely generated by S1 as compared to S2.

The general mathematical description of this choice-based strategy classification can be extracted from this example. From the assumed data generating process, it follows that the likelihood for observing a certain number of correct choices n_{jk} in line with the prediction of a strategy k for cue patterns from type j can be summarized by a binomial distribution for modelling choices between two options:

$$L_{k(C)} = p(n_{jk} | k, \varepsilon_k) = \prod_{j=1}^{J} \binom{n_j}{n_{jk}} (1 - \varepsilon_k)^{n_{jk}} \varepsilon_k^{(n_j - n_{jk})}. \tag{23.1}$$

The single free parameter ε_k can be estimated using standard statistical software packages and in this simple case also as average error rate, by:

$$\hat{\varepsilon}_k = \left[\sum_{j=1}^{J} (n_j - n_{jk}) \right] \div \left[\sum_{j=1}^{J} n_j \right] \tag{23.2}$$

If a strategy does not differentiate between two options for a specific type of items, individuals are assumed to guess and ε_k is assumed to be .5 for this type.

Comparing cognitive models is easily possible based on Bayesian Information Criterion (*BIC*) (Schwarz, 1978; Wasserman, 2000) or other measures that correct the likelihood for model flexibility (Davis-Stober & Brown, 2011; Heck, Hilbig, & Moshagen, 2017; Myung, Navarro, & Pitt, 2006; Pitt, Myung, & Zhang, 2002). The cognitive model that explains the data of a person best is the model with the lowest *BIC* indicating the highest likelihood for generating the data taking into account model flexibility according to:

$$BIC = -2\ln(L) + \ln(N_{obs})N_p, \tag{23.3}$$

in which L is the likelihood from Equation 23.1, N_p is the number of free parameters (in this example $N_p = 1$ for ε_k), and N_{obs} as number of observations.

When applying this method, it is recommended to restrict the error rate ε_k to a reasonable amount below chance level, standard recommendations are below .30 (Glöckner, 2009). This is important due to the symmetric property of the binomial distribution. Otherwise, also models with systematically wrong predictions receive a high likelihood. In the previous example, for instance, a third strategy S3 that makes exactly the opposite predictions to S1 would otherwise receive the same likelihood (i.e., observing three out of ten and one out of ten with .2 correct strategy application is also .054). Extensions of this method to the multinomial (three-option) case and useful tools for calculations in Excel are described in Bröder (2010).

To identify whether a reasonably well fitting model is included in the set of models at all, a test against a saturated model is recommended (Moshagen & Hilbig, 2011). The same authors generalized the outcome-based strategy classification method based on the earlier mentioned MPTs to potentially account for various other constraints on errors (Heck et al., 2017; Hilbig & Moshagen, 2014). A further direct Bayesian extension of this approach is described in Lee (2016), which was already introduced earlier. From this sequence of improvements it also becomes clear that all three classes of methods (i.e., simplified outcome-based strategy classification, MPTs, and Bayesian methods) are highly related, share core mathematical parts (likelihood functions), but differ in some refinements (for a direct comparison, see Heck et al., 2017). Often, they will consequently lead to similar qualitative results in strategy classification. Two further promising approaches that allow accounting for model flexibility when quantifying model fit should be mentioned. The first is based on normalized maximum likelihood. In judgment and decision making, the method has been applied to model mixtures of strategies and errors within each strategy (Davis-Stober & Brown, 2011). Second, QTEST (Regenwetter et al., 2014) provides a powerful method for testing models for binary choices by relaxing the error models further by allowing essentially any systematic definition of errors in multidimensional predictions spaces. Still, due to the complexity of the calculations, computations can take very long and simplifying assumptions are necessary.

Adding Further Measures

The multiple measure maximum likelihood (MMML) method for strategy classification also has been developed as an extension of the choice-based strategy classification method by Bröder and Schiffer (2003). The basic aim of the MMML is to provide a relatively simple approach to estimate model fits to multiple dependent measures that include (binomial) choice data as well as continuous data such as response times and confidence.

In essence, it estimates the likelihood of observing the choice data for each individual assuming a fixed trembling hand error as described in the previous section. Simultaneously, it estimates the likelihood of observing the continuous measures (e.g., response time, confidence) given the interval scaled model predictions for these measures and normally distributed residuals around these predictions. The former part is mathematically equivalent to the choice-based method by Bröder and Schiffer (2003). The second part is mathematically equivalent to a linear regression based on maximum likelihood estimation. The resulting log-likelihoods of these analyses are added up resulting in an overall estimation of the log-likelihood of observing the full vector of data. The principle of combining likelihoods (in the implementation used in MMML) has the advantages that a) it allows integrating results from nominal (e.g., choices) and interval scaled (e.g., confidence) data, b) results are insensitive to rescaling of the interval scaled measures, and c) in principle any further interval scaled measures for which the models make predictions (e.g., arousal, response time) can be added. Thereby, equal weighting of variables is implicitly applied, but in principle also a differential weighting of likelihoods for variables is possible (e.g., giving more weight to fitting choice than response time).

364 Glöckner and Jekel

The exact mathematical specification of MMML is described in the remainder of this section for completeness. We also think that it is educative to read, since the specification shows the math of a maximum-likelihood-based regression and how it is combined with equations from a binomial process that was already introduced earlier. Still, understanding this part is not essential for applying the method and readers not interested in the mathematical details might skip this part.

Specifically, for any interval scaled process measure for which cognitive models make predictions, the likelihood $L_{k(v)}$ for observing a vector of values x_i given the application of the strategy k and normally distributed errors of constant variance σ^2 around predictions follow from the density function of the normal distribution:

$$L_{k(v)} = p(\vec{x}|\mu, R, \sigma) = \prod_{i=1}^{I} \frac{1}{\sqrt{2\pi\sigma^2}} e^{-\frac{(x_i-(\mu+t_iR))^2}{2\sigma^2}}. \tag{23.4}$$

Thereby predictions are included in the upper right part of the equation with the variable t_i. t_i contains the predictions of the strategy for item i on the additional process measure, which should be positively correlated with the observed data.[2] If, for example, for items one, two, and three confidence is expected to be linearly decreasing, we would set $t_1 = 0.5$, $t_2 = 0$, and $t_3 = -0.5$. Often, cognitive models allow the derivation of interval scaled predictions that in principle could be directly plugged into t. The range is thereby arbitrary and does not influence likelihood as will become clear next. Still, conventionally, predictions t_i for item i are coded as contrast weights which add up to 0 and have a range of 1. Predictions are rescaled by adding to μ and multiplying by the scaling constant R, which takes out any differences in the scaling of t values.

The probability for observing a set of choices between two options and a further continuous process measure can then be calculated by combining Equations 23.1 and 23.4:

$$L_k = p(n_{jk}, \vec{x}|k, \varepsilon_k, \mu, \sigma, R) = \prod_{j=1}^{J} \binom{n_j}{n_{jk}}(1-\varepsilon_k)^{n_{jk}} \varepsilon_k^{(n_j-n_{jk})} \prod_{i=1}^{I} \frac{1}{\sqrt{2\pi\sigma^2}} e^{-\frac{(x_i-(\mu+t_iR))^2}{2\sigma^2}} \tag{23.5}$$

Further continuous or categorical dependent measures can be added in an equivalent manner. In some cases, transformations are necessary. For response times, for example, log-transformed values were used in previous work to reduce skewness of the distribution and the effect of outliers.[3] Furthermore, these were corrected for learning effects by partialling out the effect of trial number. The application of MMML is described for an example later and in even more detail in previous publications (Glöckner, 2009, 2010).

The *BIC* for model selection can then be estimated based on Equation 23.3. Thereby it has to be taken into account that the number of cue patterns j (cf., Equation 23.1) but not of items might be used as observations, since observations in one category are not independent (see Glöckner, 2009).

Lessons Learned and Tools for Implementing MMML

Before explaining the practical application of MMML using an example in the next section, we would like to reflect on advantages and disadvantages of applying the method based on experiences in previous research. MMML has been successfully applied in various contexts (Glöckner & Bröder, 2014; Glöckner, Hilbig, & Jekel, 2014; Jekel, Glöckner, Bröder, & Maydych, 2014; Söllner, Bröder, & Hilbig, 2013). Also ready-made packages are available in R (Jekel, Nicklisch, & Glöckner, 2010) and STATA (Glöckner, 2009) making MMML accessible and easy to use. Compared to the extended MPT approach by Heck and Erdfelder (2017), MMML considers response times in a continuous manner and still can be estimated per person with relatively few observations. Compared to Bayesian methods, the model shares the basic likelihood function but avoids further complexity due to assumptions concerning prior distributions of parameters (Vanpaemel & Storms, 2010; Wills & Pothos, 2012). This typically results in quick and stable convergence of the method.

One potential disadvantage of MMML is that some of the simplifying assumptions might not hold empirically. Many of such violations—for example the specification of error in the application of a strategy describing participants' choices—could, however, be easily implemented in a slightly extended version of the approach.[4] One further disadvantage is that model selection in MMML using the Bayesian information criterion may underestimate the flexibility of a model: The Bayesian Information Criterion only takes the number of model-parameters into account and ignores complexity resulting from the functional interplay of parameters as specified in the model (cf., Equations 23.3 and 23.5). Bayesian methods, instead, also account for functional flexibility of model parameters by taking flexibility through the marginal likelihoods of the data given the model parameters into account (Jefferys & Berger, 1992; Myung & Pitt, 1997). Since MMML shares aspects with Bayesian methods, it could also be extended to a (non-)hierarchical Bayesian framework to benefit from advantages of a Bayesian method.

The advantage of MMML over the classic choice-based strategy classification method is that it is more efficient in the sense that it integrates all information in a principled way. Specifically, it has been shown that MMML reduces misclassifications if sufficiently strong effects on the additional measures exist and therefore should be preferred in case that additional measures are collected (Glöckner, 2009).

Application of MMML

In the following, we exemplify the ideal steps of planning and conducting a study to comparatively test cognitive models applying MMML. We thereby use a probabilistic inference task in which one of two options has to be selected based on the predictions of four dichotomous probabilistic cues, but the method can of course be generalized to other tasks.

Step 1: Diagnostic Task Selection

One of the core requirements for efficiently comparing cognitive models is to include a sufficient number of items/cue patterns that allow differentiating between the models. This problem is already complex when considering choice prediction only. It becomes even more complicated if multiple dependent measures are included.

One possibility is to select tasks using theoretical considerations. Table 23.1 provides an example for a matrix of predictions for various prominent cognitive models in probabilistic reasoning. In the example, participants decided whether option A or B (e.g., stocks) is better on some criterion (e.g., future price) based on four binary cues (e.g., experts who give recommendations) that vary in predictive validity. After each decision, participants were asked to indicate how confident they are in choosing the better option on a continuous slider. Simulations have shown (Glöckner, 2009) that MMML can differentiate between strategies with these items when each is measured ten times, resulting in a total of six cue patterns x ten repetitions = 60 choice tasks. A reliable strategy classification with so few choices is, however, only possible, since the predictions of the strategies diverge quite a bit as can be seen in Table 23.1. A conservative approach would be to use a somewhat higher number of cue patterns or repetitions, for example using 120 choice tasks overall. If one is

TABLE 23.1 Six types of decision tasks with four binary cues and choice, time, and confidence predictions for strategies TTB, EQW, WADDcorrected, and PCS

	Types of Decision Tasks											
	1		**2**		**3**		**4**		**5**		**6**	
	A	*B*	*A*	*B*	*A*	*B*	*A*	*B*	*A*	*B*	*A*	*B*
Cue 1 (v = .80)	+	–	+	–	+	–	+	–	+	–	–	–
Cue 2 (v = .70)	+	–	+	–	–	+	–	–	–	+	–	–
Cue 3 (v = .60)	+	–	–	+	–	+	–	–	+	–	+	–
Cue 4 (v = .55)	–	+	–	+	–	+	–	+	–	+	–	+
	Choice Predictions											
TTB	A		A		A		A		A		A	
EQW	A		A:B		B		A:B		A:B		A:B	
WADD$_{corrected}$	A		A		B		A		A		A	
PCS	A		A		B		A		A		A	
	Time Predictions (contrasts)											
TTB	–0.167		–0.167		–0.167		–0.167		–0.167		0.833	
EQW	0		0		0		0		0		0	
WADD$_{corrected}$	0		0		0		0		0		0	
PCS	–0.44		–0.35		0.56		–0.16		0.07		0.33	
	Confidence Predictions (contrasts)											
TTB	0.167		0.167		0.167		0.167		0.167		–0.833	
EQW	0.667		–0.33		0.667		–0.33		–0.33		–0.33	
WADD$_{corrected}$	0.63		0.23		–0.37		0.03		–0.17		–0.37	
PCS	0.62		0.28		–0.33		–0.01		–0.19		–0.38	

Note: Six item types are presented in the upper part of the table. The cue validities v are shown beside each cue in parentheses. The cue values are "+" for "cue is present" and "–" for "cue is absent". Below, the predictions for choices are shown. A and B stand for the predicted option. "A:B" indicates random choices between A and B. The lower part of the table shows predictions for decision times and confidences expressed in contrasts (modified after Glöckner, 2009; 2010).

concerned about the fact that many repetitions of the same task might influence strategy usage, also lower numbers of repetitions are possible, which can be compensated by a higher number of cue patterns (e.g., 30 cue patterns with four repetitions each).

How could the tasks be identified that differentiate best between strategies? With the Euclidian Diagnostic Task Selection (EDTS) tool (Jekel, Fiedler, & Glöckner, 2011), an open source R-based tool has been developed that allows selecting tasks efficiently and based on a systematic approach. The tool basically selects the items for which predictions differ the most between models. To achieve this aim, model predictions are plotted for each item in a multidimensional space. Each dimension of the space depicts one dependent measure. As a criterion for selecting items, one uses the average Euclidian distance between models for an item in the prediction space. Items for which models are more distant to each other in the prediction space are preferred over items for which models are close in the prediction space. Selection of those items makes it easier to iden-tify the strategy used by the participant since even noisy applications of one strategy will unlikely lead to behavior that overlaps with predictions of another strategy. Hence, the items are identified that allow best differentiating between strategies and detecting which strategy is used. One further advantage of EDTS is that it is objective and precludes giving some of the models' advantages over others by selecting specific items that are hard to capture by alternative models and ignoring items that may challenge those models. EDTS has been successfully applied in probabilistic reasoning (Jekel et al., 2014) but can also be applied to other research domains as long as models make quantitative predictions. Other tools for the selection of items based on choices only have been developed as well (e.g., Cavagnaro, Gonzalez, Myung, & Pitt, 2013; Cavagnaro, Myung, Pitt, & Kujala, 2010; Cavagnaro, Pitt, Gonzalez, & Myung, 2013; Pfeiffer, Duzevik, Rothlauf, Bonabeau, & Yamamoto, 2015), but to the best of our knowledge none of them allows including multiple dependent measures in the standard version. Still, these other methods have other advantages in that they are often better able to take into account models with free parameters or generate optimal stimuli for comparing models where the entire set of all potential tasks cannot be easily evaluated for diagnosticity (e.g., preference between options with continuous cues).

Step 2: Design and Data Preparation

Usually, random ordering of trials is recommended. Some researchers use filler tasks between the cue patterns required for the analysis (e.g., Regenwetter et al., 2011) to reduce memory effects. In methods that do not require the usage of only a few specific cue patterns, fillers should not only be included in the presentation but also in the analysis (cf. Endnote 2). This fosters generality of the conclusion due to a more comprehensive comparative model testing that goes beyond fitting a very limited set of cue patterns or other items (e.g., Glöckner, Hilbig, Henninger, & Fiedler, 2016). For data preparations, some decisions on transforming data have to be made. This particularly concerns response times, which are usually skewed, may include large outliers, and show learning effects (i.e., faster decisions in later trials). We recommend to log-transform (e.g., Glöckner et al., 2014) or to winsorize (e.g., Jekel et al., 2014) response times and to partial out learning effects afterwards by extracting variance that can be accounted for by the trial position of a task in a study.

Step 3: Analysis and Interpretation

After the data is brought in the necessary format, the analysis can be done easily by applying the MMML function in Stata (Glöckner, 2009) or R (Jekel et al., 2010).[5] In the current example, we apply MMML that analyzes choices as well as two further dependent measures, namely confidence and response time. For reasons of simplification, we only discuss results for the two models take-the-best (TTB) (Gigerenzer & Goldstein, 1999) and the Parallel Constraint Satisfaction model of decision making (PCS) (Glöckner & Betsch, 2008b; Glöckner et al., 2014). A comprehensive analysis would present results for all models listed in Table 23.1.

In Table 23.2, the overall log-likelihoods and the Bayesian Information Criterions are shown for the models TTB and PCS for one particular participant (#4). Overall model fit is based on the integration of the three measures choices, decision times, and confidence ratings. Overall, PCS fits better than TTB with a lower BIC score of 636.8 versus 709.8. From the difference in BIC scores ($\Delta BIC = 73.1$), we can derive Bayes Factors by calculating $BF = e^{(-0.5 * \Delta BIC)} = 1.3 \star 10^{-16}$. This means that TTB is less likely the data generating model in comparison to PCS by a factor of about 10^{-16}. For educative purposes, single BICs for choices, decision time, and confidence ratings are also listed for each model. PCS has lower BICs and therefore fits better on all three measures in comparison to TTB. Differences in BICs between models are particularly strong for choices and smaller for decision times and confidence ratings. Thus, TTB is particularly bad at predicting choices in comparison to PCS. Note also that measures can compensate each other when calculating overall BICs. To compensate for a misfit on a measure, the model needs to be at least better by ΔBIC on another measure. For example, TTB can compensate the misfit on decision times in comparison to PCS (i.e., $\Delta BIC = 8.88$) by being the more likely model by a factor of 85 (i.e., $1/e^{(-.5 * 8.88)}$) on choices and/or confidence ratings.

Below the fit indices in Table 23.3, the model fits, parameter estimates (cf., Equation 23.5), significance tests, and confidence intervals for TTB and PCS are shown. For example, the strategy application error of TTB is $\varepsilon = .15$ (i.e., 85% correct predictions) for choices whereas the application error for PCS is only .017. Thus, in case the participant actually applied TTB, she was less consistent in doing so in comparison to PCS. Since in the example we use two continuous dependent measures, confidence and response time, Equation 23.5 is extended by repeating its right part to represent one regression for each of these variables. Consequently, estimated parameters μ, σ, and R from Equation 23.5 appear twice in the estimation with different indices for the different measures. Similarly, variables that contain interval scaled predictions for response time and confidence tare required for both measures.

For TTB, the scaling parameter R_{Conf} is significantly different from zero (p < .001), which means that confidence predictions t_{Conf} are significantly related to the observed data. For decision time, the scaling parameter R_{Time} is not significantly different from zero (p > .05), which means that TTB predictions for response times t_{Time} do not significantly predict observed response times for this participant. In contrast, for PCS the scaling parameter R_{Time} is significantly different from zero ($p < .01$) and therefore PCS predictions for response time are related to the observed data.

For comparing models, BICs are extracted from the MMML-function for all four models. The best model has the lowest BIC. Based on BICs for all models, each participant can be classified. For calculating the overall model-fit for all participants, a single BIC can be calculated based on the sum of individual log-likelihoods and a punishment term for model flexibility.

Discussion and Conclusion

In this chapter we reviewed approaches to use multiple dependent measures to test cognitive models for choice that also allow deriving predictions for other measures such as reactions times and confidence ratings. From the various methods suggested, the ones that include a parallel (in contrast to step-wise or separate) analysis of all relevant dependent measures seem to be the currently most promising development and have been successfully applied for comparing cognitive models.

TABLE 23.2 Output of the MMML function in R (Jekel et al., 2010) for evaluating the fit of the model take-the-best (TTB) and the Parallel Constraint Satisfaction network model of decision making (PCS) for participant 4. Estimates of parameters, significance tests of parameters, confidence intervals, log-likelihood, the Bayesian information criterion (BIC), and the difference of BICs between TTB and PCS (ΔBIC) integrating all dependent measures (i.e., choices, decision times, and confidence ratings) and for each single measure are shown

	Participant #	TTB				PCS			
		Choices	Time	Confidence	Overall	Choices	Time	Confidence	Overall
Log Lik.	4	−23.06	−16.88	−304.86	−344.80	−2.78	−12.44	−293.04	−308.27
BIC	4	47.91	39.13	615.10	709.83	7.36	30.25	591.46	636.76
ΔBIC	4	40.55	8.88	23.64	73.07				

	Participant #	Strategy	Coef.	Std.Err.	z	$P > |z|$	CI 2.5%	CI 97.5%
$\varepsilon_{(TTB)}$	4	TTB	.15	.05	3.25	< .001	.06	.24
$\mu_{Time\,(TTB)}$	4	TTB	8.55	0.04	206.54	< .001	8.47	8.63
$\sigma_{Time\,(TTB)}$	4	TTB	0.32	0.03	10.95	< .001	0.27	0.39
$R_{Time(TTB)}$	4	TTB	< .001	0.01	< .001	≈1.00	−0.11	0.11
$\mu_{Conf(TTB)}$	4	TTB	14.93	5.03	2.97	< .001	4.92	24.95
$\sigma_{Conf\,(TTB)}$	4	TTB	38.94	3.55	10.95	< .001	32.89	47.10
$R_{Conf(TTB)}$	4	TTB	79.12	13.49	5.87	< .001	52.25	106.00

	Participant #	Strategy	Coef.	Std.Err.	z	$P > |z|$	CI 2.5%	CI 97.5%
$\varepsilon_{(PCS)}$	4	PCS	.017	.016	1.01	.031	−.015	.049
$\mu_{Time\,(PCS)}$	4	PCS	8.55	0.04	222.41	< .001	8.47	8.62
$\sigma_{Time\,(PCS)}$	4	PCS	0.30	0.03	10.95	< .001	0.25	0.36
$R_{Time(PCS)}$	4	PCS	0.33	0.11	3.09	< .01	0.12	0.55
$\mu_{Conf(PCS)}$	4	PCS	14.93	4.13	3.62	< .001	6.71	23.16
$\sigma_{Conf\,(PCS)}$	4	PCS	31.98	2.92	10.95	< .001	27.01	38.68
$R_{Conf(PCS)}$	4	PCS	104.48	11.68	8.94	< .001	81.21	127.75

Most of the complex recent developments in comparative modelling have, however, focused on testing predictions for choices only. This concerns particularly Bayesian models and normalized maximum likelihood approaches. Although these approaches are generally capable of including further measures, this has not often been done, with some noteworthy exceptions (Lee & Newell, 2011; Ravenzwaaij et al., 2014). Another promising development is the extension of multinomial processing trees to continuous measures by Heck and Erdfelder (2017). The multiple measure maximum likelihood estimation (MMML) is a related but somewhat simplified method to both of these accounts. MMML describes the data generating process for choices based on a binomial distribution with a constant error specification. Continuous measures (such as response time, confidence, or any other) are assumed to result from a systematic component plus normally distributed noise as implemented in a maximum likelihood regression. Strategy classification in MMML is based on the Bayesian Information Criterion. This method has repeatedly been applied and is easy to adapt for one's own research. It, however, has to be acknowledged that the MMML method involves simplifying assumptions concerning error distributions, relative weighting of dependent measures (and also independence of observations), which might be violated under some circumstances. We recommend researchers to double-check the robustness of the results with the respective extensions or modifications of the equations as briefly described in this chapter or using the more complex methods mentioned earlier in case of serious concerns.

Since MMML provides multiple measures of fit for all dependent measures (i.e., error rates, R parameters as measure of covariation with model predictions, BIC for each dependent measure; see Table 23.2), checking the plausibility of the overall result is possible. MMML provides reasonable estimates for overall model fit and model classifications seem to converge with results from cross-prediction (Glöckner et al., 2014) and (in a cross-study comparison) with results from an MPT analysis including response times (Glöckner & Bröder, 2011, 2014; Heck & Erdfelder, 2017).

More generally, to make progress in developing better cognitive models that can predict multiple facets of behavior, there is an increasing need for methods that allow comparing how well these models can account for multiple dependent measures in parallel. Such broader comparison can counteract the increasing problem of an accumulation of coexisting and specialized theories, which become increasingly similar in their predictions for some of these measures. Comparing models on multiple dependent measures simultaneously allows testing models in a most general sense and circumvents the problem of cherry picking for some of the measures. It can also foster the development of more general theories that increase the empirical content of theories (Glöckner & Betsch, 2011; Popper, 1934/2005) and their ability to predict behavior across multiple situations. The methods described in this chapter make this possible. Their increased application to various kinds of judgment and decision tasks, beyond the usage in probabilistic inferences, seems promising for future research. Thereby, researchers might pick any from the three classes of methods for parallel investigation discussed in this chapter according to their prior experiences with the model classes. Results will in any case be more informed and therefore more reliable than focusing on one measure alone. Future research will have to show whether any of the methods is generally superior.

Notes

1 Note that not all cue patterns that are included in the analysis have to differentiate between strategies and it can even be helpful to include cue patterns in which predictions converge since they improve estimates of the error in applying a strategy. Importantly, if data of such cue patterns is collected they should be included in the analysis to enhance estimation and avoid biased results (Jekel & Glöckner, 2018).

2 Note that there are typically multiple items i for each cue patterns j (cf., Equation 23.1), since cue patterns are repeatedly presented and their predictions might differ after partialling out learning effects (see later).

3 Alternatively, other more complex distributions can be used such as a Weibull- or Ex-Gaussian distribution (Rouder, Lu, Speckman, Sun, & Jiang, 2005).

4 For example, in order to consider that errors are not constant but contingent on further variables as argued by Hilbig and Moshagen (2014), Equation 23.5 could be extended by substituting ε_k (for choices; left part of the equation) or σ (for continuous variables; right part of the equation) by respective equation (e.g., $\varepsilon_k = a + b * Diff$ with $Diff$ as relevant variable with which error increases and a and b as free parameters).

5 An updated MMML-function for R can be found at http://coherence-based-reasoning-and-rationality.de/software.html

Recommended Reading List

- Heck and Erdfelder (2016): for a comprehensive description of recent developments for applying multinomial processing trees to multiple measures.
- Glöckner (2010): for a comprehensive introduction to the multiple measure maximum likelihood estimation method (MMML).
- Jekel et al. (2010): for applying the MMML method in research practice, for an implementation in R.
- Glöckner (2009): for applying the MMML method in research practice, for an implementation in Stata.
- Hilbig and Moshagen (2014), and Regenwetter et al. (2014): for recent developments in choice-based strategy classification.

References

Batchelder, W. H., & Riefer, D. M. (1999). Theoretical and empirical review of multinomial process tree modeling. *Psychonomic Bulletin & Review, 6*(1), 57–86.

Birnbaum, M. H. (1999). Testing critical properties of decision making on the Internet. *Psychological Science, 10*(5), 399–407.

Birnbaum, M. H. (2008). New paradoxes of risky decision making. *Psychological Review, 115*(2), 463–501.

Bröder, A. (2010). Outcome-based strategy classification. In A. Glöckner & C. L. M. Witteman (Eds.), *Foundations for tracing intuition: Challenges and methods* (pp. 61–-82). London, UK: Psychology Press & Routledge.

Bröder, A., & Gaissmaier, W. (2007). Sequential processing of cues in memory-based multiattribute decisions. *Psychonomic Bulletin & Review, 14*(5), 895–900.

Bröder, A., & Schiffer, S. (2003). Bayesian strategy assessment in multi-attribute decision making. *Journal of Behavioral Decision Making, 16*(3), 193–213.

Cavagnaro, D. R., Gonzalez, R., Myung, J. I., & Pitt, M. A. (2013). Optimal decision stimuli for risky choice experiments: An adaptive approach. *Management Science, 59*(2), 358–375.

Cavagnaro, D. R., Myung, I. J., Pitt, M. A., & Kujala, J. V. (2010). Adaptive design optimization: A mutual information-based approach to model discrimination in cognitive science. *Neural Computation, 22*(4), 887–905.

Cavagnaro, D. R., Pitt, M. A., Gonzalez, R., & Myung, J. I. (2013). Discriminating among probability weighting functions using adaptive design optimization. *Journal of Risk and Uncertainty, 47*(3), 255–289.

Davis-Stober, C. P., & Brown, N. (2011). A shift in strategy or "error"? Strategy classification over multiple stochastic specifications. *Judgment and Decision Making, 6*(8), 800–813.

Dummel, S., Rummel, J., & Voss, A. (2016). Additional information is not ignored: New evidence for information integration and inhibition in take-the-best decisions. *Acta Psychologica, 163*, 167–184.

Erdfelder, E., Auer, T. S., Hilbig, B. E., Assfalg, A., Moshagen, M., & Nadarevic, L. (2009). Multinomial processing tree models: A review of the literature. *Journal of Psychology, 217*(3), 108–124.

Garcia-Retamero, R., Hoffrage, U., Dieckmann, A., & Ramos, M. (2007). Compound cue processing within the fast and frugal heuristics approach in nonlinearly separable environments. *Learning and Motivation*, *38*(1), 16–34. doi:10.1016/j.lmot.2006.05.001

Gigerenzer, G., & Goldstein, D. G. (1999). Betting on one good reason: The take the best heuristic. In G. Gigerenzer, P. M. Todd, & The ABC Research Group (Eds.), *Simple heuristics that make us smart* (pp. 75–95). New York, NY: Oxford University Press.

Glöckner, A. (2009). Investigating intuitive and deliberate processes statistically: The multiple-measure maximum likelihood strategy classification method. *Judgment and Decision Making*, *4*(3), 186–199.

Glöckner, A. (2010). Multiple measure strategy classification: Outcomes, decision times and confidence ratings. In A. Glöckner & C. L. M. Witteman (Eds.), *Foundations for tracing intuition: Challenges and methods.* (pp. 83–105). London, UK: Psychology Press & Routledge.

Glöckner, A., & Betsch, T. (2008a). Do people make decisions under risk based on ignorance? An empirical test of the Priority Heuristic against Cumulative Prospect Theory. *Organizational Behavior and Human Decision Processes*, *107*(1), 75–95.

Glöckner, A., & Betsch, T. (2008b). Modeling option and strategy choices with connectionist networks: Towards an integrative model of automatic and deliberate decision making. *Judgment and Decision Making*, *3*(3), 215–228.

Glöckner, A., & Betsch, T. (2011). The empirical content of theories in judgment and decision making: Shortcomings and remedies. *Judgment and Decision Making*, *6*(8), 711–721.

Glöckner, A., & Bröder, A. (2011). Processing of recognition information and additional cues: A model-based analysis of choice, confidence, and response time. *Judgment and Decision Making*, *6*(1), 23–42.

Glöckner, A., & Bröder, A. (2014). Cognitive integration of recognition information and additional cues in memory-based decisions. *Judgment and Decision Making*, *9*(1), 35–50.

Glöckner, A., Hilbig, B. E., Henninger, F., & Fiedler, S. (2016). The reversed description-experience gap: Disentangling sources of presentation format effects in risky choice. *Journal of Experimental Psychology: General*, *145*(4), 486–508. doi:10.1037/a0040103

Glöckner, A., Hilbig, B. E., & Jekel, M. (2014). What is adaptive about adaptive decision making? A parallel constraint satisfaction account. *Cognition*, *133*(3), 641–666.

Heck, D. W., & Erdfelder, E. (2016). Extending multinomial processing tree models to measure the relative speed of cognitive processes. *Psychonomic Bulletin & Review*, *23*(5), 1440–1465. doi:10.3758/s13423-016-1025-6

Heck, D. W., & Erdfelder, E. (2017). Linking process and measurement models of recognition-based decisions. *Psychological Review*, *124*(4), 442–471.

Heck, D. W., Hilbig, B. E., & Moshagen, M. (2017). From information processing to decisions: Formalizing and comparing psychologically plausible choice models. *Cognitive Psychology*, *96*, 26–40.

Hilbig, B. E., Erdfelder, E., & Pohl, R. F. (2010). One-reason decision-making unveiled: A measurement model of the recognition heuristic. *Journal of Experimental Psychology: Learning, Memory, and Cognition*, *36*(1), 123–134.

Hilbig, B. E., & Moshagen, M. (2014). Generalized outcome-based strategy classification: Comparing deterministic and probabilistic choice models. *Psychonomic Bulletin & Review*, *21*(6), 1431–1443.

Jefferys, W. H., & Berger, J. O. (1992). Ockham's razor and Bayesian analysis. *American Scientist*, *80*(1), 64–72.

Jekel, M., Fiedler, S., & Glöckner, A. (2011). Diagnostic task selection for strategy classification in judgment and decision making. *Judgment and Decision Making*, *6*(8), 782–799.

Jekel, M., & Glöckner, A. (2018). Meaningful model comparisons have to include reasonable competing models and also all data: A rejoinder to Rieskamp. *Journal of Behavioral Decision Making*, *31*(2), 289–293. doi:10.1002/bdm.2076

Jekel, M., Glöckner, A., Bröder, A., & Maydych, V. (2014). Approximating rationality under incomplete information: Adaptive inferences for missing cue values based on cue-discrimination. *Judgment and Decision Making*, *9*(2), 129–147.

Jekel, M., Nicklisch, A., & Glöckner, A. (2010). Implementation of the Multiple-Measure Maximum Likelihood strategy classification method in R: Addendum to Glöckner (2009) and practical guide for application. *Judgment and Decision Making*, *5*(1), 54–63.

Kämmer, J. E., Gaissmaier, W., & Czienskowski, U. (2013). The environment matters: Comparing individuals and dyads in their adaptive use of decision strategies. *Judgment and Decision Making*, *8*(3), 299–329.

Kellen, D., Pachur, T., & Hertwig, R. (2016). How (in) variant are subjective representations of described and experienced risk and rewards? *Cognition, 157*, 126–138.

Kruschke, J. (2014). *Doing Bayesian data analysis: A tutorial with R, JAGS, and Stan.* New York, NY: Academic Press.

Lee, M. D. (2016). Bayesian outcome-based strategy classification. *Behavior Research Methods, 48*(1), 29–41.

Lee, M. D., & Newell, B. R. (2011). Using hierarchical Bayesian methods to examine the tools of decision-making. *Judgment and Decision Making, 6*(8), 832–842.

Lee, M. D., & Wagenmakers, E.-J. (2014). *Bayesian cognitive modeling: A practical course.* Cambridge, UK: Cambridge University Press.

Moshagen, M., & Hilbig, B. E. (2011). Methodological notes on model comparisons and strategy classification: A falsificationist proposition. *Judgment and Decision Making, 6*(8), 814–820.

Myung, I. J., Navarro, D. J., & Pitt, M. A. (2006). Model selection by normalized maximum likelihood. *Journal of Mathematical Psychology, 50*(2), 167–179.

Myung, I. J., & Pitt, M. A. (1997). Applying Occam's razor in modeling cognition: A Bayesian approach. *Psychonomic Bulletin & Review, 4*(1), 79–95.

Pachur, T., & Galesic, M. (2013). Strategy selection in risky choice: The impact of numeracy, affect, and cross-cultural differences. *Journal of Behavioral Decision Making, 26*(3), 260–271. doi:10.1002/bdm.1757

Payne, J. W., Bettman, J. R., & Johnson, E. J. (1988). Adaptive strategy selection in decision making. *Journal of Experimental Psychology: Learning, Memory, and Cognition, 14*(3), 534–552.

Pfeiffer, J., Duzevik, D., Rothlauf, F., Bonabeau, E., & Yamamoto, K. (2015). An optimized design of choice experiments: A new approach for studying decision behavior in choice task experiments. *Journal of Behavioral Decision Making, 28*(3), 262–280.

Pitt, M. A., Myung, I. J., & Zhang, S. B. (2002). Toward a method of selecting among computational models of cognition. *Psychological Review, 109*(3), 472–491.

Platt, J. R. (1964). Strong inference. *Science, 146*(3642), 347–353.

Popper, K. R. (1934/2005). *Logik der Forschung* (11th ed.). Tübingen: Mohr Siebeck.

Ravenzwaaij, D., Moore, C. P., Lee, M. D., & Newell, B. R. (2014). A hierarchical Bayesian modeling approach to searching and stopping in multi-attribute judgment. *Cognitive Science, 38*(7), 1384–1405.

Regenwetter, M., Dana, J., & Davis-Stober, C. P. (2011). Transitivity of preferences. *Psychological Review, 118*(1), 42–56.

Regenwetter, M., Davis-Stober, C. P., Lim, S. H., Guo, Y., Popova, A., Zwilling, C., … Messner, W. (2014). QTest: Quantitative testing of theories of binary choice. *Decision, 1*(1), 2–34.

Regenwetter, M., & Robinson, M. M. (2017). The construct-behavior gap in behavioral decision research: A challenge beyond replicability. *Psychological Review, 124*(5), 533.

Riedl, R., Brandstätter, E., & Roithmayr, F. (2008). Identifying decision strategies: A process- and outcome-based classification method. *Behavior Research Methods, 40*(3), 795–807.

Rouder, J. N., Lu, J., Speckman, P., Sun, D. H., & Jiang, Y. (2005). A hierarchical model for estimating response time distributions. *Psychonomic Bulletin & Review, 12*(2), 195–223.

Scheibehenne, B., & Pachur, T. (2015). Using Bayesian hierarchical parameter estimation to assess the generalizability of cognitive models of choice. *Psychonomic Bulletin & Review, 22*(2), 391–407.

Scheibehenne, B., Rieskamp, J., & Wagenmakers, E.-J. (2013). Testing adaptive toolbox models: A Bayesian hierarchical approach. *Psychological Review, 120*(1), 39–64.

Schwarz, G. (1978). Estimating the dimension of a model. *The Annals of Statistics, 6*(2), 461–464.

Söllner, A., Bröder, A., & Hilbig, B. E. (2013). Deliberation versus automaticity in decision making: Which presentation format features facilitate automatic decision making? *Judgment and Decision Making, 8*(3), 278–298.

Swets, J. A. (1961). Is there a sensory threshold? *Science, 134*(3473), 168–177.

Tversky, A. (1969). Intransitivity of preferences. *Psychological Review, 76*(1), 31–48.

Vanpaemel, W., & Storms, G. (2010). Abstraction and model evaluation in category learning. *Behavior Research Methods, 42*(2), 421–437.

Wasserman, L. (2000). Bayesian model selection and model averaging. *Journal of Mathematical Psychology, 44*(1), 92–107.

Wills, A. J., & Pothos, E. M. (2012). On the adequacy of Bayesian evaluations of categorization models: Reply to Vanpaemel and Lee (2012). *Psychological Bulletin, 138*(6), 1259–1261.

24

USING PROCESS TRACING DATA TO DEFINE AND TEST PROCESS MODELS[1]

Joseph G. Johnson and Mary E. Frame

The authors of other chapters in this Handbook have done an excellent job of identifying the virtues and considerations of a wide variety of process tracing techniques. For example, they demonstrate how eye-tracking can reveal information about visual attention (Chapters 1–5), how motor movements can indicate intention (Chapters 8–10), and how these claims and others are supported on even a neuronal level (Chapters 14–16). Across these methods, process tracing creates a vast amount of rich, dynamic data. While this allows for utilization of more sophisticated analytic techniques (Chapter 22) to draw sharper conclusions, it can also serve as a significant practical challenge. This chapter illustrates the benefits of using computational models as a framework for organizing and interpreting process data to its fullest potential.

We propose that the use of computational cognitive models (CCM) allows for direct specification of cognitive processes that is different than—and arguably superior to—relying on differences across group means and other methods to learn about behavior. We will introduce the general pursuit of computational modeling, then cover work that has implemented and/or verified CCMs using a variety of process data types, ranging from movements of the hands and eyes to 256-channel electrodes measuring brain activity. Our goal is to demonstrate unique application of CCMs to process data in enough detail to serve the new researcher who desires to develop and apply CCMs in their research to better understand and relate constructs of interest.

Developing Computational Cognitive Models (CCMs)

There may be no definitive standard for what classifies a theory or model as a CCM, but reviews of such models and how they relate to traditional decision theories, such as variants of utility theory, are covered by Johnson and Busemeyer (2010; Busemeyer & Johnson, 2008). Here, we consider the key properties of a CCM to be 1) clear specification of basic information processing mechanisms that interact to produce specific behaviors, and 2) implementation as formal routines which generate quantitative predictions. Information processing mechanisms may include perception, attention, memory, calculation, or other processes that lend the "cognitive" label to CCMs, whereas the ability to clearly specify how these processes operate in a procedural or algorithmic way is what makes them "computational". In contrast, some cognitive accounts of behavior may describe general postulates, principles, and/or relationships among variables without precisely specifying how to implement these formally. For example, one might claim that familiarity with a product would lead to higher evaluations of the product and/or increased purchase intentions, and a relevant theory might hypothesize this is due to positive affect associated with increased ease of memory retrieval. However, an associated CCM would specify exactly how memory retrieval processes would contribute to a formal evaluation mechanism to allow for specific predictions of rating or choice responses.

In addition to providing a process explanation of particular cognitive constructs, CCMs can provide a more formal framework to theoretical models. For example, there are several general claims for how "dual processes" may operate in a variety of psychological domains. These verbal or theoretical models can be problematic since they are often vague or ill-specified, especially compared to, e.g., a CCM by Diederich and Trueblood (2018) which provides a formal mechanism for the operation of such dual processes.

CCMs have also been successfully leveraged in decision research. The most popular CCMs for decision making typically come in one of several forms: decision strategies built in production rule systems that specify operations such as "read information", "compare values", etc. (Johnson & Payne, 1985); simple decision heuristics built from search, stopping, and decision rules (Gigerenzer & Todd, 1999); neural networks defined by concept nodes and relationships among them (Glöckner & Betsch, 2008; Usher & McClelland, 2004); or evidence accumulation models that describe how sampled information contributes to the development of preference over time (e.g., Busemeyer & Townsend, 1993; Diederich, 1997; Johnson & Busemeyer, 2005; Roe, Busemeyer, & Townsend, 2001; Stewart, Chater, & Brown, 2006; Trueblood, Brown, & Heathcote, 2014). We focus on this last class of models for further exposition to illustrate exactly how one might go about constructing and testing CCMs in practice.

Using Evidence Accumulation Models to Illustrate CCM Construction

The first step in constructing a CCM is to identify the basic operational units, whether these be the conceptual nodes in a neural network, the "elementary information processing units" in Johnson and Payne's (1985) production rule system, or some other building blocks. In most evidence accumulation models, the units consist of an initial state/preference to start the decision process, a decision rule for terminating the process, and an intervening deliberation process that is determined by procedures for information sampling, evaluation, and integration (see Figure 24.1). The *initial state*, as the term suggests, determines the starting point of the model based on previous experience, bias, or other factors. *Information sampling* procedures simply suggest that attention shifts over time across relevant dimensions of a decision task, such as product attributes in a consumer choice setting, or possible outcomes in a risky choice task. The momentary focus of attention produces an *evaluation* of each of the different options, or courses of action, which favors those that excel on the attended dimension (e.g., products with better features, or actions with better outcomes). As attention shifts to a new dimension, the options are reevaluated accordingly and an *evidence integration* procedure determines how these momentary evaluations are integrated over time to affect a dynamic overall preference value for each option. Finally, a *decision rule* determines when the "leading" option is ultimately chosen. We will refer to these design decisions as the set of *structural elements* in a CCM.

The next step in developing a CCM is to determine how each of these basic structural elements is instantiated—what we will call the *procedures* associated with each structural element. For example, one must commit to a specific method of evaluation for the currently attended information— maybe only the option with the highest attribute value is perceived favorably, or perhaps instead all options are scaled according to their relative excellence on the attended dimension. Another

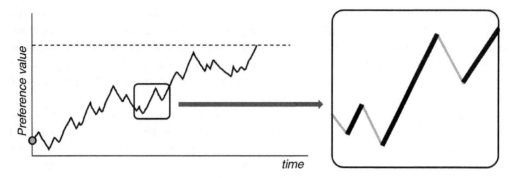

FIGURE 24.1 Illustration of an evidence accumulation CCM. Overall preference value over time is shown for a single option in a choice task, beginning at the initial state (shaded dot) and proceeding until a decision rule is implemented (shown here as a constant value threshold, dashed line). Each increment/decrement in the trajectory is determined by momentary information sampling. Dark lines (inset) represent moments of attention to features that favor the option, producing positive evaluations; light lines (inset) represent attention to features that produce negative evaluations.

example would be whether the decision rule is determined by an option that reaches some absolute threshold of attractiveness (as in Figure 24.1), or by appearing consistently better than the next-best option. Finally, CCM *parameters* control exactly how the procedures are realized for any given application of the model. For example, one might specify a threshold decision rule, but the exact value of this threshold may be a parameter that is subject to variation across people, tasks, or situational variables. An evidence integration procedure may assume that momentary evaluations are summed over time, but a parameter may determine how much relative weight to give to earlier/later evaluations to capture primacy/recency effects.

A CCM is thus developed by considering how different cognitive structural elements interact to produce behavior, formalizing the procedures that specify how these processes operate, and selecting parameter values that allow for a reasonable enactment of those procedures. In turn, we can test the model by evaluating the design decisions that are made at each of these steps—process tracing data is uniquely beneficial in each of these pursuits. First, process data can be used to identify whether proposed structural elements are indeed in operation during a task, or to determine which among several candidate sets of structural elements are most likely. Second, process data can be used to compare different procedural implementations for any given structural element. Finally, one can determine which procedural parameter values provide the best predictive accuracy or fit to process data. We now turn to illustrating each of these through examples from the extant literature.

Testing Computational Cognitive Models with Process Data

CCMs are powerful tools that have been used quite extensively across various psychological domains with considerable success. Process tracing techniques are likewise very advanced empirical methods that can reveal much more about psychological phenomena than outcome measures alone. Combining these two research endeavors thus allows decision researchers to develop a deeper understanding of decision behaviors than afforded by more common approaches. Typical analysis of process data in the literature often simply involves a comparison across conditions on the associated measurement variables. That is, one might see whether visual attention patterns, mouse movements, brain activity, or reaction times vary along with systematic differences in some dimension of the task or situation, such as the number of options, the degree of time pressure, or whether one faces gains versus losses. However, there are limitations inherent in this analytic approach—there is only so much we can learn by comparing summary variables such as means or medians across conditions. While we might be able to better understand the relationship between these variables, they do not directly verify claims made about the cognitive processes that are presumed to produce these results, especially when several competing explanations are viable. The use of CCMs, in contrast, provide the framework required to make these more meaningful connections to cognitive processes. We illustrate this potential by reviewing efforts that focus on two specific process tracing methods: eye-tracking and neural data. In doing so, we show how one might test the structural elements, procedural implementations, or parameter values of CCMs.

Evaluating Structural Elements in CCMs Using Eye-Tracking Data

The main distinction across specific CCMs is the set of structural elements from which each is constructed. Process data can be used to evaluate the empirical validity of a CCM's set of structural elements, or even whether individual elements seem to be manifest in decision behavior. Considerable work has begun to amass that compares competing behavioral accounts from different CCMs and other theories using process data such as eye-tracking (e.g., Fiedler & Glöckner, 2012; Glöckner & Betsch, 2008). For example, Fiedler and Glöckner (2012) evaluated seven distinct CCMs, including an evidence accumulation model, by comparing their predictions about how information search in a gambling task is affected by variables such as the stakes involved or choice difficulty. They then assessed the model predictions based on empirical data about attention and information search (eye-tracking), arousal and effort (pupil dilation), and reaction time. They found, among many results, that an evidence accumulation CCM correctly predicted many attentional patterns, but not an attentional shift over time towards the ultimately chosen option. Such results can lead to refinement of the structural elements and/or associated procedures in candidate CCMs; in this case, suggesting an influence of preference state on attentional shifts in evidence accumulation CCMs. In similar work, Stewart, Hermens, and Matthews (2016) used eye-tracking to monitor attention to either the win probability or win amount of two separate gambles while participants were asked to choose among them. The authors provide a detailed assessment of five different CCM approaches based on their predictions regarding factors such as fixation duration, frequency, and changes in process variables over the course of a trial (non-stationarity). In this way, they are able to evaluate in one application several of the most popular contemporary CCMs, on a single data set, using a dozen dimensions that address their component elements and/or the procedures that define them. Furthermore, they develop a statistical (regression) model that is able to very accurately predict eye-gaze transition frequencies (e.g., from "win amount" of one option to "win amount" of the other) based on the process data. These transition frequencies can be especially useful for evaluating CCMs that make claims about comparative processes.

Ultimately, no single CCM that Fiedler and Glöckner (2012) or Stewart et al. (2016) consider "passes the test" across all the data characteristics, leaving plenty of room for refining the structural elements or procedures of CCMs. This work also affords the ability to contrast the use of CCMs with purely statistical treatment of process data. The latter reduces to predicting choice outcomes based off variables in a statistical (regression) model, compared to CCMs that lend an understanding of the processes themselves—how the individual brain actually goes about making the decisions that are being predicted. That is, most authors would not argue that individuals actually perform Bayesian calculation or weighted linear integration that underlies statistical models, although these "processes" may combine relevant variables to make very accurate predictions. In this sense, they can be very useful in identifying which process data measures might be useful for more intentionally implementing through procedures in CCMs.

Krajbich, Armel, and Rangel (2010; Krajbich & Rangel, 2011) follow a different CCM assessment strategy in applying an evidence accumulation CCM to choices among two or three consumer products presented as images on a display while collecting eye-tracking data. Their contributions have proven influential in linking work on simple, perceptual value-based decision making (e.g., dot motion discrimination; Shadlen & Newsome, 2001, among many others) to multiattribute choice settings (e.g., consumer choice) through a very successful type of evidence accumulation CCM known as the drift diffusion model (DDM; Ratcliff, 1978; see Ratcliff & Smith, 2004, for discussion of this and related models). The version implemented by Krajbich et al. (2010) assumes that the evaluation procedure is biased in favor of the attended option, which determines the evidence accumulation rate. The series of attention shifts over time were modeled as a stochastic process that alternated between options based on properties of the empirical distribution of fixations. They were able to identify parameter values that allowed this model to accurately predict choices, response times, and patterns in the eye-tracking data. Thus, they showed how process data can be used to verify a specific CCM procedural assumption (evaluation biased by option fixation), and also determine the most appropriate parameter values (the degree of such bias).

Correspondence Between CCMs and Neural Data

There has been a growing interest in using neural data to support mathematical and computational models of cognition, as evidenced in part by a special issue in the *Journal of Mathematical Psychology* (see Palmeri, Love, & Turner, 2017, for the introduction). Neural data has increasingly informed various models of decision making including evidence accumulation CCMs like those described in this chapter, and especially the DDM mentioned in the previous section and the closely related linear ballistic accumulator (LBA; Brown & Heathcote, 2008). This work provides another stream of converging evidence for such models with process data. Turner, Forstmann, Love, Palmeri, and Van Maanen (2017) describe and compare various approaches for linking CCMs to neural data and offer some prescriptive advice for doing so. For example, one might use neural data to constrain the structural elements or procedures of the CCM; conversely, one might adjust CCM parameters to predict the neural data. Alternatively, one might consider neural and behavioral data simultaneously in a "joint modeling framework", which Turner and colleagues have used to successfully relate the choice threshold and accumulation rate parameters of the LBA model to data obtained from fMRI (Turner et al., 2013).

EEG data lends itself especially well to linkage with process modeling due to its high temporal resolution (see Chapter 14). One sophisticated example of linking the DDM with EEG data was conducted by van Vugt, Simen, Nystrom, Holmes, and Cohen (2012) in a perceptual decision-making task. They focused on oscillations of electrical brain activity in the theta band (4–9 Hz), which is typically associated with cognitive engagement. They found that over the course of each trial this activity correlated with dynamics modeled in the DDM. The DDM parameters obtained from behavioral data were used to predict the EEG data, which is characterized by a "ramp up" of activity that increases over the course of a trial. The shape of this neural signature was determined by parameters of the DDM using regression, where the height of the activity ramp was modulated by the threshold parameter (e.g., dashed line in Figure 24.1), and the slope was modulated by the rate of accumulation in the DDM (e.g., average rise of trajectory in Figure 24.1). Ramp onset, indicating when activity begins to rise, was delayed by a parameter describing an additional structural element capturing non-decision processing time (e.g., a rightward shift in the entire trajectory in Figure 24.1). Taken together, the CCM accounted for between 58–73% of the neural variance in ramp-like (theta activation) activity.

Turner, Van Maanen, and Forstmann (2015) have further linked CCMs and neural data by developing a modified DDM which they evaluated using their joint modeling framework applied to fMRI data and behavioral data from a dot-motion decision-making task. They successfully leveraged a CCM approach using prestimulus brain activity to predict behavioral response accuracy as well as response time and found that their modified DDM performed quite well. This serves as a preliminary demonstration of how neural data and modeling can be used to evaluate and modify the structural elements, procedures, and/or parameters of existing CCMs. More generally, this also provides a stronger link between abstract models of cognition and neuroimaging results.

Finally, efforts have also used CCMs to predict neural data even on the order of individual populations of neurons. Cassey, Heathcote, and Brown (2014) were able to link the LBA to both behavioral and neural spike data (recorded by Heitz & Schall, 2012) in a decision-making task. They found that their CCM was able to account for key patterns of both behavioral and neural data by allowing the initial CCM model analyses to be informed by the neural data. The findings of Cassey et al. (2014) and other contemporary studies linking behavioral and neural data to decision-making CCMs underscore the importance of utilizing data from both behavioral and neural sources. This facilitates models to have the flexibility to predict either data source in isolation, or simulate neural and behavioral data of subsequent participants. In this way, rich behavioral data from common process tracing methods such as eye-tracking or response dynamics may be used in conjunction with neural time series data to better inform mathematical and computational models of decision-making.

These studies have largely used neural data to fit the parameter values of well-established CCMs (rather than comparing the predictive accuracy of CCMs with different structural elements or procedures). It is exciting to realize that assumptions made in theoretical models can be linked directly to activity in the human brain. However, inferences drawn from neural data are not without potential pitfalls. Although there has been extremely promising initial research linking neural data to CCMs for decision-making, many of these studies have relied on either finding correlations between behavioral and neural data, or fitting CCM parameters to neural data. The latter risks post hoc interpretation of model parameters at best, or potential lack of falsifiability or identifiability at worst. Despite these concerns, the previously discussed findings and other contemporary studies represent a crucial first step in connecting neural data to models of decision making. Neural data is highly complex and can be parsed into numerous meaningful units. Knowing significant correlations or promising starting models provides a roadmap for the most potentially fruitful future analyses and paves the way for formalization. Eventually, perhaps the neural data can directly inform a specific formalization of decision process models, as in some of the following applications using more common process data types.

Directly Specifying Computational Cognitive Models with Process Data

The most sophisticated means of jointly employing the theoretical (CCM) and empirical (process tracing) innovations covered in this chapter involves directly specifying CCM procedures and/or parameters using process data. The studies reviewed in the previous section identified significant trends in the process data, and then evaluated which CCMs possessed the necessary features to produce them, or involved fitting CCM parameters to the process data. These are both worthwhile pursuits that contribute to the development of CCMs and a better understanding of process data,

380 Johnson and Frame

but they do not directly implement process-level empirical data into the CCM, as the examples in this section show.

Using Process Data to Encode Attention Weight in CCMs (and Utility Models)

Most cognitive process models include some notion of the "weight" afforded to different dimensions, features, or potential outcomes. This may be manifest in very different ways across models, such as representing the likelihood of the shifting attention proposed by the choice accumulator CCM, or a more perceptual effect of subjectively biased valuation in a utility-based approach (i.e., applying "more weight" to some gamble outcomes, e.g., Tversky & Wakker, 1995; or to some product dimensions, e.g., Keeney & Raiffa, 1993). The most common approach for estimating these weights is by determining which weighting assumptions (or parameters in specific functional forms) best account for choice data (e.g., Gonzalez & Wu, 1999). Alternatively, one can use the process data to determine the weights *a priori* in a CCM, and then evaluate how well the resulting model predicts choice behavior.

Zhang (2015) employed this pre-specification strategy by having participants make hypothetical choices among several different apartments described by common features (e.g., distance from campus, amenities), the values of which were determined by interval-scaling realistic values from the local area based off pretest ratings. During the choices in the main task, the decision moving window was used (Chapter 7) to determine the attention to each of the features of each apartment option. Additionally, participants were asked to provide the importance rating of each feature as they perceived it to impact their choices. Thus, Zhang (2015) could derive three different measures of "decision weight" in this experimental design. First, she relied on self-reports from the participants by calculating a subjective weight for each dimension, $W_s(i)$, based on a measure of the reported importance for dimension i relative to the sum of reported importance weights across all dimensions. Second, she determined a fixation weight for each dimension, $W_f(i)$, conveying how often information about each dimension was accessed as the number of fixations to a specific dimension i relative to the total number of fixations across all dimensions. Third, she similarly calculated a weight based on the relative amount of time spent on a given dimension, $W_t(i)$, rather than discrete fixations. Although calculated similarly, note that $W_f(i)$ and $W_t(i)$ could easily produce quite different weighting schemes. One might briefly access information multiple times about one feature, but spend a very long time during a single viewing of another feature. In this case, $W_t(i)$ would reveal the increased attention afforded to the latter feature that would not be reflected (or inverted) by considering only $W_f(i)$.

Zhang (2015) compared the efficacy of these three different, empirically based, operational definitions of "decision weight". Furthermore, the author tested these different weighting schemes—individually for each participant—in two different theoretical frameworks. She assigned weights in a simple multiattribute utility (weighted additive) model, as well as attention weights in the accumulator CCM. For the utility model, it is simply assumed that the values for each option, for each attribute (e.g., the Rent for Apartment A) are summed within each option. In doing so, the values of more important attributes (e.g., Rent) are weighted more heavily. Then, the option with the largest weighted total value is selected on each trial. The weights used for this calculation were derived from each of the three metrics derived from the process data (verbal reports or eye-tracking data).

Each of the elicited weights were also used as measures of attentional weight in an evidence accumulation CCM. In this CCM, there is no explicit weighting or multiplication of perceived dimension values as in utility theories. Rather, the decision weight represents the momentary attention at any point during the process, which is (presumably) focused on a single dimension. Thus, the three different notions of decision weight articulated by Zhang (2015) represent different procedures by which the structural element of information sampling could be implemented. Specifically, she used each set of decision weights as the probability of attending to a given attribute at each moment in the information sampling process. That is, the information sampling procedure was assumed to proceed stochastically based on the associated weights. An example would be attending to Rent on every fourth sample, on average, if Rent had a weight of 0.25. The evaluation element would produce either a favorable (such as a low rent or distance value close to campus) or unfavorable assessment of each option, which would then be integrated over time to determine the momentary preference state as described at the beginning of this chapter (see also Figure 24.1). These processes were then simulated multiple times for each decision, for each participant to produce choice probabilities for each option on each trial.

With this design, Zhang (2015) was able to not only compare relative performance of a weighting scheme independent of the theoretical model (by comparing metrics within a given model), but also similarly compare relative model performance for each metric. For example, she found that the accumulator CCM outperformed the expected utility model, regardless of the weighting scheme used, with the latter performing nearly at chance levels. Furthermore, for both models, determining decision weights using the amount of time spent on each dimension resulted in the most accurate choice predictions. However, for the accumulator CCM, the other weighting schemes did not significantly decrease performance, and in the utility model self-reports of dimension weighting produced choice accuracy equal to the use of acquisition time. These results suggest that the other processes in the CCM are able to successfully account for choice behavior as long as the weights sensibly reflect an agent's importance weights (indeed, the sets of weights were all positively correlated). The fact that self-report weights could produce the best utility model may support the policy-capturing role of such models, but the overall performance of utility models in this multiattribute task were no better than chance.

Further research in this vein may help to better and more fully explore the appropriateness of the connection between visual attention and covert attention as manifest in notions of "decision weight". This could result both from more work examining the "minds-eye" assumption linking visual attention to cognitive processing (e.g., Orquin & Mueller Loose, 2013), as well as development of CCMs that better capture how this processing produces an ultimate choice. In the Zhang (2015) study and other applications of CCMs to decision making, it is commonly assumed that the weights produce a "random draw" of attention at each moment over a choice (i.e., mathematically a zero-order stochastic process, where attention at one moment is independent of attention at the previous moment). This is done out of mathematical convenience and produces model behavior that has been clearly sufficient for producing a variety of empirical results (e.g., Rieskamp, Busemeyer, & Mellers, 2006; Roe et al., 2001). Still, more sophisticated attempts could produce better measures of attention to define the CCM information sampling procedure such as using a "moving average" or "running average" of attention weight based on visual attention. Instead, sufficient process data could be used to specify the attentional process *a priori* as well as to produce the attention stream that is used in process models (see next section for examples from Glöckner, Heinan, Johnson, & Raab, 2012, and Koop & Johnson, 2013). Other CCM approaches to modeling the attention process itself include work by Diederich (1997) and Johnson and Busemeyer (2016). The latter is especially relevant in that it uses notions of immediate attention, salience, and dwelling to produce momentary attention (in lieu of a "random draw")—essentially, the information sampling procedure in a CCM is itself defined by a separate CCM.

Using Eye-Tracking as a CCM Information Sampling Procedure to Predict Choice

Glöckner et al. (2012) developed an accumulation CCM in order to predict decisions of professional handball players who were faced with video footage of a mock game situation (Raab & Johnson, 2007). Their eye-fixations were recorded as they viewed the play developing, and their responses were verbally recorded at the end of the video, while viewing the last frame. Verbal recording was used to prevent the constrained nature of predetermined responses in a more discrete response format (see Chapter 17). For analyses, responses were simply coded according to the region of the viewing area, such that "lob pass to the left" and "fake shot to the left" would be coded the same among Left, Middle, Right.

Glöckner et al. (2012) assumed that the time spent viewing a particular spatial region during the play produced accumulation for options in that region. They directly calculated total duration for each region as eye-fixations shifted over the course of the trial. For example, suppose the eyes shifted left for 500 msec, then central for 200 msec, then left for an additional 100 msec, then right for 200 msec. This would result in total accumulation of 600 msec for the L option, 200 for the M option, and 200 for the R option. Critically, the authors also allowed for primacy or recency effects such that the impact of earlier information either grew or diminished over time, respectively. In other words, the impact of the 200 msec to R would be greater than the impact of the 200 msec to M if there were recency effects that more strongly considered fixations immediately preceding choice (or less if primacy effects favored the first regions viewed). This allows for a more dynamic use of the fixation data rather than looking at summary variables calculated at the end of each trial—although these more common metrics such as total duration per region could easily be captured in a process that assumed simple additive accumulation.

Glöckner et al. (2012) implemented these assumptions as an accumulation CCM in the following way. The formulation $E_i(n) = b \times E_i(n\text{-}1) + e_i(n)$ was used, where the evidence for a particular region $E_i(n)$ was calculated separately for each region $i = \{L, M, R\}$. It represents a weighted (by b) addition of new evidence that accrued in region i during the nth fixation, $e_i(n)$, to the running total of evidence for that region, $E_i(n)$. They assumed that $e_i(n)$ was equal to the time (in msec) spent on the nth fixation, and b was a parameter fit to individual participants that controls the primacy ($b>1$), recency ($b<1$), or neutral ($b=1$) effects.

The total attention accumulated for each region over time, as measured by eye-tracking, was thus used to predict the choice region for each trial. In the example eye-fixation sequence, where 600 out of 1000 msec were focused in the left region, this would produce a 60% probability of choosing L (assuming no primacy/recency). This was compared to a baseline choice model that simply used the total proportion of a participant's choices for each region to predict the choice probability on each trial. Although Glöckner et al. (2012) compared several versions of the accumulator CCM, the best-performing model accurately predicted an average of two-thirds of a participant's choices, outperforming chance (one-third) and the baseline model even in cross-validation (i.e., fitting the model to a subset of data, then using it to predict a different subset). Even when constraining the model to eliminate primacy/recency effects and rely on simple summation (i.e., fixing $b = 1$), it accurately predicted 57% of participants' choices.

Using empirically collected attention data during a task to predict empirically generated choices at the end of the trial represents the type of direct CCM modeling that can be achieved using process data of various types. Although this approach necessarily involves certain assumptions (e.g., attention necessarily represents an advantage for each option, precluding visual fixations to "rule out"), these can also be verified or modified through other experiments and model building. It is also important to note that this general technique can be applied to develop and test other CCMs

Defining and Testing Process Models **383**

as well. Glöckner et al. (2012) also considered neural network models driven by spreading activation which used the same data as the accumulator models but supposed very different structural elements (Glöckner & Betsch, 2008). The essentially equal performance of these two approaches reported by the authors also provides a challenge for finding other process measures to tease apart these different possible explanations.

Using Eye-Tracking in CCMs to Predict Mouse-Tracking

Koop and Johnson (2013) use a CCM with a similar attentional accumulation process to not only predict choices, but also to directly drive momentary changes in preference predicted to occur. Essentially, this amounts to predicting the relative preference at each movement of the eye to a new fixation compared to just the relative proportion at the end of each trial. For the earlier example that resulted in total accumulation of 600 msec for the L option after four fixations, the model in Koop and Johnson (2013) could additionally predict the preference after each fixation, such as 71% preference for L after only the second fixation (resulting from L fixation for 500 msec out of 700 msec). Then, this relative preference state at each time point was compared to the location of the mouse cursor as it proceeded towards each option (see Chapters 8–10). Of course, this nicely tests the direct accumulation process over time by assuming it is revealed in motor (reaching) movements as well.

Koop and Johnson (2013; Experiment 3) had participants make a series of choices among probabilistic outcomes with a single positive outcome (else nothing), such as a 90% chance to win $50. Inspecting just the eye-tracking data, there was relatively equal overall attention to the different dimensions (outcome, probability) of the two options (risky, safe), making it hard to draw conclusions on the basis of aggregate fixation data. Looking just at the response movement data, there was more movement towards an option as it was attended, but also movement towards the safe option when fixations compared its favored attribute (winning chances) and, to a much lesser extent, movement towards the risky option when the larger winning outcome was considered. Importantly, the authors go beyond such comparisons across conditions for each process measure separately, and build a CCM to formalize the relationship between the two measures.

As in Glöckner et al. (2012), Koop and Johnson (2013) presumed that information accumulated directly for an option as a direct function of longer fixation duration. A key difference in Koop and Johnson (2013) is the differential evaluation that could be triggered by information of differing quality or support for each option. That is, attending to an outcome of $90 should provide more "evidence" for selecting the associated option than attending to an outcome of $50, as would attending to a probability of 90% compared to 50%. The degree of evidence was weighted by fixation duration to determine the CCM evaluation provided by each eye fixation. Following the earlier notation, $e(n)$ was not just equal to the time (in msec) spent on the nth fixation, but rather the time multiplied by the perceived evidentiary value of the information fixated. These were assumed to drive response movements by relating $E(n)$, the accumulated evidence in the CCM, directly to the corresponding mouse position after the nth fixation. Specifically, they correlated $E(n)$ in the CCM with the mouse position for the sequence of fixations within a trial to compute a correlation for each trial of each individual. Referencing Figure 24.1, this would suggest that the increments/decrements in the trajectory produced by the model would be reflected by mouse movements towards/away from the selected option. They allowed for each participant to have a different value scheme to reflect how much of a difference, say $90 versus $50, affected evaluations in producing $e(n)$. They also allowed for individual variability in the primacy/recency effects in driving preferences as in Glöckner et al. (2012). Overall, they found their CCM produced correlations of

384 Johnson and Frame

around 0.80 between the predicted preferences and mouse positions, explaining nearly two-thirds of variability in mouse movements with the eye-fixation data. Importantly, this model far surpasses a baseline model that presumed stochastic eye fixations proportional to the overall acquisition rates.

Koop and Johnson (2013) represent the most direct implementation of an accumulator CCM using process data. Furthermore, their approach allows one to explore additional results that are achieved by the model's theoretical interpretations. For example, all of their participants were best described by a recency effect that gave more influence to eye fixations that occurred later in the sequence, or closer to the choice point. Many also showed systematic and interpretable, although variable across individuals, treatment of outcome and probability information, as reflected in the value schemes used to produce $e(n)$. For example, it seemed that four participants responded as if the value of the outcomes were equally influential (i.e., attractive) in driving preferences; another 13 seemed to systematically respond only to the top few outcome values among all the stimuli (see Koop & Johnson, 2013, Figure 15, p. 177).

The Next Steps

In this chapter, we have argued for directly implementing the processes captured by process tracing techniques covered in this Handbook in computational cognitive models (CCMs). The current practice predominantly seeks to identify how experimental conditions produce changes in the metrics associated with different measures. Although useful, this does not as fully allow us to understand the underlying cognitive mechanisms responsible for such behavioral trends. Instead, we have shown how such processes can be understood by verifying with process data the assumptions about structural elements and procedures in CCMs, or correlating CCM parameters with process data variables. Perhaps most innovative are recent examples, covered in the last section, of using process data to directly inform such models, such as by *a priori* setting decision weights, rather than fitting them to choices; or using eye-tracking fixations to "hard wire" attentional mechanisms, rather than relying on simplifying assumptions about stochastic attention processes.

The survey of applications provided here does not exhaust the possibilities for implementing process data in formal models. In particular, this chapter has focused almost exclusively on accumulator CCMs that represent the choice process as a series of attention shifts, focal processing, and preference updating. Other models such as heuristic choice processes are just as amenable to the type of direct modeling advocated in this chapter. For example, eye-tracking data could substitute for a simplifying "search rule" in lexicographic heuristics that either assume some predetermined (e.g., take-the-best, Gigerenzer & Goldstein, 1996) or stochastic (e.g., elimination-by-aspects, Tversky, 1972) information search pattern, in order to test other properties of such theories. It may even allow researchers who favor such theories to address the "selection problem" by allowing for a way to empirically identify which heuristic is being applied to a particular task. Similarly, just as we have covered several process data types including eye-tracking, mouse-tracking, verbal report, and neural data, there are certainly other ways that process data can inform CCMs and other models. For example, Hoffrage and Reisen (Chapter 22) show how to use participants' verbal descriptions of strategies to formulate models that subsequently predict choices.

In any case, we would argue that direct computational modeling of process data provides the researcher with several benefits. First, it offers a level of precision that is often missing when simply comparing across empirical conditions. Second, it allows one to develop novel predictions based on data in hand, rather than relying on (potentially dubious) simplifying assumptions. Third, it allows one to retain the time series of process tracing data by incorporating it directly in dynamic models, rather than looking at trends averaged over time. Fourth, such applications generally treat the data on an individual level rather than averaged across several trials and dozens of participants; this is generally more precise and also affords the ability for hierarchical modeling. Finally, it provides an opportunity for simultaneously considering multiple data sources for simultaneously considering, such as in the application by Koop and Johnson (2013) predicting movement data from eye-tracking data.

In closing, we would encourage researchers to consider relevant computational cognitive models when attempting to make sense of the vast array of data that is generated with most process tracing techniques. Admittedly, getting started in this regard may be a daunting task, but there are several resources available to assist the novice. Schulte-Mecklenbeck et al. (2017) even offer a simple guide for getting started with process tracing data in decision research, and several excellent introductions to formal cognitive computational modeling are available as well (e.g., Busemeyer & Diederich, 2010; Sun, 2008). We strongly believe that the pay-off is well worth the effort to develop and understand these models in the context of process tracing studies, to give researchers more bang for their buck.

Note

1   This research was funded in part by a National Science Foundation grant #0851990 to the first author.

Recommended Reading List

- Koop and Johnson (2013) use eye-tracking data to directly specify attention shifts in an evidence accumulation CCM, the resulting predictions of which are verified by mouse-tracking data.
- Turner et al. (2017) distinguish between various approaches to jointly considering CCMs, behavioural data, and process tracing data; the latter is focused on neurophysiological data but the concepts can be more broadly applied.
- Busemeyer and Diederich (2010) provide a thorough yet accessible introduction to cognitive computational modeling.

References

Brown, S. D., & Heathcote, A. (2008). The simplest complete model of choice response time: Linear ballistic accumulation. *Cognitive Psychology, 57*(3), 153–178.

Busemeyer, J. R., & Diederich, A. (2010). *Cognitive modeling.* Sage.

Busemeyer, J. R., & Johnson, J. G. (2008). Micro-process models of decision making. *Cambridge Handbook of Computational Psychology, 302,* 321.

Busemeyer, J. R., & Townsend, J. T. (1993). Decision field theory: A dynamic-cognitive approach to decision making in an uncertain environment. *Psychological Review, 100*(3), 432–459.

Cassey, P., Heathcote, A., & Brown, S. D. (2014). Brain and behavior in decision-making. *PLoS Computational Biology, 10*(7), e1003700.

Diederich, A. (1997). Dynamic stochastic models for decision making under time constraints. *Journal of Mathematical Psychology, 41*(3), 260–274.

Diederich, A., & Trueblood, J. S. (2018). A dynamic dual process model of risky decision making. *Psychological Review, 125*(2), 270–292.

Fiedler, S., & Glöckner, A. (2012). The dynamics of decision making in risky choice: An eye-tracking analysis. *Frontiers in Psychology, 3,* 335.

Gigerenzer, G., & Goldstein, D. G. (1996). Reasoning the fast and frugal way: models of bounded rationality. *Psychological Review, 103*(4), 650–669.

Gigerenzer, G., & Todd, P. M. (1999). Fast and frugal heuristics: The adaptive toolbox. In *Simple heuristics that make us smart* (pp. 3–34). Oxford University Press.

Glöckner, A., & Betsch, T. (2008). Modeling option and strategy choices with connectionist networks: Towards an integrative model of automatic and deliberate decision making. MPI Collective Goods Preprint, No. 2008/2.

Glöckner, A., Heinen, T., Johnson, J. G., & Raab, M. (2012). Network approaches for expert decisions in sports. *Human Movement Science, 31*(2), 318–333.

Gonzalez, R., & Wu, G. (1999). On the shape of the probability weighting function. *Cognitive Psychology, 38*(1), 129–166.

Heitz, R. P., & Schall, J. D. (2012). Neural mechanisms of speed-accuracy tradeoff. *Neuron, 76*(3), 616–628.

Johnson, E. J., & Payne, J. W. (1985). Effort and accuracy in choice. *Management Science, 31*(4), 395–414.

Johnson, J. G., & Busemeyer, J. R. (2005). A dynamic, stochastic, computational model of preference reversal phenomena. *Psychological Review, 112*(4), 841–861.

Johnson, J. G., & Busemeyer, J. R. (2010). Decision making under risk and uncertainty. *Wiley Interdisciplinary Reviews: Cognitive Science, 1*(5), 736–749.

Johnson, J. G., & Busemeyer, J. R. (2016). A computational model of the attention process in risky choice. *Decision, 3*(4), 254–280.

Keeney, R. L., & Raiffa, H. (1993). *Decisions with multiple objectives: preferences and value trade-offs*. Cambridge University Press.

Koop, G. J., & Johnson, J. G. (2013). The response dynamics of preferential choice. *Cognitive Psychology, 67*(4), 151–185.

Krajbich, I., Armel, C., & Rangel, A. (2010). Visual fixations and the computation and comparison of value in simple choice. *Nature Neuroscience, 13*(10), 1292–1298.

Krajbich, I., & Rangel, A. (2011). Multialternative drift-diffusion model predicts the relationship between visual fixations and choice in value-based decisions. *Proceedings of the National Academy of Sciences, 108*(33), 13852–13857.

Orquin, J. L., & Mueller Loose, S. M. (2013). Attention and choice: A review on eye movements in decision making. *Acta Psychologica, 144*(1), 190–206

Palmeri, T. J., Love, B. C., & Turner, B. M. (2017). Model-based cognitive neuroscience. *Journal of Mathematical Psychology, 76*(B), 59–64.

Raab, M., & Johnson, J. G. (2007). Expertise-based differences in search and option-generation strategies. *Journal of Experimental Psychology: Applied, 13*(3), 158–170.

Ratcliff, R. (1978). A theory of memory retrieval. *Psychological Review, 85*(2), 59–108.

Ratcliff, R., & Smith, P. L. (2004). A comparison of sequential sampling models for two-choice reaction time. *Psychological Review, 111*(2), 333–367.

Rieskamp, J., Busemeyer, J. R., & Mellers, B. A. (2006). Extending the bounds of rationality: evidence and theories of preferential choice. *Journal of Economic Literature, 44*(3), 631–661.

Roe, R. M., Busemeyer, J. R., & Townsend, J. T. (2001). Multialternative decision field theory: A dynamic connectionst model of decision making. *Psychological Review, 108*(2), 370–392.

Schulte-Mecklenbeck, M., Johnson, J. G., Böckenholt, U., Goldstein, D. G., Russo, J. E., Sullivan, N. J., & Willemsen, M. C. (2017). Process-tracing methods in decision making: On growing up in the 70s. *Current Directions in Psychological Science, 26*(5), 442–450.

Shadlen, M. N., & Newsome, W. T. (2001). Neural basis of a perceptual decision in the parietal cortex (area LIP) of the rhesus monkey. *Journal of Neurophysiology, 86*(4), 1916–1936.

Stewart, N., Chater, N., & Brown, G. D. (2006). Decision by sampling. *Cognitive Psychology, 53*(1), 1–26.

Stewart, N., Hermens, F., & Matthews, W. J. (2016). Eye movements in risky choice. *Journal of Behavioral Decision Making, 29*(2–3), 116–136.

Sun, R. (Ed.). (2008). *The Cambridge handbook of computational psychology*. Cambridge University Press.

Trueblood, J. S., Brown, S. D., & Heathcote, A. (2014). The multiattribute linear ballistic accumulator model of context effects in multialternative choice. *Psychological Review, 121*(2), 179–205.

Turner, B. M., Forstmann, B. U., Love, B. C., Palmeri, T. J., & Van Maanen, L. (2017). Approaches to analysis in model-based cognitive neuroscience. *Journal of Mathematical Psychology, 76*, 65–79.

Turner, B. M., Forstmann, B. U., Wagenmakers, E. J., Brown, S. D., Sederberg, P. B., & Steyvers, M. (2013). A Bayesian framework for simultaneously modeling neural and behavioral data. *NeuroImage, 72*, 193–206.

Turner, B. M., Van Maanen, L., & Forstmann, B. U. (2015). Informing cognitive abstractions through neuroimaging: The neural drift diffusion model. *Psychological Review, 122*(2), 312–336.

Tversky, A. (1972). Elimination by aspects: A theory of choice. *Psychological Review, 79*(4), 281–299.

Tversky, A., & Wakker, P. (1995). Risk attitudes and decision weights. *Econometrica*, 1255–1280.

Usher, M., & McClelland, J. L. (2004). Loss aversion and inhibition in dynamical models of multialternative choice. *Psychological Review, 111*(3), 757–769.

van Vugt, M. K., Simen, P., Nystrom, L. E., Holmes, P., & Cohen, J. D. (2012). EEG oscillations reveal neural correlates of evidence accumulation. *Frontiers in Neuroscience, 6*, 106.

Zhang, R. (2015). Multialternative Decision Field Theory Model Fitting Using Different Measures of Attribute Weighting (Master's Thesis). Retrieved January 20, 2018, from OhioLink.

INDEX

Active information search: AIS, 302–306, 308–311, 341–344; answers, 303–304, 306, 308–310; basic version, 303, 305, 309–310; children, 310; coding system, 309; computerized versions, 306; concurrent thinking aloud, 309; list version, 303, 305–306, 310; logit analysis, 308; prefrontal brain damage, 310; procedure, 305–306, 308–309; questions, 303–310

Area of interest 31, 67, 103, 252; AOI, 31–32, 38, 55–61, 67–71, 99, 103, 105–106

Attention 14–21, 27–28, 30–33, 36–46, 53, 62, 78–79, 85–86, 89–91, 96–102, 105–107, 161–162, 220–221, 238–239, 338, 374–378, 380–385

Attribute 8–9, 12–13, 79–80, 187–188, 193–194, 330–333, 335–336, 338, 341–342, 344–347, 349–350, 352–354, 358–359

Bayesian 92, 195, 358, 360–363, 368–370
BIC 57, 362, 364, 368–370

Classification 195, 198–205, 360–363, 370–373
Cue 20, 36, 92, 102–103, 149–151, 154, 186–187, 189, 191–193, 198, 237, 270–271, 273, 280, 296, 344, 361–362, 364–367, 370–371

Drift Diffusion Model 16, 18, 92, 218, 221–222, 224–225, 229, 326, 333, 378; DDM, 218, 221–222, 225–226, 378–379

Electro Electroencephalogram: activity, 2, 29, 34–35, 45, 48, 96, 104, 156, 161–163, 165–169, 171–173, 175–179, 198–200, 217–224, 229, 231, 234, 236, 239, 249, 251–252, 254–258, 260–265, 287, 292, 294, 331–333, 374, 376, 378–379; bands 217, 219–222; beta 219, 221–222, 229, 231; EEG 1–2, 17, 106, 156, 198, 217–219, 221–225, 227, 229, 231, 378; ERP 2, 217–219, 221–225, 227, 229, 231, 249; lateralized 222–224, 231; spectral 217, 219–221, 229; theta 219–222, 232, 250, 262, 267, 378–379

Emotion: decision making 2–4, 12, 17, 32, 35–36, 38, 49, 53–55, 62–65, 74–75, 92–96, 98–99, 101–102, 149, 162, 167, 184–186, 189, 191, 193–199, 217–225, 227, 229, 236–240, 243, 251, 253, 256–258, 265–266, 270, 274, 279–280, 286, 292–294, 297–303, 307, 309, 322, 328, 338, 347, 356–361, 363, 368–369, 375, 378–379, 381; skin conductance 2, 48, 161–168, 170, 172, 174–179, 273; social behavior 50, 155, 157, 258

Eye–tracking 2, 39, 63, 102, 319; dwell 31, 55, 60; eye–tracker 4, 6, 20, 27–31, 33–35, 38, 46–47, 53, 57–60, 62, 68, 72; eye–tracker mobile 27–29, 34–35, 38; gaze 6–7, 14–16, 18–20, 27–39, 46–47, 59–60, 63, 68, 70, 72, 98, 106, 319, 335–336, 377; movements 4–7, 21, 28–29, 31, 33–39, 53–56, 58, 60, 62, 68, 71–72, 77, 91, 96–102, 106–107, 133, 147, 290, 326, 333, 335, 338, 343, 350

Facial expression: AFFDEX 200–204, 207, 210–213; classification 49, 58, 62, 186, 189, 198–205, 207, 209, 213, 243, 358, 360–363, 365, 370, 371; emotion 2, 34, 37, 149, 154–155, 161, 167, 198–207, 209–210, 212–213, 236, 238–239, 243, 246–247, 259, 275, 279, 282; FACS 198–201, 204, 212–213; iMotions 200–204, 207–214

Fixations: distribution of fixations 7–8, 378; experts 7, 67–68, 174, 271, 291, 293, 295–300, 309, 349, 365; frequency of fixations 9, 16; object of regard 5, 7, 12, 14, 19; order of fixations 8, 60; pair comparisons 11, 13, 17, 19; predicted fixations 7; reading 5–6, 8, 11, 19, 21, 37, 49, 53–55, 63, 97–99; sequences of fixations 11, 13

Functional magnetic resonance imaging: block design 236; BOLD 172–173, 234, 262, 264, 332, 338; fMRI 17, 48, 50, 149, 154–156, 161, 166, 172–173, 183, 217, 234, 236–238, 240, 244, 249, 252–253, 255, 258, 262–265, 326, 332, 338, 378–379; hemodynamic response 234, 235–236

Heuristic 15–17, 56, 76–79, 90, 189, 195–197, 242, 273, 292–293, 346–347, 359–360, 375, 384

MouselabWEB: data cleaning 81; design 16, 34, 36, 38, 46–47, 49, 53–57, 60–62, 68, 70–73, 76, 79–80, 90, 99, 105–107, 115–117, 119, 125, 127–128, 132, 138, 140–141, 162, 172–173, 185, 188, 191, 207, 209, 212, 231, 234, 236, 249, 252, 261, 263, 268, 270–275, 277–278, 281–282, 291, 298, 322, 345, 367, 375–376, 380–381; evaluation 12–13, 16, 19, 31, 36, 38–39, 71, 76, 90–91, 104, 149, 168, 181, 187–188, 205, 207, 225, 279–283, 295, 297, 310–311, 343, 352–353, 375–376, 378, 381, 383; extracting process measures 81

Mousetracking: categorization 113, 147, 149–156, 189, 196, 199, 281; category 9, 12, 111–113, 116, 120, 128, 149–155, 199, 205–206, 243, 271, 279, 281–282, 304, 306–308, 326, 360, 364; cluster 90, 133–138, 140–145; curvature 120, 122–123, 125–126, 131, 140–142, 144, 227; gender 149–156; MouseTracker 118, 128, 146; mousetrap 111–112, 117–120, 122–123, 125–129, 134, 136, 143; OpenSesame 111–115, 117–119, 127–129; prototype 125, 138–140, 142–143, 149; trajectories 2, 116–117, 119–121, 123–129, 227, 229–230

Multilevel Model 12, 83, 86, 89, 92–93

Multinomial 358–360, 363, 370, 371

Noncompensatory 186, 189, 191–194, 347–348, 350, 352–354

Prefrontal cortex: dorsolateral 237, 239, 251, 253; dorsomedial 237, 239; ventromedial 180, 182, 237, 241, 245–246, 253, 310

Pupil dilation 37, 45–53, 70–71, 98, 100, 106, 356, 377

Reproducibility 62–63, 65–71, 73–74, 290

Response time: exemplar models 191; feedback 7, 115, 164, 186, 191–192, 206, 218, 220–222, 263, 315, 336; guessing 50, 56, 257, 359; processing order 189, 191; systems factorial technology 187, 189, 195–196; weighted additive strategy (WADD) 194

Sampling: accumulator 224, 229, 331, 333, 336, 338, 378, 380–384; description 313–316, 319–322; experience 314–325, 328; gap 314–316, 319–325; lotteries 283, 314–322, 330; multialternative 333, 336, 338; rare event 316–317, 320

Skin conductance: acquisition parameters 168, 179; amplitude 5, 98, 164, 170, 174–175, 198, 219, 223–225, 227, 230, 264; baseline 46–48, 50, 71–72, 164, 171–172, 208–212, 223–224, 235, 251, 256, 260–261, 289, 382, 384; block designs 236; choice models 167, 321, 360; data management and analysis 174; electrodes 166, 170–172, 179, 199, 250, 253, 374; event markers 170–171; experimental design 16, 46–47, 49, 53–55, 57, 60–61, 90, 138, 162, 172, 185, 234, 236, 252, 275, 380; filters 120, 168, 174–175, 179; frequency 6, 8–9, 12, 16, 47, 65, 79–85, 89, 101, 111, 125, 127, 134, 138, 142, 164, 174–175, 179, 182, 198, 218–222, 231, 252–253, 256, 258, 263, 265, 307, 315–317, 326–329, 349, 352, 359, 377; interstimulus intervals 172; measurement window 174, 176–177, 180; onset latency 164, 176, 179, 223–225; recovery half time 164; rise time 164; sampling rate 20, 29, 68, 114, 119, 168, 170, 174, 179; task structure 102, 149, 153, 168, 172, 189, 207; tonic and phasic 162, 182

Strategy 84–86, 90–92, 100–102, 104–105, 181, 185–187, 191–195, 240–244, 263, 265, 279, 287, 290–292, 320–322, 341, 344–353, 357–373; comparison 99–102, 194, 282, 287, 302, 310, 315, 326, 328, 330–333, 335, 338, 346, 350–351, 358, 363, 368, 370; selection 294–295, 297, 304, 307, 315, 345, 353, 360, 364–365

Transcranial magnetic stimulation: control conditions 139, 142, 236, 252, 265, 293, 297; safety guidelines 252–253; sham stimulation 250, 252, 256–258, 260

Take the best (TTB) 185–189, 192–194, 346–348, 368–369

Verbal reports: "why" questions 279; action replay 278; coding scheme 271, 281, 305, 307; combined with nonverbal measures 271; complete process models 282; componential analysis 281; everyday activities 34, 38, 292; expert performers 294, 297; free response 276–277, 279; instructions to participants 276, 278; probe questions 275; retrospective reports 274, 278, 291, 343; sequential analysis 281–282; stimulated recall 278–280; structured response 275, 277, 280; structuring plans 282; theoretical framework 17, 288, 290, 380; units of analysis 281

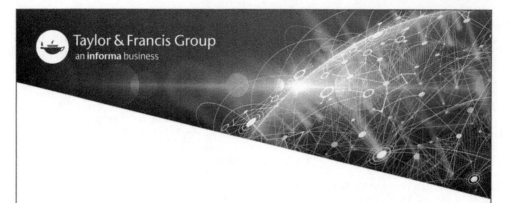

Taylor & Francis eBooks

www.taylorfrancis.com

A single destination for eBooks from Taylor & Francis with increased functionality and an improved user experience to meet the needs of our customers.

90,000+ eBooks of award-winning academic content in Humanities, Social Science, Science, Technology, Engineering, and Medical written by a global network of editors and authors.

TAYLOR & FRANCIS EBOOKS OFFERS:

- A streamlined experience for our library customers
- A single point of discovery for all of our eBook content
- Improved search and discovery of content at both book and chapter level

REQUEST A FREE TRIAL
support@taylorfrancis.com